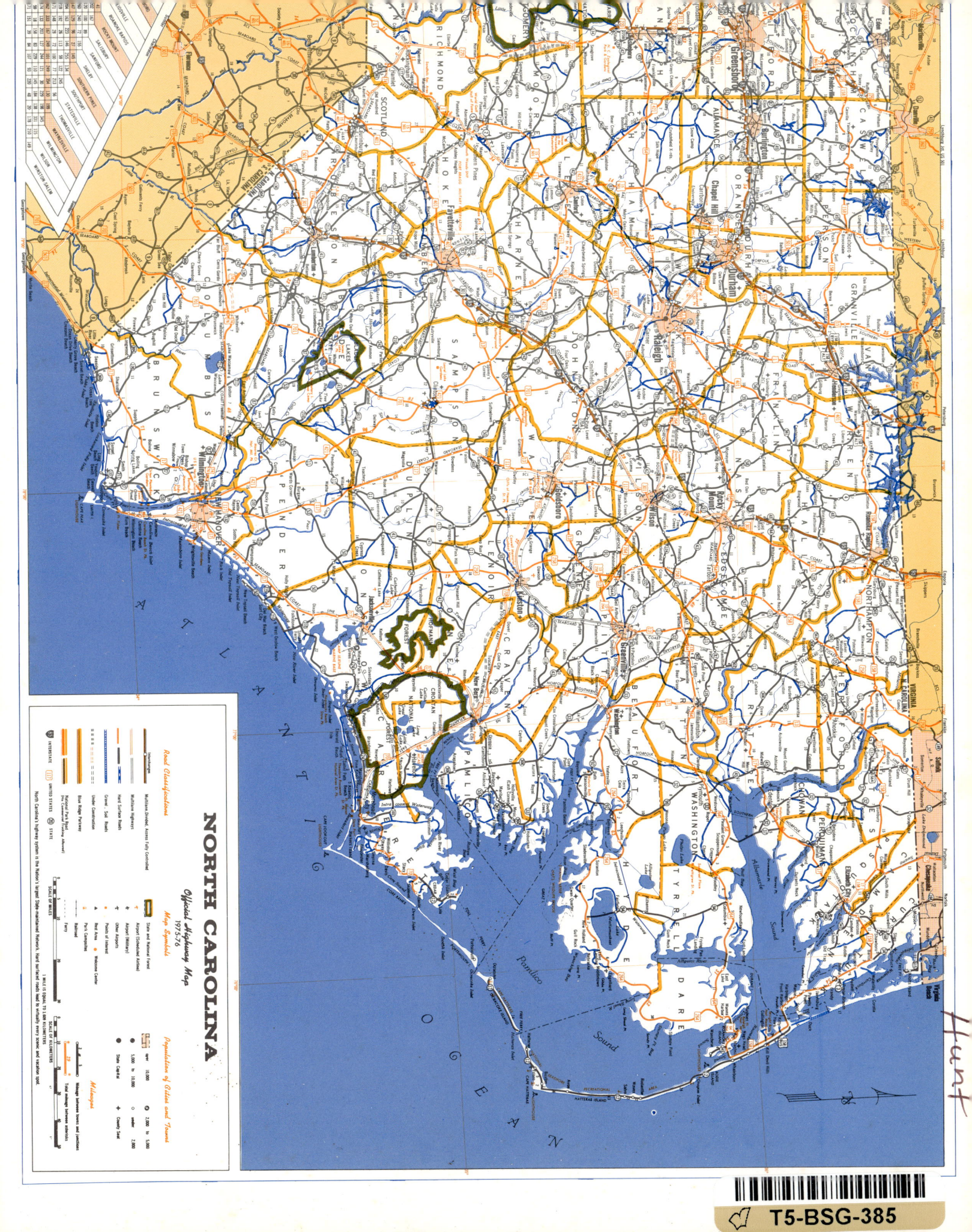

NORTH CAROLINA ATLAS

NORTH CAROLINA ATLAS

PORTRAIT OF A CHANGING SOUTHERN STATE

Edited by
JAMES W. CLAY
DOUGLAS M. ORR, JR.
ALFRED W. STUART

Foreword by JAMES E. HOLSHOUSER, JR.

The University of North Carolina Press · Chapel Hill

Chief Cartographer
JAMES W. CLAY

Staff Cartographer
JEFFERSON L. SIMPSON

Cartographic Assistants
Gary Addington
Brice Auten
David Brown
Teresa Brown
Ed Price
Richard Reiman
Kathy Walters

Randy Allen
Marc Armstrong
Graham Gilley
Cynthia Hanchar
Janet Hince
Charlie Kelly
Penni McCall
Patricia Meeks
Lola Olsen
Sally Olson
Graham Reed
John Root
Mercer Tyson
Bruce Willis

Research Assistants
Gary Brown
Alan Guggenheim
Alex Richardson
Robert Vogel

Copyright © 1975 by
The University of North Carolina Press
All rights reserved
Manufactured in the United States of America

Library of Congress Catalog Card Number 75-6984
ISBN 0-8078-1244-7

Library of Congress Cataloging in Publication Data
Main entry under title:

North Carolina atlas.

   1. North Carolina—Maps. 2. North Carolina.
I. Clay, James W. II. Orr, Douglas Milton.
III. Stuart, Alfred W.
G1300.N7 1975   912'.756   75-6984
ISBN 0-8078-1244-7

Contents

Foreword by James E. Holshouser, Jr.   ix

Acknowledgments   xi

Part I: INTRODUCTION   2

JAMES W. CLAY, Department of Geography and Earth Sciences,
The University of North Carolina at Charlotte

DOUGLAS M. ORR, JR., Department of Geography and Earth Sciences,
The University of North Carolina at Charlotte

ALFRED W. STUART, Department of Geography and Earth Sciences,
The University of North Carolina at Charlotte

Part II: HUMAN SETTLEMENT AND PROFILE

1. History   12

WILLIAM S. POWELL, Department of History,
The University of North Carolina at Chapel Hill

2. Population   32

JOHN C. CATAU, Department of Geography and Earth Sciences,
The University of North Carolina at Charlotte

A. C. DAVIS, Department of Sociology and Anthropology,
North Carolina State University

WILLIAM B. CLIFFORD, Department of Sociology and Anthropology,
North Carolina State University

R. DAVID MUSTIAN, Department of Sociology and Anthropology,
North Carolina State University

3. Urbanization   53

CLYDE E. BROWNING, Department of Geography,
The University of North Carolina at Chapel Hill

FRANCIS H. PARKER, Department of City and Regional Planning,
The University of North Carolina at Chapel Hill

4. Government and Politics   70

SCHLEY R. LYONS, Department of Political Science,
The University of North Carolina at Charlotte

WILLIAM J. McCOY, Department of Political Science,
The University of North Carolina at Charlotte

Part III: PHYSICAL RESOURCES AND ENVIRONMENTAL QUALITY

5. Climate and Air Quality   92

RICHARD J. KOPEC, Department of Geography,
The University of North Carolina at Chapel Hill

JAMES W. CLAY, Department of Geography and Earth Sciences,
The University of North Carolina at Charlotte

6. Physiography, Geology, and Mineral Resources   112

STEPHEN G. CONRAD, Office of Earth Resources,
State of North Carolina

P. ALBERT CARPENTER III, Office of Earth Resources,
State of North Carolina

WILLIAM F. WILSON, Office of Earth Resources,
State of North Carolina

7. Vegetation and Soil Resources   128

ARTHUR W. COOPER, Department of Natural and Economic Resources,
State of North Carolina

RALPH J. McCRACKEN, Agricultural Research Service,
Washington, D.C.

LOUIS E. AULL, Department of Soil Science,
North Carolina State University

8. Water Resources   150

RALPH C. HEATH, United States Geological Survey,
Raleigh, North Carolina

NATHAN O. THOMAS, United States Geological Survey,
Raleigh, North Carolina

HAROLD DUBACH, Beaufort Technical Education Center,
Beaufort, South Carolina

Contents

Part IV: THE ECONOMY

9. Income and Labor   180

EDWIN L. ROGERS, Department of Economics, The University of North Carolina at Charlotte

CHARLES R. PUGH, Department of Economics, North Carolina State University

10. Agriculture   188

JAMES G. MADDOX, Department of Economics, North Carolina State University

11. Manufacturing   202

ALFRED W. STUART, Department of Geography and Earth Sciences, The University of North Carolina at Charlotte

WAYNE A. WALCOTT, Department of Geography and Earth Sciences, The University of North Carolina at Charlotte

12. Trade, Finance, and Communications   214

D. GORDON BENNETT, Department of Geography, The University of North Carolina at Greensboro

CHARLES R. HAYES, Department of Geography, The University of North Carolina at Greensboro

JOSEPH E. JOHNSON, School of Business and Economics, The University of North Carolina at Greensboro

13. Transportation and Energy Utilities   225

W. JOHN CAMERON, Ernst and Ernst, Raleigh, North Carolina

GEORGE T. LATHROP, Creighton-Hamburg Associates, Inc., Chapel Hill, North Carolina

C. E. VICK, JR., Kimley-Horn and Associates, Inc., Raleigh, North Carolina

Part V: SERVICES AND AMENITIES

14. Education   250

RICHARD C. PHILLIPS, School of Education, The University of North Carolina at Chapel Hill

BENJAMIN H. ROMINE, JR., Office of Planning and Institutional Studies, The University of North Carolina at Chapel Hill

15. Health Care Resources   273

HARVEY L. SMITH, Social Research Section, Division of Health Affairs, The University of North Carolina at Chapel Hill

SHANNON P. HALLMAN, Social Research Section, Division of Health Affairs, The University of North Carolina at Chapel Hill

16. Outdoor Recreation   291

LELAND L. NICHOLLS, Department of Geography, Appalachian State University

17. Cultural Arts   304

MORTON SHAPIRO, Department of English, The University of North Carolina at Charlotte

Part VI: RETROSPECT AND PROSPECT   314

JAMES W. CLAY, Department of Geography and Earth Sciences, The University of North Carolina at Charlotte

DOUGLAS M. ORR, JR., Department of Geography and Earth Sciences, The University of North Carolina at Charlotte

ALFRED W. STUART, Department of Geography and Earth Sciences, The University of North Carolina at Charlotte

H. DANIEL STILLWELL, Department of Geography, Appalachian State University

Index   327

Foreword

At no time in the history of North Carolina has sound planning been more necessary to preserve our cultural and environmental heritage than it is in the 1970s. Unprecedented forces of change confront every region of North Carolina. As we continue to develop a modern and vigorous state, we need expert analysis of our growth, and we must strive to understand the broad trends and patterns of change.

This handsome book addresses these needs at a crucial time in the life of our state. By bringing a diversity of important topics under one cover and illustrating them with a multitude of clarifying maps and charts, the editors have made a unique contribution to the understanding of the problems and opportunities that face the people of North Carolina. Such an awareness is a logical prelude to planning the state's orderly development.

The public official, the business decision maker, the involved layman, or those who simply love the "Old North State," will find between these covers a wealth of incisive analysis as well as handy factual information. Beyond its utility to the citizenry of North Carolina, this analytical atlas could serve as a model to other states as they too prepare to meet the challenge of an uncertain future. Surely we all can benefit from taking stock of where we have been and where we seem to be going before we head into the last quarter of the twentieth century. *North Carolina Atlas: Portrait of a Changing Southern State* provides that perspective and I recommend it to all of my fellow citizens.

JAMES E. HOLSHOUSER, JR.
Governor of North Carolina

Acknowledgments

This book flows out of a recent strong tradition of atlases in North Carolina. In 1967, under the leadership of Richard E. Lonsdale, the very useful *Atlas of North Carolina* was published by The University of North Carolina Press. Two of us were privileged to participate in that project, and then later, at the new university campus in Charlotte, we brought into reality a new kind of atlas, one with a thematic organization and an analytical text—the *Metrolina Atlas*, published by The University of North Carolina Press in 1972. Encouraged by the success of that approach and its relevance to various contemporary concerns, the editors of this volume embarked on the even more ambitious project of applying the same techniques to an atlas of the entire state.

Dean W. Colvard, chancellor of The University of North Carolina at Charlotte, and William Britt, vice-chancellor for development, lent enthusiastic support to the project. This support was augmented by that of the General Administration of The University of North Carolina, including that of President William Friday. Without their encouragement and good offices the project would never have materialized.

That it did happen is due to the generous material support of a number of North Carolina foundations. Among them they granted the funds necessary for the preparation of the manuscript and the hundreds of maps and charts. We received substantial support from the Z. Smith Reynolds Foundation and the Smith Richardson Foundation. Very timely funding came from the Burlington Industries Foundation and the Foundation of The University of North Carolina at Charlotte. On-campus support was also provided by the Institute for Urban Studies and Community Service, at that time under the direction of Norman W. Schul.

The Southern Growth Policies Board, headquartered in North Carolina's Research Triangle Park, has been helpful to this project from the beginning. We are indebted to William L. Bowden, the board's executive director, and David E. Gillespie, director of intergovernmental affairs, for their thoughtful interest and assistance. We make special acknowledgment to James G. Maddox, contributor to the chapter on agriculture, who died before the book was finished.

A key ingredient in the production of this book has been the small army of student/staff cartographic and research assistants at The University of North Carolina at Charlotte. Their names are indicated on a previous page, and they gave a full measure of time and talent to this project. Also of critical importance was the typing and general administrative assistance contributed by Jean Beaver, Deborah Blackmon, Cathy Bost, Mickey Gregory, and Scotty Williams, all of whom worked long and with meticulous care on various phases of the project.

A special thanks is due to our colleagues in the Department of Geography and Earth Sciences for their patience as we subordinated many other worthy needs for the completion of this project. That the department grew in quantity and quality during that period is testimony to their loyal cooperation.

The close cooperation and excellent assistance provided by the staff members of our publisher, The University of North Carolina Press, deserve particular mention. Such efforts too often are overlooked, and their contributions since the inception of the project have been invaluable.

A final thanks goes to our families who had to do without us many times or, perhaps worse, live with us when the complexity of the whole effort seemed beyond us. Our wives, Fran Clay, Mary Lou Orr, and Mary Louise Stuart, suffered, usually in silence, and now are entitled to their share of the credit.

JAMES W. CLAY
DOUGLAS M. ORR, JR.
ALFRED W. STUART

INTRODUCTION

PART I

N.C. needs honest criticism—rather than the false, shallow "we are the-finest-state-and-greatest-people-in-the-country"—kind of thing. An *artist* who refuses to accept fair criticism of his work will never go far. What of a state?

—*Thomas Wolfe*

Introduction

JAMES W. CLAY
DOUGLAS M. ORR, JR.
ALFRED W. STUART

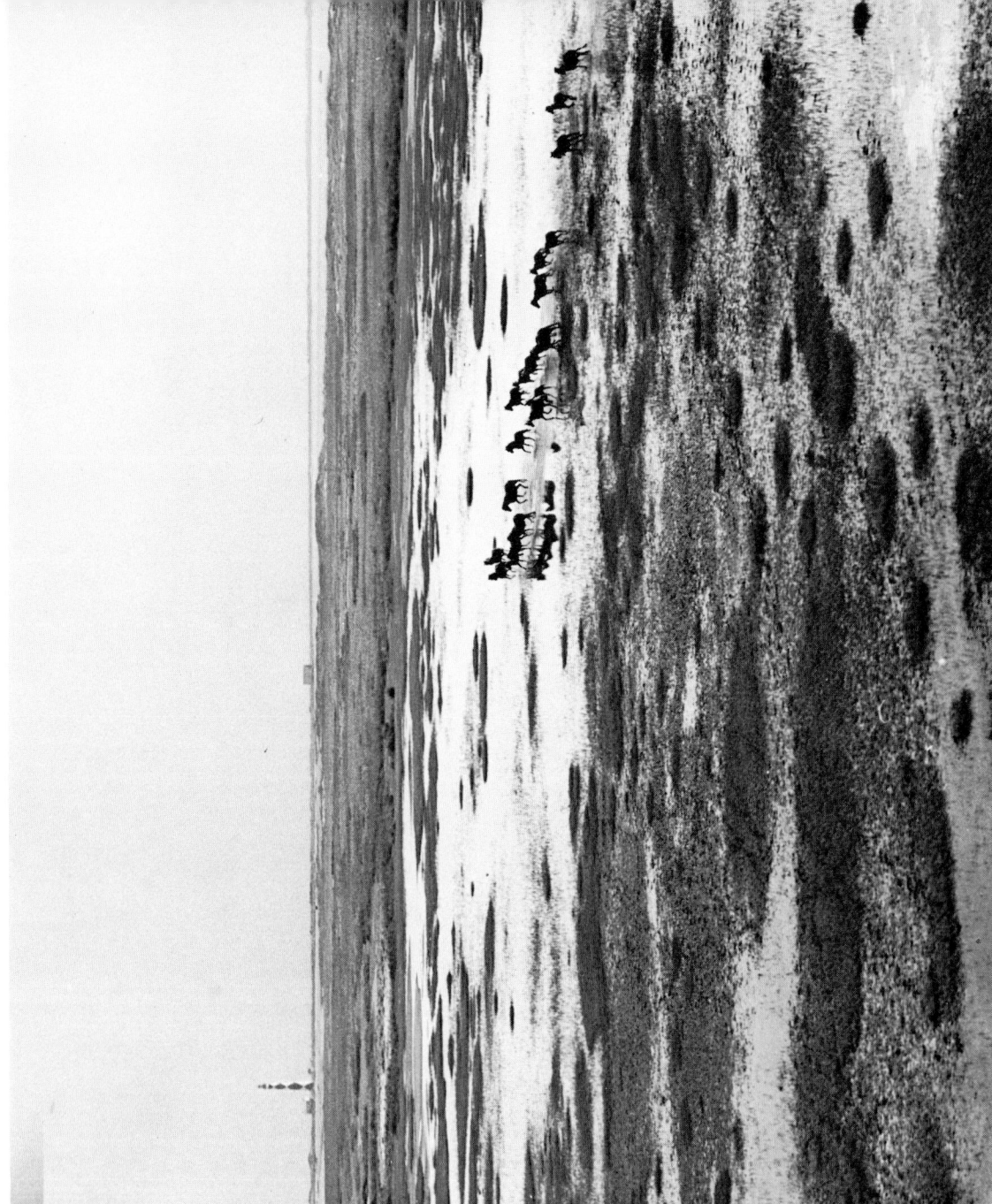

That slice of the North American continent that is North Carolina is a 503-mile-long mosaic of many patterns and dimensions. Its expanse begins at the Atlantic front with the ragged fringes of a long chain of narrow sand reefs called the Outer Banks and ends at the Tennessee border along the mile-high crests of the Great Smoky Mountains. The state's flanks are framed by two imposing Herculean "pillars" of its own: the 138-foot-high Jockey's Ridge sand dune overlooks the Atlantic Ocean at Nags Head and is the highest on the Atlantic coast, while Mount Mitchell at 6,684 feet above sea level in the North Carolina Blue Ridge is the highest peak in eastern North America. Tucked within this cross section of almost 53,000 square miles—about the size of England—are the three major regions of striking diversity: the river-fed lowland of the Coastal Plain, the rolling Piedmont plateau, and the slopes and coves of the Mountain region.

Like North Carolina's physical contours, the human profile of the Tar Heel state wears many expressions, sometimes contradictory but always intriguing. Perhaps this is the reflection of a colorful past. For one thing, North Carolina frequently has been a land of "beginnings." It was in 1585 that Sir Walter Raleigh's colonists landed on Roanoke Island to plant England's first American colony, and there the first child of English parentage was born in the new country—yet all vanished without a trace. Much later the Wright brothers would come to these same Outer Banks at Kitty Hawk and usher in the air age with the first airplane flight. And at about the same time, again on nearby Roanoke Island, R. A. Fessenden was conducting a form of wireless telegraphy experiment that became the basis for the development of radio broadcasting.

The phenomenon of the gold rush was first introduced to the young nation after the discovery of America's first gold nugget in 1799 in a small stream near the little village of Concord. Among other notable beginnings was that of the first state university to open its doors to students—the University of North Carolina in 1795, the first state-supported symphony in 1946, and the first state museum of art in Raleigh, which opened to the public in 1956.

Figure A. The State of North Carolina

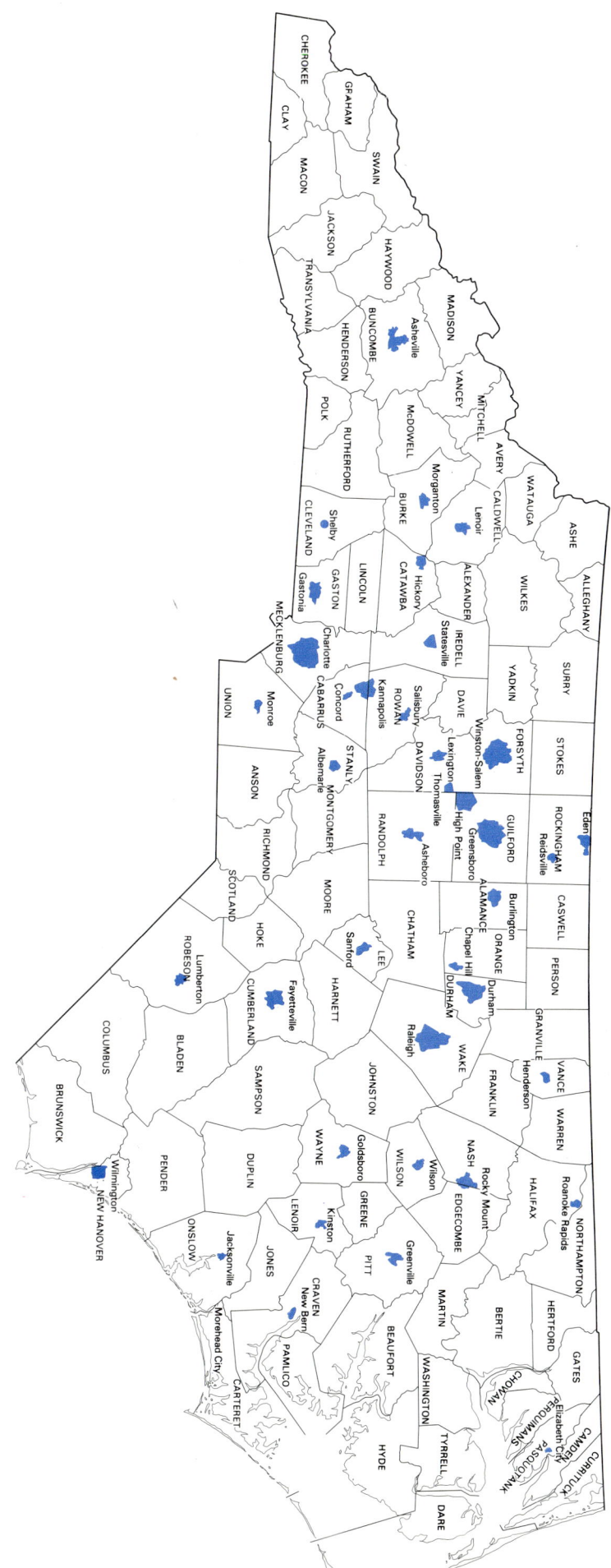

The past also helps understand that quality of ingrained independence that also gives the state identity. Perhaps the early physical—as well as psychological—isolation of the state's people from the rest of the country might be a responsible factor. Indeed, the state became so remote and uninvolved with the outside that at one point in the early nineteenth century it became known as the "Rip Van Winkle state." This stubborn streak of independence has been evidenced in many ways. The first formal sanction of American independence from England by any American colony occurred in North Carolina, but then the colony steadfastly refused to join the new Union until the Constitution had a Bill of Rights. Later, secession from the Union was strongly resisted and the state was the last to join the Confederacy in 1861. Once committed to the cause of "Southern independence," however, North Carolina fought on nearly all battlefields, suffering more casualties than any other state of the Confederacy. And one of the last surrenders of the war occurred in North Carolina when Confederate General Joseph E. Johnson surrendered to Union General William T. Sherman on 26 April 1865 at the James Bennett farmhouse near Durham. Today, North Carolina alone among the fifty states denies the governor veto power, and it is the only state east of the Mississippi that continues to turn down referenda on liquor-by-the-drink.

Then there are the enigmas: North Carolina is one of the South's more industrialized states, yet it has the nation's largest rural farm population; North Carolina is the home of some of the nation's oldest and most distinguished colleges and universities, yet its public kindergarten system has only just begun; political voting habits in North Carolina more and more defy predictability; and so it goes. To the outsider, it may all seem incongruous, but it represents some of the character and flavor distinct to North Carolina.

And yet the essence of North Carolina is so much more than all of this. It is a never-ending series of vignettes, painted in richly varying hues and tones. It is the people—the Hatteras fisherman, the claw-hammer banjo player and mountain clogger, the Piedmont industrial executive, the old tenant farmer, the new wave of youthful government leaders, the often forgotten Cherokee, and the mountain craftsman. And, of course, it is the places—the seemingly out of place but dignified classical Greek revival lines of the capitol; the Appalachian coves and hollows where "you have to lie down and look up to see out"; the Gothic spires and arches of Duke University and the "Southern Part of Heaven" that is Chapel Hill; the "profile of Grandfather"—as the Indians identified one of the world's oldest mountains; the typically medium-sized cities and towns splayed across the Piedmont landscape; the pristine tranquility of Joyce Kilmer Memorial Forest; the little Outer Banks village of Rodanthe where old Christmas is still celebrated on the Twelfth Night; and the Brown Mountain lights.

3

And all the while there is the juxtaposition of the old and new, for while North Carolina is among the oldest of the states, it is also youthful in many ways. Like much of the South with its peculiar heritage, it is a land of "late beginnings" as well as "early beginnings." As a result, the pervasive element of change seems far more apparent in the character of North Carolina and the South than in other parts of the nation.

Indeed, large parts of the South remained an American frontier until the 1830s. Later the Civil War and absence of meaningful reconstruction deprived the region from sharing the progress and abundance of the nation as a whole. As Wilbur J. Cash wrote in 1941 in *The Mind of the South*, the region was generally a closed society, immune to change. The outsider's stereotype of one-crop agriculture, the sharecropper, one-party politics, the poll tax, and Jim Crowism was difficult for the South to refute. But in the years since World War II there has been frequent reference to a "New South": joining the mainstream of the rest of the country in a kind of "Americanization of the South." It has frequently been debated whether the new age has fully arrived. Nevertheless, there is little doubt that immense changes are at work throughout the South and rapid transformations are taking place. The evidences are everywhere. For example, the 1960s was the first decade since the 1870s when more people moved into the region than moved out, so that the region showed a net gain of 6.6 million people. Urbanization is taking place in the South at twice the rate that it is in the North. The South is moving up faster in average income, housing starts, and education than any of the other three Census Bureau regions of the nation. Large-scale agricultural diversification has been accompanied by a decline in farming population to the point that only approximately 5 percent of the South's population today is engaged in farming. And perhaps most revealing of all, the South has moved ahead of the rest of the country in school desegregation, with a higher percentage of all its black pupils attending desegregated schools.

Correspondingly, however, the net in-migration, rapid urbanization, and other facets of growth are bringing problems so familiar in other parts of the country. Just at the time when growth and change in the South have come in full force, serious questions are being raised about the widespread implications of the whole growth syndrome.

Figure B. N.C. and the Eastern U.S.

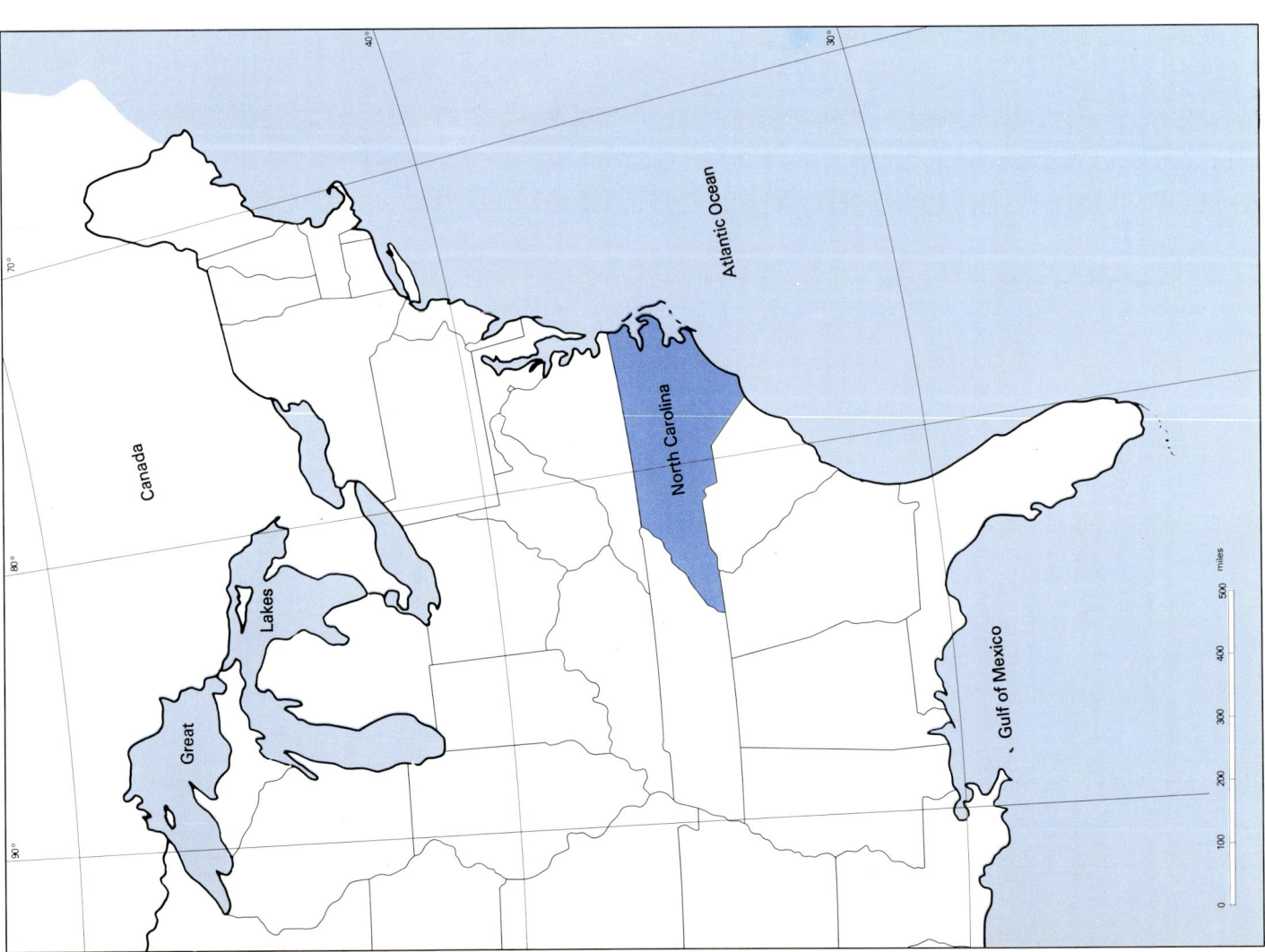

The winds of change that are sweeping through every corner of the Old South are having a major impact upon the land and life-style of North Carolina. The spread of metropolitan regions, rural to urban migrations, more diversified industrial growth, overloading of environmental systems, and political realignments are only a few of the manifestations of change. And the momentum of change seems to quicken with each year and threatens to overwhelm attempts to guide and control it.

It is clearly a time for taking stock and closely identifying the problems and trends set in motion throughout North Carolina. Effective planning is built upon such a foundation, and it is a continuous process never to be taken for granted. Certainly there exists already a considerable awareness concerning many of the features of the state's growth and change. But frequently they are seen as isolated phenomena rather than as parts of a broader, multifaceted process.

Herein is the rationale for this book. It is our intent that an analytical state atlas might be one way to analyze and display under a single cover the broader patterns of change in North Carolina. To piece together such an interdisciplinary portrayal, specialists in each subject throughout the state have agreed to participate in this undertaking. They represent a cross section of education, government, and business and come literally from the broad expanse of the state—from coast to mountains.

It is important to recognize at the outset that this atlas is not intended to be all-inclusive, touching upon every feature of the state's character. No book could accomplish that, especially when the subject is as richly diverse as North Carolina. Selected references are included at the end of each chapter for additional information. But in a generally comprehensive way, the chapters draw upon information that (1) helps depict significant patterns or trends, and (2) lends itself in most cases to visual display through the maps and other graphics. The volume is, after all, first and foremost an atlas.

In a work of this sort statistical information is used extensively. It may seem that in some places the statistics are not as recent as one would like them to be. This happens for two reasons. First, there is a considerable delay between the collection of data and its reporting, as long as two years in some cases. Compounding this difficulty is the practice of collecting certain kinds of data only occasionally. The Census of Manufactures, for example, are taken only every five years and, most significantly of all, the Census of Population and Housing is taken only at the beginning of each decade.

The second source of delay stems from the need to analyze the data before they are included in a study. The text and figures in a study such as this have to be developed, checked, and set months before the book is printed. Even if fresh data became available before printing time, their inclusion would cause significant delays because changing data is not a simple matter of replacing one set of numbers with another. The data would have to be analyzed to ascertain any possible changes in conclusions, they would have to be cross checked with related items and, sometimes, graphs and maps would have to be redone. To make matters worse, new data trickle in almost constantly. A cut-off must be established and maintained.

The truth is that the general patterns do not change much from year to year. Mecklenburg is going to be the most populous county for some years to come and the distribution of tobacco cultivation is not apt to change very quickly. It is well to remember that this book is intended to be a study of long-term trends and patterns rather than the most current factual reference work.

The interested reader can find the very latest data in the myriad information sources that undergo almost ceaseless updating. Enough of these sources are mentioned in the various chapters of this book to give the reader an indication of what sources exist. Finally, there are many activities for which statistical data are nonexistent or inadequate. The editors sympathize with the reader who is disappointed by the omission of some subject for this reason.

The *North Carolina Atlas* is divided into six parts, with chapters compatible in subject matter grouped together in each of the major parts. Following this introductory section (Part I), the *Atlas* begins most appropriately with Part II, "Human Settlement and Profile." Its chapters examine the state's historical heritage, population characteristics, rapid urbanization, and patterns of government and politics as a way of looking at the state first through the personality of its people. Part III, entitled "Physical Resources and Environmental Quality," reviews the extraordinary physical resources of the state, but also points to those environmental threats to this "goodliest land." The forces of change in the state are displayed nowhere more vividly than in the five chapters of Part IV that deal with North Carolina's economy. Never-ending economic alterations keep transforming the landscape of a state that has historically been one of the nation's most rural and agricultural. North Carolina's "quality of life" is especially highlighted in Part V—"Amenities and Services." Perhaps a mirror of the character of all the rest, the chapters on the state's education, health care resources, outdoor recreation, and cultural arts examine the current status and outlook in these endeavors so critical to the betterment of the state and its people. The final part, "Retrospect and Prospect" is an attempt by the coeditors to highlight major trends in the state's growth and change, to note some new geographic patterns that are evolving throughout the state, and to discuss the various planning efforts that are underway. Throughout the *Atlas*, it is hoped that the reader will look for the many interrelations that reoccur among these major parts and from one individual chapter to another.

Finally, considerable effort has been made to refrain from shaping this treatment into a portrayal of a North Carolina we would ideally like to see. The Tar Heel state, as any other, has its strengths and weaknesses, and we have tried to present them in an objective and balanced manner. But most of all, we hope the following chapters will provide new insights to this fascinatingly diverse state as it confronts the changes that carry it into the last quarter of the twentieth century.

Geographic Units of North Carolina

Many of the changes taking place throughout the state have been reflected in the evolution and alteration of North Carolina's various types of geographic units. Any state has its internal regionalisms, and North Carolina in particular is no exception. Several of the most significant categories of units that have emerged through time in the state are used throughout the *Atlas* to map or chart data and thereby provide a means of depicting internal spatial patterns. Those units selected—the three physiographic divisions, county units, Standard Metropolitan Statistical Areas (SMSAs), and the Multicounty Planning Regions—are described below.

The Three Physiographic Divisions The most distinctive regional differences in North Carolina, even up to present day, are found in the three physiographic divisions known as the Coastal Plain, the Piedmont, and the Mountain region. (These physiographic boundaries follow a path that crosses county lines; however, for displaying data by county throughout the *Atlas*, the boundaries are adjusted to conform to county lines.) The differences are much more than merely physical, however. As early settlers funneled into each area, often by different routes and from different sources, human variances began to match the diversities in the physical landscape. Each region developed its own human imprint, socially, economically, and politically, and in the process became contrasting cultural regions as well.

The Coastal Plain, once the bottom of an ancient ocean, extends inland an average of 150 miles as a flatland traversed by a string of broad rivers—the Chowan, the Roanoke, the Tar, the Neuse, and the Cape Fear. Massive old white oaks often draped with Spanish moss, cypress, and longleaf pine all flourish in the humid warm air of this low-lying country. The outer periphery of the Coastal Plain, affected by the ocean tides in its sounds and rivers, is the Tidewater area (sometimes depicted as an additional region in parts of the *Atlas*), comprised largely of treeless savannas, marshes, and swamps—the most notable being the impenetrable Great Dismal Swamp in the northeast extremity. It has been the South of river plantations, little towns with wide shaded streets, some counties predominantly black, and the endless flat fields of tobacco, peanuts, and cotton. Sectionalism is strong here. The English and Scottish peoples who first settled this area were intent on maintaining firm political control of the colony. The "down east" political power has flavored North Carolina politics to the present, though it has been somewhat diluted in recent years because of reapportionment. But if the North Carolina Coastal Plain and its people are always within close reach of their past, the force of change is beginning to blur that visibility on the landscape. The thousands and thousands of farms that dotted the Coastal Plain in the 1930s have been more than halved in number. The population has become increasingly "rural nonfarm" as many commute to the nearest industrial plant. The state's Old South region is being transformed just as is its larger counterpart.

North Carolina's "midland," commonly known as the Piedmont, rises from its fall line contact point with the Coastal Plain. It is characterized by a rolling topography cut sharply by swift-moving streams that became choice sites for the early textile mills dependent on water power. Some of the first settlers pushed inland from the outer Coastal Plain by using the rivers as transportation funnels. However, many more, particularly Scotch-Irish and German, made their way into the Piedmont by way of a Great Wagon Road through Pennsylvania and Virginia. Thus the North Carolina Piedmont took on a different ethnic character from the very beginning of European settlement. Farming was somewhat more difficult in the red rocky soils here than in the Coastal Plain, although the new settlers found this midland section could be very productive. But with the coming of textile mills to the region, the Piedmont began to evolve as a kind of complement to the east—more industrialized, larger and more numerous towns and cities, a faster growth and pace of life, and a closer identification with the "New South." Forming the backbone of this region is the so-called Piedmont Crescent, an elongated, curved urban area that follows the axis of the old North Carolina Railroad. Today a major expressway links its threefold urban clusters of the Research Triangle area (Raleigh–Durham–Chapel Hill), the Piedmont Triad (Greensboro–High Point–Winston-Salem), and Metrolina (Charlotte and neighboring counties). Indeed, this is the urban core of the state and a key urban region in the South. And with its medium-sized urban centers and evenly spread population distribution, this region still has the opportunity to be a model of contemporary urban development—or it can simply grow into a sprawl of coalescing urbanization like so many others.

The "Land of the Sky" was what author Christian Reid in 1876 called North Carolina's strikingly picturesque Mountain region. A part of the long Appalachian chain that runs from Quebec to Alabama, it begins with the escarpment wall of the Blue Ridge and extends to the state's western boundary as the purple-hazed Great Smokies. The region is indeed a rooftop of eastern North America, with more than forty mountain peaks above six thousand feet elevation. Within their sheltered valleys and coves developed North Carolina's most isolated and distinct culture. Fierce loyalties were a trademark of the mountaineer people who were not much inclined to be closely associated with the peoples to the east. Sympathies were not particularly strong, for example, toward the Southern cause during the Civil War. Schools for a long time were inaccessible and infrequent. It is not surprising that old folk customs are best preserved in this region of the state. Some words and accents are a throwback to early English and Scottish speech, and strains of Old English folk songs can be heard in the mournful mountain ballads. Some traditional symbols of this land are the split-rail fence, patchwork quilts, the moonshine still, gourd dippers, log cabins, and the fiddler. Although efforts are made to preserve some of the old customs, if not the life-style itself, the forces of change finally worked their way to this western third of North Carolina. New symbols brought about by the impact include vacation land development promotions, golf courses, ski lodges, and of course, belated growth of towns and cities.

County Units The most significant political subdivision below the state level in North Carolina has been the county. Although this type of geographic unit does not have the same measure of importance throughout the country, it has deep roots in North Carolina and the South, where it was installed by the English settlers in the southern colonies. Southern states underwent a proliferation of county units in the late eighteenth and early nineteenth centuries, and today most states in the South have a disproportionately large number of counties.

Because North Carolina had been largely rural, people were able to identify most easily with their county. It has been the territorial base for representation to the General Assembly and the basic building block for constructing legislative and congressional districts. Counties ordinarily are assigned important administrative functions by the state. For example, an elected board of county supervisors or commissioners has responsibilities that may include assessing and levying of taxes; the administration of public education, public health, law enforcement, and justice; planning and zoning of county

Figure C. Physiographic Regions of N.C.

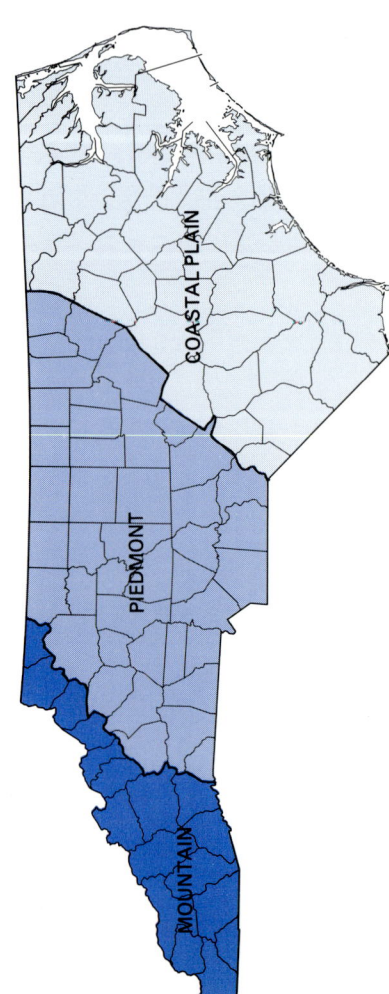

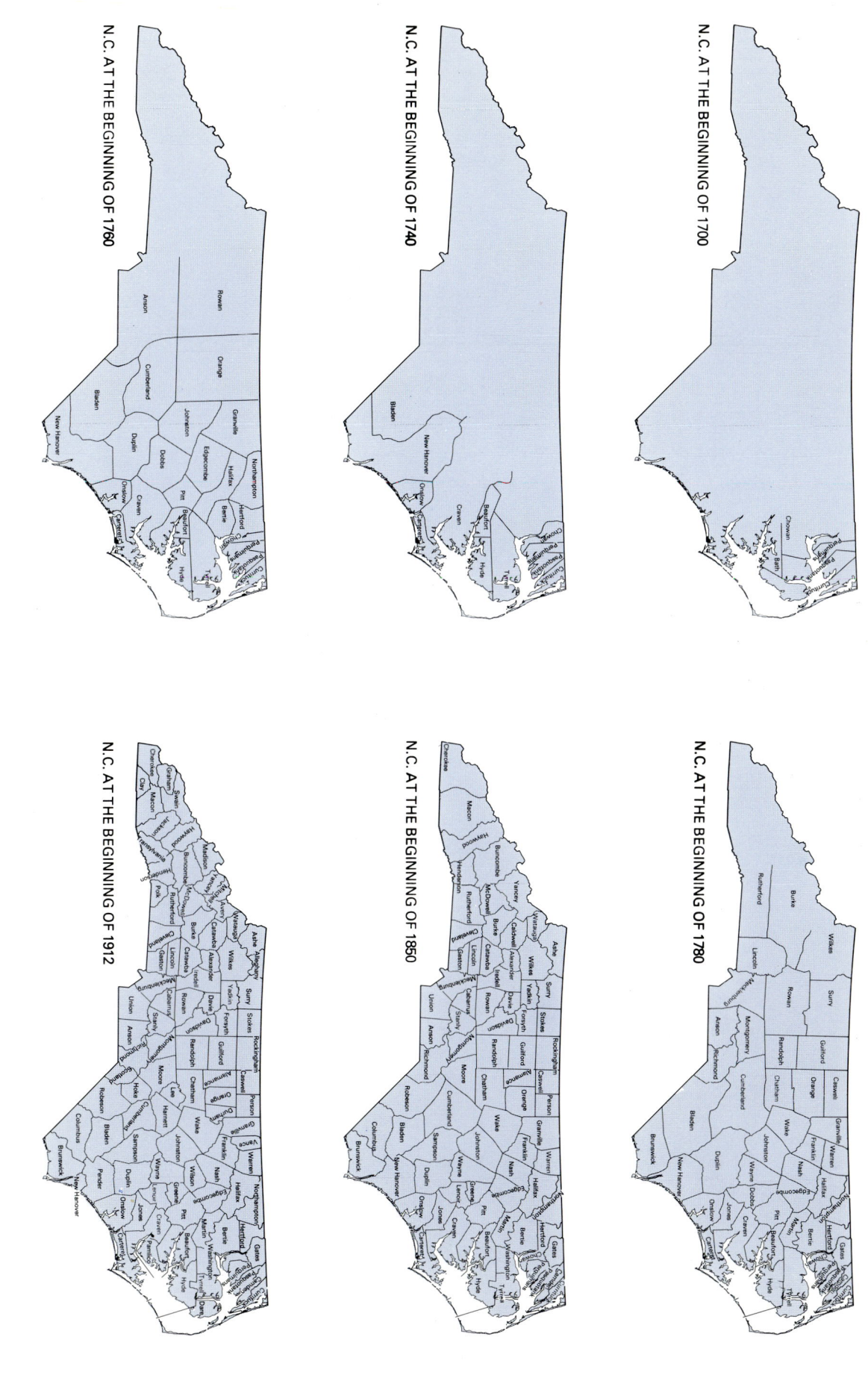

Figure D. Evolution of N.C. Counties

Source: David L. Corbitt, *Formation of the North Carolina Counties, 1663-1943*, 2nd ed. (Raleigh: N.C. Archives, 1969).

property; and construction and maintenance of roads. But like all the other spatial units within the state, the role and importance of counties is in a state of flux.

The nature of the county in North Carolina can be traced to the state's early beginnings. Since the Raleigh colonization of North Carolina had no permanent settlement effects, the first lasting settlement spilled over from the Virginia Tidewater area and concentrated around the Albemarle Sound region; "Ye Countie of Albemarle" was created in 1663 in that area. Five years later it was subdivided into the four precincts of Chowan, Currituck, Pasquotank, and Perquimans as allowed under the proprietor's Fundamental Constitutions. South of the Albemarle Sound region the county of Bath was created and in 1705 it too was subdivided into precincts. And so it went until finally in 1739 the precincts were recognized as counties by the legislature and original county divisions were dropped. The term *county* has been used ever since for North Carolina's major political subdivisions. As new counties were created during the colonial period, the location of a county seat became a major point of contention. Considerable power was at stake because the function of county government was placed largely in the hands of the county court's justices of the peace. They had authorization to raise funds, levy taxes, purchase land, and erect a courthouse at the county seat. The formative outlines of North Carolina's political geography and structure were evolving.

When settlement followed the water courses on an axis to the west, and as wagonloads of settlers from Pennsylvania and Virginia arrived, new counties were created to allow a spatial framework for local government. However, the eastern counties, in order to maintain their power base in the legislature, often insisted upon carving a new eastern county from an old one in return for the creation of a Piedmont or Mountain county. The frequent repetition of this tactic compounded the tendency toward county proliferation.

As depicted in the accompanying maps (Figure D), North Carolina completed its county structure in successive periods, with the Mountain region filling out last. There were a few occasions when the establishment of a new county was authorized by the legislature and the affected population failed to vote in favor of the act.

Figure E. Standard Metropolitan Statistical Areas of N.C., 1974

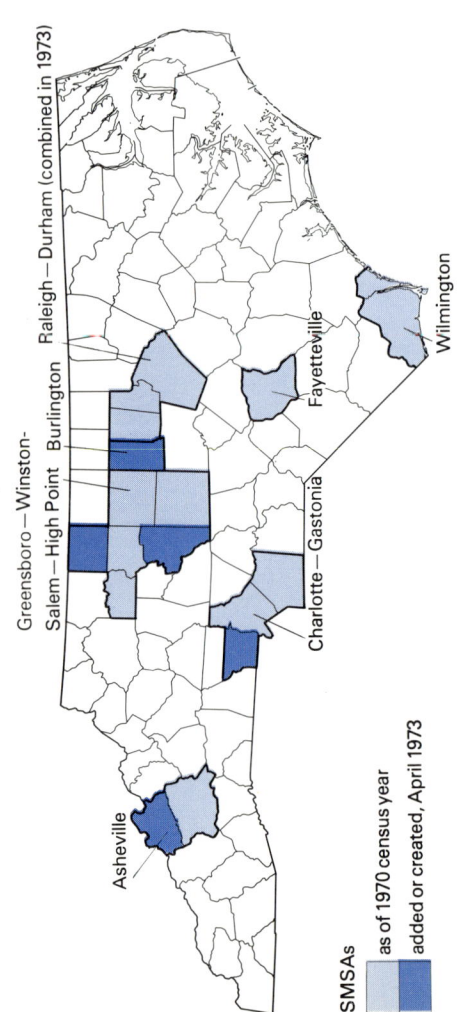

SMSAs
- as of 1970 census year
- added or created, April 1973

Figure F. Multicounty Planning Regions in N.C., 1974

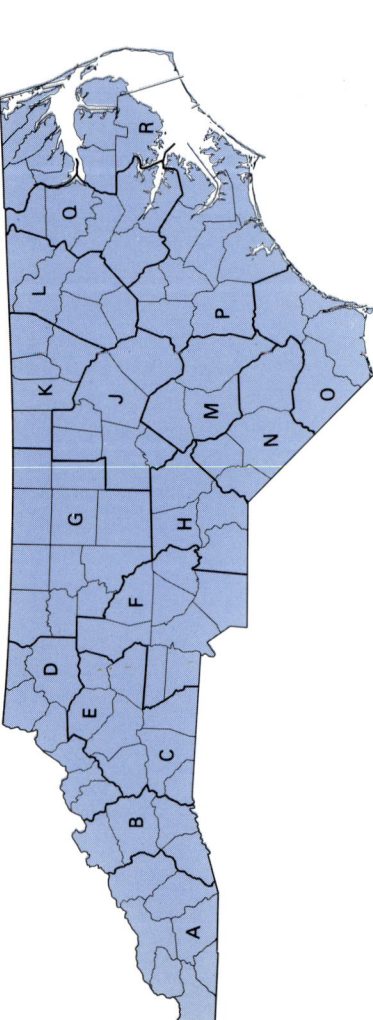

Source: N.C. Department of Administration, State Planning Division, July 1970.

The most intense single period of county formation was during the Revolution years from 1775 to 1780 when fourteen new counties were created. A major reduction of territory and counties occurred in 1789 when the legislature passed an act ceding the state's western lands to the United States. This land included seven Tennessee-area counties. The formation of new counties began to slacken by the end of the nineteenth century, and ended completely with the creation of Avery and Hoke counties in 1911. Since then only minor boundary adjustments have taken place. In the long process a total of 116 counties existed at one time or another, but the state finally peaked at what must be a statistician's ideal—one hundred counties.

Today's one hundred counties vary in size from the 180 square miles of Chowan on the Albemarle Sound to Robeson County's 944 square miles at the South Carolina border. The range of county populations is enormous, from Mecklenburg at 351,670 in 1970 to Tyrrell with 3,716. Thirty-two counties have less than 20,000 people and most of them—like Tyrrell—are declining in population. In fact, Tyrrell's 17.8 percent loss in population after the last census was the most drastic in the state, but it was typical of a trend that characterized a number of Coastal Plain counties.

Because of the disparities in county size and population, the resulting lack in many counties of a sufficiently large tax base to carry out the functions of county government, and the overabundance of counties in North Carolina, it has been suggested that a consolidation of counties would seem appropriate. Such a move is legally possible under a 1933 legislative act providing for the consolidation of contiguous counties. However, the act requires approval by popular vote in the geographic areas affected, and no counties have ever been consolidated accordingly. Also, the few attempts at city-county government consolidation have been rejected by the voters. Meanwhile, many counties are declining in importance in relation to other special units of government below the state level. A plethora of districts, from school districts to municipal corporations, has grown to meet burgeoning civic requirements.

Nevertheless, in North Carolina and in much of the South, the county should remain for some time a widely popular and identifiable geographic unit below the state level. And in many maps throughout this volume the one hundred North Carolina counties are utilized as a useful geographic base for depicting statewide patterns.

Standard Metropolitan Statistical Areas (SMSAs)

The SMSAs are defined according to criteria established by the United States Bureau of the Budget. Although they were intended originally only to present federal statistical information, they have come to be the definition of metropolitan areas most widely used by both business and governmental agencies.

SMSAs are composed principally of cities of 50,000 people or more, their surrounding county, and other contiguous counties that qualify in terms of specific measures of both metropolitan character and interaction with the core county. After each decennial census the SMSAs are modified when the new data indicate that changes should be made. Figure E shows the North Carolina SMSAs in use before 1970 and the new alignments that were defined after the 1970 census. The most recent definitions will remain in use until after the 1980 census.

The increase in the size and number of these units over the last several years in North Carolina is a clear expression of the state's steady trend of urbanization.

Multicounty Planning Regions

By the late 1960s it was becoming apparent that the state government had developed a maze of overlapping spatial units for a variety of specific purposes. In fact, the state had been divided more than seventy different ways, ranging from economic development districts to law enforcement planning units. To allow for a more orderly approach to multicounty planning, the 1969 General Assembly passed legislation authorizing the North Carolina Department of Administration and its Planning Division to work with towns, cities, counties, and federal agencies to develop a system of multicounty planning regions.

To determine where to draw the new boundaries, the Planning Division devised a set of criteria: certain economic and social interrelationships between urban centers and the surrounding areas, existing cooperative programs between counties and between counties and municipalities, a minimum of three counties in each region, a base population of at least 100,000, and major topographic divides such as a river or mountain barrier. Tentative multicounty regions were then drawn up and presented to the public through a series of meetings across the state and mailings to over 2,000 public officials. Thereafter, a revised final plan was developed and on 7 May 1970 the governor issued an executive order establishing the seventeen Multicounty Planning Regions throughout North Carolina (Figure F).

By the end of 1973, a Lead Regional Organization (LRO) had been recognized for each region, with the mandate to coordinate comprehensive planning. The state has also delegated to each LRO the responsibility for reviewing federal grants that may influence regional development. Of the seventeen LROs, the majority are Councils of Governments (COGs) and the remainder are Planning and Economic Development Commissions. All have a regional office with full-time director and staff, funded by member municipalities rather than by any direct state subsidy.

It is noteworthy that many other states have implemented the multicounty planning region concept including the neighboring states of Virginia and South Carolina. These new geographic units could very well be of considerable significance in North Carolina's future.

The existence of just these aforementioned geographic units within the state underscores the fact that North Carolina's internal configurations come in many forms. And even the boundaries of these particular units are becoming subject to challenge and possible change. The evolution of new spatial patterns is taking place continuously—as the following pages attempt to portray.

9

North Carolina is a state of towns and small cities rather than one of large cities. This remains true today despite the recent emergence of significant metropolitan areas. Even if a megalopolis does develop in the Piedmont it is unlikely that it will bear much similarity to more famous examples in the northeastern United States. Although there are some distinct advantages in the North Carolina pattern, the state has not escaped national problems associated with the conversion of land to urban uses. If anything, urban sprawl is an even greater problem in North Carolina because of the dispersed pattern of cities and towns. While the state may not have "big city" planning problems to face, there is perhaps a greater need for planning at a multicounty level that sometimes transcends local interests. In short, rather than lacking urban development problems, North Carolina seems to have a somewhat different set of problems from those of more urbanized areas.

North Carolina government and politics draw deeply upon the state's historical heritage. The earliest colonists brought to the area a distrust of government that is still apparent today, leaving a legacy of integrity of government juxtaposed with a cautiousness of operation. The state's "web of government," which has undergone some recent reorganization, has qualities that differentiate it from any other state. And Tar Heel voting habits are rooted also to the past—with a montage of "tender sectional sensibilities" reflecting the Mountain–Piedmont–Coastal Plain regionalization. On the other hand, such clear-cut patterns are breaking down as politics in North Carolina becomes more unpredictable, impacted upon by the forces of increasing urbanization, in-migration to the state, a growing third-party momentum, and the mixed tendencies toward a two-party system. Indeed, like other topics presented in the rest of this book's chapters, North Carolina's government and politics can be understood only in the context of the state's total changing character.

This portrait of North Carolina begins with a consideration of several basic characteristics of its people: their historical heritage, their demographic profile and settlement patterns, and the manner in which they govern themselves and elect their public officials. Certainly these are key building blocks to gaining a full insight into the nature of North Carolina, and in Part II the Tar Heel portrait begins to emerge.

North Carolina's history has unfolded in a fascinating pattern, with periods of rapid progress and creative outpouring counterbalanced by occasional setbacks and stagnation. At different time periods, for example, North Carolina has been referred to as the "Dixie Dynamo" and "the Rip Van Winkle state." And perhaps the 1677-79 Culpepper's Rebellion, called the first popular uprising in any of the colonies, is symbolic of a notion of regional self-identity that has grown and flowered. The reader no doubt will note that the pace of events has so quickened over the years that the last several decades have revealed an unparalleled evolution of progress—a kind of progress that all the while has been uniquely North Carolinian.

The population of North Carolina has increased slowly but steadily throughout its history and passed five million by 1970. Within that trend there have occurred other important trends. There has been a strong growth of population in the Piedmont and either decreases or very slow growth in the Mountain and Coastal Plain sections; the racial composition of the state has changed the rural farm population has plummeted while the rural nonfarm population has multiplied; urbanization has increased so steadily that North Carolina may join the rest of the nation by having a majority of its residents classified as urban by the 1980 census. Despite increasing urbanization the state's population remains relatively dispersed throughout the state; a steady trend of net out-migration that characterized most of the twentieth century shows signs of having reversed itself in the late 1960s and early 1970s. The analysis of these and many other trends is the substance of the chapter on population.

PART II

HUMAN SETTLEMENT AND PROFILE

> ... Tar Heels adopted the somewhat invidious motto "Esse Quam Videri," and took perhaps excessive pride in referring to their state as "a vale of humility between two mountains of conceit." We were mighty proud of not being proud. We did, however, in such a historical setting, become independent, courageous, resourceful, democratic, gregarious and individualistic, although we would use plainer words than these Latin terms to describe ourselves.
>
> —William T. Polk

1. History

WILLIAM S. POWELL

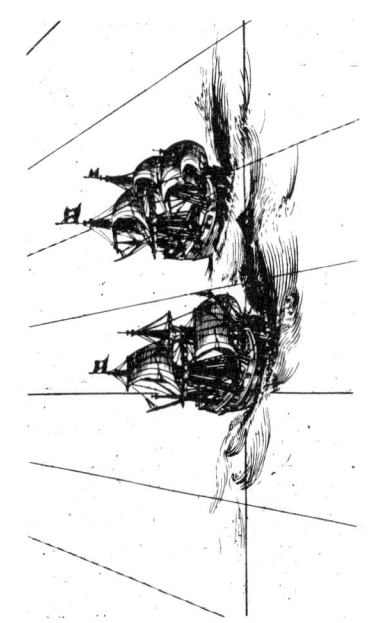

Indians

The Indians settled in North Carolina centuries before the first exploration by Europeans. Eventually they were a significant influence in the colonization of the state as well as an important factor during subsequent periods. Yet, it has always been difficult to shed light on these earliest inhabitants of the area.

The Indian occupation of America is divided into two logical periods: protohistoric and historic. Since the Indians had no written alphabet, all that is known of those who occupied the land prior to the arrival of Europeans is based upon archaeological evidence. The historic Indian, however, is known through the writings and drawings of Europeans who observed him as well as through archaeological remains, yet comparatively little archaeological research has been completed in the southeastern United States. Scattered Indian sites have been opened by untrained individuals for years and much valuable evidence has been destroyed. Few reports have been prepared from these spasmodic diggings. Joffre L. Coe in 1936 undertook the first systematic study of the Piedmont, and his report on a Keyauwee Indian site was published the following year. Before World War II forced the abandonment of the work, sites of Occaneechi and Saponi towns on the Roanoke River and of the Cheraw or Saura on the Dan River were partially excavated. It is apparent in the Piedmont that sites were occupied and abandoned and occupied again at later dates. Often artifacts from widely varying times will be found side by side. Mr. Coe has concluded that the Piedmont was occupied by Indians for at least ten thousand years before they first made any pottery.

The Outer Banks and the eastern Coastal Plain, on the other hand, appear to have been occupied for only about a thousand years before contact with Europeans.

In North Carolina, with the exception of very brief glimpses of the natives reported by Verrazano in 1524, De Soto in 1540, and Pardo in 1566-67, the historic period begins with the arrival of Walter Raleigh's explorers, Philip Amadas and Arthur Barlowe, in 1584. All of these early visitors to the region found the Indians to be friendly and generous. They appeared to welcome the visits of the strange white men who brought them gifts of paper, mirrors, small bells, and other trinkets. In due time some venturesome young Indian men, Manteo and Wanchese, consented to accompany Raleigh's men to England where they were viewed with great interest and created much support for Raleigh's undertaking. Thomas Hariot spent much time learning their language and teaching them some English. Gradually a body of information was built up by the succession of explorers and settlers who soon displaced the Indian. Initially settlers took advantage of the knowledge the Indians had accumulated through the centuries. From the natives they learned much, including a new method of agriculture; instead of clearing a field and sowing their seed broadcast as they had done in England, in America they began to cultivate in rows and hills, thereby keeping down the weeds that flourished so much more luxuriantly here. They discovered corn, squash, and some new kinds of beans as well as other useful plants. Indian names for many unfamiliar items were also added to their vocabulary: hickory, persimmon, opossum, moccasin, canoe, and hurricane, among others. The Indians' mode of warfare in which they took cover behind trees, rocks, and other natural cover was also learned and put to good advantage at a later date against the British who fought in a more conventional manner with troops advancing against an objective, side by side in good order.

Lawson recognized different dialects spoken by the Indians and on this basis he reported that there were twenty-two tribes in the colony, but he was not aware of the Cherokees in the mountains (Figure 1.1). Subsequent studies of the Indians in North Carolina have described a total of thirty-four tribes that lived there at one time or another. The earliest Indians described by the English were the Hatteras or Croatan Indians who lived along the Outer Banks in the vicinity of Cape Hatteras. The friendly young Manteo, who went to England and who was baptized on Roanoke Island in 1578 and made Lord of Roanoke at Sir Walter Raleigh's direction, was from that tribe. The Chowanoc Indians who lived primarily on the west side of the Chowan River in present Bertie and Hertford counties received some of the Roanoke explorers very kindly in the 1580s, and it was from these Indians that much important information was gleaned. In due course the Chowanoc Indians became good neighbors to the colonists. They adopted the white peoples' dress, became good farmers and dairymen, and engaged in trade.

The Tuscarora, first encountered by the English who came from Virginia in the 1650s, lived between the Neuse and Pamlico rivers and claimed a vast portion of the Coastal Plain between what is now the Virginia line and the Cape Fear River. They were probably the most numerous Indians in the region and certainly the most fierce. They engaged in war against the colonists for several years beginning in 1711 and almost succeeded in wiping out the settlement in and around New Bern. Troops from South Carolina aided in defeating them, and after a treaty in 1715, most of the Tuscaroras left for New York, the region from which they had come a number of years before. The Catawbas in the southern Piedmont,

It was only after the publication in 1709 of John Lawson's book, *A New Voyage to Carolina*, that a considerable body of information about the Indians of North Carolina became available. Lawson was concerned for the welfare of the native and thought that "every Englishman ought to do them justice, and not defraud them of their land . . . for if we do not shew them Examples of Justice and Vertue, we can never bring them to believe us to be a worthier Race of Men than themselves." Lawson described the skill with which Indians built houses, made canoes, and provided for their families. Their concern for widows and orphans and their care of the aged in their midst was commented upon. On the other hand, he noted that many were lazy and thievish; adultery and prostitution were not unknown. Indians often were cruel to prisoners of war and practiced "the most inhumane Butcheries" that they could devise.

centered in the present Mecklenburg and Union County area, were visited by Spanish explorers in the 1560s, and after the settlement of Virginia, traders made frequent visits to them to exchange English goods for skins and furs. The Catawbas were friendly to the whites and joined them on several occasions in battle against mutual enemies. The last large band of Indians to be encountered in the movement of settlers to the west were the Cherokees living in the Appalachian mountains. Like the Catawba, they had been visited by Spanish explorers in the sixteenth century and were found to be hospitable; traders from South Carolina made contact with them before the end of the next century. During the intercolonial wars in the eighteenth century the Cherokee were incited by the French against the colonists, while during the American Revolution they were suspected of being under the influence of the English. In 1838-39 the United States used the army to drive the Cherokee out of the mountains and across the Mississippi River. A few succeeded in remaining behind, however, and formed the nucleus of the present-day band of Cherokee Indians in southwestern North Carolina.

There are, of course, other Indians still residing in North Carolina, but numerous tribes have perished, victims of their own warfare and of white men's diseases—chiefly smallpox and tuberculosis. These original inhabitants, nevertheless, in assisting the early colonists, contributed a great deal to the establishment of the modern state. They also left their mark on the land in a host of names such as Waccamaw, Mattamuskeet, Perquimans, Currituck, Tuckasegee, and others now borne by rivers, lakes, mountains, and counties.

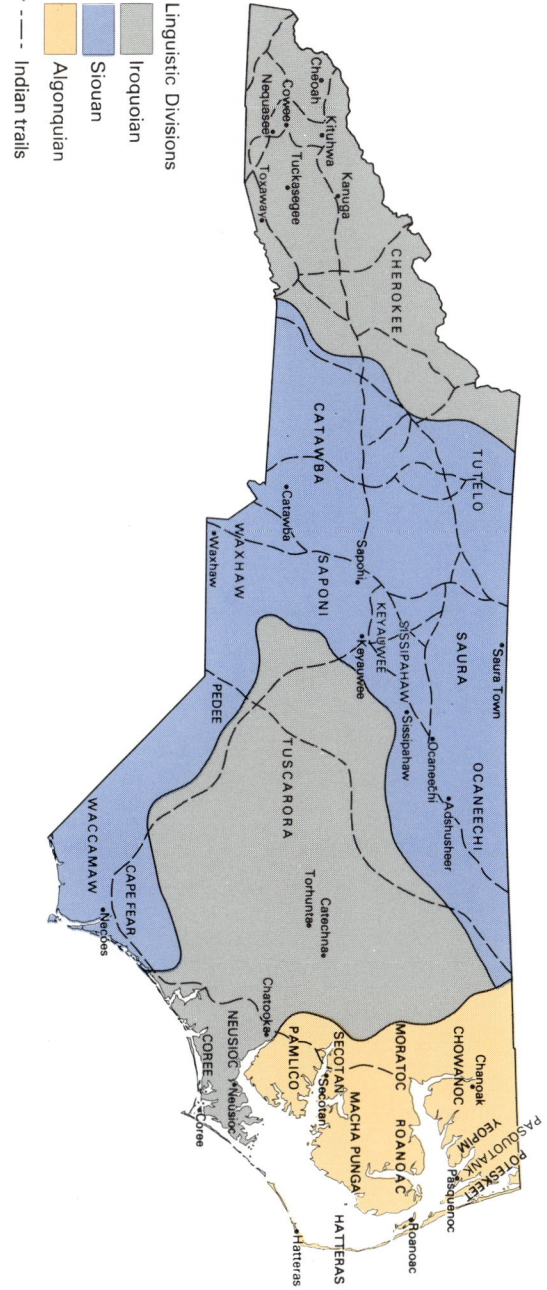

Figure 1.1. The Indians of N.C.

Linguistic Divisions
- Iroquoian
- Siouan
- Algonquian
- --- Indian trails

Note: Modified from maps in Richard E. Lonsdale, ed., *Atlas of North Carolina* (Chapel Hill: University of N.C. Press, 1967).

13

Figure 1.2. Early European Colonization in N.C.

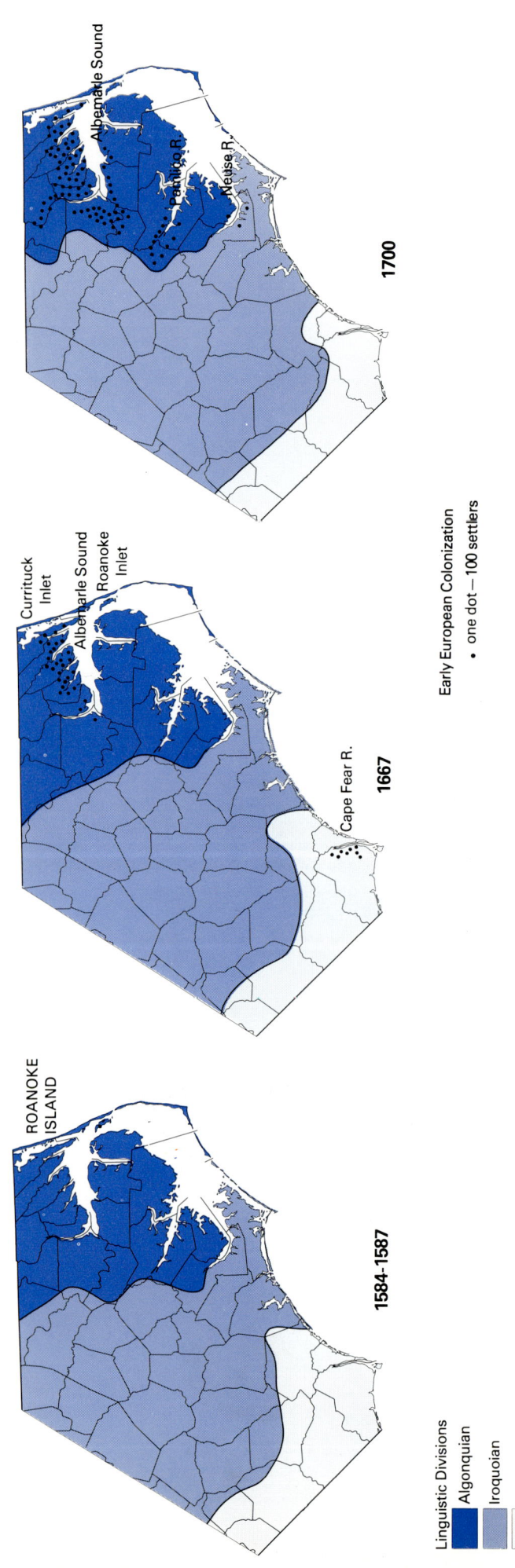

Note: Modified from maps in Richard E. Lonsdale, ed., *Atlas of North Carolina* (Chapel Hill: University of N.C. Press, 1967).

European Settlement

North Carolina has been called a state without a birthday. The date of the first permanent European settlement is unknown, but the region excited considerable interest among outsiders for perhaps more than a quarter of a century before anyone arrived to remain. From the small outpost at Jamestown, which was England's first successful American colony, John Pory set out in 1622 to explore the area along the Chowan River. He discovered vast tracts of luxuriant pines that held the promise of abundant supplies of tar, pitch, and turpentine, which might well free England from her dependence upon the Scandinavian countries for these essential naval stores. Pory also described fertile land there on which two crops could be grown in a single season; from kindly Indians he received a bit of crude copper, and they inquired about the possibility of opening trade routes with the English. In 1636 a visitor from Bermuda to the Chowan region reported that he discovered a large number of men there busily producing "sperrits of rosin." Within a dozen years Sir William Berkeley, governor of Virginia, sent a military expedition into the area to demonstrate to the Indians the strength that might be brought to bear should they attempt to resist the occupation of that region by whites. Virginians began to purchase land from the natives, and the government of the colony started to issue grants for land along the Chowan River. By 1653 the first permanent settler had arrived. At the west end of Albemarle Sound, Nathaniel Batts built a two-room house, twenty feet square, with a large chimney, and from this frontier outpost he opened a trade with the Indians. Before long he was followed by others, and the number had grown so large by 1662 that in October of that year Governor Berkeley appointed Samuel Stephens to be commander of the "Southern Plantation" and authorized him to appoint a sheriff.

Word of the promise that this region held reached London and was discussed in influential circles. Six men who had helped restore the monarchy following the civil war in England joined forces with Governor Berkeley and with Sir John Colleton of Barbados (who was familiar with the Chowan area and who, like Berkeley, had been loyal to the Crown) to secure a charter for this territory. King Charles II issued a charter to these eight Lords Proprietors of Carolina in March 1663, and he renewed it in 1665 to give them still more land. The proprietors promptly set about establishing a government, attracting settlers, and making their new possession profitable. A governor was appointed and a legislature authorized. Land grants were made, taxes levied, and trade encouraged. Yet within a few years it became apparent to the proprietors that this landlocked section of their grant was less likely to prove profitable than a new settlement with direct outlet to the sea begun in 1670 some three hundred miles down the Atlantic. From that time on, the proprietors appeared to neglect their Albemarle colony, as the northern region was called, in favor of the new settlement that eventually became South Carolina. Albemarle and subsequent settlements that developed within the future North Carolina were not tightly controlled by the proprietors, and they seemed to thrive on neglect. The expansion of North Carolina outside the bounds of the original Albemarle section occurred without any fanfare just as the movement south from Jamestown had. By 1689 settlers must have moved across the sound and down into the Pamlico River region, as the governor commissioned that year was not described as the governor of Albemarle but as the governor of the territory "north and East of Cape Feare." The County of Bath was formed in this new area in 1696, and in 1706, Bath, the first town in North Carolina, was chartered. The search for new land and choice sites along rivers and other navigable streams lured colonists south to the mouth of Neuse River by 1703. On this river, at the mouth of Trent River, in 1710, the town of New Bern was established as the focal point for a colony of Swiss, Germans, and French who settled in the midst of the earlier arrivals (Figure 1.2).

An abortive attempt was made to settle along the lower reaches of the Cape Fear River in 1664 when a colony composed of people from New England, Barbados, Virginia, and elsewhere in Carolina established Charles Town and Clarendon County. Even though it had a governor, an assembly, and a population of around eight hundred, dissension (created largely by the New Englanders) tore the colony apart and it was abandoned in 1667. Permanent settlers did not reach this region until 1724, although officials in South Carolina had issued grants for land there ten years previously. The town of Brunswick on the banks of the Cape Fear River was established in 1725, and the region was soon recognized as a most promising one for planters and merchants. Within a few years it became a flourishing center of culture, trade, and government. The town of Wilmington, established about 1733 at a more promising site a few miles upriver, soon displaced Brunswick as the center of Cape Fear life.

In 1729 the Crown purchased the proprietary rights in the colony when all but one of the original eight shares was transferred to King George II. The Carteret family, soon to acquire the title of Earl Granville, retained its interest in the land but not in the government of an eighth share of the original grant. As a royal colony North Carolina took a new direction. Instructions from London were more positive. The colony became a member of the Empire and was expected to contribute to the common cause and to share expenses proportionate to the benefits received. Royal governors were in a better position to encourage settlement, and under their steady urging the Cape Fear River valley soon filled up. Settlers began to push the line of settlement farther and farther west (Figure 1.3). North Carolina was regarded as a frontier region by all of the other colonies, and crowded conditions elsewhere produced new settlers for North Carolina. By the eve of the Revolution settlement approached the foothills of the Blue Ridge, and some hardy pioneers had pushed through the mountain gaps to open the Tennessee and Kentucky country to settlement. The Revolution temporarily halted much of the steady flow of settlers into the backcountry, but afterward it resumed again. With the signing of treaties with the Cherokee Indians in 1785, 1791, and 1798 nearly the whole mountain region was opened to white settlers. In 1784

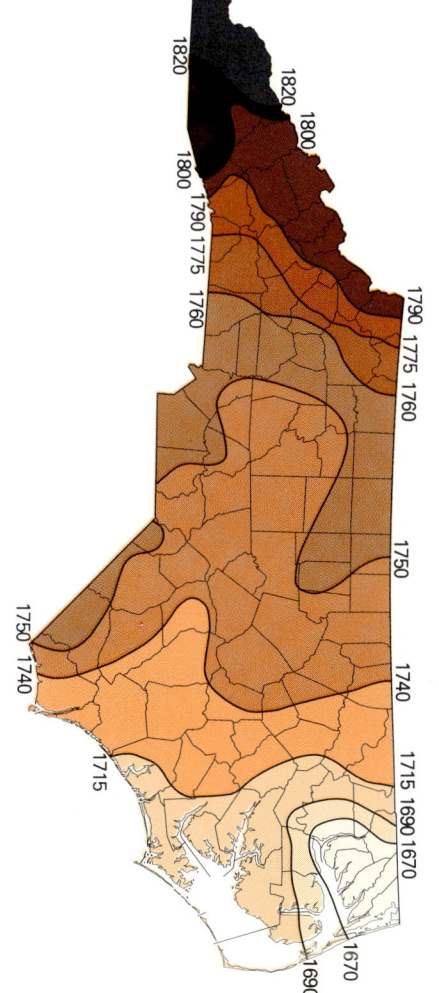

Figure 1.3. The Development of the N.C. Frontier, 1657-1835

Source: Albert Coates, ed., *Talks to Students and Teachers* (Chapel Hill: Creative Printers, 1971).

Samuel Davidson settled in the Swannanoa valley; and although he was soon murdered by Indians, he was shortly followed by others. There were so many people in the area that in 1797 Asheville was incorporated to serve as the seat of a county created not many years before and as a center of trade.

National Origins

As if to set the pattern for events to come, there were among the various explorers and colonists based at Roanoke Island between 1584 and 1590 nearly twenty-five who were not English. At least nine other nationalities were represented. The leaders in these and subsequent expeditions were English, as were the majority of people who accompanied them. So many of the earliest settlers were of English origin or descent that it was their heritage that prevailed. These people dominated most of the eastern portion of the colony and were also scattered throughout the Piedmont, where they most often lived in the county seats. The language, of course, the nature of government, and various forms of culture were English, and these characterized the major heritage of North Carolina. So natural was this and so common were Englishmen that no one took any special note of it. So all-pervasive did this culture become that others were simply swallowed up by it.

But almost nowhere were the English entirely alone. Among the new arrivals just before the beginning of the eighteenth century were many Lowland Scots who appeared in small numbers in many counties and communities. In a number of places these thrifty Scots became the most wealthy inhabitants and some of them, the Pollocks, for example, also held important positions of leadership in the government. William Drummond, the first governor of Albemarle, was a Lowland Scot from Virginia.

The earliest of the Highland Scots to arrive in the colony received grants for land on the Cape Fear River in 1732, and they were soon followed by wave after wave of their countrymen escaping the harsh climate of the Highlands and a bit later the cruel treatment of the English following the Scottish defeat at the Battle of Culloden Moor in 1746. By the beginning of the Revolution the Highlanders in North Carolina may have numbered 12,000. These people proved to be good farmers, growing various kinds of grain, peas, flax, and sweet potatoes. They also raised livestock, and many of them provided essential services for their neighbors by working as millwrights, shoemakers, weavers, carpenters, storekeepers, and at other crafts or occupations. While these Scots were filling up much of the southeastern section of the colony, other people were moving into the backcountry. Most of the newcomers there were Scotch-Irish and Germans.

Figure 1.4. Avenues of Early N.C. Settlement

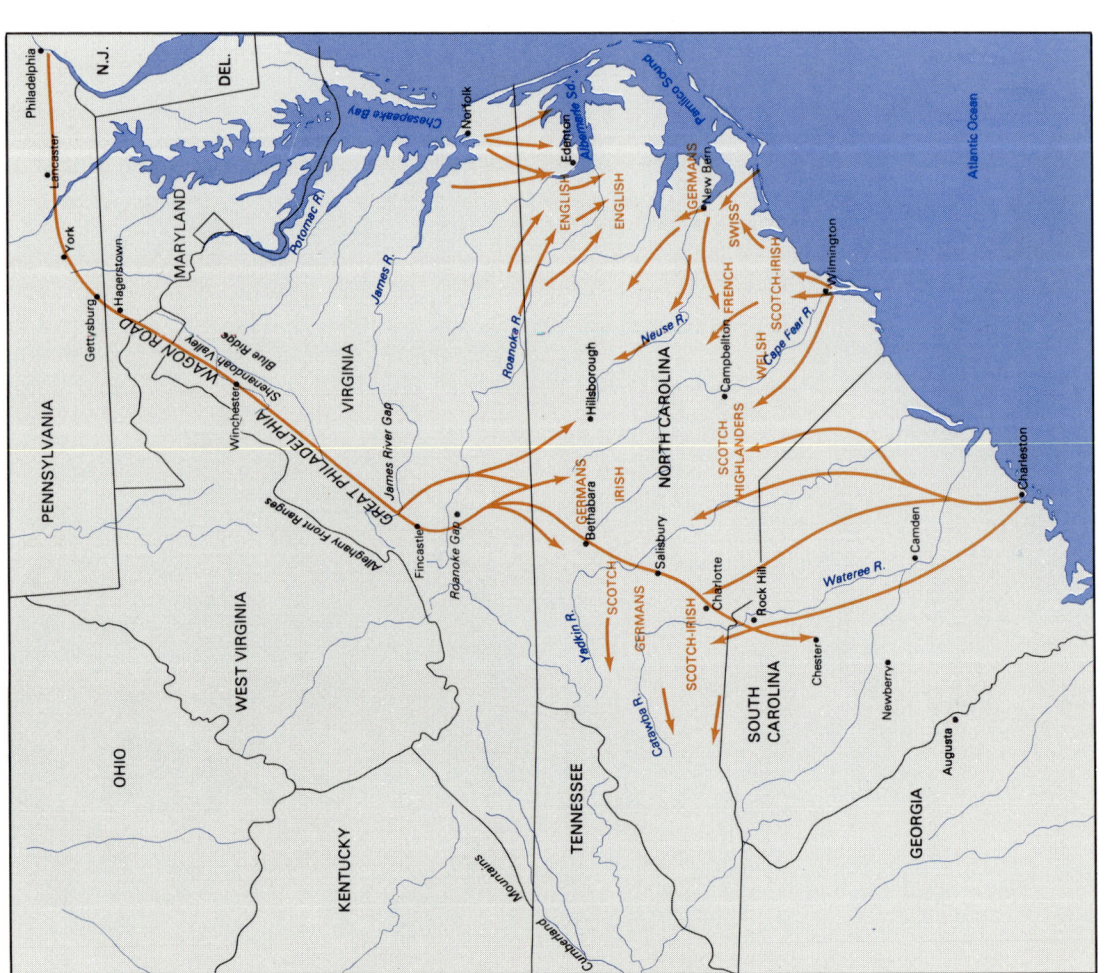

Source: Cordelia Camp, ed., *Influence of Geography upon Early North Carolina* (Raleigh: Carolina Charter Tercentenary Commission, 1963).

The former were descendants of Lowland Scots who had been moved in Northern Ireland by James I, and they were staunch Presbyterians, hard-working, conscientious people who possessed the qualifications necessary to subdue the frontier. The Germans were members of various Protestant denominations who had suffered persecution in Europe but who had also been victims of several very harsh winters and poor growing seasons. Members of both of these groups arriving in North Carolina had set out from Pennsylvania. In some cases they had recently landed there, but in others they were the children or grandchildren of immigrants. A few of the Scotch-Irish established themselves as far east as modern Duplin and Johnston counties, in Orange and Guilford counties and elsewhere, and a few Germans acquired land in the Guilford County area, but most of them settled considerably farther west—in the old Rowan and Anson counties that comprised most of the western Piedmont section. Also, a large and influential group of Moravians settled in the vicinity of present-day Winston-Salem beginning in 1753. Backcountry settlers generally followed the Great Wagon Road that ran from Philadelphia through the valley of Virginia and along the Yadkin River near Salisbury, and many of their friends and relatives stopped off at various places along the way (Figure 1.4). This influx was responsible for the creation of many new counties during the ten years following 1746.

There were Negroes in the colony certainly by 1694 when five persons claimed rights to extra land for having brought in eight Negroes. In 1709 there were 211 Negroes in Pasquotank, and the next year Currituck County had 97. By 1712 it was reported that the colony had 800.

There were several other small groups who found their way to the colony. A few French Huguenots settled around Bath before 1709, and there were a few at New Bern with the Von Graffenried colony of 1710. Between 1730 and 1734 a number of Welsh from Pennsylvania settled along the lower Cape Fear River in what is now Pender County, but they simply took up land in the midst of other settlers and except for their family names left no mark in the area (Figure 1.5).

Environmental Influences

Perhaps more than any other colony or state, North Carolina has been influenced in its pattern of settlement, its government, and its economic conditions by the physical environment. The long chain of narrow Outer Banks extending down the Atlantic coast with their shallow and shifting inlets blocked much of the mainland from ocean-going shipping. The sounds behind the banks are shallow, and the rivers emptying into them

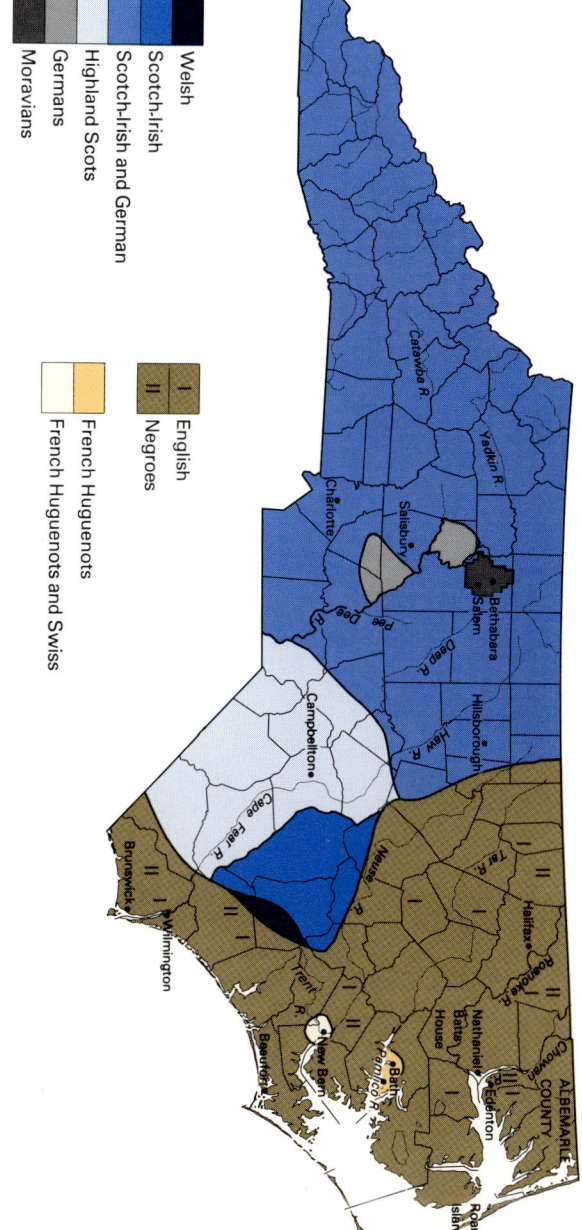

Figure 1.5. The Pioneer People of N.C.

Source: Albert Coates, ed., *Talks to Students and Teachers* (Chapel Hill: Creative Printers, 1971).

17

Figure 1.6. Transportation and Settlement in N.C., 1660-1775

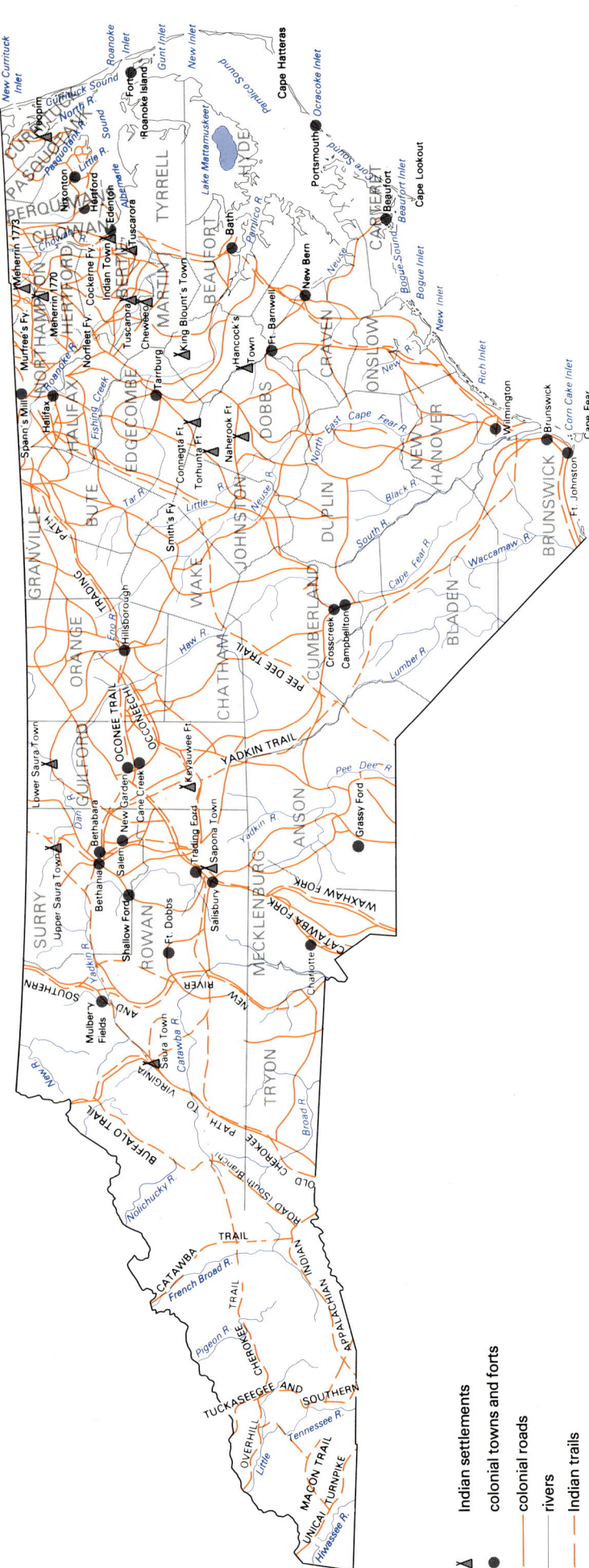

△ Indian settlements
● colonial towns and forts
— colonial roads
— rivers
--- Indian trails

Note: Modified from maps in Richard E. Lonsdale, ed., *Atlas of North Carolina* (Chapel Hill: University of N.C. Press, 1967).

deposit silt, making it necessary to clear and mark channels for shipping. Except for the Cape Fear River, none of the major rivers in the state flow directly into the Atlantic. Many of the Piedmont rivers rise in the mountains but they turn southeast to flow through South Carolina. The earliest settlers in the colony drifted south from Jamestown, Virginia, and the adjacent region. Except for the Scottish Highlanders, most of whom came direct from Europe and landed along the Cape Fear River, almost none of the colonists came direct from abroad. Those who originated in Virginia maintained contact with their old community, engaging in trade and frequently following the political trends there. Those who arrived in the backcountry from Pennsylvania, Maryland, or New Jersey by way of the Great Wagon Road often returned by the same route to sell their farm produce or livestock and to buy supplies. Others in the Piedmont found the Yadkin and Catawba rivers convenient to follow and turned their attention to South Carolina instead of to eastern North Carolina where the colony's center of population and government lay.

This pattern of settlement and economic isolation also affected the government of the colony. Provincial government developed quite naturally in the Coastal Plain with men trained in English political ideals firmly in control. When the backcountry began to fill up the easterners were reluctant to share power with men from the new section. Each county (with few exceptions) was entitled to two representatives in the assembly, but in order to retain their hold on the assembly, easterners were reluctant to create new western counties. Sheriffs, justices, and other local officials were appointed by the governor, and frequently men from the Coastal Plain were appointed to lucrative posts in frontier counties. This led to much local unrest.

Economic development in North Carolina was influenced by the physical environment in other ways than those affecting the pattern of marketing. Climate and the nature of the soil played critical roles. The loose fertile soil of the Coastal Plain tempted men to seek grants for tremendous tracts of land. The pine trees that flourished there were relatively easy to cut in clearing large fields for cultivation. Slave labor became essential to many of these planters; such labor could be used in plowing, planting, and harvesting in season and then used in the naval stores and lumber industries that flourished in the pine forests for the remainder of the year. The rivers and sounds provided means of floating goods to market on rafts or small boats to some point at which large cargoes might be assembled. The Coastal Plain, then, became the center of large-scale farming with self-sufficient plantations whose owners were little concerned with other areas of the colony so long as they offered no competition.

The red, rocky, clay soil of the Piedmont with its tough hardwoods did not tempt men to acquire more land than they could clear and cultivate themselves. Small farms developed and slave labor was relatively unimportant. Transportation to market was difficult and often involved long journeys over poor roads. The rivers, however, swift and shallow as they often were, provided a means of power that was soon adapted at gristmills throughout the area. Flour and meal were more valuable and easier to ship than loose grain, and these became important products of the Piedmont. The presence of waterpower also contributed to early attempts at industrialization in the region and to eventual success. The first cotton mill in the state and perhaps the first south of the Potomac was built near Lincolnton in 1813.

The physical environment was also responsible for a communications problem that plagued North Carolina for a great many years. The difficulty of direct contact by sea with the outside world has already been mentioned. The people of the Coastal Plain and Piedmont sections of the colony, in addition to being hampered by rivers channeling commerce elsewhere, also had the problem of crossing wide sluggish rivers and sounds in the Coastal Plain and swift Piedmont streams with rocky beds. Road and bridge building were arts little understood in the colony; men with a knowledge of engineering or skill in building were rare. Swamps and pocosins in the Coastal Plain and slick clay hills in the Piedmont delayed passage for all but the most determined couriers. Postal service was unheard-of for most of the colonial period, although several private systems intended as substitutes were tried for brief periods of time. On the eve of the Revolution a post road was opened that passed through the Coastal Plain, but even this inadequate service disappeared after a few years, and it was not until 1789 that the United States postal service offered modest relief (Figure 1.6).

Political Boundaries and Units

Of the original three counties, Albemarle, Clarendon, and Craven, only Albemarle took root in the North Carolina area, while Craven developed into South Carolina. Albemarle County, with its own governor and assembly, was divided into four precincts by 1668 and these precincts, Chowan, Currituck, Pasquotank, and Perquimans developed into the modern counties of those names. The Fundamental Constitutions, drawn up by the Lords Proprietors in 1669, provided among other things for the creation of additional units of local government. They were first called precincts but soon came to be known as counties when the original county of Albemarle gave way to the broader name—North Carolina. Bath County was created south of Albemarle Sound in 1696

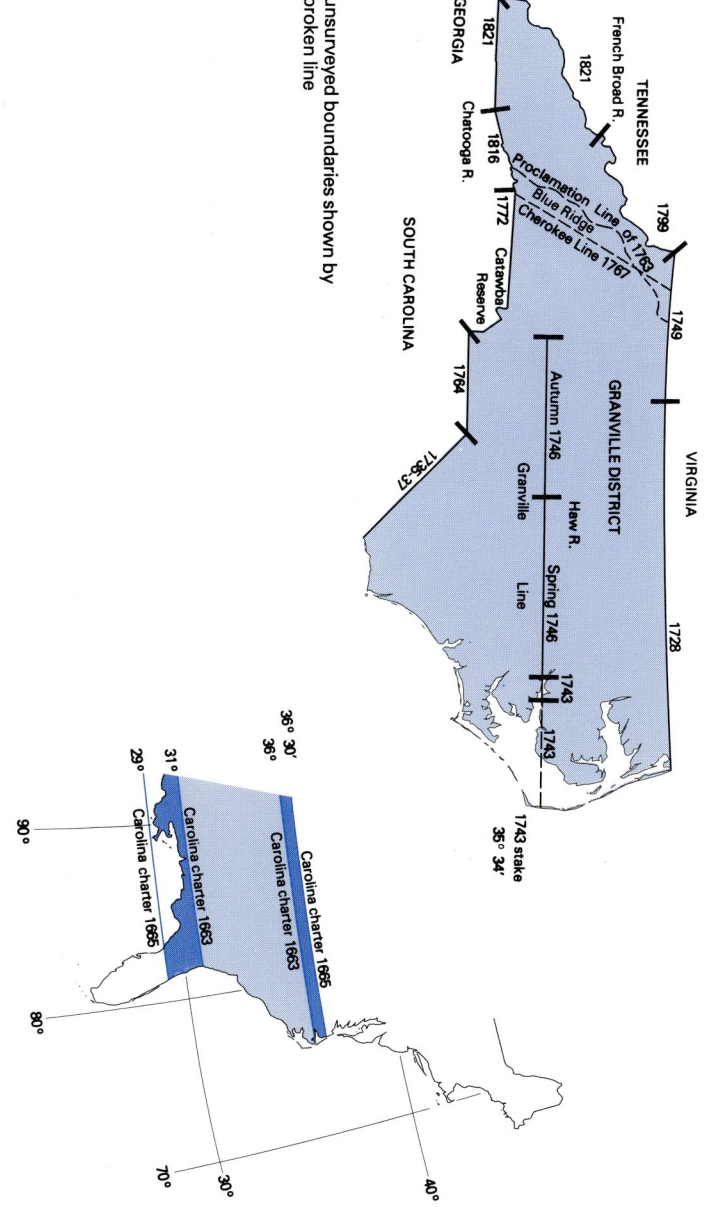

Figure 1.7. Formation of N.C. Boundaries

unsurveyed boundaries shown by broken line

and had become so populous by 1705 that it was made into three new precincts that soon came to be known as Hyde, Craven, and Beaufort counties. In 1722 Carteret County, south of the Bath region, was created, and the original Albemarle area had extended westward so that Bertie County was created there.

When settlement expanded south of Albemarle Sound the proprietors ceased to designate the chief executive of their northern colony as the governor of Albemarle; instead he was commissioned governor of "That Part of the Province of Carolina That Lies north and east of Cape feare." This designation continued in use until 1712 when Edward Hyde was commissioned governor of "North Carolina."

In 1729 Tyrrell County was created from land along the southern shore of Albemarle County and named for Sir John Tyrrell who a few years before had purchased one of the proprietary shares in Carolina. It is interesting that it was named for a proprietor in the very year that the Crown purchased Carolina. In the same year the Lower Cape Fear county of New Hanover was also created, and it was named to honor the royal family who came from Hanover. Three years later the governor and his council created three new counties, but the assembly disputed their right to do so since these new counties would then acquire seats in the legislature. The question was submitted to the Crown, and in the future the assembly participated in the creation of counties. As population increased new counties were created for the convenience of the people, but sometimes pressure had to be applied to a reluctant legislature to get it to do so.

The boundaries of the colony were of little concern for many years (Figure 1.7). The charter of 1665, of course, had set the northern boundary at 36° 30′ north latitude and the western limit as the South Sea. The boundary with Virginia was surveyed by a party under the leadership of William Byrd in 1728. As time passed and men

Note: Modified from maps in Richard E. Lonsdale, ed., *Atlas of North Carolina* (Chapel Hill: University of N.C. Press, 1967).

Figure 1.8. N.C. at the End of the Eighteenth Century

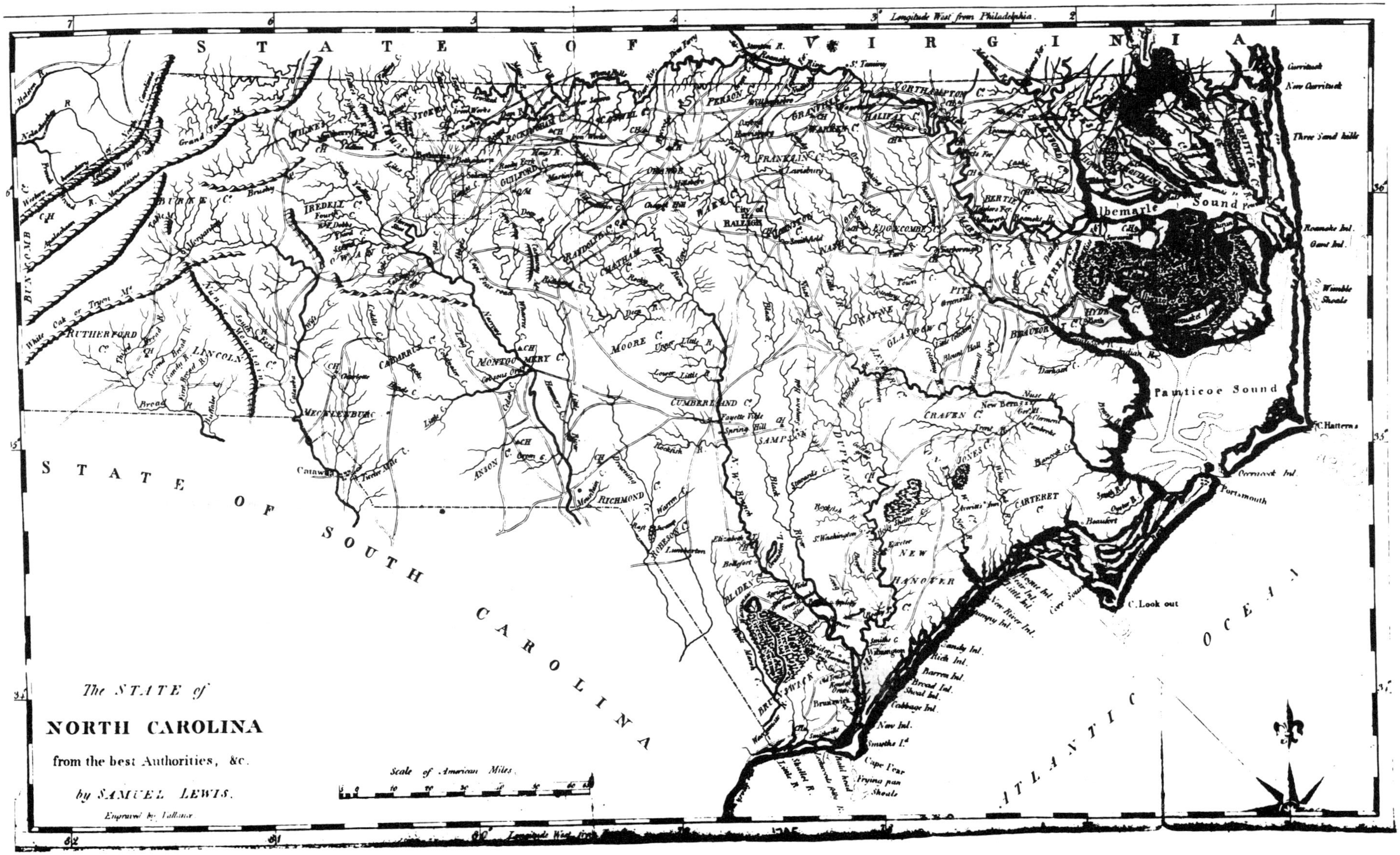

came to realize how wide a tract this was, the Mississippi River was regarded as a suitable western boundary. In a Royal Proclamation in 1763 King George III decreed that no whites should settle beyond the crest of the Blue Ridge, but this was only temporary and negotiations with the Cherokees subsequently pushed the limit of white settlement farther west. By mutual understanding with South Carolina the line between the two Carolinas should be not closer than thirty miles to the mouth of the Cape Fear, but many years passed before an agreement could be reached to survey the line.

With the cessions of the western territory to the United States in December 1789, the boundaries of North Carolina assumed their present form, although final surveys were not completed until 1799 and 1821. Tennessee was created from the ceded western region and admitted to the Union in 1796.

Political Development

The form of government that developed in North Carolina was modeled on the one that people had come to know in Virginia. A governor and council, generally appointed by the proprietors (later the Crown), composed the resident executive authority, and they represented power centered in London. An assembly composed of elected representatives spoke most often for the mass of people. The president of the council stood to succeed the governor in an emergency; the speaker of the assembly was the highest officer of government in whose election the people had any voice. Higher courts also functioned, composed at first of the governor and council, but as population spread a general court composed of appointed justices began to operate. For a brief time this form of government was permitted, indeed encouraged, but in 1669 the proprietors promulgated the Fundamental Constitutions, which they drew up to establish a feudal society consonant with the great powers accorded them by their grant from King Charles II. Orders of nobility were described, and a few men were created caciques and landgraves. Landowners with perpetual right to a seat in the local Parliament, a class of freemen with limited rights, leetmen bound to the land, and slaves were envisaged in the scheme of society. A proprietary court meeting in London would pass upon legislation adopted in the colony. A grand council in the colony would advise the proprietary governor.

The proprietors adopted these and other provisions, they said, in order to prevent the erection of a "numerous democracy" in Carolina, but they waited too long. The taste of freedom that people had enjoyed in the peaceful and fertile land bordering Albemarle Sound since their first arrival in the 1650s was too sweet to abandon in 1669. A few of the provisions of the Fundamental Constitutions were tried but found to be entirely unworkable, and before the end of the century, after having altered the document a number of times, the proprietors dropped all pretense of abiding by them. A simple government with executive, legislative, and judicial offices plus necessary administrative aides and financial officers provided all the leadership and direction that was required.

At the local or county level the sheriff was the primary officer. County courts composed of around six justices appointed by the assembly served many functions in the counties. They tried minor cases, saw to the registration of land titles, ordered the settlement of estates, recorded livestock marks, directed the laying out and maintenance of roads, bridges, and ferries, saw that orphans and poor widows were cared for, and in other ways supervised public affairs.

Two political factions arose quite early in the colony. One was composed of the governor and council and their friends—people who owed their positions to or otherwise supported the proprietors or the Crown. This was called the proprietary or the prerogative group. Opposing it was the popular party composed of those who protested the sometimes arbitrary acts of the governor and his advisers. The prerogative faction

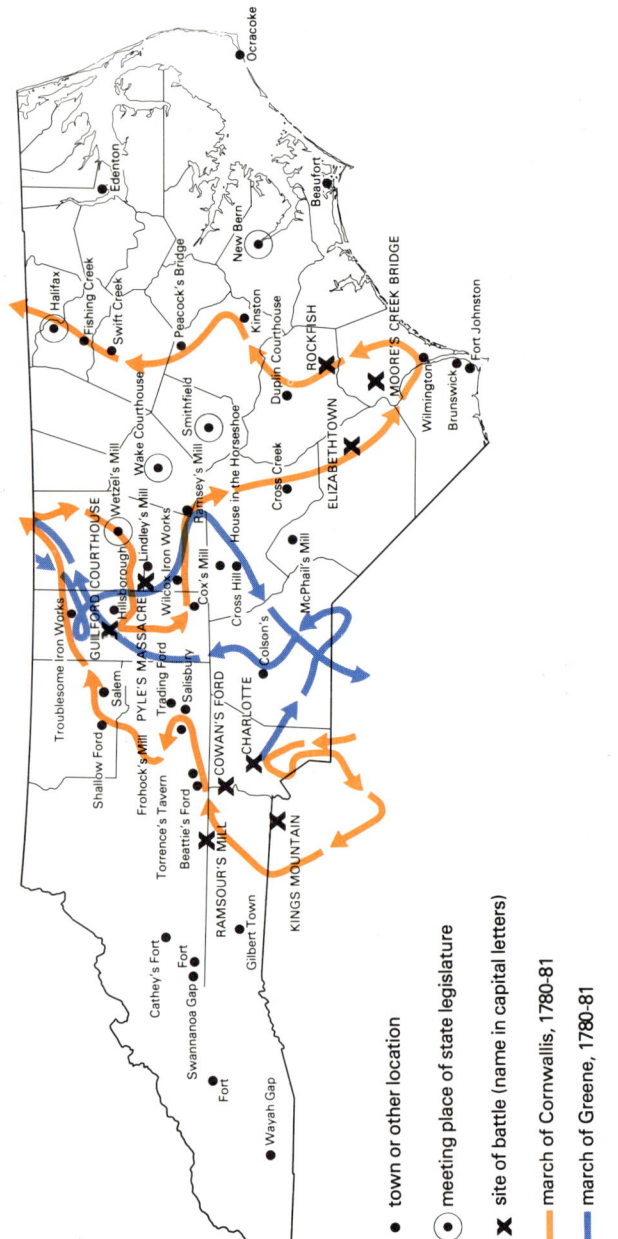

Figure 1.9. The Revolutionary War in N.C.

- town or other location
- ⊙ meeting place of state legislature
- ✗ site of battle (name in capital letters)
- ━━ march of Cornwallis, 1780-81
- ━━ march of Greene, 1780-81

Note: Modified from maps in Richard E. Lonsdale, ed., *Atlas of North Carolina* (Chapel Hill: University of N.C. Press, 1967).

thought that government should be just as independent of the people as possible, while the popular faction thought that the will of the majority should predominate and that it found expression in the assembly. The clash of interests brought about by these differences resulted in several rebellions in North Carolina during the colonial period. Culpeper's Rebellion (1677-79) has been called the first popular uprising in any of the American colonies. It occurred because of the arbitrary actions of a governor who ran roughshod over the people. His zeal in enforcing trade regulations implemented in London oppressed the people in many ways and also denied them a free market for their tobacco, so they drove him out of office and established their own government. Nearly a century later backcountry residents who were oppressed by governor-appointed local officeholders banded together as Regulators. Determined to seek relief from unfair taxes, excessive fees, and oppressive treatment at the hands of local officials sent from outside, they sought legal redress of their grievances; when that failed they resorted to arms. But they were defeated at the Battle of Alamance in 1771 by the royal governor and his well-trained militia. The American Revolution intervened and many of the Regulators laid aside their complaints for the moment and joined their former oppressors in securing independence from Great Britain. Afterward they renewed their struggle for justice in the west and finally attained victory in the constitutional Convention of 1835.

The American Revolution

Most North Carolinians came reluctantly to support the American Revolution. Many were quietly Tory or Loyalist in sympathy and many more were actively so. Men trained in English law and government merely wanted their rights as Englishmen recognized. These rights had been guaranteed to them by the charter of 1663 and by subsequent documents, and they petitioned King George III to intervene with Parliament on their behalf to have restored to them the right to levy their own taxes and not to pay taxes improperly required by Parliament. It was the Stamp Act of 1765 that began to unite the people, and in North Carolina resistance was so successful that Governor William Tryon was never able to secure any stamped paper even though ships bearing it were anchored in the Cape Fear River. By the time hostilities began in Massachusetts in the spring of 1775, a change had been worked in the minds of most of the people. So long as the king protected them, they reasoned, they owed him allegiance, but when he ceased to protect them, their obligation ended. The king had already declared the colonies to be in rebellion, and he was recruiting forces at home and abroad to subdue them. Patriots in New Bern kept royal governor Josiah Martin under such close surveillance in his palace there that he fled in the early summer of 1775 and took refuge aboard a British warship in the Cape Fear. For a time the government was in the hands of the Provincial Congress, which held sessions in New Bern, Halifax, and Hillsborough. Loyalists in the province, largely Highland Scots of the upper Cape Fear valley, expected to join British forces due to arrive in Wilmington early in 1776. Marching to this rendezvous, they encountered well-organized Patriot militiamen on 27 February at Moore's Creek Bridge, north of Wilmington, where the Loyalists were decisively defeated. When the British later reached North Carolina, they learned of the Loyalists' defeat and abandoned their plans to attack. This battle forestalled any serious action in North Carolina for several years and prevented the British from capturing the southern states at the very beginning of hostilities.

A Provincial Congress in session at Halifax on 12 April 1776 adopted a resolution instructing the delegates from North Carolina in the Continental Congress "to concur with the delegates of the other colonies in declaring independency." This was the first formal sanction of American independence adopted by any colony.

North Carolina was free from invasion for four years, but her troops served with distinction in a number of battles elsewhere. Many were with Washington during the terrible winter at Valley Forge. There were partisan bands continually on the move in the state, attacking foraging parties from British posts in South Carolina. Militia companies were used to keep Tories within the state from providing information or assistance to the enemy. A North Carolinian, Major General Robert Howe, the state's highest ranking officer, commanded the Southern Department in 1776-78.

Having met with little success in the North, the British decided to transfer their major action to the South in the summer of 1780. To meet this threat, the American general, Horatio Gates, assumed command of the Southern Department in Hillsborough on 25 July. With troops from North Carolina and elsewhere, units under his command fought at the Battle of Camden in South Carolina. Many of them took part in the significant victory at Kings Mountain, just three miles south of the North Carolina state line. In the face of an expected invasion of

North Carolina by the British under General Cornwallis, Washington sent one of his most able generals, Nathanael Greene, to replace Gates. Greene assumed command in Charlotte on 2 December 1780, and planned his strategy carefully. With the British only about twenty-five miles behind him, Greene began a masterful retreat across North Carolina during which he was followed by the enemy (Figure 1.9). In the middle of winter, Greene and his men suffered greatly, but they took advantage of muddy roads and swollen streams to escape the British and to lure them away from their base of supplies in South Carolina. The British, in an attempt to gain on the Americans, discarded much of their equipment and supplies. Greene and his men crossed North Carolina into Virginia where they rested briefly before returning to Guilford Courthouse. There, at a site of their own choosing, they engaged in battle with the British on 15 March 1781. Although Cornwallis held the field, his losses were so serious that he was greatly weakened. Greene left Guilford Courthouse and moved into South Carolina to drive the enemy out of a number of strong points there. The British moved east to Wilmington and from there north to Virginia where they surrendered at Yorktown on 19 October 1781. The war was over, and the last British troops left Wilmington on 18 November.

Between the Wars

When the Revolution ended, it was said that the people of North Carolina were in poverty, society was in disorder, and morals and manners were almost prostrate. The people rejected the federal Constitution in 1788 because they feared a strong central government. Their individualism and devotion to democracy made them fear a document that had no bill of rights. Following a campaign of education and with the knowledge that a bill of rights was being considered, the Constitution was approved the next year. North Carolina was a state of small farmers, and her leaders joined them in the belief that the best government was the one that governed least. That such a government should protect life and property was all they desired. Two forward-looking steps, almost unique in this period, were taken, however. The University of North Carolina was chartered in 1789, and in 1792 land was purchased in Wake County for a new state capital. But for the most part the period before 1835 was extremely bleak. Most of the state was undeveloped and backward, most people were indifferent to its condition, and outsiders came to regard North Carolina as the "Rip Van Winkle state."

There was little manufacturing in the state, but there were numerous home industries, many gristmills, a few establishments making hats and guns and a few other products, and some whiskey and turpentine distilleries.

The promise that the swift streams of the Piedmont held for industrialization was not realized for many years. Agriculture was the primary occupation of the people, yet few of them were aware of recent improvements in this field. They knew little or nothing of conservation or of fertilizers; they worked a field until it was exhausted and then cleared new land. There were few schools in the state, very limited banking facilities, inadequate means of transportation, and few publishers of newspapers or books. Control of the government was still centered in the Coastal Plain.

Such distressing political, social, and economic conditions were responsible for the departure of thousands of people from the state. From fourth place in population among the states in 1790, North Carolina dropped to fifth in 1820 and to twelfth in 1860. Richer soil and better transportation facilities lured many people away; some moved to escape the evils of slavery, while others took their slaves and moved to states in the Deep South. Many of those who left North Carolina became leaders elsewhere. For example, three—Jackson, Polk, and Johnson—became presidents of the United States. Three others were cabinet members, two were speakers of the House of Representatives, seven became governors of other states, and others were leaders in such diverse fields as the church, education, agriculture, and creative writing.

A few forward-looking men followed the lead of Archibald D. Murphey in pointing out essential changes to be made if the state were to throw off the bad reputation it had acquired. These men drew up plans for new and improved transportation facilities, the stimulation of manufacturing, the promotion of education, and the development of the vast human and natural resources that were at hand. The most urgent step in the direction of reform involved amending the constitution that had placed control of the state in the hands of the wealthy and conservative easterners. Western agitation for a constitutional convention succeeded in 1835 because Craven County joined the west in seeking a change in the religious qualification for officeholding. People there wanted a favorite son, William Gaston, a Roman Catholic, to be "eligible" to hold the office to which he had recently been elected. Cumberland County also joined the west as an expression of appreciation for western support when efforts were made to remove the capital to that county after the capitol burned in Raleigh in 1831. Only with the vote of representatives from these two eastern counties was it possible for the convention bill to pass.

Figure 1.10. Internal Improvements in N.C., 1776-1860

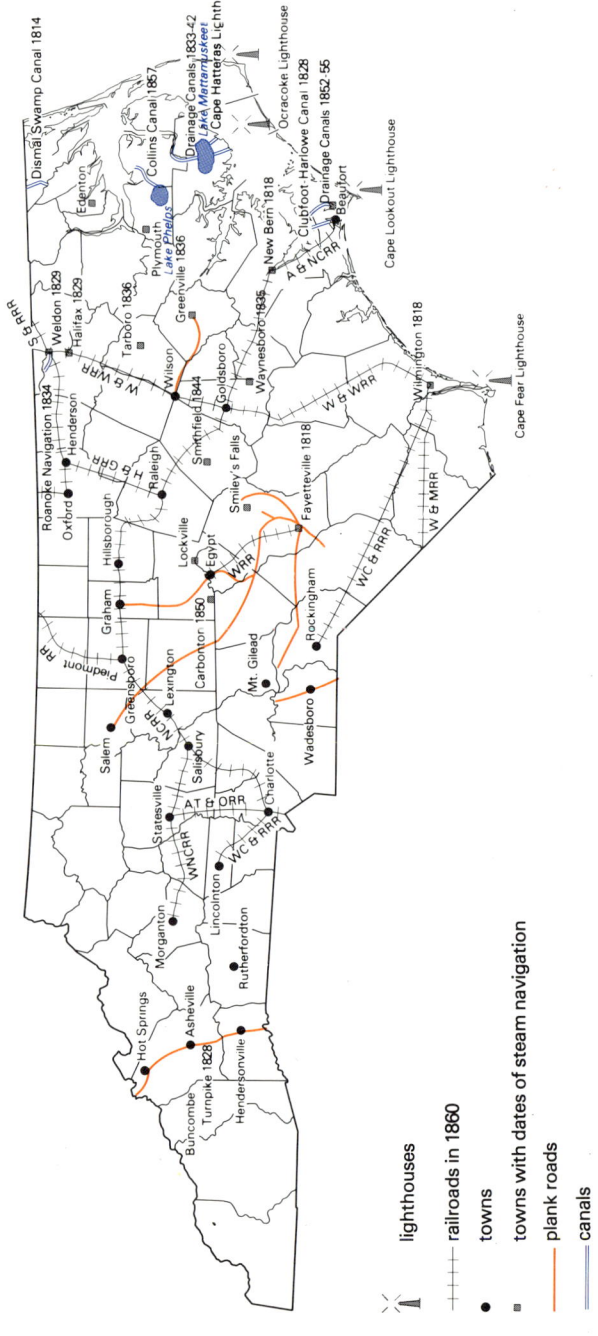

Source: Albert Coates, ed., *Talks to Students and Teachers* (Chapel Hill: Creative Printers, 1971).

The Convention of 1835 produced a more democratic government under which the political power of the people might be exercised. During the succeeding twenty-five years enormous changes were instituted. A splendid new capitol was erected in Raleigh; financial aid was provided for the building of a statewide system of railroads and plank roads (Figure 1.10); support was made available to local communities for the establishment and operation of schools; institutions for the care of the blind, deaf, and insane were opened, the tax system was reformed, and the criminal law liberalized. The university flourished and many new colleges and academies were opened. There was a great increase in the number and circulation of newspapers, and North Carolina authors began publishing books. Agricultural conditions improved, factories opened, and trade increased. In much of this development the state government played a leading role.

The Civil War

Union sympathizers in North Carolina tried in vain to avert the inevitable confrontation that took the state out of the Union. Many people felt a strong attachment for the United States, but the course of events beyond their control was such that they had no reasonable choice but to join their Southern neighbors in resisting Northern aggression. Even so, North Carolina was next to the last to secede, and it took this step only because of outside events. Zebulon Vance wrote that he was "pleading for the Union with hand upraised when news came of Fort Sumter and Lincoln's call for troops. When my hand came down from that impassioned gesticulation, it fell slowly and sadly by the side of a Secessionist." Delegates to a convention that met in Raleigh on 20 May 1861 adopted a secession ordinance. Troops were recruited and trained, and the best efforts of the state were put forward to equip them.

Figure 1.11. The Civil War in N.C.

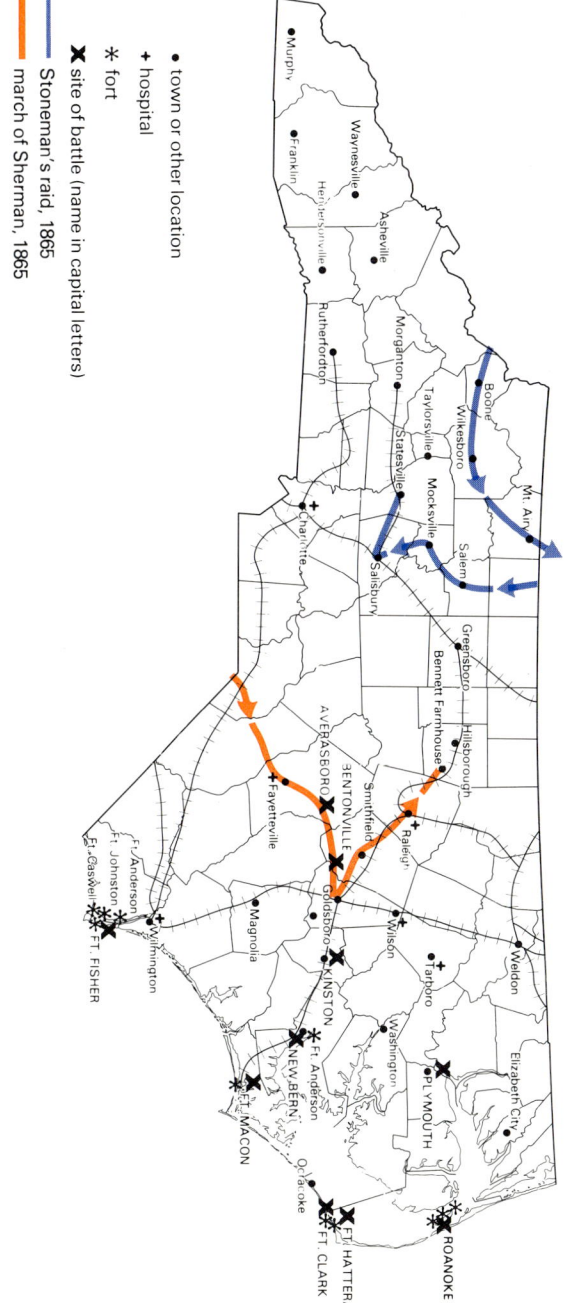

- town or other location
- + hospital
- * fort
- ✕ site of battle (name in capital letters)
- ━━ Stoneman's raid, 1865
- ━━ march of Sherman, 1865

Note: Modified from maps in Richard E. Lonsdale, ed., *Atlas of North Carolina* (Chapel Hill: University of N.C. Press, 1967).

Following two days of heavy naval bombardment, Fort Hatteras and Fort Clark on the Outer Banks fell to federal forces on 29 August 1861, giving them control of Hatteras Inlet. Much bitter fighting occurred in eastern North Carolina during 1862, and the enemy succeeded in capturing Roanoke Island on 8 February, New Bern on 14 March, Washington on 21 March, Fort Macon on 26 April, and Plymouth on 13 December (Figure 1.11). Lincoln appointed Edward Stanly as governor of the conquered portion of North Carolina with offices in New Bern, but by January 1863, Stanly had become so disgusted with the conduct of federal troops in the area that he resigned. Attempts to establish a "loyal government" in the occupied territory failed.

Confederate General D. H. Hill, a native of the state, directed operations against New Bern and Washington in March and April 1863. Although neither town was retaken, many small engagements took place at various points in the eastern section of the state. During the year troops from North Carolina were also operating elsewhere. Many fought bravely at Chancellorsville, while at Gettysburg they reached "the pinnacle of military greatness."

Another unsuccessful attempt was made to take New Bern from the enemy early in 1864. Attention was next turned to Plymouth on the Roanoke River, and both land and naval forces were engaged. The ironclad ram *Albemarle* that had been built up the river was moved down, although still under construction, to take part in the attack. On 24 April the town was freed by General Robert F. Hoke, and federal troops were also forced to evacuate nearby Washington, which they burned before retreating. Hoke turned toward New Bern but was recalled to Virginia before reaching his destination. He was needed by General Lee for service there against Grant.

Fort Fisher at the mouth of the Cape Fear River fell in mid-January 1865. This fort had protected the entrance to the river and made it possible for blockade runners to bring in supplies badly needed by the Confederacy. Wilmington fell very soon afterward.

Meanwhile Sherman was moving toward North Carolina from the south, and in March he entered and occupied Fayetteville. Having cut himself off from his base of supplies at Savannah, Sherman was now living off the land. Foraging parties from his army became roving bands of robbers, and they were responsible for widespread destruction along their route of march. General William J. Hardee delayed Sherman briefly in an encounter at Averasboro on 16 March. In the action taking place 19-21 March, Sherman defeated General Joseph E. Johnston at Bentonville in the largest battle ever fought in North Carolina. Sherman turned to Goldsboro and from there he marched to Raleigh, which had been evacuated by Confederate troops and was surrendered peacefully on 13 April.

During March and April, General George Stoneman of the federal army engaged in a "raid" through western North Carolina, attacking Boone, Wilkesboro, Mount Airy, Salem, Mocksville, Salisbury, Statesville, and other towns and communities. Federal prisoners in the Confederate prison at Salisbury were removed before Stoneman rode into town.

With the surrender of General Lee to General Grant in Virginia, the Confederacy was defeated. In North Carolina on 26 April 1865, at Bennett farmhouse near present-day Durham, General Johnston surrendered to

Sherman. Fighting continued for two more weeks in the western part of the state, and it was not until 6 May that General J. G. Martin surrendered the last of the Confederate forces in North Carolina near Waynesville.

The war destroyed much of the state's wealth, took the lives of more than 40,000 men, left a heritage of defeat, and blighted almost every phase of the state's life. Railroads, factories, public buildings, bridges, roads, schools, homes, and barns were destroyed or badly in need of repair. The abolition of slavery wiped out a capital investment of over $200 million. Confederate bonds and currency were worthless and state bonds suspect. Returning soldiers were penniless, often hungry and with little more than the clothes on their backs. With hardly more than their land, labor, and memory of defeat, these soldiers and their families bravely set to work to make a living from the soil and to rebuild their fortunes and the state.

President Andrew Johnson wanted the Confederate states to return to the union rapidly, but his moderate plans were discarded by Congress in favor of military reconstruction. The South was divided into five military districts with military forces in charge. After adopting a new constitution and ratifying the Fourteenth Amendment to the federal Constitution, North Carolina was readmitted to the union on 20 July 1868, but political reconstruction continued for a number of years. Federal troops were finally withdrawn from the South in 1877. The bitter taste of defeat in war, the unpleasant experience of military occupation, and many unhappy political actions directed by "outsiders," produced an attitude on the part of North Carolinians that was long in dying. Only those who shared the same fate could understand it.

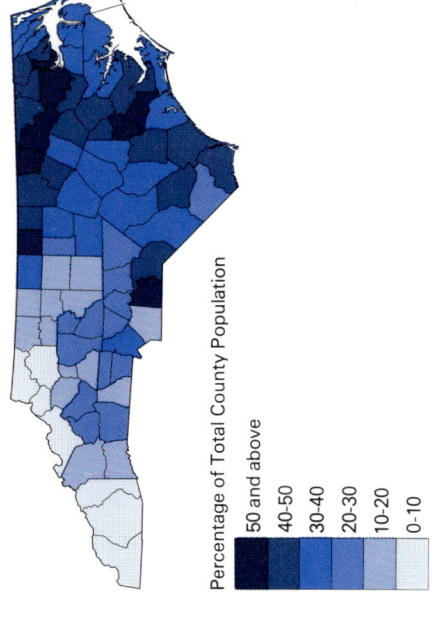

Figure 1.12. N.C. Slave Population, 1850

Percentage of Total County Population
- 50 and above
- 40-50
- 30-40
- 20-30
- 10-20
- 0-10

Note: Modified from maps in Richard E. Lonsdale, ed., *Atlas of North Carolina* (Chapel Hill: University of N.C. Press, 1967).

Note: Total number of slaves — 288,548 (33% of N.C. population).

Slavery and the Plight of the Black Man

The earliest instrument of government drawn up by the Lords Proprietors, the Concessions and Agreement of 1665, mentioned both servants and slaves and provided that land might be granted to a master for every slave he had. Several versions of the Fundamental Constitutions adopted between 1669 and 1682 gave every freeman of Carolina "absolute authority over his Negro slaves." In the latter year, however, the right of slaves to "be of what church and profession any of them shall think best, and thereof be as full members as any freemen" was guaranteed. Nevertheless no slave was thereby exempted from the civil dominion of his master and he was to be "in all other things in the same state and condition he was in before."

The earliest reference to Negroes in the colony occurs in 1694 when five persons claimed rights to extra land for having brought in eight Negroes. The lack of suitable ports prevented the direct importation of Negro slaves from Africa; they had to be bought in Virginia or South Carolina and higher prices frequently had to be paid than if they had been bought direct from a New England slave trader. In 1709 there were 211 Negroes in Pasquotank County and next year there were ninety-seven in Currituck. In 1712 there were eight hundred in the whole colony, and within five years the number had grown to more than a thousand. Slavery was strongest in the eastern counties and by 1767 in some counties Negroes outnumbered whites. There were also free Negroes in the colony as early as 1701 when several of them were permitted to vote in an election, but a law of 1715 denied them this right and also prohibited them from intermarrying with whites.

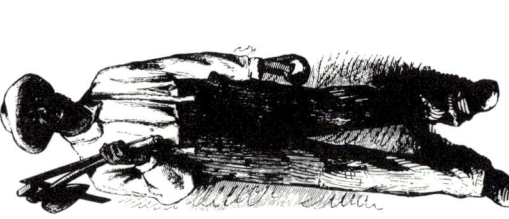

Slaveholding was never as widespread in North Carolina as in other states. Of the eleven Confederate states North Carolina ranked eighth in the ratio of slaves to whites. In 1860 only 28 percent of the families owned slaves, and 67 percent of these held fewer than ten. Those who owned few slaves worked in the fields with them, but in the case of planters an overseer might direct the laborers in the field or one of the slaves might serve as a foreman or driver. It was expected that for each slave the owner might cultivate between fifteen and twenty acres, although one progressive farmer in 1854 recommended six hands to work each fifty acres. The busiest season was from April to August, but tasks were usually found for slaves throughout most of the year. Some were used in producing naval stores, in cutting timber, or in operating gristmills during the off-season. Other slaves were trained as blacksmiths, coopers, bricklayers, or in other crafts (Figure 1.12).

The workday in season began at daybreak and sometimes continued until "first dark." On some plantations, however, the task system was used and when an assigned task was completed the slave was at liberty for the remainder of the day—often several hours. Overtime work was frequently rewarded with money, extra holidays, or a special issue of molasses, tobacco, or a barbecue. Most planters agreed that a system of rewards worked better in disciplining slaves than harsh punishments. Brightly colored head cloths for women and chewing tobacco for men were popular forms of rewards. One planter won the affection of his slaves by placing mirrors in each of their quarters. Another provided an enclosed ground for the burial of their dead and joined in mourning the death of a slave. Serious crimes and breaches of discipline, however, were subject to severe punishment. Branding or other marking was used in the eighteenth century but the practice declined by the early nineteenth. Leg irons were used, as was lashing. Dr. John Brickell, writing in the 1730s, reported that he had seen Negroes whipped until large pieces of skin hung down their back but had never seen one so treated shed a tear.

By the end of the eighteenth century the master's complete control over his slave was considerably restricted. In 1791 an act of the General Assembly made the malicious killing of a slave subject to the same punishment as the killing of a freeman. This act was expanded in 1817 to protect slaves still further and to place them "within the peace of the State."

Slave conspiracies, threatened and real, terrified many sections of the state for a number of years. In many counties slaves were suspected of plotting against their masters and they were tried in local courts. Sometimes no evidence was found to sustain the charges, but in other cases convictions resulted in punishments ranging from whipping to hanging. Such fears reached a climax in 1831 with the Nat Turner insurrection in Virginia and thereafter diligence on the part of slaveowners assured that no such uprising would occur in North Carolina. A system of patrollers was operated in most counties to insure that only slaves authorized to do so appeared off their owner's plantation.

The price a master paid for a slave varied, of course, from time to time and was often affected by the age or sex of the slave. Prices ranged from very modest sums to a thousand or more dollars. Slaves represented a heavy investment and they were housed, fed, and cared for at considerable expense. Medical care was provided and in old age they were humanely maintained. Many slaves were permitted plots of ground for their own use and they frequently produced vegetables or eggs which they sold in the neighborhood. Sometimes they accumulated enough money to buy their freedom.

Many planters recognized both the social and the financial drawbacks to slavery, but they were saddled with this source of labor and had no ready substitute. Nevertheless, hundreds of planters freed their slaves in their wills. Slaves often were freed as a reward for some particularly outstanding service such as saving a man from drowning or rescuing someone from a burning house. Children took the status of their mother and those born to free women were free. By these means and others there were 30,463 free Negroes in North Carolina in 1860, comprising just over 3 percent of the total population. In that year there were 311,059 slaves who represented 33.3 percent of the total population.

Recovery and Progress

A new state constitution was adopted in 1868 as one of the conditions under which North Carolina was readmitted to the Union. Many of its provisions were modern, progressive, liberal, and democratic; it eliminated all property qualifications for voting and officeholding and provided for the popular election of state and county officials. A Board of Charities and Public Welfare was created and "a general and uniform system of Public Schools" required. But Reconstruction was not at an end, and a few native whites joined carpetbaggers and Negroes in control of the state during an "orgy of extravagance and corruption." Violence and crime were rampant. Political activity by the Freedman's Bureau and the Union League and the presence of federal troops disrupted the return to stability. Secret societies flourished among the Republicans who controlled government at all levels as well as among the dissatisfied whites. The Ku Klux Klan became the most effective weapon of the Conservatives (Democrats). Misrule by Republicans, a growing state debt, outbreaks of violence and threats came to a head in 1870 and 1871 with the impeachment of Governor W. W. Holden. The Conservatives gained control of state government with the exception of the governor's office, and in 1875 thirty amendments were added to the constitution that, among other things, declared secret political societies illegal, prohibited marriages between whites and Negroes, provided separate schools for the races, raised residence requirements for voting, and authorized the legislature to appoint justices of the peace. Control of county government was placed in the hands of the legislature, insuring white and Democratic control.

Agriculture continued to be the primary source of income for most North Carolinians after the war as it had before. The wartime destruction of property, poor growing seasons in 1865 and 1866, and the changes in the system of labor were handicaps that were soon overcome. By 1870 the production of cotton and oats had reached prewar levels, and tobacco, potatoes, corn, hogs, milk cows, and beef cattle soon followed. Some attempts were made to bring in farm laborers from Europe, but this was not generally successful. Large plantations were broken up into small farms and a system of tenancy developed, both white and Negro. Between 1860 and 1900 the average acreage per farm decreased from 316 to 101, and North Carolina soon became a state of small farms.

Declining prices for farm products, high freight rates, and the scarcity of money worked to the disadvantage of farmers. Banks were reluctant to lend money with either farm land or projected crops as security, and many farmers were forced to turn to merchants for supplies purchased on credit at 20 to 50 percent higher prices than those charged for cash. Farmers came to realize that they were being exploited, and they demanded the regulation of railroads, corporations, and trusts, a lowering of the tariff, and a fairer land tax. Various organizations such as the Patrons of Husbandry or the Grange, and the Farmers' Alliance were formed to help improve the farmers' lot. Educational programs were conducted, cooperative purchasing was tried, and finally demands were made of political leaders in the Democratic party that relief be provided.

In the meantime, while the farmers were struggling against such great odds, an important change was taking place elsewhere in the state. A spirit of optimism prevailed among some forward-looking citizens who realized that North Carolina produced much of the raw material needed for successful manufacturing enterprises, that a source of abundant, reliable labor was at hand among those who had been forced off the farm by the upheaval of the war, and that the streams of the state could supply adequate power. By 1870 there were thirty-three cotton mills in operation whose output exceeded the value of the state's mills in 1860. At the same time, tobacco manufacturing was rapidly approaching the prewar level, while within the decade both cotton and tobacco surpassed all previous records. After 1880 rapid industrialization took place largely through local initiative, with local management. The Dukes incorporated the American Tobacco Company in 1890, and in 1888 the first furniture factory in the state was opened in High Point, although a factory established earlier in Mebane for another purpose later converted to the making of furniture. Shortly after the turn of the century there were more than a hundred such factories in nearly thirty-five different towns. In 1898 the state's first hydroelectric plant was installed on the Yadkin River and Salem became the first town in which electricity was used in homes. Most of these new industries were marked by low wages, child labor, night work, long hours, and in some cases they were responsible for the growth of mill villages and the dependence of many people on the company store where credit was extended against future wages. The owners of mills and the managers opposed labor organization; they supported the Democratic party and were able to make their sentiments felt. The regulation of manufacturing, they proclaimed, would retard the state, and until after 1900 they made huge profits from cheap labor and the consuming public. Yet all of this activity spurred the growth of towns, and from 1870 to 1900 the number of towns in excess of ten thousand inhabitants increased from one to six (Figure 1.13).

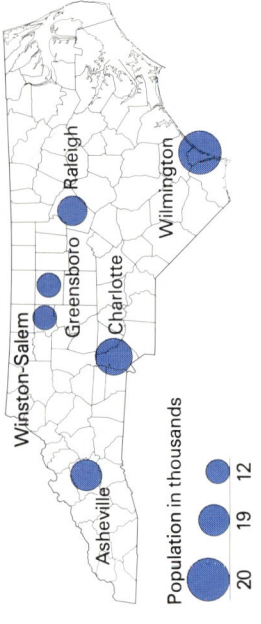

Figure 1.13. N.C. Towns in 1900 with Over 10,000 Population

Source: U.S. Department of Commerce, *1900 Census of Population and Housing*, 1900.

During the Civil War many miles of railroads in North Carolina were destroyed, and ordinary roads and bridges were damaged either by war or neglect. Following the railroad bond scandals of the Reconstruction period, the policy of state aid to railroads was abandoned and after 1870 private development and exploitation became the accepted course. State-owned rail lines were either sold or leased and consolidation into three major lines—Southern, Seaboard Air Line, and Atlantic Coast Line—took place, giving North Carolina a statewide network with interstate connections and access to the national network. A law of 1872 provided for the use of convict labor to construct and maintain roads, but few counties had the resources necessary for highway construction. The colonial scheme whereby men turned out for a few days each year to maintain roads prevailed until the twentieth century. The state's first telephone exchanges opened in Raleigh and Wilmington in the autumn of 1879, and in 1896 the first rural free delivery of mail began from China Grove in Rowan County.

Education suffered greatly during the Civil War when most of the colleges and many of the academies and schools were forced to close for lack of funds or students or both. Wake Forest, Trinity, and Davidson colleges were closed before the end of the war, but the University of North Carolina managed to survive until 1870 when it was obliged to close for lack of confidence after it had been merged with the public school system by the 1868 constitution. With the return of Conservatives to political control, a constitutional amendment of 1873 again vested control of the university in a board of trustees appointed by the General Assembly, and it opened in 1875 under an able president and a new faculty.

Before 1860 North Carolina had had a model system of common or public schools, ably directed by Calvin H. Wiley as superintendent. Early in Reconstruction, however, the system collapsed. In 1869 a new law was passed not unlike the old one, but because of a lack of confidence in the carpetbaggers who headed the system, the shortage of financial support, the poor condition of school buildings, and the fact that "mixed schools" were operated, the schools were not widely patronized. The first Democratic legislature in 1871 cut the salary of the state superintendent and effected his resignation. With the appointment of Alexander McIver to that post and the levying of a tax to support public schools, enrollment began to increase. Provision was made for a special municipal tax and many cities and towns soon established graded schools. Yet poverty, scattered population, bad roads, a large school-age population, and the necessity for maintaining a dual system of schools (in accordance with the constitutional amendment of 1875) prevented the establishment of an effective system for a number of years.

The election of Zebulon B. Vance as governor in 1876 and the removal of federal troops in 1877 marked the return of home rule to the state. Democratic domination of state government then continued for the remainder of the century except for a brief Republican-Populist fusion interlude in the mid-1890s. From Reconstruction the state inherited a debt of $30 million, a large part of which was for special-tax railroad bonds. Much of this debt was regarded as fraudulent and unconstitutional, and in due course the legislature repudiated a large portion of it and scaled down the remainder by 60 to 85 percent. The settlement of the old debt eventually made possible the financing of a program of state development. Political realignment and a "white supremacy" campaign returned control of government to whites and the Democratic party swept the 1900 election and remained in power for more than seventy years.

New Foundations

Charles B. Aycock was elected governor after a campaign in which he stressed universal education in the state. His administration coincided with the beginning of a period of material expansion and economic prosperity throughout the country, and it marked the opening of a new era in the state. Political bitterness declined and racial antagonism all but disappeared. With new leaders, the dominant Democratic party undertook to promote educational and social programs that were long overdue. By rendering public service the party gained popular favor. The government recognized the social and economic needs of its citizens, and the old laissez-faire policy was abandoned. This program gradually transformed North Carolina into a modern progressive social commonwealth.

Governor Aycock joined the superintendent of public instruction in a statewide campaign on behalf of education. With the aid of newspaper editors, clergymen, and a host of volunteers from all walks of life, the need for education was widely discussed, and the people of the state became convinced of the value of public education. Annual appropriations for public schools more than tripled within ten years. During that same period nearly three thousand new schoolhouses were constructed—an average of about one a day. Special taxes were levied for education, the school term was lengthened, a compulsory school law was enacted, and teacher training schools were established. The percentage of illiteracy dropped dramatically.

Progress was also made in higher education. A remarkable expansion occurred in the physical plants, teaching staffs, and breadth and quality of educational programs at the state-supported colleges and universities. The University of North Carolina during the 1920s achieved leadership in the South and distinction in the nation in the field of higher education. In 1931 the General Assembly consolidated the State College of Agriculture and Engineering at Raleigh, the North Carolina College for Women at Greensboro, and the University at Chapel Hill into the University of North Carolina. As a result of the establishment of the Duke Endowment of $40 million in 1924 (which was later more than doubled), Trinity College at Durham became Duke University. Davidson College and Johnson C. Smith University for Negroes at Charlotte also shared in the Duke Endowment. Salem Academy and College, Wake Forest College, and Meredith College, among others, raised substantial sums of money to qualify for matching grants by 1914.

In 1897 Durham established the first tax-supported library in the state; shortly after the turn of the century Greensboro, Charlotte, and Winston followed Durham's lead. The state also began to offer modest assistance to communities in establishing school libraries and through the Library Commission of North Carolina it took the lead in reorganizing and improving existing libraries and the establishment of new ones. Boxes of books—"traveling libraries"—were shipped from Raleigh to communities that did not have public library service.

Between 1900 and 1908 temperance forces in the state conducted a vigorous drive to prohibit the legal sale of liquor. An act of 1903 prohibited the manufacture and sale of spiritous liquors except in incorporated towns, while a statewide referendum in 1908 approved prohibition throughout the state. In this the state anticipated national approval in 1919 of the Eighteenth Amendment; although this amendment was repealed in 1933, North Carolina remained dry legally until 1937.

During 1917-18, while the United States was engaged in World War I, North Carolina turned aside from all other matters. Factories of many kinds began the production of war materials, shipyards were busy around the clock, victory gardens flourished on nearly every available plot of ground, draftees and volunteers joined the state guard and the regular army in accomplishing the task at hand. More than 86,000 North Carolinians saw military service, while over 2,300 of them lost their lives. Training camps were established in Charlotte, Raleigh, and near Fayetteville, the latter developing into Fort Bragg, now the largest of its kind in the nation. Among the North Carolinians who held national positions of importance were Josephus Daniels, secretary of the navy, and Furnifold M. Simons, chairman of the Senate Finance Committee.

During the war women worked diligently in various volunteer services and nearly two hundred from the state served as nurses with the armed services. At the end of the war women of the state played active roles in the move for "women's rights." Although the state Democratic party refused to endorse woman's suffrage, a number of individual leaders of the party did openly support the idea. With the adoption of the Nineteenth Amendment in 1920 the electorate of North Carolina was doubled.

Other significant changes soon came to be evident in the state. A $50 million bond issue for road construction brought unprecedented growth of hard-surfaced, sand-clay, and gravel roads to all parts of the state. Rapid industrialization also swept the state. The value of manufactures by 1920 was double that of agriculture.

The state became the nation's leading producer of cotton textiles, tobacco products, and wood furniture. Other industries were also growing in importance: lumber, flour, cottonseed oil and meal, and fertilizer. The production of building materials, particularly granite, brick and tile, sand and gravel, and cement products came to assume national importance.

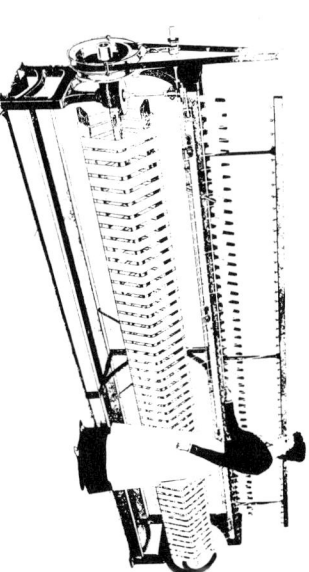

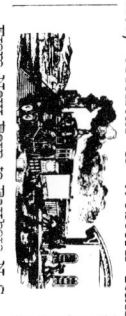

Partly as a reaction to the postwar period of adjustment, farm products dropped in value between 1920 and 1922 before they began a slow upward trend. The cost of manufactured goods increased at a faster rate while industrial wages rose slowly. The cost of living became a serious problem. When Angus D. McLean became governor in 1925 North Carolina had one of the heaviest per capita debts in the nation. It became necessary for the state to economize without curtailing such programs as public schools, the development of port facilities, road construction, and care of the unfortunate. Under Governor McLean a state budget bureau was authorized in 1925. This was one of the most important moves made by the state in the twentieth century. It directed the governor to initiate and prepare for each session of the General Assembly a balanced budget of the state's revenues and expenditures. Immediate savings were made by the consolidation of some state departments. A Salary and Wage Commission was created to fix salaries among the growing number of state employees. The old Geological and Economic Survey of 1905 was recognized as the Department of Conservation and Development, and an Educational Commission was authorized to make a complete survey of public schools and the state-supported institutions of higher learning. The next assembly created a Tax Commission to make a thorough study of the tax structure and report to the governor and assembly. These steps toward a responsible fiscal policy for the state came at a good time. Governor O. Max Gardner was inaugurated in January 1929 and the stock-market crash came in October. His program was colored by the state of economic affairs, but the program and the changes he proposed have been cited as basic to the progress the state made following the Great Depression. In addition to consolidating the state's three leading institutions of higher education, Gardner was responsible for the establishment of a Division of Purchase and Contract. Under his leadership the state pioneered in taking over the maintenance of county roads. He stabilized the credit of the state's counties and towns, making their bond issues more attractive. The General Assembly also accepted responsibility of public schools by providing that the constitutional six-months term should be supported from state rather than local revenues. By its road and school legislation the assembly reduced the tax burden on property by $12 million and altogether it reduced the cost of government by $7 million.

The Road to the Present

A new governor, J. C. B. Ehringhaus, took office in January 1933 when economic conditions were at their worst. He proposed further measures of economy which were adopted. He also took the lead in the creation of a Parole and Pardon Commission and a State School Commission, the merger of the State Highway and Prison departments, and the formation of a Utilities Commission to replace the old Corporation Commission. Largely as an emergency measure to save public schools, a 3 percent sales tax was levied. Salaries of teachers and state employees were reduced for the second time since the autumn of 1929, but the minimum school term was extended from six to eight months. By these measures and others state services were continued and the state emerged from the financial crisis in moderately good condition.

Federal relief measures were the salvation of many North Carolina families while public works programs provided new state and municipal buildings even though North Carolina received less per capita than any other state from the New Deal. Aid to farmers took the form of benefit payments to those who improved the fertility of their land or engaged in other conservation practices. Crop control was implemented to reduce production and thereby raise prices. Financial aid was extended to many tenants to enable them to become landowners. Controls on business and labor raised wages, reduced hours of work, eliminated child labor, checked waste, and protected the right of labor to organize and strike. Perhaps more lasting changes came to North Carolina through these federal programs than through any other force in the history of the state.

World War II also worked extensive and lasting changes in the state. The national defense program resulted in an enlarged base at Fort Bragg and the creation of several other camps, some of which became permanent establishments. Over 360,000 young men and women entered the armed services and saw action around the world. More than seven thousand were killed and many thousands were wounded. Of the survivors many chose to live elsewhere after the war; those who returned home brought new ideas and their experiences elsewhere made them see their home state through different eyes. The changes they wrought in the state were great and many.

The depression was another fatality of the war. Unemployment ceased to be a problem when the draft and recruiters had taken their toll. The urgent need for war materials of all kinds brought new demands to established manufacturing enterprises as well as new factories. Industries appeared in unaccustomed places in the state, and the old mill village all but ceased to exist. People of all social classes and all races were associated in a common cause, often working side by side with someone whom they would otherwise never have acknowledged. The war was a catalyst in a great leveling process among the people of the state.

With the return of peace North Carolina entered a period of unprecedented change. The face of the state was altered by the rapid growth of towns and cities; the construction of new highways, particularly a vast system of interstate highways; the establishment of new state parks and recreational areas; the construction of a number of dams that created vast lakes on several rivers in various sections of the state; the opening of many state historic sites, some with museums and visitor centers; and the construction of private recreational facilities with golf courses, ski lifts, and other features.

The "tourist industry" became a prime source of income for many people. Motels and restaurants mushroomed along the new highways, and natural and manmade attractions lured visitors to Variety Vacationland. Outdoor dramas, following the pattern set in 1937 by "The Lost Colony" on Roanoke Island, were opened in various parts of the state.

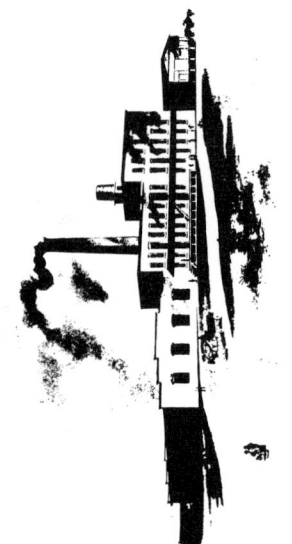

New industry moved into North Carolina, some as a result of conscious effort on the part of state or local agencies created for that purpose, while native industry simply enlarged its operations. The Piedmont Crescent, largely extending along the line of the old North Carolina Railroad from Raleigh and Durham through Greensboro and Winston-Salem to Salisbury and Charlotte, became a new concept. The Research Triangle between Raleigh, Durham, and Chapel Hill flourished as the site of research laboratories for private industry and government. Both industry and research brought many new people into the state from other parts of the nation as well as from abroad. These people brought new ideas and attitudes into their new communities, and their presence soon made itself felt at the ballot box, at the local P.T.A., at the League of Women Voters, at the American Civil Liberties Union, at the local historical society, and in countless other organizations. Entrenched Democrats soon discovered that "outside" Democrats with different ideas or even Republicans had either to be embraced or opposed. A new interest in political campaigns arose, especially after the election of a Republican governor and senator in 1972. North Carolina had a viable two-party system for the first time in three-quarters of a century.

Following World War II North Carolinians appeared more and more frequently in the forefront on the national scene. Kenneth Royall was secretary of war in President Truman's cabinet and with the creation of the Department of Defense Royall became secretary of the army. O. Max Gardner was under secretary of the treasury and James Webb was director of the budget and later under secretary of the treasury. From 1949 until 1951 T. Lamar Caudle was assistant attorney general. Luther H. Hodges, who had been governor of North Carolina from 1954 to 1961, was secretary of commerce in the cabinets of presidents Kennedy and Johnson.

After a brief period of moderate resistance, North Carolina came to accept integrated schools. In 1957 the schools of Charlotte, Greensboro, and Winston-Salem admitted Negroes to formerly all-white schools; two years later the schools of Craven and Wayne counties did the same. Gradually and with little or no difficulty in most communities the entire school system of the state was desegregated. In February 1960 the nation's first lunch counter "sit-in" took place in Greensboro, and in the years since, in part on a voluntary basis and finally in response to federal action, segregation has been virtually eliminated throughout the state.

Such changes and others in recent years have been so numerous and so all-pervasive in the life of the people of the state that an assessment of their influence may not yet be properly made. It is evident, nevertheless, that late twentieth-century North Carolina is going to be quite different than anyone in the state before World War II might have anticipated. The following chapters examine this ongoing momentum of change that is found in every facet of the life-style of the Tar Heel State.

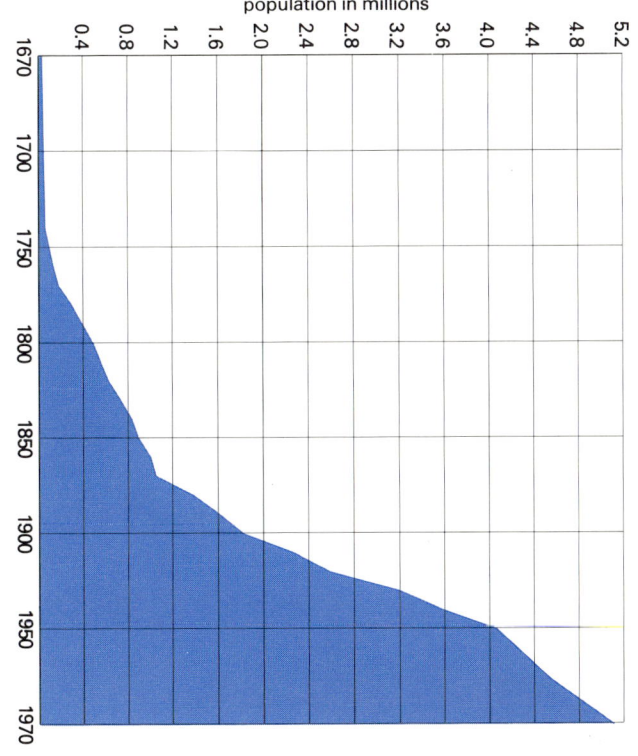

Figure 1.14. N.C. Population Growth, 1670–1970

Source: U.S. Department of Commerce, Census of Population, 1790-1970. E. B. Greene, American Population before the Federal Census of 1790 (New York: Columbia University Press, 1932).

SELECTED REFERENCES

Barrett, John G. The Civil War in North Carolina. Chapel Hill: University of North Carolina Press, 1963.

Durden, Robert F. The Dukes of Durham. Durham, N.C.: Duke University Press, 1975.

Evans, William McKee. Ballots and Fence Rails: Reconstruction on the Lower Cape Fear. Chapel Hill: University of North Carolina Press, 1967.

Franklin, John Hope. The Free Negro in North Carolina, 1790-1860. Chapel Hill: University of North Carolina Press, 1943.

Gatewood, Willard B., Jr. Eugene Clyde Brooks: Educator and Public Servant. Durham, N.C.: Duke University Press, 1960.

Gatewood, Willard B., Jr. Preachers, Pedagogues, and Politicians: The Evolution Controversy in North Carolina, 1920-1927. Chapel Hill: University of North Carolina Press, 1966.

Hammer, Carl, Jr. Rhinelanders on the Yadkin. Salisbury: Rowan Printing Company, 1965.

Jenkins, John W. James B. Duke, Master Builder. New York: George H. Doran Co., 1927.

Johnson, Guion G. Ante-Bellum North Carolina: A Social History. Chapel Hill: University of North Carolina Press, 1937.

Lee, Lawrence. The Lower Cape Fear in Colonial Days. Chapel Hill: University of North Carolina Press, 1965.

Lefler, Hugh T., and Newsome, Albert R. North Carolina: The History of a Southern State. 3d ed. Chapel Hill: University of North Carolina Press, 1973.

Lefler, Hugh T., and Powell, William S. Colonial North Carolina: A History. New York: Charles Scribner's Sons, 1973.

Merrens, Harry R. Colonial North Carolina in the Eighteenth Century. Chapel Hill: University of North Carolina Press, 1964.

Meyer, Duane. The Highland Scots of North Carolina, 1732-1776. Chapel Hill: University of North Carolina Press, 1961.

Orr, Oliver H., Jr. Charles Brantley Aycock. Chapel Hill: University of North Carolina Press, 1961.

Ramsey, Robert W. Carolina Cradle: Settlement of the Northwest Carolina Frontier, 1747-1762. Chapel Hill: University of North Carolina Press, 1964.

Rights, Douglas L. The American Indian in North Carolina. Winston-Salem: John F. Blair, 1957.

Rouse, Parke, Jr. The Great Wagon Road from Philadelphia to the South. New York: McGraw-Hill Book Co., 1973.

2. Population

JOHN C. CATAU
A. C. DAVIS
WILLIAM B. CLIFFORD
R. DAVID MUSTIAN

This book is concerned with the people of North Carolina—past, present, and future. Every chapter deals with either some aspect of human endeavor or with the physical setting in which people live. This chapter focuses rather sharply on an analysis of basic population information, especially the size, distribution, and composition of the state's population.

POPULATION GROWTH AND DISTRIBUTION

Total Population Growth

North Carolina was the twelfth most populous state in the nation in 1970. As Figures 2.1 and 2.2 indicate, this development was the product of a long-term trend of consistent but relatively slow population growth. From the 393,751 residents recorded in the first official census in 1790, North Carolina has grown to the level of 5,082,059 inhabitants in 1970. In the process, the state's rate of growth has generally been slower than the South's, and in turn, the South's rate has generally been slower than the nation's. In only four of the eighteen decades since 1790 has North Carolina's rate of population growth exceeded that of the nation.

In the early decades, from 1790 to 1900, the state population increased slightly less than fivefold. The national increase during this same period was nearly twentyfold. Since the beginning of the twentieth century, however, the growth differentials have been negligible. Whereas North Carolina has gained 3,188,249 inhabitants, for an increase of 168 percent, the entire country has increased 167 percent.

More recently, with the exception of the decade immediately following World War II, the populations of the nation, the South, and North Carolina have been increasing at a decreasing rate. Although net migration losses have been partially responsible for diminishing growth rates in the South and North Carolina, the primary cause in all three cases has been lower fertility.

Ironically, in North Carolina, the declining rates of population growth have not produced declining absolute increases. During the 1940s the state's population

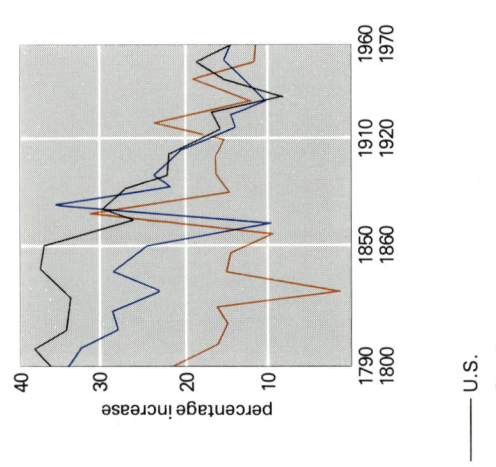

Figure 2.2. Decennial Population Change, 1790–1970

Source: C. Horace Hamilton, *North Carolina Population Trends: A Demographic Sourcebook*, vol. 1 (Chapel Hill: Carolina Population Center, 1974).

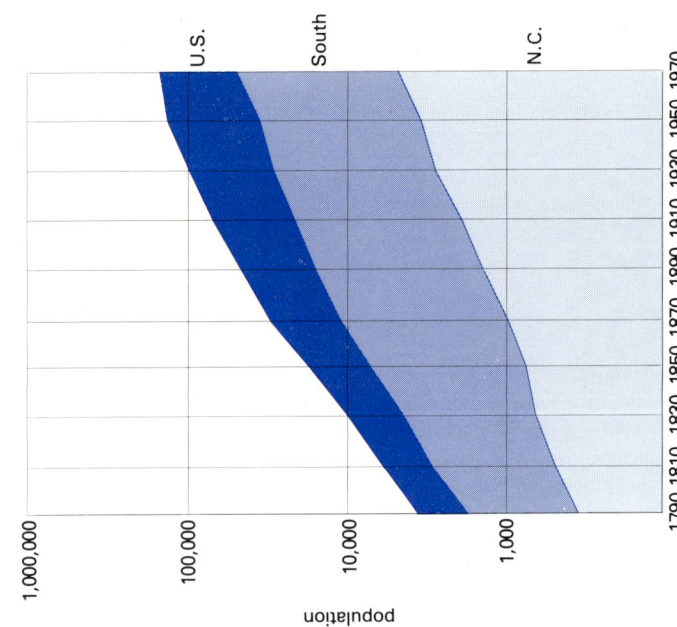

Figure 2.1. Total Population of the U.S., the South, and N.C., 1790–1970

Source: U.S. Department of Commerce, *1970 Census of Population, 1970*.

Figure 2.3. Changing Regional Distribution of Total Population in N.C., 1790-1970

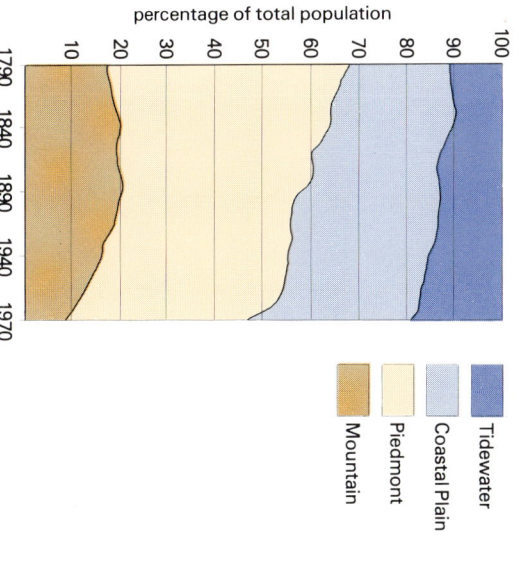

Source: C. Horace Hamilton, *North Carolina Population Trends: A Demographic Sourcebook*, vol. 1 (Chapel Hill: Carolina Population Center, 1974).

Figure 2.4. Total Population of N.C., 1970

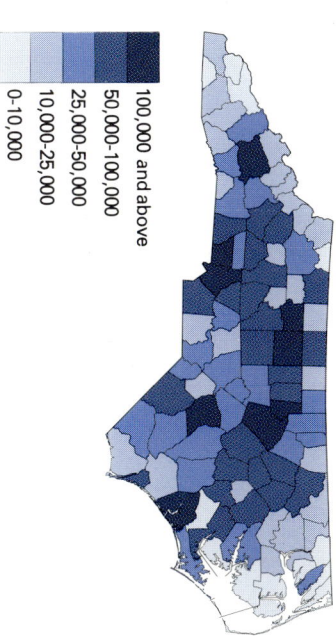

Source: N.C. Department of Administration, *North Carolina Population: A Statistical Summary*, 1971.

Figure 2.5. Change in County Share of N.C.'s Total Population, 1910-1970

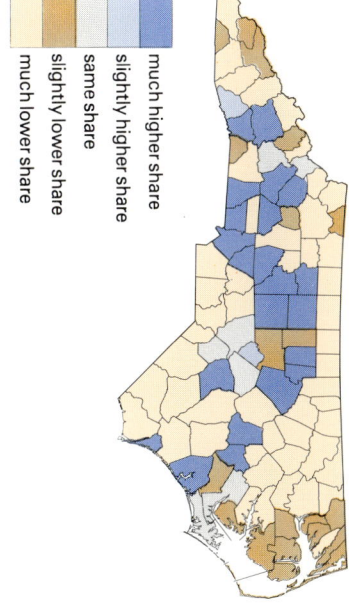

Source: U.S. Department of Commerce, *1970 Census of Population*, 1970.

increased by 490,306 people or 13.7 percent. Between 1950 and 1960, although the relative gain declined to 12.2 percent, the absolute increase rose to 494,226 inhabitants. In a similar manner, the 1960s experienced an even greater total growth of 525,904 people, yet the relative gain was only 11.5 percent. This was the lowest rate of growth in the last one hundred years, but the second largest absolute increase in state history.

Total Population: Distribution

Regional Distribution A general indication of the distribution of North Carolina's population can be gained by examining the four major physiographic regions. As is shown in Figure 2.3, the Piedmont has always had the largest concentration of population. Additionally, since the turn of the century, the extent of this dominance has been increasing. By 1960 over half (50.7 percent) of the state's population resided in the thirty-four Piedmont counties; and just ten years later, the proportion had increased to 53.0 percent.

Although the other three regions have experienced consistent population increases, they have been unable to match the Piedmont's growth. Hence, each has had a declining proportion of the state total. The twenty-three counties in the Coastal Plain have always comprised the second most populous region. In 1900 they accounted for 26.4 percent of the population but by 1970 they had fallen to 22.9 percent. The Mountain region, with twenty-five counties, declined from 19.4 percent in 1900 to 15.0 percent in 1970; and the smallest region, the Tidewater (eighteen counties), fell from 11.5 percent to 9.1 percent in the same period. These relative changes are primarily the result of differential migration patterns.

County Distribution A more detailed view of the distribution of population can be obtained through an analysis of county patterns. The 1970 spread was such that the most populous county (Mecklenburg) had only 7.0 percent of the state total. And yet, as Figure 2.4 indicates, the distribution was not even.

Of the ten most populated counties, seven are in the Piedmont. Together, they accounted for 28.8 percent of the state's population. The other three regions each had one representative in the top ten: Cumberland (Coastal Plain); Buncombe (Mountain); and Onslow (Tidewater) counties. The overall concentration in the ten largest counties was 37.9 percent of the state total.

Figure 2.5 shows the extent to which the county patterns have changed since 1910. Of course, some counties

Table 2.1. N.C. Counties with the Greatest Relative Growth, 1960-1970

County	Geographical Region	Percentage Change
Cumberland	Coastal Plain	+42.9
Wake	Piedmont	+35.1
Orange	Piedmont	+34.3
Watauga	Mountain	+33.5
Mecklenburg	Piedmont	+30.3
Alexander	Piedmont	+24.6
Catawba	Piedmont	+24.2
Randolph	Piedmont	+24.2
Union	Piedmont	+22.5
Jackson	Mountain	+20.3

Source: N.C. Department of Administration, *North Carolina State Government Statistical Abstract,* 1973.

Table 2.2. N. C. Counties with the Greatest Relative Decline, 1960-1970

County	Geographical Region	Percentage Change
Warren	Piedmont	-19.6
Tyrrell	Tidewater	-15.8
Bertie	Coastal Plain	-15.7
Jones	Tidewater	-11.1
Greene	Coastal Plain	-10.6
Northampton	Coastal Plain	-10.5
Yancey	Mountain	- 9.8
Perquimans	Tidewater	- 9.0
Martin	Coastal Plain	- 8.9
Halifax	Coastal Plain	- 8.6

Source: N.C. Department of Administration, *North Carolina State Government Statistical Abstract,* 1973.

have increased their share of the total population, and others have had a relative decline. The overall impact, however, has been one of greater concentration in a few counties. Over two-thirds (68) of the counties had a smaller proportion of the state's population in 1970 than in 1910. Although some of these experienced an actual population loss, others simply grew too slowly to maintain their relative position. Fifteen of the twenty-four counties that experienced relative gains are in the Piedmont, further demonstrating the trend for population to concentrate in that region.

A better indication of more recent changes in the distribution of the population is furnished in Figure 2.6. Once again, the Piedmont is revealed as the most rapidly growing region. Only six Piedmont counties experienced declines between 1960 and 1970. These were more than made up for by the gains registered in the remaining counties. In fact, as Table 2.1 indicates, seven of the fastest-growing counties in the state are situated within the Piedmont.

The other three regions display a larger proportion of declining counties but several significant patterns of growth are also apparent. In the Mountain region, a substantial area of expansion extends from Alleghany and Surry counties in the north to a rapidly growing cluster in the southwest comprised of Macon, Jackson, Transylvania, and Henderson counties. Included within the Mountain region is Watauga, the fourth fastest-growing county in the state. Another concentration with relatively large percentage increases appears along the Tidewater coastline. Within the Coastal Plain, the primary area of growth was centered around Cumberland County, the fastest-growing county in the state.

As has been implied, most of the thirty-eight counties experiencing population decreases during the last decade are situated in the eastern half of the state. Of the six with losses amounting to at least 10 percent, all but one (Warren) are located in the Coastal Plain and Tidewater regions (Table 2.2). The only substantial concentration of population decline in the western part of the state appears along the Tennessee border.

Rural-Urban Distribution Perhaps the most striking fact regarding the distribution of North Carolina's population is that it is one of the few states that has always been predominantly rural. (By definition, rural persons are those living outside of places with 2,500 or more inhabitants.) The first official urban residents did not appear until 1820. Since then, the proportion has increased steadily, but for many years the rate of growth was extremely slow (Figure 2.7). When the entire country reached an urban majority in 1920, North Carolina was still overwhelmingly rural (80.8 percent). By 1970, the

Figure 2.6. Percentage Change of Population in N.C., 1960-1970

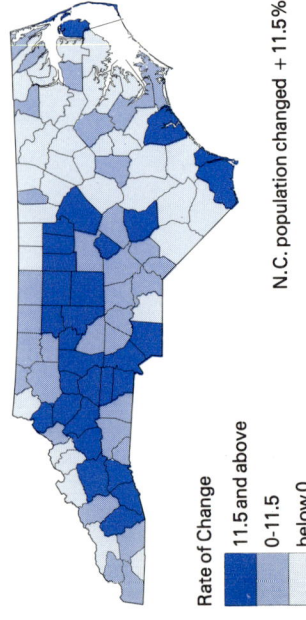

N.C. population changed +11.5%

Rate of Change
- 11.5 and above
- 0-11.5
- below 0

Source: U.S. Department of Commerce, *1970 Census of Population,* 1970.

Figure 2.7. N.C. Population by Residence, 1830-1970

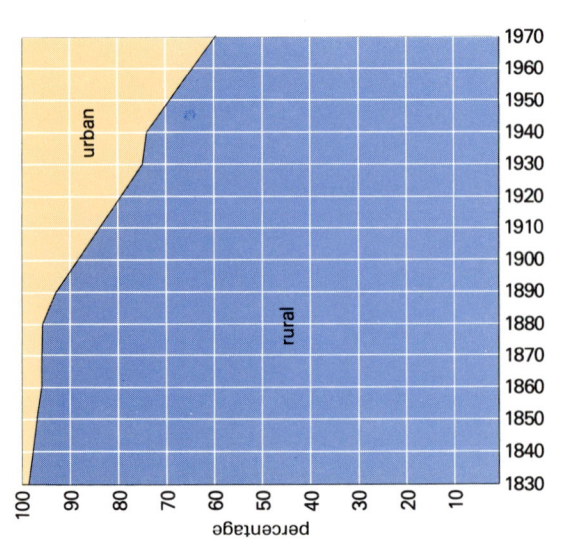

Source: C. Horace Hamilton, *North Carolina Population Trends: A Demographic Sourcebook,* vol. 1 (Chapel Hill: Carolina Population Center, 1974).

state had its largest number and proportion of urban residents ever, yet with 45 percent so classified, it was still well behind the national proportion of 73.5 percent. It appears that North Carolina may become predominantly urban by the 1980 census.

One of the logical consequences of increased urbanization is the relative decline of the rural population. For many years in the United States, as the urban segment grew, and as the rural population declined as a percent of the total, the actual number of rural residents continued to increase. This was possible because the urban rate of growth exceeded the rural rate. During the past two decades, this relationship changed and the total number of rural residents began to decline.

In the case of North Carolina, the latter change has yet to occur. Between 1960 and 1970, the actual number of rural residents increased by slightly more than 42,000. This represented a 1.5 percent increase, the lowest rate of growth since 1840. Since the urban rate of expansion was 26.8 percent, the proportion of rural residents declined from 60.5 percent to 55.0 percent.

These statistics conceal a very important differential. Specifically, if the rural component is subdivided into its two major parts (rural farm and rural nonfarm), two very different trends emerge. In 1960, North Carolina led all of the other states in the number of rural farm dwellers. The 808,379 people in this category represented 17.7 percent of the total population. This compared with a proportion of only 7.5 percent in the South, and 10.8 percent in the nation. By 1970, the number of North Carolina residents in this category had fallen to 374,692, a decrease of more than 430,000 people. Translated into relative terms, the proportion of the total population classified as rural farm dropped to 7.4 percent, a figure that more closely matched the proportions in the United States (5.2 percent) and the South (6.4 percent).

The concomitant trend for the rural nonfarm population was an increase amounting to approximately 470,000. Since this component is comprised of people residing in rural areas but not on farms, it includes such diverse elements as the residents of small (less than 2,500 people) villages and towns, open-country people not on farms, and the residents of the rural fringe areas of cities. A large proportion of the rapid growth in this sector was contributed by the processes of suburbanization and urban sprawl. By 1970, almost nine out of every ten rural residents were located in a nonfarm environment.

A similar distinction is meaningful within the urban population. With such tremendous variety in the size and importance of urban places, it is advantageous to differentiate between metropolitan and nonmetropolitan areas. As defined by the Census Bureau, there are currently seven Standard Metropolitan Statistical Areas (SMSAs) in North Carolina (Figure 2.8). Although they encompass a total of just seventeen counties, their significance is very apparent. Well over two-fifths of the total state population resided in these counties in 1970. (The same proportion for the entire United States was 68.6 percent.) Nine of the ten most populous counties in the state are metropolitan. Additionally, most of the fastest-growing counties are included within an SMSA. These and other characteristics are demonstrated more fully in chapter 4.

It is important to note that twelve of the seventeen metropolitan counties are in the Piedmont region. This is consistent with the fact that in 1970 the Piedmont accounted for 63.7 percent of the total urban population. It was 1890 before the Piedmont had a majority of the state's urban residents. It has maintained this position ever since. However, the number of urban residents in each of the four regions has continued to grow.

The regional distribution of the rural population has been less concentrated but more stable than the urban distribution (Figure 2.9). The Piedmont has always possessed the largest proportion of rural people, yet it has never fallen below 40 percent or exceeded 45.5 percent of the state total. In 1970, the Piedmont's

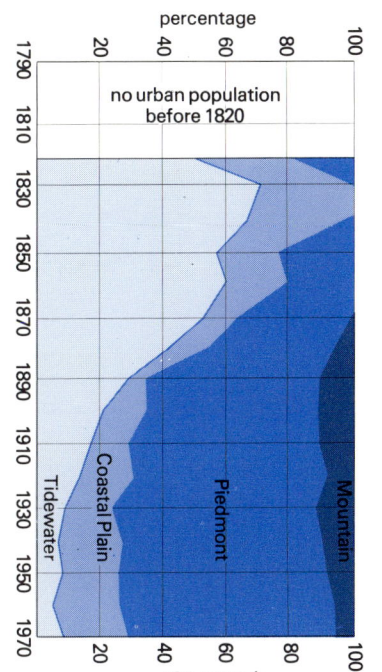

Figure 2.8. Changing Regional Distribution of Urban Population in N.C., 1790-1970

Source: C. Horace Hamilton, *North Carolina Population Trends: A Demographic Sourcebook*, vol. 1 (Chapel Hill: Carolina Population Center, 1974).

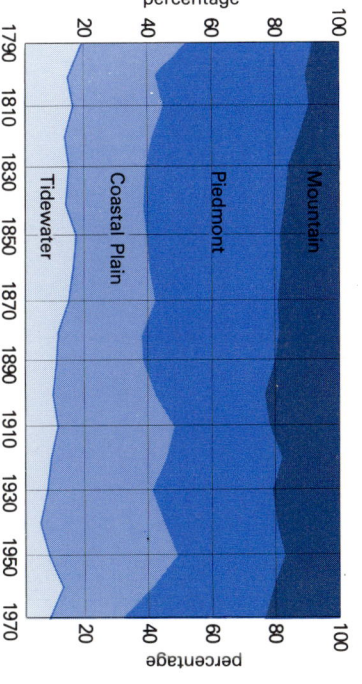

Figure 2.9. Changing Regional Distribution of Rural Population in N.C., 1790-1970

Source: C. Horace Hamilton, *North Carolina Population Trends: A Demographic Sourcebook*, vol. 1 (Chapel Hill: Carolina Population Center, 1974).

proportion was 44.2 percent. In a similar manner, the Coastal Plain has also maintained a very consistent percentage of the state total. Since 1790, when it reached its highest proportion (32.8 percent), the Coastal Plain has never had more than 30.8 percent (1930) or less than 25.5 percent (1970) of the state's total rural population. The areas showing the greatest change are the Mountain region, with its steady increase from 8 percent in 1790 to slightly more than 20 percent in 1970, and the Tidewater region, which has decreased from almost 19 percent in 1790 to slightly less than 10 percent of the state total in 1970.

From an absolute standpoint, between 1960 and 1970, only in the Piedmont and the Mountain regions did rural population continue to grow. Consequently, they both achieved their largest rural populations in 1970. The Coastal Plain, on the other hand, peaked in 1950 and the Tidewater region experienced its first decennial rural population loss between 1960 and 1970.

Figure 2.10 depicts several interesting features of the county level distribution of rural and urban residents in 1970. The significance of the rural component is brought into sharp focus. Nearly half of the counties (forty-nine) had less than one-fourth of their residents classified as urban. Thirty-four of these had no urban residents at all, and as Figure 2.10 shows, a large proportion of this group was concentrated in the Mountain (fourteen counties) and Tidewater (ten) regions.

Only seventeen counties had at least a majority of their residents classified as urban, and together, they accounted for nearly 70 percent of the state's total urban population. As might be expected, more than half of these counties were situated in the Piedmont. This is significant since it helps to show that even the most heavily urbanized region was still very rural. The Piedmont had 63.7 percent of the state's total urban population, yet as a region, it was only 54.1 percent urban. Twenty-five of the thirty-four Piedmont counties had fewer urban than rural residents. In comparison, the Tidewater region was only 41.3 percent urban; the Coastal Plain was 38.6 percent; and the Mountain region was 24.7 percent. Just four counties in the entire state had as much as three-fourths of their population classified as urban: Mecklenburg, Guilford, Cumberland, and Durham.

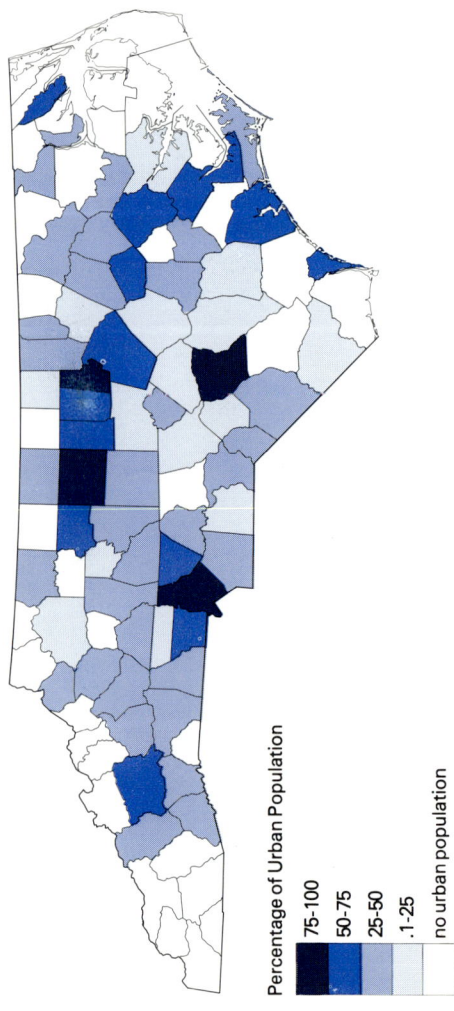

Figure 2.10. N.C. Urban Population by County, 1970

Percentage of Urban Population
- 75-100
- 50-75
- 25-50
- .1-25
- no urban population

Source: U.S. Department of Commerce, *1970 Census of Population*, 1970.

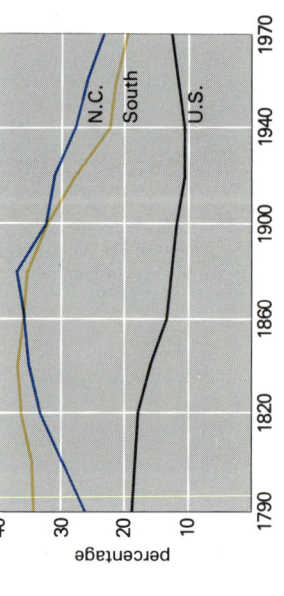

Figure 2.11. Percentage of Nonwhite Population in the U.S., the South, and N.C., 1790-1970

Source: C. Horace Hamilton, *North Carolina Population Trends: A Demographic Sourcebook*, vol. 1 (Chapel Hill: Carolina Population Center, 1974).

Growth Differentials by Race

One of the most important characteristics of the growth of North Carolina's population has been the presence of a very distinct racial differential. During the earliest years, the nonwhite population, which has always been composed almost entirely of blacks, consistently grew faster than the white population. Consequently, the proportion of the total population classified as nonwhite increased from 26.9 percent in 1790 to a state high of 38.1 percent in 1880 (Figure 2.11). At that point the situation reversed and the era of nonwhite expansion was replaced by one of nonwhite relative decline. In every decade since 1830, the white component has outgrown the nonwhite component (Figure 2.12). Thus, although the nonwhite group has continued to increase absolutely, it has still experienced a very consistent relative decline. By 1970, after a decade when the nonwhite growth was only 2.0 percent and the white growth was 14.8 percent, an ironic situation existed. Although the nonwhite population was larger than it had ever been before, as a proportion of the total, it was down to 23.2 percent, the lowest level in state history.

Figure 2.11 also depicts the impact of race differentials in the growth of the South and the United States. Except for the fact that the nonwhite decline began earlier (circa 1850), the southern trend has been closely paralleled that of North Carolina. While there were more nonwhites in the South in 1970 than ever before, the associated nonwhite component was down to 19.7 percent, the lowest level in history.

In contrast, the national experience has followed a completely different pattern. Instead of a period of nonwhite growth followed by a period of relative nonwhite decline, the United States trend has been just the opposite. Between 1790 and 1940, the nonwhite proportion gradually decreased. More recently, as the state and South have declined, the national proportion has increased. The 12.5 percent recorded in 1970 is the highest level of nonwhite representation since 1880.

The recent nonwhite expansion in the United States is largely due to the fact that the nonwhite population has had a significantly higher rate of natural increase (the excess of births over deaths) than has the white population. Although the same relationship exists in North Carolina and the South, instead of expanding, the nonwhite component has had a relative decline. This is because the nonwhite natural increase has been largely neutralized by massive out-migration. As an example, between 1960 and 1970, the black population in North Carolina recorded 196,000 more births than deaths. Most of this increase was offset, however, by a net loss of 175,000 blacks through migration. Hence, the total

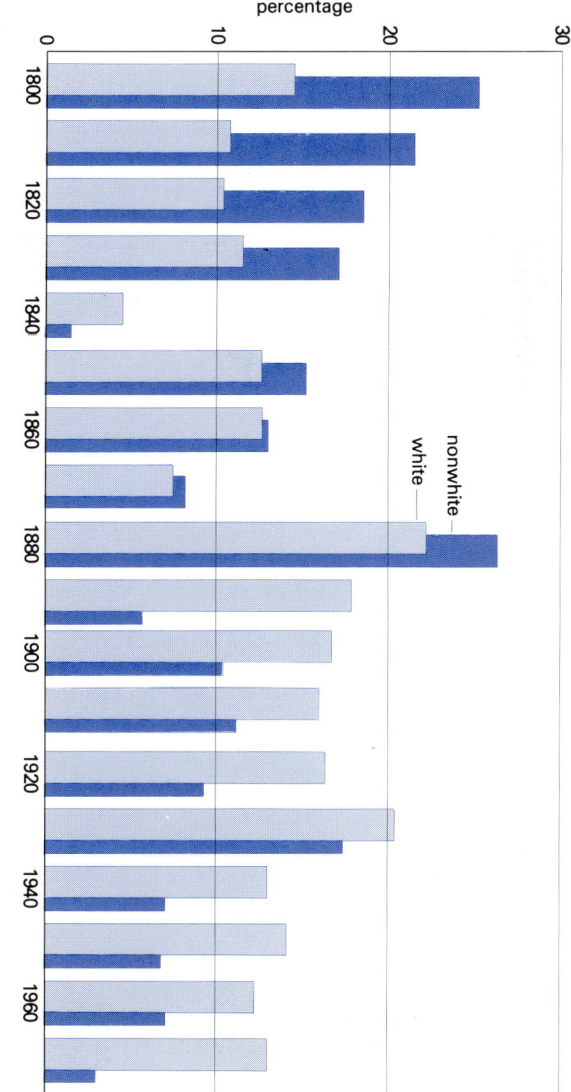

Figure 2.12. Percentage Increase in Population by Race in N.C., 1790-1970

Source: C. Horace Hamilton, *North Carolina Population Trends: A Demographic Sourcebook*, vol. 1 (Chapel Hill: Carolina Population Center, 1974).

Figure 2.13. N.C. Urban Population by Race, 1820–1970

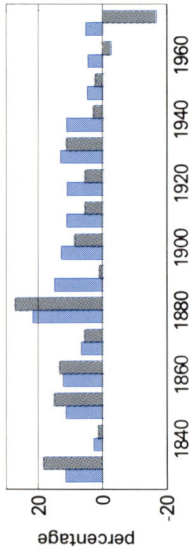

Source: Thomas E. Steahr, *North Carolina's Changing Population* (Chapel Hill: Carolina Population Center, 1973).

Note: No urban population before 1820.

Figure 2.14. Percentage Increase in Urban Population by Race in N.C., 1820–1970

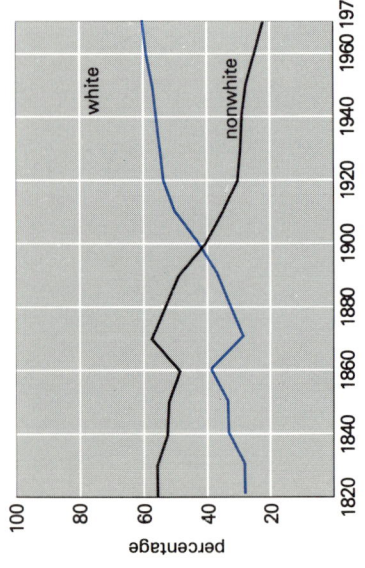

Source: C. Horace Hamilton, *North Carolina Population Trends: A Demographic Sourcebook*, vol. 1 (Chapel Hill: Carolina Population Center, 1974).

Figure 2.15. Percentage Increase in Rural Population by Race in N.C., 1820–1970

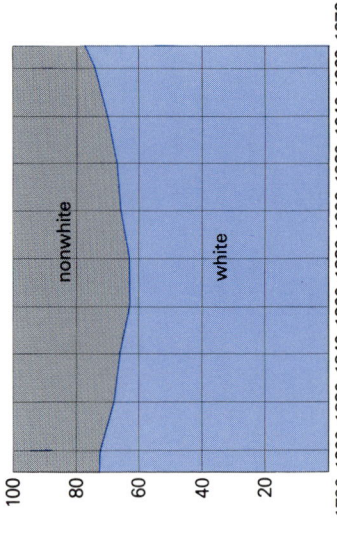

Source: C. Horace Hamilton, *North Carolina Population Trends: A Demographic Sourcebook*, vol. 1 (Chapel Hill: Carolina Population Center, 1974).

Figure 2.16. N.C. Rural Population by Race, 1790–1970

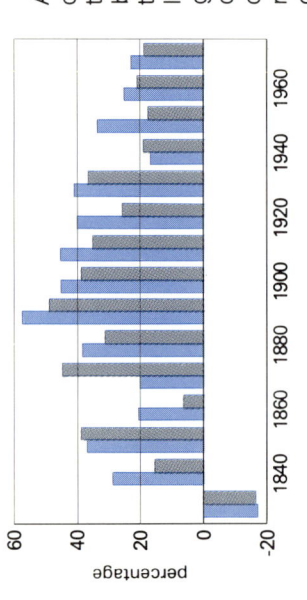

Source: C. Horace Hamilton, *North Carolina Population Trends: A Demographic Sourcebook*, vol. 1 (Chapel Hill: Carolina Population Center, 1974).

increase in the black population was just 21,000 people. The situation within the white population was very different. Instead of losing a proportion of its natural increase through migration, the white growth was supplemented by additions from net in-migration (81,000). In summary, therefore, the observed differences between the United States, the South, and North Carolina are primarily the result of migration variations.

Another intriguing discrepancy between racial growth trends of North Carolina and the nation appears in their changing rural-urban distributions. Whereas the long-term trend in both cases has been one in which the urban areas have outgrown the rural areas, a disparity exists because while the nation's cities have become increasingly nonwhite, North Carolina's cities have done the opposite and become increasingly white.

The first urban areas in the state were predominantly nonwhite (Figure 2.13). With the exception of a short period around 1860, it was not until 1890 that there were more urban whites than nonwhites. From that point until the present, although both groups have increased in each decade, the white rate of growth has almost always been the fastest (Figure 2.14). Consequently, the proportion of the total urban population classified as white has grown from 51.9 percent in 1890 to 75.5 percent in 1970. During the most recent decades, the urban growth rates for both racial groups have declined. This is consistent with the overall decline exhibited by the total population.

A comparison of Figures 2.15 and 2.16 reveals that many of the preceding urban trends are also discernible within the rural population. As an example, the growth rates of both racial groups show a long-term decline. An important difference appears, however, because during the last two decades, while the urban nonwhite group has grown, the rural nonwhite group has had an absolute decline. Specifically, between 1960 and 1970, the urban component grew by slightly more than 100,000, but the rural group declined by slightly more than 80,000. This decline, which was particularly prevalent in the rural farm areas, was caused by rural-urban shifts within the state, declining fertility, and migrations to other states.

Matching a second urban trend, North Carolina's rural areas are also becoming increasingly white. Since 1880, the white rate of growth has exceeded the nonwhite rate in every decade. This process, which has been aided especially by the recent absolute loss of nonwhites, has steadily brought the rural areas from a level of 62.5 percent white in 1880 to 77.8 percent in 1970. This white expansion has occurred in both rural farm, and more recently, rural nonfarm regions. It should be noted that the nonwhite rural farm population is declining so rapidly it may be quite negligible in ten years.

Figure 2.17. Proportion of Blacks in Total Population of N.C., 1970

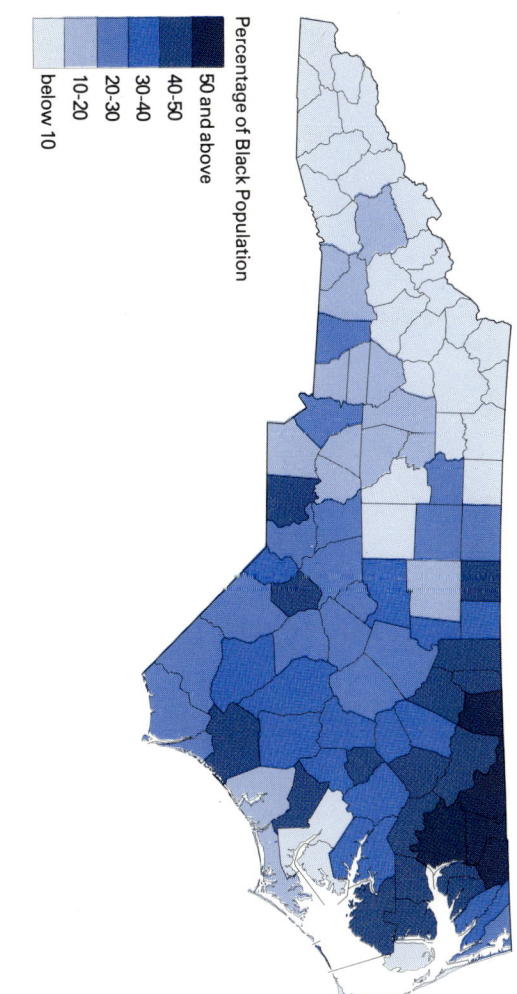

Percentage of Black Population
- 50 and above
- 40-50
- 30-40
- 20-30
- 10-20
- below 10

Both the white and nonwhite populations have become increasingly urban, yet they both remain well below the national average. The discrepancy is especially apparent among the nonwhites. While 80.7 percent of the country's nonwhites are classified as urban, the same statistic in North Carolina is just 47.5 percent. This gap is likely to increase since in recent years the nation's nonwhite group has been urbanizing faster than the state's nonwhite group.

Distribution by Race

The different racial groups are not evenly distributed throughout the state. In general, the spatial pattern established by the total population is repeated in both the regional and the county distributions of the white population. In 1970, for instance, the Piedmont predominated with 54.2 percent of the state total of whites; the Coastal Plain and Mountain regions each had approximately 18 percent; and the Tidewater had the smallest proportion of whites, approximately 9.0 percent.

The nonwhite distribution does not match the total population's pattern as well. The greatest discrepancies in 1970 occurred in the Mountain and Coastal Plain regions. Whereas the former had 22.9 percent of the total population, it had 36.8 percent of the state's nonwhites. The Mountains, on the other hand, had 15.0 percent of all the people, but only 3.9 percent of those that were nonwhite. It is also notable that between 1960 and 1970, both the Tidewater and the Coastal Plain regions experienced an absolute loss in their nonwhite components. This indicates that in these regions, the natural increase gains were exceeded by the magnitude of the out-migration losses. Although a portion of these movements had destinations within the Piedmont, many left the state entirely. Otherwise, the nonwhite population of the Piedmont would have increased dramatically.

Blacks comprise 95.4 percent of the state's nonwhites, and their distribution is shown in Figure 2.17. The Mountain region, which is 94.0 percent white, shows only three counties with more than 10 percent black. At the other extreme, the Coastal Plain includes four of the five counties that are predominantly black, and only five counties that are less than 30 percent black. With a population that is 62.6 percent white, this region is well below the state average of 76.8 percent. The remaining two regions contain counties with both high and low levels of black representation. They are much closer to the state mean. (The Piedmont is 78.6 percent and the Tidewater is 73.7 percent white.)

Although they comprise a very small proportion of the total population (0.9 percent), there are enough Indian Americans in North Carolina for the state to rank fifth among all the states. Figure 2.18 indicates that they are concentrated in very few counties. In fact, Robeson County alone contains more than half of the state total and it and the five contiguous counties have 75.6 percent of North Carolina's Indian population.

AGE AND SEX STRUCTURE

Total Population

The 1970 age and sex structure of North Carolina is portrayed in Figure 2.19. As the general slope of this profile indicates, the younger age groups predominated, with just over 40 percent of the total population being aged twenty years or less. This compares favorably with the national proportion of 39.5 percent. Within this young group, an especially notable feature is the smaller number of children between the ages of zero and four than between five and nine. The implication is clear that the fertility rates in the state declined sharply during the last half of the 1960s.

Beyond age twenty, the effects of increasing mortality are portrayed. With just two exceptions, the profile shows a consistent decline in the size of each succeeding age group. The first irregularity appears between the ages of thirty and thirty-nine. The categories comprising this interval are smaller than might be expected. These people were born during the depression of the 1930s when the birthrate was unusually low. The other discrepancy appears in the final level of the profile. It is solely the result of combining several age groups into a single category. If the five-year intervals in Figure 2.19 were continued beyond age seventy-five, the general decline would be uninterrupted.

Another notable feature of the age-sex profile is the growing predominance of females over males as age increases. At birth, males consistently outnumber females. In fact, although minor variations may occur, the sex ratio (the number of males per 100 females) among newborn babies is usually very close to 105. Consequently, during the childhood years, males always comprise the larger group. Since females experience lower mortality than males at almost every age, however, the male proportion constantly decreases.

39

In North Carolina, male dominance is maintained until between the ages of twenty-five and twenty-nine when the sexes become nearly equal. Obviously, at this point, the sex ratio is one hundred (Figure 2.20). From then on it declines, and hence, females outnumber males. The margin of difference is relatively small at first, but it increases consistently, and is down to ninety-three for the thirty-five to thirty-nine age group. The most abrupt decline occurs after age fifty. During the final years, the greater life expectancy among females really asserts itself. By age seventy-five, the sex ratio is down to sixty-two.

Figure 2.21 indicates that there were many changes in the state's age composition between 1960 and 1970. In fact, every age group was different. The two youngest categories were smaller by a total of 102,000 children. This supports the contention that the relatively high fertility rate of the previous two decades was replaced by a substantially lower rate between 1960 and 1970. In a similar manner, the comparatively low fertility of an earlier period, namely the 1930s, is also reflected in the diagram. The "depression cohorts" occupied the only other categories to show a decline in people between 1960 and 1970, those aged from thirty to thirty-nine.

Figure 2.18. Number of Indians in N.C., by County, 1970

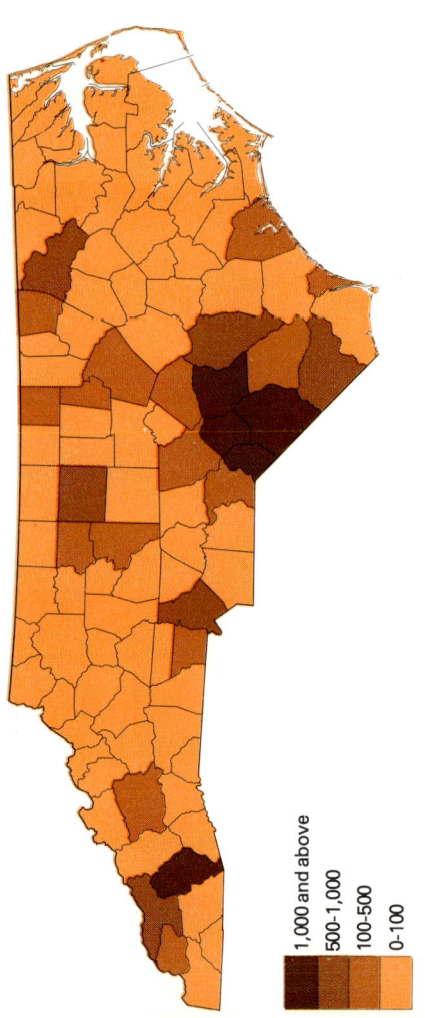

1,000 and above
500–1,000
100–500
0–100

Source: U.S. Department of Commerce, *1970 Census of Population*, 1970.

Note: Total number of Indians in N.C.—44,406.

Figure 2.19. Total Population by Age and Sex in N.C., 1970

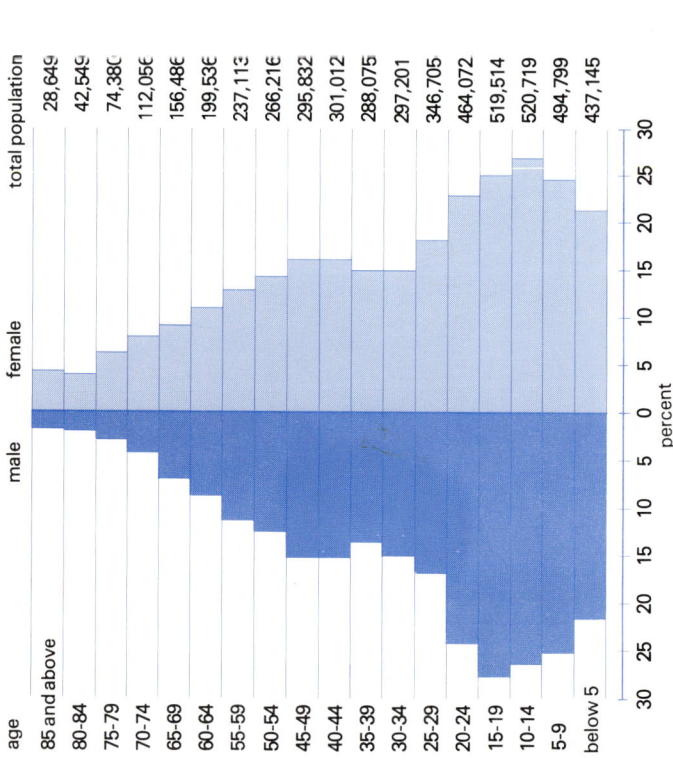

age	total population
85 and above	28,649
80-84	42,549
75-79	74,380
70-74	112,058
65-69	156,486
60-64	199,536
55-59	237,113
50-54	266,216
45-49	295,832
40-44	301,012
35-39	288,075
30-34	297,201
25-29	346,705
20-24	464,072
15-19	519,514
10-14	520,719
5-9	494,799
below 5	437,145

Source: U.S. Department of Commerce, *1970 Census of Population*, 1970.

Figure 2.20. Number of Males per Hundred Females in N.C., 1970

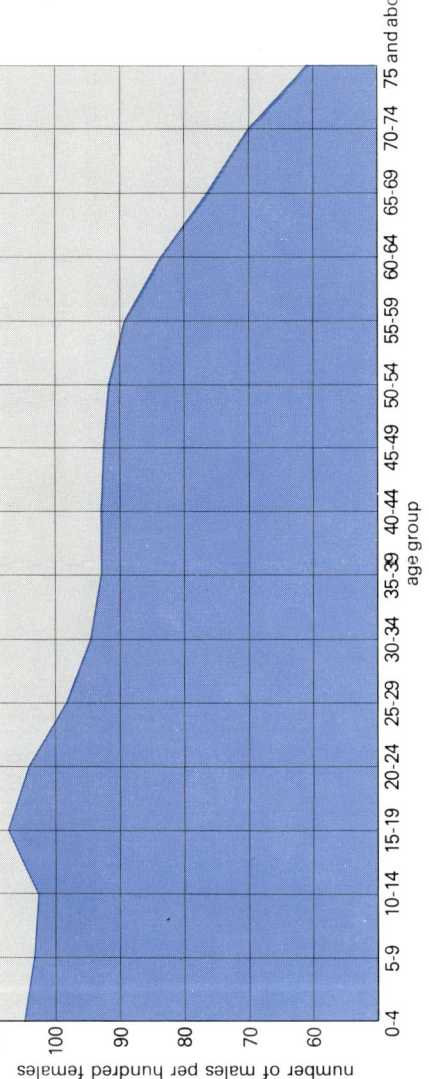

Source: U.S. Department of Commerce, *1970 Census of Population*, 1970.

Figure 2.21. Total Population by Age in N.C., 1960–1970

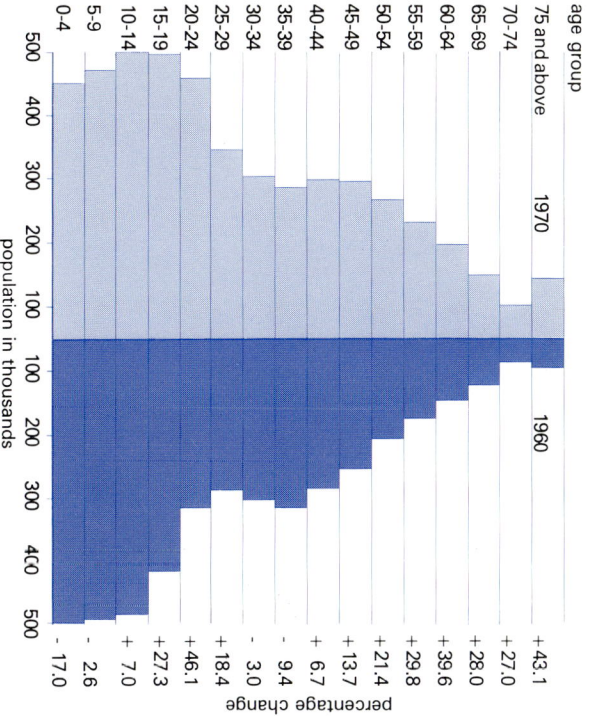

Source: C. Horace Hamilton, *North Carolina Population Trends: A Demographic Sourcebook*, vol. 1 (Chapel Hill: Carolina Population Center, 1974).

The higher fertility of the intervening decades is also clearly discernible. People born during the 1950s constituted the largest age groups in 1970 (ages ten to nineteen). Their presence surely will be felt in the next several decades as they progress through the public school system and the university system, and into the job and housing markets. Additionally, the twenty to twenty-nine age groups change occurred in the twenty to twenty-nine age groups (200, 268), which, over the course of the decade, saw the relatively small depression cohorts replaced by the post–World War II "baby boom" survivors.

Although all of the remaining age categories grew from 1960 to 1970, the most striking developments occurred in the over sixty age groups. With just one exception, the older categories displayed the largest proportional increase in the entire age spectrum. Largely explained by increases in life expectancy, this change had the overall impact of increasing North Carolina's elderly population (sixty years and over) from 9.7 percent of the total population (1960) to 12.1 percent (1970).

Racial and Residential Variations

Additional insight into the age and sex structure of North Carolina can be achieved if the population is subdivided on the basis of race and rural-urban residence (Figure 2.22). The racial differences are both distinct and consistent. In particular, the nonwhite component in all three residential categories displays substantially larger proportions of young adults and children. Consequently, whereas 36.2 percent of the white population was aged nineteen years or less in 1970, the same cohorts comprised nearly half (47.6 percent) of the nonwhite population. Although this variation is the product of a combination of factors, the most important influence appears to have been the comparatively high fertility rates that have characterized nonwhites during the last several decades.

It is interesting to note that the age pyramids for both racial groups include clear evidence of a decline in fertility during the 1960s. Consistent with the patterns of the total population, the youngest cohorts (zero through nine years) were less numerous than those born during the 1940s and 1950s. This is not to say that either group has achieved zero population growth, however, because with such large numbers of people either just entering or about to enter the childbearing years, even a comparatively low fertility rate will produce substantial increases in the absolute number of residents. In fact, with half of their population less than twenty-two years old in 1970, the nonwhite component also could continue to experience large migration losses, and yet still continue to grow. If black out-migration should slow down, however, the state's black component will increase even more.

Among the residential groups, unique age and sex structures appear in the rural farm areas. The white pyramid in this category displays the powerful influence of migration. The exaggerated indentations in the twenty to thirty-nine and the zero to nine age groups, and the uncommonly large proportions in the older age groups (forty years and above) both reflect the age-selectivity of rural out-migration. In other words, those people leaving the rural farm areas for other states, and for urban and rural nonfarm areas within the state, are overwhelmingly comprised of young adults and their families. The older cohorts are less mobile, and the comparatively large proportion of children between age ten and nineteen is probably an indication of both the high fertility during the 1950s, and the relative inertia of families with children in school.

The nonwhite rural farm pyramid also expresses the clear effects of significant net out-migrations. Although similar exaggerated indentations appear in the twenty to thirty-nine and zero to four age groups, when compared to their respective white cohorts, the older age groups are considerably smaller, and the fifteen to nineteen age groups are substantially larger. In other words, the large proportions in the younger categories, which are already large due to high fertility, are increased further when the young adults are removed through migration.

Figure 2.22. Total Population by Age, Sex, Race, and Residential Category in N.C., 1970

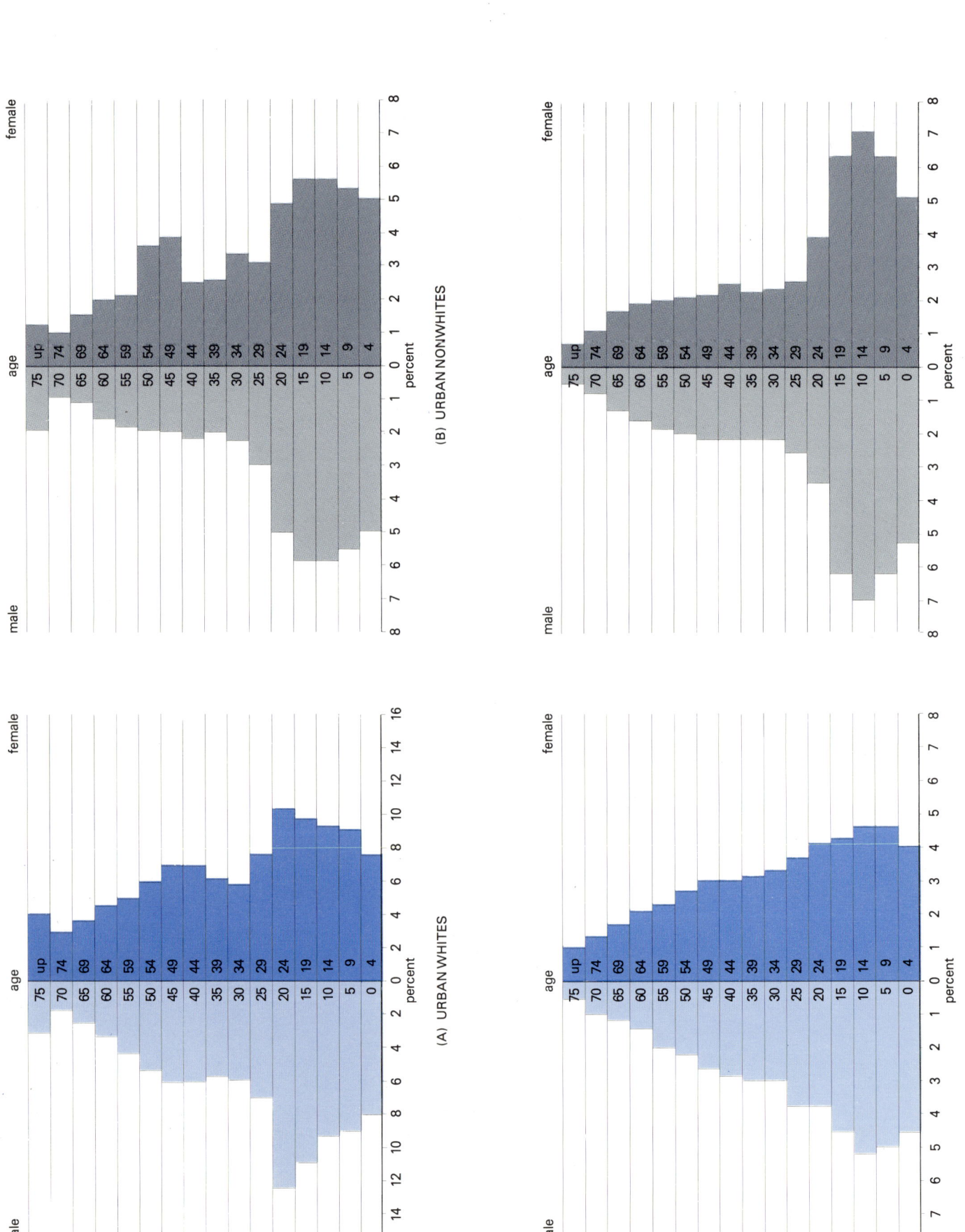

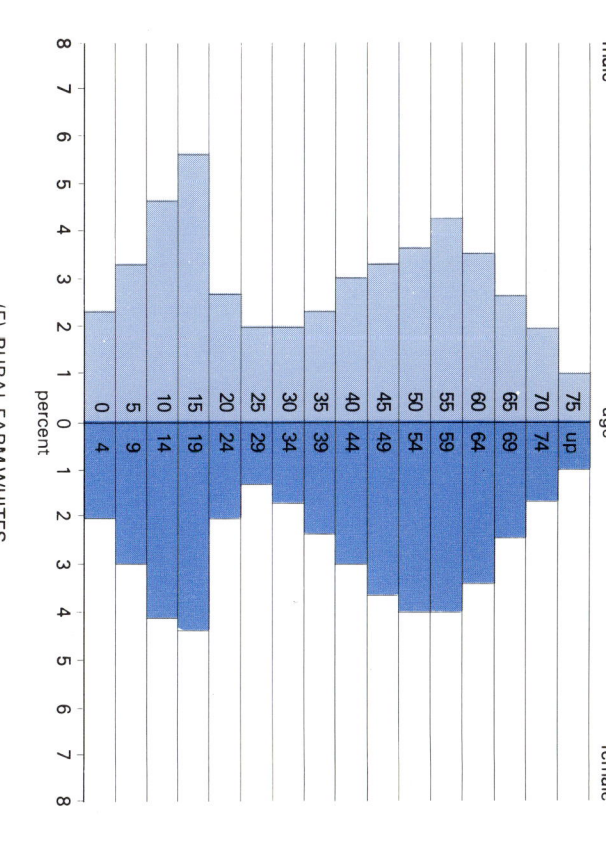

(E) RURAL FARM WHITES

(F) RURAL FARM NONWHITES

Source: C. Horace Hamilton, *North Carolina Population Trends: A Demographic Sourcebook*, vol. 1 (Chapel Hill: Carolina Population Center, 1974).

Median Age

One meaningful way to summarize changes in the age structure of a population is to examine changes in the median age. In view of the proportional increase of the elderly, and the relative decline displayed by the younger age groups, the increase from 25.5 to 26.5 years that occurred in the 1960s was to be expected.

Compared to the nation, North Carolina has always been a young state. As recently as 1960, for instance, the United States had a median age of 29.5 years, which was a full four years higher than the state's. Subsequently, however, the gap has narrowed to just 1.6 years. This is because as North Carolina has grown demographically older, the nation's median age has fallen to 28.1 years. If the same trends continue, the median ages should be nearly equal by 1980.

COMPONENTS OF POPULATION CHANGE

Every population change is determined by at least one of three major components: fertility, mortality, and migration. This includes population growth and decline, changing age and sex structures, and population redistribution. Hence, additional insight into recent North Carolina population trends can be achieved by examining the role of each of these components in greater detail.

Fertility

Trends and Differentials

The people of North Carolina have had relatively high fertility (reproduction) rates when compared with the nation and the South. As Figure 2.23 indicates, over the last three decades the state's crude birthrate (defined as the number of live births in a given year per 1,000 midyear inhabitants) has exceeded the nation's in every year; and it has been at least equal to the South's rate in all but four years.

The relatively low birthrates in 1940 were remnants of the depression era. Seven years later, after a slightly irregular increase, the crude birthrates of all three areas were at their highest levels in the entire thirty-year period. This peak in fertility, which coincides with the beginning of the popularly designated post-World War II "baby boom," was caused primarily by the creation and expansion of families that had been postponed during the war. After a slight and temporary decline, fertility remained at a consistently high level until the latter part of the 1950s. At that point a steady decline began, and it culminated in 1969 with the lowest birthrates since the depression in all three areas. The South and North Carolina were tied with 18.7 births per 1,000 midyear inhabitants, and the United States was even lower at 17.7. Each area experienced an unexpected increase between 1969 and 1970, but there are indications that this was a temporary change since the state's rate was back down to 18.6 in 1971.

Perhaps the most important feature of the preceding developments is the extent to which the crude birthrate of North Carolina has gradually converged with those of the South and the United States. Whereas the state had a substantially higher rate in 1940, by 1957 it was slightly below the South. These same two areas had identical rates in 1961, and ever since then their differences have been insignificant. In a similar manner, although the

43

Figure 2.23. Crude Birthrates for the U.S., the South, and N.C., 1940-1970

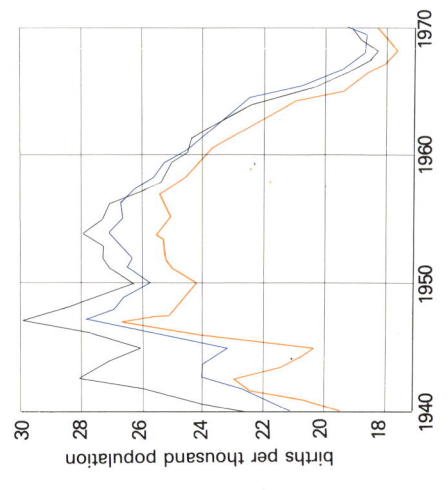

Source: U.S. Department of Commerce, *United States Vital Statistics*, 1940-68; U.S. Department of Commerce, *Statistical Abstract of the United States*, 1972; N.C. State Board of Health, *North Carolina Vital Statistics*, 1969-70.

state rate never has fallen as low as the nation's, the gap between them has narrowed considerably. Clearly, the long-term tradition of higher fertility in North Carolina is changing.

Additional support for this contention can be derived from an examination of recent changes in the fertility ratio. Defined as the number of children under five years of age per 1,000 women in the reproductive years (ages fifteen to forty-four), the fertility ratio is a better measure of actual fertility performance. Most of its advantage over the crude birthrate is the result of differences in the denominators of the two indexes. Whereas the crude birthrate reports the number of live births per 1,000 *total* population, and is therefore strongly influenced by the age and sex structure of that population, the fertility ratio considers only those components of the population that are actually exposed to the risk of pregnancy. Hence, men, younger children, and older women are not considered.

Figure 2.24. Fertility Ratios of the U.S., the South, and N.C., 1880-1970

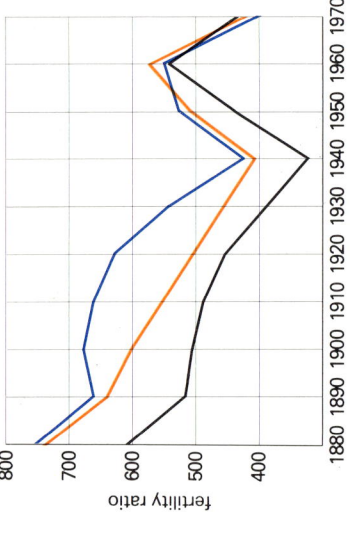

Source: C. Horace Hamilton, *North Carolina Population Trends: A Demographic Sourcebook*, vol. 1 (Chapel Hill: Carolina Population Center, 1974).

Note: Fertility ratio is defined as the number of children under 5 years of age per 1,000 women 15 to 44 years of age.

Table 2.3. Racial and Residential Differentials in the Fertility Ratios of the U.S. and N.C., 1970

	Residence		Race	
	Urban	Rural	White	Nonwhite
U.S.	391*	443	392	482
N.C.	372	412	367	486

Source: U.S. Department of Commerce, *1970 Census of Population and Housing*, 1970.
*Births per 1,000 women aged 15 to 44.

As Figure 2.24 indicates, the fertility ratios of North Carolina, the South, and the United States have followed the same general trend as the crude birthrate. The decline during the early decades of this century, the increase from 1940 to 1960, and the dramatic decline during the most recent decade are all quite clear. The convergence of fertility performance in the three areas is also obvious but, in this case, North Carolina actually fell below both the South and the nation during the 1950s. For a partial explanation of this development, as well as a clearer understanding of North Carolina fertility trends, it is necessary to subdivide the population on the basis of age, race, and residential status.

At first impression, one might conclude that North Carolina should have a higher fertility ratio than the nation. It has proportionately large rural and nonwhite populations, and two of the most consistent fertility differentials in the United States are that these two groups have substantially higher reproductive rates than their respective urban and white counterparts. As Table 2.3 indicates, these differentials were evident in both the state and the nation in 1970. How, then, can North Carolina, with 55.0 percent of its population classified as rural, and 23.2 percent classified as nonwhite, have a total fertility ratio of only 394 when the nation has one of 404?

The factors responsible for this surprising reversal must be far-reaching because, as the statistics in Table 2.3 disclose, the national ratios exceeded the state ratios in all but one category. Additionally, when the data on race and residence in 1970 are examined simultaneously rather than singularly, the whites and nonwhites in the state exhibit the lowest levels of fertility in each residential category (Table 2.4). This represents a complete reversal of their relative positions in 1950 when North Carolina consistently led the nation.

Two explanations are suggested: (1) North Carolina women may be practicing family planning more than the women in the nation; and (2) a large proportion of the women in the childbearing years in North Carolina may be concentrated in the older and less productive portion of that age level. Both of these factors deserve additional consideration.

Although it is difficult to prove conclusively that family planning is practiced more in one place than another, there is clear evidence that in North Carolina women throughout the childbearing ages were electing to have fewer children in 1970 than they did in 1960. In order to illustrate this trend, consider the birthrate of women between the ages of twenty and twenty-four. In 1960, as the most productive cohorts in the state, the women in this group delivered children at a rate of 235 for every

Figure 2.25. Birthrates by Age Groups and Race for N.C. Women, 1970

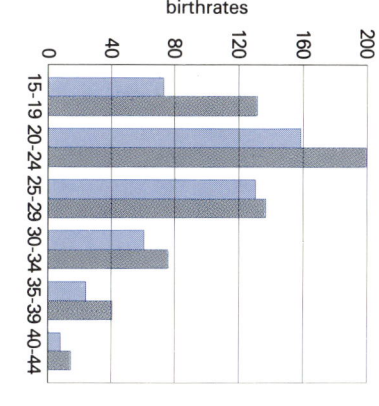

Source: Thomas E. Steahr, *North Carolina's Changing Population* (Chapel Hill: Carolina Population Center, 1973).

Table 2.4. Fertility Ratios by Residence and Race for N.C. and the U.S., 1930–1970

		1930	1940	1950	1960	1970
N.C.	Urban	358	268	391	502	372
	White	386	271	400	617	346
	Nonwhite	301	263	437	465	452
	Rural	599	494	594	576	412
	White	591	466	522	506	384
	Nonwhite	617	571	729	803	519
U.S.	Urban	315	257	422	540	391
	White	319	258	422	525	378
	Nonwhite	275	248	426	647	435
	Rural	511	442	578	621	443
	White	508	429	561	597	431
	Nonwhite	531	525	715	840	539

Source: U.S. Department of Commerce, *Census of Population*, 1930–70.

1,000 group members. Ten years later, the same age group was still the most productive in the state, but the birthrate had fallen to 167. In other words, an equal number of women between the ages of twenty and twenty-four would have delivered 28.7 percent fewer children in 1970 than in 1960. Similar declines occurred within each of the childbearing years (Figure 2.25), and among all racial groups.

A logical conclusion is that this pattern of fewer children is a reflection of an increased desire and ability to avoid unwanted pregnancies. In most cases, the desire to restrict family size has been influenced by such things as (1) an increased concern for the environmental and economic impact of population growth; (2) restricted job markets; (3) inflation; (4) increased educational attainment among young persons; and (5) changes in the norms concerning family-size preferences. Once the desires are established, the likelihood that they can be fulfilled has been increased by improvements in contraceptive technologies, and the existence and spread of local family planning programs.

The second explanation for North Carolina's unexpectedly low fertility ratios involved the age composition of the female population. Since fertility ratios are an expression of the number of children under five years of age per 1,000 women aged fifteen to forty-four, and because the individual members of this age interval have different birthrates, the fertility ratio is influenced by unusual age distributions. As an example, if women in the most productive age groups (eighteen to twenty-nine) are relatively scarce, most of the 1,000 women in the ratio's denominator will be those who are less likely to bear children. Under these conditions, a low ratio is virtually unavoidable.

This explanation applies in North Carolina because of the differential migration of females. Areas of out-migration tend to have a relative scarcity of women (and men) aged eighteen to twenty-nine; and conversely, areas of in-migration tend to have an abnormally high proportion of people similarly aged. In large part, this is because people between these ages are the most mobile group in society.

At any rate, the decline in the fertility of rural whites in North Carolina (Table 2.4) seems to be at least partially related to the fact that many of the most productive females were leaving the rural areas and heading for urban centers. This left behind relatively large proportions of females who were less likely to bear children, and thus, the rural fertility ratios declined. Moreover, as these productive rural whites moved into urban centers, they tended to inflate the ratios in those areas. This is

Figure 2.26. Fertility Ratios for N.C. Counties, 1970

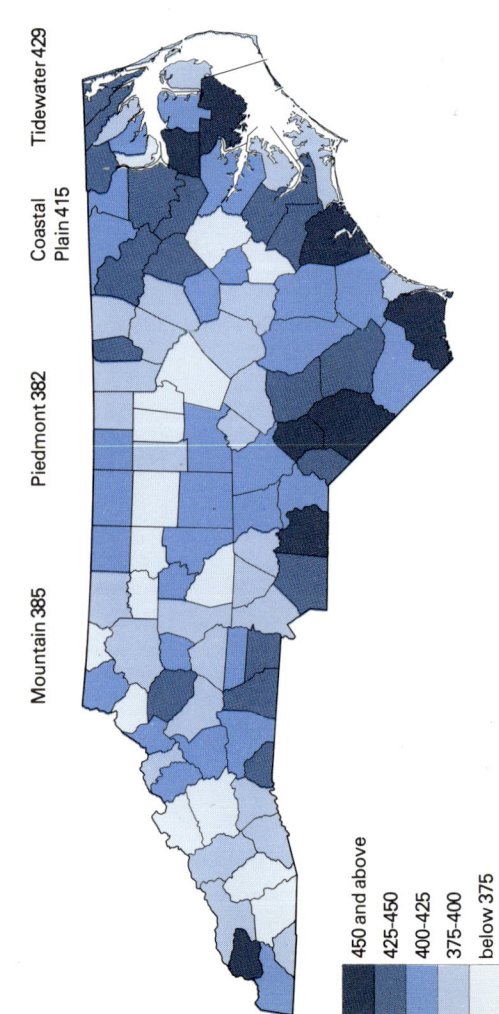

Mountain 385 Piedmont 382 Coastal Plain 415 Tidewater 429

450 and above
425-450
400-425
375-400
below 375

Source: U.S. Department of Commerce, *1970 Census of Population*, 1970.

Note: Fertility ratio is defined as the number of children under 5 years of age per 1,000 women 15 to 44 years of age.

shown in Table 2.4 by the fact that as the rural white ratio fell from 522 to 506 between 1950 and 1960, the urban white ratio increased from 400 to 617! Except for the fact that their migration flows are more likely to leave the state, the same situation exists within the nonwhite population.

One might conclude that, even though it is very difficult to project future fertility performance, North Carolina's can be expected to remain comparatively low, and perhaps decline even more, as long as (1) North Carolinians continue to urbanize; (2) the state continues to lose significant proportions of its women in the most fertile years; (3) the norms that encourage smaller families, as well as the practices that permit their realization, become thoroughly diffused throughout the state.

Current Levels of Fertility within the State Figure 2.26 can be used to assess current county and regional variations in the level of fertility. A brief glance at this map reveals that (1) fertility ratios differ widely from one section of the state to another, and more specifically, that (2) the level of fertility tends to decrease from east to west. These differences generally reflect both racial and rural-urban variations.

The Tidewater (with a fertility ratio of 429) and the Coastal Plain (415) regions are above the state average (394). Both are strongly influenced by the rural environment within which most of their population functions. Moreover, the nonwhite population is proportionately abundant, and itself, very rural. Given these conditions, therefore, the high fertility rates are not surprising.

The Piedmont (382) and the Mountain regions (385) have the lowest levels of fertility. Although there is virtually no difference between their ratios, the conditions producing these low levels of reproduction are quite different. On the one hand, the Mountain region is characterized by disproportionately high percentages of elderly people, a relative scarcity of women in the reproductive years, and very few nonwhites. The Piedmont region, on the other hand, is the most highly urbanized part of the state, and thus its residents are strongly influenced by urban fertility norms and practices.

Mortality

Trends and Differentials

When compared with the recent changes in fertility, those in mortality have been much less dramatic. Since 1940, when the crude death rate (defined as the number of deaths per 1,000 population at midyear) was 9.0, only minor fluctuations have occurred. After a gradual decline produced a low of 7.5 in 1955, the crude death rate increased just as slowly until 1970. The 8.8 deaths per 1,000 people recorded in that year was below the rates of both the nation (9.4) and the South (9.5).

Since the crude death rate does not control for variations in the age structure, the preceding changes must be interpreted with considerable caution. As an example, the lower death rate in the state, when compared to the region and the nation, is largely the result of a younger age distribution and a lower median age. Additionally, it can be shown that instead of increasing from 8.4 to 8.8 between 1960 and 1970, the crude death rate in North Carolina would have declined to 7.9 if the age structure had remained unchanged throughout the decade.

An examination of age-specific death rates further reveals why the age composition of the population is such an important consideration in interpreting levels of mortality. Defined as the total number of deaths in a specific age interval per 1,000 people in the same interval, age-specific death rates are not affected by variations in age composition. As Figure 2.27 demonstrates, they change considerably. After high death rates during the first year of life, mortality normally declines until approximately age fourteen when it begins a steady increase that continues throughout the older ages.

Figure 2.27 also depicts several very clear racial and sexual differentials in mortality. In general, whites have lower rates than nonwhites, and females have lower rates than males. Consequently, at every age level except one (the eighty years and over group), white females possess the lowest death rate, and nonwhite males possess the highest death rate. The relative positions of the remaining two groups are not as clear-cut. From birth until age forty-five, white males generally have lower rates than nonwhite females. Beyond that point, however, the situation reverses. This indicates that while race is a more important influence than sex during the early years, as one moves into the later years, women of both races outlive men.

Figure 2.27. Average Death Rates by Age, Race, and Sex in N.C., 1971

— white male
— white female
— nonwhite male
— nonwhite female

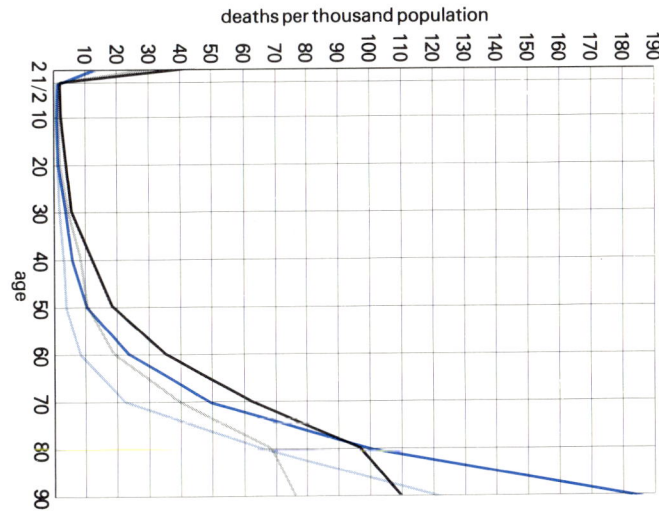

Source: N.C. State Board of Health, *North Carolina Vital Statistics*, 1971.

Figure 2.28. N.C. Crude Death Rate by County, 1970

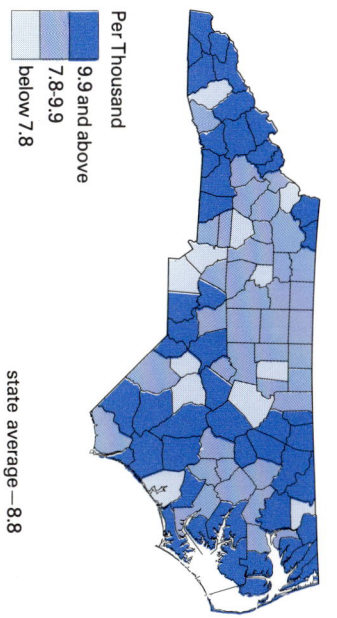

Per Thousand
- 9.9 and above
- 7.8-9.9
- below 7.8

state average—8.8

Source: N.C. State Board of Health, *North Carolina Vital Statistics*, 1971.

Current Levels of Mortality within the State County and regional variations in the crude death rate were not very large in 1970 (Figure 2.28). Only nine counties had rates that were at least three points above the state average of 8.8 deaths per 1,000 residents. Each region had a representative in this group but the Tidewater and the Mountain areas predominated with four and three counties, respectively. At the other extreme, only three counties had rates that were at least three points below the state average. These appear in every region except the Mountain region.

The existence of both of these "extreme" groups is related to differences in the age structure, race, and residential status of the population. In particular, the influence of age is especially clear. As an example, two of the three counties with low death rates are the sites of large military installations, namely, Fort Bragg in Cumberland County and Camp Lejeune in Onslow County. The other county in this group (Orange) includes the university town of Chapel Hill.

Migration

Trends and Differentials
If fertility and mortality were the only factors influencing population growth, North Carolina would be considerably more populous than it is today. The just over one million babies that were added to the population between 1960 and 1970 were only partially counterbalanced by 412,000 deaths. Hence, on the basis of these two components alone, the state would have increased by more than 620,000 people. The fact that the actual growth was only 526,000, however, is clear evidence that a third factor, migration, was also in operation.

The net loss of 94,000 people through migration during the 1960s was consistent with a trend that has existed in every decade since 1900. Experts generally agree that most of the massive outflows during this period were motivated by lack of sufficient economic opportunities in the state. The peak outflow occurred during the 1940s when the net loss exceeded 250,000 people. Since that decade, however, the state's economy, and especially its industrial base, has grown. Concomitantly, the migration losses have declined steadily. In fact, census statistics show that between 1965 and 1970, the state actually had a net migration *gain* of 21,428 people. (This information is derived from the 1970 census, and unfortunately, it is only a partial accounting of the entire decade's flows. The statistics only refer to those people who lived in one state in 1965 and another in 1970. They do not consider any intervening moves that might have occurred, and even more importantly, they disclose nothing about the first half of the decade.) If a similar pattern continues through the 1970s, North Carolina will experience its first decade of positive migration in this century.

One of the most intriguing aspects of this recent development is a very distinct racial differential. While the white component grew by 81,000 people through migration between 1960 and 1970, the nonwhite group declined by 175,000. Hence, the net loss of 94,000 people was entirely the result of nonwhite mobility. Their net loss was so large, it nearly neutralized their rapid growth via natural increase. With a surplus of 196,000 births over deaths, the nonwhite growth actually amounted to just 21,000 or 2.0 percent when migration adjustments were included. It is important to note that there are clear indications that the black outflow may be slowing considerably. Of the net loss of 175,000 nonwhites, just 25,000 occurred in the last half of the decade. This would be another very important change if it continues. In particular, if more nonwhites decide to remain within the state, and yet continue to shift from rural to urban areas, the impact on the state's larger urban places, and especially those in the Piedmont, will be monumental and far-reaching.

Figure 2.29. Origins and Destinations of Population Migrating to and from N.C., 1969-1970

Figure 2.29, which depicts the general flow of migrants to and from North Carolina between 1965 and 1970, reveals several other racial differences. The origins of the black migrants to the state are heavily concentrated in just two regions, the Middle Atlantic, which contributed 26.8 percent of the total, and the South Atlantic, which contributed 44.2 percent. Many of the individual states in these two regions were very important source areas in themselves. In fact, if the forty-nine other states and the District of Columbia are ranked on the basis of the number of migrants they sent to North Carolina during the period in question, the top nine, led by New York (16.1 percent of the total), South Carolina (13.5 percent), and Virginia (10.0 percent), would fall into one of these two regions.

The origins of the white migrants, on the other hand, were more diverse. At first glance, this may seem unlikely since the neighboring South Atlantic states were just as predominant (contributing 42.5 percent of all white migrants) as they were for the black migrants. But the next largest contribution, which happened to come from the Middle Atlantic region, was only 12.9 percent of the total. Similar proportions came from the East North Central states (11.3 percent), the East South Central states (9.1 percent), and the Pacific (7.8 percent). In addition to specific states in the South Atlantic region, especially Virginia (13.4 percent), South Carolina (8.9 percent), Florida (8.4 percent), and Georgia (5.8 percent), substantial proportions of white migrants also came from such widespread places as New York (5.6 percent), California (5.5 percent), Tennessee (4.3 percent), Ohio (3.7 percent), and Texas (3.5 percent).

Additional racial discrepancies are apparent in the movement of migrants away from the state. Among the majority of black out-migrants, the decision to leave North Carolina was concomitant with a decision to leave the South. The 43.2 percent who remained in the South, however, were highly concentrated in the South Atlantic states. In fact, the two South Central regions together only attracted 4.8 percent of all the black migrants. Those with South Atlantic destinations displayed a distinct northward orientation. Virginia, Maryland, and the District of Columbia accounted for three-fourths of the entire 38.4 percent who remained in this region. A proportion almost equal to those who elected to remain in the South chose to move to the Northeast (42.2 percent), and especially to the Middle Atlantic states (35.2 percent). New York was the most popular destination in the United States (18.3 percent), and New Jersey (10.5 percent) ranked third behind the District of Columbia (11.3 percent). The only other regions to attract more than 5.0 percent of the state's black out-migrants were New England (7.0 percent) and the East North Central

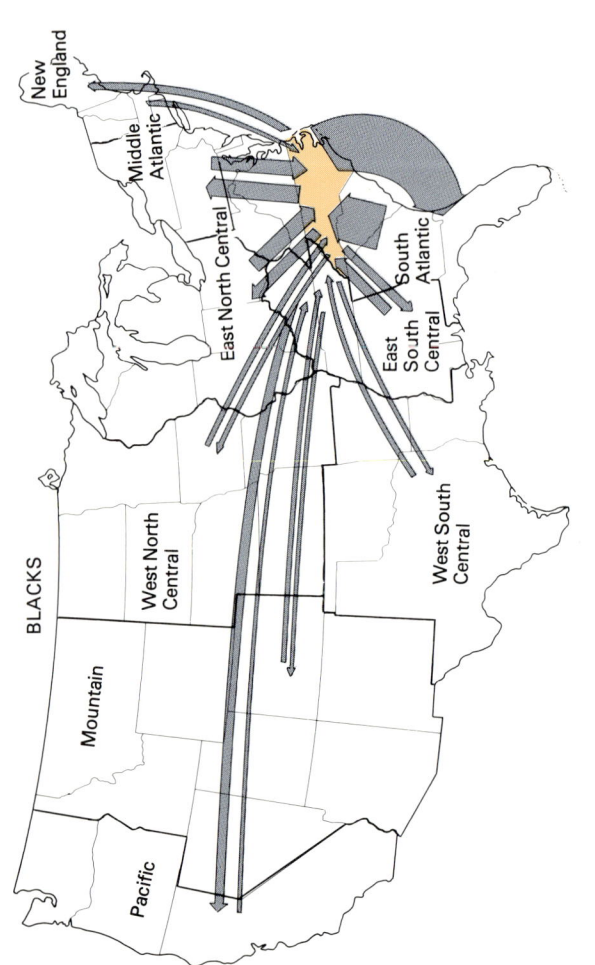

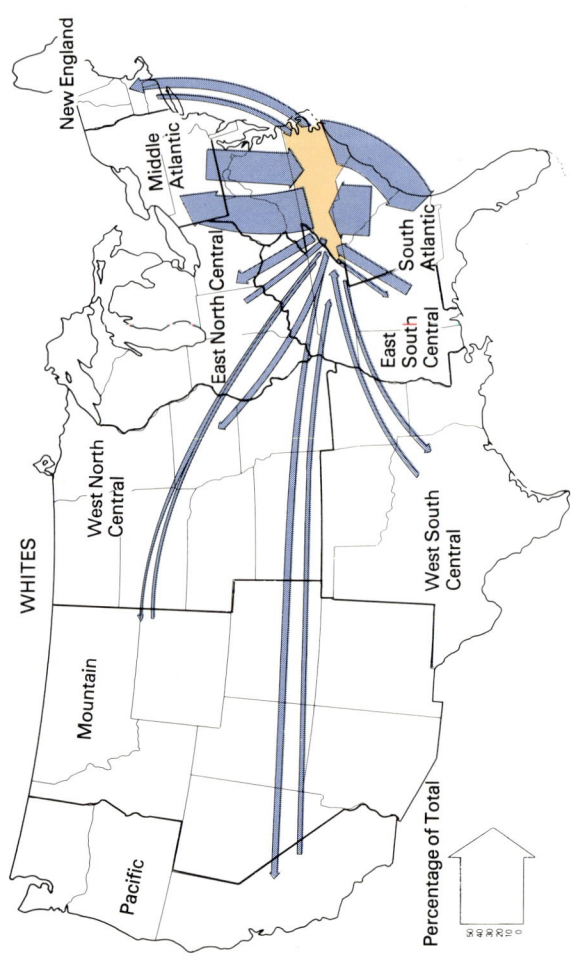

Source: U.S. Department of Commerce, *1970 Census of Population*, 1970.

area (7.1 percent). Clearly, the black movements were not oriented in either a southward or a westward direction.

In contrast to the pattern of black destinations, those of the white migrants show a stronger preference for the South and a greater aversion for the Northeast. Almost two-thirds of the whites who left the South between 1965 and 1970 remained in the South. The South Atlantic states were far and away the most attractive, accounting for 49.5 percent of all the migrants. And the South Central regions pulled in another 14.6 percent. Within the South, the leading destinations were the neighboring and nearby states of Virginia, South Carolina, Georgia, and Florida. Together, they attracted 44.3 percent of the state's white migrants. The Northeast, on the other hand, was the destination for just 12.0 percent. This contrasts sharply with the strong black attraction to this region. Other regions with more than a 5.0 percent appeal were the East North Central (8.8 percent) and the Pacific (9.1 percent). California was the fifth most important destination in the entire United States. Obviously, the southern and western orientation of white out-migrants is very different from the northern orientation of the blacks.

The influence of age on interstate movements is another differential that deserves recognition. Between 1965 and 1970, the state experienced a net in-migration of 21,000 people, but significantly, all age groups did not share in this growth equally. In fact, three intervals actually decreased as a result of net out-migration. Young adults, who were between the ages of 25 and 29 by the end of the decade, declined by a total of 17,700 people. Since it can be safely assumed that some of these people were married, and hence, that some had started families, it is not surprising that the other two decreases occurred among children aged five to nine and ten to fourteen in 1970. Additionally, because people between the ages of twenty-five and twenty-nine have one of the highest fertility rates in the state, the fact that such a large decline occurred is doubly important.

The influence of age-selective migration on fertility becomes even clearer when the migration flows are subdivided on the basis of sex. The previous discussion of age-specific fertility revealed that the highest rates occur among women in the twenty to twenty-nine age group, and especially among those between the ages of twenty and twenty-four. It is significant, therefore, that both these groups declined through migration between 1965 and 1970. Females in the younger, more productive group decreased by 3,340 (or 1.5 percent when compared to their numbers in 1965); and those in the more mature group fell by 5,140 (or 3.0 percent). Hence, there was a net loss of 8,480 women in the midst of their most productive years. This helped to deflate the state's fertility ratio, especially since the other age groups between the productive years (fifteen to forty-four) either grew or remained virtually unchanged due to migration.

It is instructive to note that while women of both races shared in the decline between the ages twenty-five and twenty-nine, entire loss in the twenty to twenty-four age group was caused by black out-migration. In fact, since white women of this age increased through migration, the black loss was much larger than the statistics for the total population indicate. Specifically, the net decline among black women aged twenty to twenty-four years was 6,861. This represented the largest relative decline (-15.8 percent) in any racial-sexual group in the state. The implications of this trend are important when one considers the fact that this particular group is the single most fertile group in the entire state.

Differential migration also has had an impact on several other North Carolina age groups, specifically: (1) all black female groups experienced net out-migration; (2) up until age fifty-five all black male groups also declined through migration, but beyond that age there were across-the-board net increases; (3) white males between the ages of fifteen and nineteen increased by more than 15,000 (5.9 percent), and those between twenty and twenty-four grew by nearly 17,000 (7.8 percent), partially illustrating the strong pull created by the state's military installations; and (4) there are indications that the state is becoming an attractive retirement center since, with the exception of black females, all other groups above age fifty-five increased through migration.

Current Levels of Migration within the State

In order to understand fully the role that migration plays in the changing population structure of North Carolina's counties and regions, it is necessary to recognize that more than interstate shifts are involved. Of the more than 4.6 million state residents who were at least five years old in 1970, nearly 1.9 million, or 40.5 percent, were living in a different house in the United States in 1965. A large majority of these movers (59.5 percent) did not cross a county boundary when they changed homes. Hence, their moves had very little, if any, impact on county level population changes. The remaining 40.5 percent, on the other hand, were intimately involved in the processes of change. Either they moved to North Carolina from another state (21.5 percent) or they moved within the state to a different county (19.0 percent). Together with those who left the state, these migrants produced several interesting changes in North Carolina's population patterns.

Figures 2.30 and 2.31 show the influence of each component of population change between 1960 and 1970. Since no county had more deaths than births, however, only three types of changes were possible. First, the natural increase (the excess of births over deaths) may have been supplemented by net in-migration, usually producing strong growth. Second, the natural increase may have been only partially neutralized by net out-migration, resulting in modest increases. And finally, the natural increase may have been exceeded by net out-migration, thus causing a population loss. The occurrence of these possibilities is depicted at the county level in Figures 2.30 and 2.31. The counties with in-migration are subdivided into those with large gains (10 percent or more) and those with moderate or small gains.

As Figure 2.30 indicates, when the total population is considered several distinct patterns emerge. Perhaps the most striking feature is the fact that only thirty counties experienced net in-migration. The Piedmont was the only region in which as many as one-half of its counties (seventeen) attracted more migrants than they lost during the 1960s (Table 2.5). The other regions ranged from 28 percent of the counties in the Mountain region, where seven of twenty-five counties grew through migration, and 25 percent in the Tidewater, where five of twenty counties increased, to an extremely low 5 percent in the Coastal Plain, where only one of the twenty counties (Cumberland) had a net in-migration.

A glance at the specific counties in this category suggests that two main streams of movement were in operation: (1) the flow of people out of rural areas and into urban centers, and (2) the flow of people into several of the counties with amenity and recreational attractions. Fourteen of the seventeen metropolitan counties experienced net in-migration, and five of these had gains that exceeded 10 percent of the 1960 population. Amenities appear to have been an important influence in the Tidewater and Mountain regions. The fastest migration increase in the state occurred in Watauga County, the mountainous site of both a major university and substantial recreational facilities.

The thirty-nine counties that lost population between 1960 and 1970 are concentrated largely in the eastern part of the state. Together, the Coastal Plain and Tidewater regions accounted for two-thirds of the counties in this category. The plight of the Coastal Plain is particularly notable since twenty of its twenty-one counties experienced net out-migration, and seventeen of these lacked sufficient natural increase to prevent an overall population loss. The only counties with a population loss in the western one-third of the state are situated along the North Carolina-Tennessee border.

United States Census Bureau estimates show that the patterns of migration changed considerably between 1970 and 1973 (Figure 2.32). The number of counties experiencing net in-migration nearly doubled from thirty to fifty-eight. Most of these (thirty-one) had very modest gains (2.0 percent or less), but particularly large percentage increases occurred in Currituck (20.3 percent); Brunswick (19.3 percent); Watauga (10.8 percent); Orange (10.4 percent); and Dare counties (10.1 percent). Whereas the Piedmont region displayed the most consistent pattern of increase with twenty-seven of its thirty-four counties experiencing net in-migration, at the other extreme, the Coastal Plain region remained the most hard-hit by net out-migration. This latter trend was tempered somewhat, however, since the number of counties with migration losses large enough to cause an overall population decrease declined by more than one-half. Although Cumberland County was the fastest-growing county in the state between 1960 and 1970, it actually lost almost 10,000 people through net out-migration between 1970 and 1973. Since the largest migration loss in the state occurred in Onslow County (-16,300), one might assume that a major influence in both these cases was reductions in military manpower at Fort Bragg and Camp Lejeune.

Additional insights into the patterns of population change in the state can be derived from Figure 2.30. The movements of the nonwhite population (Figure 2.31) are closely related to changes in the total population. In fact, many of the same patterns are duplicated in a more distinct manner. As an example, the dilemma of population loss in the eastern half of the state is closely linked with a massive outflow of nonwhites. Only five of the forty-one counties in the Coastal Plain and Tidewater regions did not lose a portion of their nonwhite population between 1960 and 1970 (Table 2.6). Of the exceptions, two had out-migration but still managed to grow through natural increase, and one was impossible to classify and evaluate since the necessary information was unavailable. Ironically, the two remaining counties, Cumberland and Onslow, were the only ones in the entire state to grow by more than 10 percent through migration.

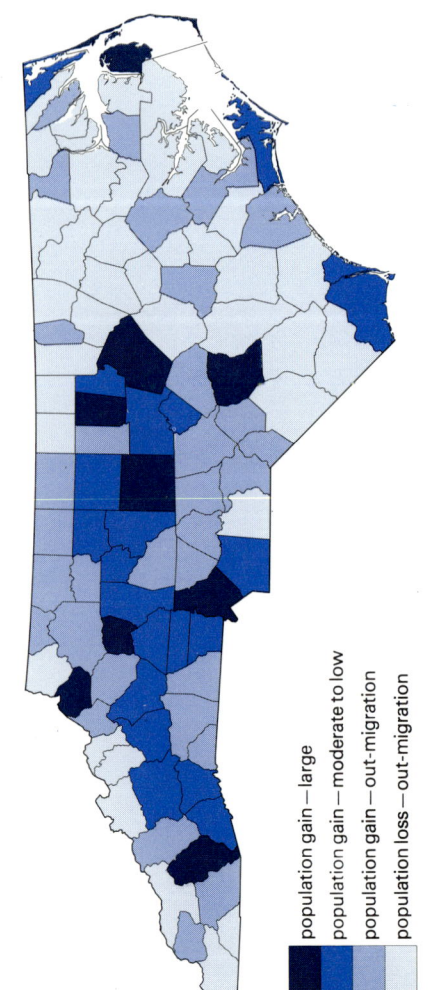

Figure 2.30. Components of Population Change by County for the Total Population of N.C., 1960-1970

- population gain — large
- population gain — moderate to low
- population gain — out-migration
- population loss — out-migration

Source: U.S. Department of Commerce, *Current Population Reports*, Series P-25, no. 464, 1971.

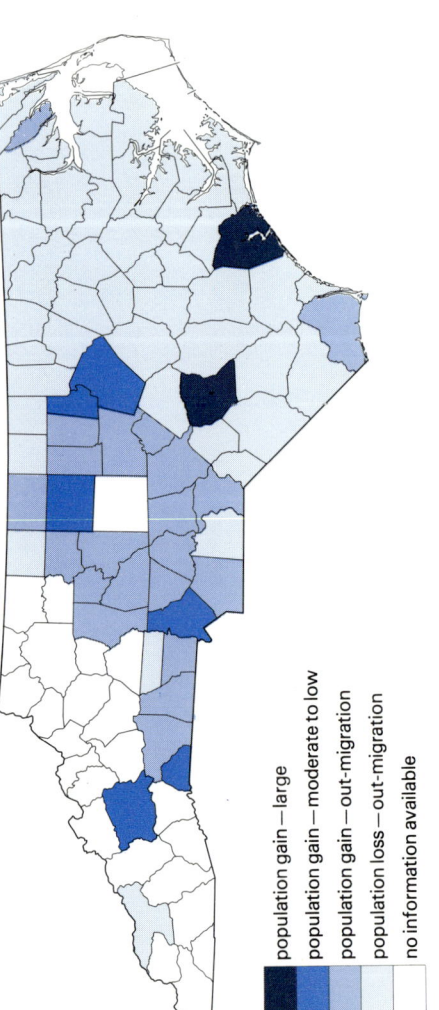

Figure 2.31. Components of Population Change by County for the Nonwhite Population of N.C., 1960-1970

- population gain — large
- population gain — moderate to low
- population gain — out-migration
- population loss — out-migration
- no information available

Source: U.S. department of Commerce, *Current Population Reports*, Series P-25, no. 461, 1971.

Note: No information available for counties with less than 10 percent or 10,000 nonwhites in 1960.

It is apparent that some of the outflows from the surrounding counties were funneled into these areas. In each case, part of the attraction may have been caused by the existence of a large military installation. Cumberland County is the site of Fort Bragg and Pope Air Force Base, while Onslow County is the location of Camp Lejeune.

Although the lack of information about the migration of the nonwhite population for many of the counties in the Mountain region makes it difficult to evaluate the western half of the state, one trend is very clear. Some of the outflow from the east was also funneled into the large metropolitan centers of the Piedmont and the Mountain regions. Five of the six counties that grew through in-migration are the sites of large metropolitan central cities. The significance of this trend is obvious when one recalls the extent to which black out-migration from the state declined between 1965 and 1970. If blacks continue to leave the Coastal Plain and Tidewater regions, but switch to destinations within the state, the Piedmont metropolitan areas can expect to experience substantial nonwhite growth in the future.

Population Projections

Although it is virtually certain that North Carolina's total population will continue to grow over the next several decades, it is literally impossible to predict the exact magnitude of the growth. To do so would require the ability to look into the future and anticipate any forthcoming fluctuations in fertility, mortality, and migration. Nonetheless, information concerning the future size and structure of a society's population is crucial to successful public and private planning. In view of these needs, but with a full understanding of the inherent limitations, demographers have developed several very sophisticated population projection techniques.

Based upon certain assumptions about future trends in fertility, mortality, and migration, the population scientist can identify the logical consequences of these assumptions, and thus, project growth. If the assumptions are faulty, the projections will also be faulty. Consequently, severe social or economic shifts in the society or state during the projection period surely will lead to inaccurate projections. This would include such unpredictable events as wars and economic depressions. Additionally, a less historic change such as one in the norms or attitudes concerning fertility performance also could detract from the projection's accuracy.

Table 2.5. Components of Population Change for the Total Population of N.C. by Region, 1960-1970

Region	Counties with Population Gain and Large In-Migration	Counties with Population Gain and Moderate to Small In-Migration	Counties with Population Gain and Out-Migration	Counties with Population Loss and Out-Migration	Total
Mountain	2	5	11	7	25
Piedmont	5	12	11	6	34
Coastal Plain	1	0	3	17	21
Tidewater	1	4	6	9	20
Total	9	21	31	39	100

Source: U.S. Department of Commerce, *Current Population Reports*, Series P-25, no. 461, 1971.

Table 2.6. Components of Population Change for the Nonwhite Population of N.C. by Region, 1960-1970

Region	Counties with Population Gain and Large In-Migration	Counties with Population Gain and Moderate to Small In-Migration	Counties with Population Gain and Out-Migration	Counties with Population Loss and Out-Migration	No Information	Total
Mountain	0	2	1	1	21	25
Piedmont	0	4	18	9	3	34
Coastal Plain	1	0	0	20	0	21
Tidewater	1	0	2	16	1	20
Total	2	6	21	46	25	100

Source: U.S. Department of Commerce, *Current Population Reports*, Series P-25, no. 461, 1971.

Note: No information available for counties with less than 10 percent or 10,000 nonwhites in 1960.

Figure 2.32. Estimated Population Change, 1970-1973

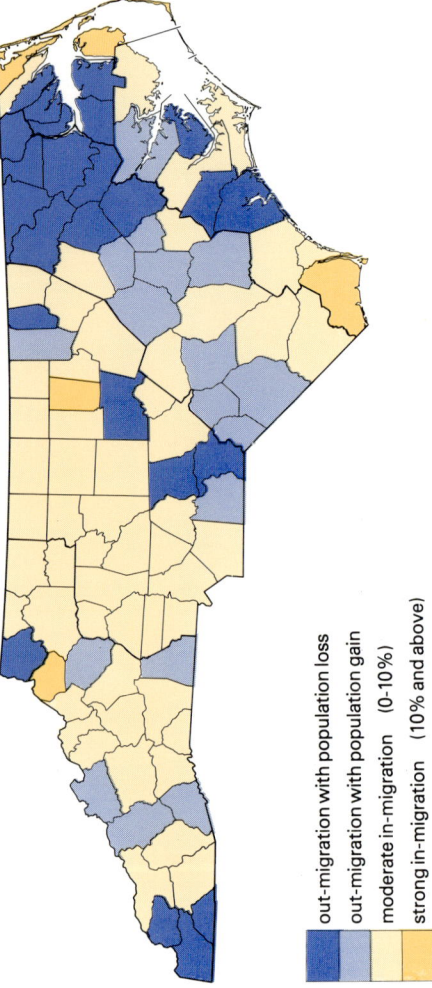

- out-migration with population loss
- out-migration with population gain
- moderate in-migration (0-10%)
- strong in-migration (10% and above)

Source: U.S. Department of Commerce, *Current Population Reports*, Series P-26, no. 68, 1974.

One of the best sources of these projections is the U.S. Census Bureau. Using sophisticated methodologies and four different types of assumptions concerning patterns of interstate migration and national fertility trends, the Census Bureau has developed four projections of each state's total population for the years 1980 and 1985. The North Carolina predictions are ranked below in descending magnitude:

	Total Population	
Projection Series	1980	1985
Census II-B	6,048,000	6,497,000
Census I-B	5,993,000	6,386,000
Census II-D	5,637,000	5,902,000
Census I-D	5,888,000	5,801,000

The highest projections, which resulted from Series II-B, were based upon the assumptions that (1) recent interstate migration rates will change so as to result in no net migration among states; and (2) there will be a moderate increase in fertility. In the case of North Carolina, the migration assumption is an especially important factor in producing the projected growth since it is assumed that the state's traditional net out-migration will stop.

The lowest projections (Series I-D), on the other hand, resulted from the assumptions that (1) recent interstate migration rates will continue; and (2) there will be a continued decline in fertility.

When these maximum and minimum values are considered together, the range of projected growth can be determined. In 1980, for instance, the difference between the highest and lowest projections is 460,000 people. Thus, the total population growth in North Carolina from 1970 to 1980 is projected to be between 19.0 percent and 10.0 percent. It may be recalled that the growth from 1960 to 1970 was 11.5 percent.

The range in 1985 is 696,000 people. This amounts to a fifteen-year projected growth of between 27.8 percent and 14.1 percent. The difference of 13.7 percent is quite substantial and illustrates the fact that variations in the projection assumptions have a greater impact for long-term predictions.

It is important to remember that variations in fertility, mortality, and migration during the next ten to fifteen years will determine which of the preceding projections comes closest to the actual North Carolina population growth. However, perhaps the central message is that regardless of how fertility and migration rates may vary within reasonable ranges, North Carolina will have a substantially greater population within the near future. The implications of both past growth and the virtually certain growth of the future are a primary concern of the rest of this book.

SELECTED REFERENCES

Carolina Population Center and N.C. Department of Administration. *County Population Trends: North Carolina, 1790-1960.* Raleigh: The Center and The Department, 1969.

Clifford, William B., and Mustian, R. David. *Projected Population Growth in North Carolina by Age, Sex, and Color: 1970-1980.* Department of Sociology and Anthropology Progress Report no. 57. Raleigh: North Carolina State University, 1972.

Hamilton, C. Horace. *North Carolina Population Trends: A Demographic Sourcebook*, vol. 1. Chapel Hill: Carolina Population Center, 1974.

Stearn, Thomas E. *North Carolina's Changing Population.* Chapel Hill: Carolina Population Center, 1973.

U.S. Department of Commerce, Bureau of the Census. *Census of Population: 1970*, vol. 1, *Characteristics of the Population: Part 35, North Carolina.* Washington, D.C.: The Department, 1973.

U.S. Department of Commerce, Bureau of the Census. "Components of Population Change by County: 1960 to 1970." *Current Population Reports: Population Estimates and Projections,* Series P-25, no. 461. Washington, D.C.: The Department, 1971.

3. Urbanization

CLYDE E. BROWNING
FRANCIS H. PARKER

THE PATTERN OF URBANIZATION

One very useful definition of "urbanization" is that it is the proportion of a population that lives in places classed as urban. It is one of the simplest statistics about areas and yet one of the most significant because the level of urbanization is often highly correlated with key economic and social aspects of areas. For the United States, the Census Bureau considers places with a population of 2,500 or more as urban (plus the unincorporated fringe of metropolitan areas). In this chapter, urbanization will also be used in a broader sense to include the general urban development and urban pattern of the state.

North Carolina is an urban anomaly. Less than half (45.0 percent) of the state's people live in urban places, a figure far below the national average for 1970 of 73.5 percent. The state ranks forty-fifth in the nation in degree of urbanization. Those states ranking below North Carolina are largely agricultural (the Dakotas, Mississippi, and Vermont) or mining (West Virginia), and their low standing in urbanization is understandable. But North Carolina is a highly industrialized state. Historically, industrialization has been associated with, or even responsible for, urbanization. This has not been the case in North Carolina.

Thus, the major questions are: How has this unique problem of urbanization come to be? What are the advantages and disadvantages of such a low level of urbanization and lack of large cities?

Evolution of the Urban Pattern

North Carolina's low level of urbanization has been a long-lasting condition (Figure 3.1). During the colonial period the colony had only about a dozen towns, small in size and generally undistinguished in appearance, whose total population was estimated to be less than 5,000. Although one of the most populous of the colonies, North Carolina's urban development was hampered by the lack of a good port (especially compared to Norfolk and Charleston), poor roads (in a time of universally primitive roads, North Carolina's were invariably the butt of critical comment by visitors), an overwhelmingly agrarian society, and a generally low income level. When the first census was conducted in 1790 the state had no place with a population of over 2,500 and therefore—officially at least—no urban population.

Not until 1820 did the state officially register any urban population; four places were so designated with a combined population of 12,502. About this time, the United States began to urbanize, especially after 1840. North Carolina, however, actually regressed slightly, from a proportion of 2.5 percent urban in 1820, the state declined to 1.4 percent in 1830 and 1.8 percent in 1840. The number of places qualifying for urban status dropped from four to three. The most striking aspect of North Carolina's urbanization curve (Figure 3.2) is the essentially level line until 1880. For contrast, the urbanization curve of Massachusetts has been included to demonstrate further how retarded was the urban development of North Carolina. In today's largely urban national setting, it is difficult to realize how rural the state was; of North Carolina's nearly one million people in 1860, only 24,554 (less than 2.5 percent) lived in urban places.

About 1880, the pace of urbanization in the state finally began to quicken in response to the growth of industry, particularly textiles and tobacco manufacturing. The general slope of the trend line established then has continued to the present, with the exception of a pause during the Great Depression of the 1930s. Note the more accelerated growth for the South since 1940 in contrast to the relatively constant growth of North Carolina. The South has begun to close the gap in urbanization between it and the nation while the gap between North Carolina and the nation has remained roughly the same (about thirty percentage points).

Turning from the urbanization pattern in general to the growth of particular cities, it is not surprising that the largest towns in North Carolina in the colonial period were in the Coastal Plain (Table 3.1). Not only did some of the population arrive and spread westward from the coast, but water was by far the easiest mode of transport. Virtually all of the early towns were on the coast or one of the larger rivers.

New Bern was the early leader as the capital of the colony but by 1840 Wilmington had taken the lead. Its natural situation, at the mouth of the largest river in the state, gave it an advantage. None of the North Carolina cities, however, could match the size of Charleston, South Carolina, whose 16,359 inhabitants made it the fourth largest city in the nation in 1790. By 1840 Norfolk, Petersburg, Richmond, and Savannah had joined Charleston among the South Atlantic cities over 10,000. No North Carolina city had even 5,000; Wilmington had 4,744 in 1840 and did not pass the 10,000 mark until 1870.

The development of the urban pattern in North Carolina is portrayed in a series of maps beginning in 1860 (Figure 3.3). The 1860 map shows only a scattering of

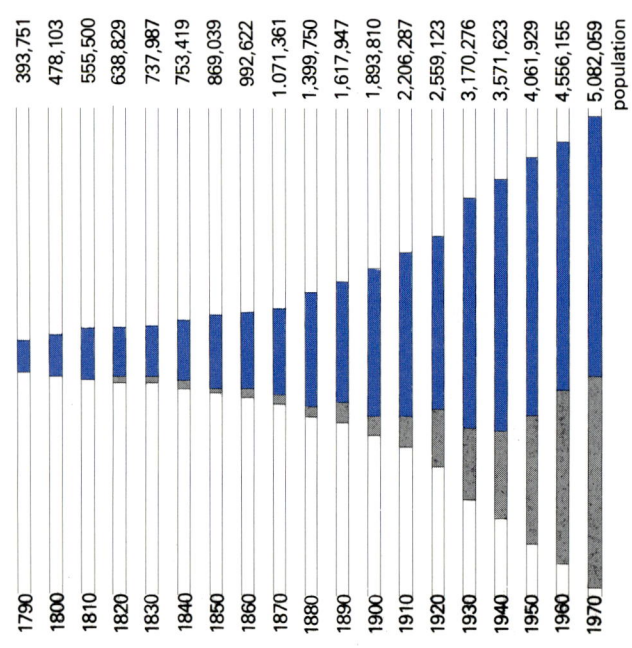

Figure 3.1. Urbanization Trends in N.C., 1790-1970

Source: N.C. Department of Administration, *County Population Trends North Carolina 1790-1960 State Region County*, 1969. U.S. Department of Commerce, *1970 Census of Population*, 1970.

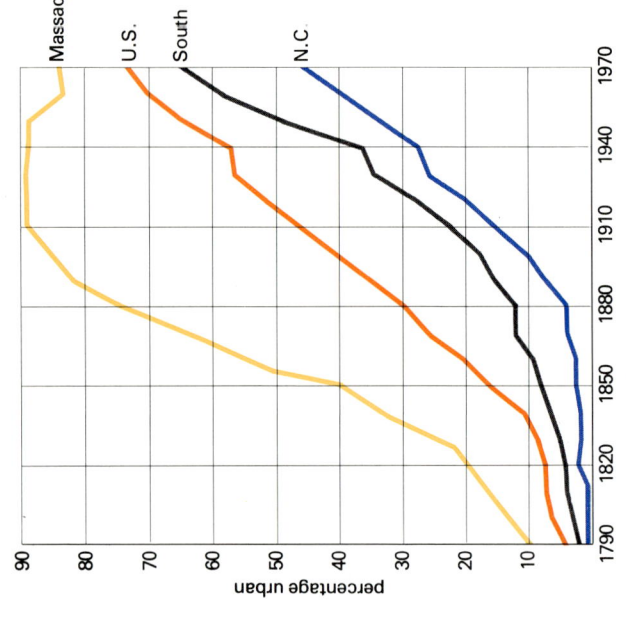

Figure 3.2. Growth of Urbanization in the U.S., South, Massachusetts, and N.C., 1790-1970

Source: U.S. Department of Commerce, *Census of Population* and *Census of Population and Housing*, 1790-1970.

Table 3.1. N.C.'s Ten Largest Cities, 1860-1970

Rank	1860	Population	1880	Population	1910	Population	1940	Population	1970	Population
1	Wilmington	9,552	Wilmington	17,350	Charlotte	34,019	Charlotte	100,899	Charlotte	279,530*
2	New Bern	5,432	Raleigh	9,265	Wilmington	25,798	Winston-Salem	79,815	Fayetteville	161,370*
3	Fayetteville	4,790	Charlotte	7,094	Winston-Salem	22,700	Durham	60,195	Raleigh	152,289*
4	Raleigh	4,780	New Bern	6,443	Raleigh	19,218	Greensboro	59,319	Greensboro	152,252*
5	Salisbury	2,420	Winston-Salem	4,194	Asheville	18,762	Asheville	51,310	Winston-Salem	142,589*
6	Charlotte	2,265	Fayetteville	3,485	Durham	18,241	Raleigh	46,897	Durham	100,769*
7	Kinston	1,335	Goldsboro	3,286	Greensboro	15,895	High Point	38,495	High Point	93,597*
8	Wilson	960	Salisbury	2,723	New Bern	9,961	Wilmington	33,407	Asheville	72,451*
9	Goldsboro	885	Asheville	2,616	High Point	9,525	Rocky Mount	25,568	Wilmington	57,645*
10	Greenville	828	Elizabeth City	2,315	Concord	8,715	Fayetteville	17,428	Gastonia	47,142

Source: U.S. Department of Commerce, *Census of Population* and *Census of Population and Housing*, 1860-1970.

*Urbanized Area definition (not incorporated city).

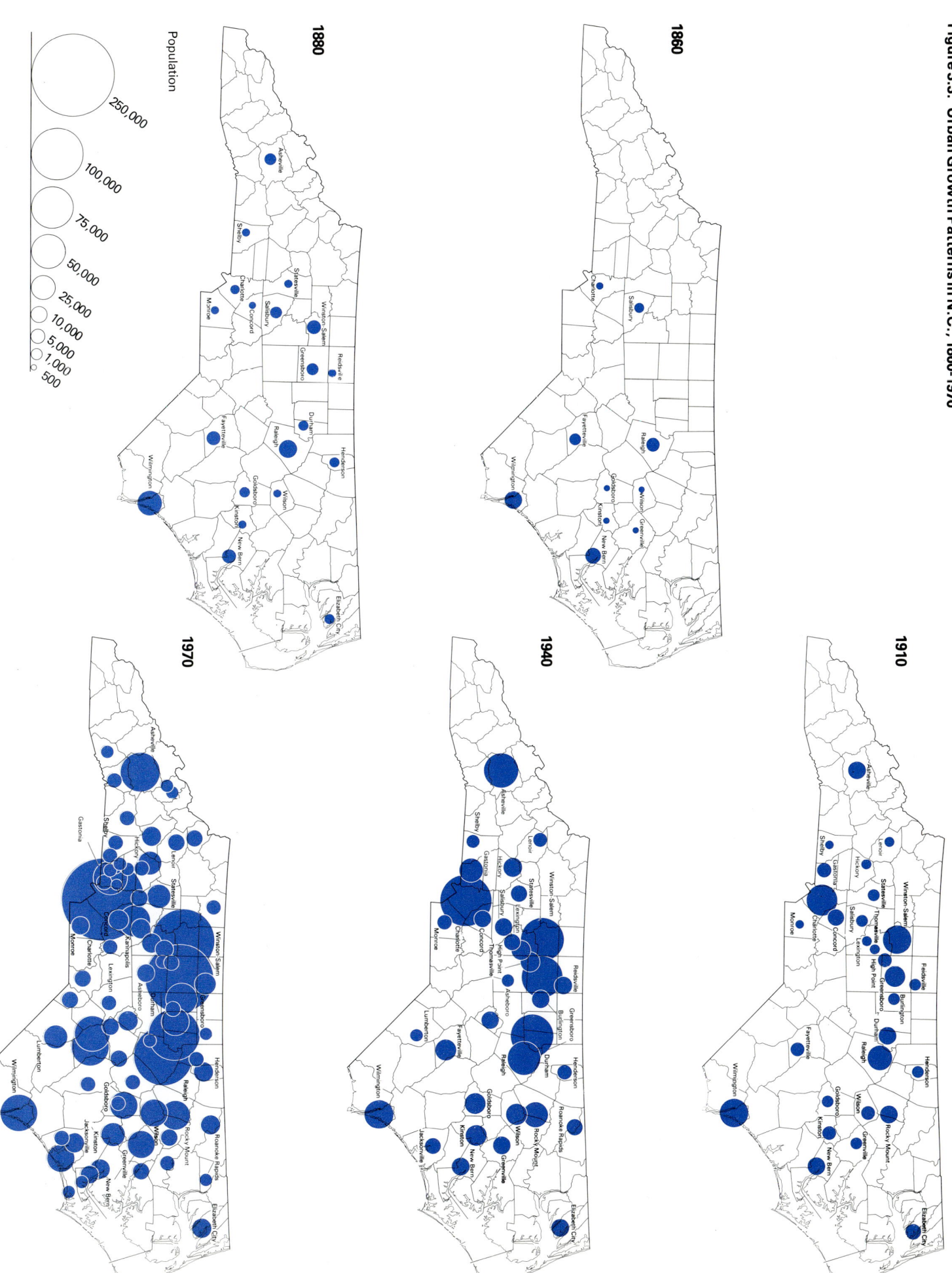

Figure 3.3. Urban Growth Patterns in N.C., 1860–1970

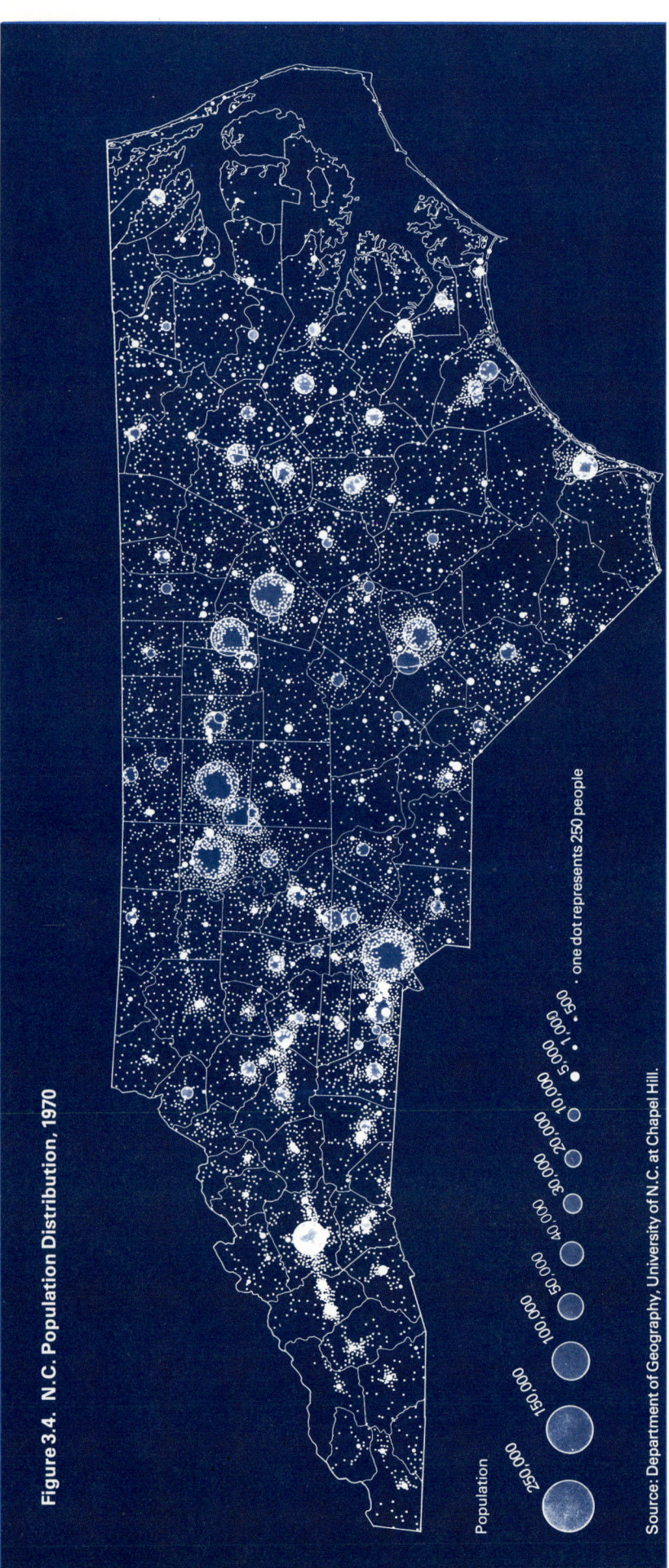

Figure 3.4. N.C. Population Distribution, 1970

Source: Department of Geography, University of N.C. at Chapel Hill.

small cities; in fact, plans to map earlier time periods were discarded because of the lack of cities. Wilmington had a rather commanding lead over New Bern. Fayetteville, due mainly to its importance as a river port, edged Raleigh for third place. Salisbury at this time was slightly larger than Charlotte.

Between 1860 and 1880 the urban population doubled and the number of cities increased considerably, even though the level of urbanization increased only slightly. The shape of the Piedmont Urban Crescent emerged, spurred on by the building of the state-owned railroad from Raleigh to Charlotte. Wilmington retained its lead, but Raleigh and Charlotte replaced New Bern and Fayetteville as the challengers. In fact, Fayetteville lost population from 1860 to 1880. The union of Winston and Salem gave the new city fifth place and New Bern was beginning to assert itself as the urban center of the Mountain region.

By 1910, the basic pattern that has continued until the present is clearly visible on the map. Only a few sizable towns of today, like Jacksonville and Morganton, are not on the map. Charlotte had assumed first place and the growing importance of industry in the Piedmont was reflected not only in the rapid rise of the larger manufacturing cities—Durham, Greensboro, Winston-Salem, and High Point—but also in the growth of a series of smaller mill towns.

Despite a slowdown during the depression, North Carolina cities grew rapidly from 1910 to 1940. The urban dominance of the Piedmont Urban Crescent was fully manifest. It had six of the seven largest cities in the state and contained many small towns and cities as well. The once dominant Coastal Plain cities could not keep pace; Wilmington fell to eighth place and New Bern was no longer in the top ten. The 1970 map demonstrates that even though North Carolina cities continued their rapid growth after 1940 the basic pattern remained unchanged and, in fact, the dominance of the Piedmont became even more pronounced.

The Present Pattern

One of the best ways to observe the urban pattern of an area is to fly over it at night. The lights of the cities and roadways clearly distinguish the urban areas from the rural areas shrouded in darkness. Figure 3.4 is an attempt to convey this vivid impression.

The most striking feature of the map is the arc of urban settlements extending from Raleigh around to Charlotte. This urban region, the Piedmont Urban Crescent, continues through South Carolina to Anderson, near the Georgia border. The Piedmont Urban Crescent is one of the best examples of a polynucleated urban region in the country. No single city dominates the crescent, but its aggregate population (over 2.5 million) is second only to the South Florida urban region in the Southeast. The crescent shape was originally influenced by the state railroad line. Its form has now been reinforced by the location of U.S. Interstate Highway 85.

The North Carolina portion of the crescent in turn is made up of three distinct clusters: the Research Triangle, Raleigh–Durham–Chapel Hill; the Triad, Greensboro–Winston-Salem–High Point; and the Metrolina area, centered on Charlotte. It is an interesting happenstance that the first two clusters are comprised of three cities. In each case there are two cities that have vied for leadership and a third city in a definitely subdominant category. Furthermore, over time the once-largest city in each cluster—Durham and Winston-Salem—has seen its population surpassed by the urban rivals—Raleigh and Greensboro. The early lead of Durham and Winston-Salem, originally dependent on manufacturing, has been eclipsed by cities with more diversified economies. Metrolina is a twelve-county region that extends into nearby South Carolina. Charlotte is the unquestioned leader of this region, but there are a number of subdominant cities, including three in the 25,000–50,000 population range.

Aside from the crescent, other linear urban patterns include the east-west line from Statesville to beyond Asheville and the line of cities south of Roanoke Rapids. Blank spaces are either rough or swampy land, parks, or military bases. The map graphically reveals why Wilmington could not retain its early population lead—the immediate hinterland is sparsely settled because of poor soils.

The Piedmont is the most urbanized region (54.1 percent) in the state, followed by the Tidewater (43.1 percent), Coastal Plain (38.6 percent), and Mountain region (24.7 percent). Take away the cities in the crescent, however, and the Piedmont is surprisingly devoid of urban places of 10,000 or more. Although North Carolina, compared to some states, has a relatively dispersed urban pattern, the distribution of cities is generally uneven. Only in the midsection of the Coastal Plain are the cities relatively evenly distributed.

The level of urbanization of an area gives valuable clues to the nature of that area but it does not necessarily reveal much about the size of the communities in which people live. A given level of urbanization could mean that the urban dwellers reside in many small cities or in a few large ones. However, it makes a great deal of difference whether a person lives in a small town or in a giant metropolis. Size of community is related to such factors as the life-style of the people; the job opportunities available; the variety of educational, recreational...

Table 3.2. Cities in N.C. Ranked According to City Population Size (10,000 or More Population), Incorporated and Unincorporated

Rank	City	1970 Population	Percentage Change 1950-60	1960-70
1	Charlotte	241,178	50.4	19.7
2	Greensboro	144,076	60.7	20.5
3	Winston-Salem	132,913	26.6	19.6
4	Raleigh	121,577	43.0	29.4
5	Durham	95,438	9.8	21.9
6	High Point	63,204	55.3	1.8
7	Asheville	57,681	13.6	-4.2
8	Fayetteville	53,510	35.7	13.6
9	Gastonia	47,142	61.6	26.5
10	Fort Bragg (U)	46,995	—	—
11	Wilmington	46,169	-2.3	4.9
12	Kannapolis (U)	36,293	21.8	4.8
13	Burlington	35,930	35.2	8.2
14	Camp Lejeune Central (U)	34,549	—	—
15	Rocky Mount	34,284	16.1	6.6
16	Wilson	29,347	25.0	2.1
17	Greenville	29,063	36.7	27.1
18	Goldsboro	26,810	34.6	-7.1
19	Chapel Hill	25,537	37.0	103.1
20	Salisbury	22,515	5.9	5.7
21	Kinston	22,309	35.4	-10.1
22	Hickory	20,569	31.0	6.4
23	Statesville	19,996	17.4	0.4
24	Concord	18,464	8.0	3.7
25	Lexington	17,205	18.6	6.9
26	Lumberton	16,961	66.6	10.8
27	Shelby	16,328	14.1	-7.7
28	Jacksonville	16,328	240.7	18.8
29	Eden	15,871	—	—
30	Thomasville	15,230	36.2	0.3
31	Lenoir	14,705	30.0	43.4
32	New Bern	14,660	-0.6	-6.7
33	Elizabeth City	14,069	10.9	0.4
34	Henderson	13,869	15.9	9.1
35	Reidsville	13,636	21.9	-4.4
36	Morganton	13,625	10.5	48.3
37	Roanoke Rapids	13,508	63.3	1.4
38	Cherry Point (U)	12,029	—	—
39	Sanford	11,716	22.4	-4.4
40	Monroe	11,282	7.3	3.7
41	Albemarle	11,126	3.9	-9.3
42	Asheboro	10,797	22.7	14.3
43	North Belmont (U)	10,759	110.9	29.2

Source: N.C. Department of Administration, North Carolina State Government Statistical Abstract, 1973.

Note: (U)=unincorporated.

Table 3.3. N.C. Urbanized Areas, 1970

Urbanized Area	Population 1960	Population 1970	Percentage Change 1960-70
Asheville	68,592	72,451	5.6
Asheville city	60,192	57,681	-4.2
Outside central city	8,400	14,770	75.8
Charlotte	209,551	279,530	33.4
Charlotte city	201,564	241,178	19.7
Outside central city	7,987	38,352	380.2
Durham	84,642	100,764	19.0
Durham city	78,302	95,438	21.9
Outside central city	6,340	5,326	-16.0
Fayetteville	—	161,370	—
Fayetteville city	—	53,510	—
Outside central city	—	107,860	—
Greensboro	123,334	152,252	23.4
Greensboro city	119,574	144,076	20.5
Outside central city	3,760	8,176	117.4
High Point	66,543	93,547	40.6
High Point city	62,063	63,204	1.8
Outside central city	4,480	30,343	577.3
Raleigh	93,931	152,289	62.1
Raleigh city	93,931	121,577	29.4
Outside central city	—	30,712	—
Wilmington	—	57,645	—
Wilmington city	—	46,169	—
Outside central city	—	11,476	—
Winston-Salem	128,176	142,584	11.2
Winston-Salem city	111,135	132,913	19.6
Outside central city	17,041	9,671	-43.2

Source: U.S. Department of Commerce, *1970 Census of Population and Housing*, 1970.

Note: There were no Urbanized Areas delineated for Fayetteville and Wilmington for the 1960 census. Losses outside central cities were the result of expansion of central cities through annexation.

tional, and shopping facilities; the stability of the local economy; and the probability of whether the community will grow or decline. Some types of economic activity need the manifold facilities of large cities, other industries seek the smaller places. In sum, the size of the community has tremendous ramifications, both for individuals and the community as a whole. Table 3.2 lists all the North Carolina cities that had a population of 10,000 or more in 1970.

The U.S. Census Bureau has long realized that the political definition of the city may be a poor representation of the actual size of a city. A number of alternative definitions have evolved, one of which is the Urbanized Area. The Urbanized Area is essentially the central city of 50,000 population or more and the surrounding, built-up contiguous area (incorporated or unincorporated) that meets certain population-density criteria. The Urbanized Area is often considered the best measure of urban size because it neither "underbounds" the city (by taking just the political city) or "overbounds" it (including peripheral, largely rural areas). Table 3.3 lists the state's Urbanized Areas. The other major alternative definition is the Standard Metropolitan Statistical Area (SMSA). This is the definition based on county units. It includes the county containing a central city, usually of 50,000 population or more, and any adjacent counties economically and socially linked to the central county (Table 3.4). After the 1970 census, new SMSAs were defined that, under new criteria, did not necessarily require a central city population of 50,000.

North Carolina's community-size pattern is dramatically different from the rest of the United States. In addition to being predominantly rural, the state has a set of cities that are generally small or medium-sized. Figure 3.5 also divides the urban portion of the population into the Urbanized Areas and those communities outside Urbanized Areas. This arrangement avoids counting the enormous number of small suburban places that are really parts of the larger metropolitan areas.

Some urban experts believe that true metropolitan status begins when a community has reached the size of 250,000 population. The Census Bureau's metropolitan definition, they maintain, is set too low. If this larger definition is used, and it is remembered that the Urbanized Area definition results in a smaller population than the SMSA definition, how does North Carolina compare with the United States? For the nation nearly half of the population resided in Urbanized Areas of 250,000 or more in 1970. The comparable proportion for North Carolina was 5.5 percent. In 1960, no North Carolinians lived in places of 250,000 or more and in 1970 none lived in Urbanized Areas with populations of over 500,000.

Those urban places outside Urbanized Areas, such as Concord, Lexington, or Lumberton, were relatively more important in North Carolina than they were in the nation as a whole. Predictably, North Carolina contrasts strongly with the nation in the high proportion of the state's population that is found in towns with populations of less than 2,500 or in truly rural areas.

Another distinguishing feature of North Carolina's urban pattern has been the lack of suburban communities on the fringe of the metropolitan areas. In North Carolina (1970), only 21.2 percent of the population of Urbanized Areas resided in the urban fringe (that part outside the central city). For the nation, nearly half (46.0 percent) of the Urbanized Area population was in the urban fringe. Furthermore, two-thirds of the people in the North Carolina urban fringe did not reside there in urban places (there were only nine such places in all) but were dispersed in the thickly settled peripheral countryside. Conversely, in the nation only about a quarter of the fringe area population lived in the countryside, the remaining three-quarters living in the 2,914 fringe area suburban communities.

This pattern was even more evident in 1960 when there were only three urban places in the fringes of North Carolina's Urbanized Areas and those three contained only 6.2 percent of the population in the urban fringe. North Carolina law easily permits municipalities to annex adjacent areas (without the consent of the inhabitants) and this has been instrumental in avoiding the extreme political fragmentation that has plagued many large metropolitan areas.

The Size of the Leading City

One important part of the community-size pattern of North Carolina is the relatively small size of its leading city. Charlotte's Urbanized Area population was only 5.5 percent of the state total in 1970. This was the next to lowest percentage among the fifty states and except for a statistical quirk associated with Newark, New Jersey, North Carolina would have ranked last (Figure 3.6). Charlotte's small share is in dramatic contrast to Providence, New York, or Chicago. Southern cities, especially those in the old Confederate South, generally rank rather low, but Charlotte's share is considerably below most of them. While its share is tending to increase, it has always been low; in 1950 it was 3.5 percent and in 1960, 4.6 percent.

Figure 3.5. Percentage of Population by Size of Area, 1970

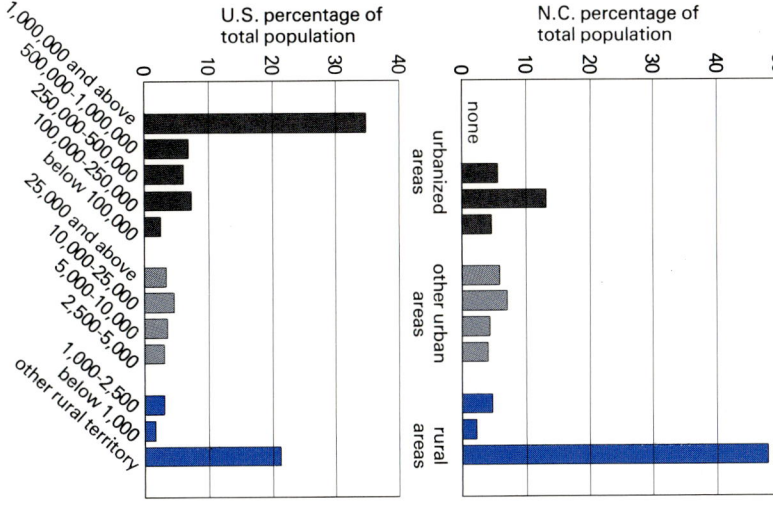

Source: U.S. Department of Commerce, *1970 Census of Population and Housing*, 1970.

Table 3.4. N.C. Standard Metropolitan Statistical Areas (SMSAs)

1. Asheville SMSA
   Asheville (Buncombe County), Madison County
   Population (1970):
   Asheville city 57,681
   Outside central city 103,378
   Total 161,059

2. Charlotte–Gastonia SMSA
   Charlotte (Mecklenburg County), Union County, Gastonia (Gaston County)
   Population (1970):
   Charlotte city 241,178
   Gastonia city 47,142
   Outside central cities 269,465
   Total 557,785

3. Raleigh–Durham SMSA
   Raleigh (Wake County), Durham (Durham County), Orange County
   Population (1970):
   Raleigh city 121,577
   Durham city 95,437
   Outside central cities 201,827
   Total 418,841

4. Fayetteville SMSA
   Fayetteville (Cumberland County)
   Population (1970):
   Fayetteville city 53,510
   Outside central city 158,532
   Total 212,042

5. Greensboro–Winston-Salem–High Point SMSA
   Greensboro (Guilford County), High Point (Guilford County), Winston-Salem (Forsyth County), High Point (Guilford County), Stokes County
   Population (1970):
   Greensboro city 144,076
   High Point city 63,204
   Winston-Salem city 132,913
   Outside central cities 287,484
   Total 627,677

6. Wilmington SMSA
   New Hanover County, Brunswick County
   Population (1970):
   Wilmington city 46,169
   Outside central city 61,050
   Total 107,219

7. Burlington–Alamance SMSA
   Burlington (Alamance County)
   Population (1970):
   Burlington city 35,930
   Outside central city 60,432
   Total 96,362

8. Norfolk–Portsmouth SMSA
   Chesapeake, Norfolk, Portsmouth, Virginia Beach, Currituck County, N.C.
   Population (1970):
   Chesapeake 89,580
   Norfolk 307,951
   Portsmouth 110,963
   Virginia Beach 172,106
   Currituck County (N.C.) 6,976
   Total 687,576

Source: U.S. Department of Commerce, *1970 Census of Population and Housing*, 1970, and verbal communication with the Bureau of the Census.

Note: SMSA definitions are those of 1973–74, which are different from those of 1970. Population, however, is for 1970.

If the Charlotte-Gastonia SMSA is used in place of the Urbanized Area, its share of the state's population would only go to 11 percent. Substituting for North Carolina's first city the multiple-city Triad SMSA would only raise the leading city share to 12 percent of the state's population. Even the generously defined "Metrolina" area, the twelve-county area that includes and surrounds Charlotte, would still not account for much more than a fifth of the state's population. Therefore, however the urban cake is sliced, the fact remains that the leading city in North Carolina has a remarkably small share of the state's population.

The condition is partially a legacy of the past. The state has never had a dominant city. The early leaders, New Bern and Wilmington, did not have sufficiently advantageous natural situations either to compete with other South Atlantic ports or to extend their domain within the state. Charlotte did not assume the lead until 1910, and it has never eclipsed its urban rivals in the Piedmont. The dominantly rural character of the state would automatically limit the share of the state's population. But even if the urban population is substituted for the total population in calculating Charlotte's share, the low standing among the states is still maintained. The major reason may be the dispersed pattern of population and industry, so long a feature of North Carolina. Beginning in about 1880 the growth of textile mills in many small towns gave many North Carolinians an economic alternative to farming and allowed them to maintain a small town or even rural residence. Thus some of the classic rural-urban migration was cut off at the source.

Even when all the reasons for the lack of primacy have been considered, there is still an unexplained remainder. Why is the largest city's proportion so very low and why has its increase been so modest? Charlotte has had a rapid population growth. Its location, practically astride the border, makes it deserving of the slogan, "Queen City of the Carolinas." Charlotte performs certain wholesaling and metropolitan functions for parts of South Carolina. It thus handles some urban functions for South Carolina in the manner of Kansas City, Missouri, for the state of Kansas. This would imply that Charlotte's size would be enhanced somewhat and a larger city would be the result.

Undoubtedly in the future Charlotte's share will increase. This will be due not only to its more rapid growth than the state but to a changing definition of the urban area. This is particularly true if the metropolitan area (SMSA) definition is used, since it seems only a matter of time before a number of additional counties will be added to the Charlotte SMSA, materially boosting the population.

Figure 3.6. Percentage of Each State's Population Contained in Its Largest City, 1970

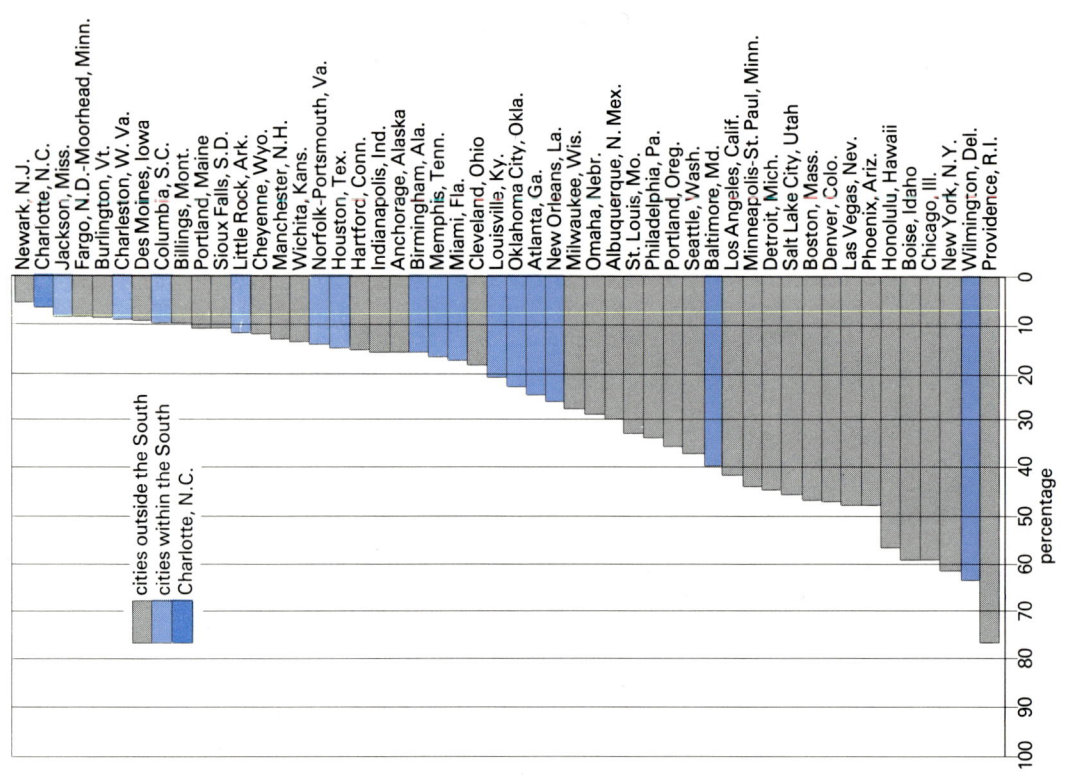

Source: U.S. Department of Commerce, *1970 Census of Population and Housing*, 1970.

The Small Town in North Carolina

The decline of the small town has been a major feature of the changing settlement pattern in the United States since the turn of the century. There is no consensus as to what constitutes the upper limit of the small town—it has been set anywhere from 5,000 to 25,000. However defined, there is no doubt that the smaller places in the countryside have declined in importance. Some maintain that the small towns in America are slowly dying, that they are becoming an anachronism in the modern economy and society.

The role of the small town has been undermined by such trends as (1) the decline in the rural population of their trading area, (2) improvement in roads and vehicles that made it easy to bypass the smaller places in favor of larger but more distant centers, (3) the shift to an industrial-based economy, and (4) the tendency of youth to seek their fortunes in the larger cities. The main exceptions to this pattern are those small towns within commuting distance of the larger cities and those located in amenity areas (for example, coastal locations).

Although it is difficult to compile the necessary information from the census reports, it appears that the smaller towns in North Carolina have fared better over the last fifty years than have their counterparts in other sections of the country. Nevertheless, as Table 3.5 indicates, there is the tendency for the smaller places to grow more slowly, if not to lose population. The proportion of places losing population increases as the size decreases (with the exception of the 10,000-25,000 class). The decline in some medium-sized cities is misleading. The decline occurred only in the central city, but the entire urban area increased. This was the case with Asheville. From 1960 to 1970, the city of Asheville lost, but the Urbanized Area gained.

North Carolina: An Urban Anomaly

North Carolina, in a variety of contexts, is indeed an urban anomaly. However, the question still remains, Why? Major possible reasons include the following:

The Nature of North Carolina Industry
The industrial composition of North Carolina is still dominated by textiles. It is a characteristic of this industry that economies of scale are not important; in other words, large plants are no more efficient than small plants. This is also true of such other important industries as apparel and furniture. Even within the same community, the same company may have a number of mills rather than one large plant.

The Locational Tendencies of North Carolina Industry
Large plants, employing thousands of workers (as in the auto industry), are rare in North Carolina. Rather, the pattern is many small plants. These small plants are often, especially in apparel and textiles, located in small towns or rural areas to tap the surplus farm labor. Because prevailing wage levels are higher in the larger towns, these industries may often avoid these areas. Even the newer industries will often seek a site in the countryside.

Residential Preference of North Carolinians
Unlike people in other parts of the country, many rural North Carolinians prefer to commute rather than to move closer to work. Precisely why this is so has not been studied, but it would appear to be a result of such factors as (1) preference for country versus town living, (2) desire to be near kin folk, (3) the cheaper housing and living costs in the country, and (4) the reluctance to stop farming entirely, especially if a tobacco allotment is involved.

The Type of Agriculture
North Carolina's agriculture has traditionally been dominated by tobacco. This is an intensively cultivated crop with high monetary yields per acre. This has led to high farm densities, especially in the inner Coastal Plain. Generally, agricultural areas of this type are associated with small or medium-size towns. Conversely, the extensive (or highly commercial) agriculture of the west has led to larger towns. North Carolina's agriculture is beginning to mechanize and this should spur further urbanization.

The Lack of a Superior Situation for Cities
In the discussion of the growth of North Carolina cities, it was noted that no city was so well situated that it could dominate the state. This was true for the early time period of water-oriented transportation and it is also true today when road and rail movement are most important. North Carolina has no major rail focus, and it lacks sites like Atlanta and Indianapolis at which interstate routes converge. The state has not been blessed with superior situational features, whether they be natural (good harbors) or manmade (rail junctions), and this has left its mark on the urban pattern.

Table 3.5. Percentage Change in Population of N.C. Towns, 1960-1970

Percentage Change, 1960-70	Number of Towns in Each Size Range in 1960					
	Below 2,500	2,500 to 5,000	5,000 to 10,000	10,000 to 25,000	25,000 to 100,000	100,000 and Above
Gain						
100 or over	15	2				
50-99	24	1				
20-49	57	10	2	2	3	1
10-19	46	8	4	2	1	2
0-9	82	14	12	9	6	
Total Gain	224	35	18	14	10	3
Loss						
0-9	59	12	6	5	2	
10-19	39	3		1		
20 or more	21	2				
Total Loss	119	17	6	6	2	0
Percentage Loss	35	33	25	30	17	0

Source: U.S. Department of Commerce, 1970 Census of Population and Housing, 1970.

AN ASSESSMENT OF NORTH CAROLINA'S URBAN PATTERN

The urban pattern of North Carolina is characterized by a small-town orientation, a polynucleated urban region, the lack of a dominant single city, and a high rural nonfarm population. Since this pattern differs from most states it may be instructive to give a brief review of the pros and cons of the North Carolina pattern.

Advantages of North Carolina's Urban Pattern

Environmental Quality Current news reports indicate that the Environmental Protection Agency suggests that it may be necessary to severely restrict vehicular travel in some of the large metropolitan areas (by 63 percent in northern New Jersey to virtual elimination in Southern California). Big cities have the biggest pollution problems—air, water, waste disposal, and noise. Although North Carolina's urban pattern does not eliminate environmental stress, it avoids the high concentrations of pollution that make solutions for the major metropolitan areas so difficult.

Preferred Community Sizes Gallup polls indicated that most people prefer small towns (even while living in larger ones because of economic necessity). The troubles in the big cities have tarnished their image and made the smaller places more attractive by comparison. Preference for living in the open countryside—in the style of the rural nonfarm—has become more popular recently. North Carolina's pattern is in keeping with this trend.

Reduced Congestion and Crowding High density living produces crowding and congestion that may be psychologically damaging. Rural or small-town slums may be no more justified than big-city slums but living conditions are less oppressive.

Less Traffic Congestion Although North Carolina workers frequently commute over unusually great distances, they do not have large-city traffic problems to contend with.

Somewhat Lower Cost of Living The cost of living is lowest among small Southern towns. This advantage may be purchased, however, at the price of fewer facilities and services. Lower taxes are one reason for the lower costs, but this often results in poorer schools, fewer parks, and substandard municipal services.

Disadvantages of North Carolina's Urban Pattern

Less Diversity and Stability in the Local Economy The economic support of the small North Carolina town has traditionally been the textile mill. Many places are thus virtually one-industry towns, almost wholly dependent upon the often-fluctuating fortunes of the local mill. Job opportunities are limited, both in variety and wage levels. Reportedly, some companies attempt to block industrial diversification in order to avoid competition for labor.

Fewer Consumer Choices Consumers must often pay higher prices for a limited selection of goods because the small-town merchants' low volume does not permit a wider selection or more competitive pricing. As it becomes easier to travel to the larger centers, this disadvantage has become less critical.

Fewer Educational, Cultural, and Recreational Opportunities Smaller towns cannot offer the range of educational, cultural, and recreational opportunities that the large-city residents take for granted. Generations of novelists have attacked the conformist and provincial atmosphere of small towns.

High Energy Consumption A dispersed urban pattern implies long driving distances to jobs, to shopping, and for social interaction. Dependence on the automobile for transportation is almost total. Recent and dramatic increases in the price of gasoline add a substantial new cost to maintaining the present dispersed pattern.

The Contrast Between Georgia and North Carolina

Another way to evaluate North Carolina's urban pattern is to contrast it with Georgia's, which is increasingly dominated by Atlanta. Compared with cities in other states, Atlanta's share of Georgia's population is not remarkable (25 percent), but nevertheless it is five times larger than Charlotte's share (5 percent) of North Carolina's population. Atlanta is one of the most dynamic, fast-growing, large metropolitan areas in the country. Capitalizing on a carefully cultivated image as the "Spearhead of the New South," Atlanta's share of Georgia's wealth is considerably greater than its share of the population. Its rapid rise has been the principal reason that Georgia's per capita income has now passed North Carolina's.

The metropolitan population of Atlanta is less than the North Carolina part of the Piedmont Urban Crescent, but its national "visibility" is much higher. Its role as the regional capital of the South has induced most large corporations to establish a distribution center or branch office there, and they often employ relatively highly paid personnel. These events have helped make Atlanta's airport one of the busiest in the country, and this in turn has helped to make Atlanta more attractive to national conventions. Although Georgia's population is smaller than North Carolina's, Atlanta has become a "big league town" in more than just a sports context.

No place in North Carolina can match the attractions and facilities of Atlanta. Lacking a large city, the state must provide such facilities as an art museum, symphony orchestra, and zoo. Unquestionably, from the viewpoint of economic advantages, Georgia's urban pattern, centered on Atlanta, has brought more benefits than North Carolina's.

In terms of the broader perspective of the overall quality of life, the scale is not tipped as much in Atlanta's favor. In the future Atlanta is certain to become bigger than its current 1.5 million, but not necessarily better. Size will cease being an advantage and will become a handicap.

North Carolina's cities, on the other hand, should still be able to benefit from some of the economies of larger size and the greater range of opportunities it affords. Because of the polynucleated form of much of North Carolina's urban pattern, the state has the opportunity to have its urban cake and eat it too. This is especially true in the Piedmont Urban Crescent, particularly the Research Triangle, Triad, and Metrolina areas. They may be able to combine the advantages of small or medium-size centers with the facilities normally found only in large metropolitan areas. This may also be possible in the areas containing Hickory–Lenoir–Morganton or the Rocky Mount–Wilson–Goldsboro–Greenville-Kinston area.

To realize the full potential inherent in these polynucleated clusters, however, requires a high degree of intergovernmental cooperation and a lessening of the traditional urban rivalries. The failure of a regional airport to be realized in the Rocky Mount area, and the uncertain fate of a proposed Triad regional park illustrate how difficult cooperative endeavors are to achieve. Once the citizens fully realize that the whole is much greater than the sum of the parts, the task might be easier. In many ways North Carolinians have a virtually unique urban opportunity.

The Conversion of Land to Urban Uses

Urbanization consumes large amounts of land, converting it from agricultural or natural conditions into a manmade network of roads, shopping areas, places of work, and residential neighborhoods. At the same time, these urban uses themselves change, through the gradual workings of the real estate market or through dramatic public actions such as urban renewal or highway construction. The process of change is an important one, because it shapes the urban pattern in which North Carolinians will live for decades to come.

In absolute terms, the amount of land devoted to urbanization in North Carolina is rather small. In 1967, only 4.7 percent of North Carolina's land area was actually devoted to urban uses. This may be misleading, however, because urban uses are not distributed evenly. Five counties had less than 1 percent of land in urban use while three had more than 20 percent of their land urbanized. In general, the high percentages of urban land use are found in the Piedmont counties, with the Mountain and Coastal Plain counties less heavily urbanized (Figure 3.7).

Although the absolute amount of urbanized land in North Carolina is still low, trends indicate a dramatic increase in the rate at which land is used for urbanization. Between 1958 and 1967, the amount of land in North Carolina devoted to urban uses increased by 83 percent, from 1,249 to 2,283 square miles. During this same period, North Carolina's population only increased about 12 percent. The rate of urban land expansion outran the population increase by a factor of six! Another way of putting this is that while every 100 persons in 1958 required 15 acres of urban land, each addition of 100 members to the population required 110 acres. This reflects the fact that most population increase is in fact urban-oriented, and also reflects the changing nature of urban land uses to serve new needs. Even allowing for a certain lack of comparability between 1958 and 1967 figures, it is clear that population growth in the future will consume much more land than was true in the past.

The pattern of urban land conversion is interesting, because it does not coincide simply with the existing pattern of urbanization (Figure 3.8). Individual county increases ranged from modest 3 or 4 percent increases up to jumps of 500 percent and more. Some of the most dramatic increases were recorded in coastal counties where urbanization had been very low, and where the surge of recreational growth has sparked a boom in second-home development.

Two observations may be made about urban land conversion. The first is that urbanization is producing a rapid increase in land consumption, at a rate that exceeds the rate of population growth. Even if North Carolina's population were to stop growing, there would still be a substantial increase in urban land area to serve the needs of the population already there. The second observation is that this increase is not confined to the existing urban area. Some of the most rapid growth in urban land is occurring in areas that historically have been the least urban. By the same token, these are areas that typically are ill prepared to guide and direct growth. Some of the most significant problems of land management in North Carolina occur where rapid urbanization strikes an unprepared rural area. The scenic resources of an area encourage urbanization and compound the problem, for unplanned urbanization can rapidly destroy the very environment that brings it into being. North Carolinians familiar with certain areas in the mountains and along the coast can readily observe this process at work.

URBAN POPULATION DENSITY

As pointed out previously, North Carolina is an urban anomaly. Only 45 percent of the population is classed as urban, compared with a national figure of 73.5 percent in 1970. Less of the population that does live in cities is congregated in a single dominant city. Instead, North Carolinians live in a dispersed pattern of small and medium-sized cities. Because of their size, these cities tend to have low population densities. The typical urban dweller in North Carolina lives in a smaller city and at a lower density than his counterpart in many other states.

There are, according to the 1970 census, 138 urban places in North Carolina with a population of 2,500 or more. The population density in these urban places ranges from 624 to 5,116 persons per square mile. Only 9 of these places, however, have densities below 1,000 persons per square mile, and only 13 have densities above 3,000 per square mile. The other 116 fall into the range of 1,000 to 3,000 persons per square mile, as shown in Figure 3.9. By contrast, 29 cities in New Jersey have densities above 10,000 persons per square mile, and New York City has an overall density of 26,000 persons per square mile.

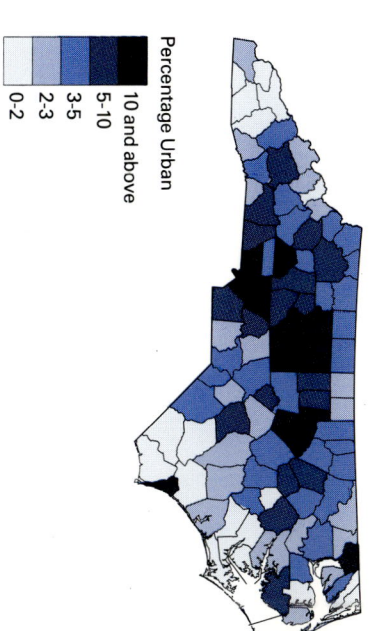

Figure 3.7. Land in Urban Uses in N.C., 1967

Percentage Urban
- 10 and above
- 5-10
- 3-5
- 2-3
- 0-2

Source: N.C. Department of Administration, *North Carolina State Government Statistical Abstract*, 1968.

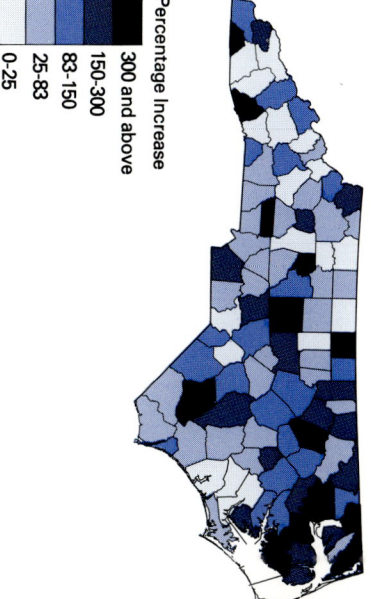

Figure 3.8. Rate of Conversion of Land to Urban Uses, 1958-1967

Percentage Increase
- 300 and above
- 150-300
- 83-150
- 25-83
- 0-25

statewide percentage increase: 85

Source: North Carolina Conservation Needs Inventory, 1971.

Figure 3.9. Population Density in N.C. Urban Areas, 1970

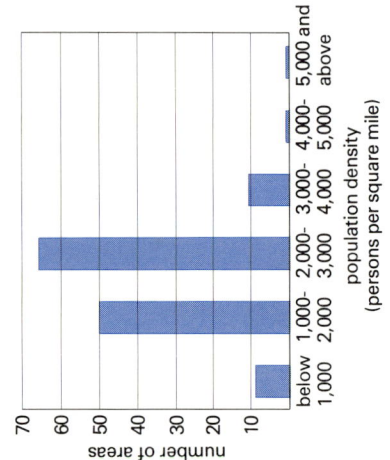

Source: U.S. Department of Commerce, *1970 Census of Population and Housing*, 1970.

The population density in North Carolina's 9 Urbanized Areas ranges from 1,796 to 2,645 persons per square mile for the entire area, and from 2,052 to 3,173 persons per square mile within the city limits of the central city of the Urbanized Area. This is shown in Figure 3.10. There is only a weak correlation between size and density within this group of cities, although the largest city does appear to have the highest density within the group. Compared with all 138 urban places, however, it can be seen that the density of North Carolina's larger cities is little higher than the density for all urban places. Even North Carolinians in larger cities live at a reasonably low population density. In the portions of the Urbanized Areas outside the city limits, density is quite low, generally around 1,000 persons per square mile. The exception is Fayetteville, where military bases outside the city raise the density to over 2,000 persons per square mile.

banized Area, despite significant population gains in most cases. Only one central city (Asheville) actually lost population during the decade. In all cases, including Asheville, the low density in 1970 is primarily due to annexation of low density surrounding areas. As North Carolina cities grow, they tend to become less dense in population and much more land-consuming.

This is a significant fact, with implications for everything from transportation to environmental quality. The automobile, with its ease of access and its seemingly insatiable demand for parking space, helps to maintain the low density pattern. As density decreases, however, it becomes increasingly difficult for public transportation to serve the population adequately. Public transport decreases or in some cases disappears altogether, leaving no alternative *but* the private automobile. The subject of transportation is a complicated one, but it is worth noting that the density pattern contributes in part to the problem.

The environmental aspect of this low density urbanization is the high rate at which land is consumed per person, thereby taking land out of other uses. North Carolina has probably not reached the point where urban land conversion threatens the agricultural base or the food supply. Nevertheless, there is pressure on agriculture, and much of the agriculture on the urban fringe is in fact in speculative rather than purely productive uses. It has been observed that at a rather low population density—perhaps as low as 100 persons per square mile, population pressures begin to conflict with agricultural uses. Soon agriculture becomes uneconomical and land is forced, often prematurely, into the urban land market, creating a costly and inefficient pattern of urban development.

Low density is not necessarily bad. Many North Carolinians feel pleased that they are able to live without the crowding and congestion that are typical of northeastern cities. Low density only becomes a problem when it interferes with other valuable goals, such as efficient transportation or sound land use. North Carolinians may have to ask themselves at some point whether too high a price is being paid for a low density on the urban periphery.

Within the central cities, of course, population densities are still somewhat higher, particularly in low income sections. These high density areas tend to be restricted in size to an area that was once within walking or streetcar distance of the central business district. Through a combination of abandonment, conversion, and urban renewal, these high density areas are now somewhat smaller than before. A study done in Greensboro, for example, found that in 1940 the population

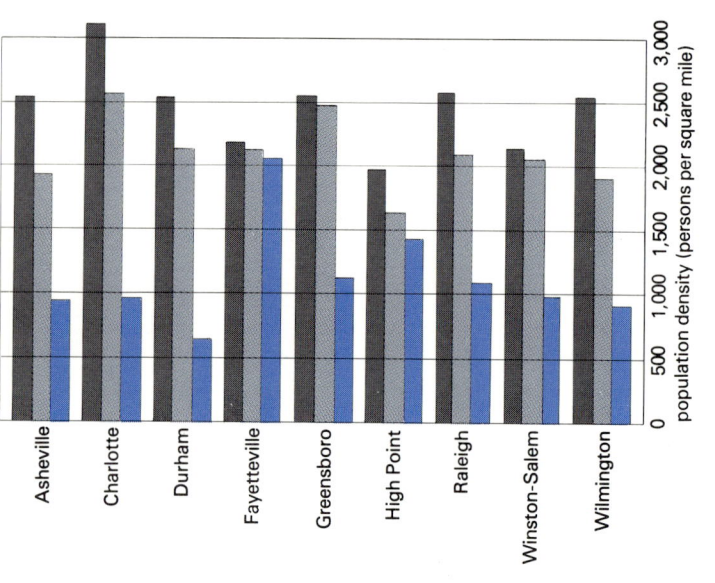

Figure 3.10. Population Density for Major Urbanized Areas in N.C., 1970

Source: U.S. Department of Commerce, *1970 Census of Population*, 1970.

density was 12,000 persons per square mile in the area within one-half mile of the city center. Density fell sharply beyond this point, however, so that one mile from the center the density was down to 2,000 persons per square mile (Figure 3.11). By 1960, the central area density remained about the same, but the break was not quite so sharp. Density at one mile from the center was estimated to be 4,000 persons per square mile, falling to under 2,000 within the next mile. During this period, better transportation had filled in some of the areas at the edge of the former walking and transit city, and the full effect of urban renewal had not yet been felt.

It is difficult to compare population densities over time since the boundaries of Urbanized Areas and of the central cities have changed from year to year. It is noteworthy, however, that in most of the Urbanized Areas, population density actually fell from 1960 to 1970, both in the central city and in the surrounding area. Greensboro and High Point had increases in density within the city limits, while Charlotte and High Point had increases in density outside the central city. The result of extending boundaries, however, was that no Urbanized Area registered a density increase for the entire Ur-

Looking at current trends, however, the Greensboro planners projected still another population distribution curve for 1980. In this case, only slight increases in density were expected in the areas outwards of one mile from the city center, but density within this radius was expected to drop, confining high density areas to smaller and smaller portions of the city core.

This flattening of the population distribution curve is probably typical of all North Carolina cities. In Charlotte, for example, densities on the periphery of the city increased sharply between 1960 and 1970 while in the inner city the number of census tracts that had densities of over 12,000 persons per square mile dropped from six to two. Charlotte may be more typical than Greensboro because Greensboro was the one city to show density increases between 1960 and 1970. The automobile and the highway network have the effect of blurring the distinction between urban and suburban areas, while natural processes of change tend to reduce densities in the urban core. Density within particular areas on the urban fringe increases as vacant portions are filled in, but the density for the entire Urbanized Area falls as the land area increases.

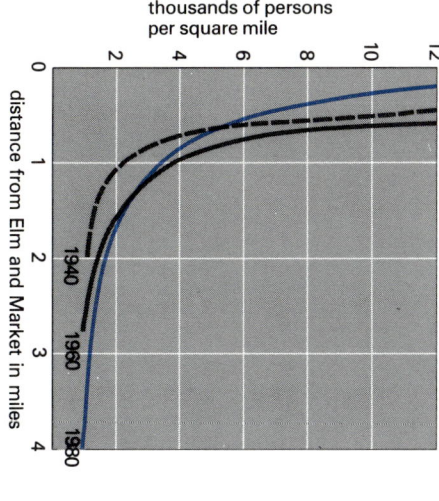

Figure 3.11. Average Population Distribution of Greensboro, N.C., 1940, 1960, and 1980.

THE USE OF URBAN LAND

Although urban land has hundreds of specific uses, it can be grouped into five categories: residential land, commercial land, industrial land, public and institutional land, and transportation land. Residential land is used for living quarters from detached single-family homes to high density apartment complexes. Industrial land is used primarily by manufacturing plants and utilities. Retail and wholesale businesses of all types and office buildings use commercial land. Public and institutional land is used by churches, schools, hospitals, government buildings, universities, parks, and other public agencies. Transportation land is devoted primarily to streets, highways, and related spaces, and to railroad land.

Land use is surveyed periodically by city planning departments, although there is little uniformity in the frequency, the extent, or the coverage of these surveys. Figure 3.12 indicates the distribution of land uses in eight of the nine Urbanized Areas of North Carolina. The area of each chart is proportional to the amount of developed land in each city. These figures are not strictly comparable because of differences in coverage and in the date of the survey. The proportional distribution of land, however, is comparable.

It is interesting to note the consistent proportions of land devoted to each category of use in the eight cities. Homes and residences consume the greatest amount of land, between 42 and 53 percent of the total. Transportation, primarily streets and highways, is the next highest, with 17 to 29 percent of the developed land. Public and institutional land varies from a low of 10 percent in Greensboro to a high of 34 percent in Raleigh, reflecting the many state government facilities and the university in that city. The second highest figure, in Durham, probably reflects the extensive holdings of Duke University.

It may seem surprising that commerce and industry are consistently small users of urban land. The explanation is that commercial and industrial land, while small in actual area, is highly visible because it is located along the main arteries of travel in urban areas. It is apparent that these land uses affect the image and the appearance of the urban scene out of all proportion to their actual area. Many cities have in fact zoned much more land for these uses than will actually be needed in the foreseeable future. Since these uses often require special sites and special facilities it might be appropriate to reserve suitable sites for them rather than zoning large but sometimes unsuitable portions of the urban area for them. This would be one element in an active land management policy.

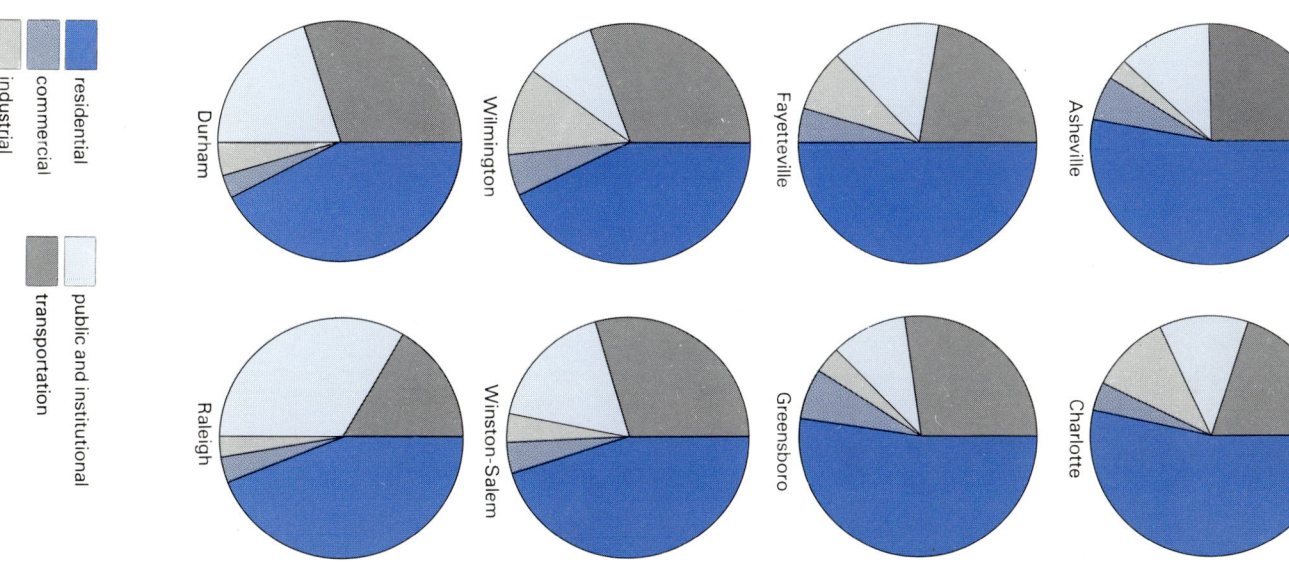

Figure 3.12. Proportion of Developed Urban Land in Specified Uses for Selected N.C. Cities

65

Figure 3.13. Projected Changes in Urban Land Use in Selected N.C. Cities

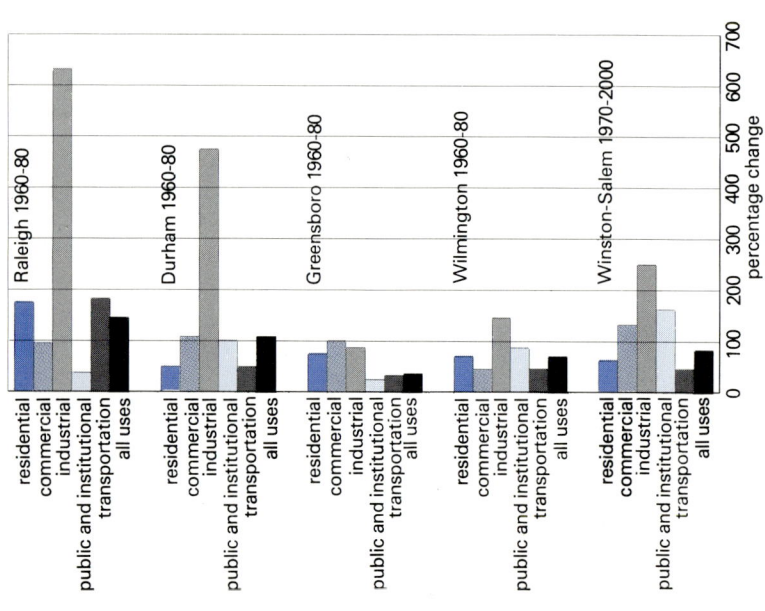

Source: Individual city land-use surveys.

In addition to these developed land uses, most of the areas surveyed contained large amounts of vacant or undeveloped land, up to 59 percent of the total land surveyed in the case of Asheville. Some of this land is currently agricultural land or woodland. Other portions are unsuitable for development because of steep slopes, location in floodplains, or division into small or isolated portions not subject to economical use. The supply of sites suitable for such large uses as industries or schools may be much more limited than this vacant land resource would seem to indicate.

CHANGES IN URBAN LAND USE

As the urban area expands, changes also occur in the individual land uses. These changes take two forms: (1) changes in the relative amount of land devoted to each use, and (2) changes in the typical location and arrangement of the individual uses. Figure 3.13 indicates some of the projected changes of the first type, based upon land-use surveys and plans for selected North Carolina cities. For the time periods used (1960–80 in all cases except 1970–2000 for Winston-Salem and Forsyth County), the overall amount of developed urban land was expected to increase by amounts ranging from 39 percent (Greensboro) to 143 percent (Raleigh). Within these overall increases, however, there were marked differences in the extent to which each category of land use was expected to expand.

Residential Land

Residential land, the largest single component of urban land use, showed a mixed pattern of expected percentage increases in the selected cities. It appears that the dominance of residential land use will not be significantly altered in any of the cities.

There are several trends at work with respect to residential use of land. One factor is of course the large-lot size that goes with most new single-family houses. As the houses themselves spread out rather than up, as they include more parking and garage space, and as lifestyles emphasize outdoor living, the typical new household requires more land for its single-family house than did those in previous generations. The greater-lot frontage, in turn, requires greater lengths of streets and utilities to service each house. More land is used, perhaps wastefully, and the costs per unit increase.

Perhaps in reaction to this expansion, another trend has been the significant increase in multifamily units as a percentage of all new residences. Rental apartments, condominiums, and town houses require less land per unit than the traditional single-family house. In 1960, units in multifamily structures accounted for only 11 percent of all building permits issued in the state. By 1969, their share had increased to 37 percent. In three SMSAs, multifamily units accounted for over 50 percent of the permits issued in 1969.

The use of mobile homes has also increased, from 1.5 percent of total North Carolina housing stock in 1960 to 5.4 percent of total stock in 1970. While the bulk of this increase occurred in rural areas, particularly in the Mountain region and the Coastal Plain, mobile homes accounted for over 3 percent of the housing stock of all North Carolina SMSAs by 1970. In Fayetteville, due to the presence of Fort Bragg, mobile homes accounted for over 10 percent of all housing. Mobile homes are frequently grouped in densities typical of multifamily structures. An eyesore when improperly situated, they are important as one of the few forms of new housing that are available to moderate and low income families. Planning policies should work to improve the appearance and the environmental quality of mobile home neighborhoods, rather than relegating them to "catch-all" or other undesirable areas.

Both of these recent trends may have an impact on urban land use. Both multifamily units and mobile homes consume less land per individual unit of housing, and this may slightly reduce the overall rate at which land is converted for residential uses. Also important is the opportunity they provide for new patterns of neighborhood living. Through planned unit developments, con-

Industrial Land

The most striking percentage increase projected for the chosen time periods was the increase in industrial land. In part this reflects the very small industrial land component at the beginning of the time period.

The high projected increases in industrial land reflect the suburbanization of industry as it moves from cramped downtown locations to fringe locations with room for truck loading, employee parking, and more economical production processes. The typical older pattern of industry, still visible in most North Carolina cities, is a pattern of two- and three-story mills grouped in corridors along central city railroad lines. The newer pattern is more dispersed. There is still a tendency for some factories to locate along railroad lines, but they now occupy much larger sites. Other factories locate along interstate highway corridors, or on other sites that afford convenient truck access. The typical plant is now single story, with generous space suitable for arranging machinery in efficient production patterns. Room for future expansion is built into the plans, and the plant is usually landscaped. This is particularly true of research and other "prestige" industries, such as those visible along interstate highways or grouped in the Research Triangle Park.

Commercial Land

The projected increases for both residential and commercial land are mixed; some are above and some below the projected percentage increases for all urban land. Unlike residential land, commercial land accounts for a very small proportion of total urban land area, although the nature and location of these uses is such that they are visible out of all proportion to their actual area.

The commercial pattern has, of course, followed the overall suburbanization of land uses. Historically, the pattern was one of a compact and tightly grouped central business district, accessible primarily by public transportation. Secondary commercial land was located along the major thoroughfares leading to the central business district.

This pattern has broken down at an accelerating rate since World War II. Expanding population and low densities made it less convenient to get to the central business district, while its compactness and congestion, designed for pedestrians, made it less convenient for the typical shopper in an automobile. Neighborhood, and then regional, shopping centers diverted retail business from the central city. The larger regional shopping centers came in fact to serve as substitute downtowns, sometimes losing out in their turn to newer and still larger centers.

Important efforts have been made, and should continue to be made, to improve the competitive attractiveness and convenience of downtown areas. Nothing, however, is going to restore their retail primacy. The commercial pattern of the North Carolina city will continue to be one of multiple centers.

Somewhat less efficient are the lengthy strip commercial areas lining many urban highways in the state. Unlike the large shopping centers, the individual businesses must compete strenuously for the attention of the passing motorist. The result can be visual chaos. Multiple access points impede the traffic flow and decrease the safety of the highway, until the entire area must sometimes be bypassed to restore the original purpose of traffic flow.

Present land-use controls, especially zoning, have had little impact on slowing this type of commercial development. Alternatives are available, including a much stronger public role in designating commercial areas,

A special category of commercial land use is office space, which is the only commercial space still concentrated to any degree in the central business district (CBD). Most new construction in the CBD is in fact devoted to this use, so that the central city is tending to become a specialized office and financial center, with auxiliary retail services. This is especially apparent in Charlotte where numerous office buildings have been constructed since 1970, including three in the 35 to 40-story range.

Public and Institutional Land

This category, comprising a mixture of land used for governmental, religious, educational, and health purposes, and other public or semipublic land, has been projected for generally slow expansion in four of the five cities shown in Figure 3.13. In Greensboro, in fact, the total acreage devoted to social and cultural uses actually fell 8 percent between 1960 and 1965, while other uses were increasing 19 percent. Only in Winston-Salem–Forsyth County were increases for social and cultural uses projected substantially above the overall land-use increase.

Some public land is spread throughout the urban area and its expansion keeps pace with suburban residential growth. New schools in outlying areas tend to be large land users because of recommended national standards for facility size. Other large land users, including hospitals, government buildings, and probably churches, do not expand outward quite as fast because of their large fixed investment in older locations. Urban renewal, as a special catalyst of land-use change, tends to favor the use of redeveloped land in the central city for public institutional activities.

A special category of public land is land for parks, open space, and recreation. Most cities have not been aggressive in acquiring land for these purposes to keep pace with general urban growth. Special opportunities exist in the form of flood plains and other areas that are not suitable for intensive development. Public acquisition of flood plain areas, for example, could provide for open-space parks with recreation areas, bicycle paths, and open-air theaters, while simultaneously saving the cost of expensive dams or facilities needed to avert flooding. Occasional flooding would cause little harm or inconvenience to such areas. The alternative is expensive and improper private construction in these areas,

followed by appeals to public agencies such as the Corps of Engineers to "do something" about the flooding. Sound planning, implemented by active public land acquisition, can prevent such misallocation of resources.

Transportation Land

Highways are, of course, the major component of transportation land. Highway land includes the access roads required to serve new residential lots, industries, or other uses, and also improvements and extensions to the arterial highway networks. Within existing built-up areas, the percentage of land devoted to these uses has increased as cities completed expressways or built their portions of the interstate network. This increase has typically been at the expense of residential land and inner city parkland.

Within the expanding urban area, however, transportation land is generally projected for slower than average growth, reducing slightly the percentage of all developed land committed to this use. Despite that projection, the amount of transportation land per person will probably grow.

Transportation growth is obviously needed to serve the expanding urban area. The question is, How much is needed? New forms of residential development, for example, can cluster homes so that shorter access roads are needed, and the land saved can be used instead for open or recreation space. Problems of pollution and possibly chronic fuel shortages make dubious the wisdom of relying totally on the private car for urban transportation, and they may promote some diversion to more space-saving modes of transportation. Given the nature of North Carolina cities today, however, it would be difficult to predict any radical shift in transportation modes. The nature of the land-use pattern and the low overall density make it difficult for public transportation to succeed. Unless land-use policies change dramatically, the automobile, with all of its attendant space demands, will continue to be the dominant form of transportation in North Carolina cities.

NEW URBAN FORMS

A recent urban phenomenon is the growth of large-scale planned developments, projects containing a range of urban facilities and frequently consisting of one square mile or more. These projects include planned unit developments (typically residential, but with some commercial or industrial facilities and common open space), special-purpose recreation or retirement complexes, and fully self-sufficient new communities, with a balanced population, employment opportunities, and community services. Figure 3.14 shows the general location of nearly fifty such planned developments in North Carolina. At least fourteen of these projects already involve 1,000 acres or more, with total projected sizes ranging up to 15,000 acres and 10,000 housing units.

These projects pose both an opportunity and a challenge for orderly urban development. Their size and the long-term nature of their financing frequently mean that their planning and design quality is above average. They are able to achieve sound land use, with clusters of housing, open space, and commercial facilities properly organized and laid out. They are often an improvement over the common piecemeal or strip development adjacent to urban areas.

The challenge of the large-scale developments is that they bring urban development to areas unaccustomed to it, and to areas often ill prepared to handle a new urban population. Figure 3.14 shows that while planned unit developments cluster around existing urban areas, the new communities and recreational retirement communities occur largely in heretofore modestly urbanized regions, especially around the mountain ski areas and along the coast. Because they are large, these projects can provide some of the needed urban services for their own residents, but they also demand substantial public improvements in highway access and waste treatment facilities. Surrounding towns and counties may not be prepared to provide these services. They may also not be prepared to control the adjacent surrounding areas. Attracted by the major project, secondary growth, which is often less well-planned and less desirable, begins to develop. The result detracts from the value of the original project, creates environmental problems, and develops a new form of "instant urbanization."

These new urban forms pose a challenge to the state. At present the initiative on such projects rests entirely with the private sector, and the state comes in only after the fact, when additional highway capacity is desired or when environmental problems emerge. It has been suggested that North Carolina should play a more active role with respect to large-scale development, analogous to roles now played by some other states. For example, the state could regulate the location and quality of developments, could assist and facilitate development in appropriate locations, and could function directly as a developer itself for projects of statewide importance and benefit. The model for this type of activity already exists in the New York State Urban Development Corporation, a state entity that functions, either by itself or in cooperation with local governments and private developers, as a sponsor of large-scale developments, ranging from low income housing and industrial parks to complete new towns. Whether this precise model is followed or not, it appears that only the state government can adequately meet the challenge of these large-scale developments.

Two examples illustrate the latter problem. Figure 3.16 illustrates the Research Triangle area. Originally composed of three distinct urban areas (Raleigh, Durham, and Chapel Hill), there are now strong pressures for development of the area between them. The Research Triangle Park is a high-employment magnet centrally located in this area, and the Raleigh-Durham airport and the Interstate 40 highway provide high accessibility to it. Pressures are already increasing: by the year 2000 this entire center portion could well be a low density urbanized area. Fingers of development reach out along all the linking highways, and Chapel Hill and Durham are already joined by continuous highway development.

A second example exists in the Piedmont Triad of Winston-Salem, Greensboro, and High Point (Figure 3.17). Highways and airports again encourage urban infilling of the region between the existing cities. In this case the problem is compounded by the fact that the catchment area for the municipal water supply for Greensboro is located in the direct path of the urbanization. Construction in this area leads to siltation and pollution that, if unchecked, could destroy the utility of the reservoirs.

These are two examples of urban land-use crises that cannot be solved by individual cities. In both these regions there exist multicounty regional planning councils (the Triangle J Council of Governments for Raleigh-Durham-Chapel Hill, and the Piedmont Triad Council of Governments for Greensboro-Winston-Salem-High Point). Each planning body is trying to make the public aware of the problems and the possibilities of urbanization. The Piedmont Triad Council has presented a plan to preserve critical open-space areas, or buffers, between the existing built-up areas in its region. Public awareness will be one prerequisite, but it appears that the regional planning councils will also require greater statutory power than they now possess if they are to effectively manage urbanization within their regions. This power can only be granted by the state, and it will probably need to be backed with certain review authority and control by the state government. Much land for open space, for recreation, and for environmental protection will need to be publicly acquired, and here too the state will have to play a significant role, either directly or by acting through the regional planning councils.

URBAN LAND MANAGEMENT

It is clear that urban development extends beyond municipal boundaries and even beyond the borders of Urbanized Areas and SMSAs in the census definition. Urbanization is becoming a pervasive phenomenon, and is affecting the use of land in all parts of the state. One estimate has been made that once population density reaches 100 persons per square mile, the land is subject to pressures for urbanization and becomes less valuable for other uses. Figure 3.15 indicates the areas of the state where this density now exists, and those areas where it will probably be true by the year 2000. It can be seen that the entire center portion of the state is under pressure to fill in the spaces between existing urban areas.

This poses problems for land management that go beyond the individual municipality. Urban planning for North Carolina's future must deal with two major questions: (1) What is the best mix of various town and city sizes across the state and within its several subregions? (2) What is the best use of land between expanding urban areas?

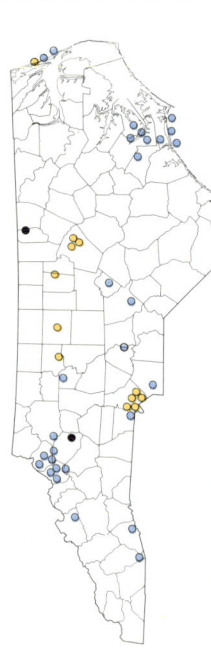

Figure 3.14. New Communities and Large-Scale Developments in N.C., 1972

Type of Development
- planned unit development
- recreation/retirement communities
- new communities

Source: David R. Godschalk, ed., *New Communities and Large-Scale Development: Alternative Policies for North Carolina* (Raleigh: N.C. Office of State Planning, 1972).

Figure 3.15. Present and Future Areas That Are Likely to Experience Urban Development

Population Density of 100 People per Square Mile (Density at Which Urban Development Begins)
- 1970
- 2000

Source: Richard R. Wilkinson, ed., *Critical Environmental Areas of North Carolina* (Raleigh: N.C. Office of State Planning, 1972).

There is much in North Carolina's present pattern of urbanization that is not only attractive but perhaps unique. There is also time to insure that the desirable parts of this pattern can be preserved. North Carolina should not be lulled, however, into thinking that this will happen automatically. There are problems already evident and more will become evident as present trends continue. Planning for a desirable urban pattern takes time. This planning must proceed now, and it must involve not only the cities but also the multicounty regions and state government. The challenge of urbanization is at hand.

The Pattern of Urbanization—Clyde E. Browning
The Use of Urban Land—Francis H. Parker

SELECTED REFERENCES

Godschalk, David R. *New Communities and Large Scale Development: Alternative Policies for North Carolina.* Raleigh: N.C. Office of State Planning, 1972.

N.C. State Conservation Needs Committee. *North Carolina Conservation Needs Inventory.* Raleigh: The Committee, 1971.

N.C. State Department of Administration. *Statewide Development Policy.* Raleigh: The Department, 1972.

Parker, Francis H. *Land Policy Alternatives for North Carolina.* Raleigh: N.C. Office of State Planning, 1972.

Sumka, Howard J., and Stegman, Michael A. *The Housing Outlook in North Carolina: Projections to 1980.* Raleigh: N.C. Office of State Planning, 1972.

Wilkinson, Richard R. *Critical Environmental Areas of North Carolina.* Raleigh: N.C. Office of State Planning, 1972.

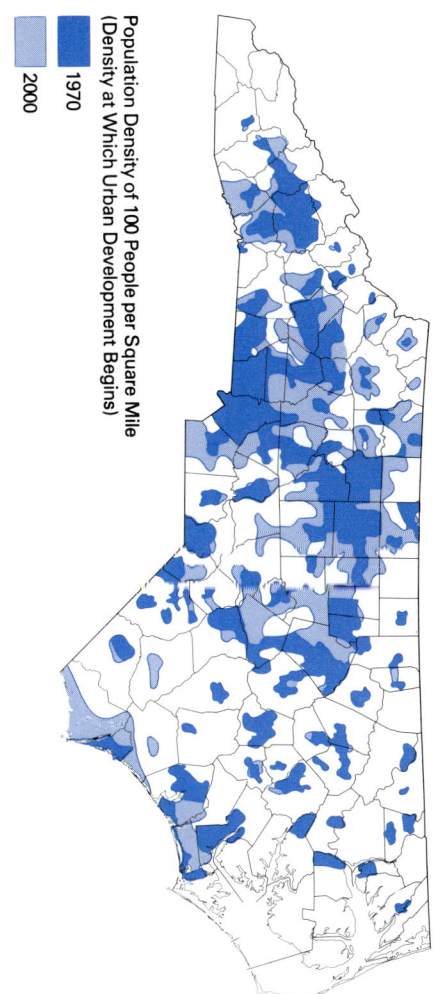

Figure 3.16. N.C. Research Triangle Region—Projected Urban Development

Source: Research Triangle Regional Planning Commission, *Research Triangle Regional Development Guide,* 1969.

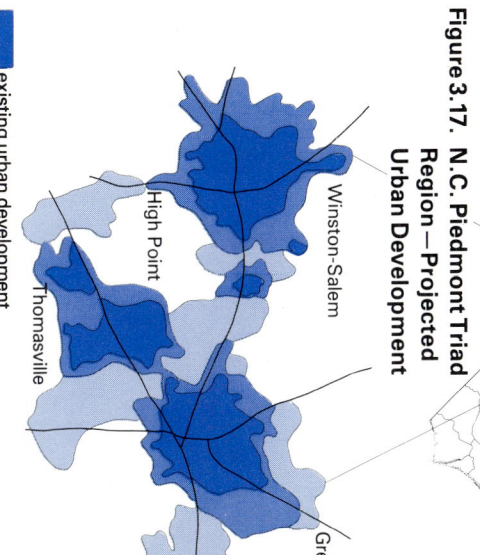

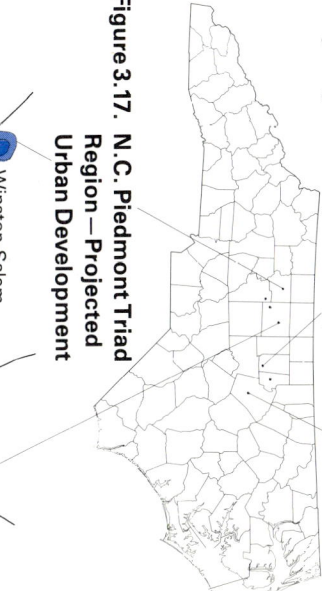

Figure 3.17. N.C. Piedmont Triad Region—Projected Urban Development

- existing urban development
- future urban development (2000 A.D.)
- planned management (open space) area

Source: Piedmont Triad Council of Government, *Piedmont Triad Regional Development Guide,* 1972.

4. Government and Politics

SCHLEY R. LYONS
WILLIAM J. McCOY

The government of North Carolina has been described as something of a paradox. Only in the last decade have any substantial reforms been made in the administrative and judicial structures of this "charter member" of the federal Union since the adoption of its state constitution in 1868. The General Assembly lags behind the other state legislatures in providing itself with reference bureaus and professional staff upon which it can depend for technical and research assistance. But compared with neighboring states in the southern region, North Carolina enjoys reasonably good government. An opinion shared by many students of state government is that North Carolina government, while not spectacular, has been for the most part honest, efficient, and effective. Describing and explaining this governmental and political paradox are the primary objectives of this chapter.

GOVERNMENT IN NORTH CAROLINA

The Web of Government

In describing the activities and powers of North Carolina government it must be remembered that state and local government in the United States functions within the constraints of the American federal system. A common view of federalism is that it resembles a layer cake with local government at the base, state government in the middle, and the national government at the top. In practice, however, American government has never operated in this fashion. The federal system always has been characterized by far more cooperation and shared responsibilities than by separation.

Another view of the American governmental system portrays national and state powers at the opposite ends of a seesaw—if national powers are increased, then state power declines. Evidence also refutes this belief. During the years since the Great Depression, national power and activities have multiplied manifold, but so have the power and activities of North Carolina government. For the citizens of North Carolina, state and local governments continue to bear the major responsibility for domestic affairs.

The breadth of state and local government activities is reflected in the fact that in 1974 North Carolina government cost $4 billion a year, of which the state spent $3 billion and local government the remainder. This pattern, in which the state is the dominant fiscal partner, is not generally found in other states. Only thirteen of fifty state governments expend over two-thirds of total state and local taxes (Figure 4.1).

During the decade preceding 1974, total state government expenditures increased 335 percent. It was a decade in which the expenditures of national government also spiraled upward at an unprecedented rate. Over three-fourths of the 1974 state budget was allocated for three critically important domestic programs, education (42 percent), health and welfare (19 percent), and transportation (16 percent). Compared with other states, however, North Carolina is categorized as a low expenditure state. In 1972 North Carolina state and local governments spent $563.45 for every man, woman, and child, placing it forty-ninth among the fifty states in per capita spending (Table 4.1).

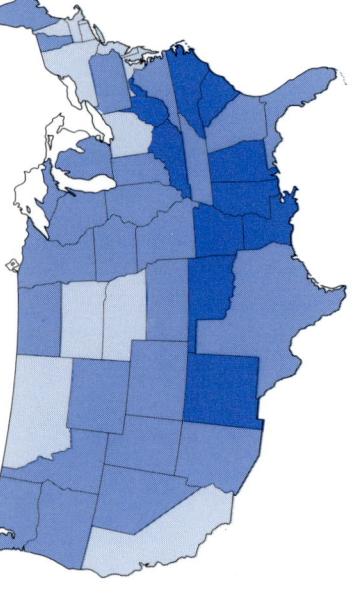

Figure 4.1. State Share of State and Local Tax Systems, 1972

over 66.6% (state dominant fiscal partner)
50% to 66% (state strong fiscal partner)
under 50% (state junior fiscal partner)

Source: Advisory Commission on Intergovernmental Relations, *American Federalism: Into the Third Century*, 1974.

Table 4.1. Per Capita Direct General Expenditure of State and Local Governments, for Selected Items, for N.C. and Other Selected States, 1972

State	Total	Education	Transportation	Public Welfare	Health and Hospitals
Median state	$ 740.68	$315.67	$ 98.99	$ 74.20	$ 49.63
North Carolina	563.45	240.41	78.22	55.72	43.20
Alaska	2,146.63	727.98	388.79	104.54	62.18
Arkansas	512.38	200.44	82.27	71.95	40.12
California	979.66	338.91	76.22	188.23	65.25
Florida	657.22	264.28	81.06	48.23	62.59
Illinois	794.12	313.19	95.52	107.94	48.83
Mississippi	630.44	226.78	108.63	83.17	69.20
New York	1,238.72	407.71	80.92	180.74	139.75
Ohio	636.86	264.50	75.39	65.84	48.98
South Carolina	567.24	252.15	64.50	36.55	61.47
Tennessee	606.76	228.26	83.52	59.69	61.21
Virginia	637.53	275.86	89.87	56.47	39.48

Source: Council of State Governments, *The Book of the States, 1974-1975* (Lexington, Ky.: The Council, 1974), p. 221.

Table 4.2. Chief Functions and Services Authorized for City and County Governments in N.C.

A. Services and Functions Authorized for Counties Only

1. Agricultural extension
2. Community colleges
3. County home
4. Juvenile detention homes
5. Public schools
6. Register of deeds
7. Social services
8. Soil and water conservation

B. Services and Functions Authorized for Both Cities and Counties

9. Ambulance services
10. Animal shelters
11. Art galleries
12. Beach erosion control
13. Bus lines and mass transit
14. Civil defense
15. Community action
16. Community appearance
17. Fire protection
18. Historic preservation
19. Hospitals
20. Human relations
21. Industrial promotion
22. Inspections
23. Jails
24. Law enforcement
25. Libraries
26. Manpower
27. Mental health
28. National Guard
29. Off-street parking
30. Open space
31. Parks
32. Planning
33. Public health
34. Public housing
35. Recreation
36. Refuse collection and disposal
37. Rescue squads
38. Sewerage
39. Urban redevelopment
40. Veterans services
41. Water
42. Watershed improvement programs

C. Services and Functions Authorized for Cities Only

1. Auditorium
2. Cable television
3. Cemeteries
4. Electric systems
5. Gas systems
6. Sidewalks
7. Storm drainage
8. Street lighting
9. Streets
10. Traffic engineering

Note: Both units have authority to undertake the necessary supporting functions and activities: finance, tax collection, personnel, purchasing, etc., and to construct buildings and other facilities needed to provide the listed services and functions. The authority cited in the above list is qualified in some cases. In a few cases, only units of a certain size have the authority. In others, state policy may restrict or limit the authority. And in some cases one unit's action may limit the other's. The list does not include regulatory authority.

Source: Institute of Government, *Popular Government* (Chapel Hill: Institute of Government, University of N.C., 1974), p. 27.

The bulk of the revenues (64 percent) to fund the state's extensive spending programs are derived from state taxes, including state income, corporate taxes, and sales taxes. But a full one-fourth of the state's revenues are obtained from the national government, primarily through categorical grant-in-aid programs and the more recent general revenue sharing plan. The remainder of the revenues are derived from miscellaneous sources such as the State Treasurer's investments, fees from regulatory functions, and court costs.

The expansive nature of North Carolina government can be seen also in its role as an employer. In 1972 the state government employed 65,941 full-time persons and local governments 148,375 full-time persons, which combined is 13 percent of the total employment in the state. Government in North Carolina is impressive not only in regard to the size of its budget and employment rolls but also in the magnitude of its responsibility. Over thirty licensing and examining boards regulate many of the service workers, including architects, barbers, hearing aid dealers and fitters, opticians, certified public accountants, chiropractors, dentists, pharmacists, and real estate agents. State agencies such as the North Carolina Milk Commission, the State Banking Commission, and the State Board of Alcoholic Control supervise and regulate important segments of the state economy.

At the local level Tar Heel citizens are served by 800 units of government—100 counties, 435 active cities and towns (approximately another 50 are inactive), and some 265 special districts, authorities, and independent boards and commissions. In 1970 a little less than 43 percent of the state's population lived inside incorporated and active towns and cities. The rest resided outside municipalities, and most of these voted for the members of only one local governing body, the Board of County Commissioners. North Carolina's relatively simple and uncluttered local government structure has been admired by students of government and held up as a model for others to follow.

From a constitutional point of view local governments in the United States are part of state government. Communities have no constitutional right to self-government and all of their governmental powers flow from state government. Counties, municipalities, special districts, and school districts are creatures of the state, subject to the obligations, privileges, and powers and restrictions that state government imposes upon them. To the extent that local governments can collect taxes, regulate their citizens, and provide services, they are actually exercising state powers delegated to them by the state either in its constitution or laws.

Table 4.2 lists the chief functions and services of city and county governments as authorized by the North Carolina state government. The table indicates that county governments have principal responsibility for health, education, and welfare, while cities have principal responsibility for streets, utilities, and transportation. All other functions and services may be shared through arrangements that vary from one county to another (Table 4.2).

Local Government in North Carolina

The major units of local government in North Carolina are counties and municipalities. Although they are uniform in governmental structure, considerable variation exists among the counties in terms of power because of the General Assembly's habit of dealing with problems through local legislation. The Board of County Commissioners is the central governing body in the one hundred North Carolina counties, but considerable authority over important governmental functions has been delegated to other bodies at this level, e.g., special district governments and school boards. Industrialization, shifts in population, and growing demands by citizens have had a substantial effect on the scope of county government in recent decades. Some counties now support libraries, hospitals, and fire and police departments, and maintain water and sewer systems and a myriad of other activities usually associated with cities. In fact, recent revision of the North Carolina General Statutes provides counties with many of the basic powers available to cities.

In North Carolina, as in every other state, a town or city is a municipal corporation and, as such, shares some of the attributes commonly associated with a private business corporation. Cities possess a dual character in a legal sense. On the one hand, municipalities have a governmental capacity; they act as an agent of the state for the promotion of the health, safety, security, and general welfare of their citizens. In this capacity a municipality may regulate the conduct of persons and their property, levy and collect taxes, take land for public purposes, and provide streets, parks, fire and police protection, and buildings. However, a municipality may also act in a proprietary capacity for the private advantage of the body politic. Although this distinction is not always clear in practice, a municipality, unlike a county, may engage in business and provide services of the type that are normally associated with private corporations. Thus, in the ownership of power plants, bus and railway systems, and other services supported by users' fees the municipality is said to be exercising its proprietary powers.

Municipal home rule in North Carolina is of the statutory rather than constitutional variety. It consists largely of the authority given to towns and cities to amend their existing charters. Either the governing body of a city or a prescribed number of qualified voters within a city may initiate the procedure for making a change that, in turn, becomes effective after it receives a favorable vote from a majority of persons in an election conducted for that purpose. In practice, however, municipalities are more inclined to use special legislative enactments of the General Assembly to obtain changes in governmental organization and functions.

One of the most discussed local problems in recent decades is that of "fragmented government," or the proliferation of governments in metropolitan areas with a resulting lack of coordination of public programs. Various commentators have described government in metropolitan areas as a "patchwork," a "governmental maze," and similar to a "stack of pancakes." Although this problem tends to be less severe in North Carolina than in other states, Tar Heel voters have been in the vanguard of the metropolitan reform movement by approving a constitutional amendment in 1972 prohibiting the incorporation of a new town or city closer than one mile from a city with a population of 5,000 to 10,000; three miles from a city with a population of 10,000 to 25,000; four miles from a city with a population of 25,000 to 50,000; and five miles from larger cities. The state legislature can disregard these limits only by a three-fifths vote. In 1973 the General Assembly took an additional step by enacting a new law applicable to counties that may reduce the demand for new incorporations in the future. This new law empowered counties to provide water and sewer facilities, fire protection, and solid waste collection and disposal for newly created service districts. The need for such services is often the impetus to incorporation and if the new act facilitates the providing of these services by counties, the need for new municipal incorporation may lessen. These progressive acts may aid in preventing the proliferation of governments in North Carolina's major metropolitan areas.

Although North Carolina cannot boast of any successful city-county consolidations, there has been a long-standing interest in this particular reform. City-county consolidation has been seriously proposed in several counties over the last forty years, most recently in Mecklenburg and Durham counties. But Tar Heel voters have consistently rejected such proposals by substantial margins. Consequently, major changes in local government patterns and functions are likely to take place in a structure that includes counties, cities, and towns.

The Major Institutions of State Government

Aside from sharing a common constitutional framework and cultural background all the states of the Union divide governmental authority among legislative, executive, and judicial branches. In the following sections some of the distinguishing characteristics of North Carolina state government are examined.

The State Legislature
"Making the laws of the state" is the way most citizens would describe the major activity of the North Carolina General Assembly. The description is accurate in the sense that the legislature considers and passes thousands of bills and resolutions every session. These bills and resolutions touch upon almost every facet of human behavior and during the 1974 legislative session ranged from such complex issues as no-fault insurance, child abuse, legislative ethics, obscenity, state land-use management, election reforms, revision of the criminal code, and expansion of the state's medical schools to the more mundane questions of regulating massage parlors and bingo playing at the state fair.

In terms of organization and procedure the North Carolina General Assembly is rather typical. It is composed of two houses, the Senate and House of Representatives with a membership of 50 and 120, respectively (Figures 4.2a and 4.2b). Meeting the constitutional requirements for membership in these two bodies is a simple matter. A state senator must be at least 25 years of age, a resident of the state for two years, and a resident of the district he represents for one year immediately preceding the election. A member of the House of Representatives must be a qualified voter and a resident of the district he is elected from for one year immediately prior to the election. There are, of course, many extraconstitutional requirements that a citizen must satisfy in order to be a state legislator. A composite profile of the 1975–76 membership of the General Assembly indicates that state legislators are disproportionately selected from a well-educated professional and managerial stratum of North Carolina society. The typical legislator was Caucasian (96 percent) and male (91 percent). He was born in North Carolina (88 percent) and completed college (64 percent). About half the legislators (48 percent) have earned an advanced degree, most likely a law degree. The largest single occupational category represented was that of lawyer (25 percent); 40 percent were businessmen, including owners and managers; 20 percent were in service occupations such as teaching, medicine, banking; 12 percent were farmers and 2 percent were retired persons. A typical legislator was likely to be either a Methodist (36 percent), a Baptist (31 percent), or a Presbyterian (13 percent). The average age of a legislator was 50.6 years, with the youngest being 29 and the oldest 77. He tended to have had prior governmental experience before becoming a state legislator, usually at the local level and was a "joiner," as evidenced by the large number of organizations in which he held membership.

One of the most important leaders in the General Assembly is the Speaker of the House of Representatives. He makes all the committee assignments and presides over the deliberations of the House of Representatives. A two-thirds vote of the membership is required to override his ruling, an eventuality that rarely occurs. Although not a member of the Senate, the lieutenant governor is the presiding officer of that body. He has the power to appoint the membership of the Senate committees but unlike the Speaker, he can vote on pending legislation only in case of a tie.

In each house groups of standing committees are used to expedite the work of the General Assembly. Standing committees attempt to become expert in various categories of legislation; some of the more important standing committees are Agriculture, Appropriations, Banking, Education, Finance, Judiciary, and Local Government. When any bill is introduced that touches on a subject matter that falls within the jurisdiction of a particular committee, the rules of the General Assembly require that it be referred to that committee before any action is taken by the full legislative body. The purpose of the committee system is to bring as much expertise as possible to bear on subjects under consideration and to reduce the legislative workload to manageable proportions by providing for a division of labor. During the 1975–76 biennium there were twenty-four standing committees in the Senate and forty in the House of Representatives.

Like most state legislatures the North Carolina General Assembly is a part-time institution. Prior to 1973 the legislature convened in January during odd-numbered years following the general election. Beginning in the 1973 session the General Assembly met in annual sessions as a result of a decision to appropriate money for only one year at a time. At the time of this writing it has not yet been determined whether the 1973, 1974, and 1975 annual sessions are only an experiment or the beginning of annual sessions. Regardless of the disposition of the annual session issue, most legislators must earn a living in an occupation outside of legislative service. Legislators receive only nominal compensation. During 1973-74 they received a biennial salary of $4,800 or a total estimated compensation of $9,525 including food and travel allowance. Since this level of compensation cannot provide full support for a legislator and his family he must be either independently wealthy or have some other income. This unwritten qualification for legislative service explains to a large degree the preponderance of lawyers and self-employed businessmen in the General Assembly, occupations flexible enough to allow absences of approximately six to eight months every two years.

Textbooks on state government have for years depicted legislatures as inept organizations suffering from few staff assistants, rapid turnover of membership, short legislative sessions, and low pay for its members, but the North Carolina General Assembly seems to suffer from these ills more than most. In a recent study (1971) conducted by the Citizens Conference on State Legislatures, the North Carolina General Assembly was ranked forty-seven among the fifty state legislatures in terms of efficiency and effectiveness. Obviously evaluating performance on the basis of such factors as salary levels and length of session is hazardous and fraught with the danger of extending generalizations beyond the limits of the data, but evidence is persuasive that the North Carolina General Assembly is hampered by an often inexperienced, understaffed, part-time membership. Although the state legislature must confront and hopefully resolve twentieth-century problems, it does so with an organization and procedures that had their origins in the eighteenth and nineteenth centuries.

The Chief Executive

The spectacular growth in government in the twentieth century has disproportionately advantaged the nation's chief executive officers including the governor of North Carolina. The governor is the central figure of state government, yet the office remains best known for its limited powers. In all likelihood the one thing known about the governor of North Carolina by most of the nation's schoolchildren is that he alone among the fifty state governors lacks the veto power.

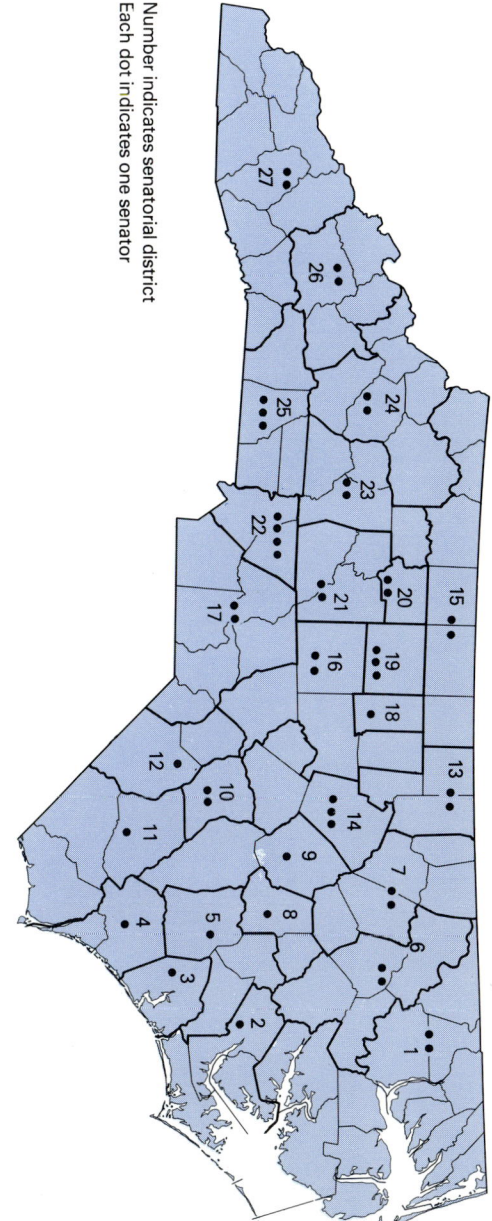

Figure 4.2(a) N.C. Senatorial Districts, 1974

Number indicates senatorial district
Each dot indicates one senator

Source: Hugh T. Lefler and Albert R. Newsome, *North Carolina: The History of a Southern State*, 3d ed. (Chapel Hill: University of N.C. Press, 1973).

Note: The apportionment is for elections of 1972 and subsequent years, the number of senators is 50, and the average population per senator (norm) is 101,641.

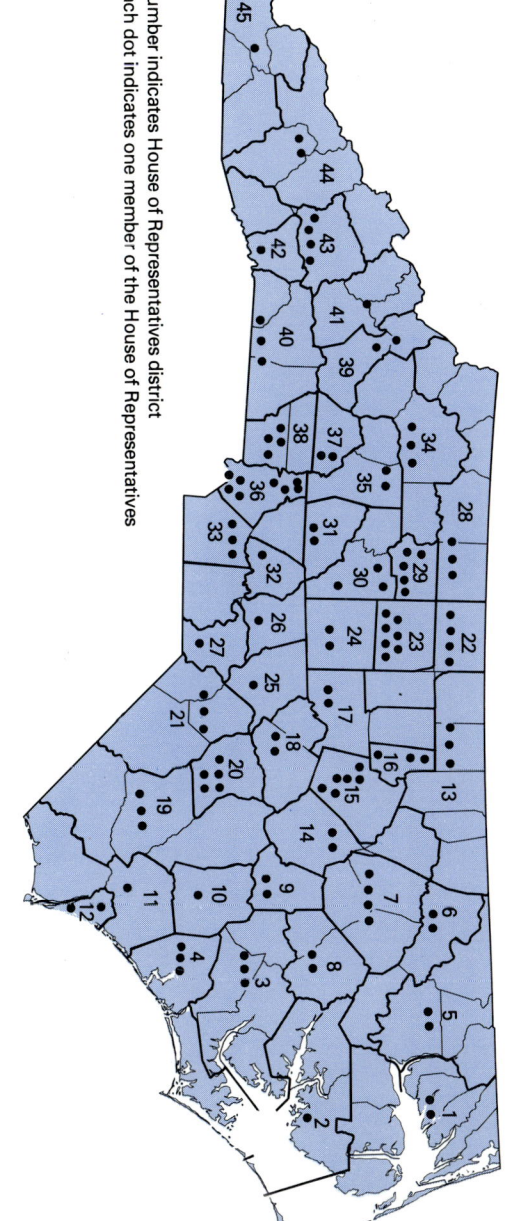

Figure 4.2(b) N.C. House of Representatives Districts, 1974

Number indicates House of Representatives district
Each dot indicates one member of the House of Representatives

Source: Hugh T. Lefler and Albert R. Newsome, *North Carolina: The History of a Southern State*, 3d ed. (Chapel Hill: University of N.C. Press, 1973).

Note: The apportionment is for elections of 1972 and subsequent years, the number of representatives is 120, and the average population per representative (norm) is 42,350.

73

among the governor, eight popularly elected department heads, and some 160 boards, commissions, councils, committees, and other bodies. In the words of the Committee on Economic Development, that division represents "unfortunate organizational patterns."

Reacting to the problem of diffused power in the executive branch, the General Assembly in 1971 enacted the Executive Organization Act that empowered the governor to reorganize the state's administrative structure. Most of the existing two hundred or so bureaus, boards, and commissions were redistributed within one of seventeen functional departments. The hoped-for effect of the reorganization was to clarify the governor's lines of authority through either popularly elected or appointed departmental secretaries. Theoretically, the new organizational structure provided clearer channels of control, responsibility, and accountability. However, the verdict as to whether these reforms accomplished the above-stated goals must await further experience with the new administrative structure (Figure 4.3).

Although law making is the primary function of state legislatures, governors in all fifty states share in the exercise of this power. They do this through the constitutional provisions empowering them to call special sessions, give messages, veto legislative enactments, and adjourn legislative sessions. The North Carolina governor has only the first two constitutional powers mentioned above, which, comparatively speaking, makes him a moderate to weak legislative leader among the fifty governors. Nevertheless, the governor has assumed responsibility for initiating major legislative proposals largely by default. The part-time General Assembly controlled by the dominant Democratic majority for most of the twentieth century acquiesced in the legislative leadership of a Democratic governor. With the election in 1972 of a Republican governor, James E. Holshouser, Jr., the Democratic majority attempted to reassert its leadership in the legislative process. The result was a standoff during the first two years of the Holshouser administration. But the governor's influence was noticeably diminished during the 1975 legislative session due to the virtual Democratic sweep of state legislative seats in the 1974 election. However, a governor with very little party support in the legislature still has an important role in establishing the agenda for public decision making. As a central figure in state government he can focus public attention on those issues he deems important, a powerful weapon in his political arsenal. In the final analysis the North Carolina governor's real power rests on his abilities of persuasion. To accomplish his objectives the present governor must persuade administrators over whom he has little control, legislators who are jealous of their own prerogatives and who disproportionately are members of the opposition

history. In that election six Democrats and four Republicans sought the governorship in the primaries and general election and reported spending a total of $2,740,505 in their quest for the state's highest political office. This staggering campaign expenditure indicates the high esteem in which the office is held by the small and select group of would-be governors in the state.

The governor's powers of supervision and appointment have expanded along with the general growth in the size and activities of state government. However, his newfound formal powers are a mixed blessing. These formal powers are not sufficient to allow him to meet the expectations that people have of the office. Although he is held responsible for everything that occurs in the executive branch, his administrative powers are restricted because many departments are headed by other elective executive officials. The governor also confronts many independent policy-making and advisory boards and commissions. Although he appoints the members of many of these boards and commissions, his control after their appointment is nominal. In fact, recent studies have suggested that North Carolina's administrative structure was not a model to emulate. The Committee on Economic Development stated in 1967 that the administrative structure of North Carolina was one of the least efficient and accountable administrations to be found among the fifty states. Executive authority was divided

To be governor one must meet only the constitutional requirements of age, residence, and citizenship. A person could satisfy these minimal requirements by being thirty years of age, a citizen of the United States for five years, and a resident of North Carolina for two years. If elected, a governor serves a four-year term and is prohibited from succeeding himself by the somewhat unusual constitutional provision that permits him to serve no longer than four years out of any given period of eight years.

These constitutional requirements for being governor are deceptively simple To seek the first office of the state is a demanding and expensive undertaking. North Carolinians expect a gubernatorial candidate to wage vigorous campaigns, not only in the general election but also in the primaries. Candidates must make campaign trips to all corners of the state, expend large sums of money on television, radio, and billboards, and appear informed on all facets of state government. Although it is impossible to estimate precisely the total amount of money necessary to campaign for the governorship because of the unevenness in the reporting of campaign expenditures by the candidates, the cost would certainly run into the hundreds of thousands of dollars. Observers of the North Carolina political scene have commented that the 1972 campaigns were the most expensive and probably the most honest and completely reported in the state's party, federal and local officials over whom he has no authority and, finally, the general public who views the limited office of governor as a position of power that has virtually no boundaries.

The Judiciary

In an address to the American Bar Association, Warren Burger, chief justice of the United States Supreme Court, declared that "in the supermarket age we are with few exceptions operating the courts with cracker barrel corner grocery methods and equipment, vintage 1900." That kind of criticism was applicable to North Carolina courts as late as 1965, but in that year the General Assembly rewrote the judicial article of the state constitution and initiated a judicial reform movement still in progress today. A key provision of the 1965 judicial article stated that "the general court of justice shall constitute a unified judicial system for purposes of jurisdiction, operation and administration and shall consist of an appellate division, a superior court division, and a district court division." The change to a unified court system occurred because of the proliferation of special courts and the inefficiency of the justices of the peace, including the potential for wrongdoing inherent in the fee system of remuneration.

The hierarchy of courts established under the new judicial article included at the lowest level the district courts that replaced a variety of special courts—the recorder's court, the juvenile court, the mayor's court, and the above-mentioned justice of the peace courts. The task of the district courts is to try less serious criminal cases such as traffic violations and civil cases involving less than $5,000 in property. In most cases that come before the district courts a jury is not used and a person can appeal any judgment to the North Carolina Superior Court. Each of the state's thirty judicial districts has a district court on which from two to six judges serve. The district court judges are elected by popular vote for four-year terms (Figure 4.4).

The major trial court of general jurisdiction in North Carolina is the superior court. This is the court of original jurisdiction for the more serious civil and criminal cases. For most citizens the superior court is not only a court of original jurisdiction but also the court of last resort. A very small percentage of cases are ever appealed from this court to higher levels. Each of the thirty judicial districts has a superior court that is served by one or more judges who are elected by popular vote for eight-year terms. In addition to the elected judges, the governor appoints eight special superior court judges for four-year terms. Before the superior court the state is represented by a district attorney who is elected in each judicial district by popular vote for a four-year term. In criminal cases it is the job of the district attorney to present the state's case against the defendant.

At the top of the judicial hierarchy are the appeal courts. In North Carolina there are two appeal courts, the North Carolina Supreme Court and the North Carolina Court of Appeals. The supreme court is the highest state court, composed of seven justices popularly elected for eight-year terms. The General Assembly authorized the creation of the court of appeals in 1967 to assist the supreme court in hearing appeals from the lower courts. The popularly elected nine-man court of appeals hears cases on appeal deemed to be less important than those presented before the state supreme court.

Figure 4.3. Organizational Chart of Political Executives in N.C.

Popularly Elected Officials
1. State Auditor
2. State Treasurer
3. Commissioner of Agriculture
4. Commissioner of Insurance
5. Attorney General
6. Commissioner of Labor
7. Superintendent of Public Instruction
8. Secretary of State
9. Lieutenant Governor

Governor

Gubernatorially Appointed Executives
1. Secretary of Commerce
2. Commissioner of Revenue
3. Secretary of Natural and Economic Resources
4. Secretary of Transportation and Highway Safety
5. Secretary of Military and Veterans' Affairs
6. Secretary of Art, Culture, and History
7. Secretary of Social Rehabilitation and Control
8. Secretary of Human Resources

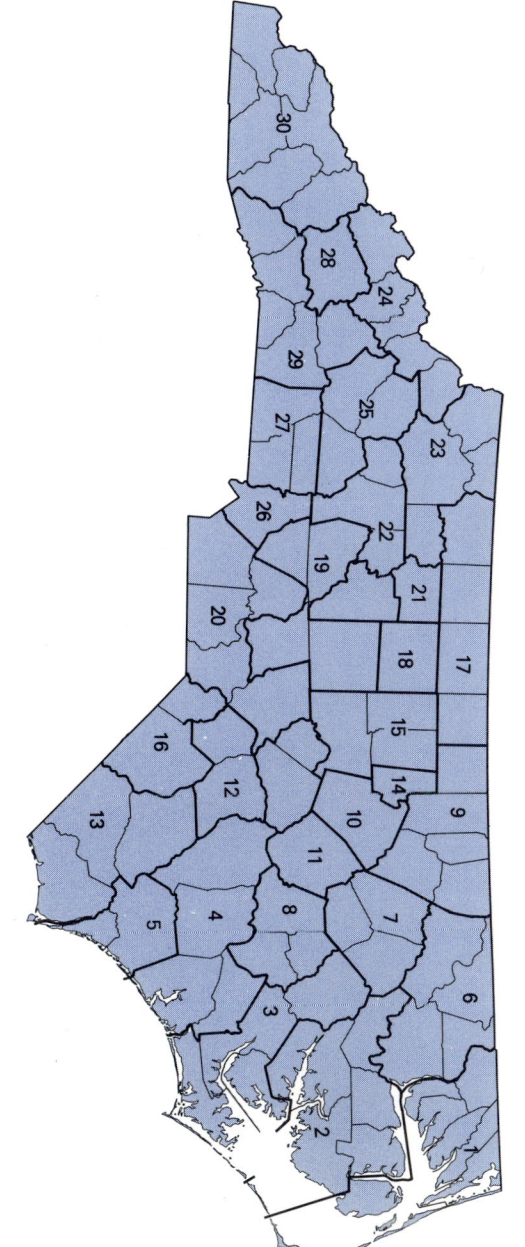

Figure 4.4. N.C. Judicial Districts, 1974

Source: Hugh T. Lefler and Albert R. Newsome, *North Carolina: The History of a Southern State*, 3d ed. (Chapel Hill: University of N.C. Press, 1973).

Although courts are "political" institutions because they attempt to resolve conflicts among men, a strong argument can be made for isolating judges from direct political involvement. Critics of the elective method of selecting judges claim it forces judges into political relationships and compromises their independence. In contrast, supporters of an elective judiciary state that if voters are competent to select legislators and governors, why not judges as well? At the highest level of the judicial hierarchy such debate is often superfluous. In practice most of the appellate judges come to the bench through appointments rather than by elections. This paradox comes about because the governor has the power to make interim judicial appointments on the occasion of vacancies caused by death or retirement. An interim-appointed judge is expected to seek the office in the next regular election and by that time he has the prestige and status of an incumbent judge. Although North Carolina elects its judges, in 1973 all seven of the supreme court judges and all nine court of appeals judges came to the bench initially by appointment.

PARTY POLITICS IN NORTH CAROLINA

Approximately two decades ago V. O. Key, Jr., observed in his classic *Southern Politics* that the Republican party did not endanger Democratic control of North Carolina. However, in 1972 it was evident to even the most casual follower of Tar Heel politics that such a situation no longer existed. The election in North Carolina of a Republican governor and a United States senator, both firsts in the twentieth century, and the landslide victory of an incumbent Republican president broke a Democratic dominance begun in 1900. Describing and explaining the changes leading to this political reversal provide the focus for the following section. The inquiry includes an analysis not only of interparty competition but also of levels of political participation and interest by Tar Heel citizens, their political beliefs and attitudes, and the impact of third party movements on statewide voting patterns.

Voting Trends: 1948-1974

Political analysts have long recognized that North Carolina had "more tender sectional sensibilities than any other state in the South." For the first half of the twentieth century, Republican territory tended to be restricted to a few counties wedged in along the spine of the Blue Ridge Mountains. With a few exceptions the rest of the state routinely delivered votes to Democrats, especially in the Coastal Plain counties with their heavy concentration of blacks. By the 1970s sectional sensibilities, although still important, had diminished as the appeal of the Republican party spread from its historical Mountain base into the growing middle class of the urban, industrial Piedmont.

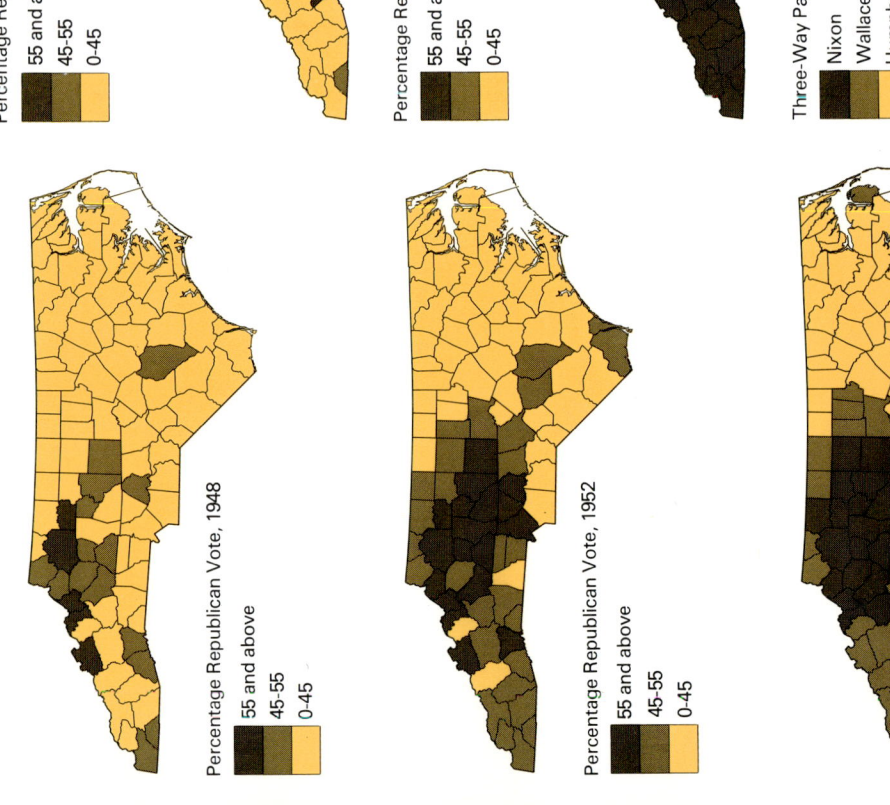

Figure 4.5(a). Republican Percentage of Presidential Vote in N.C. Counties, 1948-1972

Source: N.C. Secretary of State, *North Carolina Manuals*, 1949, 1953, 1957, 1961, 1965, and 1969. 1972 data were provided by the N.C. State Board of Elections.

Using 1948 as a point of departure the strong sectional character of the Republican vote is clearly demonstrated. Dewey received 45 percent of the Mountain vote, 34 percent of the Piedmont vote, and only 17 percent of the vote in the Coastal Plain counties. The Republican gubernatorial candidate ran even less well but the strong sectional nature of the vote was evident. Sectional differences in voting remain today with Richard Nixon being the only statewide GOP candidate who polled a majority of the popular vote among the Coastal Plain electorate during the period under review (Figures 4.5a and 4.5b).

Although North Carolinians expressed approval of Herbert Hoover in 1928 when the state Democratic party split over the candidacy of the "wet," Catholic, New York City-born Al Smith, it was not until 1952 when Eisenhower received 46 percent of the vote, up from Dewey's 32.7 percent, that Democrats encountered any serious, sustained opposition from the GOP. With the exception of Goldwater's candidacy, GOP presidential candidates have run strong since 1952 and won the state's electoral votes in 1968 and 1972. Some observers of the Southern political scene suggest that the recent success of Republican presidential candidates is not due to any shifting of Tar Heel voters to the GOP but rather to a rejection of the civil rights and welfare policy orientations of the national Democratic party. Such a proposition is supported by the fact that the national Democratic ticket received the support of only 29.2 and 28.9 percent of the popular vote in 1968 and 1972, respectively. When given an alternative other than the Republican party in 1968, 31 percent of the electorate rejected both major parties. The competitive nature of the presidential elections over the last twenty years has enhanced the image of the state GOP and made Republicanism a more respectable political allegiance in a once solid Democratic state, at least until the Watergate debacle of 1974.

At the gubernatorial level, Republicans did not become competitive until 1960 when their candidate received 45.5 percent of the vote against the relatively liberal, self-styled national Democrat, Terry Sanford. Throughout the 1960s Republican gubernatorial candidates were able to make respectable showings against their Democratic opponents. But it was not until 1972 that a Republican, James E. Holshouser, Jr., won the office by the thin margin of 51 percent of the popular vote. In winning the governorship, the moderate Holshouser was aided by the landslide nature of Nixon's victory and by being teamed on the ballot with the self-professed ultraconservative Jesse Helms, the first Republican to be elected to the United States Senate from North Carolina in this century. Helms, a former Raleigh news broadcaster, ran well in many of the normally Democratic Coastal

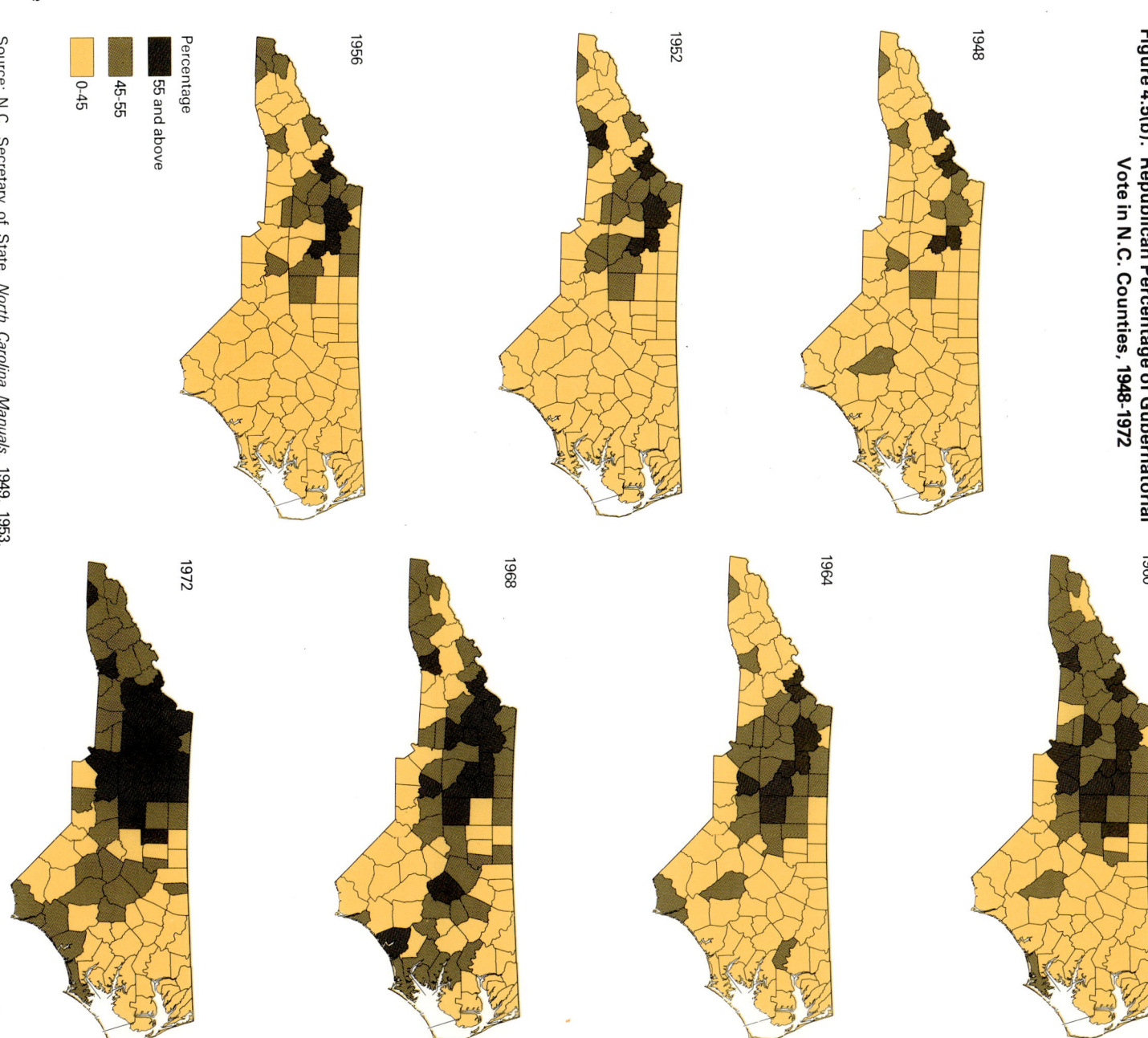

Figure 4.5(b). Republican Percentage of Gubernatorial Vote in N.C. Counties, 1948-1972

Source: N.C. Secretary of State, *North Carolina Manuals*, 1949, 1953, 1957, 1961, 1965, and 1969. 1972 data were provided by the N.C. State Board of Elections.

Plain counties that had been serviced by his programs and he probably held some "eastern" votes for Holshouser. By winning the two top political offices in the state, the GOP at the beginning of the 1970s was in position to improve on its record at the lower levels of the ballot.

At the time V. O. Key, Jr., made his favorable prognosis of the political health of the Democratic party in North Carolina there were no Republican members among the state's delegation to the United States Congress. Three years later in 1952 Charles Jonas broke the solid Democratic hold on the congressional delegation. Jonas was elected from the tenth congressional district and was the first Republican congressman from North Carolina since his father was elected in 1928. Surviving several attempts by the Democrats to gerrymander him out of office, he retired in 1972 after serving twenty years in Washington. Republicans increased their share of the congressional delegation by winning additional seats in 1962, 1966, and 1968. Offering candidates in nine of the eleven congressional districts in 1972, they came very close to winning a fifth seat as they lost a tight contest in the fourth congressional district amid charges of ballot box tampering on the part of Democratic electoral officials (Figure 4.6). But in the 1974 elections the GOP lost two of its four congressional seats. Voters reacting to the Watergate scandal, the resignation and pardon of former president Richard Nixon, and persistent inflation returned Republicans to Congress in only the ninth and tenth congressional districts. Although the Republican party in 1975 controlled only two of eleven congressional seats, this level of the ballot was one of the GOP's biggest success stories during the 1960s (Figure 4.7).

A more reliable measurement of interparty competition may be obtained by examining electoral contests of less visibility and intensity than presidential, gubernatorial, and congressional elections. Statewide races that have relatively low visibility among the electorate—elections for state auditor, secretary of state, and commissioner of agriculture, for example—are less susceptible to intervening considerations such as the appeal of exceptionally popular candidates. Controlling for the impact of candidate popularity, as in the special case of Dwight Eisenhower, is virtually impossible in highly visible presidential and gubernatorial races. In analyzing aggregate data there is no way to separate party appeal from candidate appeal. Since candidates for the Council of State offices are usually less well known, it can be assumed that party identification is a much stronger factor in determining how citizens will vote in these elections. The mean percentage of the vote for Republican candidates in nine statewide executive office races from 1948 to 1972 shows a persistent upswing in the electoral power of the GOP. A curious aspect of the data,

Figure 4.6. N.C. Congressional Districts, 1974

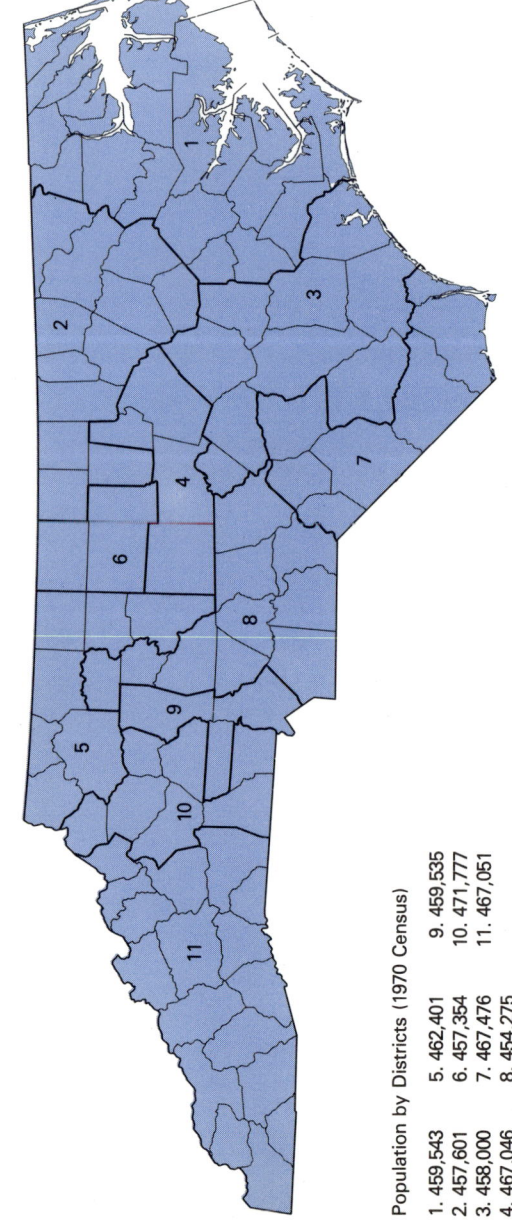

Population by Districts (1970 Census)

1. 459,543	5. 462,401	9. 459,535
2. 457,601	6. 457,354	10. 471,777
3. 458,000	7. 467,476	11. 467,051
4. 467,046	8. 454,275	

Source: Hugh T. Lefler and Albert R. Newsome, *North Carolina: The History of a Southern State*, 3d ed. (Chapel Hill: University of N.C. Press, 1973).

Table 4.3. Percentage of Republican Vote in N.C. for Nine Statewide Executive Offices, 1948-1972

Office	1948	1952	1956	1960	1964	1968	1972
Lieutenant Governor	26	32	33	41	39	45	43
Secretary of State	28	32	33	39	38	45	44
State Auditor	28	32	33	39	39	45	44
Treasurer	28	32	33	39	39	44	45
Attorney General	28	32	34	39	39	44	41
Commissioner of Agriculture	28	32	33	39	38	44	43
Superintendent of Public Instruction	28	32	34	39	uncontested	44	43
Commissioner of Insurance	28	32	33	39	38	44	42
Commissioner of Labor	28	32	33	39	38	44	44

however, is that the success the Republican party enjoyed at the top of the ballot in 1972 was not reflected in the races for these more obscure offices. Since 1968 it appears that a Republican candidate for a statewide executive office can count on approximately 44 percent of the popular vote (Table 4.3).

As of 1972 the Democrats remain in firm control of the North Carolina General Assembly. With few exceptions, primarily in the Mountain counties, Democrats enter candidates in all legislative races. Facing a more difficult recruiting task, especially in the eastern counties, the GOP is unable to match the Democrats candidate for candidate and usually permits at least one-third of the state legislative seats to go to the Democrats by default. A high point in contested elections was reached in 1968 when Republicans entered candidates in 79 percent of the Senate and 68 percent of the House races. Surprisingly, the GOP contested only 63 percent of the seats in 1972, a year when the omens for Republicans were quite good. Although running less and winning more, the Republicans in 1972 won a record number of seats for the 1973-74 legislative sessions, fifteen in the Senate and thirty-five in the House. But these Republican gains were totally wiped out in the Democratic landslide of 1974. Tar Heel voters returned only one Republican to the state senate and nine Republicans to the lower house, an electoral rejection of the GOP reminiscent of the 1940s (Figure 4.8).

Even though the Republicans have become competitive at the top of the ballot during the last quarter of a century, the voters of the state retain a lopsided Democratic identification. In 1972, 74.6 percent of the eligible voters were registered as Democrats and only 21.9 percent as Republicans. This division makes it extremely difficult for the Republicans to be competitive for all political offices. First, it limits the pool of candidates available for the Republicans and, second, it retards party organizational efforts, particularly in those races for the less visible offices such as state legislator, county commissioner, sheriff, and district attorney. The low Republican registration will probably act as a brake on any dramatic Republican upswing in these particular offices.

The Tar Heel state has moved from its once solid Democratic moorings to more competitive interparty competition. Significant gains were made by the GOP during the sixties and early seventies, especially in the urbanizing Piedmont. At the top of the ballot—in the presidential, gubernatorial, and until 1974 the congressional offices—the Republican party has been a strong and vigorous competitor for offices once considered safe for the Democratic party. Below this level, gains in recruiting candidates and winning elections have been less spectacular. In state legislative races the draw-

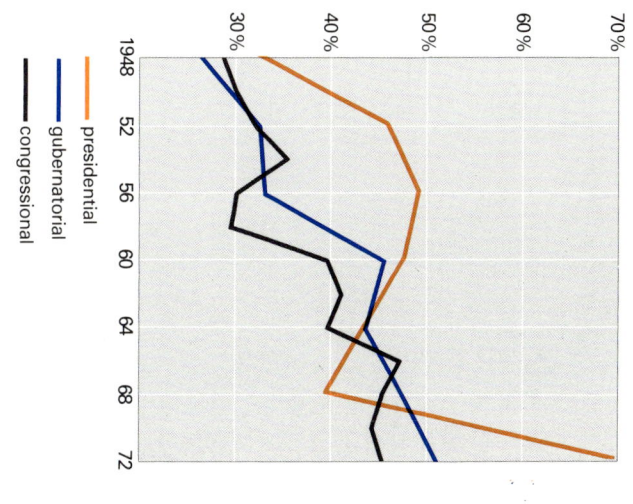

Figure 4.7. Republican Percentage of Presidential, Gubernatorial, and Congressional Vote for N.C., 1948–1972

Source: N.C. Secretary of State, *North Carolina Manuals,* 1949, 1953, 1957, 1961, 1965, and 1969. 1972 data were provided by the N.C. State Board of Elections.

backs of being identified with the minority party and being on the outside in legislative decision making are keenly felt and are obstacles not easily overcome. Party politics in North Carolina is changing but changing unevenly at different levels of the ballot.

A Sociodemographic Analysis of Interparty Competition

What are some of the factors associated with the shifting of North Carolina from a one-party Democratic state to one with increased interparty competition? The literature on party competition suggests that a heterogeneous society is a necessary prerequisite for competitive parties because it is this type of society that can support at least two different perspectives on public policy questions. Scholars who have investigated the lack of two-partyism in the South usually conclude that there has

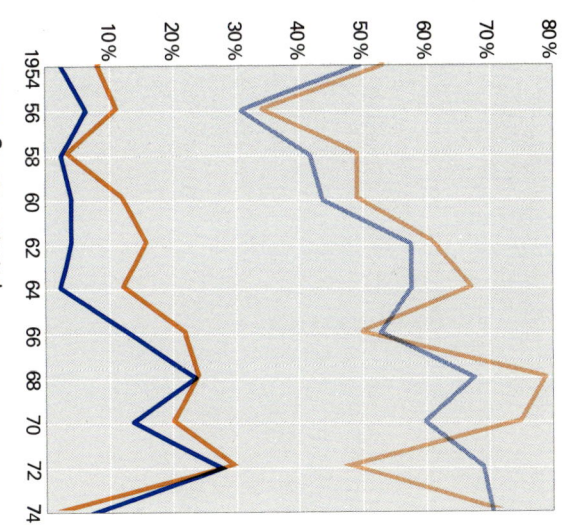

Figure 4.8. Percentage of N.C. Legislative Seats Contested and Won by Republican Party, 1954–1974

Part of the riddle of North Carolina politics is that the state has undergone few massive demographic changes during the past two decades. To be sure the state has experienced the influx of new industry and increased urbanization, but North Carolina remains one of the least urbanized states in the nation and population growth has lagged behind the average of eleven southern states. In 1970 only 45 percent of the population lived in urban areas of 2,500 or more residents (the Census Bureau

been a superficial homogeneity to southern society because one issue—the race question—tended to override all other concerns. The southern voter looked to the Democratic party as the defender of white supremacy. Consequently, increased party competitiveness in North Carolina may be related to a growing diversity among the state's population and a movement away from the doctrine of white supremacy by the Democratic party.

79

definition of an urban place). This figure is misleading, however, because some parts of the state have experienced rapid urbanization while other parts of the state have remained rural. In general, the Piedmont is urban, the eastern Coastal Plain is the stronghold of rurality, and the Mountain region is typified by a traditional folk rurality in which ownership of marginal farms is common.

Because the growth of Republican strength in the South occurred at the same time many parts of the region were urbanizing, many political analysts concluded the two phenomena were related. Such a conclusion seems appropriate only for the Eisenhower years. The apex of urban Republicanism in North Carolina occurred in the presidential election of 1956 and the gubernatorial election of 1960. Since then there has been little difference between urban and rural voters and the way they react to Republican candidates at the top of the ballot (Figure 4.9). Consequently, evidence does not support the often postulated relationship between growth of Republicanism and urbanization.

Another important political fact is that North Carolina has been losing population to other states to an extent that many do not realize. The massive exodus of population from rural areas brought on by agricultural mechanization and industrialization hit the state particularly hard because it had been heavily involved in agriculture. In 1940, 33.6 percent of the labor force was employed in agriculture compared to only 5.2 percent in 1970. Whites and blacks have left the state's agricultural regions in large numbers in approximately the same ratio. Between 1960 and 1970 thirty-six of the one hundred counties lost population, and most of these were located in the east. Of major political significance is that while a large percentage of white migrants moved to towns and cities within North Carolina, most black migrants who usually identified with the Democratic party moved to metropolitan areas in the North and Midwest. This trend has been evident for at least forty years as the black population has declined from 32 percent in 1910 to 22.2 percent in 1970 (Figure 4.10).

In-migration patterns since 1950 have also tended to erode the Democratic advantage. It has been suggested by various analysts that the North-to-South migration is selective along partisan lines. The nonsoutherners moving into the South are actually more Republican than the nonsoutherners they leave behind. This fact means that interregional convergence in partisanship is correspondingly speeded up, for the departure of these Republicans leaves the non-South more Democratic than it would otherwise be at the same time the South becomes more Republican.

Without a doubt, however, the most critical variable in understanding the growth of party competition in North Carolina as well as in the South as a whole is race. Twenty-five years ago V. O. Key, Jr. discussing the relatively progressive nature of North Carolinians on the race question, stated that the black man had already won his electoral spurs in some locales, and as black participation spread throughout the state, it might not seem as traumatic to Tar Heel citizens as it would to those who lived in other areas of the South. But election and census data statistics reveal that a high concentration of blacks severely depressed two-party competition from 1948 to the mid-1960s. During this period North Carolina adhered to the typical Southern pattern in that the higher the percentage of blacks living in a county, the more likely the county would vote a straight Democratic ticket. In counties with a large black population, whites apparently coalesced around the Democratic party to preserve their control over county politics. Such a finding supports the proposition that during most of this century race has had the impact of creating an artificial Democratic solidarity in North Carolina. But in 1968 a basic change in the structure of party competition occurred—party competition was more likely to occur in those counties with a high concentration of blacks.

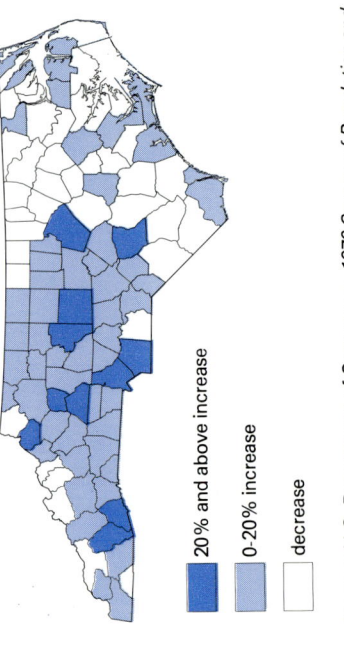

Figure 4.10. Population Change in N.C. Counties, 1960-1970

- 20% and above increase
- 0-20% increase
- decrease

Source: U.S. Department of Commerce, *1970 Census of Population and Housing*, 1970.

Figure 4.9. Republican Percentage of the Vote in Presidential and Gubernatorial Elections in Metropolitan and Nonmetropolitan Areas of N.C., 1940-1972

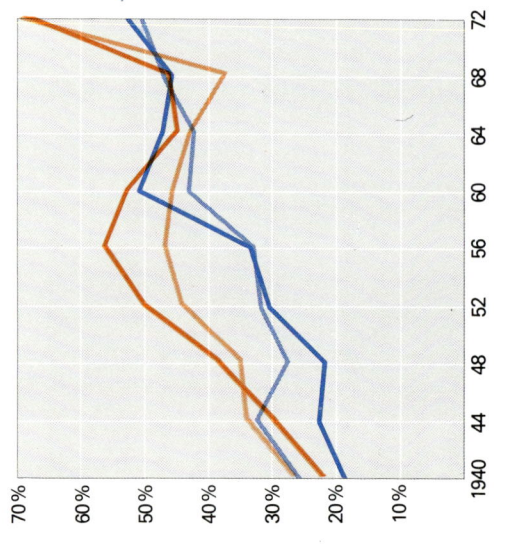

- presidential elections—metropolitan areas
- presidential elections—nonmetropolitan areas
- gubernatorial elections—metropolitan areas
- gubernatorial elections—nonmetropolitan areas

Source: The 1940-64 data are taken from Jack D. Fleer, *North Carolina Politics: An Introduction* (University of N.C. Press, 1968). 1968 data are from N.C. Secretary of State, *North Carolina Manual*, 1969. 1972 data were provided by the N.C. State Board of Elections.

Note: Metropolitan—Buncombe, Durham, Forsyth, Guilford, Mecklenburg, and Wake counties.

Probably the long-term reason for this change is that the Democratic party abandoned the historic prop of white supremacy, thus making it easier for thousands of Tar Heel voters to shift to GOP candidates. However, a more immediate reason for the reversal of trends in 1968 was the three-way presidential race among Nixon, Humphrey, and Wallace. In counties where the difference between the Republican and Democratic vote was the narrowest the black population was the largest. Wallace received his strongest support among whites who normally voted for Democrats, thus denying Humphrey those votes. Consequently, the Democratic standard-bearer made his best showing in counties with a large black turnout. In 1972 there apparently was a strong reaction among many white traditional Democrats to the civil rights and prowelfare positions of George McGovern. Rather than support a national Democrat who endorsed such positions for president, many Tar Heel voters either stayed home or deserted to the Republican candidate. Whether this new relationship between interparty competition and black concentration will continue is not easily predicted and depends primarily on the future politics of the national Democratic party.

At the gubernatorial level black concentration is still related to a lack of two-party competition. Gubernatorial contests prior to 1960 were more or less extensions of historic partisan divisions with the GOP candidates running well in the middle Mountain region and western midsection of the Piedmont. Beginning with the 1960 gubernatorial contest and continuing through 1972, Republican strength has extended rather rapidly up and down the Piedmont corridor and into a few sections of the Coastal Plain. Pockets of Republican strength have begun to emerge in a few Coastal Plain counties, notably New Hanover, Dare, and Brunswick. The Republican party is extremely strong in Sampson, an eastern county. In Sampson County, Populist forces at the turn of the century were so bitter toward the Democratic party that they refused to support it when their own party expired. Consequently, the GOP has always done well in Sampson. Nevertheless, interparty competition continues to lag in the eastern portion of the state, which is where the heaviest concentration of black voters is located (Figure 4.11). The number of counties in the eastern region in which the two parties compete within a ten percentage point margin of each other in gubernatorial races has climbed very slowly from 1952 to 1972; in 1952 it was 17 percent; in 1956, 17 percent; in 1960, 32 percent; in 1964, 27 percent; in 1968, 39 percent; and in 1972 it was 34 percent. Moreover, the congressional elections also evidenced little switching in party allegiances as the three Democratic candidates from districts in the Coastal Plain had either nominal or no opposition from the Republicans in the last three elections.

The Characteristics of North Carolina Voters

All of the observations presented above are based on the analysis of census and election data. Such analysis is useful in describing and explaining group behavior, but it cannot inform the reader about the beliefs and behavior of individuals. For example, how do Tar Heel citizens classify themselves politically? What proportion of the electorate considers itself to be politically independent? Who are the ticket-splitters? Who are the liberals and conservatives? How much trust do North Carolinians have in their political institutions? And what proportion of the electorate participates in the political process in ways other than by voting? Answers to such inquiries can be obtained only through survey analysis.

In the following section the beliefs, attitudes, and participation levels of the state's citizenry are examined. The data were taken from the survey of North Carolina conducted in 1971 by the Institute for Research in Social Science, The University of North Carolina at Chapel Hill, with the cooperation of The University of North Carolina at Charlotte. A random sample of 1,440 North Carolinians stratified by region of the state and size of community was selected. Of these 1,130 (78.5 percent) were successfully interviewed. In analyzing the survey, special attention was given to such factors as region of state, size of community, race, education, income levels, and age.

Although registration figures indicate that three out of four North Carolinians register as Democrats, voting patterns belie such a lopsided identification. In order to test how citizens perceive their partisanship at the national and state levels, the sample was asked whether they usually thought of themselves as Republicans, Democrats, or Independents. At the national level 46 percent identified themselves as Democrats, 16 percent as Republicans, and 31 percent as Independents. Within the context of state politics there was only a modest shifting of personal party identification. Sixteen percent viewed themselves as Republicans, the Democratic identifiers increased to 50 percent, and the Independents decreased to 24 percent. Such a split among the electorate strongly suggests that as the Democratic dominance of the state relaxes there is very little reason to believe it will be replaced by an era of GOP hegemony.

The survey data reinforced the proposition that the North Carolina Democratic party relies heavily on the support of black voters. Seventy-three percent of the black respondents classified themselves as Democrats in national politics and 76 percent in state politics compared to 40 and 44 percent, respectively, among white respondents. Approximately one-third of the white respondents considered themselves Independents com-

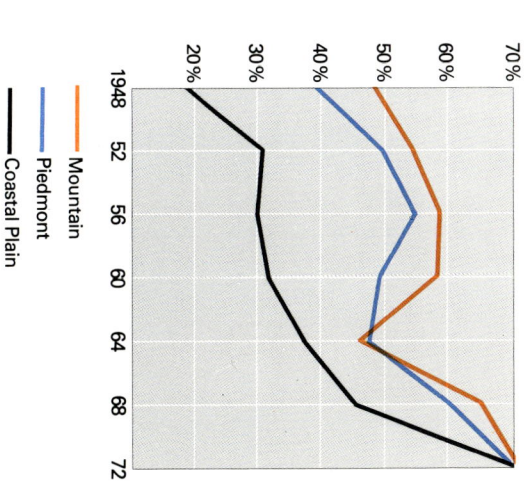

Figure 4.11. Republican Percentage of the Vote in Presidential Elections in the Three Major Regions of N.C., 1948-1972

Source: N.C. Secretary of State, *North Carolina Manuals*, 1949, 1953, 1957, 1961, 1965, and 1969. 1972 data were provided by the N.C. State Board of Elections.

Note: The 1968 vote is the division of the vote between the two major parties. When Wallace's American party is considered the vote is as follows:

	Mountain	Piedmont	Coastal Plain
	50.4	42.7	26.0 Republican
	20.0	28.2	32.1 Democrat
	21.7	29.1	41.9 American

In 1948, when the Dixiecrat party is considered

	44.9	34.5	17.0 Republican
	49.6	53.5	75.0 Democrat
	5.5	12.0	7.9 Dixiecrat

pared to only about one out of every ten blacks (Figure 4.12).

In terms of social class, Democrats, Republicans, and Independents are very heterogeneous. Although class is a poor predictor of partisanship, there was a tendency for the upper-middle class, those with incomes of over $15,000 per year, to disproportionately identify themselves as Independents rather than Democrats. But in even the upper-middle income categories there were more Democrats than Republicans (Figure 4.13). Regional differences in the North Carolina polity, however, were revealed. Although a preponderance of citizens think of themselves as Democrats in all three major regions of the state, those who reside in the Coastal Plain counties tend to disproportionately identify with the Democratic party (Figure 4.14).

An examination of the relationship between partisanship and age indicated that those under forty years of age disproportionately viewed themselves as Independents. It appears that as these younger voters become part of the potential electorate they are more willing than former generations to disassociate themselves from both major parties. Although the Democratic share of the electorate is declining, the gains are not accruing to the Republican party. Of course, it is possible that an Independent status may be a halfway point in the conversion from the Democratic to the Republican party, but survey data ranging back to the 1930s show that the proportion of Independents among young voters has always been substantially higher than for the electorate as a whole. Young voters generally have a lower level of political involvement and need time to form strong party loyalties. Consequently, it is unknown whether the youthful Independents will become more partisan as they grow older and, if so, how they will divide their loyalties (Figure 4.15).

It is generally known that the proportion of the electorate voting a straight party ticket has been declining since the end of World War II. In his 1968 postelection study, George Gallup found that only 43 percent of the American voters said they had voted a straight party ticket. The trend toward split-ticket voting is attributable to several factors, including the decline of strictly one-party areas throughout the United States, higher levels of education among the citizenry, and improved sources of political information for the voter, especially the electronic media. Such changes increase the options available to the voter and enable him to consider things other than party identification when making an electoral choice.

Figure 4.12. Political Partisanship and Race in N.C.

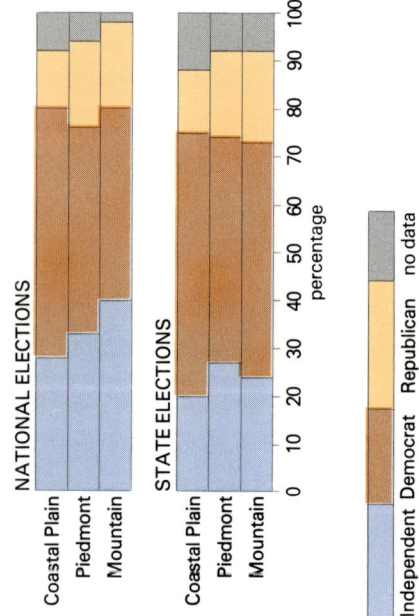

Figure 4.13. Political Partisanship and Income in N.C.

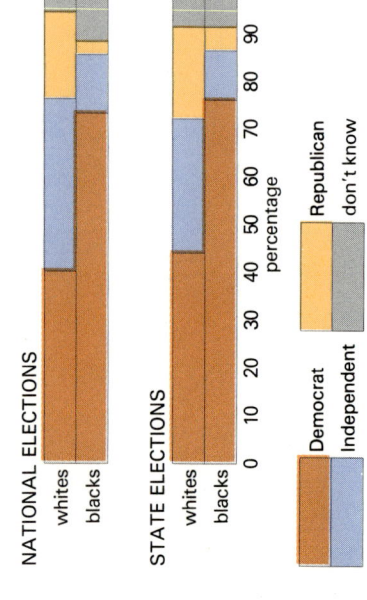

Figure 4.14. Political Partisanship and Regions in N.C.

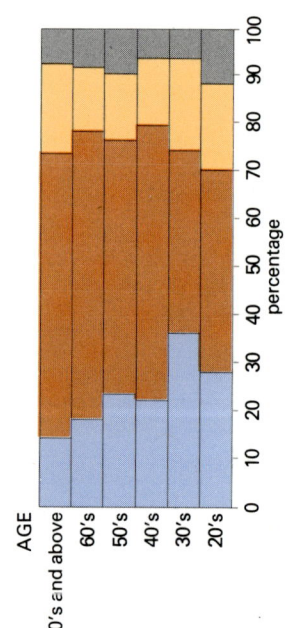

Figure 4.15. Political Partisanship and Age in N.C.

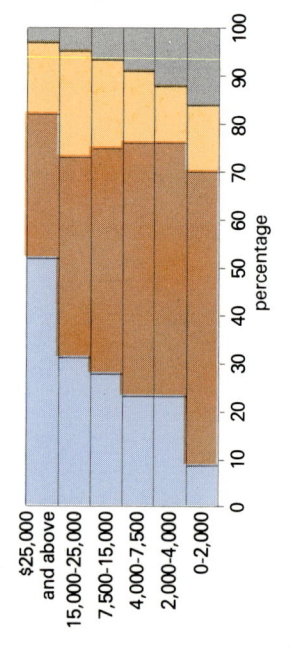

In order to measure the size of the North Carolina electorate that regularly splits the ballot between Democratic and Republican candidates the responses to the following two questions were analyzed: "In general, when voting, how often have you split your ticket, that is, voted for Republicans and Democrats in the same election?" and "When you consider voting for congressman, how important is the candidate's political party?"

In response to the first question 21 percent of the respondents stated they almost always split their tickets and an additional 15 percent claimed they often did so. On the other hand, 24 and 21 percent, respectively, stated they seldom or never split their tickets. The remaining respondents either had never voted or were unable to answer the inquiry. Overall, it appears that approximately one-third of the potential North Carolina electorate split their ballot on a regular basis compared to a little less than half who do so rarely or never. Roughly the same proportions materialized in the responses to the second question. In voting in congressional races 40 percent of the respondents did not think the candidate's political party was an important consideration in making an electoral judgment, compared to 26 and 28 percent, respectively, who felt it was either a very important consideration or somewhat important. The conclusion that seems inescapable is that for a very large minority of Tar Heel voters, roughly one-third, party affiliation is of only modest consequence in making a vote choice. Electoral judgments are based on other considerations such as issues, personalities, or random events.

Do the ticket-splitters have any characteristics that distinguish them from the straight-ticket voter? By exploring this question it may be possible to glimpse the future tide of partisan politics in North Carolina. First, the ticket-splitter is far more likely to be white than black. Forty-three percent of the whites either always or often split their ballots compared to only 10 percent of the blacks. In addition, 47 percent of the whites stated that the candidate's political party was not an important consideration in deciding for whom to vote in congressional elections. On the other hand, only 12 percent of the blacks were willing to discount party affiliation in making electoral judgments.

The class variables were strongly associated with the tendency to be a split-ticket voter. Over one-half the respondents who had at least some college training claimed to split their ballots either always or often. Almost 50 percent of the college-trained voters stated that partisanship was not important in congressional elections. Likewise, the higher the income level the less likely the respondent voted a straight ticket and felt the political party affiliation of congressional candidates to be important.

Residents of the Coastal Plain counties were the least likely to split their tickets. However, the response patterns among those who lived in the three regions of the state varied only slightly. Thirty percent of the Coastal Plain respondents stated they split their ballots regularly compared to 42 and 40 percent among the Mountain and Piedmont samples. There was also very little regional difference in regard to discounting the importance of party in congressional elections.

The association between age and ticket-splitting strongly suggests a political future in which straight-ticket voting will become less prevalent. Among Tar Heel voters over forty years of age, a majority stated they usually voted a straight-party ticket compared to less than a third among those who were younger. The data also make evident the fact that younger citizens participate at much lower rates in the electoral process than their elders. Forty-five percent of the respondents under thirty years of age stated they had never voted compared to only 12 and 8 percent in their thirties and forties. The younger the respondent the more likely his stated party affiliation was not an important consideration in voting for congressmen. If the political attitudes of these younger voters remain stable as they become older, party loyalty as a factor in North Carolina elections will decline in importance and election outcomes will probably become less predictable (Figure 4.16).

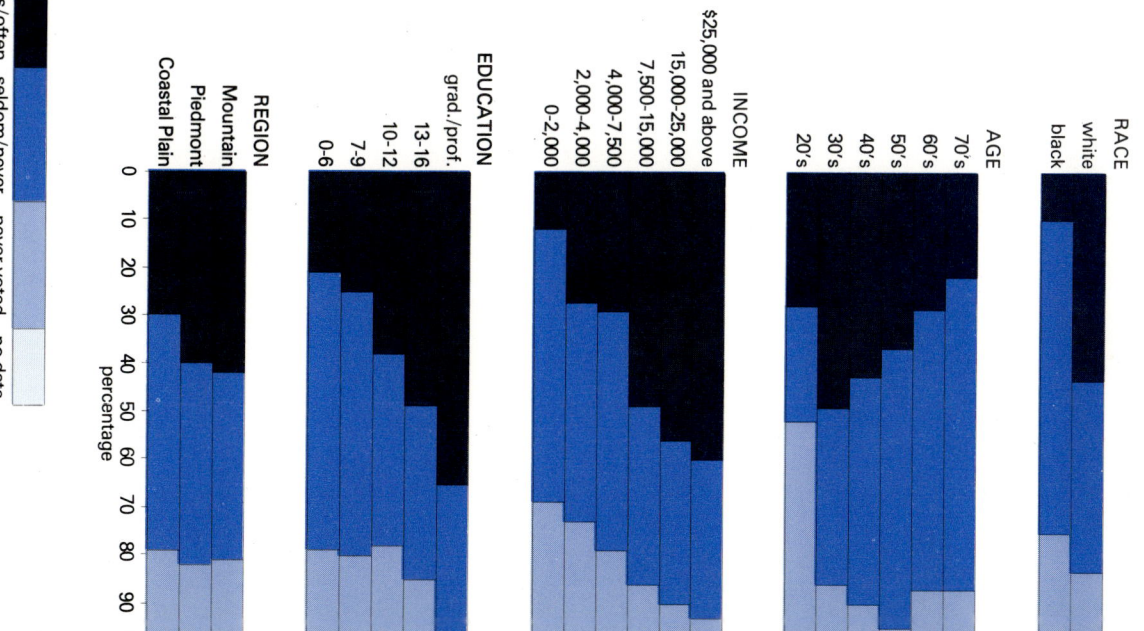

Figure 4.16. Ticket Splitters and Selected Population Characteristics in N.C.

Source: Institute for Research in Social Science, University of N.C. at Chapel Hill, N.C., Survey, 1971.

Figure 4.17. Political Ideology and Partisanship in N.C.

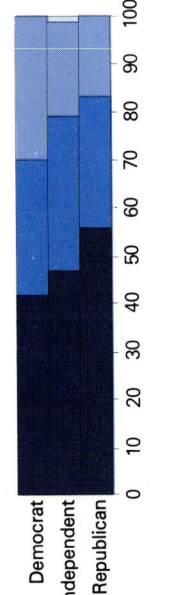

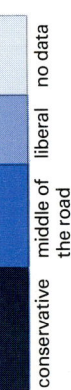

Source: Institute for Research in Social Science, University of N.C. at Chapel Hill, N.C., Survey, 1971.

Figure 4.18. Political Ideology and Selected Population Characteristics in N.C.

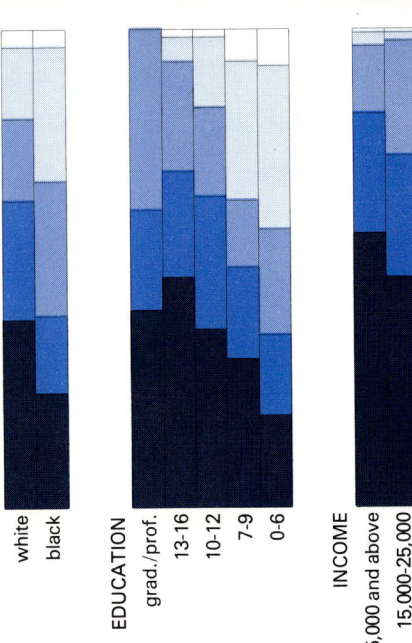

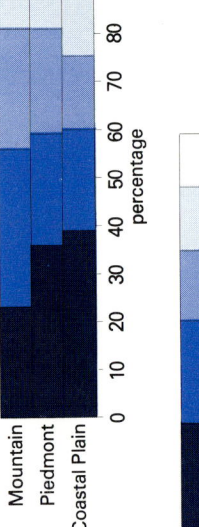

Source: Institute for Research in Social Science, University of N.C. at Chapel Hill, N.C., Survey, 1971.

Political Beliefs Most commentators on the American political scene attempt to describe political realities in terms of liberalism and conservatism. Political analysts tend to place such ideological labels on candidates, parties, and policy positions. On the other hand, researchers who study the importance of ideology in politics suggest that relatively few members of the electorate evaluate candidates or select parties in conformity with an ideological commitment. In the minds of most voters liberal-conservative labels are vague and confusing. The lack of a strong relationship between party identification and self-professed political philosophy within the North Carolina sample supports the above proposition (Figure 4.17).

Nevertheless, when Americans are asked to identify themselves as liberals or conservatives, most are able to do so. Such labels do have meaning but are not necessarily good predictors of specific attitudes or behavior. A Gallup poll based on a national sample in 1972 reported that 37 percent of the respondents stated they were either very or fairly conservative; 26 percent were very or fairly liberal; 35 percent were middle-of-the-road; and 4 percent had no opinion. Overall, the North Carolina electorate closely approximates the national pattern. Among Tar Heel voters 35 percent classified themselves as conservative, 21 percent as liberal, 23 percent as middle-of-the-road, and 21 percent had no opinion.

In the national sample there was a tendency for blacks, the college educated, the young (those in their twenties), and those who lived in metropolitan areas to be more likely professed liberals than others. Generally, the same pattern held true in the North Carolina sample. However, among white Tar Heels only graduate school or professional education had a positive association with liberalism. Otherwise, education through the baccalaureate level was related to increasing conservatism. Unlike the national sample in which income did not appear to have any relationship to political ideology, the North Carolina sample showed an association between high income levels and professed conservatism. In order to place the above observations in perspective, however, it is necessary to indicate that Tar Heel conservatives outnumbered liberals in almost every category. The exceptions included the very old, blacks, residents of the Mountain region, and those with the lowest education and income (Figure 4.18).

The "sectional sensibilities" that Key referred to over twenty years ago remained evident in the response patterns to the liberal-conservative question. The proportion of the electorate who claimed to be conservative increased as one moved west to east across the state. Twenty-three percent of the sample claimed to be conservative in the Mountain region, 36 percent in the Piedmont, and 39 percent in the Coastal Plain counties. Finally, age was not as significant a factor in predicting liberalism in North Carolina as it was nationally. Among Tar Heel respondents there was very little association between age and ideology. Young Tar Heels were more likely to resemble their elders in regard to liberalism-conservatism than were their counterparts across the country.

No government has the support and loyalty of all its citizens. Some citizens will always suspect the motives of political leaders and emphasize the injustices in society whether real or imaginary. Distrust of government and public leaders is probably a first step toward political alienation and perhaps an active resistance to prevailing governmental institutions. Although a problem for all governments, the voluntary acceptance of duties and obligations of citizenship is especially acute in a democracy. A democratic system requires a great deal of self-discipline and a willingness to accept the policies and programs of government. Democracy's guiding ideal is the substitution of mutual understanding and agreement for coerciveness and arbitrary authority in all phases of social and political life. The existence of distrustful citizens who are convinced that the government serves the interests of a few rather than the interests of all is a barrier to the realization of this ideal.

To depict the proportion of Tar Heel citizens who are distrustful of government the responses to the following two questions are reported: "If, in person, you told your local government officials what you wanted the community to do about some public question, do you think they would listen to you or not?" and "Do you think they would try to get what you wanted done, or do you think they would do nothing but listen?" Thirty-two percent of the sample felt that government officials would listen and 21 percent felt they would try to do something. Approximately 50 percent of the sample stated the officials would not even listen to them and close to 60 percent claimed they would make no effort to implement a citizen suggestion. Of course, we cannot be sure that such questions tap deeply seated cynicism or more superficial attitudes. However, on the surface it is apparent that a majority of North Carolinians are unwilling to give government officials the benefit of the doubt (Figure 4.19).

In analyzing those characteristics associated with distrust we find that such an attitude is not affected by size of community, region of the state, race, or age. There is a modest association between the class variables—education and income—and political trust. The higher the education and income levels the more likely the respondents felt government officials would pay attention to their demands. It must be emphasized that these associations were not strong, and a large proportion of the respondents in every education and income category felt public officials were not responsive.

Citizen Participation One of the most persistent complaints about the American electoral process is the failure to achieve the high rates of political participation found in some other countries. Only in presidential elections does turnout exceed 60 percent of the potential electorate. In the past, however, the South has lagged behind this national turnout rate. Various reasons have been offered to explain this condition but two of the more important are (1) the lack of two-party competition in southern states for most of the twentieth century and (2) the systematic disfranchisement of blacks begun in the latter part of the nineteenth century and continued to relatively recent times.

Research has demonstrated that high turnout is closely related to high levels of political interest, a condition usually found in presidential elections. During the last twenty years approximately one-half the potential North Carolina electorate has participated in these elections. In off-year elections interest dwindles and so does turnout. Overall, the voting rate falls twenty percentage points in off-year congressional elections so that only about 30 percent of the North Carolina electorate votes in these nonpresidential-year elections (Figure 4.20).

Turnout rates also vary from one region to another. Data show that from 1948 to 1972 turnout declined in moving west to east across the state. Although regional differences are narrowing in more recent years, turnout rates are declining in all three major regions of the state. One possible explanation for the low rate of voting in 1972 (46 percent of those eligible) was the lowering of the voting age to 18, bringing into the electorate a large bloc of young persons who were not accustomed to voting (Figure 4.21).

Citizen participation in the political process can be measured also by asking individuals to describe their political activities. The 1971 survey data yielded the following profile of the North Carolina electorate. Fifty-two percent of the respondents stated they almost always voted in elections, 15 percent often voted, 16 percent seldom voted, and 14 percent never voted. This latter percentage supports the notion offered in several national studies that roughly 15 percent of the potential electorate are habitual nonvoters and virtually outside the political process.

Certain social characteristics—education and income levels, for example—are rather strongly associated with voting. Over one-third of those with a high school education or less stated they seldom or never vote in elections compared to 18 percent with some college and 7 percent who had graduate or professional training. Among those making less than $7,500 per year approximately 40 percent indicated they seldom or never voted while over 80 percent of those having incomes higher than $7,500 almost always or often voted. As has been suggested earlier, young persons do not participate in the electoral process at the same rate as older citizens. Approximately one-half of the sample under thirty years of age stated they had either seldom or never voted. As would be expected when one considers the political history of the South, blacks participate in elections at lower rates than whites. Thirty-nine percent of the black respondents stated they seldom or never voted compared to 27 percent of the whites. Finally, turnout rates in the eastern Coastal Plain counties were lower than in the Piedmont or Mountain counties (Figure 4.22).

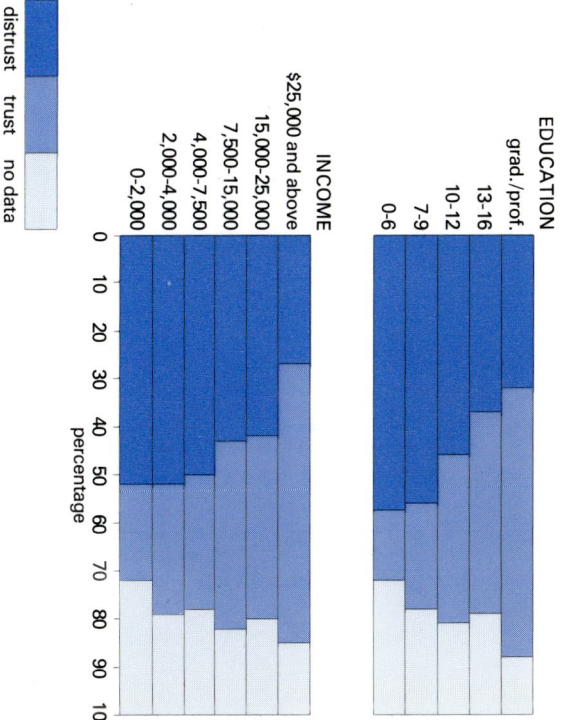

Figure 4.19. Political Distrust and Education and Income Levels in N.C.

Source: Institute for Research in Social Science, University of N.C. at Chapel Hill, N.C., Survey, 1971.

85

Figure 4.20. N.C. Voting Participation in Presidential, Gubernatorial, and Congressional Elections, 1948-1972

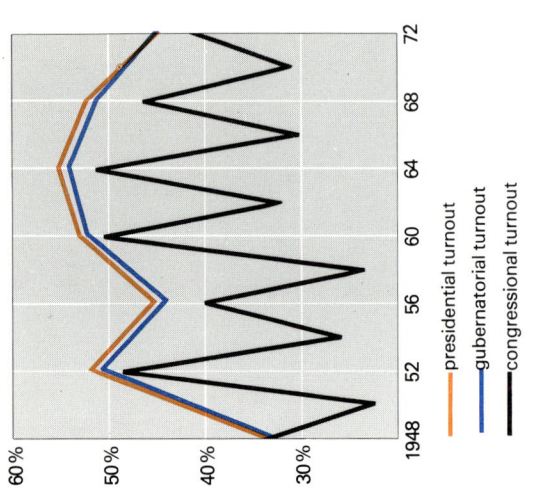

— presidential turnout
— gubernatorial turnout
— congressional turnout

Source: N.C. Secretary of State, *North Carolina Manuals*, 1949, 1955, 1957, 1961, 1965, and 1969. 1972 data were provided by the N.C. State Board of Elections.

Note: Turnout rate in 1974 congressional election was 28 percent.

The relationship between turnout and such characteristics as education, income, age, and race seem to hold for all elections and in all parts of the nation. But aside from analyzing the social composition of the active electorate, it is also important to note that voting is about all most people do in the political process. When asked about other political activities, Tar Heel citizens indicated the following: 60 percent seldom or never talk to anyone about politics; 84 percent seldom or never try to convince anyone to vote for a certain candidate or party; 93 percent seldom or never write to political leaders; and 98 percent seldom or never join in public demonstrations. Less than 2 percent of the North Carolina sample claimed to be very active in politics in ways other than by participating in conversations touching on political topics and voting. Such a political portrait is probably equally applicable to the electorates of the other forty-nine states (Figure 4.23).

Figure 4.21. Voting Turnout in Presidential Elections in the Three Major Regions of N.C., 1948-1972

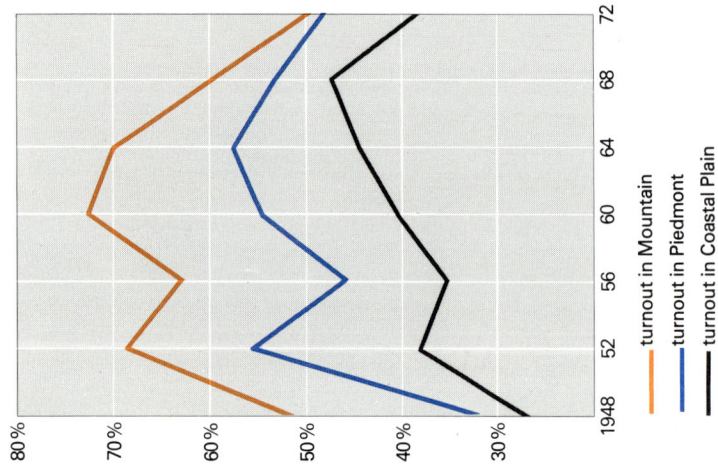

— turnout in Mountain
— turnout in Piedmont
— turnout in Coastal Plain

Twenty years later Wallace electors garnered 31.2 percent of the popular vote, eight percentage points behind the slate of Republican electors but two percentage points ahead of the Democrats. The Wallace appeal was a strongly concentrated one, centered almost entirely in a wide belt of Coastal Plain counties stretching from the Virginia to the South Carolina border. The sectional pattern of the vote has several important implications. First, the distribution of the vote suggests that loyalty to the Democratic presidential candidate in the Coastal Plain counties is very precarious. All the counties won by Wallace were carried by the Democrats in 1964 and, with the exception of Alamance, in 1960. Although black voters in these counties provided Humphrey with a major portion of his support, white voters generated enthusiasm for Wallace partially because of his racist appeal. Such a situation suggests the white-black Democratic coalition is on shaky ground in its last remaining bastion of strength.

Second, it is not at all clear that the Republican party can successfully advance its position through a similar racist appeal in the absence of a third party candidate such as Wallace. This observation derives from a comparative analysis of the 1964 and 1968 election returns. There had been widespread speculation about a so-called southern strategy in the Republican presidential campaign of 1964 with some commentators equating the Goldwater voters with those who would have supported Wallace had he entered the 1964 race. The accompanying map (Figure 4.25) identifies the upper third (by percentages) of Goldwater's strongest counties in 1964 and of Wallace's strongest counties in 1968. There is absolutely no overlap; the two candidates were appealing to different clientele. This interpretation is buttressed by more recent national survey data gathered by the Survey Research Center of the University of Michigan which points out that, if anything, Wallace was a "poor man's Goldwater." His demagogic appeal was attractive to the "redneck"-populist electorate but somewhat repugnant to the more educated and middle-class conservative. Although a Wallace-type candidate may indirectly aid the Republican cause by bringing about a deterioration of Democratic strength, a similar Republican candidate will probably not be equally successful because of the internal tensions among potential GOP voters who are reluctant to support such a racist-populist appeal.

Third Party Movements in North Carolina

Although third party candidates do not win office in North Carolina, they do influence the trend of interparty competition. Between 1948 and 1972 two third party movements, the Dixiecrat candidacy of South Carolina's Strom Thurmond in 1948 and the Wallace bid for the presidency in 1968, were supported by some North Carolina voters. The Dixiecrat movement was markedly unsuccessful in North Carolina as a whole with the best showing coming in Cabarrus County where 27 percent of the vote was won by the Thurmond ticket. Identification of the upper quartile of those counties where the Dixiecrats made their greatest impact reveals a pattern that might be best characterized as a "friends and neighbors" vote. Except for a few Piedmont counties in the north, all of the strongest Dixiecrat counties were located on the South Carolina border or contiguous to border counties (Figure 4.24).

The differential impact of the Thurmond and Wallace candidacies underscores the extent to which Democratic dominance of North Carolina politics has eroded. In the late 1940s it would have been unthinkable for the Democratic candidate to run third in a three-way race. It is likely that one of the more lasting consequences of the Wallace candidacy was getting many Democratic straight-ticket voters to break the habit. Many of these

Figure 4.22. Voting Turnout and Selected Population Characteristics in N.C.

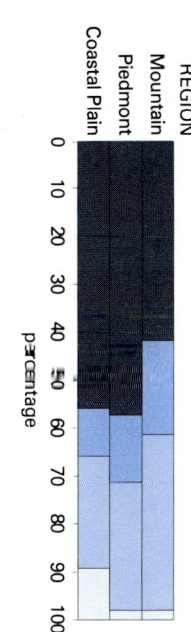
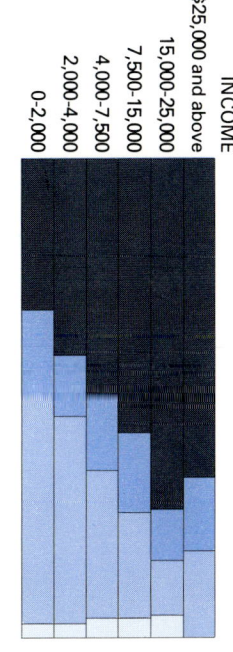
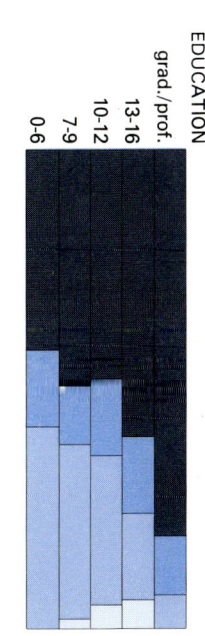
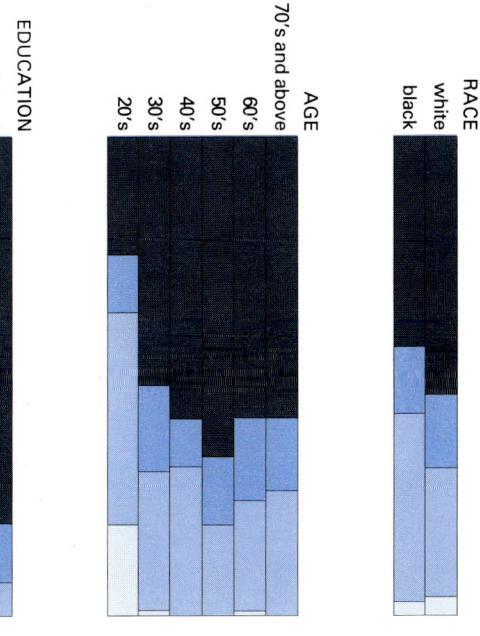

Figure 4.23. Participation Rates in Selected Political Activities in N.C.

Source: Institute for Research in Social Science, University of N.C. at Chapel Hill, N.C., Survey, 1971.

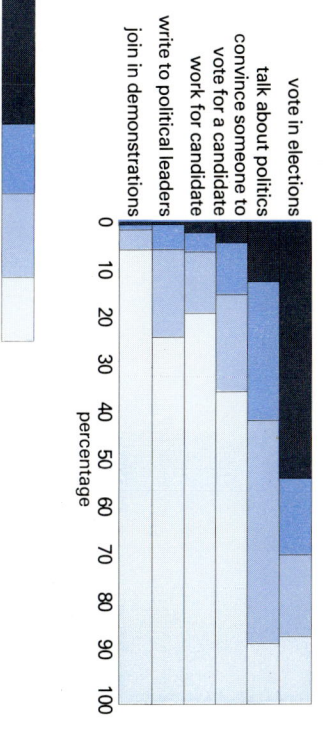

Figure 4.24. Thurmond Presidential Vote in N.C. Counties, 1948

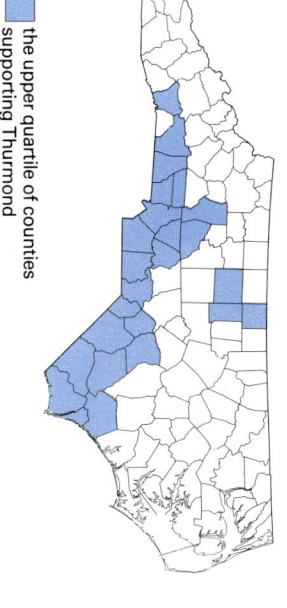

Source: N.C. Secretary of State, *North Carolina Manual*, 1949.

percent of the Tar Heel electorate claim to be Republican compared to 27 percent nationally. In terms of actual registration, 21.9 percent of the state's citizenry has registered as Republicans (Figure 4.27).

It is true that North Carolina Republicans have been winning more elections in the last decade, but a range of factors other than party realignment aid in the explanation. First and foremost is the Democratic party's major unresolved problem, racial conflict. Both nationally and in North Carolina the black versus white confrontation is one of the politically important ethnic cleavages remaining in American politics. Throughout the South for most of the twentieth century, race was the issue that caused voters to coalesce around the Democratic party. However, the strong civil rights stand of the national Democratic party in recent years has now resulted in the race issue's causing white voters to desert the party. Ironically, the blacks who had been systematically disfranchised by southern Democrats in the past now provide the most consistent support for Democratic candidates. It is in the South and the nation's cities that racial confrontation most directly threatens the Democratic coalition and until that problem is resolved Democratic fortunes will wax and wane with the intensity of the conflict.

Second, many analysts are more concerned with party decomposition than with realignment. Data presented above show no systematic defection of Tar Heel voters to the Republican party but a rejection of the Democratic party. Many citizens have decided to live outside both major parties. Certainly the Wallace candidacy demonstrated that upward of a third of the North Carolina electorate would desert both parties if given the opportunity. Survey data collected in 1971 also indicated that Wallace would receive approximately the same portion of the vote in a three-way race between himself, Richard Nixon, and a Democrat, regardless of who that Democrat might be! This "Wallace electorate" was spread throughout the state but tended to be disproportionately located in the rural, Coastal Plain counties characterized by relatively low education levels.

In the more urbanized counties there is also a tendency to discount the importance of party. A generalized rise in education and affluence coupled with an expansion of political information sources have made the middle-class Tar Heel feel more capable of evaluating candidates and issues without the help of party organizations. The political consequence of this development is an increase in political independence and a proclivity to vote a split ticket. To date, it has been the Republican party that has been advantaged by these trends.

But the ascendancy of the GOP in North Carolina is a fragile thing, as was demonstrated in the 1974 elections.

voters ended up in the Nixon, Helms, and Holshouser columns in 1972. For example, Jesse Helms, Republican candidate for the United States Senate, carried twenty-four of the forty counties won by Wallace in 1968, counties that were safe for Democrats prior to 1968.

A Speculative Summary

During the 1950s journalists, politicians, and scholars speculated about a fundamental realignment of the American party system, with the Republican party being the primary beneficiary. The enlargement of the middle class and the growth of the suburbs were the most frequently cited factors that were to sweep the GOP to dominant party status. Advantaged by hindsight, we now know that upwardly mobile suburbanites took their party identification with them as they poured into the fringe areas surrounding the nation's major urban centers. The assumption that the depression era relationship between class and Republicanism would persist into the post-World War II period proved to be unfounded.

A decade later the Goldwater debacle stimulated a spate of analyses that concluded that the demise of the Republican party was at hand. James Reston wrote in the *New York Times* that Senator Goldwater had wrecked his party for a long time to come. The Survey Research Center, after analyzing the 1964 election data, observed that the United States was quite possibly entering "a period of party realignment which will increase the prevailing Democratic advantage in the party balance."

The above premature hypotheses notwithstanding, the party identification of the American electorate during the postwar era has remained stable. Citizens do shift partisanship but not easily. Party identification is apparently handed down from parent to child in much the same way people identify with a Ford or Chevrolet and with about the same intensity. In any particular election voters engage in a certain amount of electoral crossover but with about the same compunction as they engage in switching to a new car model.

Historical patterns suggest that some epoch-making social or economic change such as the Civil War or the Great Depression is necessary for a major party realignment. Survey data indicate that in the postwar era such fundamental change has not occurred. From 1947 to 1974 the only noticeable pattern has been a slight increase in the percentage of the electorate who identify themselves as Independents, and most of the increase has occurred since 1968 and may be short-term in nature (Figure 4.26).

Therefore, as the last quarter of the twentieth century begins, it is not surprising that North Carolina remains less Republican than the rest of the nation. Only 16

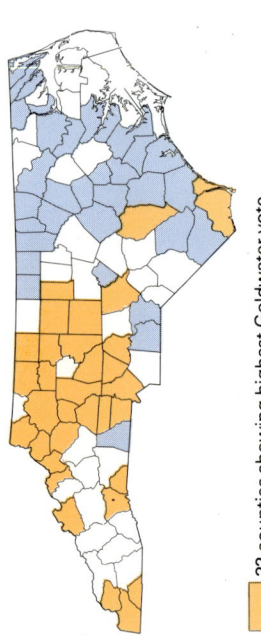

Figure 4.25. Comparisons of Goldwater and Wallace Vote in N.C. Counties

■ 33 counties showing highest Goldwater vote
■ 33 counties showing highest Wallace vote

Source: N.C. Secretary of State, *North Carolina Manual*, 1965 and 1969

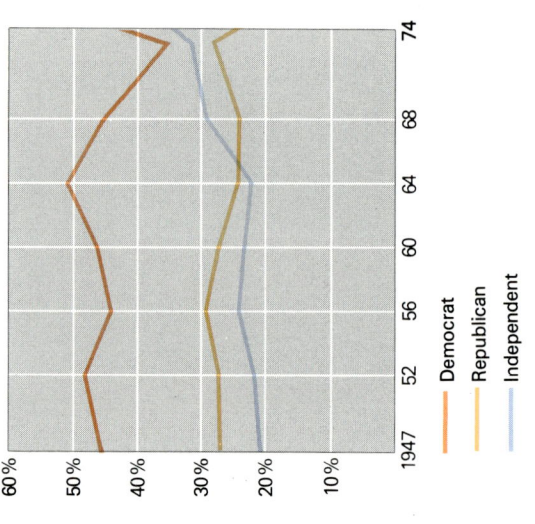

Figure 4.26. Party Identification of the National Electorate, 1947–1974

— Democrat
— Republican
— Independent

Source: William H. Flanigan, *Political Behavior of the American Electorate* (Boston: Allyn & Bacon, 1972), and Gallup poll data.

Figure 4.27. Comparison of Party Registration and Political Self-Designation of the N.C. Electorate, 1971-1972

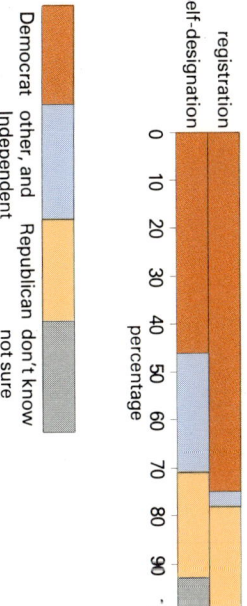

Source: Institute for Research in Social Science, University of N.C. at Chapel Hill, N.C., Survey, 1971.

Figure 4.28. Voting Turnout in Presidential Elections for the U.S., the South, and N.C., 1948-1972

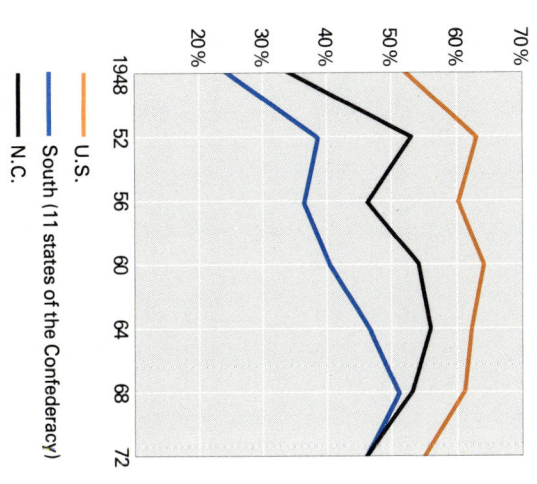

It is due more to the woes of the Democrats than to the growing appeal of the Republican party. No more than 5 percent of the black population identifies with the GOP. New voters who are entering the party structure for the first time identify with the Democrats by a 2½ to 1 margin. Then too the stigma of being a long-term minority party is difficult to overcome. Most North Carolinians are registered as Democrats primarily because in the past the "real" election was the Democratic primary. Although evidence has been presented above showing that voting behavior does not necessarily coincide with nominal party membership, candidate recruitment and party organization are adversely affected by the low level of Republican registration. A major problem facing the Republicans in North Carolina is finding attractive candidates to seek office at the lower level of the ballot. All of these factors will probably weigh heavily against any short-term upturn in Republican fortunes at the state legislature and "county courthouse" levels.

Perhaps a more fundamental question than which party will gain control of the formal institutions of government is the size and characteristics of the electorate that determines who will govern. A phenomenon that has confounded political analysts is why the United States consistently has a poorer voting record than any other major democracy in the world. National survey data in 1972 indicated that nearly 40 percent of the nonvoters did not go to the polls because they could not meet residency requirements or had not bothered to register. Nearly a third stated they were not interested in politics. This problem is more acute in North Carolina and the South because the citizens in this section lag behind the rest of the nation in turnout and have done so consistently over the last quarter century (Figure 4.28).

Nonvoters are not randomly distributed in the population. Blacks, the lower class as measured by education and income, and the young disproportionately comprise the nonparticipating electorate. Political action beyond the simple act of voting is frequently engaged in by no more than 2 percent of the potential electorate. Politics in North Carolina, as well as elsewhere, is an activity reserved for an elite, not by design but by default. One can only speculate about the impact of such a condition on public decision making but it is likely to be of major importance in some policy areas.

In terms of political philosophy, the North Carolina electorate closely resembles its national counterpart, tending to be more conservative than liberal. Although it is unclear what this means in regard to public support for specific policies, it does suggest that political leaders must conform to public expectations in terms of style and rhetoric. Another attitude prevalent among Tar Heel citizens is distrust of government officials. It is likely that this feeling toward the political system contributes to the relatively low rate of participation. If citizens feel the governmental system is basically unresponsive, then there would be little motivation to expend time and energy in attempting to influence it.

The evidence is persuasive that North Carolina's political elite is aware of citizen disenchantment with the state's political institutions. Discussions concerning the reform of the state bureaucracy, the governor's office, the legislature, and the courts have ranked high on the governmental agenda in recent years. The impact of such reforms on citizen attitudes is difficult to gauge but it is unlikely to be of major consequence. Factors beyond the control of government are of more fundamental importance. The perceived inadequacy of the individual is affected more by the increasing complexity of society. The rise of the urban, technological, bureaucratic state and the frequent inability of the political system to cope with the problems it spawns are probably the primary cause of citizen cynicism. Over the short-run it is difficult to foresee any major breakthrough in regard to these kinds of problems.

North Carolina politics has entered a new era. No longer can Democrats consume most of their energies confronting one another in the primaries. Republicans, especially at the top of the ballot, are competitive and when conditions are favorable they will win major political offices. However, the importance of party in candidate selection is declining, particularly among the young and middle and upper classes. A full one-third of the Tar Heel electorate display only a nominal interest in party labels. Therefore, it is unlikely that the GOP or the Democrats will win consistently in statewide races. Such an electorate will be more interested in personalities and issues than in supporting a new political dynasty. Margins of victory between the parties are likely to shift dramatically from one election to another. More ticket splitting by voters resulting in divided government in terms of party control appears to be part of North Carolina's political future.

Other factors difficult to control and predict must also be considered. First, a major unresolved question is whether the tendency to identify as an Independent by the upper class and youth segments of the electorate is a halfway point in a conversion to Republicanism. Second, the success of government and the party system in coping with such societal problems as race relations, the distribution of wealth, the protection of the environment, and the humanization of a depersonalized, bureaucratic state will loom large in determining whether citizens retain their high levels of political distrust, low levels of participation and tendency to discount the importance of

The adequacy and quality of air, minerals, land, water, and other naturally occurring resources are among the most crucial problems of our time. The availability and quality of these resources place constraints on the size, density, and standard of living that a population can enjoy. Although these resources are commonly available, there is an increasing awareness of their limited quantity, the variation in their abundance and quality, and their great sensitivity to abuse.

North Carolina has truly been favored, for although it is not without environmental problems, it does not show the intensity of environmental deterioration that now characterizes the more industrialized sections of our country. Logic and instinct suggest that, as the state continues its economic development, those responsible for guiding that development should possess an increased awareness of and concern for related environmental consequences. With sound guidance, compassionate stewardship, and resolved leadership the state can improve the social and economic welfare of its citizenry without a parallel deterioration of its physical environment.

North Carolina occupies a most favorable climatic position. It experiences neither the frequent drought nor early frost that characterizes the American Midwest, nor does it suffer the severe winter common to the American North or the continuously oppressive summer of the Deep South. This climatic advantage is increasingly relevant as a more mobile America searches for comfortable living areas and as agricultural production increases are sought. On the negative side, frequent air stagnation and a high propensity for temperature inversion limit the natural ability of the atmosphere to absorb emissions from human activities.

With an average annual precipitation ranging from 45 to 70 inches, the state has a generous natural supply of water. Resulting streams and their channels have provided opportunities for many dams and reservoirs throughout the Piedmont and Mountain sections of the state. Considerable economic development and recreational opportunities have accrued to the state as a result of these developments. The state is also favored with a large supply of high-quality groundwater and an immense estuary area. From coastal estuaries to mountain trout streams, however, water resources are exhibiting their sensitivity to abuse.

Stretching from the Blue Ridge Mountains across three physiographic provinces to the Atlantic Ocean, North Carolina possesses one of the most varied and interesting landscapes in the United States. To the delight of rock and mineral collectors all major classes of rocks—sedimentary, igneous, and metamorphic—and hundreds of minerals are common to North Carolina. The distribution of these rocks strongly relates to physiographic features, soil patterns, and drainage characteristics. Further, they provide for a mining industry that is becoming increasingly important as an economic activity. The nature of mining, however, is such that unless proper constraints are exercised great environmental damage can result in the form of water, air, and land pollution.

With many of North Carolina's leading industries dependent upon her forests and soils, these resources are among the state's greatest assets and they also contribute to a natural beauty that has brought renown to the state. More than 153 species of trees and untold hundreds of species of other plants grow naturally. Although most North Carolina soils require application of lime and fertilizer, with treatment they provide an excellent base for agricultural production. The massive erosion and topsoil losses of the nineteenth and early twentieth century are behind us; however, erosion and related problems continue at a great cost to the state. An increased attention to use compatibility, particularly uses in urban areas, is needed to minimize soil-related problems.

It is the purpose of Part III to provide an inventory of North Carolina's physical resource base, to analyze problems and opportunities related to the use of these resources, and to generate a sense of awareness of and concern for their sensitivities and limitations.

parties. And finally, short-term factors including candidate charisma, scandal as exemplified by Watergate and the resignation of former president Richard Nixon, and the policy orientations of the national Democratic and Republican parties must be weighed in the balance when contemplating the political future of North Carolina.

SELECTED REFERENCES

Burnham, Walter Dean. *Critical Elections and the Mainsprings of American Politics.* New York: W. W. Norton & Co., 1970.
Campbell, Angus; Converse, Philip; Miller, Warren; and Stokes, Donald. *The American Voter.* New York: John Wiley & Sons, 1960.
Campbell, Angus; Converse, Philip; Miller, Warren; and Stokes, Donald. *Elections and the Political Order.* New York: John Wiley & Sons, 1965.
Converse, Philip; Miller, Warren; Rusk, Jerold; and Wolfe, Arthur. "Continuity and Change in American Politics: Parties and Issues in the 1968 Election." *American Political Science Review* 63 (December 1969): 1083-1105.
Cosman, Bernard. "Presidential Republicanism in the South, 1960." *Journal of Politics* 24 (May 1962): 303-22.
DeVries, Walter, and Tarrance, V. Lance. *The Ticket-Splitters: A New Force in American Politics.* Grand Rapids: William B. Eerdmans Publishing Co., 1972.
Ferrell, Joseph S. *Law and Government: County Government in North Carolina.* Chapel Hill: Institute of Government, University of North Carolina, 1968.
Fleer, Jack D. *North Carolina Politics: An Introduction.* Chapel Hill: University of North Carolina Press, 1968.
Free, Lloyd A., and Cantril, Hadley. *The Political Beliefs of Americans: A Study of Public Opinion.* New York: Simon and Schuster, 1968.
Havard, William, ed. *The Changing Politics of the South.* Baton Rouge: Louisiana State University Press, 1972.
Key, V. O. Jr. *Southern Politics in State and Nation.* New York: Random House, 1949.
Ladd, Everett Carll, Jr; Hadley, Charles; and King, Lauriston. "A New Political Realignment?" *Public Interest* 23 (Spring 1971): 46-63.
Lefler, Hugh T., and Newsome, Albert R. *North Carolina: The History of a Southern State.* 3d ed. Chapel Hill: University of North Carolina Press, 1973.
Leiserson, Avery, ed. *The American South in the 1960's.* New York: Frederick A. Praeger, 1964.
Matthews, Donald R., and Prothro, James W. "Social and Economic Factors and Negro Voter Registration in the South." *American Political Science Review* 57 (March 1963): 24-44.
Orr, Douglas M., Jr. *Congressional Redistricting: The North Carolina Experience.* Chapel Hill: Department of Geography, University of North Carolina, 1970.
Rankin, Robert S. *The Government and Administration of North Carolina.* New York: Thomas Y. Crowell Co., 1955.
Sindler, Allan P. *Change in the Contemporary South.* Durham, N.C.: Duke University Press, 1963.
Strong, Donald S. *Urban Republicanism in the South.* University, Ala.: Bureau of Public Administration, University of Alabama, 1960.

PART III

PHYSICAL RESOURCES AND ENVIRONMENTAL QUALITY

When we consider the Latitude and convenient Situation of Carolina, had we no farther Confirmation thereof, our Reason would inform us that such a Place lay fairly to be a delicious Country, being placed in that Girdle of the World which affords Wine, Oil, Fruit, Grain and Silk, with other rich Commodities, besides a sweet Air, moderate Climate and fertile Soil.

—John Lawson

5. Climate and Air Quality

RICHARD J. KOPEC
JAMES W. CLAY

CLIMATE

Very sensitive to the condition and quality of the atmosphere, man views climate not only as a fundamental resource but also as his natural adversary. Despite notable advances in technology, mankind remains subject to the whims and vagaries of the weather, and humanity's ever-increasing numbers only intensify the negative impact of climate on man and his activities. As the production of food becomes more critical to his growing needs, man is made acutely aware that agriculture is climate-controlled and that floods or prolonged droughts result in losses measurable in lives as well as in dollars and cents. With civilizations becoming ever more complex, the extent of death and damage wrought by storms and abnormal weather multiplies. Tidal inundation and destruction along densely settled coasts, disruption of communications and transportation due to heavy snowfalls, and power shortages resulting in "brownouts" and "blackouts" brought on by spells of unusually hot or cold temperatures are constant reminders of the influence that climate exerts on our lives. An increasing awareness of and concern for air quality problems have also heightened man's interest in atmospheric processes and patterns.

Climatic influences, however, are not primarily catastrophic. To the contrary, the atmosphere should be viewed as a resource essential to man's existence. As such, it exists as an impartial component of the natural fundament and, carefully considered, can be utilized as are other resources.

It has long been recognized that climate exerts important influences on such activities as settlement patterns and agricultural specialization. The fastest-growing population densities in the United States are in those areas where climate is considered to be an environmental amenity: California, Florida, and Hawaii, for example. Man has judiciously exploited the climate to his own advantages by farming such agricultural entities as corn belts, wheat belts, and fruit belts. By capitalizing on his knowledge of climatic characteristics, by living in harmony with its regimes, and by refraining from abusing atmospheric quality, man can optimize his benefits from the utilization of this natural resource.

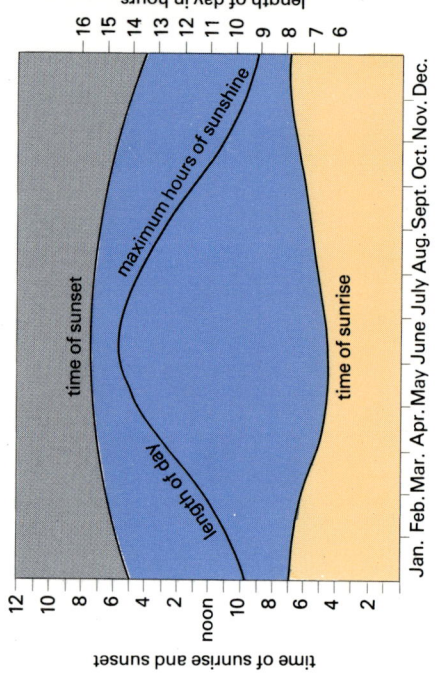

Figure 5.1. Hours of Sunshine by Months for Raleigh, N.C.

Source: U.S. Naval Observatory, *Nautical Almanac*, 1973.

Dominant Climatic Controls

There are four primary controls responsible for the nature and variation of North Carolina's climate: latitude, altitude, proximity to the Atlantic Ocean, and positional location on the continent. An examination of each of these variables will help in understanding North Carolina's climatic pattern.

Latitude The significance of latitude is essentially one of sun control. As it accounts for 99.98 percent of the energy at the earth's surface, the sun is the force underlying all weather processes. Variations in latitudinal receipt of radiant energy from the sun cause temperature inequities in the lower atmosphere that in turn cause pressure differences. As it attempts to equilibrate these pressure differences, the atmosphere moves and, in doing so, carries with it water vapor and moisture as well as its unique thermal conditions. Hence the atmosphere, propelled by the sun's energy, remains in a constant state of flux in order to moderate the impact caused by differences in solar energy received.

Aside from the amount of cloudiness, fogginess, or degree of pollution, the latitudinal variation in radiation results from two fundamental factors: the angle at which the energy from the sun reaches the earth's surface, and the length of time that the earth is exposed to this radiation. Both of these considerations are a function of a place's position north or south of the equator. The higher the sun is in the sky, the more directly energy is delivered to the earth's surface—both by passing through less atmosphere and by concentrating more energy per unit area. The length of the daylight period is equally important, for it determines the amount of energy that will be received.

As illustrated in Figure 5.1, at Raleigh, North Carolina, in mid-June, the noon sun is approximately seventy-two degrees above the southern horizon, and the length of the daylight period is approximately fourteen and one-half hours. At this time of year, a location on the equator has a maximum sun angle of only sixty-six degrees, and a daylight period of twelve hours. Thus, during summer months, Raleigh receives more solar radiation than does an equatorial position.

In winter, the sun is much lower in the southern sky, and the daylight period is only nine hours long at Raleigh. Consequently, because less solar energy is being received at this time, temperatures are reduced to their annual minimums. Compared, however, with such cities as New York and Miami, Raleigh has relatively moderate temperature regimes. Warmer than New York in the winter and cooler than Miami in the summer, temperatures at Raleigh reflect the intermediacy of its latitude between the two cities.

In winter, with low sun angles and very short days, temperatures drop markedly in the high latitudes of North America. Large masses of surface air, chilled by contact with the cold earth, move equatorward across the northern and central United States, causing great temperature contrasts within the country. In the summer, the thermal differences between those places in the United States where the sun is highest and the polar regions of the continent where daylight prevails continuously are much reduced, and latitudinal temperature gradients show an average of 12° F. from Florida to Canada. While Raleigh, North Carolina, is normally 17° F. warmer than Albany, New York, in January, it is only an average of 5° F. warmer in July.

Altitude It is a climatic axiom that the atmosphere is fueled from below; or, in other words, the earth's surface is the atmosphere's primary source of heat. Absorbing the sun's shortwave radiation, the earth converts this energy to long wave length. Through the transfer processes of radiation, conduction, convection, and evaporation and condensation, this reformed energy is diffused into the lower atmosphere. Hence, air temperatures are generally highest at the surface in the troposphere (the layer of air adjacent to the earth), and decrease as altitude increases. Normally, this decrease, called the lapse rate, amounts to about 3.5° F. for every one thousand feet increase in altitude.

The effects of elevation on air temperatures are significant in North Carolina. The range of elevation within our state is the greatest of any eastern state—almost seven thousand feet—and it affects temperatures in North Carolina in several ways. Areas having high elevations experience markedly colder temperatures than low-lying eastern sections of the state. North Carolina's mountains also serve to block and modify incursions of cold, polar air from the north and west. In the same latitudes as Tennessee, North Carolina had January temperatures averaging some 5° F. warmer because of its position to the east of the Blue Ridge Mountains.

There are additional climatic effects resulting from the influence of mountains and their high elevations. Because the mountains provide a barrier to the surface flow of air, the air is forced to rise or move around the mountains. In rising over the highlands, the air is chilled. The ability of the atmosphere to evaporate and maintain water as a gas is based mainly on its heat content; the ability is reduced when air is raised, for energy is consumed in the lifting process, and the temperature of the air is lowered. If raised sufficiently, the cooled air will condense its water vapor and form clouds. The ultimate result of this orographic process is precipitation. Measured against the yearly precipitation total in the country (except for Hawaii and the northwestern states) North Carolina's western counties have a high percentage of cloudy and wet days. However, air upon crossing the mountains is diverted downward. Descension causes the air to compress and its temperature to rise. This process is the antithesis of the precipitation-producing process, and settlements on the lee or sheltered side of mountain barriers are usually drier and warmer than places along the windward slopes. Asheville, North Carolina, located to the lee of the Appalachians, has an average annual precipitation of thirty-seven inches and a January mean temperature of 44° F., which contrasts notably with its wetter, cooler surroundings.

Oceanic Influence

Land and water surfaces react differently to the receipt and release of solar energy. Being opaque, immobile, and a relatively poor conductor of heat, ground surfaces, when exposed to sunlight, absorb solar radiation only to shallow depths. Because of this, the energy is concentrated and soil temperatures rise rapidly. Similarly, at night, land temperatures are quickly reduced as the soil radiates heat to the atmosphere, and lower soil depths are unable to keep the cooled-surface layer heated. The result is a large variation in soil temperatures from day to night, which is reflected in the behavior of air temperatures adjacent to the ground. For the same reasons, continents heat rapidly in the summer, when energy from the sun is delivered more directly and days are longer; in winter, they lose heat rapidly and become centers of low air temperatures.

A water surface characteristically responds more slowly in absorbing and radiating heat energy. Water is comparatively transparent and mobile. Its transparency permits solar radiation to penetrate deeply, causing heat to be distributed throughout a much greater volume than in opaque soils. The mobility of water, both as horizontal and vertical currents, further redistributes heat and reduces its concentration per unit volume. Also evaporation, an enormous consumer of heat, is more pronounced over water than land and contributes additionally to slowing the rate at which large water bodies warm. For these and other reasons, water surfaces heat more slowly than land surfaces. However, eventually warmed, oceans and other large water bodies stand as vast reservoirs of heat and when land temperatures recede, they help ameliorate the air temperature of nearby coastal regions.

This physical difference is evidenced in the temperature regimes of places influenced by large water bodies. Where prevailing wind systems are conducive, the retarded heating and cooling rates natural to oceans serve to temper climatic extremes. Air temperatures associated with maritime influences are relatively cooler in summer and warmer in winter than temperatures modified by continental surfaces, and daily and seasonal ranges of temperature are moderated.

Unlike wind patterns in states along the Pacific Coast, winds over North Carolina work against maximizing the maritime effect. During the winter season, when the warm Gulf Stream might significantly modify temperatures across the state, the winds are basically offshore, confining the ocean's moderating influence to the coastal counties. Due to the dominance of westerly winds, most of North Carolina lies under the influence of continental air masses. Nevertheless, in the Coastal Plain, winter temperatures are warmer, and the summer's heat and high humidities are alleviated by the predominance of sea breezes. Precipitation totals are higher nearer the coast and the percentage falling as snow in the cold season is noticeably lower.

Positional Location

Situated in the middle latitudes and in the extreme east of the North American continent, North Carolina is subject to other climatic controls that relate to this position and are periodically important. As do all states, North Carolina cyclically comes under the influence of moving cells of high and low pressure. High-pressure cells are masses of diverging air associated with fair weather conditions. Low-pressure areas originate in conflict zones between air masses having significantly different temperature and humidity characteristics and develop into cyclonic storm systems. These storm systems move quite rapidly across the nation and bring about changes in weather to areas over which they pass. During the winter when temperature contrasts are greatest, cyclonic storms are most numerous and affect North Carolina's weather every few days. However, in the summer, cyclonic activity is not an important feature of North Carolina's climate, as the pattern of cyclonic storm systems has shifted well to the north. Warm season precipitation usually results from thunderstorms that predominate at this time.

To the east of North Carolina well out over the Atlantic Ocean there exists a source region of high pressure called the Bermuda High. It is an enormous system of clockwise-circulating winds that varies seasonally and vacillates in position and size. During the summer, its western edge periodically covers the southeastern United States, and its influence is physiologically debilitating. Winds from the Bermuda High reach North Carolina from the south and southwest, and introduce high temperatures and humidities to the state. Daytime temperatures soar to near-record heights and both days and nights are uncomfortably sultry. When this source of hot, moist air affects the weather of the eastern United States—and the Bermuda High's influence can last for several weeks at a time—it is a period of high climatic stress for elderly and infirm people. Fortunately, the Bermuda High's effect is frequently interrupted by invasions of mild, dry air emanating from Canada.

North Carolina's Climate Type

North Carolina lies within a climatic region that can be typed as a *humid subtropical climate*. Corresponding in dimension to the southeastern states, this climate region is found on the eastern sides of all continents between the latitudes of twenty degrees and forty degrees. As the title implies, those areas or states within this climate region have short, mild winters, long, hot, and humid summers, and very pleasant transitional seasons. Precipitation is normally adequate for agriculture, with the warm season generally receiving the larger amounts. Except for two or three snowfalls each winter, precipitation is largely in the form of rainfall.

There is, however, considerable climatic variation within the state. In the mountains, annual and monthly mean temperatures are lower, precipitation extremes greater, and snowfalls heavier than in the rest of the state. Yet, everywhere the climate is marked by its temperateness. Temperatures seldom drop to zero in the winter, and only occasionally reach beyond 100° F. in the summer. Seasonality is sufficiently pronounced to cause contrasts in vegetation and provide other environmental variations for the residents of the state.

Seasonal Changes in Climate

Winter The alternate passage of low- and high-pressure systems over the state during winter months results in changing weather conditions. Moisture and warmer temperatures are characteristically associated with frequently passing low-pressure cells. Lows are followed by polar highs, which bring lower temperatures and clear skies. However, even when under the influence of these polar highs, temperatures seldom fall below 10° F., and midday temperatures reach into the forties, making the winter season very tolerable by northern standards.

January average temperatures shown in Figure 5.2 illustrate the mildness of winters. Only at the highest elevations do temperatures average below freezing. The mean temperature for January at Mount Mitchell is 28.7° F., the lowest in the state. Yet, at Asheville, located on the lee side of the mountains, temperatures for January average 39.4° F.

Nowhere else in North Carolina is the local contrast in temperatures as great as in the western counties. Temperature contrasts are least where the climate is mildest. Hatteras, on the Outer Banks, has a January mean of 48.0° F., and only thirteen days each year when temperatures of 32° F. and below are recorded.

The tendency for January isotherms to parallel the coast shows the influence of the Atlantic Ocean. Wilmington, in southeastern North Carolina, the most subtropical area in the state, exemplifies the maritime effect. This coastal city has a January mean temperature of 47.8° F., and an average of only eight days during January when temperatures dip to 32° F. or less, as compared with eighteen days at Raleigh and nineteen at Asheville.

In the Piedmont, latitude is the primary control on temperature, and the isotherms maintain a zonal pattern. As might be expected, temperature averages lie between those exhibited by the surrounding regions. Charlotte has a mean January temperature of 42.3° F., Greensboro, 39.0° F., and Raleigh, 42.7° F.

However, whereas Asheville averages eighty-three days each year when temperatures drop below freezing, Winston-Salem has freezing temperatures eighty-eight days annually, and Greensboro has eighty-four days with freezing temperatures.

Figure 5.2. Average January Temperatures in N.C.

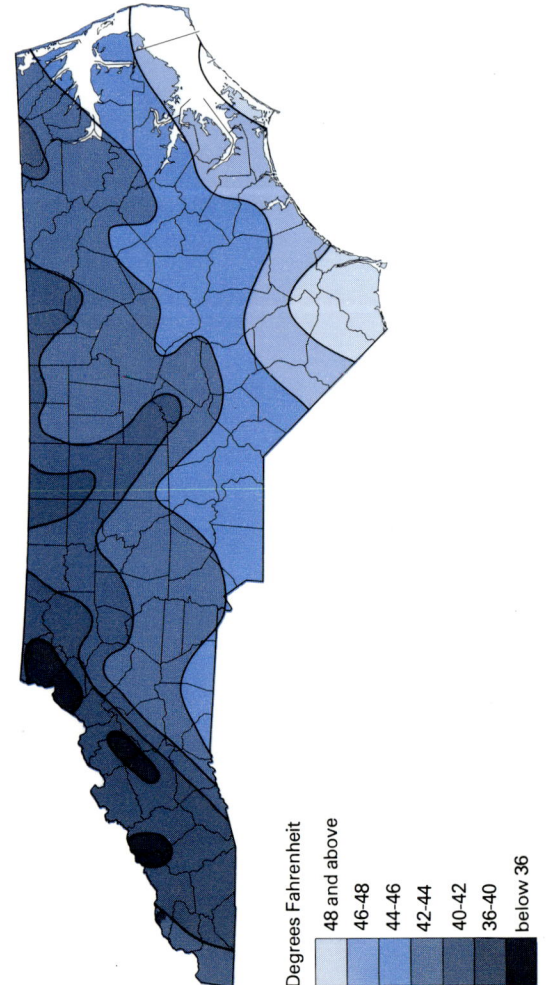

Degrees Fahrenheit
48 and above
46-48
44-46
42-44
40-42
36-40
below 36

Source: U.S. Department of Commerce, *Weather and Climate in North Carolina*, 1972.

Figure 5.3. Mean Maximum Temperature in N.C.

JANUARY

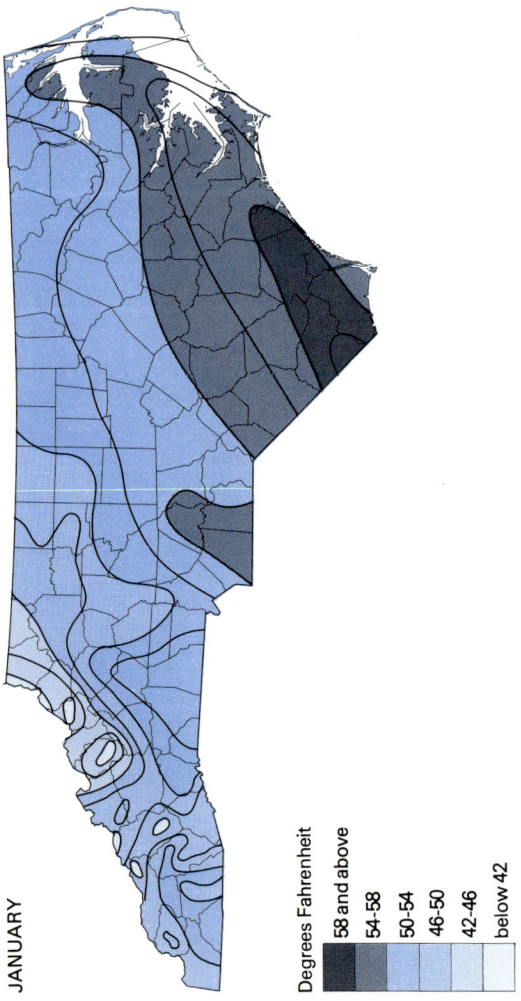

Degrees Fahrenheit
58 and above
54-58
50-54
46-50
42-46
below 42

Source: U.S. Department of Commerce, *Weather and Climate in North Carolina*, 1972.

January Mean Maximum and Minimum Temperatures

Figure 5.3 illustrates the temperature pattern across North Carolina on a typical afternoon of the coldest month. The cool waters of the East Coast are responsible for the isotherms taking an abrupt inland turn to the north before resuming the northeast-southwest pattern usually found on temperature maps. This distribution indicates that midday temperatures in January are highest a short distance inland from the coast unlike the pattern of mean temperatures that indicates a smooth gradient from the coast westward. Also, in the mountains, isotherms of mean maximum temperature are more numerous and some "islands" or "pockets" of cool temperatures exist. The greater ranges of temperature are associated with mountain valleys where nights are cold and days are warm, causing patterns of maximum temperatures to contrast significantly with mean temperature distributions.

The moderating effect of the ocean becomes evident in Figure 5.3, where January mean minimum temperatures are shown. Isotherms on this map reflect characteristic nighttime temperatures. The pattern reveals that temperatures are milder along the coast and decrease inland fairly rapidly. Once again, the temperature pattern is more complex in the highlands region. Generally, mean minimum temperatures are well below freezing in the Mountain region, at freezing levels throughout the Piedmont, and above freezing in the Coastal Plain. A comparison of Figures 5.3 and 5.4 indicates that during January the daily range of temperature is about 20°F. everywhere in the state.

Average Annual Heating Degree Days

There are climatically significant measurements of heat energy variation other than the direct determination of temperature, the cyclical occurrence of certain temperature levels, or the periodicity of temperature realms. These measurements relate to temperature efficiency in terms of human comfort or plant growth. One of these less common indexes is the *heating degree day*. This measurement is a cold season index and is based on the assumption that a temperature of 65°F. within a building is the minimum thermal threshold for normal human comfort. The negative departure of daily mean temperature from this standard figure is recorded as heating degree day units. For example, a daily temperature average of 40°F. would be listed as twenty-five heating degree days. Developed by heating engineers, this index permits a relatively accurate measurement of fuel consumption, and removes the guesswork from the calculation of fuel needs. The accumulation of heating degree day units at given locations is totaled annually and averaged for a period of years. To those persons interested in climate, this indirect measurement of heat energy provides additional insight into the thermal environment.

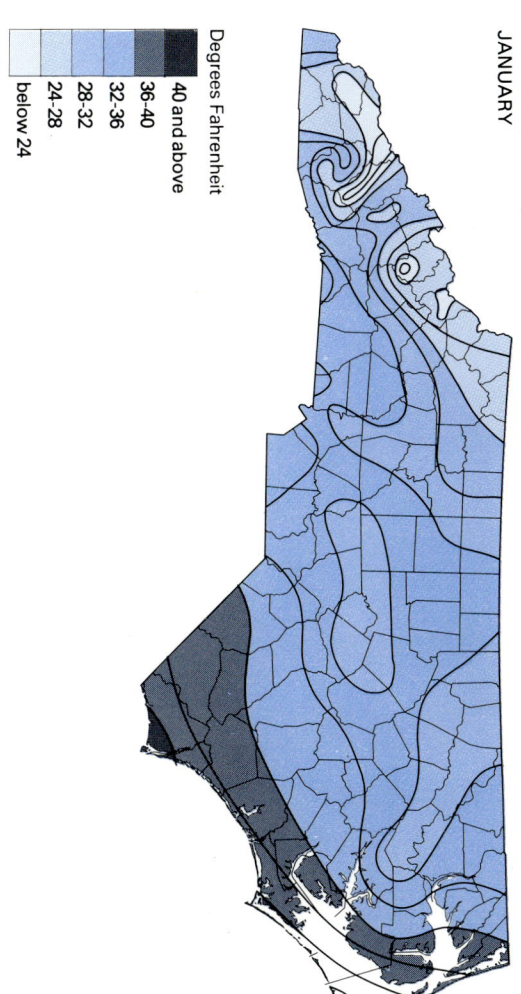

Figure 5.4. Mean Minimum Temperature in N.C.

JANUARY

Degrees Fahrenheit
- 40 and above
- 36-40
- 32-36
- 28-32
- 24-28
- below 24

Source: U.S. Department of Commerce, *Weather and Climate in North Carolina*, 1972.

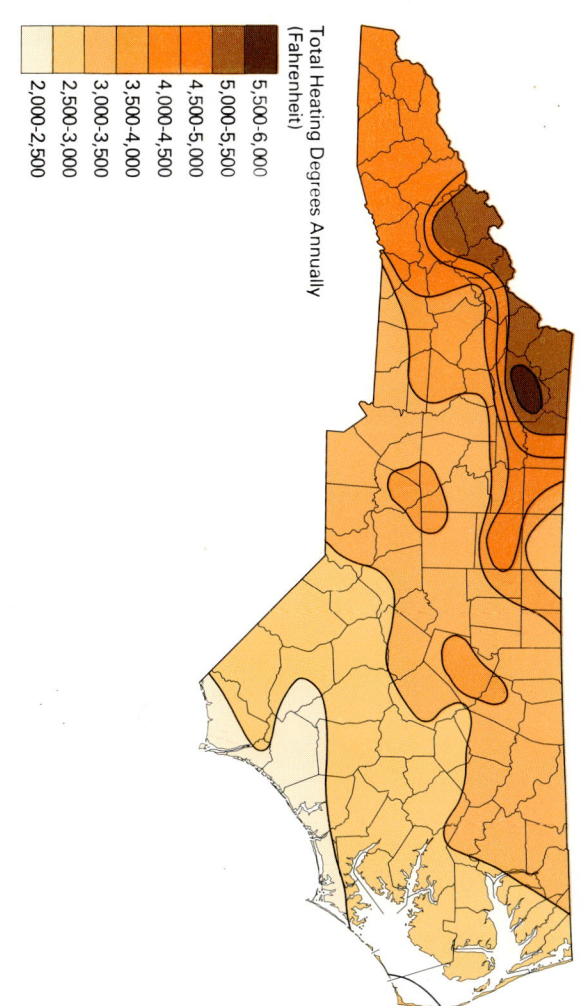

Figure 5.5. Average Annual Heating Degree Days in N.C.

Total Heating Degrees Annually (Fahrenheit)
- 5,500-6,000
- 5,000-5,500
- 4,500-5,000
- 4,000-4,500
- 3,500-4,000
- 3,000-3,500
- 2,500-3,000
- 2,000-2,500

Source: U.S. Department of Commerce, *Weather and Climate in North Carolina*, 1972.

Figure 5.5 is a very generalized map showing the distribution of heating degree days in North Carolina. Figure 5.6 shows the variation through time for three North Carolina cities. Values increase from 2,347 units at Wilmington to 3,805 at Greensboro, and in the Mountains more than 4,000 heating degree days are common for certain valleys and higher elevations. However, because of generalization on the map, actual figures in many of the higher areas are undoubtedly much greater. Compared with the eastern and central parts of the state, the values in the Mountains appear extreme and the cost of home heating expensive. However, in contrast with northern states such as North Dakota and Minnesota, where values in excess of 10,000 units are accumulated, heating costs in North Carolina's Mountain region can be seen in a different perspective.

Winter Precipitation For the winter months of January, February, and March, precipitation ranges from 3 to 4 inches per month for the Piedmont and Coastal Plain, and from 4 to 6 inches per month for the Mountains. In the middle and eastern counties, precipitation in excess of 0.01 inches usually falls ten to eleven days each month. In the western counties, the number of wet days is somewhat higher, with some places in the Mountains having as many as sixteen days with precipitation.

Cold season precipitation is related to the passing of low-pressure cells (cyclones) and usually occurs as rainfall. Snowfall amounts are small almost everywhere in the state. Using a water equivalence ratio of 12 inches of snow to 1 inch of water, only a few Mountain stations record as much as one-third of their winter precipitation totals as snowfall. As illustrated in Figure 5.7, snowfall totals increase dramatically as one moves in a westward direction. Mount Mitchell, reporting an average snowfall of 58 inches annually, leads the state in this category. Laurinburg, in the southeast, shows an average of only half an inch of snow per year. Unlike northern states, which are attuned to the problems accordant with heavy deposits of snow and sleet, unexpectedly severe winter storms cause considerable inconvenience and even disaster in the Piedmont and Coastal Plain. Hatteras, which averages 1.1 inches of snow yearly, has received as much as 12 inches in one day. Likewise, Raleigh, normally getting 7 inches each year, has had 17.8 inches dropped on it in a twenty-four hour period, and Winston-Salem has received up to 21 inches of snow during December, a month when no more than 1.9 inches are expected. Fortunately, however, the snow cover seldom remains longer than a week before melting.

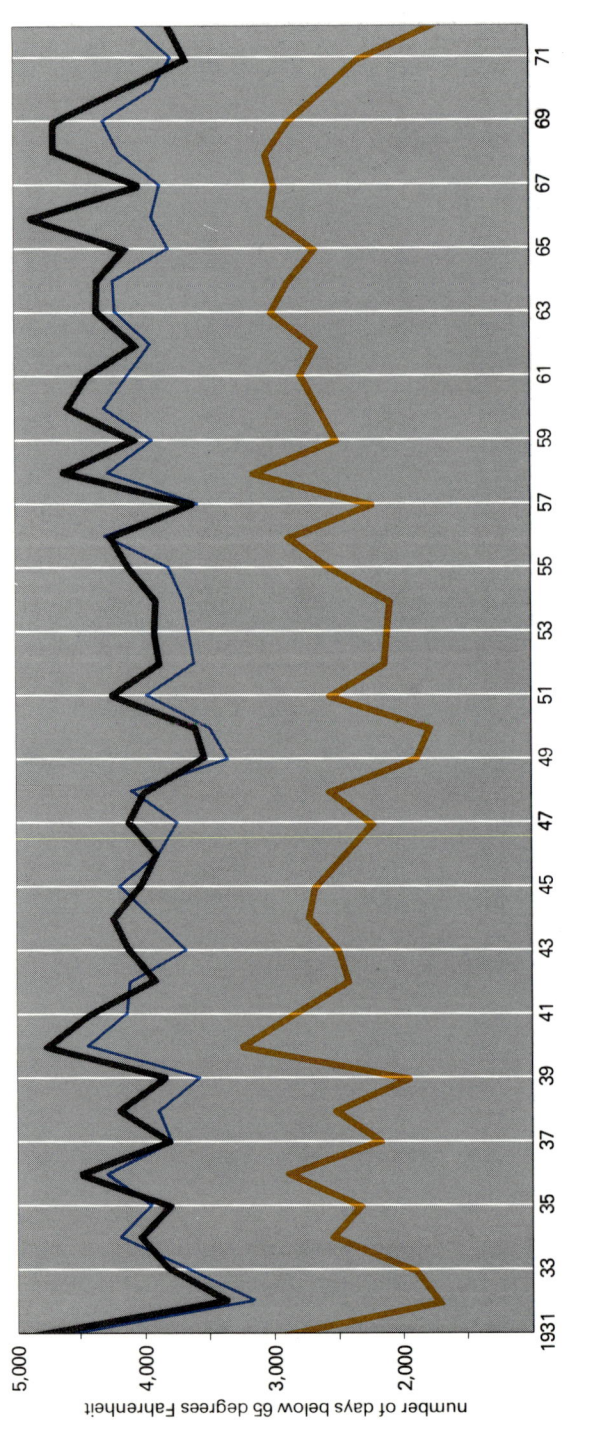

Figure 5.6. Annual Heating Degree Days at Cape Hatteras, Greensboro, and Asheville, N.C., 1931–1973

Source: U.S. Department of Commerce, *Climatological Summary*, 1972.

When high-pressure systems (anticyclones) dominate, clear to partly cloudy weather prevails. Receiving, on the average, 50 to 60 percent of total possible sunshine, North Carolina receives more hours of winter sunshine than do states to the north and to the immediate west. Sunshine is more prevalent in the southeast around Wilmington, and diminishes rapidly as the Mountains are approached. The Mountains receive about one-third less sunshine than does the rest of North Carolina.

Spring For many North Carolinians, this season is the most preferable of all. With the northward shifting of the noon sun, the storm track normal to North Carolina during the winter retreats northward and fewer and fewer cyclonic storms occur. Cold spells are less numerous and periods of high temperatures and balmy days become longer and more pronounced. Rainfall diminishes slightly in April, but increases toward the summer as cyclonic activity gives way to thundershowers and their heavy downpours. Although more precipitation is received in the state during May and June, there are fewer hours and days in which rainfall occurs, indicating a higher precipitation intensity.

Mean temperatures range from the fifties in April to the seventies in June for all places save those at high elevations. The days are marked by cool nights and warm afternoons with relative humidities at optimal levels for human comfort. As the daylight period lengthens, sunshine percentages and totals increase to their highest values for the year. For the eastern two-thirds of the state, sunshine curing April, May, and June is received approximately 70 percent of the time and in amounts exceeding three hundred hours for the latter part of the season.

Average Date of the Last Freeze in Spring As illustrated by Figure 5.8, the beginning of the freeze-free season varies across the state from 1 March to 10 May, a difference in time of over two months. As expected, the milder climate along North Carolina's coast engenders early dates, whereas the more severe climate of the Mountains retards the start of the freeze-free period longer than elsewhere. In most areas of the Coastal Plain, the last spring freeze generally occurs by the first of April. The Piedmont has its last freezes between 1 and 10 April, or about ten to fifteen days later than the Coastal Plain. In the Mountains, there is greater variation in mean dates for both the beginning and the end of the freeze season. Because cold air chills more quickly at higher elevations, and because air is denser than warm air, the cold air drains into the valleys where it is contained and continues to lose heat by radiation. The result of this process is that in certain Mountain areas some valleys are more often colder than their slopes at intermediate altitudes. Lying between the below-freezing temperatures of the valleys and the higher elevations are "verdant" or "thermal" belts.

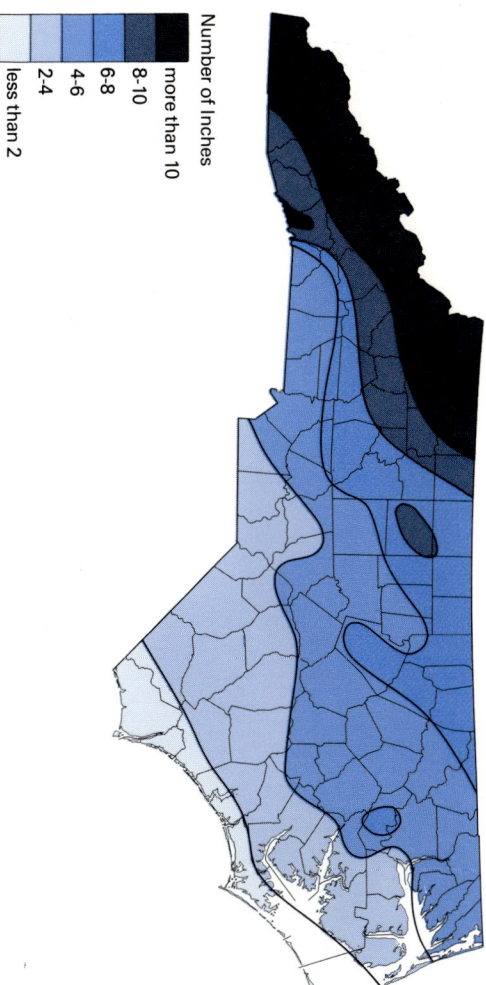

Figure 5.7. Average Annual Snowfall in N.C.

Number of Inches
- more than 10
- 8-10
- 6-8
- 4-6
- 2-4
- less than 2

Source: U.S. Department of Commerce, *Climatological Summary*, 1966.

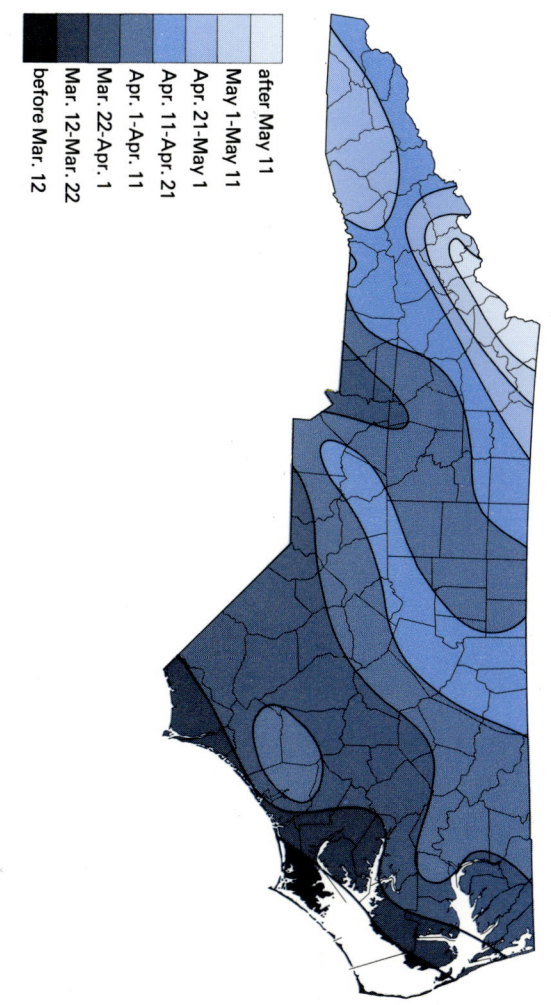

Figure 5.8. Average Date of Last Freezing Temperature in N.C.

- after May 11
- May 1-May 11
- Apr. 21-May 1
- Apr. 11-Apr. 21
- Apr. 1-Apr. 11
- Mar. 22-Apr. 1
- Mar. 12-Mar. 22
- before Mar. 12

Source: U.S. Department of Commerce, *Weather and Climate in North Carolina*, 1972.

These strip-like regions have longer freeze-free seasons and thereby show earlier dates for the end of the freeze period than their surroundings. They support frost-susceptible vegetation long after the greenery has disappeared in nearby areas. Often in early winter or even in midwinter a contrasting belt of green flanked above and below by brown may be seen. These green belts are characteristically located along slopes that face the winter sun, are protected from cold northern winds, and have cold air drainage to lower valleys. The blossoming of dogwood and redbud moves across the state in a pattern similar to that of the end of the freeze season to blanket North Carolina with color and beauty.

Summer   Summer is characterized by its high temperatures, high humidities, high amounts of rainfall, and high physiological stress. Except for the amelioration of these climatic elements in the Mountains, and the relief afforded by sea breezes along the coast, elsewhere in the state summer is a season of extremes. Mean monthly minimum temperatures for July and August are in the upper seventies and eighties and mean maximum temperatures reach into the nineties.

However, to quote a popular adage, "it's not the heat but the humidity," and North Carolina's temperatures in combination with the high water vapor amounts prevalent during the summer months are definitely uncomfortable. In addition, high sunshine percentages and a predominance of southerly winds tend to aggravate an already unpleasant climatic condition. Only the periodic passage of cool, dry air masses from the north and sea breezes in the coastal areas alleviate the discomfort of summer weather for North Carolina's low-lying counties.

July Average Temperatures   The pattern of mean temperatures in July is similar to the pattern in January (Figure 5.9). However, in the Piedmont and Coastal Plain, isotherms are fewer in number and farther apart. In the Mountains, the reverse is true. The widespread isotherms east of the Mountains indicate that temperature averages across central and eastern North Carolina exhibit little contrast. From the western Piedmont to the coast, the difference in mean temperatures is only 4°F. Although the influence of the ocean is not evident in the arrangement of isotherms, the high temperatures of the Coastal Plain are made less severe by the cooling power of the sea breeze. Hatteras, on the Outer Banks, records a temperature of 90°F. on the average of only one day each year, while Wilmington, a short distance from the coast, has an occurrence of 90°F. temperatures about twenty-four days annually. In contrast with these locations, Raleigh and Winston-Salem mean temperatures for July are slightly lower, but the average number of days on which a temperature of 90°F. or above is experienced increases to more than forty.

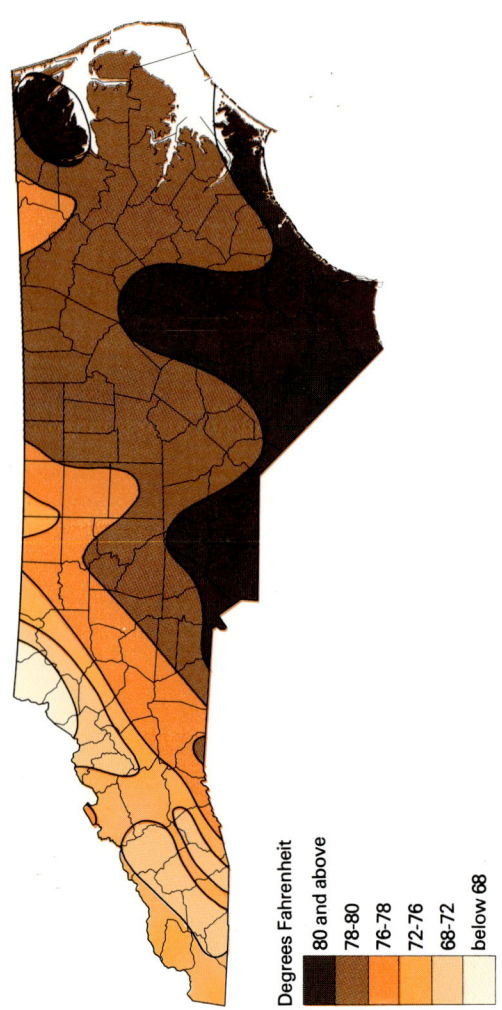

Figure 5.9. Average July Temperature in N.C.

Degrees Fahrenheit
- 80 and above
- 78–80
- 76–78
- 72–76
- 68–72
- below 68

Source: U.S. Department of Commerce, *Weather and Climate in North Carolina*, 1972.

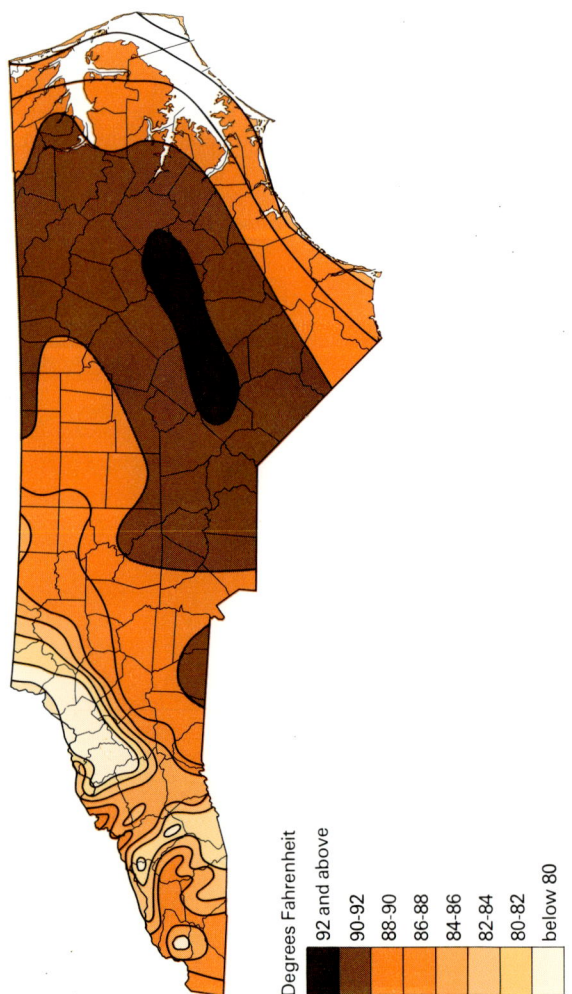

Figure 5.10. Mean Maximum July Temperature in N.C.

Degrees Fahrenheit
- 92 and above
- 90–92
- 88–90
- 86–88
- 84–86
- 82–84
- 80–82
- below 80

Source: U.S. Department of Commerce, *Weather and Climate in North Carolina*, 1972.

In the Mountains, the effects of altitude reduce mean temperature values sharply. The temperature gradient in July is even steeper than in January. East to west across Caldwell County, mean temperatures drop from 76°F to 68°F. and Mount Mitchell remains the coolest site in the state with a July average of 59°F. At Asheville, the warmest month averages 73.8°F. and only seven caves during the summer show temperatures reaching to 80°F. With daily minimum temperatures in the fifties and sixties during the summer months for summer recreation becomes evident.

July Average Maximum and Minimum Temperatures

The temperatures typically recorded during an afternoon in July are shown in Figure 5.10. In the Coastal Plain, isotherms representing mean maximum temperature are aligned parallel to the shoreline, signifying the effect of the cool ocean and sea breeze. At Cape Hatteras, the summer daytime maximum is 84°F. Inland, temperatures increase and reach their highest values in the Fayetteville area where scorching temperatures in excess of 92°F. are experienced. In the Piedmont, maximum temperatures average between 88°F. and 92°F. Toward the Mountains, midday highs drop to more pleasant levels. In Swain and Haywood counties, afternoon temperatures are generally in the low seventies and most western counties record mean July maximums under 80°F.

Although isotherms of mean minimum temperature exhibit a pattern similar to the pattern of maximum July temperatures, in the outer Coastal Plain absolute temperature values are reversed (Figure 5.11). Minimum temperatures represent nighttime conditions and their distribution indicates that the effect of the ocean is to warm adjacent areas. Farther inland, the more rapidly cooling land causes the temperatures to be lower. Thus the maps showing average July maximum and minimum temperatures portray the daily relative change in influence from ocean to land and back again along the coastal fringe of North Carolina. Over the Piedmont and the Inner Coastal Plain, July average minimums show little change with distance, ranging only 4°F. from 66°F. to 70°F. In the Mountains, 50°F. and 60°F. temperatures indicate the characteristically cool weather associated with this region during summer nights.

Summer is the season of greatest precipitation in North Carolina. Thunderstorms are the predominant mechanism for precipitation delivery and occur mainly in the afternoon or evening. They come on an average of ten to twelve days per month. July and August show the highest rainfall amounts with many sections of the state reporting 5 to 7 inches of rain for each of these months. The coastal region around Wilmington and the southwestern counties are the rainiest areas in the state

having over 8 inches of precipitation and an average of fourteen rain days in July. By August the hurricane season has arrived and these storms may contribute a significant percentage of rainfall to monthly totals and continue to do so well into the fall.

Average Growing Degree Days

Similar in its derivation to the heating degree day concept, the *growing degree day* is based on the positive departure of mean daily temperature from an established temperature value representing the start of the active growth period for plants.

Although each plant has its own base temperature for seed germination and active growth, a mean daily temperature of 40°F. will represent the beginning of the growth period for most crops. To determine growing degree day units for example, a daily mean temperature of 50°F. will indicate ten growing degree days or a 10°F. departure from the base minimum of 40°F. These units are then accumulated for the year and averaged over a period of time to provide us with the data for preparing Figure 5.12. Since each plant requires a certain amount

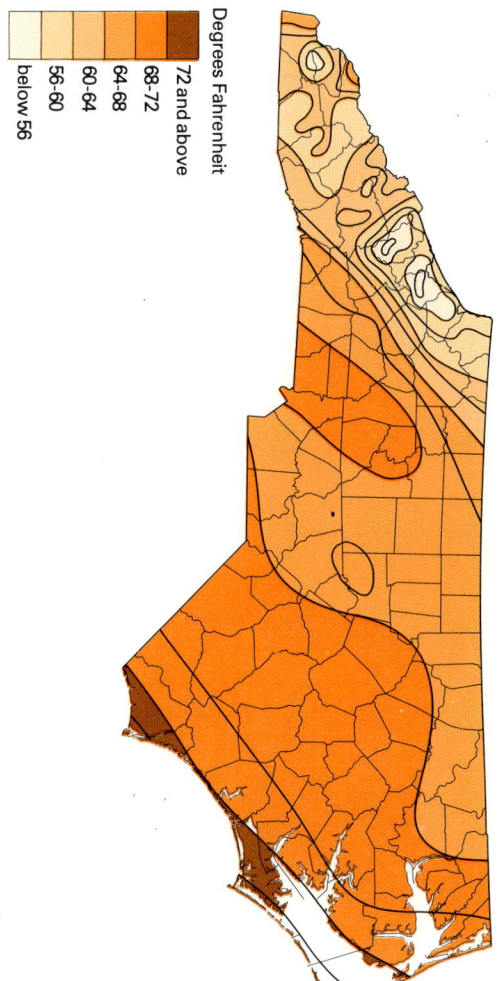

Figure 5.11. Mean Minimum July Temperature in N.C.

Degrees Fahrenheit
- 72 and above
- 68–72
- 64–68
- 60–64
- 56–60
- below 56

Source: U.S. Department of Commerce, *Weather and Climate in North Carolina*, 1972.

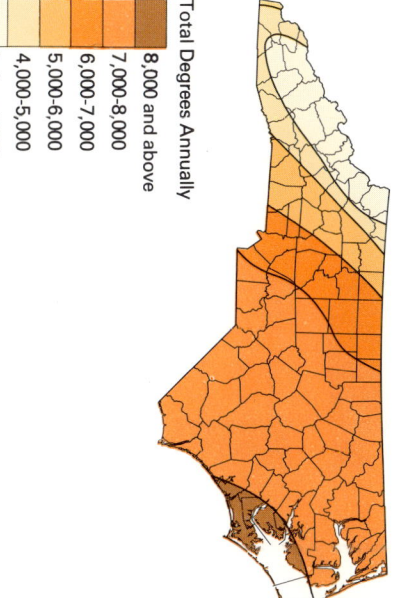

Figure 5.12. Average Annual Growing Degree Days in N.C.

Total Degrees Annually
- 8,000 and above
- 7,000–8,000
- 6,000–7,000
- 5,000–6,000
- 4,000–5,000
- below 4,000

Source: U.S. Department of Commerce, *Climatological Summary*, 1966.

of heat energy units to reach maturity, the accumulation of growing degree day units is a means of determining crop maturation. For instance, when 1,500 units have accumulated, peas are ready to be harvested. Therefore, the growing degree day index is a measure of a region's thermal efficiency in enhancing plant growth.

Once again, spatial patterns relating to heat energy show maximum values along the coast and lowest values in the Mountains. Coastal North Carolina has twice the accumulation of growing degree day units than are found in the Appalachians. The pattern across the Coastal Plain and eastern Piedmont indicates surprising uniformity. Variation in the growing degree day index amounts to less than 1,000 units throughout this area. As the highlands are approached, growing degree day totals diminish rapidly. Most middle-latitude crops requiring a lengthy growth period can be easily accommodated by the temperature regime of the eastern two-thirds of North Carolina. However, the western third of the state shows a thermal efficiency comparable to that of New England, central Wisconsin, or eastern Montana. Since most vegetable crops reach maturity within a limit of 4,000 growing degree day units, each year North Carolina's thermal climate permits at least one harvest of vegetables in the Mountains and two harvests of vegetables in the eastern sections of the state.

Average Length of the Freeze-Free Season Known also as the frost-free period and somewhat erroneously as the growing season, the freeze-free season refers to that segment of time between the mean date of the last day in the spring when a low temperature of 32° F. occurs, and the first day in fall of the same occurrence. Of particular interest to agriculturalists is that the length of this thermal phenomenon partially dictates the type of crops that may be cultivated. Since freezing temperatures are destructive to most domestic plants, the beginning and the length of the growth period are regulated by the freeze-free season. In North Carolina, this season is of sufficient duration to accommodate most middle-latitude crops. A look at Figure 5.13 will show that the freeze-free period varies from almost 300 days at Hatteras to 150 days in the Mountains. Throughout the Piedmont, an average of 200 days is representative.

Autumn Gradually the heat and humidities of summer give way to the mild and comfortable weather of fall. Like the spring season, the fall is a very pleasant time for North Carolinians. Days remain hot through November and nights are agreeably cool. Normal daily temperatures average 55° F. in October; 45° F. to 55° F. in November; and 35° F. to 50° F. in December. Daily temperatures range 20° F. to 25° F. for the entire season.

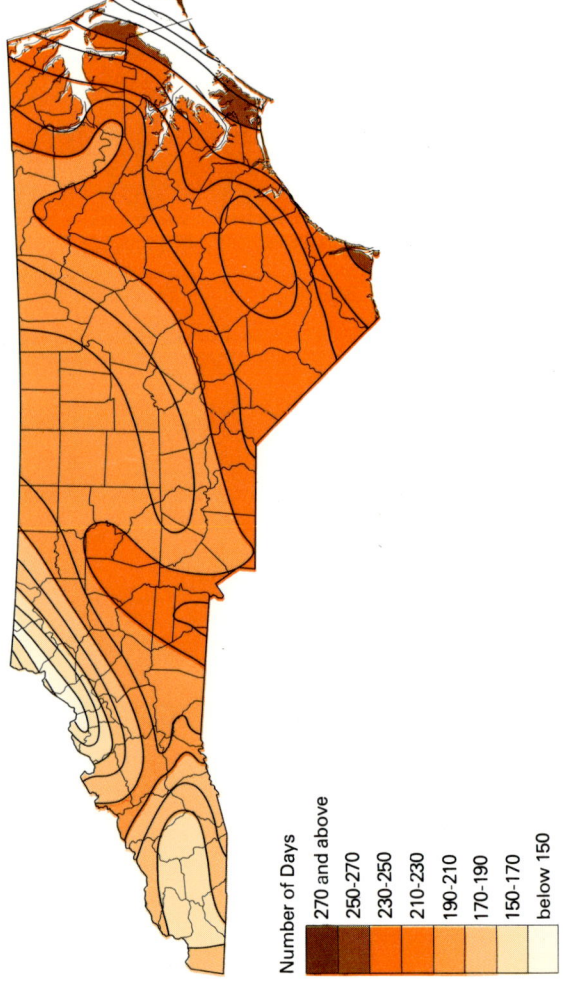

Figure 5.13. Average Length of Freeze-Free Season in N.C.

Number of Days
- 270 and above
- 250-270
- 230-250
- 210-230
- 190-210
- 170-190
- 150-170
- below 150

Source: U.S. Department of Commerce, *Weather and Climate in North Carolina*, 1972.

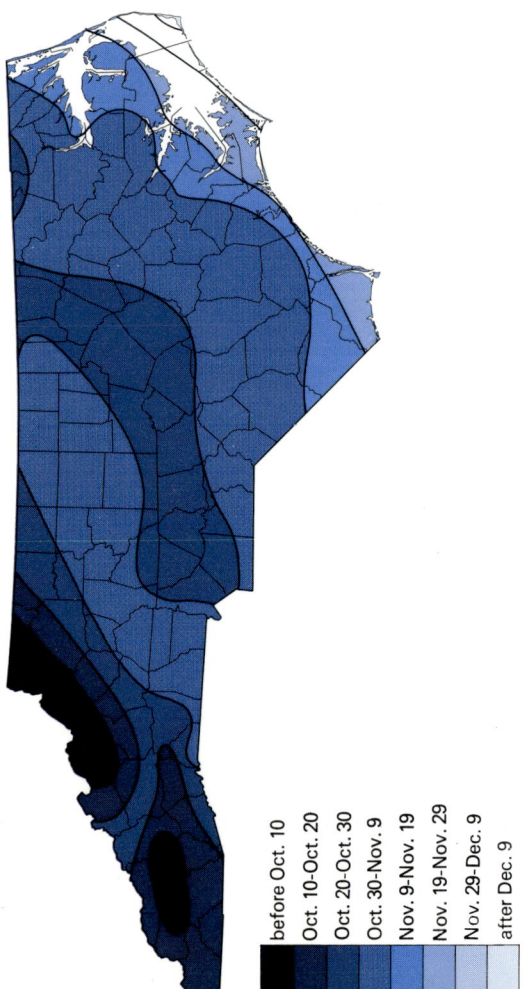

Figure 5.14. Average Date of First Freezing Temperature in N.C.

- before Oct. 10
- Oct. 10-Oct. 20
- Oct. 20-Oct. 30
- Oct. 30-Nov. 9
- Nov. 9-Nov. 19
- Nov. 19-Nov. 29
- Nov. 29-Dec. 9
- after Dec. 9

Source: U.S. Department of Commerce, *Weather and Climate in North Carolina*, 1972.

As illustrated in Figure 5.14, freezes begin early in October in the Mountains and slowly move eastward toward the coast. In early December, the freeze-free season reluctantly comes to a close in the Wilmington-Southport area. Deciduous trees begin their dormancy period and the color of the state gradually changes from the quiet greens of summer to the fiery reds and brilliant yellows of fall. By late autumn the highlands, now a mottled brown and green, show an occasional sprinkling of white as temperatures in the Mountains fall below freezing and the possibility of snow increases. However, in the Piedmont and Coastal Plain, tennis, sailing, and picnicking, for example, continue into November and football games played late in the season are often attended by fans dressed in warm-season attire.

Annual Precipitation and Humidity

Although a considerable variation in the distribution of rainfall exists throughout the state, everywhere precipitation is high (Figure 5.15). In the Coastal Plain, rainfall totals average from 44 to 55 inches; the highest amounts were received at the Outer Banks. Across the Piedmont, yearly rainfall averages range from 43 to 48 inches, with the lowest rainfall reported in the state. More commonly, average annual precipitation in the Mountains ranges from 44 to 58 inches. For the state as a whole, an average total of 50 inches is representative.

The distribution of rainfall throughout the year is reasonably uniform. Although there are no pronounced wet and dry seasons, a profile of average annual precipitat on indicates a bimodal distribution, i.e., two periods of higher rainfall separated by two periods during the year when rainfall amounts are lower than the norm. Generally, the highest precipitation totals are associated with the summer months. In the fall, the season of the least rainfall, the lowest yearly totals usually occur in October or November. Precipitation increases slightly during the winter season and then decreases to a secondary low in April. This precipitation regime is common to the state and varies only slightly from place to place.

Although rainfall is heaviest in the summer, evaporation and transpiration losses are also great. Consequently, the summer season is deficient in its supply of soil moisture and irrigation may be required to sustain crop needs.

Although it is considered to be a wet state, North Carolina nevertheless has its occasional "bout with drought." Recently, the Piedmont and Inner Coastal Plain suffered through an especially severe drought. In 1968, negative rainfall departures amounting to as much as 26 inches were computed by individual stations within this area. On the other hand, 1972 proved to be an abnormally wet year. During that year, Raleigh, which has an average annual precipitation of 46.35 inches, experienced a total rainfall of 51.74 inches. Raleigh's weather records may be used to illustrate the variations in yearly precipitation amounts. In the capital city, annual totals have varied from a low of 30 inches in 1933 to a high of 64 inches in 1936. On a monthly basis, rainfall variation for July has ranged from 12.36 inches in 1931 to as little as 0.38 inches in 1953. Yet precipitation variability in North Carolina is moderate compared with those states where rainfall totals are significantly less and consequently precipitation patterns and regimes are more unpredictable.

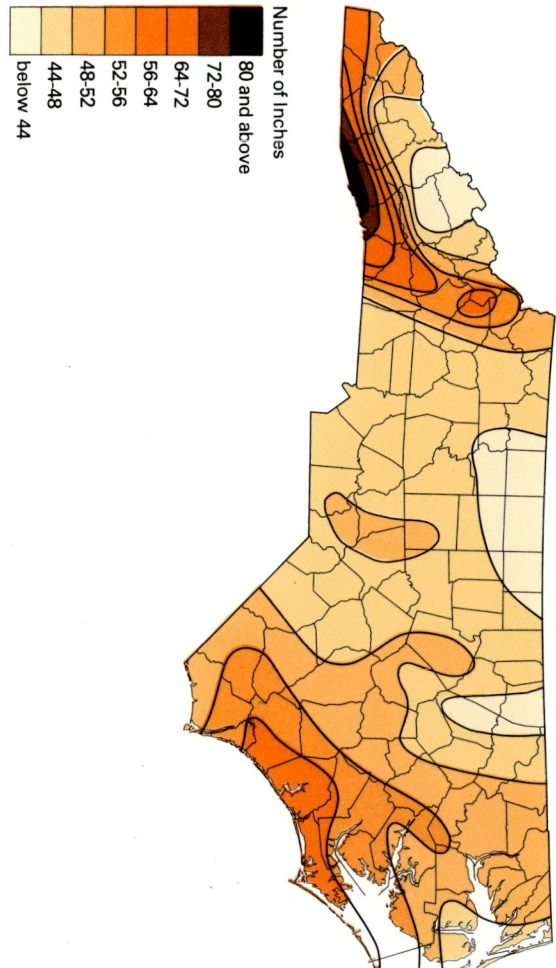

Figure 5.15. Average Annual Precipitation in N.C.

Number of inches
- 80 and above
- 72-80
- 64-72
- 56-64
- 52-56
- 48-52
- 44-48
- below 44

Source: U.S. Department of Commerce, *Weather and Climate in North Carolina,* 1972.

Average Number of Days with 0.01 Inches of Precipitation or More

Figure 5.16 shows the pattern of days with measurable precipitation in North Carolina. The Mountains have the greatest number of days with measurable precipitation, averaging 10 to 20 more rainy days per year than the southern Piedmont. In the northwest corner of the state precipitation occurs 4 out of every 10 days. By contrast, the sandhills in the Southern Piedmont experiences precipitation on only 30 percent of the days. In fact, a "tongue" of fewer rainy days penetrates the state from south to north, through North Carolina's central counties. For the state as a whole, 125 days with measurable precipitation is a representative figure.

Water Balance

The "wetness" or "dryness" of any region is mirrored by its natural vegetation. Indigenous plant life is an indicator of a region's precipitation effectiveness and its capacity to support plant growth. The minimal moisture requirements of plant communities are quite specific, and in situ vegetation reflects the amounts of water annually and seasonally available for its use. As the size of a bank account depends upon the balance between deposits and withdrawals, so precipitation effectiveness

101

Figure 5.16. Mean Number of Days with 0.01 or More Inches of Precipitation per Year in N.C.

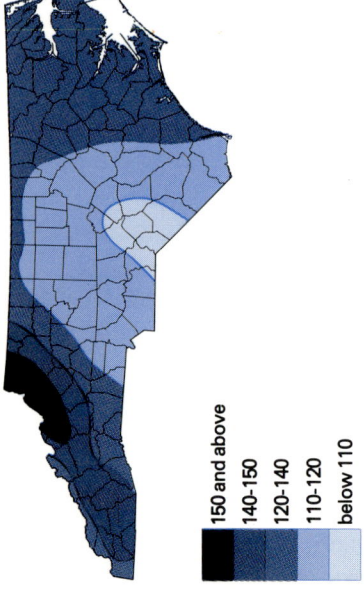

- 150 and above
- 140-150
- 120-140
- 110-120
- below 110

Source: U.S. Department of Commerce, *Climatic Summary of the U.S.*, 1972.

Figure 5.17. Water Balance, Raleigh, N.C.

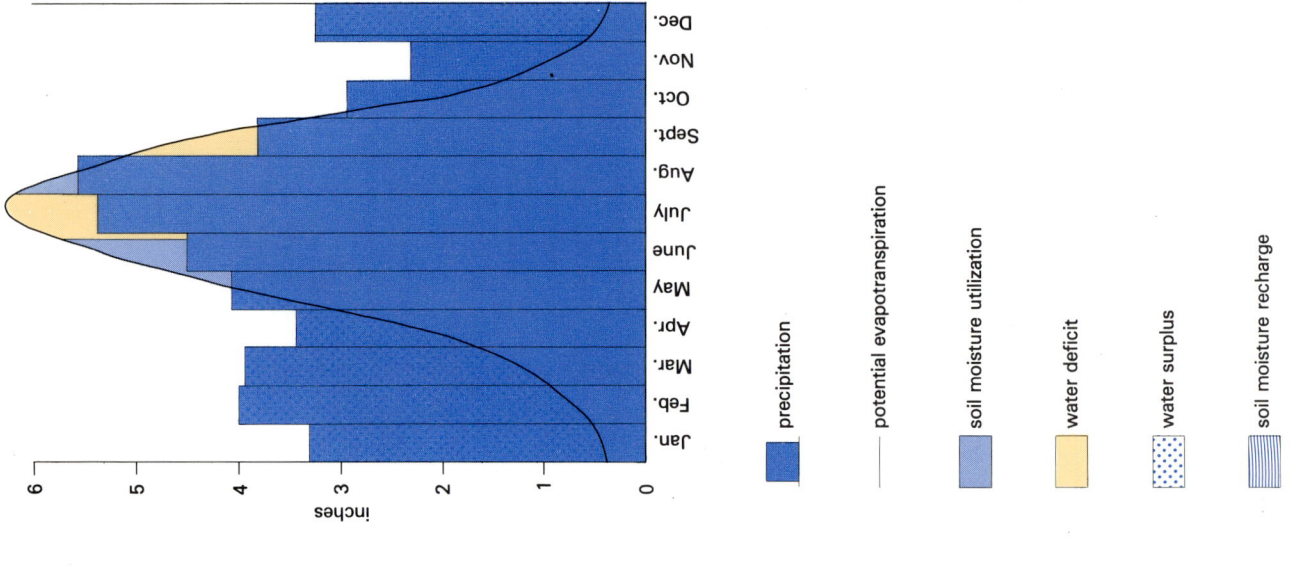

- precipitation
- potential evapotranspiration
- soil moisture utilization
- water deficit
- water surplus
- soil moisture recharge

Source: Glenn T. Trewartha, Arthur H. Robinson, and Edwin H. Hammond, eds., *Elements of Geography*, 5th ed. (New York: McGraw-Hill Book Co., 1967).

is determined by the balance between incoming precipitation and outgoing evaporation and transpiration (evapotranspiration). In temperate regions where annual precipitation exceeds evapotranspiration, forests normally flourish. Conversely, in those areas where evaporation and transpiration incur water losses greater than the supply provided by precipitation and soil moisture storage, forests give way to grasses and desert plants. This relationship between incoming and outgoing moisture is known as the *water balance concept*, and is utilized to calculate a region's water profiles and budgets as well as to classify its climate.

However, merely comparing precipitation to evapotranspiration on an annual basis is not adequate in understanding precipitation effectiveness. The efficiency of rainfall depends not only on total rainfall supply but also upon a region's temperature regime and the degree of correlation between its evaporation and rainfall regimes. Although a region may have an appreciable surplus of precipitation over evapotranspiration in terms of annual totals, nevertheless it may still show seasonal moisture deficiencies. In North Carolina, for instance, during summer months, temperatures and evaporation rates are highest and transpiration is at its peak. At this time, despite the fact that rainfall reaches its highest monthly levels, many places in the state will record moisture deficits. When such deficits occur, soil moisture is utilized until replenishment is provided by rainfall, or until depletion of soil moisture storage is complete. Beyond this point, wilting occurs and plants eventually die or go into dormancy. For domesticated crops, periods of water deficiency must be offset by irrigation to insure against soil moisture exhaustion, especially for high-value crops. Although many areas in North Carolina show water deficits during the course of the warm season, droughts are usually minor.

The water balance of individual stations can be shown graphically. Figure 5.17 is a water balance climograph showing Raleigh's annual budget of water supply and expenditure presented on a monthly basis. The climograph is based on the primary assumption that ten inches of water is required to saturate the soil in the Raleigh area. The period from January to May is a time when soil moisture storage is complete and precipitation exceeds potential evapotranspiration (the maximum loss of water possible). All precipitation during this time is listed as surplus water since none is required by the soil. From May to September, the months of greatest rainfall, water loss nonetheless is greater than water receipt and soil moisture storage is depleted. Water deficits are recorded as actual evapotranspiration drops below potential evaporation levels. From September to December, soil moisture storage is recharged and the soil is once again brought to the saturation point. When the ten-inch soil moisture requirement is satisfied, additional precipitation will drain to the underground water table or run off the land as surplus water.

Figure 5.18 provides the water balance deficits for the state and shows that everywhere except for the Asheville area and the northern Piedmont, the annual water deficit is less than one inch. By contrast, Figure 5.19 gives water balance surpluses. Being a wet state, North Carolina's water budget indicates surpluses exceeding deficits by large amounts. While most of the Piedmont and Coastal Plain have surplus water up to 15 inches, the Outer Banks and the Mountains show surpluses above 15 inches. In the southwest corner of the state, water surpluses amount to as much as 30 inches.

Mean annual evaporation for North Carolina is shown in Figure 5.20. Evaporation rates and totals are related to temperature, wind velocity, and relative humidity. Where temperatures are highest and humidities lowest, evaporation intensities will be greatest. Since temperatures throughout the Coastal Plain and the Piedmont are highest for the state and since humidity percentages are greater in the vicinity of the ocean, evaporation totals are lower in the Mountains and along the coast, and highest in the southern Piedmont and Coastal Plain. A comparison of the maps showing precipitation, evaporation, water surplus, and water deficit will provide the reader with a fairly complete picture of North Carolina's water balance.

Winds and Storms

Three types of storms and their associated winds are common to North Carolina: cyclonic and convectional thunderstorms, hurricanes, and tornadoes. These storms are integral parts of the state's climatic pattern. In analyzing the importance of winds, direction and speed are major considerations.

Although prevailing winds (winds that persist in blowing from one direction more so than any other) characterize given geographical areas, wind direction changes frequently. A northwesterly wind (coming from the northwest) will be, relatively speaking, a cooling and drying wind, whereas a southeasterly wind will bring warm, moist air to the state. The passage of cyclones and anticyclones with their characteristic wind patterns will change the wind's direction so that it may come across North Carolina from any point of the compass.

Figure 5.18. Water Balance Deficit in N.C.

1 inch and above
below 1 inch

Source: U.S. Department of Commerce, *Climatic Summary of the U.S.*, 1972.

Figure 5.19. Water Balance Surplus in N.C.

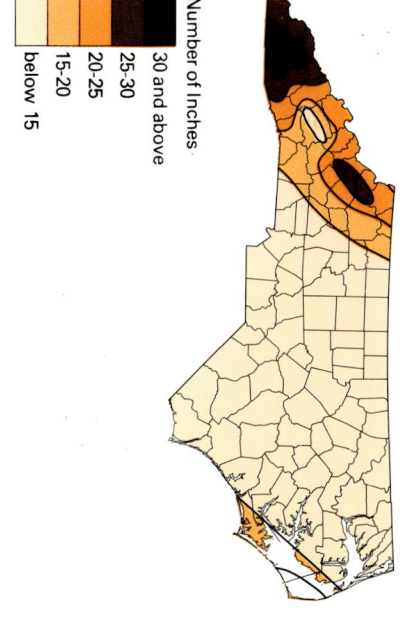

Number of Inches
30 and above
25-30
20-25
15-20
below 15

Source: U.S. Department of Commerce, *Climatic Summary of the U.S.*, 1972.

Figure 5.20. Mean Annual Evaporation in N.C.

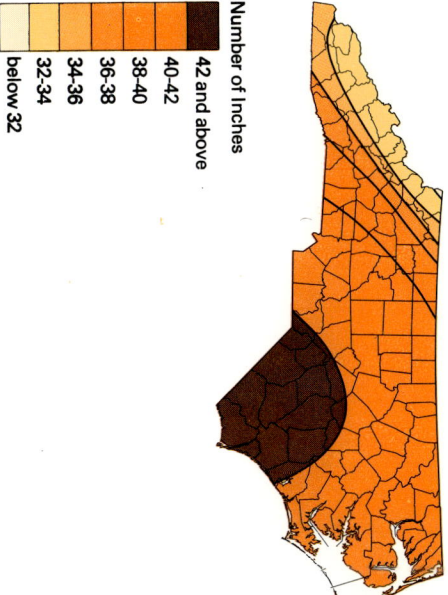

Number of Inches
42 and above
40-42
38-40
36-38
34-36
32-34
below 32

Source: U.S. Department of Commerce, *Climatic Summary of the U.S.*, 1972.

The velocity of the wind is relevant to ventilation of air pollutants, evaporation rates, and thus cooling and chilling indexes. On those occasions when winds reach gale force and higher, their velocities are of singular importance because of their destructive capabilities. Damaging winds are usually associated with infrequent hurricanes and tornadoes and, at times, with severe thunderstorms.

The prevailing winds and mean wind speeds averaged for the year are given in Figure 5.21. For the eastern two-thirds of the state, winds blow most frequently from the southwest and south. Throughout the Mountains and the western Piedmont, winds prevail from northerly directions. This annual pattern of prevailing winds persists for most months of the year except September and October when winds are dominantly from the northeast. During these months, the clockwise flow of air from seasonal anticyclones lying poleward of North Carolina, and the counterclockwise winds associated with an increased number of offshore storms cause northeasterlies to prevail across the state.

103

Figure 5.21. Prevailing Winds and Mean Annual Wind Speed in N.C.

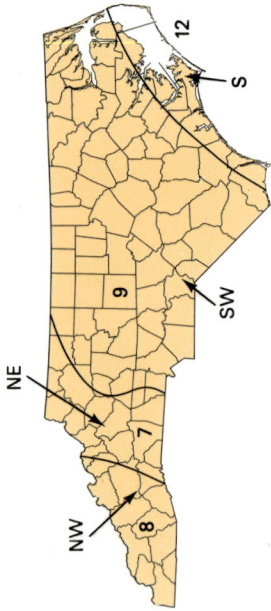

Source: U.S. Department of Commerce, *Climatic Summary of the U.S.*, 1972.

Note: Wind speeds are noted in miles per hour.

Wind speeds have been averaged for each zone of prevailing winds. Winds tend to diminish in speed westward from the coast where sea breezes and offshore storms contribute to velocities that average twelve miles per hour. Throughout the Inner Coastal Plain and the Piedmont, the mean wind speed is nine miles per hour, and in the western counties, representative wind speeds are seven and eight miles per hour. On a daily basis, wind velocities are lowest before dawn and highest around midafternoon. Seasonally, winter, with greater temperature and pressure contrasts, shows the most rapid air movement and summer is the time of lowest wind speeds.

Thunderstorms Thunderstorms are vertically developed storm systems that involve lightning and thunder. Produced by instability in the atmosphere, these storms are sustained by the conversion of water vapor into rain and hail, which causes the release of enormous amounts of energy. This energy results in vigorous updrafts of rapidly moving air. The intensity and turbulence of an individual thunderstorm is related to the degree of atmospheric instability and the supply of latent energy released by the condensing of water vapor. In structure, the typical thunderstorm is a collection of convective cells each averaging a mile or more in diameter. A cell is comprised of columns of rapidly rising air separated and counterbalanced by downdrafts of slower moving air. Associated with thunderstorms and their bulbous facade are heavy downpours of rain, hail, gusty and squally winds, and, of course, lightning and thunder.

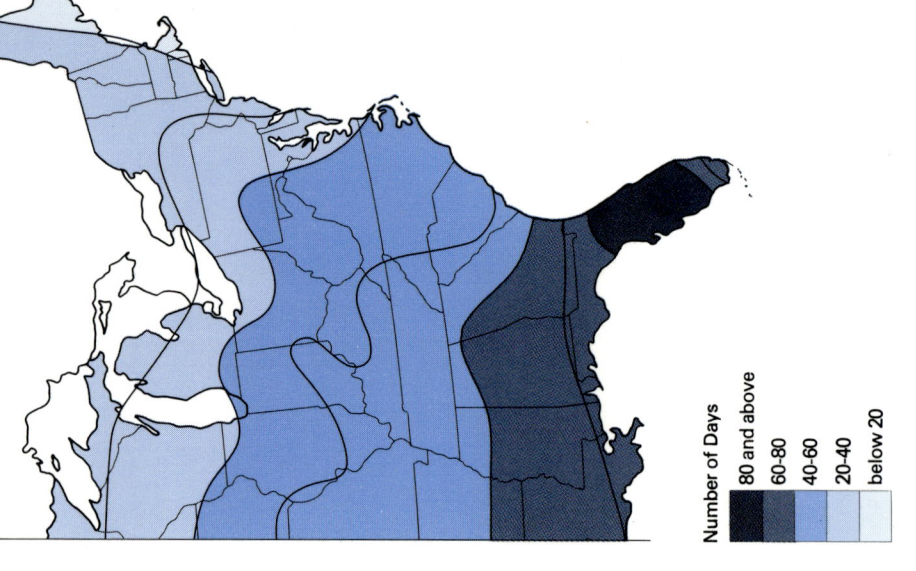

Figure 5.22. Average Number of Days with Thunderstorms

Number of Days
- 80 and above
- 60-80
- 40-60
- 20-40
- below 20

Because thunderstorm development and frequency is enhanced by (1) atmospheric instability that is linked to high surface temperatures, (2) atmospheric moisture that supplies the latent energy requirements, and (3) some triggering device to start the convection process, thunderstorms occur more frequently in regions of warm temperatures and high humidities. North Carolina's climate is conducive to thunderstorm development and the state experiences violent local storms forty to fifty days each year. For the United States, Florida and the Gulf Coast lead in the number of days with thunderstorms. Here, seventy to ninety days per year with thunderstorms is normal. In the northern states and along the West Coast, thunderstorm activity drops off because of colder temperatures over land and coastal waters. North Carolina's pattern of thunderstorm activity shows fewest storms off the northeast coast where coastal waters also are cooler. Inland, thunderstorms are more frequent, increasing to fifty days as the Mountains are approached. In the Mountains, the higher frequency of storm activity (all types) and the triggering supplied by mountain and frontal slopes results in the most thunderous area to be found in the state (Figure 5.22).

Hurricanes In the latter half of the year, the United States is visited by hurricanes. Originating over tropical oceans as small cyclones, under favorable conditions hurricanes become large, intense storm systems. Their winds exceed seventy-five miles per hour and spiral counterclockwise around an "eye" of very low pressure. Sustained by the ocean that breeds them, these storms are driven by the heat released from condensing water vapor. Covering tens of thousands of square miles, hurricanes move slowly and deliberately, at speeds between fifteen and fifty miles per hour, delivering prodigious amounts of precipitation to areas over which they pass. Moving out of the tropics, hurricanes of the Atlantic Ocean generally invade the Gulf of Mexico, or veer northward toward the middle latitudes, occasionally penetrating the continent, or skirting the coastline as far north as New England. Hurricanes are sea monsters and diminish in intensity as they move inland and away from their source of energy. Although capable of great destruction, hurricanes nevertheless benefit the southeastern states to a substantial degree. As the eastern states are subject to periodic summer droughts, the vast amounts of water delivered to this region by these giant tropical storms have served more than once to alleviate or terminate the disastrous effects of drought conditions. However, hurricanes are killer storms, and their long-range benefits are obscured by the more obvious death, destruction, and damage accompanying them. On the average, the Atlantic Ocean generates six hurricanes a year, but as many as eleven in one year have been observed. North Carolina has experienced twelve especially disastrous hurricanes since 1900. Cape Hatteras, extending as it does into the ocean, is affected by hurricanes more than any other area of North Carolina (Figure 5.23). Its low-lying sandy surface is especially vulnerable to the combined effects of high winds, high tides, and flooding associated with these storms.

Source: Glenn T. Trewartha, Arthur H. Robinson, and Edwin H. Hammond, eds., *Elements of Geography*, 5th ed. (New York: McGraw-Hill Book Co., 1967).

Tornadoes Tornadoes are the most destructive storms that occur. Associated with thunderstorm activity and hurricanes, tornadoes are violently rotating funnels of air that hang from storm clouds. Caused by extreme instability in the atmosphere, tornadoes are comprised of winds whose velocities can only be surmised as no instrument can withstand their force. It is estimated that tornadic winds may reach three hundred to five hundred miles per hour. When the funnel of a tornado reaches to the ground, debris is sucked into this rapidly whirling column of air and its color changes from a shadowy white to an ominous black. Few things can survive the fury of a tornado. Fortunately, as these storms average only three hundred to four hundred yards in width, and move at relatively low speeds, their effects are localized. Their paths average four miles in length, and seldom exceed ten miles, although one storm traveled for three hundred miles. Although they often appear in families, tornadoes usually occur singly. In 1925, one tornado was responsible for 689 persons killed, for 1,890 persons injured, and for over $16 million in damages to property.

North Carolina is fortunate to be located outside the main tornado paths. Of the 240 tornadoes recorded in the United States each year, our state experiences, on the average, only 3. Compared to Texas, Oklahoma, and Kansas, where 25 to 27 storms occur annually, or to our sister states along the Gulf of Mexico, which average 7 to 8 tornadoes annually, we are indeed fortunate to receive so few deadly storms. Although tornadoes may occur during any month of the year, in North Carolina, the months of greatest tornado frequency are March, April, and May. Most tornadoes occur in the afternoons and evenings, and in the southern Piedmont region. Seldom have they been reported in the Mountains or along the coast. Normally, North Carolina can expect at least one death per year from tornadoes.

AIR QUALITY

Although the ambient (surrounding) air throughout the larger portion of the state is of a relatively high quality, several areas are experiencing difficulties in maintaining a level compatible with public health and welfare requirements. The difficulty results from two principal factors: (1) high levels of emission related principally to the extensive use of coal as an energy source and high densities of automobile traffic in urbanized areas, and (2) meteorological conditions unfavorable for the rapid dispersion of air pollutants in the Piedmont and Mountain regions.

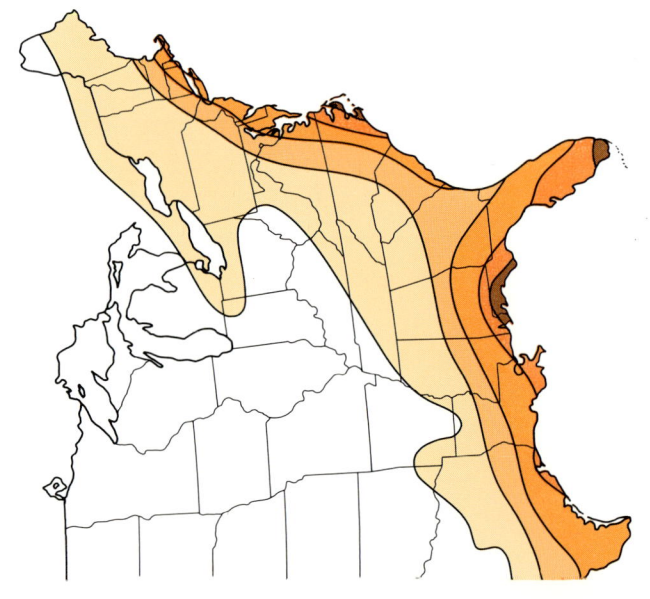

Figure 5.23. Destruction Caused by Tropical Storms, 1901-1955

Number of Destructive Storms
- 20 and above
- 15-20
- 10-15
- 5-10
- 0-5

Source: U.S Department of Commerce, *Climates of the States*, 1970.

Figure 5.24. Total Pollutants Emitted in N.C., 1970

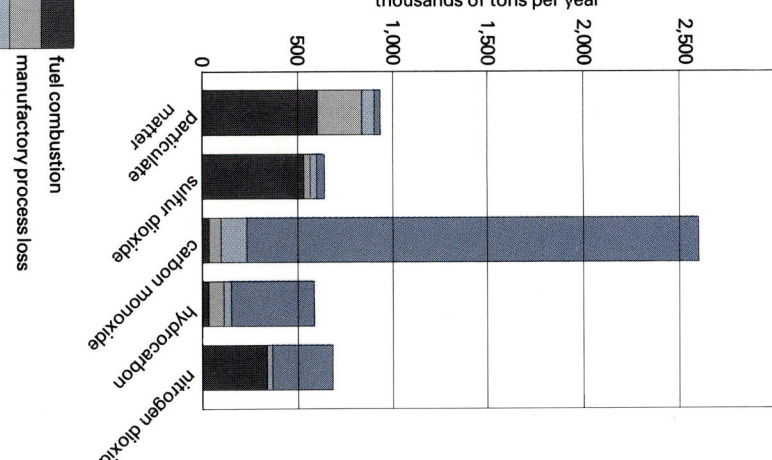

Source: N.C. Department of Natural and Economic Resources, *The North Carolina Plan for Implementing National Air Quality Standards*, 1970.

Figure 5.25. Air Quality Control Regions in N.C.

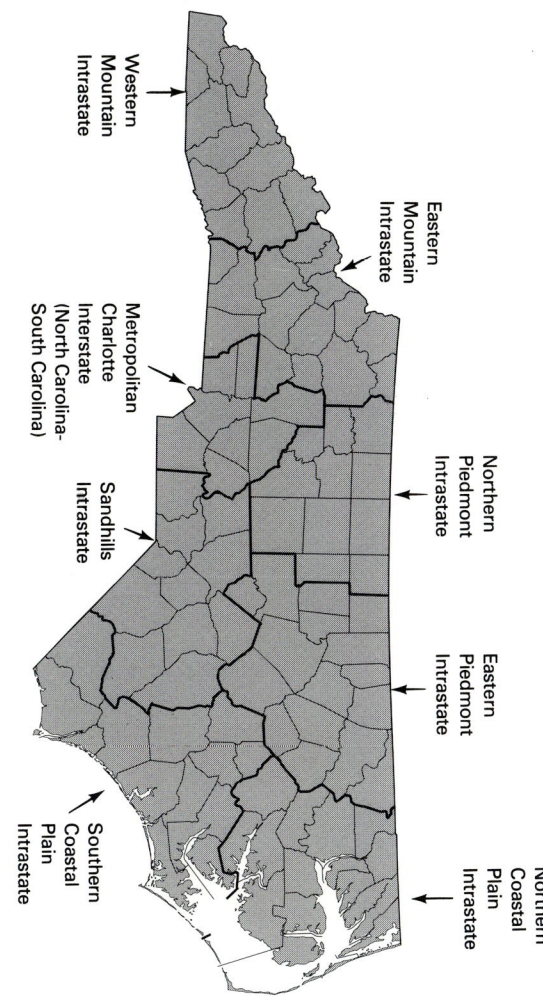

Source: N.C. Department of Natural and Economic Resources, *The North Carolina Plan for Implementing National Air Quality Standards*, 1970.

Air Pollution Emissions

Almost all human activity results in some form of air pollution, either directly or indirectly. Every house, automobile, truck, bus, factory, refuse disposal, and power plant is polluting the open air. As shown in Figure 5.24, North Carolina's air pollution derived from four types of emission in 1970: fuel combustion, industrial process, refuse disposal, and transportation. Of these, fuel combustion and transportation were by far the most important emission sources. They accounted for 94 percent of all carbon monoxide, 99 percent of the nitrogen dioxides, 95 percent of all sulfur dioxide, 75 percent of all hydrocarbons, and 64 percent of all particulates. Most of the state's fuel combustion is from the burning of coal by thermoelectric power plants.

For purposes of monitoring air quality, all of North Carolina has been divided into eight air quality control regions shown in Figure 5.25. Of these regions, one, Metropolitan Charlotte, is interstate. Figure 5.26 shows estimated emissions for each of these regions. Higher levels of emission are clearly associated with the Piedmont. Of these, the Metropolitan Charlotte area, with an annual emission of 285 tons per square mile in the North Carolina counties, is the region where the greatest effort is required to reduce or control emissions.

Dispersion of Pollutants

The earth's atmosphere is continually in motion, dispersing or scattering air pollutants from areas of emission. In urbanized and industrialized areas, emissions are characteristically high and the dispersion of pollutants vertically and horizontally results in a dilution of pollutants. There are upper limits on the dispersion capacity of the atmosphere. These limits are a function of meteorological conditions and thus vary over space and through time. The most important of these characteristics are horizontal wind speed and vertical turbulence. Unfortunately, much of North Carolina lies in an area where dispersion capability is limited.

The Piedmont and Mountain regions are characterized by a high frequency of temperature inversion and frequent stagnating migratory high-pressure cells called *anticyclones* that limit vertical mixing. Under normal conditions, temperature decreases as altitude increases for several miles above the earth's surface. When these conditions exist, air near the ground is heated and rises carrying pollutants. This upward-moving air is replaced by cooler, cleaner air from above. At night, the ground cools more rapidly than the air to cool the air near the earth's surface. Often this reverses the usual daytime *vertical temperature distribution*. Within the first

Figure 5.26. Emissions of Pollutants per Square Mile by N.C. Air Quality Control Regions, 1970

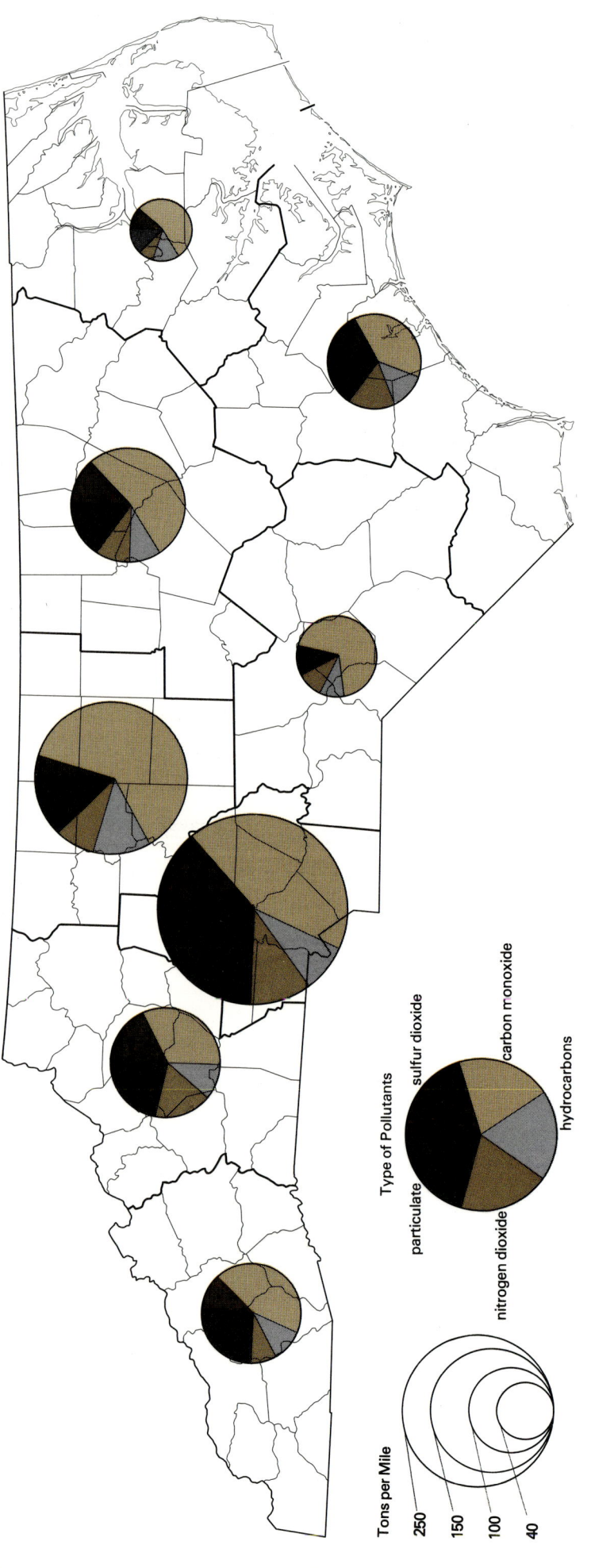

Source: N.C. Department of Natural and Economic Resources, *The North Carolina Plan for Implementing National Air Quality Standards,* 1970.

thousand feet or so, the temperature may then increase with height, a condition referred to as a *temperature inversion.* In this situation, instead of rising, the cool, pollutant-laden surface air is held near the ground by the warmer air above it. Nighttime surface inversions usually dissipate by midmorning. As shown in Figure 5.27, during the fall season the Piedmont and Mountain regions of the state experience, on the average, surface inversions 40 to 45 percent of the time. (In the Coastal Plain, low-level inversions are far less common.) They occur most commonly during clear nights when ground temperatures and air near the ground are cooled.

Inversions higher in the atmosphere may be more widespread and longer lasting. They are generally associated with anticyclones where the air is subsiding and becoming warmer. Often this air does not subside all the way to the ground, but stops at two thousand feet or so to create an inversion condition that traps cooler air with its load of pollutants below. Thus, during periods when these conditions persist for several days, pollutants accumulate in or near the surface. The intensity of the problem increases until the anticyclonic condition no longer exists. As illustrated in Figure 5.28, North Carolina lies in an area that experiences the highest incidence of stagnating anticyclones in the eastern United States. This high frequency results from the domination of the area by the western extension of the Bermuda High. As shown in Figure 5.28, during the thirty-year period from 1936 to 1965, air mass stagnation, extending over four or more days each, was noted eighty times in the Piedmont and Mountain regions. The longer the anticyclonic condition persists, the greater the pollution of the atmosphere. Thus the occurrence of stagnating anticyclones extending seven or more days on six separate occasions during the same thirty-year period is particularly alarming.

Dispersion problems resulting from these inversions are compounded by low horizontal wind speeds. Pollutants build up near their source only if they can move neither upward nor horizontally. Nighttime inversions are generally associated with low wind speed. As illustrated by Figure 5.29, the Piedmont and Mountain regions have nighttime wind speed of less than seven miles per hour 70 percent of the time. Upper level inversions associated with anticyclones are also characteristically accompanied by low horizontal wind speeds.

The ridge and valley character of the Mountain area presents another dispersion problem. When the slopes and mountaintops cool at night, mountain winds result and the cool air flows into the valley producing a strong inversion condition. The problem is compounded by ridges that limit horizontal dispersion, consequently, the winds carry pollutants through valleys like a pipe. As a result, high concentrations of pollutants may extend for twenty or more miles from the sources along valleys. Thus these natural conditions and the traditional location of industries in valley bottoms make the Mountain region particularly susceptible to air pollution problems. Clearly, then, the quantity of pollutants that can safely be put into the air in the Mountains and Piedmont is very limited.

Dispersion capability varies considerably through time, both seasonally and daily with meteorological conditions. Although day-to-day variations in the production of air pollutants are not very great, day-to-day variations in their concentration can be considerable. In Table 5.1, seven meteorological variables basic to the dispersion of air pollutants are integrated on a seasonal basis for the Metropolitan Charlotte area. Winter, fall, and summer appear to have lower dispersion capability and thus are periods when air pollution potential is highest. Day-night variations in dispersion are also substantial. As shown earlier, characteristic nighttime temperature inversions combined with low wind speeds result in a much lower nighttime potential for the dispersion of air pollutants than do day periods.

Ambient Air Quality

Of primary concern to everyone are the types and concentrations of pollutants in the ambient air, for they affect man's health, property, and the overall quality of his environment. In accordance with provisions of the Clean Air Act, as amended on 31 December 1970, the administrator of the Environmental Protection Agency (EPA) has published proposed national primary and secondary ambient air quality standards for six pollutants as shown in Table 5.2. The standards are designed to indicate thresholds above which the air is injurious to the health and welfare of people. Primary ambient

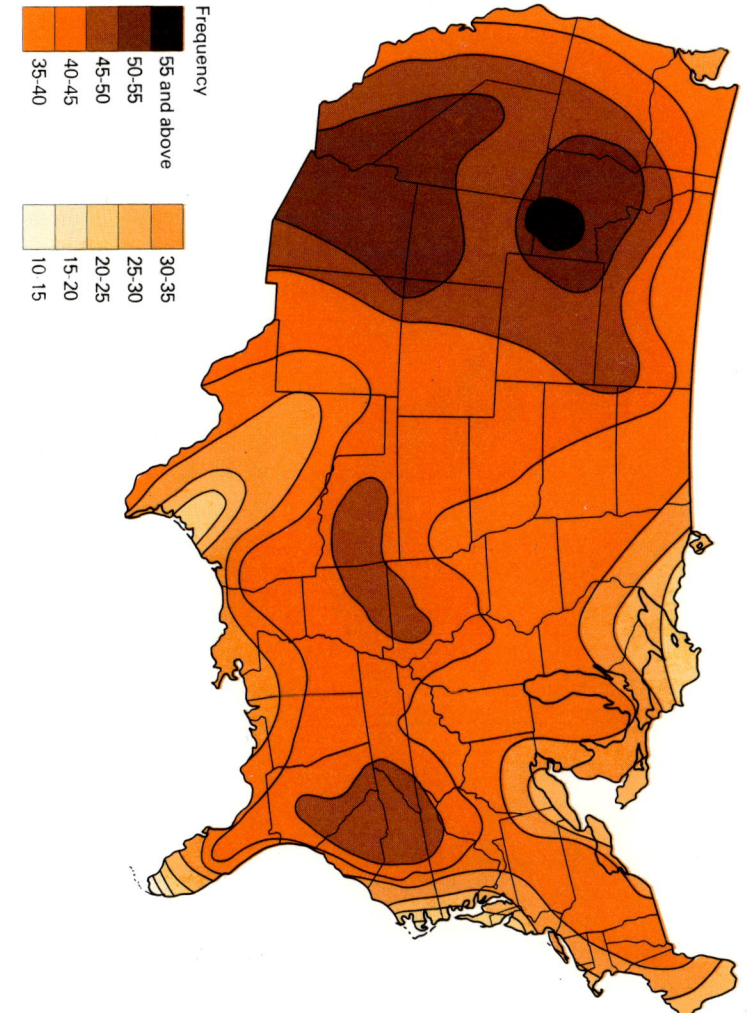

Figure 5.27. Average Daily Percentage of Hours of Low-Level Inversion during the Fall Season

Frequency
55 and above
50-55
45-50
40-45
35-40
30-35
25-30
20-25
15-20
10-15

Source: D. H. Pack, "Meteorology of Air Pollution," Science 146 (Nov. 1964) 119.

standards are designed to protect human health while secondary standards are designed to protect against effects on water, soil, plants, material, weather, visibility, and personal comfort and well-being. Each state was required by this amendment to submit an implementation plan that would result in an ambient air quality compatible with EPA standards by 1975.

Air quality is monitored at 165 stations throughout the state by the North Carolina Department of Air and Water Resources. Figures 5.30 and 5.31 indicate stations where the recommended standards were exceeded in 1973. As shown in Figure 5.30, the geometric annual mean of particulate levels exceeded EPA standards in widely scattered areas across the state. Except for two stations in port areas along the coast, high readings were restricted to the Mountain and Piedmont areas of the state. The high readings in the Mountains are largely a function of a low dispersion capacity, while the high readings in the Piedmont result from greater industrialization and urbanization coupled with a similarly low dispersion capacity. The high concentrations resulted from a variety of reasons. In several instances the location of sampling stations was very near such polluting sources as a racetrack or construction site. In other areas, high readings were related to power plants reflecting their high levels of emissions. In still other areas, stations were located in industrial areas.

Figure 5.28. Stagnating Anticyclones in Eastern U.S., 1936-1965

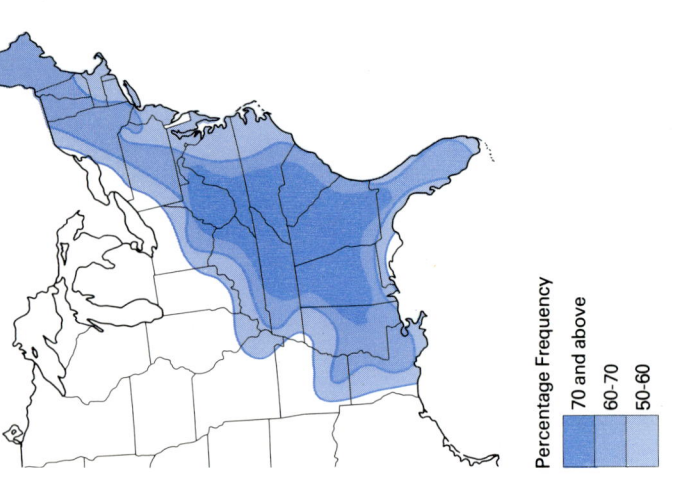

Frequency of Stagnating Anticyclones
4 Days or More between 1936 and 1965
- 70 and above
- 60-70
- 50-60
- 40-50
- 30-40
- 20-30
- 10-20
- 0-10

Total Number of Days of Stagnation between 1936 and 1965
- 350 and above
- 300-350
- 250-300
- 200-250
- 150-200
- 100-150
- 50-100
- 0-50

Figure 5.29. Percentage Frequency of Nighttime Winds Seven Miles per Hour or Less

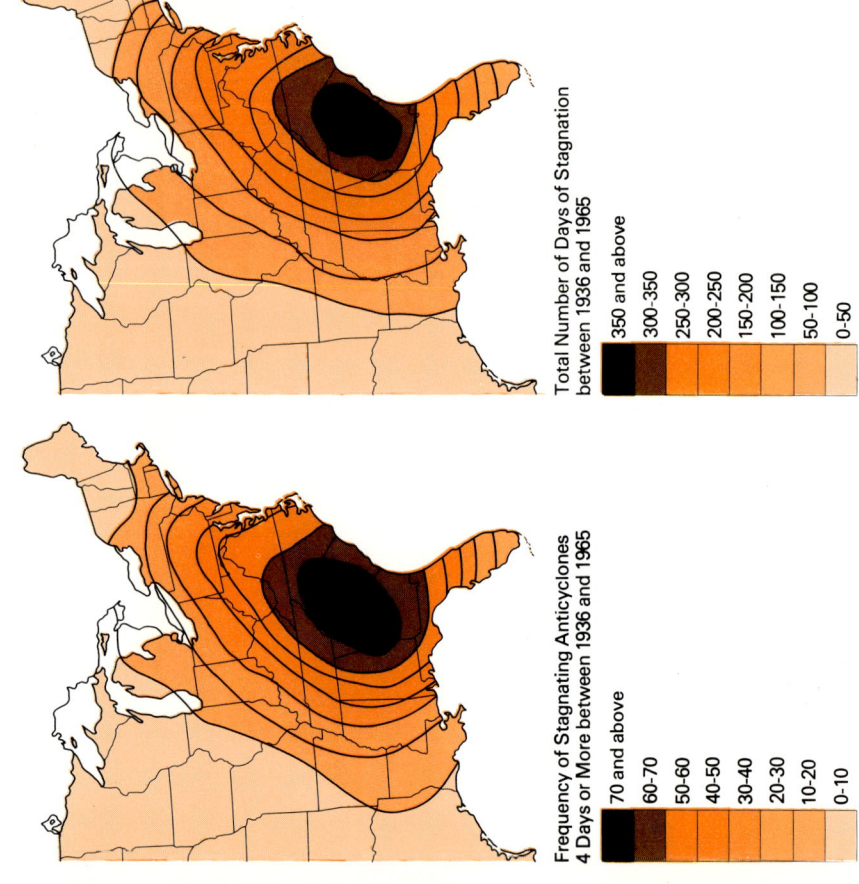

Percentage Frequency
- 70 and above
- 60-70
- 50-60

Source: *An Air Appraisal Report of South Carolina,* 1968.

Figure 5.30. Stations in N.C. Recording Annual Geometric Mean of Particulates Exceeding EPA Standards, 1973

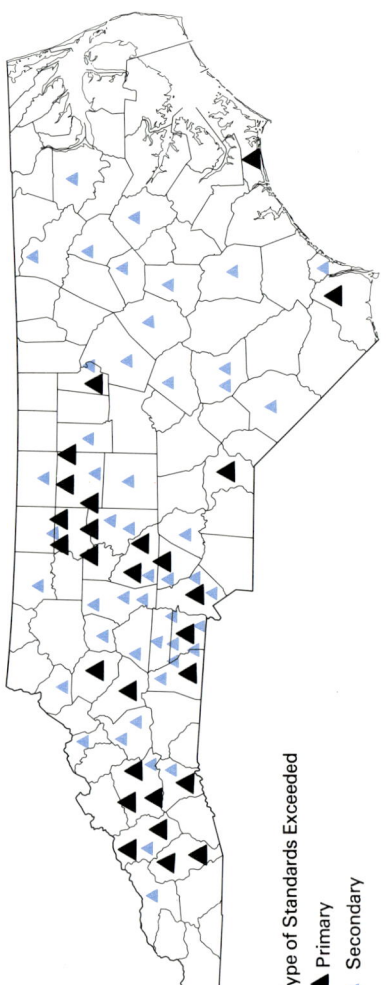

Type of Standards Exceeded
- ▲ Primary
- ▲ Secondary

Note: Data taken from the National Aeromatic Data Bank Standards.

Nitrogen dioxide concentrations exceeded the primary standards at three stations, Charlotte, Durham, and Greensboro; ozone concentrations exceeded primary standards at two stations, Charlotte and Asheville; and sulfur dioxide and carbon monoxide concentrations exceeded primary standards only at stations located in Charlotte.

Climate—Richard J. Kopec
Air Quality—James W. Clay

Figure 5.31. Sites in N.C. Recording NO₂, SO₂, CO O₃ Exceeding Primary EPA Standards in 1973

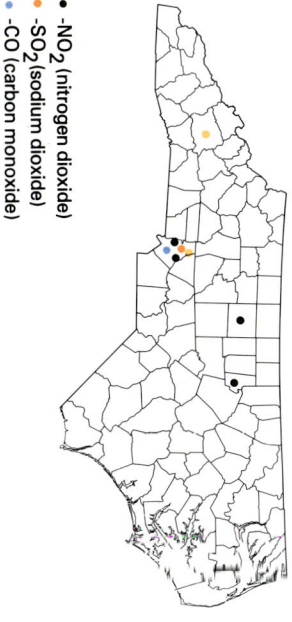

- • -NO₂ (nitrogen dioxide)
- • -SO₂ (sodium dioxide)
- • -CO (carbon monoxide)
- • -O₃ (ozone)

Note: Data taken from the National Aeromatic Data Bank Standards.

SELECTED REFERENCES

Environmental Protection Agency. "Requirements for Preparation, Adoption, and Submittal of Implementation Plans." *Federal Register* 36, no. 158, pt. 2 (August 1971).

Hardy, Albert V. "Climate of North Carolina." In *Climates of the States. Climatography of the United States*, no. 60-31. 1960. Rev. ed. Silver Spring, Md.: Environmental Data Service, Environmental Science Services Administration, U.S. Department of Commerce, 1970.

Hardy, Albert V. *Low Temperature Probabilities in North Carolina*. Agricultural Experiment Station Bulletin 423. Raleigh: North Carolina State University, 1964.

Hardy, Albert V., and Hardy, Jessie D. *Weather and Climate in North Carolina*. Agricultural Experiment Station Bulletin 395. Rev. Raleigh: North Carolina State University, 1971.

Hardy, Albert V.; Carney, Charles B.; and Marshall, Henry V., Jr. *Climate of North Carolina Research Stations*. Agricultural Experiment Station Bulletin 433. Raleigh: North Carolina State University, 1967.

Hosler, Charles R. "Climatological Estimates of Diffusion Conditions in the United States." *Nuclear Safety* 5, no. 2 (Winter 1963-64).

Hosler, Charles R. "Low-level Inversion Frequency in the Contiguous United States." *Monthly Weather Review* 89 (September 1961): 319-39.

Table 5.1. Summary of Factors Affecting Dispersion of Air Pollutants in Metrolina

Season	Frequency of Inversions (% total hours)	Ventilation (Mixing Depth X Wind Speed)	Stability (Difference between Max. & Min. Temp.) (1936-65)	Number of Stagnation Cases Extending over Days	Monthly Average Precip. (inches)	Wind Speed (mph)
Winter	43 (4.0)	4,513 (4.0)	18.3 (4.0)	7 (1.0)	11.27 (2.6)	8.4 (1.8)
Spring (2.9)	32 (1.0)	10,852 (1.0)	21.3 (1.0)	17 (2.0)	10.70 (2.3)	8.8 (1.0)
Summer (1.4)	33 (1.3)	10,863 (1.0)	19.6 (2.2)	19 (2.2)	13.94 (4.0)	7.2 (4.0)
Fall (2.5)	40 (3.2)	8,171 (2.3)	20.0 (2.7)	37 (4.0)	8.31 (1.0)	7.6 (3.3)
Annual average per season (2.7)	37	8,600	19.8	20	44.22	7.9

Source: James W. Clay and Douglas M. Orr, Jr., *Metrolina Atlas* (Chapel Hill: University of N.C. Press, 1972).

Table 5.2. Minimum Ambient Air Quality Standards and Levels of Adverse Effect on Health and Welfare

Pollutant	Proposed Federal Standards		According to Federal Criteria Levels of Adverse Effects	
	Primary	Secondary	Health	Welfare
Particulates (Micrograms/M₃) Annual geometric mean	75	60	80 (Increased death rate, persons over 50)	60 (Corrosion of steel panels)
Maximum 24-hour concentration	260	150	200 (Increased illness in industrial workers)	150 (Reduces visibility to as low as five miles)
Sulfur oxides (Micrograms/M₃) Annual arithmetic mean	80	60	115 (Increased death from bronchitis)	85 (Plant injury, excessive leaf drop)
Maximum 24-hour concentration	365	260	300 (Increased hospital admissions for respiratory disease, persons over 50)	285 (Reduces visibility to as low as five miles)
Carbon monoxide (Micrograms/M₃) Maximum 8-hour concentration	10	10	11.5 (Driving reaction impaired. Heart patients die after long exposure.)	—
Maximum 1-hour concentration	40	40	58	—
Photochemical oxidants (Micrograms/M₃) Maximum 1-hour concentration	160	160	130 (Impairs performance of student athletes)	100 (After four hours, leaf injury to sensitive plants, like petunias)
Hydrocarbons (Micrograms/M₃) Maximum 3-hour concentration, 6-0 A.M.	160	160	—	—
Nitrogen dioxide (Micrograms/M₃) Annual arithmetic mean	100	100	113 (Increased bronchitis in infants and schoolchildren)	—
Maximum 24-hour concentration	250	250	—	225 (Level of human odor perception)

Source: James W. Clay and Douglas M. Orr, Jr., *Metrolina Atlas* (Chapel Hill: University of N.C. Press, 1972).

6. Physiography, Geology, and Mineral Resources

STEPHEN G. CONRAD
P. ALBERT CARPENTER III
WILLIAM F. WILSON

PHYSIOGRAPHY

North Carolina extends across three physiographic provinces that are generally present in the eastern part of the United States: the Coastal Plain, the Piedmont, and the Blue Ridge. These provinces and their major physiographic features are shown in Figure 6.1.

The Coastal Plain

The Coastal Plain is bounded on the east by the Atlantic Ocean and on the west by the higher lands of the Piedmont. The demarcation between the two provinces is the "fall line," or a zone where the soft, sedimentary rocks give way to the harder, crystalline rocks. The Coastal Plain includes about 45 percent of the area of the state and varies in width from 100 to 140 miles. It rises in elevation gradually from sea level at the coastline to nearly 500 feet above sea level in the sandhills district. Except near the edge of the Piedmont and at the major rivers, relief is slight, resulting in slow-flowing streams and poor drainage.

A geological controversy concerning the Coastal Plain province relates to the number, nature, and age of a series of coastal terraces that rise in a step-like manner from east to west. Ideally, each terrace should be separated by a scarp (steep slope) that marks the location of the shoreline at the time the terrace was formed. However, practically nowhere is there a complete sequence of terraces, for development of some of the younger terraces may have cut away some of the older ones.

Most geologists who have studied these North Carolina terraces feel that they are marine in origin, having formed during high sea levels during interglacial or intraglacial time. Geologists recognize six terraces illustrated schematically in Figure 6.2. The scarps are low topographic features that are most easily recognized in the vicinity of major streams, such as near Fayetteville on the Cape Fear River, in the vicinity of Goldsboro on the Neuse River, and near Scotland Neck, in Halifax County, on the Roanoke River.

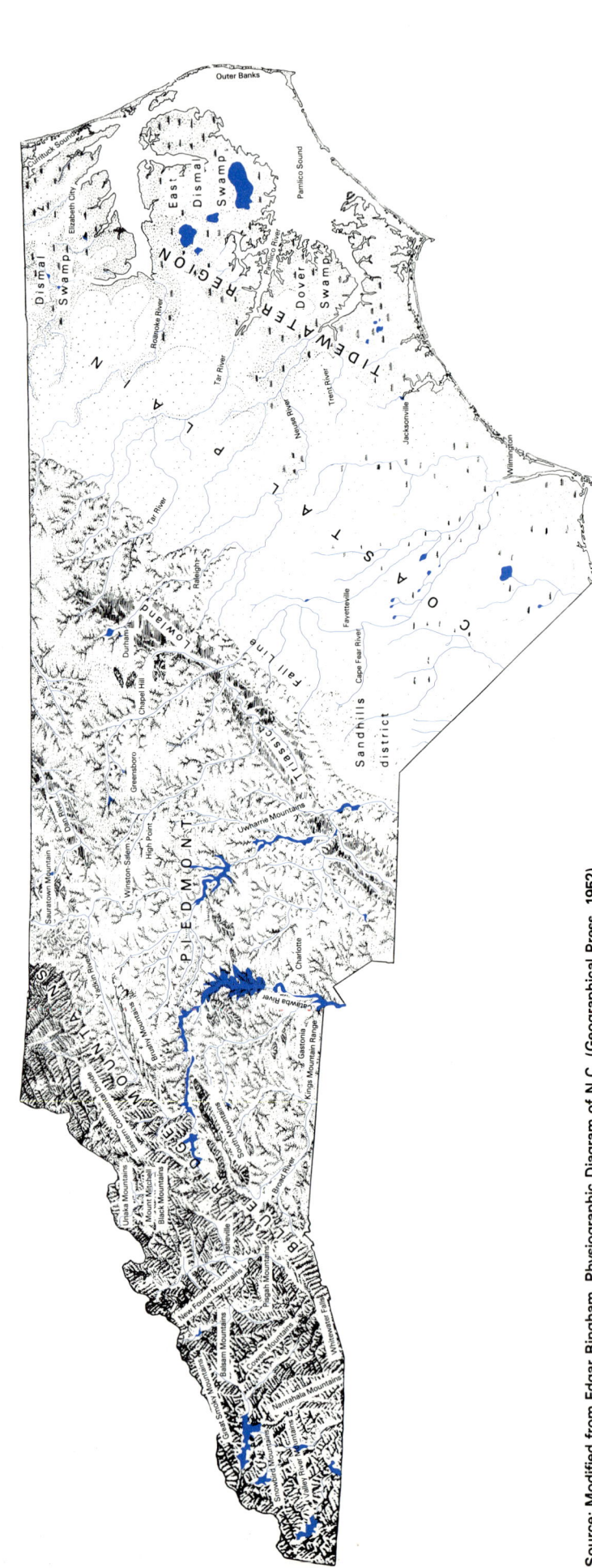

Figure 6.1. The Physiographic Regions of N.C.

Source: Modified from Edgar Bingham, Physiographic Diagram of N.C. (Geographical Press, 1952).

Figure 6.2. Schematic Illustration of N.C. Marine Terraces

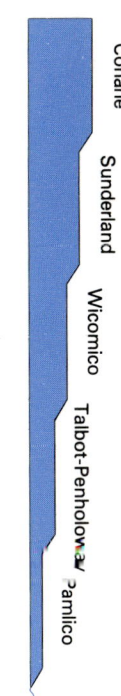

Coharie Sunderland Wicomico Talbot-Penholoway Pamlico

The Coastal Plain can be divided into two regions in accordance with relative elevation and drainage. The Outer Coastal Plain, or Tidewater region, lies closer to the ocean, is extremely flat, averages less than twenty feet above sea level and contains large swamps and lakes indicative of poor drainage conditions. The Inner Coastal Plain lies farther inland, is higher in elevation and is more dissected and better drained.

A series of shallow, elliptical depressions numbering in the thousands called "Carolina Bays," apparently because of the common occurrence in them of the evergreen bay tree, represent another interesting physiographic development in the Coastal Plain (Figure 6.3). There has also been considerable controversy as to the origin of these depressions, and even today geologists are not in agreement as to their origin.

The bays characteristically have sand rims, are located on sandy terraces, are nearly filled with peat, and are elongated in a northwest-southeast direction. They are most prominent in the southern part of the Coastal Plain.

Another significant physiographic development in the Coastal Plain is a chain of islands that extend along practically the entire coastline of the state, the "barrier islands," or as more commonly called, the Outer Banks (Figure 6.4). These islands are separated from the mainland by a fringe of salt marshes and lagoons. The islands are experiencing increasing development that is threatening their stability. Development schemes and dune stabilization have produced undesirable changes in the geomorphic and ecological processes that create and maintain these islands.

The Piedmont

The Piedmont province, lying between the Coastal Plain and the Blue Ridge Mountains, is bounded on the east by a fall line and on the west by the Blue Ridge scarp. The scarp is a prominent topographic feature generally thought to have resulted from displacement associated with faulting. In North Carolina the scarp varies in height from about 1,700 feet near the North Carolina-Virginia border to about 2,500 feet near Blowing Rock. The Piedmont is about equal in size with the Coastal Plain, occupying about 45 percent of the area of the state. Elevations range from 300 to 600 feet above sea level along the eastern border and gradually rise to the west to about 1,500 feet above sea level at the foot of the Blue Ridge scarp.

The Piedmont is an ancient erosion surface characterized by gently rolling hills with a few hundred feet of local relief. Standing above this surface are mountainous remnants of more erosion resistant rock, or monadnocks. These monadnocks are present throughout the Piedmont, but the more prominent ones are in the Uwharrie Mountains in Montgomery and Randolph counties, the Sauratown Mountains in Stokes and Surry counties, the Kings Mountain range in Cleveland and Gaston counties, the Brushy Mountains in Wilkes County, and the South Mountains in Burke and Rutherford counties.

The rolling topography with well-rounded hills and long low ridges, for which the Piedmont is noted, is the result of streams acting on rocks of unequal resistance. As shown by Figure 6.1., the northern part of the Piedmont is drained by the Dan River and its tributaries. The Tar, Neuse, and Cape Fear rivers drain that part of the Piedmont south of the Dan River drainage and east of the Yadkin River valley. The Yadkin, Catawba, and Broad rivers drain the southwestern half of the Piedmont.

The Blue Ridge Mountains

The Blue Ridge scarp rises abruptly 1,500 to 2,500 feet above the Piedmont to mark the division between the Piedmont and Blue Ridge provinces. In North Carolina, the Blue Ridge is about two hundred miles long and varies from fifteen to fifty miles wide. It contains an area of about six thousand square miles, or about 12 percent of the area of the state, and extends from the Blue Ridge scarp on the east into Tennessee on the west.

The Blue Ridge is a highly dissected mountain plateau bounded by two mountain chains (Figure 6.1). On the east are mountains that range from 3,000 to 4,000 feet in elevation, with a few peaks reaching almost 6,000 feet. The Unaka and Great Smoky Mountains are the western border and elevations range from 3,000 to 6,000 feet. Between the two bounding mountain chains are a number of cross ridges and broad intermontane valley floors that give the area its rugged mountain character.

The most prominent cross ridge is the Black Mountains, extending some fifteen miles from where it leaves the Blue Ridge Mountains and containing a dozen peaks that exceed 6,000 feet in elevation. Mount Mitchell is included in this group and has an elevation of 6,684 feet, the highest peak east of the Mississippi River. Other cross ridges from northeast to southwest are the Pisgah Mountains, New Found Mountains, Balsam Mountains, Cowee Mountains, Nantahala Mountains, Snowbird Mountains, and the Valley River Mountains.

The Blue Ridge in western North Carolina is the culminating region of the Appalachian mountain range and contains the greatest masses, the highest elevations, and the most rugged topography in the Appalachian Mountain System. Within the area are forty-three peaks that exceed 6,000 feet in elevation and eighty-two peaks that are between 5,000 and 6,000 feet.

Most of the rivers have an even gradient, but where some of them leave the Blue Ridge, spectacular waterfalls and cascades are present. The most notable of these are Toxaway Falls and Whitewater Falls in Transylvania and Jackson counties. The crest of the Blue Ridge Mountains marks the Eastern Continental Divide. Thus precipitation and streams to the west of this crest eventually drain into the Gulf of Mexico, while those streams on the east of this crest drain to the Atlantic Ocean.

GEOLOGY

All major classes of rocks—*sedimentary, igneous,* and *metamorphic*—are common to North Carolina. Sedimentary rocks have their origin mostly as nearshore deposition of marine sediments to form such rocks as shale, sandstone, and limestone. They are largely derived by erosion of older rocks. The youngest rocks are at the top and the older rocks successively lower. The geological time scale, Table 6.1, gives the traditional terminology for rocks of varying ages. In the North Carolina Coastal Plain, surface rocks represent deposition during the Cenozoic era. They consist largely of loosely consolidated to unconsolidated sediments: clays, sands, gravels, limestones, and marls.

Figure 6.3. Carolina Bays

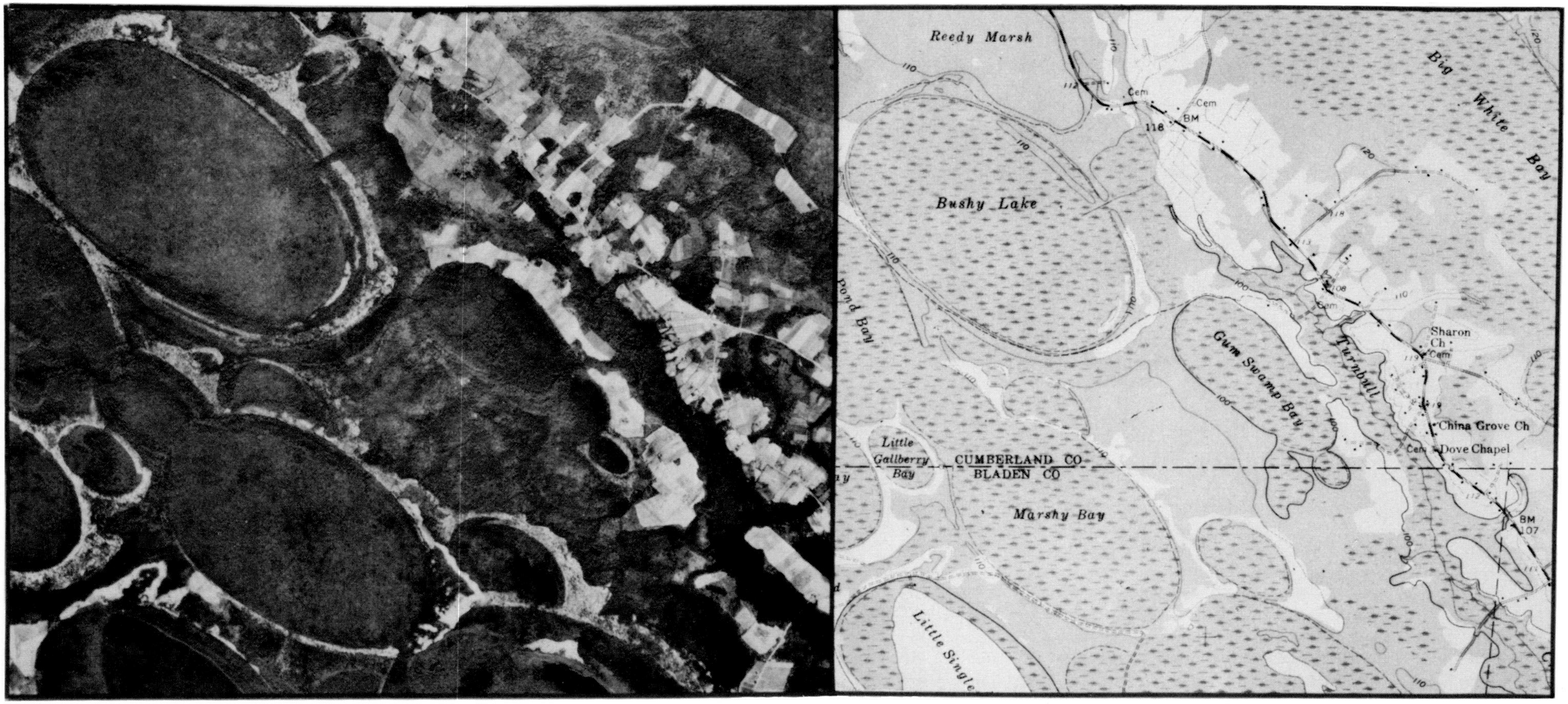

Figure 6.4. Location Map of Major Coastline Features of the Outer Banks Barrier Chain of N.C.

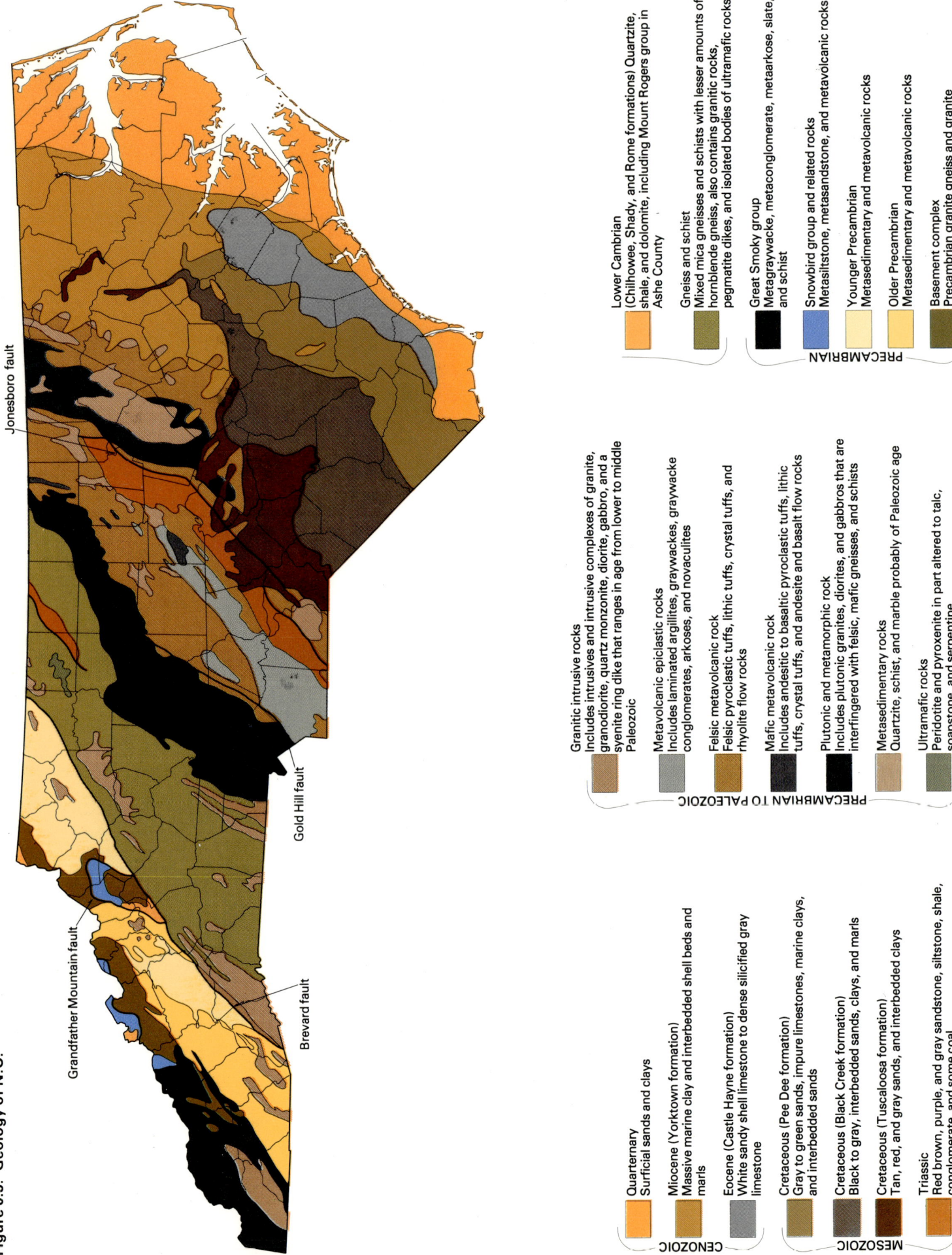

Figure 6.5. Geology of N.C.

the state near the northern boundary. Like the three major physiographic units, the major geological belts are those of the Coastal Plain, the Piedmont, and the Blue Ridge.

Coastal Plain Geology

The Coastal Plain of North Carolina is part of a much larger accumulation of Mesozoic and Cenozoic sediments that are present along the east coast of North America from southern Florida to the Grand Banks of Newfoundland. The sediments form a wedge-shaped mass that thickens from a feather edge along the fall line to 10,000 feet at Cape Hatteras. As shown in Figure 6.6, these sediments overlie older basement rocks that are similar to those found in the Piedmont.

In North Carolina, these early Cenozoic rocks crop out in broad belts that roughly parallel the coastline. The older of these formations, of Cretaceous age, crop out along the western edge of the Coastal Plain and become progressively buried deeper toward the coast (Figure 6.7). The younger Cenozoic rocks, of Tertiary (Figure 6.8) and Quaternary age, crop out southeast of the Cretaceous formations and are buried less deeply near the coast.

Cretaceous System
The outcropping Cretaceous formations are from oldest to youngest, the Tuscaloosa, Black Creek, and Pee Dee formations (Figure 6.7). The Tuscaloosa formation crops out mainly in the southeastern part of the state south of the Neuse River in Harnett, Moore, Cumberland, Hoke, Scotland, and Richmond counties. It is composed chiefly of light-colored sand and clay, with some gravel near the base of the formation. The Black Creek formation overlies the Tuscaloosa formation and crops out, or occurs near the surface in Green, Wayne, Sampson, Bladen, and Robinson counties. It is composed chiefly of beds and laminations of dark carbonaceous clays and fine to medium sands.

The Pee Dee formation overlies the Black Creek and crops out east of the Black Creek formation in Pitt, Lenoir, Duplin, Pender, and Columbus counties. It is composed of dark-gray to green glauconitic sands and clays, and locally contains impure limestone beds.

Rocks of Lower Cretaceous age are present in the subsurface throughout much of the Coastal Plain. They occur at or near the surface in Halifax County and are no doubt present in other areas within the Coastal Plain as well.

The Piedmont and Blue Ridge regions are composed of older sedimentary and volcanic rocks, many of which have been variably altered by heat and pressure associated with an earth process called *metamorphism*. As a result, the constituent minerals have been recrystallized to form new minerals aligned in a textural pattern called *foliation*. In many areas, these rocks have been intruded by igneous rocks, resulting in a complex geological pattern. Igneous rocks were once molten, but subsequently crystallized to become rock. Some igneous rocks, called *extrusive rock* (volcanic material such as ash and lava), crystallized at the surface. Others crystallize beneath the surface and are called *intrusive rock* (dikes, sills, and laccoliths). Common extrusive igneous rocks in the state include granite, diorite, gabbro, and syenite. Common extrusive rocks include tuffs, rhyolite, andesite, and basalt. Metamorphic equivalents of some common North Carolina sedimentary and igneous rocks are listed in Table 6.2.

The geology map shown in Figure 6.5 depicts the type and age of rocks found at or near the surface. The cross section, shown in Figure 6.6, schematically illustrates the surface geology. It represents an east-west profile of the state.

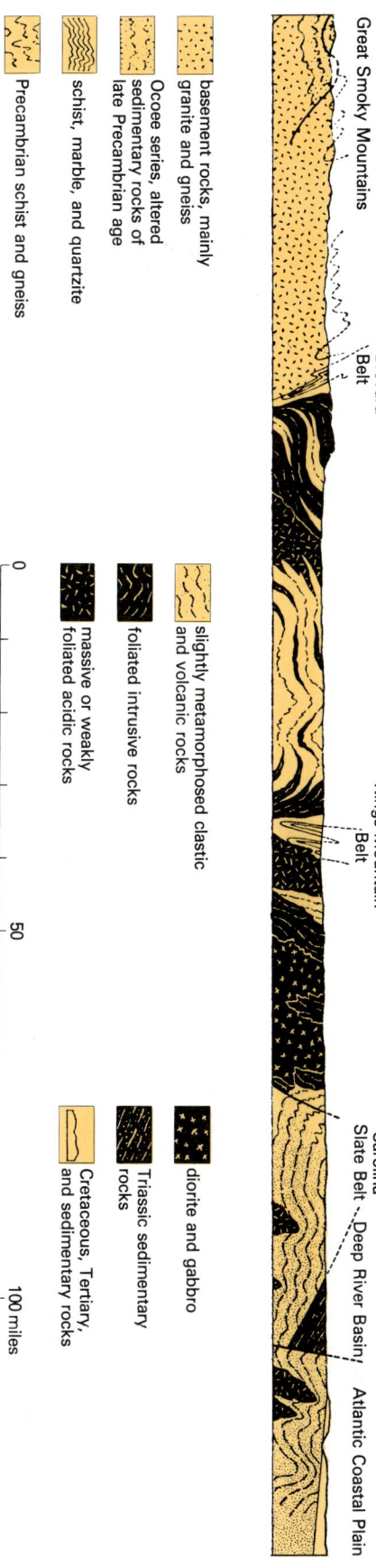

Figure 6.6. Geologic Profile of N.C.

Source: Philip B. King, *The Evolution of North America* (Princeton: Princeton University Press, 1959).

Table 6.1. Geological Time Scale for N.C.

Era	Period	Epoch	MYA*	Geologic Events in N.C.
Cenozoic	Quaternary	Recent Pleistocene Pliocene	1	Deposition of sediments in Coastal Plain and erosion of Piedmont and Appalachian mountains to their present rugged feature.
	Tertiary	Miocene	10 25	Phosphates deposited in Beaufort County. Schooley Peneplane completed and uplifted.
		Oligocene Eocene Paleocene	40 60 70	Sediments deposited. Weathering and erosion continue.
Mesozoic	Cretaceous	Upper		Formation of sediments throughout the Coastal Plain of N.C. Continued erosion of the Piedmont and Mountains.
		Lower	135	Marine sediments deposited in northern half of the Coastal Plain of N.C. Piedmont and Mountains eroded.
	Jurassic	Upper		Appalachian mountains and Piedmont plateau reduced to a peneplane known as the Fall Zone Peneplane. 1,378 feet of sediments deposited in the Cape Hatteras area of N.C.
		Middle Lower	180	Weathering and erosion of the Appalachian mountains and the Piedmont plateau.
	Triassic	Upper		Formation of the Deep River and the Dan River basins.
		Middle Lower	225	Destruction of the older rocks by weathering and erosion.
Paleozoic	Permian		270	Emplacement of granite intrusives and the formation of the Appalachian mountains accompanied by major thrust faulting.
	Pennsylvanian } Carboniferous System			Time of erosion with possible implacements of igneous intrusives.
	Mississippian		370	Time of erosion with emplacement of igneous intrusives.
	Devonian		400	Metamorphism of the slate belt rocks. Emplacement of granites and Cherryville Quartz monzonite in the western Piedmont. Long period of erosion.
	Silurian		440	Intrusion of granites. Long period of erosion.
	Ordovician		500	Taconic Revolution. Pegmatites. Intrusion of granites including Toluca Quartz monzonite. Intrusion of Periodotites. Metamorphism of older rocks. Volcanic and sedimentary rocks of Carolina Slate Belt deposited.
	Cambrian		600	Sandstone, shale, and limestone deposited.
Precambrian	Precambrian	Late		Beginning of Appalachian Geosyncline. Volcanic and sedimentary rocks formed and metamorphosed.
		Early	2,680	Sedimentary and igneous rocks formed and metamorphosed to gneisses and schists.

Source: J. L. Stuckey, *North Carolina: Its Geology and Mineral Resources* (Raleigh: N.C. Department of Conservation and Development, 1965).

*Million years ago.

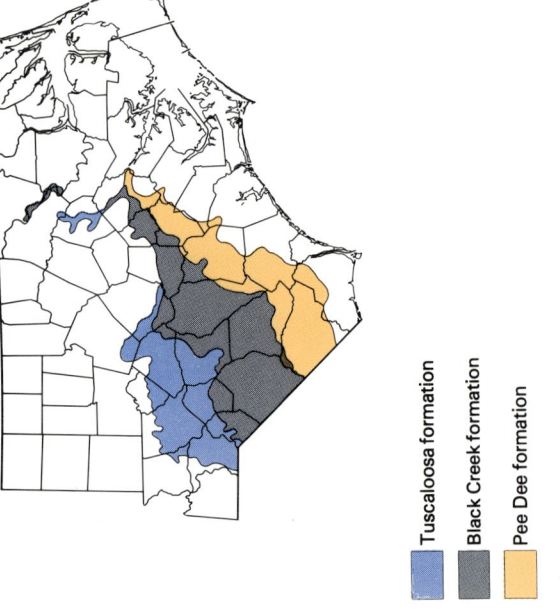

Figure 6.7. Distribution of Upper Cretaceous Rocks in N.C.

- Tuscaloosa formation
- Black Creek formation
- Pee Dee formation

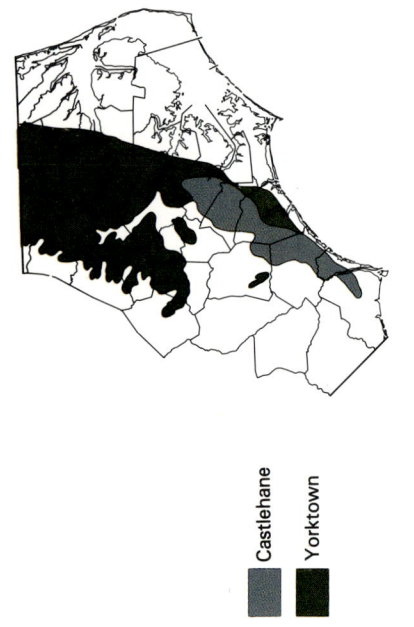

Figure 6.8. Distribution of Cenozoic Rocks in N.C.

- Castlehane
- Yorktown

Table 6.2. Principal Metamorphic Rocks

Source Material	Corresponding Metamorphic Rocks
Granite and corresponding extrusive rocks	Muscovite schist and gneiss
Shale	Phyllite
	Slate
	Phyllite
	Mica schist
Sandstone	Quartzite
Gabbro and corresponding extrusive rocks	Greenstone schists
Marls	Greenschists
	Amphibolite
Peridotite and pyroxenite	Chlorite schist
	Talc schist
Limestone and dolomite (impure)	Calcite marble
	Dolomite marble

Tertiary System

The only Tertiary formations that crop out in North Carolina are the Castle Hayne limestone of Eocene age and the Yorktown formation of Upper Miocene age, shown in Figure 6.8. Paleocene, Lower to Middle Miocene, and Oligocene sediments are present in the subsurface.

The Castle Hayne limestone is at or near the surface in a relatively narrow belt that extends through Craven, Jones, Onslow, Duplin, Pender, and New Hanover counties. It consists of marl, sand, and a distinctive indurated shell rock or shell limestone. The hard shell limestone is the only source of crushed stone in the eastern Coastal Plain region. The Castle Hayne limestone is an important aquifer in which ground waters stored and transported. The aquifer is an important source of ground water in the area.

The Yorktown formation underlies a large portion of the Coastal Plain north of the Neuse River. It varies in composition from blue massive clay to lighter-colored shell beds to sands and sandy clay.

Quaternary System

The Coastal Plain of North Carolina has a characteristic veneer of sands and clays that almost everywhere covers the older formations. These surficial deposits vary from a few feet to over forty feet thick and occur as belts ten to fifteen miles wide. As discussed earlier in this chapter, these deposits are commonly considered to be marine terraces of Pleistocene age. Each terrace is bounded on the west by a scarp that marks the presence of the shoreline at the time the terrace was formed (Figure 6.2).

Piedmont Geology

The Piedmont in North Carolina is part of the Appalachian Piedmont that lies between the Blue Ridge and the Coastal Plain from New Jersey to Alabama. At its northern extremity, the Piedmont is only 10 miles wide, but it widens to the south and reaches its maximum width of nearly 150 miles in North Carolina. The Piedmont is underlain mostly by metamorphosed crystalline rocks of late Precambrian to early Paleozoic age and intrusive rocks that range from gabbro to granite. Downfaulted basins (Triassic basins) filled with Triassic sedimentary rocks are also present. Locally, the Triassic sediments have been intruded by dikes and sills of gabbroic composition. Except along the major stream valleys, the rocks of the Piedmont are everywhere covered by a mantle of thoroughly weathered residual material, called saprolite, that in many places exceeds fifty feet in thickness.

The complex geology of the crystalline rocks of the Piedmont of North Carolina is at best only generally understood at the present time. However, because of similar rock types, structures, and areal distribution, the Piedmont is divisible into parallel geologic belts oriented in a northeast to southwest direction (Figure 6.2). From the southeast to northwest, these geologic belts are known as the Carolina slate belt, the Charlotte belt, the Kings Mountain belt, and the Inner Piedmont belt. The Brevard belt, a prominent regional structural feature, forms the western boundary of the Inner Piedmont belt and separates it from the Blue Ridge.

Triassic Rocks

Within the crystalline rocks of the Piedmont from Nova Scotia through the Carolinas are a series of downfaulted basins containing unaltered sedimentary rocks that are of Triassic age (Figure 6.9). The major part of two of these basins, the Deep River and Dan River basins, and a small subsidiary basin, occur in North Carolina.

The Deep River basin is the largest of the southern basins and extends from just over the South Carolina line through Anson County, northeastward to near Oxford in Granville County, a distance of about 150 miles. The basin varies from 5 to about 18 miles in width. Different parts of the basin have been termed the Wadesboro, Sanford, the Deep River, and the Durham basins, but these names are actually subdivisions of a single basin.

Figure 6.9. Distribution of Triassic Rocks in N.C.

The Deep River basin is bordered on the east and west sides by *normal faults* (vertical displacement) with the area between depressed in a form referred to as a graben. However, greater downward movement apparently took place along the eastern border fault. The beds in the Deep River basin dip southeastward toward the eastern border fault (Jonesboro fault) and consist of red, brown, purple, or gray claystone, shale, siltstone, and sandstone. Conglomerate and fanglomerate (a cemented fragmental rock consisting of rounded stones embedded in a finer matrix) predominate adjacent to the border fault. These rocks consist of angular to subangular rock fragments that were derived from crystalline rocks on adjacent sides of the basin. Where the Deep River basin has been studied in detail, the rocks have been divided into three formations. The Cumnock formation, a dark gray shale and coal-bearing unit, separates the lower Pekin formation and the upper Sanford formation. Reptile and plant fossils are locally abundant in the Pekin and Cumnock formations.

The Dan River basin begins near Germanton, Stokes County, and strikes northeast along the Dan River across Stokes and Rockingham counties, and continues for some distance into Virginia. The portion in North Carolina is about forty miles long and averages five to seven miles in width. The rocks in the Dan River basin are much like those in the Deep River basin in composition and stratigraphic position. However, in the Dan River basin the rocks dip to the northwest toward the western border fault.

119

Figure 6.10. Distribution of Carolina Slate Belt Rocks

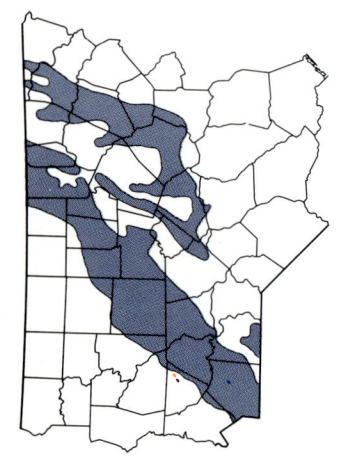

About twenty-five miles southwest of the Dan River basin, in the northwest corner of Davie County, there is a small, isolated area of Triassic rocks that dip to the northwest toward a border fault.

Carolina Slate Belt

The Carolina slate belt is the easternmost geologic belt in the Piedmont province. As shown in Figure 6.10, it occupies much of the eastern Piedmont, cropping out in two regions. The larger western region enters North Carolina in Union County on the southwest and extends northeastward through the south-central part of the state to Person, Granville, and Vance counties where it continues into Virginia. A smaller eastern region occurs in Halifax, Nash, Wilson, Johnston, Harnett, Moore, Richmond, and Anson counties. As can be seen in Figure 6.5, the eastern and western regions are separated to the north by an area of medium-grade metamorphic rocks and a large granite body, and to the south by the Deep River Triassic basin. On the west, the Carolina slate belt rocks are in contact with igneous and medium-grade metamorphic rocks of the Charlotte belt. The Gold Hill fault marks this boundary between Union and Davidson counties. On the east, the slate belt rocks continue beneath the Cretaceous and Tertiary deposits of the Coastal Plain.

The rocks of the Carolina slate belt are of volcanic and sedimentary origin, all of which have been subjected to low-grade regional metamorphism. The dominant sedimentary rock is a well-bedded, finely laminated rock that has been termed slate, volcanic slate, shale, mudstone, argillite, and siltstone. Coarser-grained sedimentary rocks that are also abundant include graywacke, siltstone, sandy siltstone, and fine sandstone. Less abundant sedimentary rocks include quartzite, conglomerate, and very rarely, limestone. Interbedded with the sedimentary rocks are extensive subaqueous and subaerially deposited volcanic rocks that range from rhyolite (acid) to basalt (basic) in composition. Both flow rocks and pyroclastic deposits are present.

Based on a few radiometric age dates and very meager fossil evidence, the Carolina slate belt is generally considered to be of early Paleozoic age.

Igneous intrusive bodies are common in the northern half of the slate belt. These intrusive bodies range in size from narrow dikes and sills to plutons several miles across. They are granitic to gabbroic in composition and some are metamorphosed and others are not. They range from early Paleozoic to Triassic in age.

Charlotte Belt

The Charlotte belt lies northwest of the Carolina slate belt and is about forty miles wide at its maximum width. It is composed mostly of plutonic, or igneous, rocks that form a complex mixture of granites, diorites, and gabbros. Toward the northeast end of the belt in Guilford County, the plutonic rocks begin to finger out in gneisses and schists of the Inner Piedmont belt.

Although plutonic rocks are much more abundant in the Charlotte belt than in the other Piedmont geologic belts, much of the area is composed of granitoid gneiss that apparently originated as sedimentary and volcanic rocks. These medium-grade metamorphic rocks may be in part equivalent in age to the sedimentary and volcanic units present in the adjacent Carolina slate and Kings Mountain belts.

One of the most interesting features of the Charlotte belt is the so-called Concord ring-dike that occurs about twelve miles northeast of Charlotte in western Cabarrus County. This is an almost circular belt of coarse-grained, massive syenite that is a mile wide and six miles in diameter. The syenite weathers to large boulders and the ring-dike forms a distinctive topographic high. The ring-dike encircles a gabbro-diorite intrusive body.

Radiometric age dates indicate that the plutonic rocks of the Charlotte belt are from 415 to 385 million years in age. Some of the plutons are metamorphosed and others are not. The granite rocks of the Charlotte belt are the principal source of commercial stone, both crushed and dimension, in the Piedmont section of the state.

Kings Mountain Belt

Beginning at the South Carolina line and continuing in a northeasterly direction for about forty miles through Cleveland, Gaston, Lincoln, and Catawba counties, is a narrow belt of low-grade metamorphic rocks of sedimentary and volcanic origin that comprise the Kings Mountain belt. Through this area the Kings Mountain belt separates the Charlotte belt and the Inner Piedmont belt.

Rocks in the Kings Mountain belt have been altered by low-grade regional metamorphism, but their sedimentary and volcanic origin is clearly evident. Rock types include slate, phyllite, quartzite, conglomerate, and marble. Especially prevalent are sericite, or muscovite, schist, and hornblende schist, parts of which are clearly volcanic in origin. Quartzite beds, some of which contain kyanite, are especially evident because they form the prominent ridges in the area such as the Pinnacle and Crowder's Mountain.

The Kings Mountain belt has been tightly compressed by folding and all of the beds dip at nearly vertical angles. The age of the rocks in the belt is not clear, but recent workers in the area suggest they may be correlative with the Carolina slate belt.

Inner Piedmont Belt

The largest of the geologic belts in the Piedmont of North Carolina is the Inner Piedmont belt. It occupies a broad area fifty to sixty miles in width across the state. The western border is marked by the Brevard belt and on the east it is in contact with the Kings Mountain belt to the south and the Charlotte belt to the north. The contact with these two belts on the east appears to be more of a change in metamorphic grade than one of rocks of different age.

The belt occupies the zone of highest regional metamorphic grade in the Piedmont of North Carolina and consists mostly of a great variety of complexly mixed mica gneisses and schists with lesser amounts of hornblende gneiss and schist. The belt is characterized by generally low and irregular dips of the foliation. Except along its margins, the dip of the gneisses and schists is rarely steep and dips of less than forty-five degrees are more common than dips of more than forty-five degrees. In Stokes County, a dome-shaped structure composed of interlayered quartzite and schist rises above the surrounding gneisses to form the Sauratown Mountains. Because of their obvious sedimentary origin, the rocks in this area have been correlated with the Kings Mountain belt, but the age and structural relationship with the surrounding gneisses remains uncertain.

Granitic rocks are abundant in the Inner Piedmont belt, but are subordinate to the gneisses and schists. Where mapped in detail, the granitic bodies consist of widely spaced sheets and lenses that intrude the gneisses and schists and represent two distinct ages of igneous activity. Commercial muscovite pegmatite dikes, some of which contain spodumene (lithium ore), are associated with the granitic rocks, particularly in the Shelby-Kings Mountain area. Ultramafic rocks, occurring as small, isolated bodies, are scattered throughout the belt.

The high regional metamorphic grade makes the origin, stratigraphic sequence, and geologic history of the Inner Piedmont belt extremely difficult to decipher. However, it is generally believed that the gneisses and schists represent upper Precambrian and lower Paleozoic sedimentary and volcanic rocks that have undergone several episodes of regional metamorphism and igneous intrusive activity.

Brevard Belt

The Brevard belt, often referred to as the Brevard fault zone, is a narrow belt of low-grade metamorphic rocks that separates the Inner Piedmont belt from the Blue Ridge belt. It is present from northern North Carolina to Alabama, a distance of more than 325 miles. It enters North Carolina in southwestern Transylvania County and strikes northeastward through Henderson, Buncombe, McDowell, Burke, Caldwell, Wilkes and Surry counties. The segment of the belt in North Carolina varies from less than one mile to over five miles in width. Although the Brevard belt marks the southeast edge of the Blue Ridge geologic belt, it does not exactly correspond to the southeast edge of the Blue Ridge physiographic province. It lies northwest of the Blue Ridge scarp from Transylvania County to McDowell County where it descends to the Piedmont province and remains in that province for the rest of its length in North Carolina.

Most of the rocks in the Brevard belt have been intensely sheared and show evidence of having been derived by retrogressive metamorphism of the bordering rocks. Others are progressively metamorphosed sedimentary rocks that locally show primary textures and structures. Crystalline limestone, or marble, lenses are common in the southwestern portion of the belt in North Carolina. Throughout most of its length, rocks in the Brevard belt are steeply dipping or vertical.

The Brevard belt is bordered on the northwest and southeast sides by faults. Where detailed studies have been conducted in areas that span the belt, significant contrasts in rocks that lie to the northwest in the Inner Piedmont belt and those to the southeast in the Blue Ridge belt have been demonstrated. Differences in metamorphic grade, structural pattern, relative proportions of schist, gneiss, and amphibolite, and abundance and character of rocks are obvious.

Because of its unique character and importance in any interpretation of the geologic history of the area, the Brevard belt has been of interest to geologists since it was first recognized early in this century. No less than nineteen theories have been advanced to explain the Brevard belt including most forms of faulting and combinations of faulting and folding. Whatever its origin, the Brevard belt is one of the most complex structural features in the southern Appalachians and has been involved in much of the tectonic development of the region.

Blue Ridge Geology

The Blue Ridge in North Carolina is part of the Blue Ridge belt that extends for more than seven hundred miles from southern Pennsylvania to northwestern Alabama. It ranges in width from less than five miles in Maryland and Pennsylvania to as much as seventy miles in North Carolina and Tennessee. The belt is composed of variously metamorphosed Precambrian rocks, and other than the Canadian shield, is one of the largest exposed areas of Precambrian rocks in North America. Because of a pronounced change in structural pattern, the Blue Ridge belt is divided into two sections. That part lying north of Roanoke, Virginia, is called the Northern Blue Ridge, and that part to the southwest where it disappears beneath the Coastal Plain in central Alabama is called the Southern Blue Ridge.

In North Carolina, the Blue Ridge belt is bordered on the southeast by the Brevard fault zone and on the northwest by Paleozoic rocks of the Valley and Ridge and Unaka belts in Tennessee and southwest Virginia. In very generalized terms the Blue Ridge belt is composed of a core of older Precambrian basement rocks unconformably overlain by a vast thickness of young Precambrian metamorphosed sedimentary and volcanic rocks. Intrusive into these Precambrian rocks are diverse types and ages of plutonic rocks. Large-scale, low-angle thrust faults have transported part, if not all, of the southern Blue Ridge belt northwestward as much as thirty-five miles over the unmetamorphosed Paleozoic rocks of the Valley and Ridge belts. Subsequent uplift and erosion have exposed the younger overridden rocks in "windows" at several places.

The basement core is composed of massive, granitic-textured rocks and layered and nonlayered granitic gneisses mixed with various proportions of biotite and hornblende schist, amphibolite, and other nongranitic rocks. The massive granitic-textured rocks have been mapped as the Max Patch Granite and Cranberry Gneiss and occur mostly on the northwest side of the Blue Ridge belt in Swain, Haywood, Madison, Yancey, Watauga, and Ashe counties. Recent radiometric age determinations on samples of Cranberry Gneiss from Ashe County have

given ages of 1,207 million years to 1,297 million years and these are also the oldest rocks thus far found in the Southern Blue Ridge. The Blowing Rock Gneiss and Wilson Creek Gneiss are granitic gneisses of the Precambrian basement complex that occur within the Grandfather Mountain Window in Avery, Caldwell, and Watauga counties. These rocks are also in excess of 1,000 million years in age. Other rocks of the Precambrian basement core occupy a large area in parts of Macon, Jackson, Madison, Haywood, and Buncombe counties and consist of a complex mixture of granitic gneiss and layered and nonlayered gneisses composed mostly of biotite, hornblende, garnet, and muscovite.

Unconformably overlying the older Precambrian basement core is a vast thickness of metasedimentary and metavolcanic rocks of younger Precambrian age. Along the west side of the Blue Ridge belt through parts of Cherokee, Graham, Swain, and Madison counties, these younger Precambrian rocks comprise the Ocoee Series. The rocks of the Ocoee Series are only slightly to moderately metamorphosed and consist mostly of *clastic sediments* that range from shale to conglomerate. The total thickness of the Ocoee may be as much as 25,000 feet. It is broken by a number of major thrust faults and is complexly involved by folds and faults with the underlying basement rocks.

In several restricted areas in the North Carolina Blue Ridge belt, sedimentary rocks of apparent lower Paleozoic age are found. The most extensive of these is the Murphy belt which begins in Graham County and strikes southwestward through parts of Clay and Cherokee counties where it continues for some distance into Georgia. Other areas in which Paleozoic rocks are exposed include the Hot Springs Window in Madison County and the Grandfather Mountain Window in Avery, Caldwell, and Watauga counties. The presence of limestone, dolomite, and marble are distinguishing features of the areas of Paleozoic rocks.

Intrusive into the older Precambrian basement core and the overlying young Precambrian rocks are numerous igneous bodies that range from Precambrian to Paleozoic in age and from mafic (basic) to felsic (acid) in composition. These include the Beech, Brown Mountain, and Whiteside granites, the Bakersville gabbro, and numerous pegmatites and "alaskite" bodies in the Spruce Pine mining district. Small bodies of metamorphosed ultramafic rocks (dunites), many of which have been mined for asbestos, olivine, vermiculite, and corundum, occur throughout the Blue Ridge belt from Clay County on the southwest to Alleghany County on the northeast.

121

Figure 6.11. Value of Mineral Production in N.C., 1950-1972

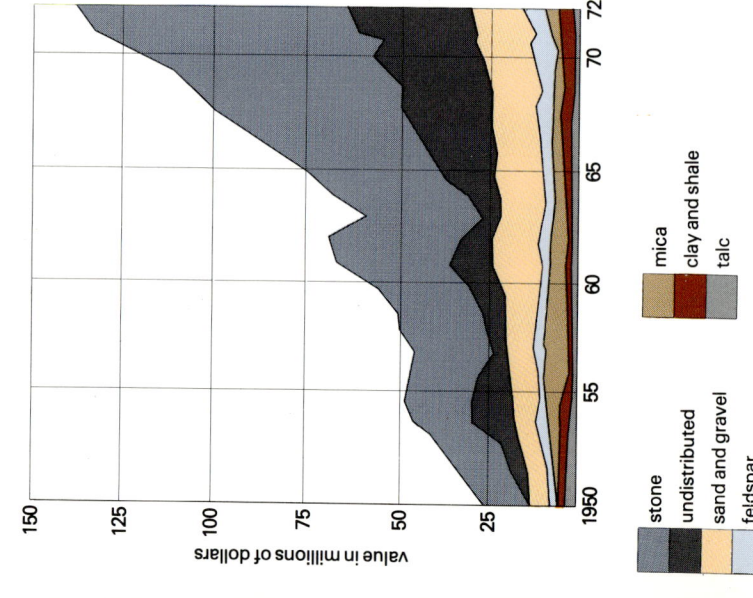

MINERAL RESOURCES

Because of its complex geological history and wide variety of rocks that were formed from Precambrian time to the present that include the products of practically every known geological and mineralogical process, North Carolina is endowed with an abundance of rocks and minerals that are of economic importance to our industrialized society. Of the over three hundred varieties of rocks and minerals known to occur in the state, over seventy have uses in commercial or industrial processes. As a result, mining has been an important factor in the state's economy since colonial days. During and immediately following colonization of the territory, emphasis was mainly on the search for base and precious metals. An iron industry, consisting of many small furnaces scattered throughout the central and western parts of the state, flourished during the eighteenth and nineteenth centuries, and was a stabilizing factor in the early development of North Carolina. The discovery of gold in Cabarrus County in 1799 is credited with ushering in the first period of major mining activity in the United States. Copper, lead, silver, and coal were also mined during this time.

The discovery of large deposits in other parts of the country resulted in a rapid decline in metal mining in North Carolina around the turn of the century. In contemporary times, only relatively small amounts of metallic ores have been produced, while the production of nonmetallic or industrial minerals has increased steadily to dominate the mineral industry of the state.

Metallic Minerals

Metallic minerals are associated principally with the igneous and metamorphic rocks of the Piedmont and Blue Ridge geologic belts. Chromite, copper, gold and silver, iron, lead and zinc, manganese, molybdenum, nickel, tin, titanium, and tungsten all occur in the state to some extent. The only metallic ore produced in North Carolina during 1972 was high-grade magnetite from the old Cranberry Mine in Avery County.

Although of little importance in the state's mining industry today, noteworthy amounts of gold, copper, iron, and tungsten have been produced in the past. In fact, North Carolina was the leading producer of gold prior to the discoveries in California in 1849, and, during the time it was operated in the 1950s, the Hamme Mine in Vance County was the largest single tungsten mine in the United States. There remain, however, prospects of future mining of metallic minerals. Considerable reserves of tungsten ore remain in the area of the Hamme Mine and as economic conditions change, the mine will undoubtedly be reopened in the future. Because of its geologic similarity to important metal mining districts in Canada, the Carolina slate belt has been the target of extensive exploration during the past few years, and is considered to have good potential for the discovery of massive sulfide (copper, lead, zinc) deposits.

Nonmetallic Minerals

Nonmetallic minerals include a wide variety of rocks, minerals, and other naturally occurring substances that are mined for their economic value, and it is this group of rocks and minerals that have dominated the North Carolina mineral industry since the turn of the century. In 1962 the total mineral production in North Carolina was valued at $54.6 million. As shown in Figure 6.11, by 1972 this value had increased to $116.3 million, over twice that in 1962, and reflects the dramatic growth that has taken place in the state's nonmetallic mineral industry during the past decade.

The nonmetallic mineral industry in North Carolina is highly diversified and is distributed throughout the state (Figure 6.11). In 1972, North Carolina continued to rank first among the states in the production of feldspar, lithium minerals, and mica; second in the production of olivine; and fourth in the production of asbestos, clays, and phosphate rock. North Carolina has been the leading producer of bricks in the nation since 1962.

Feldspar Feldspar has been mined in North Carolina since 1911. Mining began in the Spruce Pine district, which is now the principal feldspar-producing district in North America. North Carolina accounted for 60 percent of total United States production in quantity and 58 percent in value in 1972. Production amounted to 439,838 tons valued at $6 million, an increase of 12 percent in quantity and 29 percent in value over 1971. Six companies operated nine mines in Cleveland, Mitchell, and Yancey counties. Leading producers were International Minerals and Chemical Corporation, Lawson-United Feldspar and Mineral Company, and the Feldspar Corporation. Production was mainly in the form of flotation concentrate for use in the glassmaking industry.

Mica Mica mining began on a large scale in western North Carolina about 1868 and that area has since been a principal producer of mica in the United States. Sheet mica was the principal product for many years, but transistors have, to a large extent, eliminated many of the uses for sheet mica. Consequently, no significant amounts of sheet mica have been produced in North Carolina since about 1962, but scrap and ground mica are still produced in large quantities.

North Carolina accounted for 57 percent of the total United States domestic production of scrap mica by quantity and 68 percent by value. Production amounted to 91,000 tons valued at $2.9 million, an increase of 36 percent in quantity and 66 percent in value over that of 1971. Leading producers were Deneen Mica Company, Harris Mining Company, Kings Mountain Mica Company, the Feldspar Corporation, and United States Gypsum

The older Precambrian basement rocks were metamorphosed at least once prior to the deposition of the overlying younger Precambrian rocks. The Upper Precambrian rocks and the underlying basement rocks were subsequently subjected to one and probably several episodes of regional metamorphism during the Paleozoic era. These metamorphic effects, plus the folding and faulting that has taken place, make the Blue Ridge belt one of the most geologically complex areas in the country.

Company. Ground mica was produced by seven companies with nine plants in Buncombe, Cleveland, Macon, Mitchell, and Yancey counties. The major uses for ground mica are for joint cement, paint, roofing, rubber, and well-drilling muds.

Lithium Although first recognized as early as 1906, the economic significance of the spodumene-bearing pegmatites of the Kings Mountain district was not realized until 1942. Today, this relatively small area in Cleve and and Gaston counties contains more than 80 percent of the known lithium ore reserves in the United States.

From this area, two producing mines accounted for the major portion of United States production in 1972. Foote Mineral Company operated a mine and mill at Kings Mountain, Cleveland County, and Lithium Corporation of America operated a mine and lithium chemicals plant near Bessemer City, Gaston County. Output from these mines was used to produce lithium metal, the lightest of all known metals, and in various lithium chemical compounds, ceramics, greases, batteries, and many other industrial processes.

Crushed Stone and Sand and Gravel Crushed stone and sand and gravel annually account for over one-half of the total mineral value produced in North Carolina. The sandhills region in Anson, Moore, Lee, Harnett, and Richmond counties is the principal producing area of sand and gravel, but sand is mined from practically every county in the state. Granite and related crystalline rocks in the Piedmont and Blue Ridge geologic belts provide the principal sources of crushed stone in North Carolina. However, numerous quarries are located in the dense fine-grained rocks of the Carolina slate belt. Crystalline limestone and marble are quarried in limited amounts in the Piedmont and Mountain regions and shell limestone from the Castle Hayne limestone is the principal source of crushed stone in the Coastal Plain.

Deposits of sand and gravel occur throughout the state and at one time or another have been worked in every county. Sand and gravel is the second leading mineral commodity produced in the state. In 1972, production was recorded by 104 commercial and 65 government and contractor operations located in seventy-nine counties. Eighteen commercial operations in Anson, Buncombe, Cumberland, Harnett, and Moore counties accounted for 67 percent of the commercial production, which amounted to 13,485,000 tons valued at $14.6 million. Most sand production is used in building, paving, and construction work and gravel in building, paving, and railroad ballast. Some high-silica sand and gravel is used in glassmaking and for chemical purposes.

Stone has for many years been the principal mineral commodity produced in the state and annually accounts for over one-half of the total mineral production value. In 1972, there were 32,297,000 tons of stone valued at $62.4 million produced from 108 quarries located in fifty-five counties by 42 commercial operators. The Department of Transportation and Highway Safety operated one quarry. Twenty-four large quarries with individual outputs of more than 500,000 tons accounted for 69 percent of the total production. Eleven quarries in the state produce one million tons or more each year. The leading stone producers are Central Rock Company, Inc., Ideal Cement Company, Martin Marietta Aggregates, Nello L. Teer Company, and Vulcan Materials Company. Together, their forty-eight operations account for almost 90 percent of the total production.

Dimension stone is produced from fifteen granite, two slate, and three individual marble, quartzite, and sandstone quarries. The North Carolina Granite Company operates the largest granite dimension stone quarry in the United States at Mt. Airy in Surry County. Stone from this quarry has been shipped to many cities, and many of the public buildings in Washington, D.C., have been built of this stone.

Clay Clays of different kinds are found in varying amounts throughout the Coastal Plain, Piedmont, and Mountain regions of the state. These clays provide the raw materials from which over one billion bricks are produced annually in North Carolina. Common clay and shale were mined by twenty-six companies from forty-five mines located in twenty-three counties. Sixteen mines in Chatham, Lee, Rockingham, and Stanly counties accounted for 59 percent of the state's production in quantity and 51 percent in value. Production amounted to 3.86 million tons valued at $4.47 million, which was a substantial increase over 1971. Seventy percent of the common clay and shale produced was consumed by twenty-two companies in the manufacture of face bricks. Other major uses were for lightweight aggregate, cement, common brick, sewer pipe, and to a lesser extent, structural and drain tile. In 1972, North Carolina produced 1.2 billion bricks valued at $47.1 million for 15 percent of the total United States production.

Kaolin High quality primary, or residual, kaolin deposits occur in the Franklin-Sylva district and in the Spruce Pine district. These deposits were known as early as 1767, but systematic mining was not begun until 1888 near Webster in Macon County. Harris Mining Company, with two mines in Avery County, was the only producer of waterwashed kaolin, used mainly in the manufacture of china and porcelain fillers. Kings Mountain Mica Company produced unprocessed kaolin at a mine in Cleveland County for use in the production of white face brick.

Talc and Pyrophyllite Pyrophyllite, which is a high alumina mineral that occurs exclusively within rocks of the Carolina slate belt, was first mined commercially in North Carolina in about 1855 and it has been mined almost continuously since that time. Talc deposits, associated with crystalline limestones of the Murphy marble belt in Cherokee and Swain counties have been mined since 1859.

In 1972, North Carolina production of talc and pyrophyllite totaled 89,334 tons valued at $594,000, an increase of 5 percent in quantity and 14 percent in value over 1971. Talc was produced by the Hitchcock Corporation from underground mines in Cherokee County. Pyrophyllite was produced by four companies operating six mines in Alamance, Granville, Moore, and Orange counties. The major part of the production was used in refractories, ceramics, and insecticides.

Phosphate The most recent addition to the mineral industry in North Carolina is phosphate. A deposit of this material was found to underlie a large portion of Beaufort County in the early 1950s and subsequent exploration delineated a minable ore body that contains on the order of two billion tons of phosphate ore.

Phosphate is produced by Texasgulf, Inc., from a large open-pit mine located near Aurora in Beaufort County. The major portion of the output from this mine is used in nearby chemical facilities to produce phosphoric acid, triple superphosphate, and diammonium phosphate. In 1972, record-high production of phosphoric acid and dry fertilizers was achieved, and the company has recently announced major mining and chemical expansion plans that will bring the total investments in this facility to over $175 million.

Olivine Olivine is a magnesium silicate mineral that has been used principally as a refractory material but is becoming increasingly more important as a molding sand in the foundry industry and occurs extensively throughout the Blue Ridge area. Vermiculite and anthophyllite asbestos also occur in the same rocks (durites) as the olivine.

Cement Portland and masonry cement is produced by Ideal Cement Company from its plant located at Castle Hayne, New Hanover County. Most of the raw materials for this plant are mined locally from the Castle Hayne limestone, which provides the high calcium feed and clay material. Combined shipments of the products from this plant have decreased slightly in quantity and value from those of 1971.

Asbestos Amphibole asbestos was mined by Powhatan Mining Company in Jackson and Yancey counties. Production has decreased slightly, in both quantity and value, from that in 1971.

Gem Stones North Carolina has long been famous for the variety of precious and semiprecious stones found in the Piedmont and Mountain regions of the state. In 1972, there were twenty-one commercially operated collecting localities in which amateur collectors recovered emeralds, rubies, sapphires, hiddenite, garnet, and other semiprecious stones.

Other nonmetallic minerals that have been mined in the past or are considered to have potential for future mining include corundum, garnet, barite, graphite, kyanite, sillimanite, beryl, columbite-tantalite, allanite-gadolinite, monazite, illmenite, zircon, and uranium minerals.

Mineral Fuels

Mineral fuels provide the primary sources of energy currently consumed in the world and include coal, petroleum, natural gas, and uranium. North Carolina is deficient in the mineral fuels and must import these resources from outside sources in order to meet its energy requirements.

Coal The only area in North Carolina that contains coal of potentially commercial value is the Deep River coal field which lies along Deep River in Chatham, Moore, and Lee counties. The coal is associated with sandstones and shales of Triassic age and occurs in beds from only a few inches to a maximum of forty-eight inches in thickness. The Cumnock seam, which averages about forty inches in thickness, is the only minable coal present.

Coal has been mined intermittently from a number of underground mines developed in the Cumnock seam. However, the coal seam is deeply buried, badly broken by a number of faults, and there have been several major mine disasters. The most recent effort to mine coal from the Deep River field was between 1947 and 1953.

A detailed report on the Deep River coal field was published by the United States Geological Survey in 1955, and it was estimated that the Deep River coal field contained 110,337,000 short tons of coal to a depth of less than 3,000 feet of which 55,170,000 tons were recoverable under conditions existing at that time.

Petroleum and Natural Gas The only area of North Carolina that is considered to have any potential for oil and gas production is the eastern one-third of the Coastal Plain and its continuation under the continental shelf. This area is underlain by a wedge-shaped block of sedimentary rocks that are largely of marine origin.

From 1925 until the present 112 wildcat exploration wells have been drilled in the onshore area of the state in the search for oil and gas. Although traces of gas have been detected in a few of these wells there have been no commercial quantities of oil or gas found to date.

Uranium Minerals A number of the uranium-bearing minerals are known to occur as minor constituents in the pegmatites of North Carolina, principally in the Spruce Pine district and adjacent areas. Radioactive minerals have been found in schists and underlying granitic rocks in northern Burke, Mitchell, Avery, and adjacent counties. However, none of these occurrences is large enough to be of commercial value.

Associated with the phosphate deposits in Beaufort County are trace amounts of uniformly distributed uranium. If this uranium could be recovered as a by-product of the chemical fertilizer industry, North Carolina would have a significant uranium resource.

The Triassic basins and the Upper Cretaceous continental sediments may be favorable environments for the occurrence of uranium.

Trends and Developments

From 1962 to 1972 total investments for new and expanded industry in North Carolina were $5.4 billion, which is reported to be more than any state in the South. During this same period of time the mineral industry in North Carolina experienced its greatest period of growth. In 1964, a record-high mineral production of $55.7 million was reached. Every year since 1964, mineral production in North Carolina has established a new record high. It surpassed $100 million for the first time in 1971 and was valued at $116.3 million in 1972 (Figure 6.12).

Because the mineral commodities mined in North Carolina are closely related to the productivity of the construction industry, future mineral production in North Carolina will be closely related to the general economy of the state and will continue to grow in direct relationship to the overall growth and development of the state.

An overall annual growth rate of 3.5 to 4 percent is expected for most mineral commodities mined in the state throughout the remainder of the present decade.

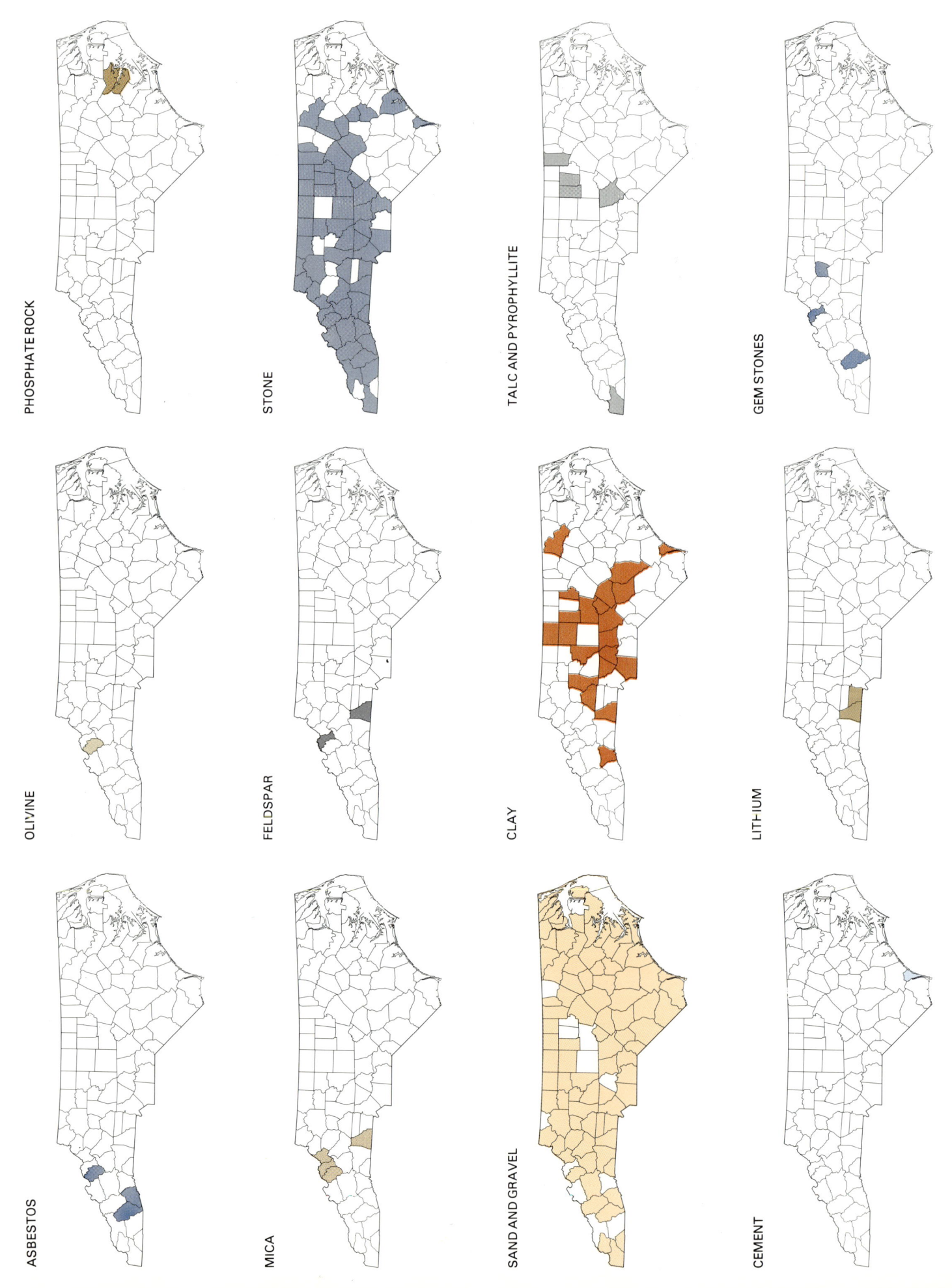

Figure 6.12. Mining by County in N.C., 1973

Mining and the Environment

Mining is an essential activity that must be conducted to provide the vast amounts of raw materials on which our economy and standard of living are based. In 1972, the United States required about 4.4 billion tons of new basic mineral and nonfood organic materials. This is equivalent to 42,500 pounds per person.

The nature of mining is such that unless proper restraints are exercised great environmental damage can result in the form of water, air, and land pollution. Some parts of the country have suffered these damages from mining in the past, particularly those areas in which coal has been mined by contour strip-mining methods. Fortunately, the mining industry in North Carolina is such that relatively small areas have been affected.

Recognizing the dangers that could result from uncontrolled mining practices, the 1971 North Carolina General Assembly enacted a surface mining control bill that requires every mining operation in the state that disturbs more than one acre of land per year to obtain a permit. The issuance of this permit is predicated upon the mining operator's submitting a reclamation plan that meets the requirements of the act and the posting of a surety bond to guarantee that the mining operation will be conducted in accordance with the terms of the permit.

In 1972, the state had issued permits for 347 mines covering a total of 10,825 acres of affected land. It is believed that this legislation will provide the necessary safeguards to assure that mining conducted in North Carolina will not endanger the environment.

SELECTED REFERENCES

Brown, P. M.; Miller, J. A.; and Swain, F. M. *Structural and Stratigraphic Framework, and Spatial Distribution of Permeability of the Atlantic Coastal Plain, North Carolina to New York.* U.S. Geological Survey Professional Paper 796. Washington, D.C.: U.S. Government Printing Office, 1972.

Fisher, G. W.; Pettijohn, F. J.; Reed, J. C., Jr.; and Weaver, K. M., eds. *Studies of Appalachian Geology: Central and Southern.* New York: Interscience Publishers, 1970.

Hadley, J. B., and Nelson, A. E. Geologic Map of the Knoxville Quadrangle, North Carolina, Tennessee, and South Carolina: Map I-654. Washington, D.C.: U.S. Geological Survey, 1971.

Merwin, R. W., and Conrad, S. G. "The Mineral Industry of North Carolina." In *1972 Bureau of Mines Minerals Yearbook.* Washington, D.C.: U.S. Department of the Interior, 1972.

Rankin, D. W.; Espenshade, G. H.; and Neuman, R. B. Geologic Map of the West Half of the Winston-Salem Quadrangle, North Carolina, Virginia, and Tennessee: Map I-709-A. Washington, D.C.: U.S. Geological Survey, 1972.

Rodgers, John. *The Tectonics of the Appalachians.* New York: John Wiley & Sons, 1970.

Russell, R. J., ed. *Guides to Southeastern Geology: 1955 Guidebook.* New Orleans: Geological Society of America, 1955.

Stuckey, J. L. *North Carolina: Its Geology and Mineral Resources.* Raleigh: N.C. Department of Conservation and Development, 1965.

7. Vegetation and Soil Resources

ARTHUR W. COOPER
RALPH J. McCRACKEN
LOUIS E. AULL

VEGETATION

The natural vegetation of North Carolina, rich in species and varied in composition, constitutes one of the state's greatest natural resources. The coastal live oak forests and the high mountain spruce-fir forests are but two extremes in a range of vegetation types unequalled in any other eastern state. Despite over four hundred years of occupation by the white man, and despite extensive modification, many areas still remain from which the essential features of the state's natural vegetation can be deduced.

Each vegetation type described here occurs over a sizable geographic area, is characterized by a general similarity in species composition and structure wherever it is found, and occupies a generally similar habitat throughout its range. Unless otherwise indicated, each vegetation type is a climax community, that is, one that would continue to occupy its habitat under the prevailing conditions of climate and geology. Each type can be recognized by any observer who can, in turn, recognize the major plant species involved. Forests are emphasized because the climax vegetation of virtually all of North Carolina's soils is some type of forest.

Coastal Vegetation

The distribution of vegetation types on the coast is influenced primarily by the effects of saltwater ocean tides, windblown sand and salt spray, and the texture and drainage of the soil.

Beaches and dunes occur in the most extreme terrestrial environment on the coast. Here sterile, windblown sands combine with strong winds, storms, and occasional inundations of salt water to produce a harsh and unstable environment. Where man has not seriously altered the form of the beaches and dunes, there typically is a gentle beach face regularly washed by the surf. Above the drift line formed by high tides, there is an upper beach bounded on its inner margin by the first line of dunes. These first dunes are usually low hummocks, often breached by openings. Behind the first dune line there is an area of lower dunes, open sand flats, and moist depressions. The inner edge of the beach and dune zone is marked by a line of withdrawn dunes, often of considerable height and extent.

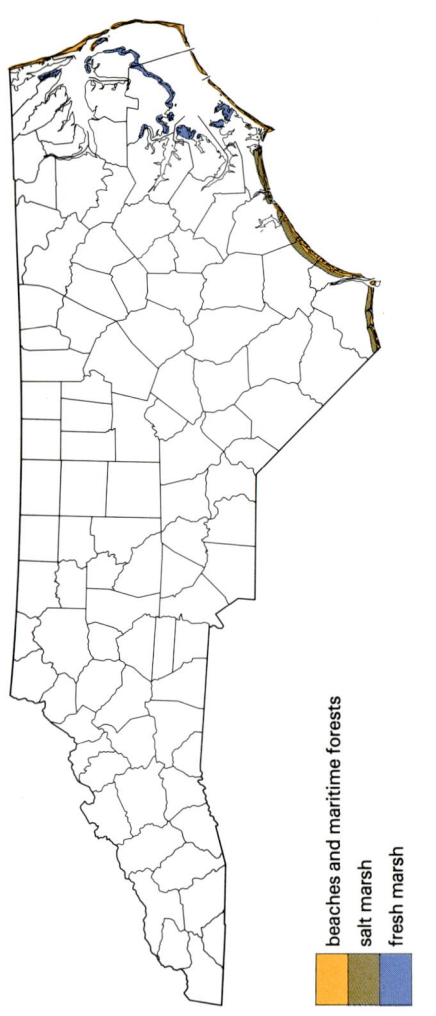

Figure 7.1. Beaches and Marshland in N.C.

beaches and maritime forests
salt marsh
fresh marsh

Perennial grasses dominate the dunes. Sea oats (*Uniola paniculata*) is the most common of these, although American beach grass (*Ammophila breviligulata*) has become very common in recent years as a result of extensive planting for dune stabilization. There is a rich dune herb flora of which beach pea (*Strophostyles helvola*), croton (*Croton punctatus*), and dune elder (*Iva imbricata*) are the most important species. Sea oats, croton, and dune elder occupy the slopes and crests of dunes, whereas other species such as broomsedge (*Andropogon* spp.), spurge (*Euphorbia polygonifolia*), and primrose (*Oenothera humifusa*) occur in the more protected areas and on "blowouts" (wind-formed depressions) between dunes. This zonation is due primarily to the relative tolerance to salt spray of the various species. Low moist areas within the dunes, which are influenced by freshwater accumulations through much of the year and by occasional accumulations of salt water, have a distinctive flora. Saltmeadow cordgrass (*Spartina patens*), a species of high salt marshes, is the dominant.

Landward near the innermost dunes and in more protected areas where the effects of salt spray are not as severe as on the dunes, the *maritime shrub thicket* community occurs (Figure 7.1). As the name implies, the community is a dense thicket of shrubs often physically bound together with vines. The crowns of the shrubs, particularly where exposed, are asymmetrical with the side toward the ocean growing very little in comparison to the leeward side. This is a result of windblown salt spray that kills off the buds on the windward side of the crown, thus producing a "pruned" effect. Yaupon (*Ilex vomitoria*), wax myrtle (*Myrica cerifera*), and red cedar (*Juniperus virginiana*) are the common plants of this zone. They are usually interlaced with thick growths of catbrier (*Smilax* spp.). In many areas, one may find shrubs overwhelmed by moving sand and it is not uncommon to find the "skeletons" of dead shrubs scattered throughout the dunes. These stand as mute witness to the harshness and instability of the habitat. It is also not uncommon to find occasional stunted individuals of tree species characteristic of inland forests such as cypress (*Taxodium distichum*) and pine (*Pinus* spp.). These are undoubtedly relicts of a time when forests occupied the site and are evidence of the general shoreline recession characteristic of the entire North Carolina coast.

Inland from the shrub zone, in areas where some degree of protection from salt spray is afforded either by distance or by dunes, a *maritime forest* develops (Figure 7.1). Live oak (*Quercus virginiana*) is the characteristic tree of this forest as it is particularly well adapted to withstand the effects of salt spray. In areas where the only protection afforded the forest is from shrubs, the trees growing closest to the ocean are small and gnarled. Behind large dunes, or farther from the ocean, a well-developed maritime forest may have a canopy over fifty feet in height. In many areas, active dunes are overwhelming the seaward edge of maritime forest as they migrate inland.

Maritime forest varies from south to north along the coast. Forests of the southern coast are strongly dominated by live oak with other species present but only locally dominant. Palmetto (*Sabal palmetto*) is common on Smith Island, indicating an affinity of such forests with those farther south in the Sea Islands. From Bogue Banks north, remaining well-developed stands of maritime forest include an intermixture of other species more characteristic of inland areas such as beech (*Fagus grandifolia*), pine, hickory (*Carya* spp.), and hophornbeam (*Ostrya virginiana*). Such areas are probably relicts of hardwood forests that extended much farther seaward during geologically recent periods of low sea level.

Coastal marshes form in protected areas behind the barrier beaches and on the edges of sounds where the substratum is periodically flooded. The flooding waters may be salt, brackish, or fresh, and the flooding may occur rhythmically, as a result of lunar tides, or irregularly. North Carolina originally had over two hundred thousand acres of these coastal wetlands and they constitute one of the state's most valuable natural resources. However, dredging and filling have reduced this acreage substantially, and as many as fifty thousand acres have been destroyed or altered in this way.

Salt marshes occur where the flooding waters are saline or brackish. *Regularly flooded salt marshes* are found primarily southwest of Beaufort Inlet. Here tides average between two and five feet, the soils are gray, soft, and silty, and tidal creeks are complexly branched. Smooth cordgrass (*Spartina alterniflora*) dominates these marshes, growing very tall along tidal creeks where drainage is good but reduced to less than a foot in height in areas away from creeks where drainage is poorer and salinity tends to increase. Clumps of black needlerush (*Juncus roemerianus*) occur scattered throughout the marsh and as a narrow fringe between the marsh and high ground. Above the approximate mean high-tide line, smooth cordgrass is replaced by saltmeadow cordgrass and saltgrass (*Distichlis spicata*) in a zone often called "high marsh." Here the soil is usually sandy and the salinity drops well below that of the regularly flooded marsh proper.

North of Beaufort Inlet and along the Outer Banks regularly flooded salt marsh becomes much less common and is replaced by *irregularly flooded salt marsh.* Vast areas of these marshes, dominated by black needlerush, occur along the inner and outer edges of Core, Pamlico, and lower Currituck sounds. Tides inundate these marshes infrequently, rarely flooding them to a depth greater than one foot. The flooding tides are wind-driven and usually brackish and the substratum is firmer and sandier than in regularly flooded salt marsh. Behind the black needlerush, beyond the effects of all but extreme storm tides, large expanses of saltmeadow cordgrass and saltgrass occur, intermixed with brackish ponds and wet openings.

Extensive *freshwater marshes* are found in upper Currituck Sound, along the fringes of Albemarle Sound, and along the Cape Fear River near Wilmington. Here the major species are bulrush (*Scirpus* spp.), cattail (*Typha* spp.), sawgrass (*Cladium jamaicense*), and big cordgrass (*Spartina cynosuroides*). The soils of these marshes are typically peaty and continually waterlogged with fresh to slightly brackish water.

All coastal marshes are very valuable and productive natural systems. Regularly flooded salt marshes produce large amounts of plant material that is washed from the marsh by the tides and, while undergoing decay in the surrounding estuarine waters, serves as a major food source for many small forms of fish and shellfish. In addition, tidal creeks serve as nursery areas for these small animals. It is estimated that over 95 percent of the fish and shellfish that are taken by commercial or sports fishermen along the North Carolina coast depend in one way or another on coastal salt marshes and their adjacent waters. Irregularly flooded salt marshes serve as major waterfowl resting and feeding areas as do fresh marshes. In many ways, the biological health of our coastal waters depends on the natural activities that occur in its adjacent marshes.

Coastal Plain

The vegetation of the Coastal Plain proper is characterized by a wide variety of plant communities of very different aspect and species composition. The distribution and ecology of these plant communities is determined primarily by the depth of the water table below the soil surface, soil texture, and fire. Superimposed upon these natural variables are the effects produced by the activities of man.

Swamp forests of two major types occur along the major rivers and lesser streams of the Coastal Plain. *Gum-cypress swamps* are best developed on floodplains of black water rivers and on flats associated with upland drainage channels. The soils in such swamps are

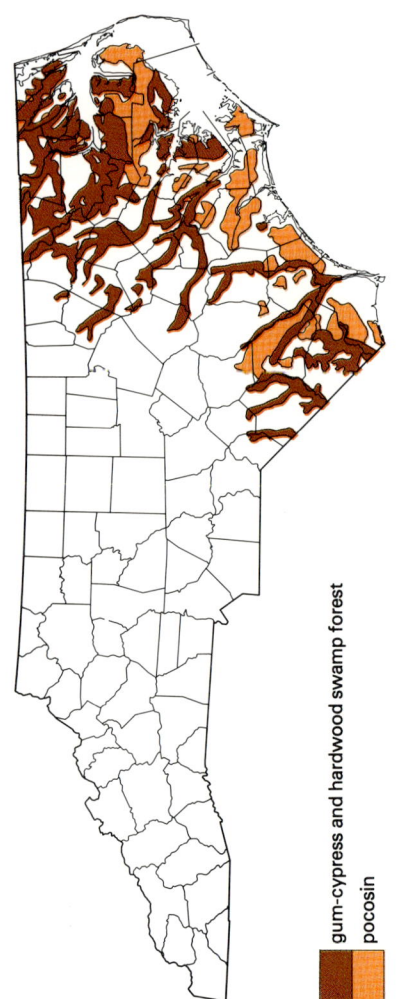

Figure 7.2. Pocosin, Gum-Cypress, and Hardwood Swamp Forest in N.C.

gum-cypress and hardwood swamp forest
pocosin

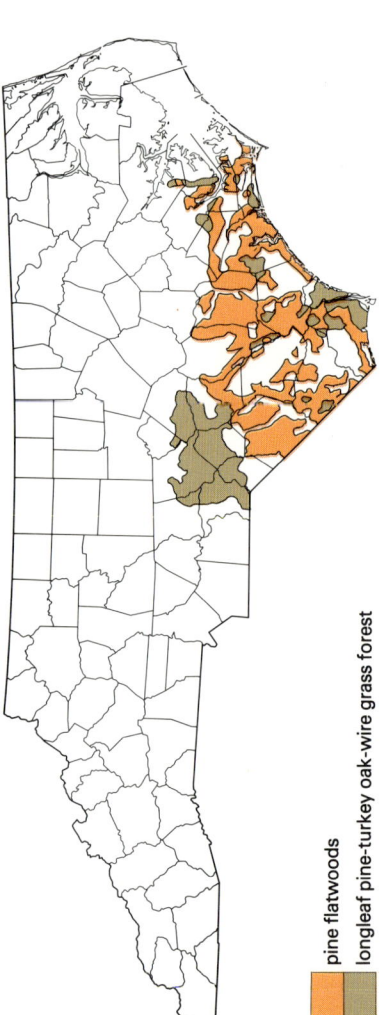

Figure 7.3. Longleaf Pine-Turkey Oak-Wire Grass Forest and Pine Flatwoods in N.C.

pine flatwoods
longleaf pine-turkey oak-wire grass forest

peaty and are usually covered with standing water throughout the growing season during years of average precipitation. Cypress occurs in the wettest portions of such swamps where the soil rarely, if ever, dries out. Tupelo gum (*Nyssa aquatica*) and swamp gum (*N. sylvatica* var. *biflora*) dominate the slightly drier sites with tupelo gum typically able to survive longer periods of flooding than swamp gum. Both the gums and cypress have swollen trunk bases, or buttresses, similar to those found in tropical rain forests. Such structures are thought to be adaptations to a constantly wet environment. In addition, the cypress trees show development of "knees," structures once thought to aid in aerating the roots but now generally agreed to have no aerating capacity, and thus they represent a growth response by the tree roots to the wet soils. Although gum-cypress swamps are flooded virtually all the time, they do dry out occasionally, for it is only under such conditions, where the soil surface is dry, that cypress seed can germinate and the seedlings become established.

The floodplains of the major through-flowing rivers of the Coastal Plain and their tributaries are dominated by *hardwood swamp forest*. Such floodplains are typically flooded only by the periodic freshets and major floods occurring during the heavy rains of winter and early spring. During the summer the soil surface is often quite dry. The major trees of these forests are willow oak (*Quercus phellos*), water oak (*Q. nigra*), cherrybark oak (*Q. falcata* var. *pagodaefolia*), sweet gum (*Liquidambar styraciflua*), river birch (*Betula nigra*), and elm (*Ulmus* spp.).

One of the most fascinating, and formidable, wet-land vegetation types of the Coastal Plain is the *pocosin* (also called "bay" or "shrub bog"). The word pocosin comes from the Indian term for "swamp on a hill," an appropriate term, for the true pocosin is much like an inverted saucer with its highest elevations in the center. These consist of dense masses of evergreen shrubs, with scattered pond pine (*Pinus serotina*), growing on highly organic peat soils. They form in three very different situations: elliptical depressions (the famous "Carolina Bays"), true pocosins of vast low upland flats in the lower Coastal Plain (Holly Shelter and Angola Bays and the Green Swamp), and in shallow sandy depressions between sand ridges ("Bay-Heads"). The peat underlying the surface varies in depth from a few inches to fifteen to twenty feet and, particularly in the extensive flats of the lower Coastal Plain, often has a distinct layer of buried logs. Pond pine is the only tree of any importance and it is usually scattered in rather open stands. On the deeper, more acid peats its growth rate is very slow. Consequently, only the shallower peats and those where acidity can be controlled by drainage are

productive forest soils. The universal occurrence of pond pine in pocosins is related to its capacity to sprout profusely at the root collar and in the crown following fire. In addition, its cones require fire before they will open and natural seeding will occur only on a cleanly burned seedbed. The major shrubs are ti-ti (*Cyrilla racemiflora*), gallberry (*Ilex glabra*), fetter bush (*Lyonia lucida*), honey cup (*Zenobia pulverulenta*), cane (*Arundinaria tecta*), and sweet pepperbush (*Clethra alnifolia*). Sweet bay (*Magnolia virginiana*), red bay (*Persea borbonia*), and loblolly bay (*Gordonia lasianthus*) often occur as large shrubs or small trees. Although the water table is near the surface throughout much of the year pocosins are not regularly flooded. Where the peat is deep and most regularly flooded, dwarf shrubs such as leatherleaf (*Chamaedaphne calyculata*) and lambkill (*Kalmia angustifolia* var. *caroliniana*) often dominate. Pocosins are very susceptible to fire and often burn extensively during dry periods. In fact, it is thought that some pocosins may have originated as a result of natural burning of gum-cypress swamps. Huge stumps and logs buried in the peat, and exposed by fire, stand as mute testimony to the existence of earlier gum-cypress swamps on many sites. For many years the peat soils of pocosins were thought to be nonproductive for agricultural purposes. However, with the development of new heavy equipment and techniques for drainage many of the shallower peats are being cleared and converted to agriculture. With proper water management and fertilization such soils can be highly productive.

Another important vegetation type of the lower Coastal Plain is the *pine flatwoods* or savanna. As the name implies, these are dominated by scattered pines and usually have a continuous ground cover of grasses and herbs. Flatwoods form both on gently sloping sand ridges and on extensive, poorly drained flatlands. Pond pine and longleaf pine (*Pinus palustris*) are the major trees. Longleaf pine is the more common and is found both on the sandy ridges and on the sandier, slightly better drained flatlands. Pond pine, on the other hand, is confined primarily to finer-textured, poorly drained flatlands. Shrubs vary considerably in their abundance, being common in some places and entirely absent in others. Gallberry, wax myrtle, and sweet bay are the most common. On the coarse, well-drained sandy soils wire grass (*Aristida stricta*) is the common savanna grass. On the flatlands with finer-textured, less well-drained soils, wire grass is mixed with other grasses. The savannas are very rich in wild flowers and this community is perhaps the most showy of all our natural vegetation types. A number of species, including orchids, pitcher plants, lilies, goldenrods, sunflowers, and asters may be in bloom at any one time from early March to late November. The unique Venus's-flytrap (*Dionaea muscipula*) occurs in grassy, poorly drained habitats

similar to those of savannas. Flytrap plants cannot survive extended competition from grasses and shrubs. Consequently, they thrive only in areas that are burned fairly regularly. In fact, it is thought that savannas, like pocosins, are produced by fire. Repeated fires destroy all accumulation of peat on the soil surface and, in addition, destroy the crowns of shrubs, thus favoring grasses. Repeated fires perpetuate grasses at the expense of shrubs, thus permitting the savanna to persist. Where savannas are protected from fire, they change rapidly into shrub and tree-dominated stands with species composition similar to that of the drier pocosins.

Deep, well-drained, coarse sands in the Coastal Plain are typically dominated by the *longleaf pine-turkey oak-wire grass community* (Figure 7.3). This vegetation type is confined principally to the southern half of the Coastal Plain, being best developed in the sandhills region along the "fall line," but also occurring on the deep sands of old dunes and terraces associated with ancient inland shorelines. These areas have a distinctive appearance, usually consisting of an open layer of scattered, large longleaf pines and a lower layer of scrub oaks, primarily turkey oak (*Quercus laevis*), bluejack oak (*Q. incana*), blackjack oak (*Q. marilandica*), and scrubby post oak (*Q. margaretta*). Dwarf huckleberry (*Gaylussacia dumosa*) is the most common shrub, supplanting wire grass in areas where the turkey oaks are thickest. Although the wire grass is the major herb, there are numerous other herbaceous species present, many of which have showy flowers. Virtually all herbs show adaptations to the extreme dryness of the habitat, as do many of the woody plants. Those who have studied this community agree that it is fire perpetuated. If it were protected from fire over long periods of time, the oaks would become dominant and longleaf pine would diminish in importance.

Some kind of *oak-hickory forest* once covered the uplands of the Coastal Plain in areas where soils are not too sandy and where drainage is adequate, but not excessive. Such soils are generally located in the northern half of the Coastal Plain. There, oak-hickory forests extended almost to sea level. In the southern Coastal Plain, however, because of the preponderance of sandy soils, most oak-hickory forests are found relatively near the Piedmont. Most of the sites once occupied by this community were desirable as farm land and thus were cleared of forest early in colonial times. Consequently, there are few examples of it now remaining and we have very little idea of its original vegetative composition. Judging from the few areas still remaining, the moist but well-drained sites supported white oak (*Quercus alba*), southern red oak (*Q. falcata*), water oak, post oak (*Q. stellata*), swamp chestnut oak willow oak,

(*Q. michauxii*), hickories (*Carya* spp.), sweet gum, tulip poplar (*Liriodendron tulipifera*), beech, black gum (*Nyssa sylvatica*), red maple (*Acer rubrum*), and pine (mostly *Pinus taeda*). Beech may become locally dominant on protected, moist sites and on highly calcareous ridges. On the drier sites, which grade into the longleaf pine community, blackjack, post, and turkey oaks are the dominants along with hickory and pine.

Piedmont

Perhaps more than in any other part of the state, the vegetation of the Piedmont shows the impact of man's treatment of the land. Three and one-half centuries of logging, farming, grazing, and increasing urbanization have converted a once-forested landscape into patches of pine and deciduous forest mixed with fields in varying kinds of cultivation and in varying stages of abandonment. Despite these massive changes in the landscape, remaining patches of forest reflect the natural variability in soils and topography that influence the pattern of Piedmont vegetation. From these, one can reconstruct what the original vegetation might have been like.

Oak-hickory forest undoubtedly covered all of the Piedmont uplands except for the extremely dry and extremely wet sites (Figure 7.4). Judging from the records of early explorers and from existing little-disturbed stands, these Piedmont forests were fine indeed, much more so than one might judge from observing the present, heavily disturbed woodlots now scattered through the area. On the rolling uplands of the Piedmont, oak-hickory forest is dominated by white, black (*Quercus velutina*), scarlet (*Q. coccinea*), southern red, and post oaks, mockernut and smooth hickory (*Carya tomentosa* and *C. glabra*), black gum, tulip poplar, and occasional shortleaf (*Pinus echinata*) and loblolly pines. Dogwood (*Cornus florida*) and sourwood (*Oxydendrum arboreum*) are the common understory trees.

The great diversity of topography and soil within the Piedmont produces much local variation in forest composition. On steep, sheltered slopes, and on the more fertile and less eroded soils, beech, northern red oak (*Q. rubra*), white oak, and tulip poplar are the major species. On such sites there is a great diversity of shrubs and low trees and one may find large numbers of spring and summer flowering herbs. Upland sites with soils that become very wet in winter and very dry in summer are dominated by post and blackjack oak with some sand hickory (*Carya pallida*) and white and southern red oak. Carolina shagbark hickory (*C. carolinae-septentrionalis*) is found on sites with similar moisture conditions, but only where such sites occur in the Carolina Slate Belt running through the center of the Piedmont. On dry, excessively drained ridges, scarlet oak and occasionally

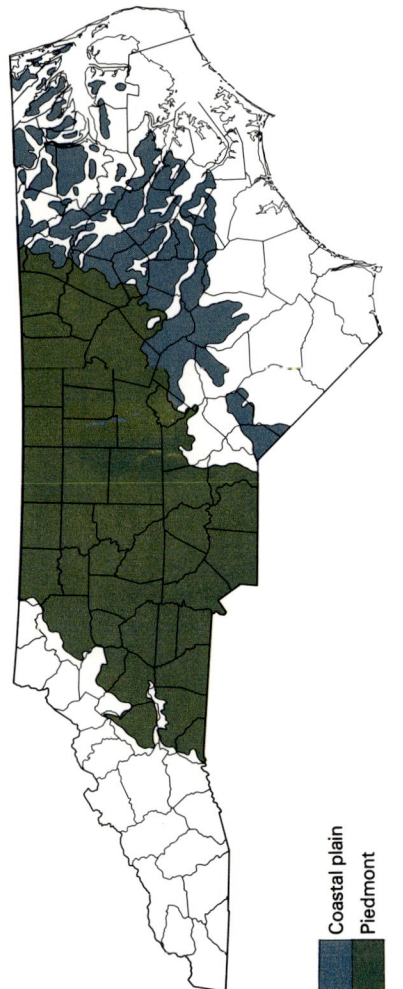

Figure 7.4. Oak-Hickory Forest in N.C.

Coastal plain
Piedmont

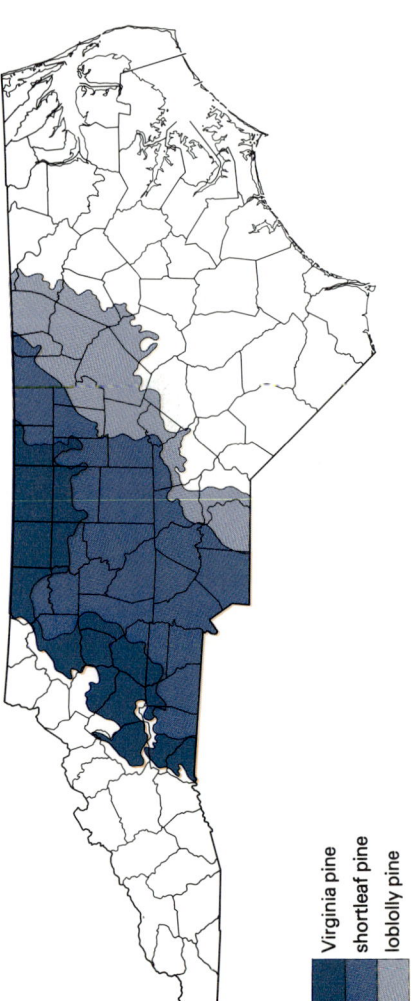

Figure 7.5. Loblolly, Shortleaf, and Virginia Pine Belts in the N.C. Piedmont

Virginia pine
shortleaf pine
loblolly pine

chestnut oak (*Q. prinus*) are common. Such stands become much more abundant in the western Piedmont nearer the Blue Ridge.

Hardwood swamp forest, similar to that of the Coastal Plain, occurs on the floodplains of the major rivers and their tributaries. The major species of this community are sycamore, river birch, ash, elm, sweet gum, willow oak, swamp chestnut oak, and tulip poplar.

There are many isolated patches of vegetation in the Piedmont of limited distribution but of considerable interest. For example, an isolated stand of hemlock (*Tsuga canadensis*) and one of white pine (*Pinus strobus*) occur in Wake and Lee counties, respectively, near the edge of the Coastal Plain. Also, there are a number of stands of purple rhododendron (*Rhododendron catawbiense*) in the Piedmont and Coastal Plain. Several areas of granite flatrock also occur and these have a number of interesting flowering herbs that occur in few other habitats. Pilot Mountain, Kings Mountain, Crowder's Mountain, and other isolated low hills in the eastern and central Piedmont are crowned with stands of chestnut oak and present a mountainous aspect in the otherwise subdued Piedmont landscape.

The sequence of communities that develops following abandonment of a cultivated field is so much a part of the Piedmont scene that one must understand it to understand the vegetation of the region. When a field is cultivated, crabgrass (*Digitaria sanguinalis*) and other weeds dominate during the first summer following abandonment. In the first summer following abandonment, horseweed (*Erigeron canadensis*) dominates and, the second year, its place is taken by white-topped aster (*Aster pilosus*). Gradually, during the next few years, the field shifts to a cover of broomsedge (*Andropogon* sp.), which is rapidly invaded by pines. Different pines dominate in different regions of the Piedmont, with loblolly, shortleaf, and Virginia (*Pinus virginiana*) characteristic of the eastern, central, and western portions, respectively. As the pines mature, a layer of young hardwood seedlings develops beneath them. These mature as the growth of the pines slows and, in time, the pines die and are replaced by hardwoods. Eventually, an oak-hickory forest is reestablished on the site. Although the stages from abandonment to a young pine forest may take place in as little as from 10 to 15 years, the entire sequence from cultivated field to a mature climax forest takes from 150 to 200 years.

Mountains

Two major vegetation systems occur within the Mountains (Figure 7.6). Deciduous forests cover the valleys

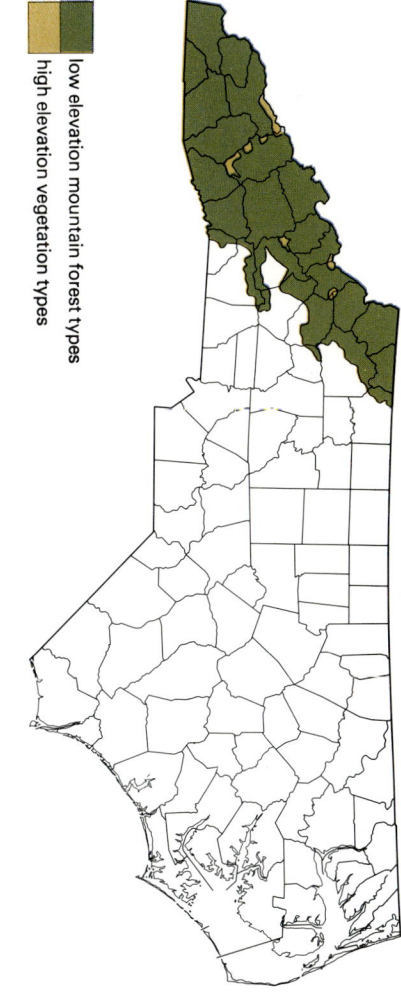

Figure 7.6. Low Elevation Mountain Forest Types and High Elevation Vegetation Types in N.C.

- low elevation mountain forest types
- high elevation vegetation types

and slopes up to 5,000-5,500 feet, whereas boreal conifer forests and related types occur above 4,500-5,000 feet. Within each of these systems there are several major vegetation types, each with its own characteristic history and habitat relationships. The seasonal changes in the appearance of the vegetation make North Carolina's mountain scenery as beautiful as that found anywhere in the world.

Deciduous Forests Five major forest types can be found in the deciduous forests that cover the lower mountain slopes and valleys. Before the white man's coming, *cove hardwood forest* (often called *mixed mesophytic forest*) occupied sheltered mountain valleys and clothed protected lower slopes and more open north- and east-facing slopes from 1,500 to 4,500 feet. Although many of these sites are now cultivated, large unbroken tracts still occur in the Great Smokies and in the national forests. Cove forests are among the richest, most magnificent deciduous forests found anywhere on earth. There are, for example, more tree species recorded in the Great Smokies than there are in all of Europe, and the bulk of these occur in cove forests. It is this richness in species composition, in fact, that characterizes cove forests. Although twenty-five to thirty species may occur in any given stand, towering specimens of six trees are especially typical: hemlock, silverbell (*Halesia carolina*), yellow buckeye (*Aesculus octandra*), white basswood (*Tilia heterophylla*), sugar maple (*Acer saccharum*), and yellow birch (*Betula lutea*). Huge tulip poplar and beech are also found in most stands. Other species frequently found are cucumber tree (*Magnolia acuminata*), fraser magnolia (*M. fraseri*), sweet birch (*B. lenta*), white ash (*Fraxinus americana*), black cherry (*Prunus serotina*), red maple, northern red oak, and bitternut hickory (*Carya cordiformis*). White oak, chestnut oak, and, before advent of the blight, chestnut (*Castanea dentata*) from the adjacent oak forests are often present. Although low trees and shrubs do not form an evident layer, a number of kinds do occur. A luxuriant herb layer is present in all cove forests, and its beauty and seasonal variety is without equal in North Carolina. In coves that have been logged, tulip poplar is the dominant tree. However, the original botanical richness of the vegetation can still be observed in herbs and tree reproduction. Toward its upper altitudinal limits, the number of species in cove forests decreases and there is a gradual rise in importance of white basswood, yellow buckeye, and yellow birch. Toward the moisture limits of cove forest on drier open slopes, the proportion of oaks increases.

Dark and somber *hemlock forest* dominates creek bottoms and ravines at low elevation. Such forests also occur in moist sites at higher elevations in ravines and on valley flats. White basswood, sugar maple, silver bell, and fraser magnolia are the most common associates of hemlock. Perhaps the most characteristic feature of these forests where they occur along streams is the dense tangle of rosebay rhododendron (*Rhododendron maximum*) with doghobble (*Leucothoe axillaris* var. *editorum*) underneath. On hemlock slopes the shrub stratum virtually disappears and a dense, varied layer of herbs and ferns is present.

Exposed slopes up to 4,500-5,000 feet are covered with forests dominated by various species of oak. These forests are continuous with those of the adjacent Piedmont.

Oak-hickory forests, very similar to those of the Piedmont, occur over the southern- and eastern-facing outer slopes of the Blue Ridge below 3,000 feet and in the interior mountain basins. These stands are typically dominated by white oak with chestnut; black and scarlet oaks are commonly the codominants. Red maple, black locust (*Robinia pseudo-acacia*), black gum, sourwood, and dogwood are the other common trees. The shrub layer is dominated by mountain laurel (*Kalmia latifolia*) and blueberries (*Vaccinium* spp.). Few herbs are present. In the Asheville basin a mixture of oaks and pine, very similar to that of the Piedmont, dominates.

The most extensive oak type of the middle and lower slopes is *chestnut oak forest*. In the early days, this was oak-chestnut forest because of the former codominant role of chestnut. Now, because of the blight fungus that invaded the mountains in the 1920s, it seems appropriate to use the more descriptive name based on the present leading dominant, chestnut oak. At lower elevations, this vegetation type occurs on long, gradual east- and north-facing slopes, whereas at higher elevations it is continuous on exposed slopes facing in any direction. Chestnut oak dominates virtually all stands but northern red oak becomes more important at higher elevations. Common associates are red maple, scarlet oak (particularly on drier sites), and sourwood. Dead snags of chestnut are commonly scattered throughout indicating the important role this species once played in this forest community. The shrub layer is always well developed. Mountain laurel is the major species and, on the driest sites, it often occurs as a dense, continuous tangle. Rosebay rhododendron is frequently important on more moist sites. The beautiful flame azalea (*Rhododendron calendulaceum*) commonly occurs scattered throughout these forests. At the extreme upper limits of chestnut oak forest, forests of northern red oak with dead chestnut snags occur widely. Such stands often have shrubs and herbs similar to those found in more moist cove forests at similar elevations.

Virtually all dry, open ridges (called "leads") and steep open south- and southwest-facing slopes are dominated by *pine forest*. Such forests are most common at low elevations but virtually disappear by 4,500 feet. Up to about 2,500 feet, Virginia pine dominates with pitch pine (*P. rigida*) often codominant. At mid-elevation, between 2,500 and 3,500 feet, pitch pine is the major species of leads. Table mountain pine (*P. pungens*) assumes dominance up to the limits of pine at about 4,500 feet. Shortleaf pine occurs throughout but in greatest numbers at lower elevations. Scarlet oak is almost always present in pine stands and it frequently becomes the dominant in the zone between the pine forest and the dry oak forest of adjacent slopes. Chestnut oak, red maple, black gum, and sourwood are virtually always present in small numbers. The shrub layer is usually a dense layer of mountain laurel and blueberry. The soils are usually shallower with higher contents of clay and rock than those downslope under hardwoods. Nutrient levels are very low due to the steepness of slopes on which pine occurs. Fire appears to favor pines and many pine stands are populations of pine that entered after fire. Once established, however, pines are self-maintaining on the steep, dry slopes and thus can be regarded as a climax type of the most extreme sites in the deciduous forest system.

Boreal Conifer Forests and Associated Types of High Elevation The high peaks and ridges of the mountains, above 4,500-5,000 feet, are usually clothed with *spruce-fir forest* of distinctly boreal aspect. The most extensive stands of spruce and fir are in the Smokies, where they occur as low as 4,500 feet and in the Black Mountains, and in the Balsam and Plott Balsam ranges where they begin at about 5,500 feet.

These forests, more reminiscent of Canada than North Carolina, are composed primarily of red spruce (*Picea rubens*) and fraser fir (*Abies fraseri*). Spruce-fir forest is best developed over 6,000 feet where spruce and fir make up over 95 percent of the canopy. The only other common trees are mountain ash (*Sorbus americana*), yellow birch, and fire cherry (*Prunus pensylvanica*). Where these reach the canopy they are usually relicts of some past disturbance such as fire or windthrow. In general, spruce dominates at lower elevations and fir increases in importance with increasing elevation. Although shrubs are rarely important in mature spruce-fir forest, the herbaceous layer is well developed. Ferns and herbs such as *Oxalis montana*, *Clintonia borealis*, *Chelone lyoni*, and *Aster acuminatus* are almost always present. Mosses and liverworts are everywhere abundant.

Large areas within the spruce-fir region have been disturbed by lumbering, fire, storms, and windthrow. Lumbering began in the early 1900s and was followed by extensive fires. Fire cherry, and often yellow birch, become established immediately following fire. Such stands are usually very dense and as they age many trees die and the canopy opens up so that blackberry (*Rubus canadensis*) forms a dense underlayer. Ultimately, fire cherry-yellow birch stands are invaded by spruce and fir seedlings. Such invasion is slow and after twenty years only occasional spruce and fir seedlings may be encountered in a badly burned area. Windthrows are very common, particularly in high elevation fir stands where the trees are shallowly rooted and the soil thin and rocky. Following overthrow of canopy trees, dense stands of fir seedlings develop, leading to pole stands of even-aged trees. Thus reproduction of many high elevation stands appears to be cyclic. At lower elevations, however, individual trees are uprooted, broken off, or die and are gradually replaced, giving rise to uneven-aged stands.

Although spruce and fir dominate the high mountain peaks, climax stands of deciduous forest are also present. Such stands range in stature from true forest to scrubby stands of gnarled trees. The major trees of these forests are beech, yellow birch, sugar maple, and yellow buckeye. The most distinctive of these forests are dense stands of low, gnarled beech trees, regenerated from root sprouts, known as *beech gaps* or *beech orchards*. Such stands are best developed on steep south-facing gaps between ridges covered with spruce and fir. The herbaceous flora of these forests is very rich, especially in spring, where dense layers of wild flowers carpet the forest floor. The origin of these gap forests is unclear. In many places they represent the uppermost extension of ravines or coves. Gap forests may also owe their origin to their ability to withstand the effects of winds that, when funneled through a gap, would uproot the more shallowly rooted spruce and fir.

There are two unique, treeless, communities also found in the same elevational zone as spruce-fir forest. Although both are called "balds," they are very different in appearance and species composition.

Heath balds, or "laurel slicks," are treeless communities dominated by evergreen rhododendrons and mountain laurel. They cover exposed areas of steep, rugged topography at elevations from 4,000 to 6,000 feet. Although at a distance they appear smooth (thus the name "slick"), within they are extremely rough, tangled, and virtually impenetrable. Although the shrubs may exceed ten feet in height, on exposed ridges they diminish to a few feet and, in places, consist of scattered mats and cushions. The steepest and most dramatic heath balds occur in the Smokies but the famous rhododendron "gardens" of the Craggies and Roan Mountain are such balds on more gentle summits. The heath balds of lower elevation are dominated by mountain laurel, rosebay rhododendron, and purple rhododendron, but at higher elevations mountain laurel drops out. Heath bald soils are thin and the sites on which balds occur are almost always on relatively steep, exposed slopes. These factors combine to make the balds very dry sites, thus virtually eliminating trees. There are no plant species confined to balds alone and the bald flora appears to be derived from that of the surrounding forest.

There is much debate as to the origin of heath balds. Some consider them to be formed as a result of catastrophic destruction of trees by fire, windfall, and landslide. The evergreen shrubs, because of their ability to sprout, can survive such disasters, and trees are prevented from entering by the dry soils, recurring fire, and severe competition from the shrubs. This concept appears to hold for large balds such as Craggy Gardens, but other balds, on very steep slopes, probably represent the climax community for such extreme sites.

Beyond all doubt the most enigmatic of all mountain vegetation types is the *grass bald*. The origin of these high mountain pastures has been a matter of speculation for years and there are almost as many theories for their origin as there are people who have visited them.

Four sorts of areas are called grass balds: forested areas dominated by widely spaced dwarfed hardwoods; areas recently cleared for fire towers; grassland occupying recently deforested sites; and the true balds presumably in existence prior to the advent of the white man in the mountains. True grass balds show no relationship to topography, as they occur on dome-shaped summits, in gaps, and on ridges. They are most common on south, southwest, and west exposures and the vast majority occur between 5,200 and 5,800 feet. Most are either surrounded by deciduous forest or lie between deciduous and spruce-fir forest. Deciduous trees at bald margins are gnarled and stunted.

Mountain oat grass (*Danthonia spicata*) is the characteristic plant of all balds, forming a dense turf over the surface and extending into the adjacent open woods. Many weeds occur in the balds as do a number of native herbs. Woody plants are common. Flame azalea, blueberry, and blackberry are common shrubs with shadblow (*Amelanchier laevis*) and hawthorn (*Crataegus macrosperma* var. *roanensis*) the most frequent small trees. Studies over the past thirty years show that the percentage of woody plants on the balds has increased and that forest has moved onto the balds themselves.

Several balds in the Smokies decreased by as much as 25 percent in area between the early 1940s and 1961.

It is difficult to suggest a satisfactory explanation for the formation and persistence of the grass balds. Some have theorized a catastrophic origin by fire, storm, or windthrow with grasses entering after elimination of the trees and persisting by excluding them through root competition. Another theory holds they were formed by Indians who cleared and maintained them as hunting openings. Whatever their origin it is clear that they were expanded and maintained by grazing during the 1800s and early 1900s. Now, with reduced grazing, many balds are reverting to forest and, without maintenance, will disappear. A final explanation suggests that the grasses have entered the zone between deciduous and spruce-fir forest as these two types migrated upward and downward in response to recent climatic changes. The grasses maintain themselves in a zone where the limits of tolerance of seedlings of many tree species are approached or exceeded.

Forest Resources

In addition to giving character to North Carolina's scenery, the state's natural vegetation is its most valuable renewable natural resource. The forests of North Carolina have been of great importance in the development of the state since the earliest colonial days. Some of the first exports from the colony were ship's timbers of oak and longleaf pine and naval stores.

Forestland In the mid-1960s, there were about 20.5 million acres of forestland in North Carolina—65 percent of the state's land area—thus placing North Carolina among the top five states in the nation in total area of commercial timberland. Although the climax vegetation of almost all sites in North Carolina is some type of forest, the state has not always had this much land actually in forest. In 1885, only 13.5 million acres—48 percent of the state's land area—was forested. This acreage increased steadily to slightly in excess of 18 million acres (59 percent) in 1938 (Figure 7.7). By the 1950s, forested land exceeded 20 million acres. Recent analyses of the state's timber resources show that forest acreage peaked in the mid-1960s and that it is now declining (Figure 7.8). Almost half of the state's 20 million acres of forest are in the Coastal Plain with 6 million more in the Piedmont and 4 million in the Mountains.

135

There are ten major commercial forest types in North Carolina (Figure 7.9). The loblolly pine, shortleaf pine, Virginia pine, and oak-hickory types are the most important, covering 60-70 percent of the state. In the Coastal Plain and Piedmont, these types occur on areas that were once covered by oak-hickory forest but which have since been cultivated, cut over, or otherwise disturbed. In the Mountains, the oak-hickory type occupies slopes that were once either oak-hickory or chestnut oak forest. The longleaf-slash pine type occurs in coarse, sandy areas that will support longleaf pine-turkey oak-wire grass forest, whereas pocosins support commercial forests of pond pine. Slash pine (*Pinus elliottii*) is not native to North Carolina, but it has been widely planted and has thrived on a variety of sites. The oak-gum-cypress type is found in areas of gum-cypress and hardwood swamp forest. Small areas of white pine-hemlock and maple-beech-birch commercial forests occur on moist slopes of the higher mountain elevations.

Forest Industry The first forest industry to develop in North Carolina—the naval stores industry—became highly developed during the nineeenth century, with the port of Wilmington being one of the largest export points in the country. *North Carolina Resources*, published by the State Board of Agriculture in 1896, indicates that "the industry of tapping the pine for resin and the distillation of that gives employment to several thousand men in this State." Furthermore, according to that source, resinous products sold from this state were in fact about one-third of the entire products of these commodities in the world. This industry practically vanished with the depletion of the original longleaf pine forests and their replacement by the loblolly pine. By 1929, the naval stores industry had declined to such a low level that the North Carolina Department of Conservation and Development publication, *North Carolina Resources and Industries*, did not even mention it in the section on forest industries.

The pine timber industry has been and still is of great economic importance in the eastern section of the state. This industry was originally based on the longleaf pine, as were naval stores, with the loblolly being used but little, and that only locally. The sawmilling developed at waterfront towns, with the logs being rafted to them from up-river. Wilmington, New Bern, Washington, Edenton, and Elizabeth City were major shipping points of lumber destined for the West Indies and England, from the first three ports, and the northeastern states, from the other two ports.

When dry kilns were introduced in the last half of the nineteenth century, they allowed the loblolly pine lumber to be seasoned without staining. The loblolly lumber then found wide acceptance for interior uses, such as

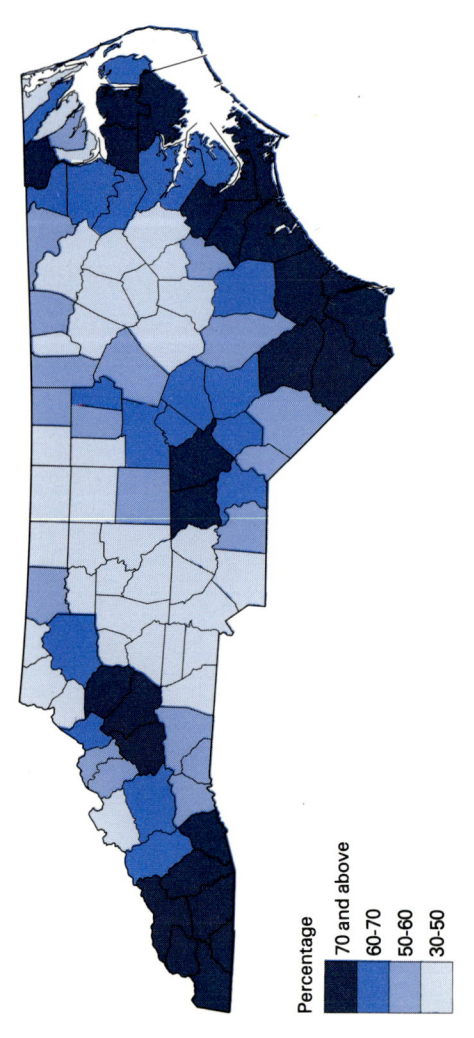

Figure 7.7. Percentage of Land in Forests by N.C. County, 1938

Percentage
70 and above
60-70
50-60
30-50

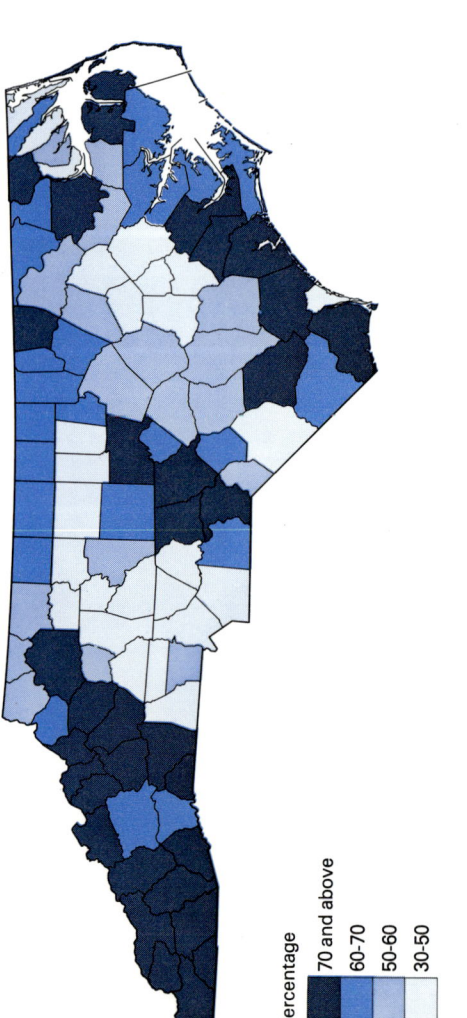

Figure 7.8. Percentage of Land in Forests by N.C. County, 1974

Percentage
70 and above
60-70
50-60
30-50

Figure 7.9. Major Forest Types in N.C.

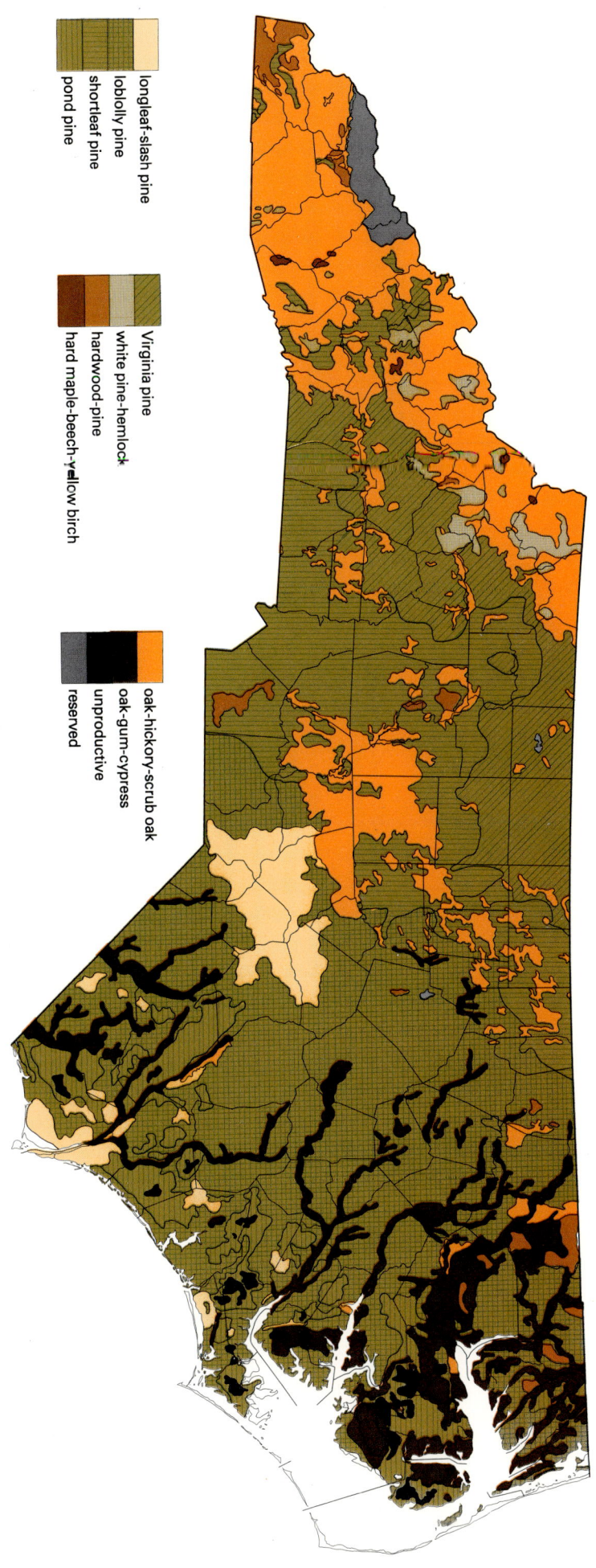

- longleaf-slash pine
- loblolly pine
- shortleaf pine
- pond pine
- Virginia pine
- white pine-hemlock
- hardwood-pine
- hard maple-beech-yellow birch
- oak-hickory-scrub oak
- oak-gum-cypress
- unproductive
- reserved

Source: Data taken from U.S. Department of Agriculture, 1955.

Note: This is a generalized map showing basic forest-type regions. In these regions the predominant forest type is indicated. A forest type grows where conditions are most favorable.

flooring, trim, and ceilings. It then took over the lumber industry, which had depleted the longleaf pine, and was widely marketed in the northeastern states as "North Carolina Pine."

The hardwood forests were somewhat later in making their impact on the state's economy, except for some oak and cypress in the coastal swamps. The oaks were heavily used for cooperage and the cypress for shingles. The upland and mountain hardwood forests did not come into their own until the railroads were established to provide adequate transportation.

One early industry in the hardwood region that was significant but now has practically ceased to exist in North Carolina was tanning. Tanneries located in most of the western counties obtained their tanning materials from the bark of hemlock and oak and from chestnut wood. Some reasons for the demise of this industry were the death of the chestnut, development of less expensive materials, and transportation that allowed for centralization of the tanneries. At this time, the *Directory of North Carolina Manufacturing Firms* lists only one tannery in the state.

Two other small items that were significant in local areas have been replaced by other materials. Shuttles for textile mills (made from the hard wood of dogwood and some persimmon) have largely been replaced by plastics, and insulator pins for telephone and electric lines (made from the rot-resistant wood of locust) have largely been replaced by treated softwoods.

The supply and quality of the fine cabinet woods available in North Carolina were in part responsible for the location of the large furniture industry around 1888. This industry has prospered and grown since that time and North Carolina now leads the nation in the production of wood furniture and the hardwood veneer used in its construction.

Forest Products Lumber of pine and hardwood, pulpwood (both pine and hardwood), hardwood veneer, furniture lumber, flooring, pine and hardwood plywood, pressure-treated timbers, and shipping and warehouse pallets are North Carolina's major forest products. At present, forest-based industries provide more than 15 percent of the employment and wages of all manufacturing in North Carolina. The wages paid by these industries amount to over two-thirds of a billion dollars and the value of the products amounts to over two billion dollars annually.

Saw logs lead all other products. In 1969, over 1,500 million board feet of lumber were cut, 850 million of pine, and 650 of hardwood. From the early 1950s to the mid-1960s the annual cut of pine lumber decreased rapidly but the decline has been reduced in the late 1960s. Hardwood lumber production remained about constant through the mid-1950s, but has increased substantially in the 1960s.

There are now seven pulp mills in North Carolina with a total daily capacity of 5,820 tons of pulp. This industry is the second largest wood consumer in the state with over 2.8 million cords of pulpwood cut in 1969 (Figure 7.11). The total annual pulpwood cut has increased from about 1.5 million cords in 1954 to its present level. The softwood cut approaches 2 million cords annually and appears to have stabilized at that level since the mid-1960s. The hardwood pulpwood cut has increased steadily for the last twenty years.

Production of veneer logs is another major forest industry. The majority of veneer plants are located in the Piedmont where they support the wood furniture industry. Present output of veneer logs exceeds 150 million board feet.

SOILS

Each category of soil users views soils differently. While the highway engineer is interested in physical properties such as the load-bearing capabilities of the soil, the farmer is concerned with properties related to agricultural productivity, and the developer may ask how well the soil handles waste from a septic tank. The primary objective here is to examine the characteristics and spatial pattern of soils within the state from these varying perspectives.

North Carolina's Soil Characteristics and Patterns

Practically all North Carolina soils require application of liberal amounts of lime and fertilizer before they are suitable for the more commonly grown row crops and pastures. This acid and infertile condition is due to a loss of mineral nutrients, especially nitrogen, potash, calcium, and magnesium by a process called *leaching*. Leaching results from an annual rainfall that is in excess of evaporation and transpiration (loss from plants). Upland soils of North Carolina are lower in organic matter and richer in iron (redder) than their counterparts in northern and midwestern states. This is due to the long, hot summers, the year-round weathering conditions, and, in part, the greater soil age in North Carolina.

Although North Carolina soils do have these common features, they differ from one another in ways that can be important in both agricultural and nonagricultural uses. More than two hundred types of soils (soil series) have been identified within the state. There are major differences on a regional basis, with soils ranging from light sands with little humus in the sandhills to the heavy plastic clays of the Piedmont, and from the black-high organic soils of the coast to the brown loams of the Mountains. There is also considerable variability within each of these regions, and as a matter of fact within a single field or lot. These local and regional differences are due to a variety of causes—differences in native vegetation, which is in part related to climatic differences, differences in the kinds of rocks from which the soils have formed, variations in degree of wetness (water saturation) resulting from the soils' topographic position, and variations in the age of soils.

Effects of vegetation differences on soils are mostly expressed in the nature of the humus layers and in their upper mineral layers, or A horizons (topsoil). Soils under pines have raw undecomposed needle litter layers and very acidic leached topsoils. Those formed under broadleaf forests, on the other hand, have well-decomposed rich humus layers and less acidic and leached A horizons. Soils of the cove forests in the mountains are richer, browner, and much less acidic than those of the oak forests, and especially contrast with the lighter-colored, very acidic soils of spruce-fir forests.

A major reason for differences among soils is the kind of parent rock or sediment from which they have formed. This is the most important factor in understanding soil variations in the Piedmont. Soils formed from disintegration of light-colored coarse granitic rocks have very coarse sandy A horizons (topsoils), are yellowish in color, and are very acidic. In contrast, those formed from the weathering of the dark "basic" or "mafic" rocks have heavy loamy horizons, dark red subsoils (if well drained), and are less acidic and infertile than those from granitic and gneissic rocks.

Figure 7.10. Lumber Production in N.C., 1954-1969

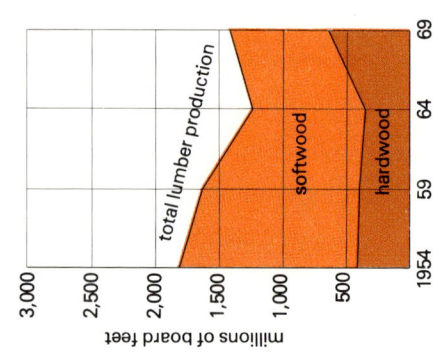

Source: U.S. Department of Agriculture, *North Carolina's Timber*, 1969.

Figure 7.11. Pulpwood Production in N.C., 1954-1969

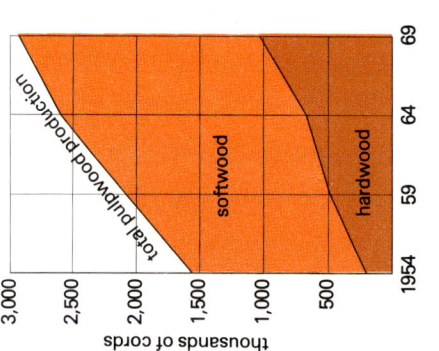

Source: U.S. Department of Agriculture, *North Carolina's Timber*, 1969.

In the Coastal Plain, depositional environment is very relevant to soil patterns. Soils formed from sediments deposited in former lagoons and sounds are very heavy, plastic soils. Sediments from environments like offshore bars, beaches, and sandy floodplains form very sandy, infertile soils.

However, the most important factor causing local soil differences in the Middle and Lower Coastal Plain is the topographic position the soils occupy on the local landscape. Those of the higher points are lower in organic matter, yellower or browner in color, have sandier surface layers, and ordinarily do not have high water tables. In contrast, those of low-lying swampy areas like swales and pocosins contain high amounts of organic matter (humus) with loamy surfaces, are gray, very acidic, and contain high water tables much of the year unless artificially drained. The association of soils formed from similar geologic materials but with great variation in soil properties, from highest point to lowest on a landscape, is called a catena (from the Latin for "chain"), as the soils are in a sagging, chain-like association downslope, across the swale, and up the next slope. Figure 7.12 illustrates two characteristic North Carolina catenas, the Norfolk-Portsmouth and the Cecil-Worsham.

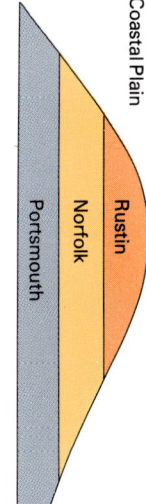
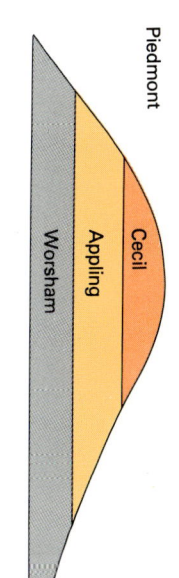

Figure 7.12. Two Characteristic N.C. Catenas

Piedmont: Cecil, Appling, Worsham
Coastal Plain: Rustin, Norfolk, Portsmouth

Source: U.S. Department of Agriculture, Soil Conservation Service, Raleigh, N.C.

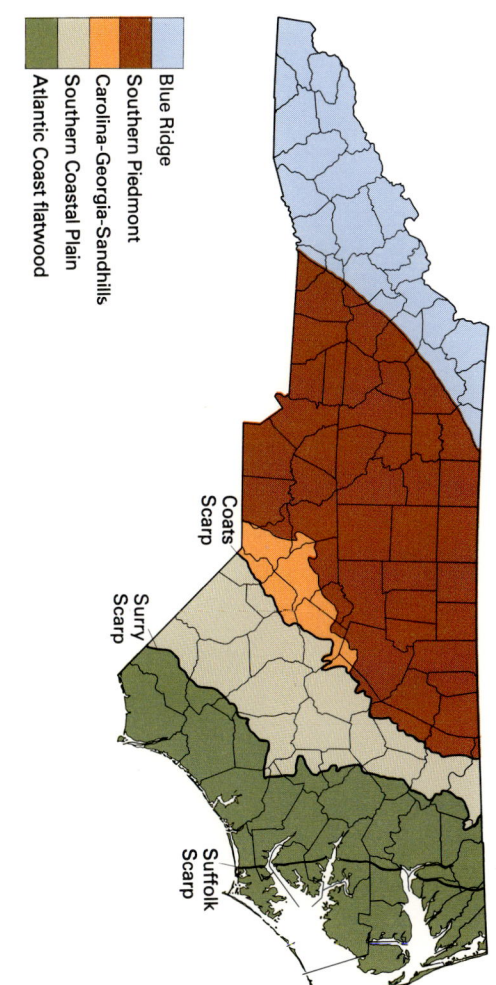

Figure 7.13. Major Land Resource Areas of N.C.

- Blue Ridge
- Southern Piedmont
- Carolina-Georgia-Sandhills
- Southern Coastal Plain
- Atlantic Coast flatwood

Source: U.S. Department of Agriculture, Soil Conservation Service, Raleigh, N.C.

Another reason for so many variations in Coastal Plain soils is the difference in ages of the landscapes on which they have formed. The Coastal Plain underwent several cycles of invasion and recession of the sea in the Pleistocene period (Ice Age). This period of sea invasion has left a series of sedimentary deposits of varying age—from more than a million to less than twenty thousand years—the oldest being in the Upper Coastal Plain and the youngest in the Lower Coastal Plain and Tidewater. If these sedimentary deposits have not been disturbed or eroded, the soils that have formed vary in their properties in accordance with the age of the sediments, with the older soils having experienced greater weathering and leaching. However, during periods in the Ice Age when sea level was much lower than it is now and when rainfall was possibly higher, there was much geologic erosion and removal of sediments, especially from hillslopes along streams in the Upper Coastal Plain—and to a lesser extent in the Middle Coastal Plain. In these places, we find soils that are much younger and less weathered than the undisturbed, uneroded soils of the adjacent smoother uplands and the broader ridge tops.

This gives rise to a complex pattern of soils of varying ages and thicknesses. West of the Coats Scarp, shown in Figure 7.13, soils on the broad ridge tops are very old, have thick very sandy A horizons, and are very deep and highly weathered. Soils on the adjacent hillslopes, below and downslope from the ridge tops, have formed on land surfaces that have undergone several periods of intense geologic erosion—the last one less than fifteen thousand years ago—related to Ice Age events. Soils on these "young" hillslopes are thin, not highly weathered, and lack thick sandy surfaces. Between the Coats Scarp and the Surry Scarp, soils of the undisturbed surfaces are younger than those undisturbed ones above the Coats Scarp. Consequently, there is less difference between soils on broad ridges and those of the adjacent hillslopes. East of the Surry Scarp and Suffolk Scarp, soils are younger and there is little or no difference in the age of soils in a local area. Here, soil differences are due largely to variations in efficiency of natural drainage.

139

Table 7.1. Soil Orders Represented in N.C.

Soil Order	Characteristics
Alfisols	Well-developed subsoils, generally brown or yellowish in color and not as acid, leached, and weathered as the more common Ultisols (formed from "basic" parent material that has more dense clayey subsoils).
Entisols	Recent or juvenile soils with little or no soil development.
Histosols	Organic soils, the peats, and the mucks of the Blacklands.
Inceptisols	Modest subsoil development formed on rather young Coastal Plain landscapes or on steeper slopes where geologic erosion nearly keeps pace with soil development.
Spodosols	Very acid, sandy soils with subsoil accumulations of humus and aluminum.
Ultisols	Soils with prominent subsoils of clay accumulation—very acid, highly leached, and weathered.

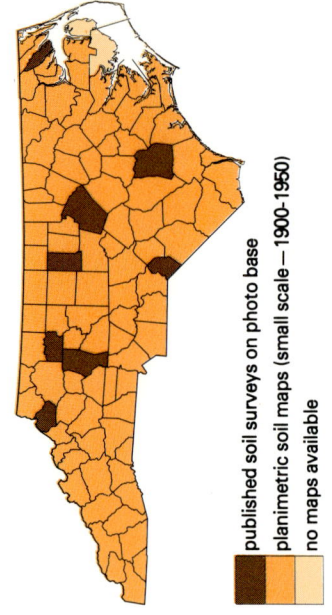

Figure 7.14. Status of Soil Mapping in N.C., June 1974

published soil surveys on photo base
planimetric soil maps (small scale—1900-1950)
no maps available

Source: U.S. Department of Agriculture, Soil Conservation Service, Raleigh, N.C.

In the Piedmont and the Mountains, there are less striking differences in the age of soils. Since the entire area has been eroded, there are no old, preserved original depositional surfaces as in the Upper and Middle Coastal Plain. Soils of the steeper hillslopes along the near drainageways are thinner and "younger" than those of the more gently rolling slopes away from the rivers, but there are not the great contrasts in properties due to age as are found in the Coastal Plain. The oldest, most highly weathered and leached soils in North Carolina are those of the old remnantal depositional surfaces on the tops of the interstream divides in the upper Coastal Plain, above the Coats Scarp.

Rainfall and temperature have some limited influence on soil variety in North Carolina, but not nearly as much as parent material, local landscape position, and soil age. Soils of the southern portion of the Mountains receive larger amounts of rainfall and are more highly leached and weathered than others, even though they are on steep hillslopes and are rather young soils. This is especially true for soils of the warmer south-facing slopes. These soils contain large amounts of gibbsite, an aluminum ore mineral generally found to a significant extent in the highly weathered soils of the warm humid tropics. In contrast, soils of northeastern North Carolina are less leached, more fertile, and browner than other soils of the state. Differences in soils from place to place in the state are not always obvious from casual examination of the land; however, they may be important to environmental, engineering, or agricultural decisions. To show these differences, soils have been described, classified, and mapped throughout the state.

Soil Classification

The problem of classifying soils is extremely complicated. Soils are formed through the interaction of five variable factors—climate, vegetation and microorganisms, parent material, slope, and time. As these variables change from place to place a very great number of combinations can result. To accommodate these many possible combinations, a comprehensive soil classification system, the 7th Approximation, was published in 1960 with a lengthy supplement added in 1967. In the new International System of Soil Classification, ten broad kinds of soil, or soil *orders*, are recognized. Each soil order is composed of soils with similar genetic layers or horizons, formed by the same kind and intensity of soil-forming factors. As shown in Table 7.1, six of these ten soil orders are found in North Carolina. Each of these orders is subdivided into successively smaller, more narrowly defined classes. That is, each of the orders is subdivided into several subclasses or *suborders*. Each of these suborders is further subdivided into a number of *great groups*. A great group is composed of soils having similar *profiles* (the same kind, arrangement, and thickness of genetic layers—A horizons or topsoil, and B horizons or subsoils). They have developed with similar soil-forming factors (similar kinds of vegetation, climate, parent rock, and landscape position).

The great groups are further subdivided into *subgroups*, these into *families*, and finally the families are each subdivided into several *soil series*, the basic soil taxonomic and map unit. Soil series are designed to illustrate and describe what soils are like in individual fields, tracts, and lots, and are ordinarily used for the detailed surveys and classifications. The soil series are composed of soils similar in color, texture, reaction, consistency, and chemical and mineralogical properties in all their genetic layers or horizons. The characteristic county soil maps display soils at the series level of classification.

Soil Resources in North Carolina

The broad soil pattern of North Carolina is illustrated in Figure 7.14. This map has been generalized from county surveys to show broad soil resource areas (soil orders) composed of combinations of certain great groups that occur together. Table 7.1 summarizes general characteristics of each of the six soil orders found in the state. Soils belonging to the same great group have generally similar kinds of physical and chemical properties, vegetation associations, agricultural and nonfarm use potentials, and utilization problems. Therefore, soil orders are probably the most feasible of units or classes for examining soil resources in broad general terms. At this scale, natural vegetation and agricultural land use can generally be correlated with soil type.

Soil Type and Vegetation By comparing Figures 7.1–7.6 with Figure 7.14, a general correlation can be demonstrated between soil and the natural vegetation patterns. Histosols and Spodosols in the Lower Coastal Plain are associated with pine flatwoods, pocosins, and savanna types of vegetation. Entisols of the sandhills are associated with longleaf pine and oak-hickory vegetation types while Entisols along the Outer Banks support maritime forests and salt marshes. Other great groups of the Coastal Plain are in wetland vegetation, upland oak-hickory, and pines. The great groups of the Piedmont are in old field pines and upland oak-hickory. Some cove forests of yellow poplar occur in the upper Piedmont and foothills.

The Dystrochrepts of the higher mountains are associated with spruce-fir, heath balds, "beech gaps," and cove forests. Other great groups of the Mountains support oak forests, old field pine, and yellow poplar in the coves.

Soil Type and Agriculture A close association can also be demonstrated between soil properties and localization of certain types of specialized agricultural production. The smooth slopes, high organic-matter content, good moisture-supplying capacity, and responsiveness of the Umbaquults and Ochraquults soils of the Lower Coastal Plain and Tidewater are in part responsible for the concentration of corn-soybean production in this area. Sloping land, highly erodible soils with acid clay subsoils, and low summer-moisture supply of the Hapludults and associated soils of the Piedmont are factors related to the greater specialization in pastures and small grain.

The North Carolina peach-growing industry is concentrated in the sandhills, mainly on the Quartzipsamment soils such as the Lakeland soil type. The good air drainage of the rolling hills, plus the early warming, ease of root penetration, and good tilth of the sands are among the factors responsible for this localization.

The North Carolina blueberry industry is concentrated on Haplaquod soils in the southern Tidewater region. The highbush type of blueberry now used for main production is adapted to these very sandy acid soils with an organic pan or hardpan in the subsoil. (Rabbiteye blueberries are suited to a wider range of soil conditions.)

Peanut production in North Carolina is concentrated in seventeen counties in the northern portion of the Middle Coastal Plain. This production is mainly on Paleudults and Hapludults, soils that have good natural drainage, a sandy loam topsoil, and a friable, sandy clay loam subsoil. The sandy loam surface soils are well suited to peanut "pegging," and the well-drained friable subsoils provide excellent soil moisture and physical conditions for peanut growth. Furthermore, these soils occur on relatively smooth land suited for the machine culture of peanuts.

Apple production is concentrated in the western part of the state, on shallow Hapludults and Dystrochrepts of the Blue Ridge and foothills. Here, the good air drainage provided by the slopes and the excellent growth and timely ripening permitted by the cooler climate combine with the good physical conditions of the soils to encourage this expanding enterprise.

Factors other than soil properties are responsible for localization of patterns of production of some other field crops in North Carolina. Cotton, for example, tends to be concentrated in three producing areas in North Carolina—two on the Coastal Plain and one in the southwestern Piedmont—and soil properties are not a major contributing factor to this localization (see chapter 10).

Pulpwood production is somewhat concentrated on the Ochraquults of the northern Tidewater, where the sandy loams provide good moisture retention without year-round high water tables to enhance site quality.

Soil Type and Nonfarm Urban Uses There is an increasing interest in nonfarm urban uses of soil resources. Although there is a store of information available on soil from an agronomy viewpoint, little has been published concerning the compatibility of soils with various urban uses. In examining the compatibility of the land with nonfarm urban uses for specific sites, a map showing soil series should be consulted, or perhaps even a field examination made. For more general planning purposes, however, *soil association maps* have proven very useful. The soil association classification is derived by grouping together several similar soil series. In compiling the maps, county surveys of soil series are checked in the field for association boundaries. A brief discussion of the feasibility of soils with urban land uses in each of North Carolina's three major physiographic regions is presented below. The spatial pattern of North Carolina's soil associations is shown in Figures 7.15, 7.16, and 7.17. Limitations and general characteristics of each soil association are summarized in Tables 7.2, 7.3, and 7.4.

Mountains The major soil characteristics affecting nonfarm land use in the Mountain area are slope and thickness of the soil mantle over rock or other impermeable layers. The most desirable soils for residential, industrial, and recreational purposes are those having slopes under 12 percent and a soil thickness greater than thirty-six inches. The greater the slope, the greater the potential for excessive sediment and erosion losses from site clearing. The effectiveness of soil areas as waste treatment systems, where public sewage disposal is not available, is mainly associated with the thickness and permeability of the soil and slope gradient. Slope, depth to hard or bed rock, support and slippage potentials of the soil, and natural drainage are strongly related to problems associated with roads and parking facilities.

Although flood-prone land in the Mountain area is not extensive, problems of sediment control and active erosion are serious where nonfarm uses would involve removal of vegetative cover. Further, watersheds are subject to flash flooding at low points within the watershed boundary. This flooding potential increases drastically as urban development increases. Thus, as in other regions of the state, hazards are involved in nonfarm uses of flood-prone areas.

Considering these limitations, approximately 18 percent of the North Carolina Mountain area is suitable for nonfarm uses when public utilities (sewer lines) are not available. With widespread public sewer lines and minimal development expenses, approximately 32 percent of the area might be compatible with nonfarm urban uses.

Piedmont Soil characteristics that affect nonfarm urban uses in the Piedmont include the following: slope, the amounts and kinds of clay, the thickness of the soil mantle over hard rock, and the presence of any impermeable strata. Considering these limitations, about two-thirds of the soil resources of the Piedmont have one or more characteristics that impose moderate to severe limitations for urban-suburban use.

In urban-suburban development of Piedmont soils, the following considerations should be noted:

1. The control of erosion and the resulting sediment is closely related to slope and the erodibility of the Piedmont soil. Nonfarm developments that require removal of vegetation and that expose soils for long periods of time lead to severe soil losses by erosion. Where slopes exceed 12 percent, nonfarm uses frequently require extensive grading, cutting, and filling.

2. The percolation of subsurface horizons in Piedmont soils is variable. Some soil areas are underlain by dense clays of very low percolation rates and thus are not suitable as waste sinks. Piedmont soils are not well adapted to high density development unless waste treatment systems are available. Percolation rates of the soils restrict their use as waste sinks. They are, however, generally satisfactory if the quantity of waste is controlled, and if soils are not subjected to saturation for long periods of time.

3. Some soil resource areas consist of clayey, plastic soils that create serious problems for foundations, streets, and all building appurtenances. The recognition and modification of these resource areas for urban-suburban uses are essential.

Figure 7.15. N.C. Soil Resources

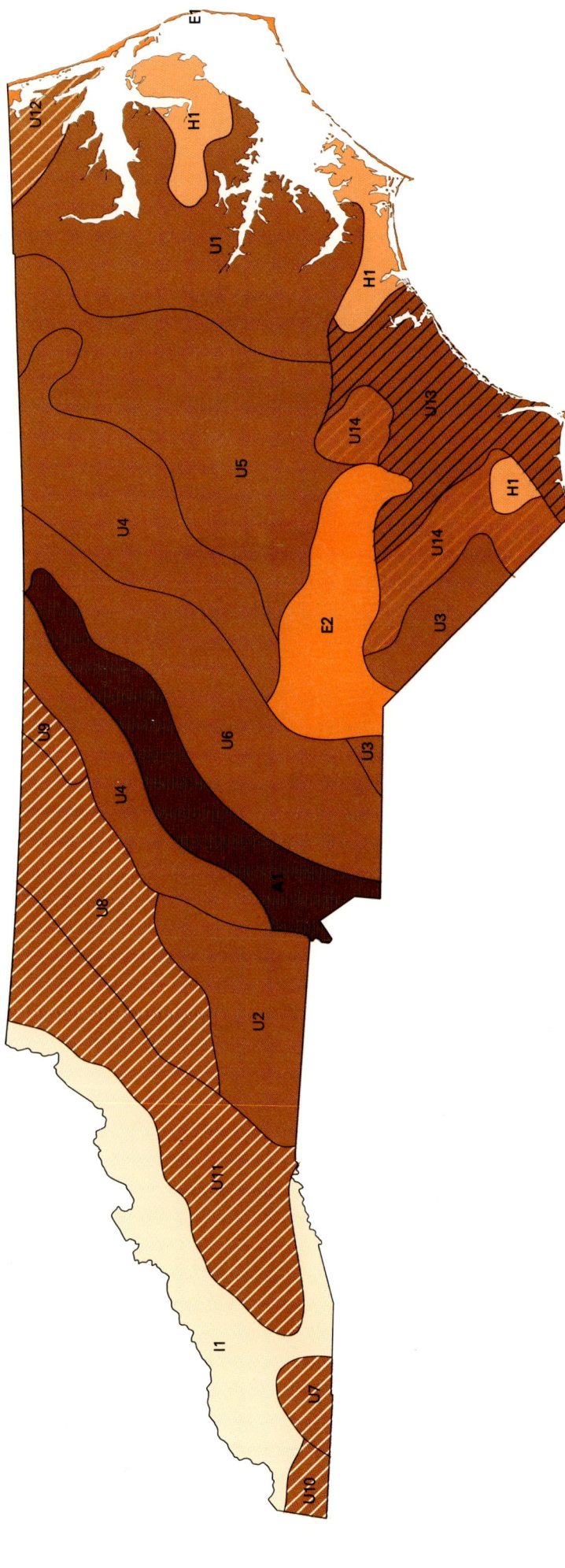

Source: S. W. Buol, ed., *Soils of the Southern States and Puerto Rico* (Raleigh: Agricultural Experiment Station, N.C. State University, 1973).

4. High density development in and close to natural drainageways is hazardous. Although flood-prone areas are not extensive, they severely restrict urban-suburban uses and their use should be restricted to recreation, green belts, and park uses. As the hydrologic characteristics in watersheds are changed by urban development, the flooding potential is greatly increased.

Coastal Plain In the Coastal Plain, physical limitations on urban-suburban development are largely related to internal and external drainage, soil texture, and the organic content. In urban-suburban development of the Coastal Plain regions, the following soil characteristics are most significant:

1. Erosion and sediment control are not major problems and are confined to the more sloping lands of the Upper Coastal Plain. Flooding, however, is a problem and floodplain land areas are generally best suited for recreational activities or farm uses.

2. Many soils are seasonally wet. This limits the usefulness of the land area as waste sinks, and generally renders the land area unstable for foundations and traffic ways.

3. Soils of either slow or rapid percolation will contribute to pollution problems where soils are used as waste sinks. Both types are present in the Coastal Plain.

4. The organic soils and soils with organic hard pans present special problems in urban-suburban development in the Coastal Plain. These soils are very poorly suited for many nonfarm uses. They are not suitable as waste disposal areas, even when intensively drained.

High water tables, clayey soils with slow percolation rates, organic soils, and soils with impermeable hard pans are the principal limitations on about two-thirds of the soils in the region. All nonfarm uses of these soils will encounter waste disposal problems and pollution hazards without extensive modification. Urban-suburban uses of these soils generally require that special measures be undertaken to correct soil limitations prior to development for failure to correct results in environmental deterioration. The other third of soil resources is well-drained and has characteristics very favorable for engineering uses. Percolation rates are favorable, providing good waste disposal areas where soils are not subject to continuous saturation.

Table 7.2. Characteristics and Use Limitations of Soils in the Mountain Region of N.C.

Soil Association	Soil Characteristics	Agriculture	Use Limitations Nonfarm Urban
Braddock-Dyke-Delanco	Gently sloping to sloping, well-drained soils. Loamy surface soils and clayey subsoils.	Highly productive soils. Major hazard is erosion. Acid soils.	Moderate percolation rates are major limitations.
Chester-Edneyville-Ashe	Sloping to steep, well-drained soils. Loamy surface soils and clayey or loamy subsoils.	Moderate to high production potential. Slope and erosion are major limitations. Acid soils.	Good percolation rates but uses limited by slopes and in places rock close to surface.
Chester-Hayesville	Sloping to steep well-drained soils. Loamy surface soils and clayey subsoils.	Moderate production potential. Slope and erosion are major limitations. Acid soils.	Uses primarily limited by slope.
Clifton-Porters	Sloping to very steep well-drained soils. Loamy surface soils and clayey or loamy subsoils.	High production potential. Slope and erosion are limiting factors. Slightly acid.	Slope and rock close to surface are major limitations.
Fannin-Watauga	Sloping to very steep well-drained soils. Micaceous loamy surface soils and micaceous clayey or loamy subsoils.	Moderate production potential. Slope and erosion are major limitations. Acid soils.	Slope and lack of stability of micaceous material limit uses. Sediment control a major problem.
Porters-Ashe	Steep and very steep well-drained soils. Loamy surface soils and loamy subsoils.	High to moderate production potential. Slope is limiting factor. Slightly acid to acid soils.	Slope and rock close to surface limit uses.
Stony land	Steep and very steep well-drained soils. Loamy soil material more than 50% stone and rock ledges.	Low production potential. Stones and slope limit use.	Stones, rock ledges, and outcrops are major limitations.
Talladega-Chandler-Tate	Sloping to very steep well-drained soils. Talladega and Chandler micaceous loamy texture and Tate nonmicaceous loamy texture.	Low production potential for Talladega and Chandler. High production potential for Tate. Slope and erosion are limiting factors. Acid soils.	Talladega and Chandler are limited by slope, unstable micaceous soils, and rock close to surface. Tate has water problems from seepage.

143

Figure 7.16. Soil Associations in N.C. Mountains

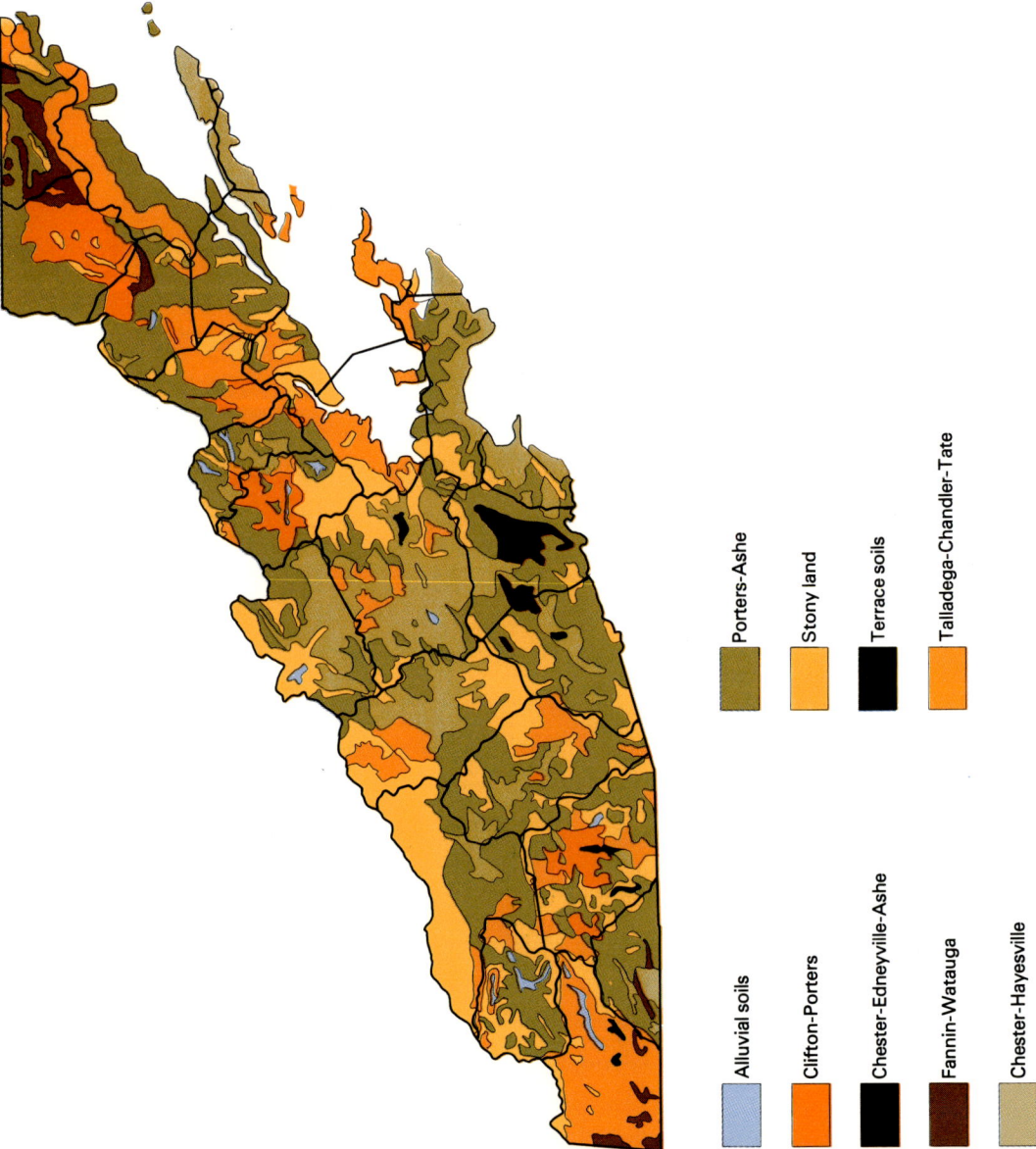

Alluvial soils
Clifton-Porters
Chester-Edneyville-Ashe
Fannin-Watauga
Chester-Hayesville
Porters-Ashe
Stony land
Terrace soils
Talladega-Chandler-Tate

Source: Modified from William D. Lee, *The Soils of North Carolina* (Raleigh: N.C. State University, 1955).

Local Soil Resources in North Carolina

To provide the public with soil information relevant to local analysis, systematic field examinations are made and their findings published as soil maps, together with careful descriptions of the soil properties. Each of the soils is fitted into the International System of Soil Classification, including the aggregation of soil series into great groups and orders. The maps are compiled at a county level, are larger in scale, and thus show much greater detail than can be shown in this publication. The maps and reports are prepared as an inventory of our soil resources by the Soil Conservation Service with the assistance and cooperation of the North Carolina Agricultural Experiment Station. Figure 7.18 shows the status of county soil mapping in the state. Copies of county maps are available in soil conservation district offices, county Agricultural Extension offices, North Carolina Agricultural Experiment Station in Raleigh, and the United States Government Printing Office.

Land Use and Conservation in North Carolina Multicounty Planning Regions

As shown in Figure 7.19a, forest is the predominant land use in the state, accounting for more than 50 percent of the total land use in each of the seventeen state planning regions in 1970. Further, the percentage of state land in forest is increasing at the expense of cropland. In the Mountains and Coastal Plain, there are large additional acreages of forest on federal lands. Urban-suburban uses are very dynamic, increasing throughout the state. The percent of land in urban and suburban uses is greater in the Piedmont where approximately 10 percent of the total land is used for urban and suburban purposes and increasing. Recreation is a significant nonfarm use for the Mountain area, increasing the percentage of total land used for urban-suburban purposes.

As illustrated in Figure 7.19b, the predominant portion of the Piedmont has potentially large percentages (70-80 percent) of good to fair agricultural land (Class 2-4). However, only in the Coastal Plain area is there a substantial area of prime agricultural land (Class 1). In contrast, more than 50 percent of the total land in the Mountain region is not well suited to agriculture (Class 5-8).

As shown in Figure 7.19c, more than three-fourths of the land in the state would benefit from drainage and erosion control. In the Coastal Plain the problem is related to poor drainage while in the Mountain region, steep slopes contribute to erosion and management problems. In the Piedmont, main resource management problems result from clayey, slowly permeable soils, short summer droughts, and subsoil acidity and lime needs. Many

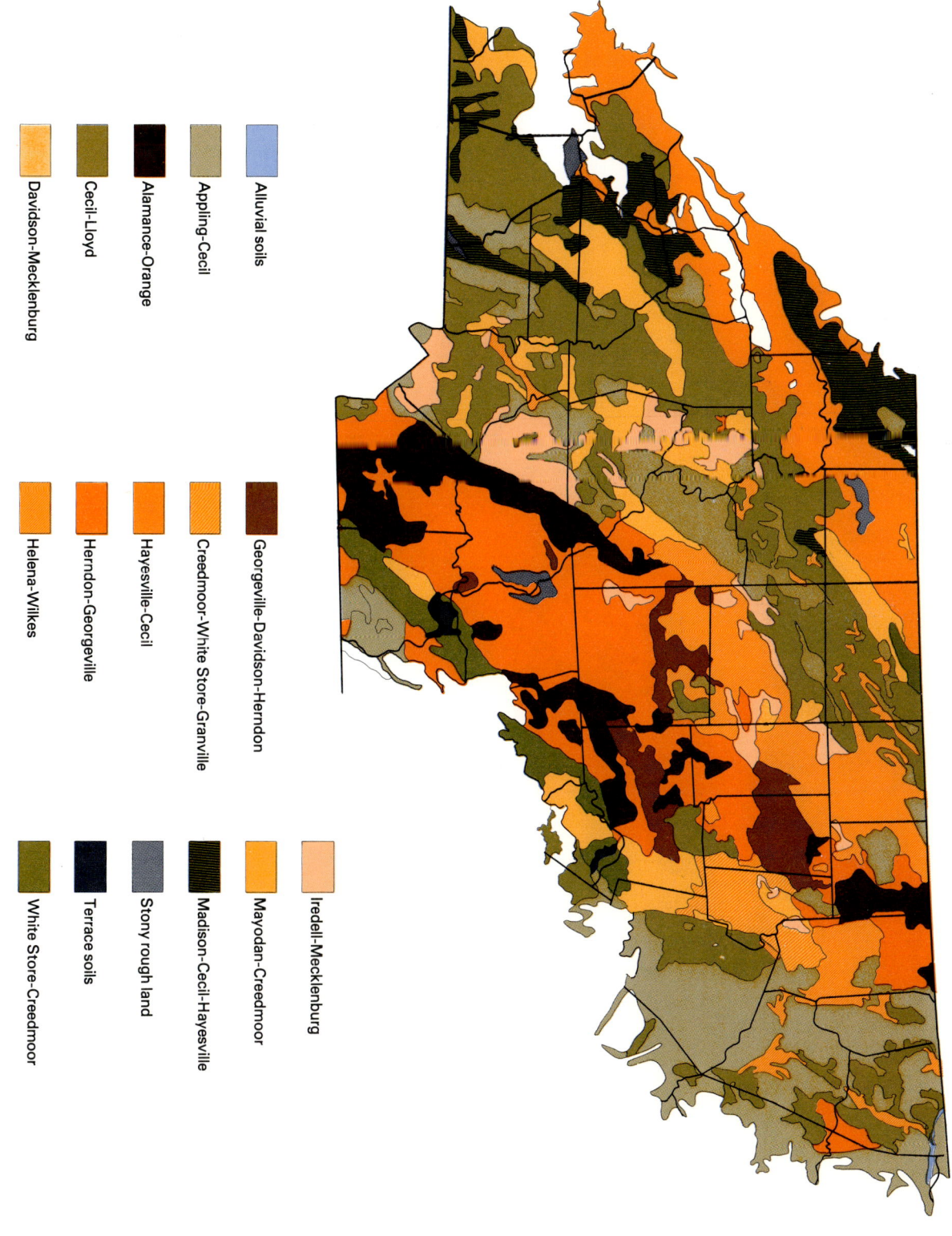

Figure 7.17. Soil Associations in N.C. Piedmont

Source: Modified from William D. Lee, *The Soils of North Carolina* (Raleigh: N.C. State University, 1955).

Figure 7.18. Soil Associations in N.C. Coastal Plain

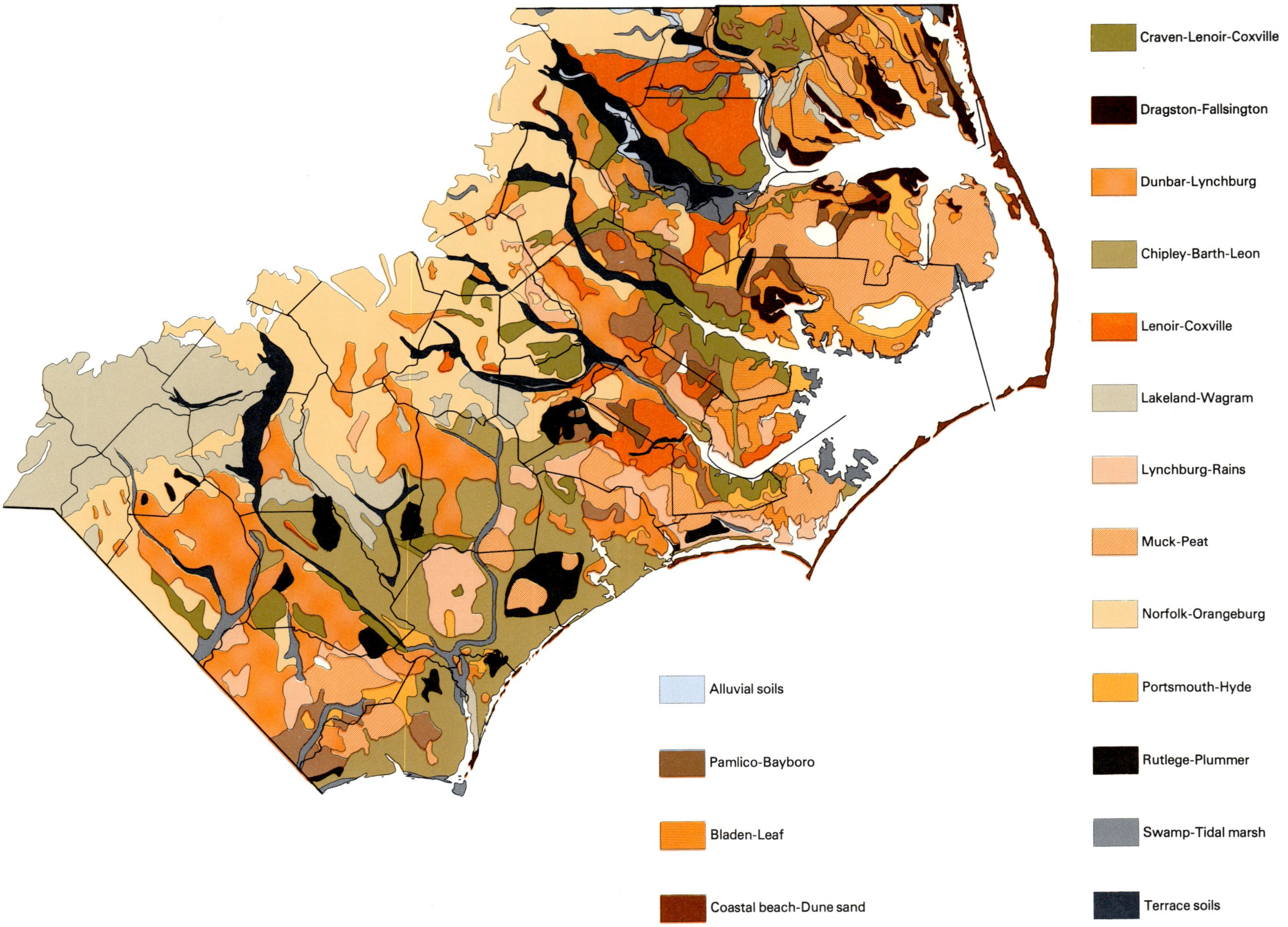

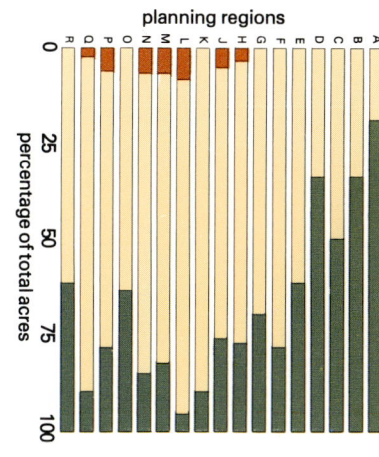

Figure 7.19(a). Land Use by N.C. Planning Regions

Source: U.S. Department of Agriculture, North Carolina Conservation Needs Inventory, 1971.

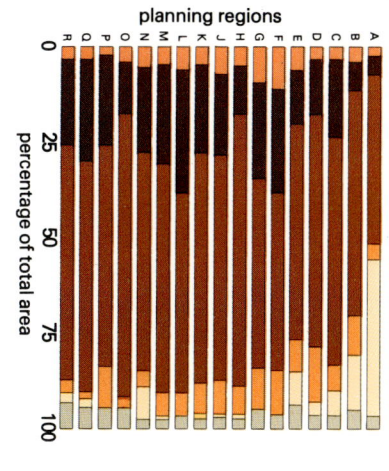

Figure 7.19(c). Erosion Control and Artificial Drainage Needs for N.C. Planning Regions

Source: U.S. Department of Agriculture, North Carolina Conservation Needs Inventory, 1971.

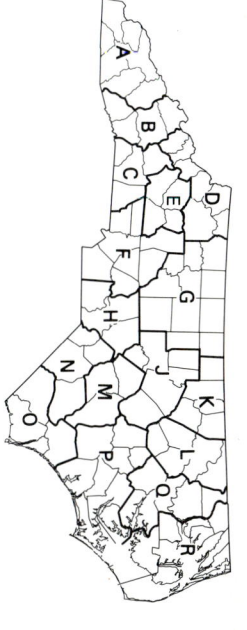

N.C. State Planning Regions

Figure 7.19(b). Potential Agricultural Land and Land Capability by N.C. Planning Regions

Source: U.S. Department of Agriculture, North Carolina Conservation Needs Inventory, 1971.

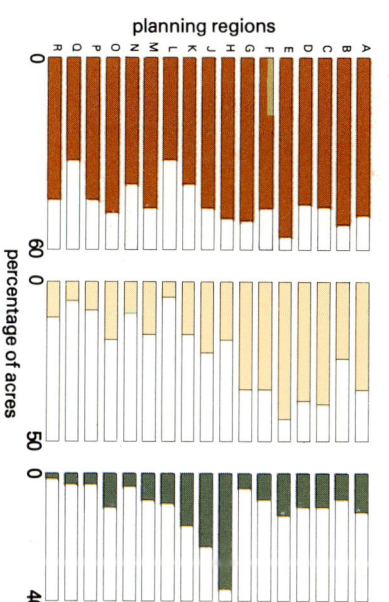

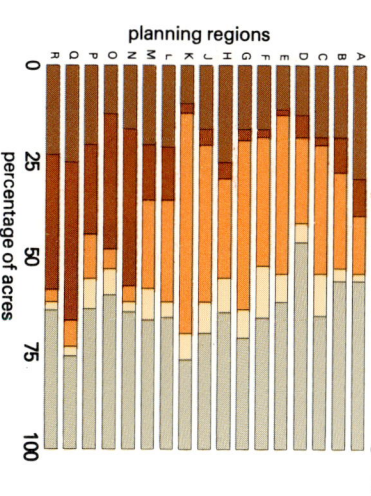

Figure 7.19(d). Lime Needs and Soil Fertility Evaluation for Multicounty Planning Regions

Source: N.C. Department of Agriculture, Soil Testing Division, 1972.

147

Piedmont areas are severely eroded and the sloping lands are very susceptible to erosion unless conservation measures are practiced.

Soil deficiencies are characteristic to all regions of the state. Thus, for the best result in agricultural activities, considerable fertilization is required. As shown in Figure 7.19d, approximately one-half of the soils need lime, one-third need phosphorus, and one-fifth need potassium. Lime requirements are relatively uniform throughout the state except for the Inner Coastal Plain where the need is not as great as elsewhere in the state. Phosphate requirements are greatest in the Mountains and potassium deficiencies are substantially greater in planning regions J, K, and L.

Vegetation—Arthur W. Cooper
Soils—Ralph J. McCracken and Louis E. Aull

SELECTED REFERENCES

Buol, S. W., ed. *Soils of the Southern States and Puerto Rico.* Southern Cooperative Series Bulletin 174. Raleigh: N.C. Agricultural Experiment Station, 1973.

Daniels, R. B.; Gamble, E. E.; and Cady, J. G. "Some Relations among Coastal Plain Soils and Geomorphic Surfaces in North Carolina." *Soil Science Society of America Proceedings* 34 (1970): 648-53.

Eaddy, D. W. Soil Test Summaries for North Carolina. Raleigh: Soil Testing Division, N.C. Department of Agriculture, 1971, 1972.

Lee, W. D. *Soils of North Carolina.* Technical Bulletin 115. Raleigh: N.C. Agricultural Experiment Station, 1955.

N.C. Agricultural Experiment Station. North Carolina Soil Association Map. Raleigh: The Station, n.d.

N.C. Conservation Needs Committee. *Soil and Water Conservation Needs Inventory: 1967.* Raleigh: Soil Conservation Service, U.S. Department of Agriculture, 1971.

N.C. Department of Natural and Economic Resources, Office of Forest Resources. *Major Forest Types–North Carolina.* Raleigh: The Department, 1955.

N.C. Wildlife Resources Commission. Wildlife Cover Map of North Carolina. Raleigh: The Commission, 1950.

Table 7.3. Characteristics and Use Limitations of Soils in the Piedmont Region of N.C.

Soil Association	Soil Characteristics	Agriculture	Use Limitations Nonfarm Urban
Altavista-Wickham-Augusta	Gently sloping soils that are well to somewhat poorly drained. Sandy and loamy surfaces with clayey subsoils.	Potential productivity high. Some drainage needed. Acid soils requiring lime and other nutrients. Some low-lying areas flood.	Well-drained soils are adapted to all uses. Other soil areas limited by high water tables and flooding potential.
Appling-Cecil-Louisburg	Gently sloping to steep soils that are well drained. Sandy to clayey surface soils with clayey subsoils or lacking subsoils.	Potential productivity high to moderate. Slope and erosion are major limitations. Acid soils.	Slope and percolation rates are major limitations.
Cecil-Lloyd	Gently sloping to steep soils that are well drained. Sandy to clayey surface with clayey subsoils.	Potential productivity high to moderate. Slope and erosion are major limitations. Acid soils.	Slope and percolation rates are major limitations.
Chewacla-Congaree	Floodplain soils that are well to somewhat poorly drained. Loamy textures.	High production potential but may have severe flooding hazard.	Flooding is major limitation. High water table limits some uses.
Creedmoor-White Store-Granville	Nearly level to steep soils, somewhat poorly to well drained. Sandy surface soils, Creedmoor and White Store have impermeable clayey subsoils and Granville a permeable loamy subsoil.	Creedmoor and White Store have low to moderate production potential; Granville moderate to high. Very acid soils and susceptible to erosion. Strongly acid soils.	Very slow percolation, high water table and high shrink-swell clay limit use of White Store and Creedmoor. Granville soils suitable for most uses.
Davidson-Mecklenburg-Lloyd	Gently sloping to steep soils with loamy surface soils and clayey subsoils. Well drained.	High to moderate production potential. Slope and erosion major limitations. Slightly acid.	Slope and percolation rates are limitations.
Georgeville-Davidson-Herndon	Gently sloping to steep well-drained soils. Loamy surface soils and clayey subsoils.	High to moderate production potential. Slope and erosion major limitations. Slightly acid to acid.	Slope and percolation rates limit certain uses.
Hayesville-Cecil	Sloping to very steep well-drained soils. Loamy surface soils and clayey subsoils.	Moderate production potential. Limited by slope and erosion. Acid soils.	Slope limits many uses.
Helena-Wilkes-Enon	Sloping to very steep well-drained soils with loamy surface soils and plastic, impermeable, clayey subsoils.	Moderate production potential, limited by slope, erosion, and plastic clay subsoils. Slightly acid to strongly acid.	Slope, very slow percolation, and shrink-swell clays limit use.
Herndon-Georgeville	Sloping to steep well-drained soils with loamy surface soils and clayey subsoils.	Moderate production potential. Slope and erosion limit use. Acid soils.	Slope and percolation rates limit uses.
Iredell-Mecklenburg-Enon	Gently sloping to steep well-drained soils. Loamy surface soils and plastic, impermeable, clayey subsoils.	Moderate potential for grass land and low for crops. Slope, erosion, and plastic clay subsoils are major limitations. Slightly acid.	Very slow percolation rates. Slopes and high shrink-swell clays limit uses.
Madison-Cecil-Hayesville	Strongly sloping to very steep well-drained soils. Loamy surface soils and clayey subsoils.	Moderate production potential. Slope and erosion limiting factors. Acid soils.	Slope and moderate percolation rates limit some uses.
Mayodan-Creedmoor	Gently sloping to strongly sloping soils that are well to imperfectly drained. Loamy surface soils and clayey subsoils.	Moderate production potential. Slope, erosion, and drainage are limiting factors. Acid soils.	Percolation rates and high water tables limit uses.
Orange-Herndon	Gently sloping to sloping soils that are well to imperfectly drained. Loamy surface soil with clayey subsoils that are impermeable and plastic or moderately permeable.	Low to moderate production potential. Slope, erosion limit Herndon; Orange limited by imperfect drainage and plastic clay subsoil.	Moderate percolation rates and slopes are limitations in using Herndon soils. Orange soils limited by high shrink-swell clays, very slow percolation, and water tables.
White Store-Creedmoor	Nearly level to gently sloping soils that are imperfectly drained. Loamy surface soils with plastic impermeable, clayey subsoils.	Low to moderate production potential. Drainage and plastic clay subsoils limit uses. Strongly acid soils.	Very slow percolation rates and high shrink-swell clays are major limitations.

Table 7.4. Characteristics and Use Limitations of Soils in the Coastal Plain Region of N.C.

Soil Association	Soil Characteristics	Agriculture	Nonfarm Urban
Barth-Pactolus-Chipley	Nearly level, imperfectly drained soils. Sandy surface soils and sandy subsoils.	Moderate production potential. Drainage and low-water holding capacity limiting factors. Acid soils.	High water tables and rapid percolation rates. Low filtering capacity for wastes.
Bladen-Leaf	Nearly level, poorly drained soils. Loamy surface soils and plastic clayey subsoils.	Moderate production potential. Drainage and slowly permeable plastic clay subsoils limit uses. Acid soils.	High water tables, very slow percolation rates, and surface water ponding limit uses.
Chipley-Barth-Leon	Nearly level, imperfectly drained soils. Sandy surface soils and sandy subsoils.	Moderate to low production potential. Drainage and low water-holding capacity are major problems. Leon soils have organic hardpan. Acid soils.	High water tables, low filtering capacity limit uses. Leon soils have restrictive hardpans.
Coastal beach-Dune sand	Nearly level to sloping soils. Excessively drained sands.	Low production potential. Very droughty and subject to salt damage. Acid to alkaline.	Erosion by wind and water is severe. Difficult to stabilize.
Coxville-Bladen-Lenoir	Nearly level, imperfectly drained soils. Loamy surface soils and plastic clayey subsoils.	Moderate production potential. Drainage and slowly permeable plastic, clay subsoils limit uses. Acid soils.	High water tables, very slow percolation rates, and surface water ponding are major hazards.
Craven-Lenoir-Coxville	Nearly level to sloping imperfectly drained soils. Loamy surface soils and plastic clayey subsoils.	Moderate production potential. Drainage, slow permeability, and erosion on sloping areas are principal limitations. Acid soils.	High water tables and very slow percolation rates are limiting factors.
Dorovan-Pamlico-Ponzer	Level, very poorly drained soils. Organic soils.	Moderate production potential. Drainage, water control are essential. Require special management. Strongly acid.	High water tables and unstable organic materials limit use. Very poorly suited for nonfarm urban uses.
Dunbar-Lynchburg	Level to gently sloping, imperfectly drained soils. Loamy surface soils and loamy to clayey subsoils.	High production potential. Drainage needed for most crops. Acid soils.	High water tables are major limiting factor. Percolation rates moderately rapid to slow.
Kalmia-Lumbee-Roanoke	Level, well to poorly drained soils. Sandy to loamy surface soils and loamy to clayey subsoils.	High to moderate production potential. Kalmia soils high production and good physical properties. Lumbee soils need drainage and Roanoke soils have plastic clay subsoils and are poorly drained. Acid soils.	Kalmia soils well suited. Lumbee soils have high water tables. Roanoke soils have high water tables, very slow percolation rates, and are subject to water ponding and occasional flooding.
Lakeland-Wagram	Gently sloping to sloping, well drained soils. Sandy surface soils and sandy subsoils.	Moderate production potential. Susceptible to drought and excessive leaching. Acid soils.	Poor filters when used for waste disposal. Other characteristics favorable.
Lenoir-Coxville	Level to gently sloping, imperfectly drained soils. Loamy surface soils and plastic, clayey subsoils.	Moderate production potential. Drainage and slowly permeable clay subsoils are limiting factors.	High water tables and very slow percolation rates limit uses.
Lynchburg-Rains	Nearly level to gently sloping, imperfectly drained soils. Sandy surface soils and loamy subsoils.	High production potential. Drainage needed. Acid soils.	High water tables are limiting factor. Percolation rates are moderately rapid.
Mantachie-Kinston-Bibb	Nearly level soils on stream floodplains. Imperfect to poorly defined and loamy textures.	High to moderate production potential. Drainage and flooding are limitations. Acid soils.	High water tables and flooding limit uses.
Norfolk-Orangeburg	Nearly level to sloping, well drained soils. Sandy surface soils and loamy subsoils.	High production potential. Erosion a moderate hazard on slopes. Acid soils.	No limitations in use.
Pamlico-Bayboro	Level, very poorly drained soils. Loamy, organic surface soils and loamy to clayey subsoils.	High production potential for adapted crops. Drainage and water control are needed. Acid soils.	High water tables and difficulty of managing waste are severe limitations. Percolation rates are moderate to slow.
Portsmouth-Hyde	Level, very poorly drained soils. Loamy, high organic surface soils and loamy to clayey subsoils.	High production potential for adapted crops. Drainage and water control are needed. Acid soils.	High water tables and water management are severe limitations. Percolation rates moderately slow.
Rutlege-Plummer	Level, poorly drained sands.	Low production potential. Wet sands with low available water when drained.	High water tables and low filtering properties limit uses.
Swamp-Tidal marsh	Level, very poorly drained soils that flood frequently.	Not suited.	Not suited.

8. Water Resources

RALPH C. HEATH
NATHAN O. THOMAS
HAROLD DUBACH

North Carolina's abundant and high-quality water resources are a key element in the state's economic health and attractive physical environment. Effective management of these resources to meet future needs and to avoid further degradation of their quality is among the most important goals of state, regional, and local planning. The material in this chapter is divided into two sections—one deals with fresh water (water resources of the land) and the other deals with the sounds and the ocean (marine resources).

WATER RESOURCES OF THE LAND

Precipitation is the basic source of water resources. North Carolina, with an average annual precipitation ranging from forty-five to seventy inches, has an ample supply of water—if it is effectively managed. An understanding of three chief parameters is particularly relevant to good management decisions. These parameters are (1) the source and availability of water resources, (2) the utilization of these resources, and (3) the limitations on utilization imposed by both resource quality and pollution. Each of these parameters is discussed in this section.

Sources of Water

Water supplies are developed either from streams or lakes (surface water sources), or from wells or springs (groundwater sources). Although surface water and groundwater resources are often viewed as separate and distinct from each other, they are inherently linked, as schematically illustrated in Figure 8.1. The endless movement of water—from the atmosphere to the land to the sea and then back to the atmosphere—is referred to as the hydrologic cycle. This is a central concept in the science of hydrology.

Water that has been evaporated from both land and ocean areas falls as precipitation. After exposed surfaces of soils, vegetation, and buildings are wet, water begins to infiltrate into the ground, replenishing both soil moisture and groundwater reservoirs. If the rate of precipitation exceeds the rate of infiltration, water fills surface depressions and runs off over the surface into nearby streams or lakes. The occurrence of overland runoff is evident from rapid increases in streamflow, in some cases culminating in destructive floods.

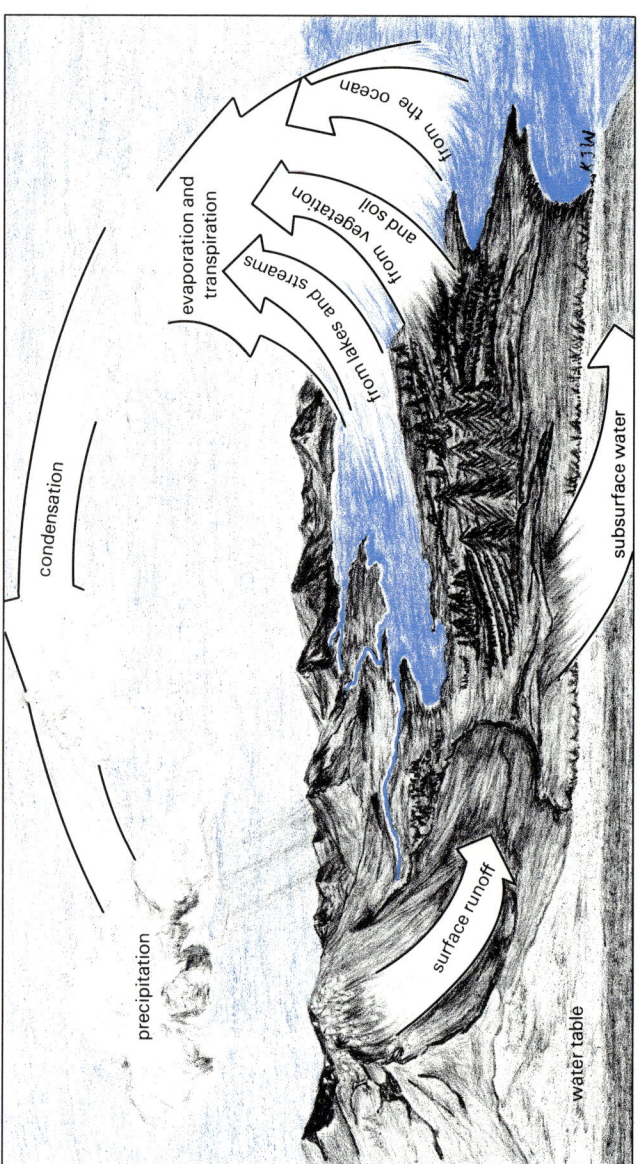

Figure 8.1. Hydrologic Cycle

After overland runoff ceases, the flow of streams is sustained by discharge from the groundwater reservoirs. Therefore, the flow of streams includes both overland runoff and groundwater discharge. This flow, however, is only a part of the water that falls as precipitation. The missing water, which is referred to as water loss, has returned to the atmosphere as vapor transpired by plants and as evaporation from land and water surfaces, thus completing the cycle.

Water Losses by Evapotranspiration

Approximately two-thirds of the precipitation falling on North Carolina is returned to the atmosphere as water vapor through evaporation from lakes, rivers, swamps, and other wet areas, and through transpiration of water by plants. The combined loss of water through these processes is referred to as evapotranspiration. The remaining one-third of the precipitation leaves the state either as streamflow or groundwater outflow. Together these comprise the water available for use.

Evapotranspiration rates vary widely and depend upon such meteorological factors as air temperature, wind speed, and vapor pressure, and upon the nature of the evaporating surface. As illustrated in Figure 8.2, evapotranspiration in North Carolina varies from more than 70 percent of total precipitation in a large portion of the Coastal Plain and Piedmont sections of the state to less than 50 percent in a portion of the Mountains. In addition to these natural losses, millions of gallons each day are evaporated or consumed in the state as a result of man's activities.

Lake Evaporation One of the more important sources of these man-related losses is lake evaporation. While evaporation of water from land areas totals fifteen to twenty inches per year in North Carolina, evaporation from perennially wet areas such as lakes, reservoirs, and streams ranges from about thirty-four inches per year in the Mountains to about forty-two inches in the southeastern part of the state (Figure 8.3). Thus, evaporation from water areas is about twice as much as from land areas. This difference will be of considerable importance in the

Figure 8.2. Evapotranspiration in N.C.

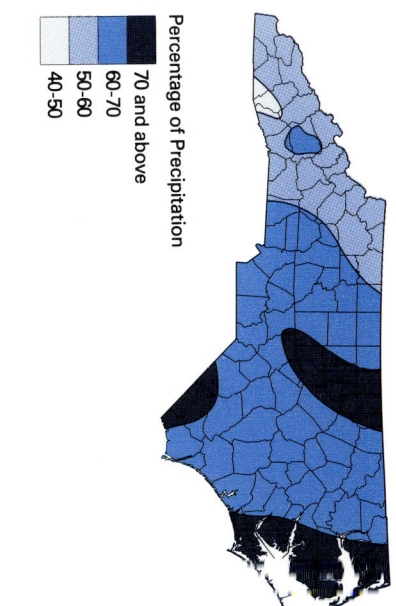

Percentage of Precipitation
- 70 and above
- 60-70
- 50-60
- 40-50

Figure 8.3. Mean Annual Lake Evaporation in N.C.

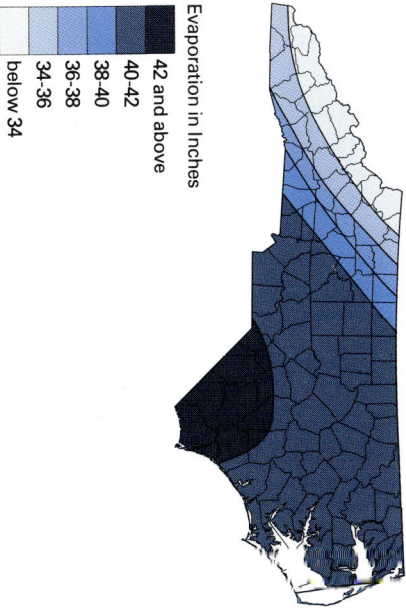

Evaporation in Inches
- 42 and above
- 40-42
- 38-40
- 36-38
- 34-36
- below 34

Source: U.S. Department of Commerce, *Climatic Atlas of U.S.,* 1968.

future management of the state's water resources. The North Carolina Office of Water and Air Resources estimated that, in 1972, freshwater lakes and reservoirs occupied about 640 of the 52,586 square miles within the state boundaries. Natural evaporation from these waters averages about 1,200 million gallons per day (mgd), or about 600 mgd more than the evapotranspiration loss from an equivalent land area. The seasonal variation in lake evaporation is of prime importance in analyzing the yield of reservoirs for water supply because the highest rates of evaporation occur in the summer when inflow is smallest and when rates of withdrawal are usually greatest.

Reservoirs are built when water supply demands exceed the minimum flow of the stream that serves as the source of supply. Excess needs are met by water stored in the reservoir from times when inflow exceeds withdrawals and downstream releases. The length of time during which storage is utilized to help meet withdrawals may range from as little as 15 days to as much as 183 days (six months). In order to determine how much storage is needed during these periods, the net evaporation—that is, the excess of evaporation over precipitation—must be added to withdrawals. However, because of differences in precipitation and temperature from year to year, the net evaporation varies. It is common practice in hydrology to express such differences in terms of *recurrence interval*. Net evaporation for lakes in the Piedmont area for different recurrence intervals is shown in Figure 8.4. For example, during any period of twenty years, net evaporation, on the average, will equal or exceed 400,000 gallons per acre during a continuous period of 183 days, or 275,000 gallons per acre during a continuous period of 60 days.

Future evapotranspiration losses from land areas may be expected to decrease as more land is covered by buildings, streets, highways, and other paved areas, resulting in an increase in volume of runoff from urban areas. On the other hand, evaporative losses will increase as more land is used for reservoir sites and crop irrigation, human and livestock consumption, and manufacturing. In long-range planning of water developments, it is essential to consider water losses associated with various alternatives, and to select those alternatives that are most effective in conserving water.

Figure 8.4. Net Evaporation from Lakes in the Piedmont Region of N.C.

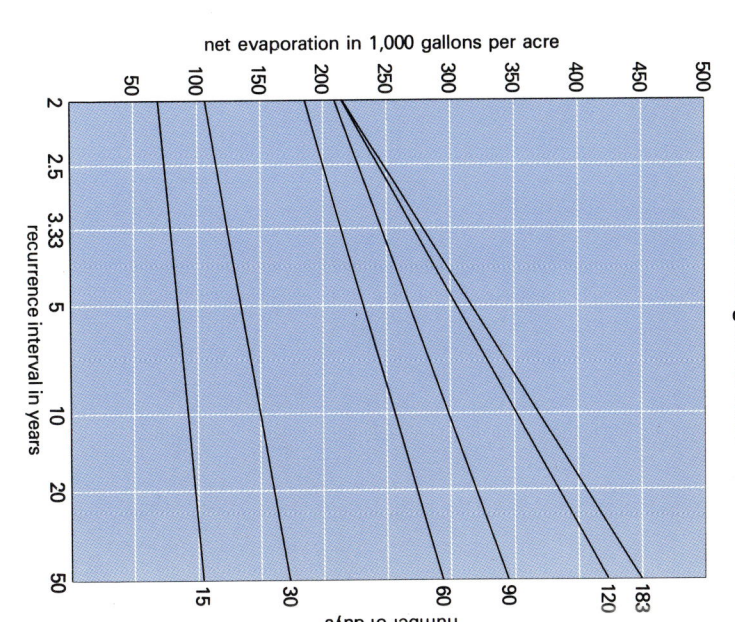

Figure 8.5. Lakes, Rivers, and River Basins in N.C., 1973

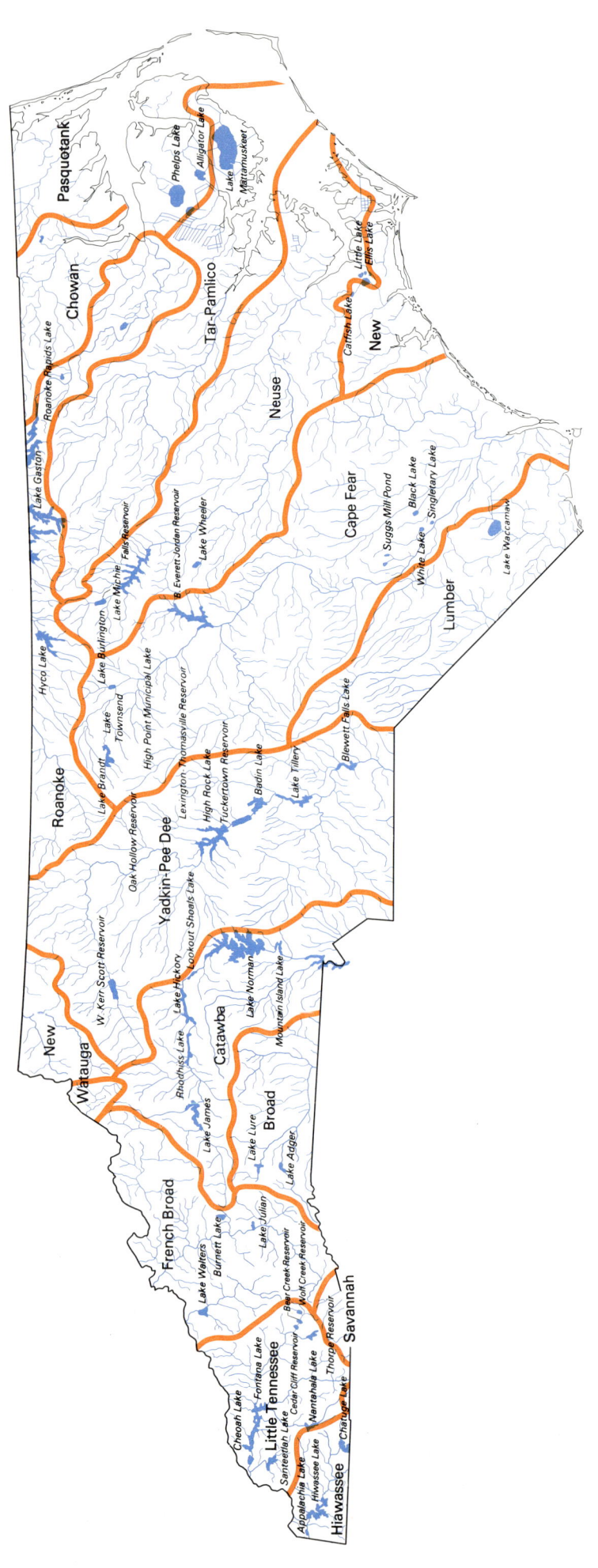

Surface Water Resources

Streams and lakes, both natural and manmade, are the most important sources of water supplies in North Carolina. They serve as sources of supply for cities and industries, provide huge amounts of water needed for hydropower generation and cooling of thermoelectric power plants, and provide the state with an important recreational resource. These streams, their drainage basins, and major natural and manmade lakes are shown in Figure 8.5.

Streamflow Characteristics The Mountain, Piedmont, and Inner Coastal Plain regions of the state are drained by a dense network of streams.

Of North Carolina's total area of 52,586 square miles (including sounds), 46,240 square miles are drained to the Atlantic Ocean through major rivers, coastal streams, estuaries, and sounds. Major rivers include the Roanoke, the Tar-Pamlico, the Neuse, the Cape Fear, the Lumber, the Yadkin-Pee Dee, the Catawba, and the Broad.

The Outer Coastal Plain, most of which is less than thirty feet above sea level, has a relatively poorly developed natural drainage system. To improve drainage in this area, thousands of miles of drainage ditches have been dug.

An area of 6,346 square miles in the western part of the state drains to the Ohio and Tennessee rivers. Major streams in this area include the New-Watauga, the French Broad, and the Little Tennessee rivers.

Variation is the most important aspect of streamflow. Streamflow not only varies from year to year and from day to day, but also from place to place. Knowledge of these variations is essential to the development of surface water supplies. Systematic collection of data on the flow of streams in North Carolina was started by the United States Geological Survey in the 1890s. By 1973, continuous records of streamflow had been collected and published for 289 locations for periods ranging in length from a few years to more than seventy-five years. From these records, the flow characteristics of North Carolina streams can be determined.

As shown in Figure 8.6, the average runoff of streams ranges from more than 2.5 mgd per square mile in parts of Jackson and Transylvania counties to less than 0.5 mgd per square mile in the northern parts of Person and Granville counties. The long-term average runoff figures indicate the maximum amount of water available for development. However, there is a diminishing return from developments that exceed about 50 percent of the long-term average runoff, and it is probably not feasible to attempt to develop more than about 75 percent. Diminishing returns are the result of increased evaporation losses from large reservoirs and the extra storage needed to insure that the reservoir has sufficient water during drought years.

Reservoirs are needed because of the large annual and daily variation in runoff. The annual variation is illustrated by Figure 8.7, which shows the annual runoff for the French Broad River, at Asheville, from 1897 to 1973. The runoff during this period ranged from a maximum of 52.74 inches (2,372 mgd) in 1901 to a minimum of 16.73 inches (754 mgd) in 1956. The daily streamflow variation is much greater. As illustrated in Figure 8.8, the maximum daily discharges for most streams exceeds the minimum daily discharges several hundred to several thousand times. During periods of heavy rainfall, there is a rapid increase in overland runoff. During periods of low rainfall, the flow of streams declines steadily, with the flow being derived chiefly from groundwater discharge and from water released from reservoir and channel storage.

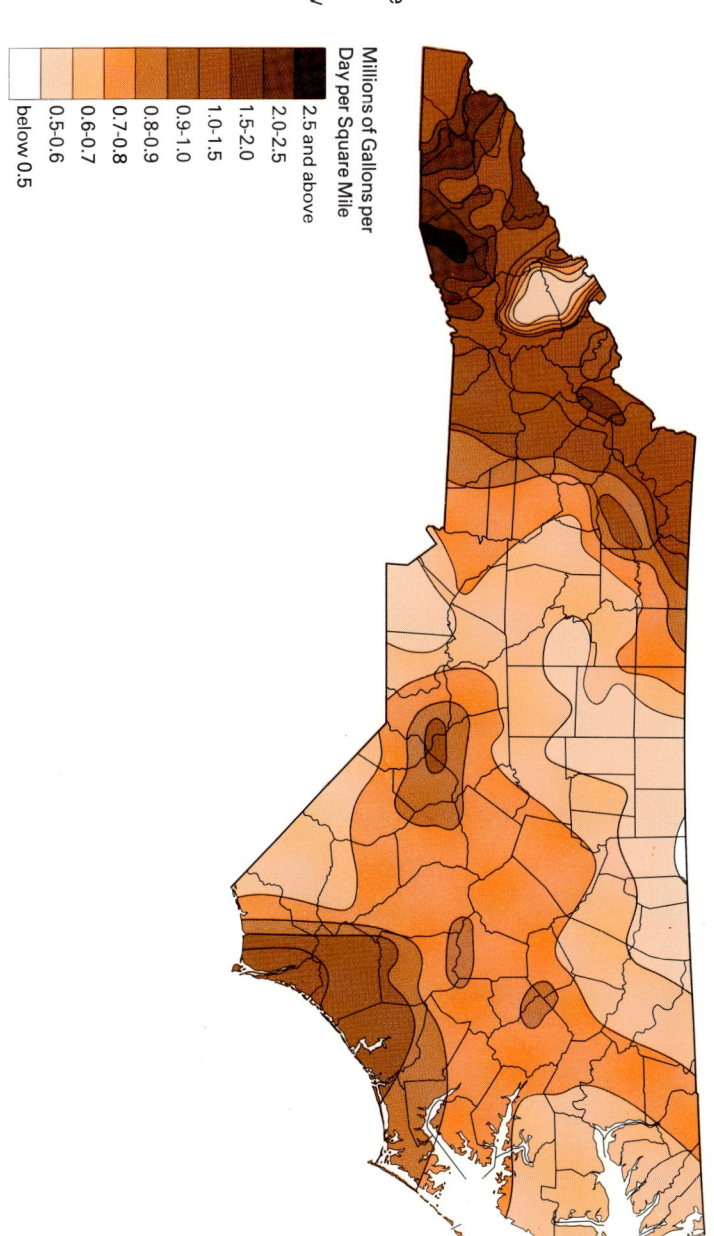

Figure 8.6. Average Runoff of N.C. Streams

Millions of Gallons per Day per Square Mile

- 2.5 and above
- 2.0-2.5
- 1.5-2.0
- 1.0-1.5
- 0.9-1.0
- 0.8-0.9
- 0.7-0.8
- 0.6-0.7
- 0.5-0.6
- below 0.5

Source: U.S. Department of the Interior, Geological Survey.

Figure 8.7. Average Annual Precipitation and Runoff in the French Broad River Basin in N.C., 1897-1972

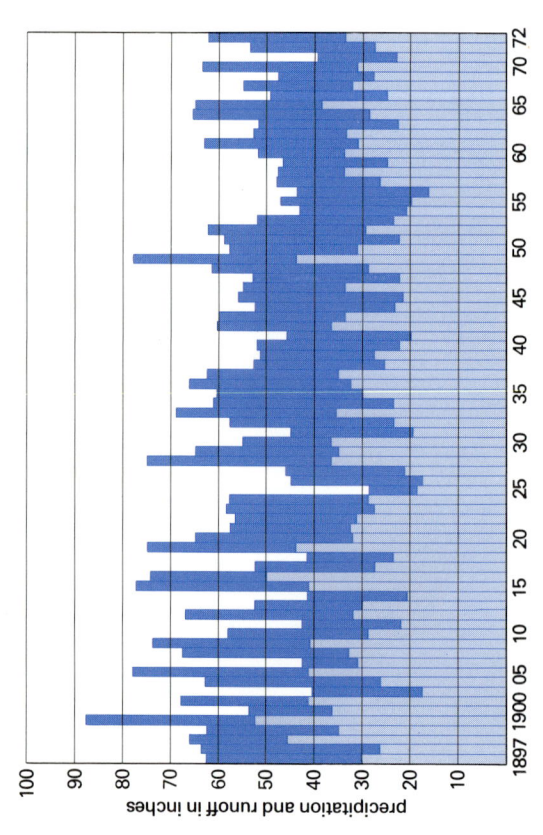

Source: U.S. Department of Commerce, National Weather Service, and U.S. Department of the Interior, Geological Survey.

Figure 8.8. Characteristic Discharge of Selected Streams in N.C.

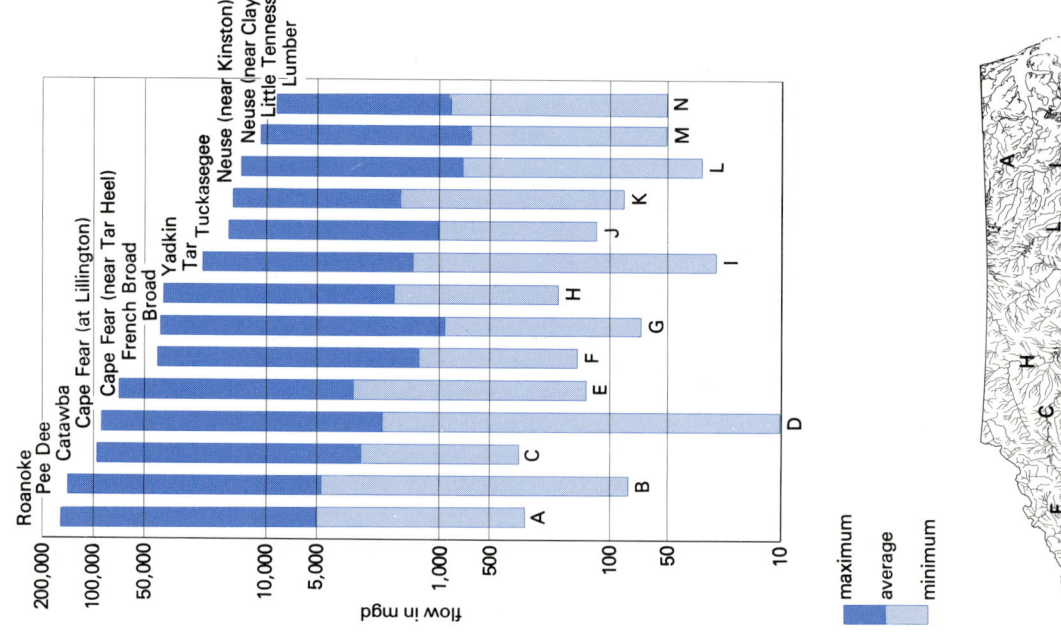

Source: U.S. Department of the Interior, Geological Survey.

Figure 8.9. Hydrograph of Daily Flow, French Broad River, at Asheville, N.C., 1941 Climatic Year

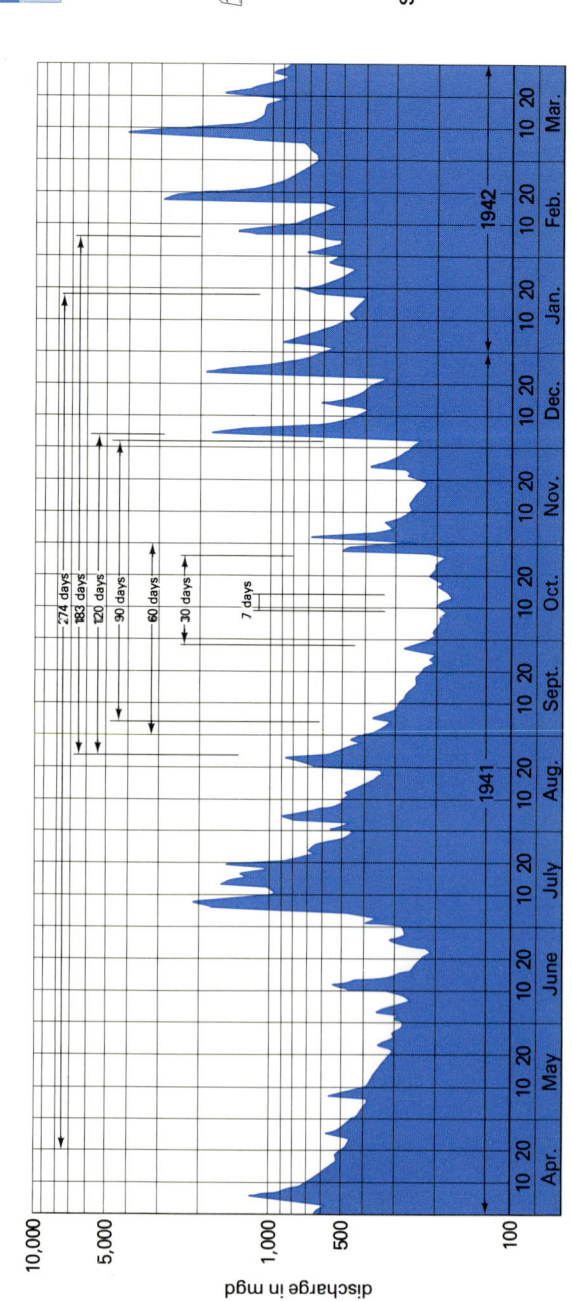

Figure 8.10. Magnitude and Frequency of Annual Low Flow of the Eno River at Hillsborough, N.C.

Data on the minimum flow of streams are essential in determining the water available both for water supplies and for waste dilution. For use in these studies, streamflow data are analyzed to determine the frequency of occurrence of low flows for different periods of consecutive days. Figure 8.9 shows selected periods ranging in length from 7 to 274 days, during which the lowest flows for those numbers of days occurred on the French Broad River, at Asheville, during the climatic year of record shown in the illustration.

Figure 8.10 indicates the full range of low runoff data for the Eno River at Hillsborough. As an aid in reading this graph, two specific flows used in waste dilution and water supply analyses are indicated. The graph shows that, on the average of once every ten years, the minimum flow for seven consecutive days will be 0.0082 mgd per square mile, for the 66.5 square miles of the Eno River drainage basin above Hillsborough. The data needed to prepare similar graphs for other long-term stream-gauging stations in North Carolina are contained in a 1973 United States Geological Survey report by Nathan O. Thomas.

Low runoff of streams for periods up to about thirty days is primarily dependent on precipitation, groundwater discharge, and evapotranspiration. Figures 8.11 and 8.12 show that the minimum runoff is greatest in the mountainous areas where precipitation is the highest, groundwater discharge is substantial, and water losses are the lowest. The lowest runoff occurs in the eastern Piedmont and in the eastern part of the Coastal Plain. The low runoff in the eastern Piedmont reflects low groundwater discharges, while in the eastern Coastal Plain, groundwater discharge is significant and evapotranspiration losses are high. Seven-day, ten-year minimum runoff of streams (Figure 8.12) is the flow parameter used in North Carolina, as well as in many other states, in the design and approval of waste treatment plants. It is also the minimum flow required to be released at all dams for the protection of fish and downstream users.

Floods occur when the water reaching streams exceeds the carrying capacity of the channels and overflows onto the adjoining floodplains. Major floods in North Carolina during this century include those of 1916, 1928, 1940, 1945, and 1955. The flood of August 1940 probably was the most extensive and caused the greatest damage. The extent of flooding depends on the amount and intensity of precipitation, the topography, and soil moisture conditions. A wet period, during which soil moisture has been replenished, followed by several hours or days of intense rain, results in the most severe floods.

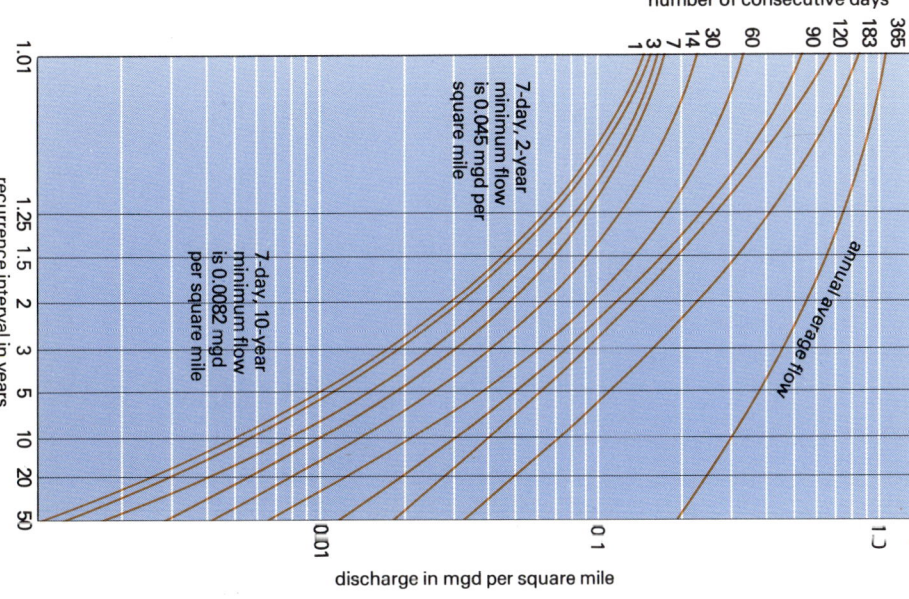

Figure 8.11. The Seven-Day, Two-Year Minimum Runoff of N.C. Streams

MGD per Square Mile
- 0.3 and above
- 0.15-0.3
- 0.05-0.15
- below 0.05

Note: Data does not apply to regulated streams.

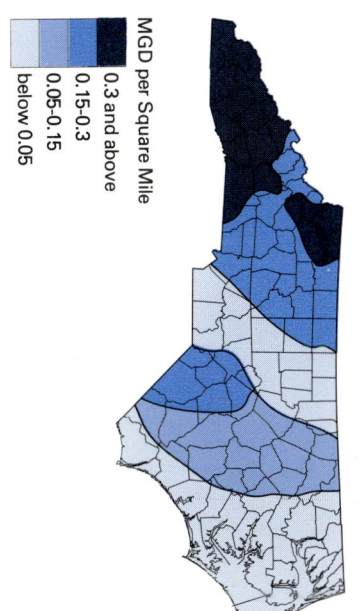

Figure 8.12. The Seven-Day, Ten-Year Minimum Runoff of N.C. Streams

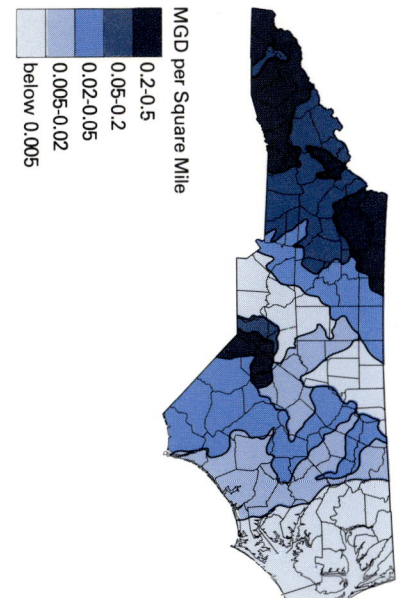

MGD per Square Mile
- 0.2-0.5
- 0.05-0.2
- 0.02-0.05
- 0.005-0.02
- below 0.005

The heights reached by flood waters are critically important to persons living near streams, and to engineers designing reservoirs, spillways, bridges, and other structures intended either to control the flows or to let them pass unimpeded. The rise in the stage of streams during floods depends on the size of the drainage area that is contributing flood waters and the physical features of the stream channel and floodplain. Figure 8.13 portrays the rise in stream level above normal low-water position for the one hundred-year flood, that flood expected to occur on the average of once every one hundred years.

The concentration of people and property in urban areas makes the flooding of these areas a matter of great public concern. Studies conducted by the United States Geological Survey at Charlotte, Durham, Lenoir, Morganton, and Winston-Salem indicate that flood runoff occurs much more rapidly in urban areas than in rural areas. Consequently, the peak discharge of floods having the same recurrence interval is much higher in urban areas than in rural areas. The effect of urbanization in the Piedmont region on the one hundred-year flood is illustrated by Figure 8.14. The higher discharges under urban conditions reflect the composite effect of two conditions. First of all, the streets, buildings, parking lots, and other structures cover a significant part of the land surface in urban areas and thus prevent infiltration of precipitation. Second, storm drains and streets permit precipitation to run off to streams much more quickly than does the land surface in rural areas. Putnam (1972) has shown that the effect of urban conditions on floods in the Piedmont can be determined if the amount of impervious cover—that is, the percent of the area covered by streets, buildings, and so on—is known. The impervious area in Piedmont cities ranges from about 85 percent in densely developed downtown areas to about 15 percent in low-density residential areas. The impervious cover in rural areas is only about 1 percent.

Damage during floods results from encroachment on floodplains. Floodplains in urban areas have remained relatively undeveloped until recent years because of the danger of flooding. There is now an increasing tendency to overlook this danger because of the need for large, relatively flat areas for shopping centers, apartment complexes, and similar urban developments. To counter this, federal, state, and many local governments have passed laws and adopted regulations to control the use of floodplains. The objective of most of these laws and regulations is to limit development in the area inundated by the one hundred-year flood to those activities and structures that will neither be damaged by flood waters nor impede their flow.

Figure 8.13. Height of the 100-Year Flood above Normal Low-Stream Level in N.C.

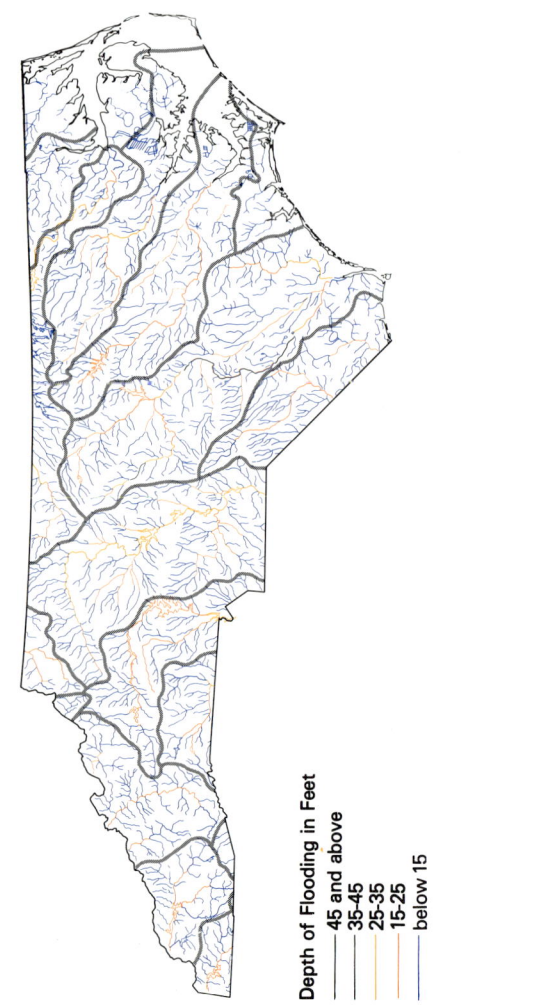

Depth of Flooding in Feet
- 45 and above
- 35-45
- 25-35
- 15-25
- below 15

Figure 8.14. Relation of Discharge of the 100-Year Flood to Drainage Area

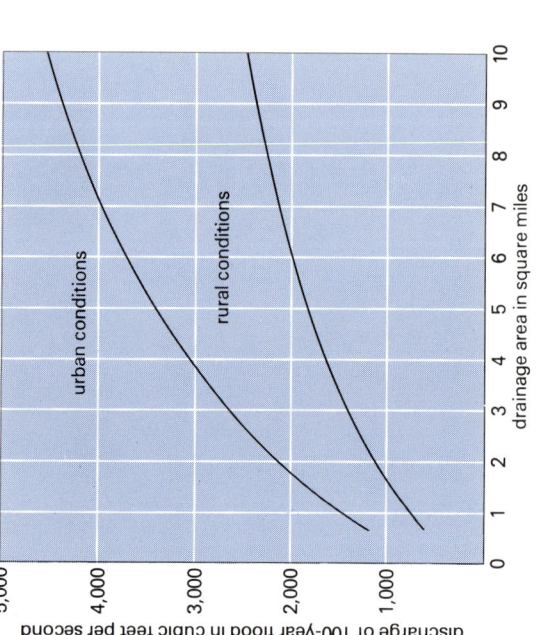

Note: This chart is based on an impervious cover of 25 percent.

The control of floods is a special concern of the United States Corps of Engineers, and, in those western portions of North Carolina that drain to the Tennessee River, of the Tennessee Valley Authority. John H. Kerr Dam on the Roanoke River and W. Kerr Scott Dam on the Yadkin River were built by the Corps of Engineers to control floods and to provide recreation and other benefits. Fontana Dam on the Little Tennessee River and Chatuge, Hiwassee, and Appalachia dams on the Hiwassee River were constructed by the Tennessee Valley Authority for flood control and other purposes.

Lakes and Reservoirs

There are approximately 48,000 lakes, ponds, and reservoirs in North Carolina. Major reservoirs and natural lakes are shown in Figure 8.5. Natural lakes in North Carolina occur only in the Coastal Plain. The largest of these are Lake Mattamuskeet (sixty-seven square miles), Lake Phelps (twenty-five square miles), and Lake Waccamaw (fourteen square miles). Smaller elliptical-shaped lakes, whose origin has been the subject of numerous scientific papers, include Black Lake, White Lake, and others in Bladen County. These lakes and other elliptical-shaped depressions on the Atlantic Coastal Plain are referred to as "Carolina Bays," or Bladen Lakes. The level of nearly all natural lakes in the state is now controlled by drainage canals and control works.

Lakes in the Piedmont and in the Mountains are all manmade. They were constructed for one or more of the following main purposes: (1) to provide storage for water-supply needs for cities and industries when natural streamflows are inadequate, (2) to protect downstream areas from floods, (3) to provide opportunity for water-related recreation, and (4) to provide water needed for hydropower generation and to cool thermoelectric power plants. The State Office of Water and Air Resources maintains a computer storage file of dams and dam sites that presently contains data on about 3,500 sites. Table 8.1 lists storage, surface area, and other data for reservoirs having a total storage of more than five thousand acre-feet.

The amount of water that must be stored in a reservoir to meet water supply needs is determined in a "draft-storage" analysis. One method of analysis involves use of the seven-day, two-year minimum flow index. This index has been calculated for North Carolina locations

Table 8.1. Larger Reservoirs in N.C.

Name of Reservoir and Stream	Drainage Area (sq. mi.)	Total Storage (acre-feet)	Dead Storage (acre-feet)	Usable Storage (acre-feet)	Surface Area (acres)	Year Completed	Use	Owner or Operator
Hyco Lake–Hyco River	189	75,480	—	75,480	3,750	1964	C	Carolina Power & Light Co.
Lake Gaston–Roanoke River	8,339	513,000	52,900	460,100	22,500	1962	FP	Virginia Electric and Power Co.
Roanoke Rapids Lake–Roanoke River	8,395	85,000	—	26,000	4,900	1955	P	Virginia Electric and Power Co.
Lake Michie–Flat River	170	13,962	1,353	12,609	550	1926	M	City of Durham
Lake Wheeler–Swift Creek	38.0	7,670	—	7,670	575	1956	M	City of Raleigh
Lake Brandt–Reedy Fork	70.0	6,750	—	6,750	787	1923	M	City of Greensboro
Lake Townsend–Reedy Fork	105	19,950	—	19,950	1,950	1968	M	City of Greensboro
Lake Burlington–Stony Creek	44.0	9,820	0	9,820	760	1960	M	City of Burlington
Oak Hollow Reservoir–West Fork Deep River	35.0	10,740	—	10,740	725	1970	M	City of High Point
High Point Municipal Lake–Deep River	61.4	5,060	—	5,060	340	1926	M	City of High Point
W. Kerr Scott Reservoir–Yadkin River	350	153,000	8,000	145,000	3,980	1962	F	U.S. Corps of Engineers
Lexington-Thomasville Reservoir–Abbotts Creek	70.3	6,520	60	6,460	650	1957	M	Lexington and Thomasville
High Rock Lake–Yadkin River	3,980	254,590	19,740	234,850	15,180	1927	P	Yadkin, Inc.
Tuckertown Reservoir–Yadkin River	4,120	42,525	35,780	6,745	2,560	1962	P	Yadkin, Inc.
Badin Lake–Yadkin River	4,180	241,000	86,088	154,912	5,355	1917	P	Yadkin, Inc.
Lake Tillery–Pee Dee River	4,600	167,000	29,800	137,200	5,000	1928	P	Carolina Power & Light Co.
Blewett Falls Lake–Pee Dee River	6,830	97,000	54,530	42,470	2,500	1911	P	Carolina Power & Light Co.
Lake James–Catawba and Linville rivers	380	288,840	47,650	241,190	6,500	1919	P	Duke Power Co.
Rhodhiss Lake–Catawba River	1,090	73,200	33,783	39,417	3,515	1924	P	Duke Power Co.
Lake Hickory–Catawba River	1,310	127,480	75,190	52,290	4,110	1928	P	Duke Power Co.
Lookout Shoals Lake–Catawba River	1,450	31,110	26,330	4,780	1,270	1915	P	Duke Power Co.
Lake Norman–Catawba River	1,790	1,092,430	474,650	617,780	32,510	1962	P	Duke Power Co.
Mountain Island Lake–Catawba River	1,860	57,300	31,313	25,987	3,235	1923	P	Duke Power Co.
Lake Julian–Powells Creek	4.8	9,005	—	9,005	320	1963	C	Carolina Power & Light Co.
Burnett Lake N. Fork–Swannanoa River	21.9	23,000	5,350	17,650	372	1954	M	City of Asheville
Lake Walters–Pigeon River	455	25,280	4,780	20,500	340	1929	P	Carolina Power & Light Co.
Nantahala Lake–Nantahala River	91.0	137,300	11,300	126,000	1,605	1942	FP	Nantahala Power & Light Co.

157

and is illustrated in Figure 8.15. The figure demonstrates the relationship between minimum flow, the storage required in acre-feet, and the yield of the reservoir in mgd. The yields derived are based on a design period of twenty years; that is, the results have been adjusted to a recurrence interval of twenty years. However, the yields shown are not adjusted for evaporation, seepage, or depletion of storage by sediment. The maximum storage shown in the figure, two hundred acre-feet per square mile of drainage area above the reservoir, represents between 40 and 50 percent of the average annual runoff.

Groundwater Resources

Saturating the pores, fractures, and other openings in sediments and rocks, groundwater is available in quantities adequate for household and small municipal and industrial needs at nearly every point in North Carolina. A valuable resource to the state, groundwater accounts for about 40 percent of water used exclusive of that used for electric power plant cooling and hydropower generation. Well yields, and thus intensity of groundwater use, vary considerably within the state—chiefly as a result of differences in rock composition and structure. As illustrated by Figure 8.16, sediments in the Coastal Plain characteristically have yields many times higher than the crystalline rocks of the Piedmont and Mountain regions.

Table 8.1.—Continued

Name of Reservoir and Stream	Drainage Area (sq. mi.)	Total Storage (acre-feet)	Dead Storage (acre-feet)	Usable Storage (acre-feet)	Surface Area (acres)	Year Completed	Use	Owner or Operator
Wolf Creek Lake—Wolf Creek	15.2	10,060	2,420	7,640	176	1955	P	Nantahala Power & Light Co.
Bear Creek Lake—Tuckasegee River	75.3	34,700	30,160	4,540	476	1953	P	Nantahala Power & Light Co.
Cedar Cliff Lake—Tuckasegee River	80.3	6,315	5,617	698	121	1952	P	Nantahala Power & Light Co.
Thorpe Reservoir W. Fork–Tuckasegee River	36.7	70,410	3,570	66,840	1,462	1941	P	Nantahala Power & Light Co.
Fontana Lake—Little Tennessee River	1,571	1,443,000	296,500	1,146,500	10,670	1944	FNP	Tennessee Valley Authority
Cheoah Lake—Little Tennessee River	1,608	35,110	27,780	7,330	595	1918	P	Aluminum Co. of America
Santeetlah Lake—Cheoah River	176	156,300	25,400	130,900	2,850	1927	P	Aluminum Co. of America
Chatuge Lake—Hiwassee River	189	240,400	18,400	222,000	7,150	1942	FNP	Tennessee Valley Authority
Hiwassee Lake—Hiwassee River	968	434,000	71,600	362,400	6,280	1940	FNP	Tennessee Valley Authority
Appalachia Lake—Hiwassee River	1,018	57,720	9,120	48,600	1,123	1943	P	Tennessee Valley Authority

Note: The purpose for which the impounded waters are used is indicated by the following symbols: C, cooling water; F, flood control; M, municipal; N, navigation; P, power.

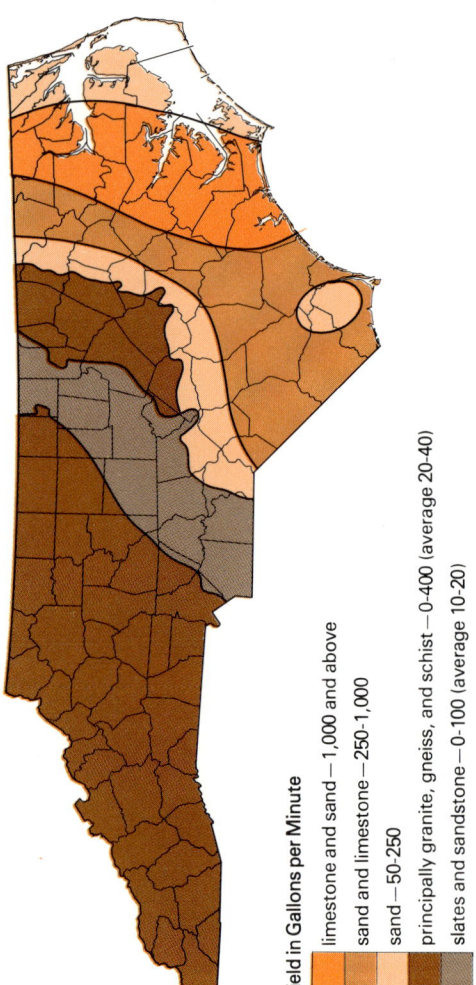

Figure 8.16. Well Yields by Aquifer Type in N.C.

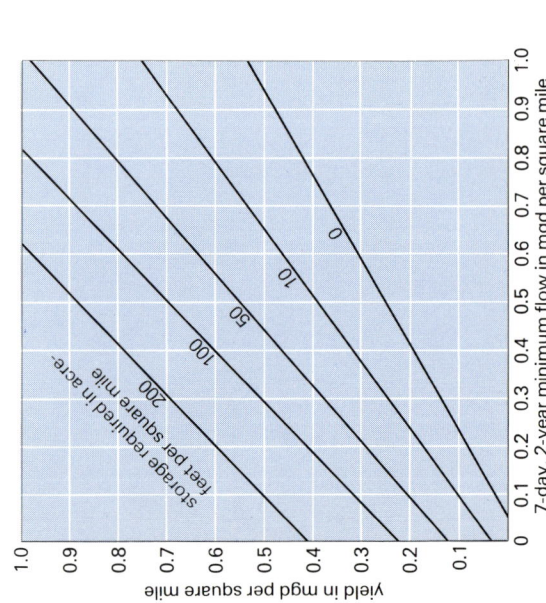

Figure 8.15. Formula for Reservoir Storage Estimates

Coastal Plain Region

The high-yielding unconsolidated sedimentary rocks underlying the Coastal Plain increase in thickness from the inner margin of the plain toward the coast, reaching a maximum of thickness, on land, of more than ten thousand feet at Cape Hatteras (Figure 8.17). From the standpoint of groundwater production, these rocks may be grouped into three major units. The uppermost of these consists of interbedded sands, silts, clays, and sandy shell beds. This unit extends from the surface to depths of about one hundred feet in the western and central parts of the Coastal Plain and to depths of several hundred feet along the northern part of the Outer Banks. The lowermost unit consists of complexly interbedded layers of sand, silt, and clay. This unit rests on bedrock and thickens toward the coast, increasing in thickness from less than one hundred feet along the inner margin of the Coastal Plain to as much as several thousand feet along the coast. The upper and lower units are separated in the outer part of the Coastal Plain by a limestone that ranges in thickness from a few feet along its western margin to more than eight hundred feet in eastern Carteret County.

The limestone is the most productive of the three units. Wells screened in this unit will yield about ten gpm (gallons per minute) for each foot of limestone penetrated by the well up to a maximum of several thousand gpm. Twelve wells drawing from this unit in an area of about one square mile in Beaufort County have been pumped continuously at rates of fifty to sixty mgd since 1965. Water is obtained from the upper and lower hydrologic units from wells screened in the sand layers that comprise roughly half of these units. Yields of more than 1,000 gpm are not uncommon from the lower unit. Yields of a few hundred gallons per minute are usually obtained from the upper unit.

Aquifers (water-producing sediments) underlying the Coastal Plain are recharged by precipitation that filters into the ground in interstream areas. The water moves downward and laterally through the sediments to discharge areas along perennial streams and the coast. The movement of water through the lower hydrologic unit is hampered by the presence of extensive and numerous layers of silt and clay.

Withdrawal of water from wells results in a drawing down of water levels in the surrounding area such that the water levels assume the shape of an inverted cone whose apex is at the pumping well. Very large withdrawals may result in a lowering of water levels to below sea level. Figure 8.18 shows the altitude of the water level in wells penetrating the middle and lower hydrologic units. Water levels are below sea level around several of the larger pumping centers.

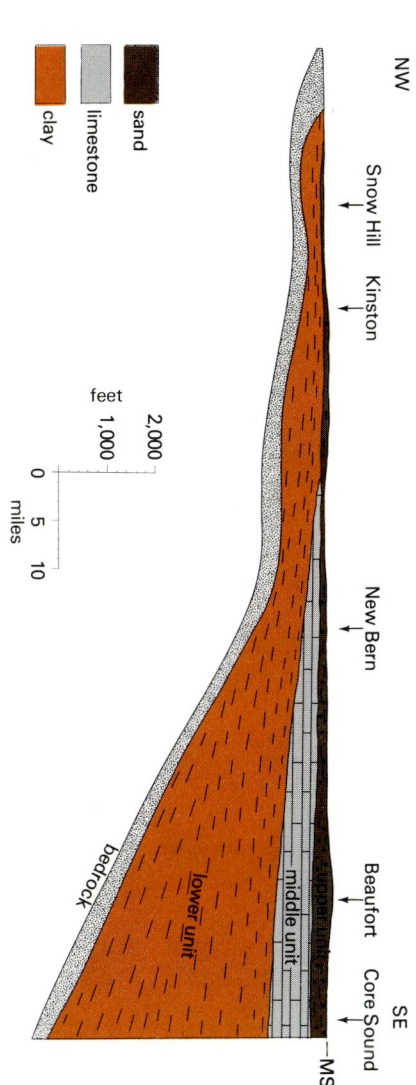

Figure 8.17. Idealized Geological Cross Section of the N.C. Coastal Plain

Source: U.S. Department of the Interior, Geological Survey.

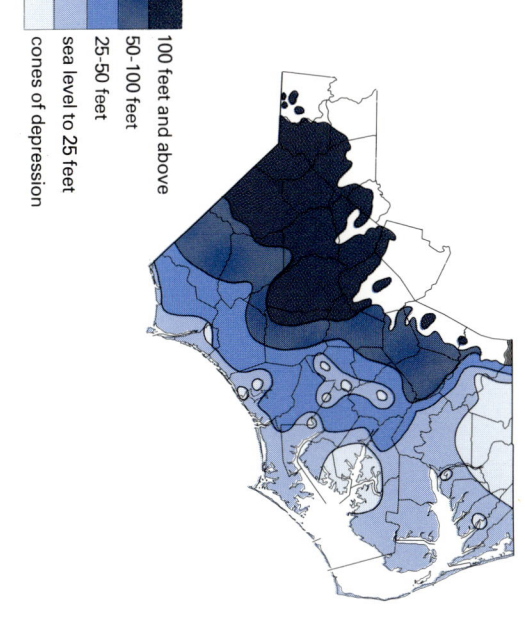

Figure 8.18. Altitude of the Water Level in Artesian Wells of the N.C. Coastal Plains

- 100 feet and above
- 50–100 feet
- 25–50 feet
- sea level to 25 feet
- cones of depression

Source: N.C. Department of Natural and Economic Resources, Water Quality Division.

Prior to the withdrawal of water through wells, the recharge and the discharge of the groundwater system were in balance. Because withdrawals are a form of discharge, they must ultimately be balanced by either an increase in recharge or a reduction in natural discharge. However, man's modification of the land surface has neither increased recharge nor decreased discharge. Recharge has been reduced by conversion of much of the area from forest to cultivated land and by drainage of recharge areas. Discharge has simultaneously been increased by the deepening of stream channels for navigation, flood control, and improved surface drainage.

Lack of knowledge of the groundwater system makes it impossible to determine the individual effect of either the groundwater withdrawals or the modifications of recharge and discharge conditions. However, in the regional decline in groundwater levels, the composite effects may be observed. Figure 8.19 shows the decline in water level in an observation well near Cove City, about midway between Kinston and New Bern. Prior to June 1968, the groundwater level was declining, presumably as a result both of withdrawals at Kinston and Grifton and of modification of recharge and discharge conditions. Since June 1968, the ground level has also been affected by pumpage from the nearby well field owned by the city of New Bern.

The future development of groundwater from the Coastal Plain groundwater system must include consideration of the effect of regional water level declines, such as that depicted in Figure 8.19, on the long-term availability of groundwater. Among potential adverse effects is the encroachment of salty water from the deeper water-bearing zones. The thickness of the freshwater-bearing sediments in the Coastal Plain is shown in Figure 8.20. Water containing more than 250 mg/l (milligrams per liter) of chloride occurs east of the dashed line. West of the dashed line, from the water table to the underlying bedrock, the sediments contain only fresh water. Prior to the beginning of significant groundwater withdrawals, the salty water in the Coastal Plain sediments was slowly being flushed from the groundwater system. Although definitive data are lacking, it is probable that regional drawdowns caused by major pumping centers have halted the flushing in most areas, causing a very slow encroachment of salt water in a few areas.

The continued economic growth of the Coastal Plain is greatly dependent upon the solution of water problems. These problems include the improvement of land surface drainage, the betterment of farming and living conditions, and the development of methods for increasing recharge of the groundwater system. Because these problems are essentially different aspects of the same problem, they provide a unique opportunity for long-range planning. For example, the development of groundwater supplies from shallow aquifers in poorly drained areas would not only increase the amount of groundwater available for use, but might also solve the drainage problems. It may also be possible to increase the yield of wells significantly in the Coastal Plain by locating production wells near perennial streams where conditions are favorable for stream infiltration.

Piedmont and Mountain Regions The Piedmont and the Mountains are underlain by igneous and metamorphic rocks such as granite, gneiss, schist, and slate. These rocks, commonly referred to as bedrock, are overlain nearly everywhere by a layer of clayey soil and granular material derived from weathering of the underlying bedrock. This layer, called saprolite, ranges in thickness from a few feet to more than 200 feet.

Groundwater in the Piedmont and the Mountains is obtained from either hand-dug or bored wells that penetrate only the saprolite and are as much as 4 feet in diameter; or from drilled wells up to about 1 foot in diameter, which penetrate the bedrock. Bedrock wells from the land surface to a few feet below the top of the bedrock, are lined with well casing and are finished with open holes extending to depths of 100 to 150 feet into the rock. In saprolite, groundwater occurs in, and moves through, the pores between rock particles. In the underlying bedrock, groundwater occurs in, and moves through, sheet-like joints and fractures.

A basic concept of groundwater hydrology is that aquifers function both as pipelines and as reservoirs. A significant feature of the Piedmont and the Mountains is that these functions are, for practical purposes, separated. As illustrated in Figure 8.21, the pore spaces of the saprolite function as the reservoir, and the fractures of the bedrock function as an intricate network of pipelines that transmit water from the saprolite to the wells.

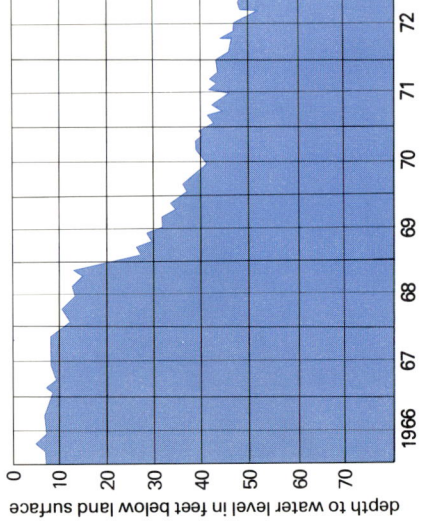

Figure 8.19. Decline of the Water Level in an Observation Well Near Cove City in Craven County, N.C.

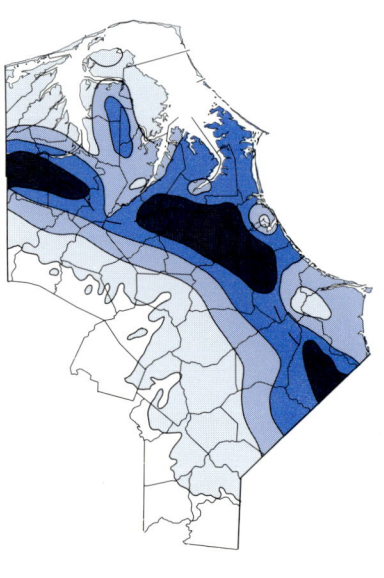

Figure 8.20. Thickness of Freshwater Zone in the N.C. Coastal Plain Sediments

Thickness in Feet
- 600 and above
- 400–600
- 200–400
- below 200
- --- western limit of water containing more than 250 mg/l of chloride

Because of the nonuniform distribution of fractures, the yield of neighboring wells in the Piedmont and the Mountains may range from nothing in the dry holes to as much as five hundred gallons per minute. Yields of only a few gallons per minute are obtained from some large-diameter saprolite wells. The largest-yielding and most satisfactory wells are those drilled in bedrock. The selection of the most favorable sites for bedrock wells is the key element in the development of groundwater supplies in the Piedmont and the Mountains.

LeGrand has shown that two land surface features, when considered together, provide a good index for selecting well sites. These features are topography and saprolite thickness. As indicated in Tables 8.2 and 8.3, LeGrand's method consists of assigning point values to different topographic conditions and to different thicknesses of saprolite, and adding the results. Through the use of the chart shown in Figure 8.22, the total point values may then be used to predict the probability of obtaining a certain yield at the selected site.

The yield of aquifers may be expressed in either of two ways: in terms of the expected yield of individual wells or in terms of the yield from a unit area such as a square mile. Relatively steep slopes in the Piedmont and the Mountains and the relatively low hydraulic conductivity of the saprolite both favor overland runoff of precipitation. Therefore, in most parts of the region, groundwater yields per unit area are probably less than two hundred thousand gallons per day per square mile. However, considerably larger yields than this can be obtained by locating wells near streams and lakes. The yield of such wells is derived both from the movement of groundwater toward the streams to discharge and from the infiltration of water from the streams and lakes into the aquifer. Yields in excess of one million gallons per day per linear mile of valley can be obtained from favorably located bedrock wells spaced five hundred to one thousand feet apart.

Water Use

Water is used, either directly or indirectly, in nearly every human activity. It is essential to all living things and, at one stage or another, to all manufacturing activities. It forms transportation arteries, cools buildings and power plants, beautifies landscapes, and serves many forms of popular recreation. Water requirements increase not only with our expanding population but also with improvements in the standard of living.

Table 8.2. Well Sites and Topography

Point Value	Topography
0	steep ridge top
2	upland steep slope
4	pronounced rounded upland
5	midpoint ridge slope
7	gentle upland slope
8	broad flat upland
9	lower part of upland slope
12	valley bottom or floodplain
15	draw in narrow catchment area
17	draw in large catchment area

Source: H. E. LeGrand, *Ground Water of the Piedmont and Blue Ridge Provinces in the Southeastern States*, Geological Survey Circular 538 (Washington, D.C.: U.S. Department of the Interior, 1967).

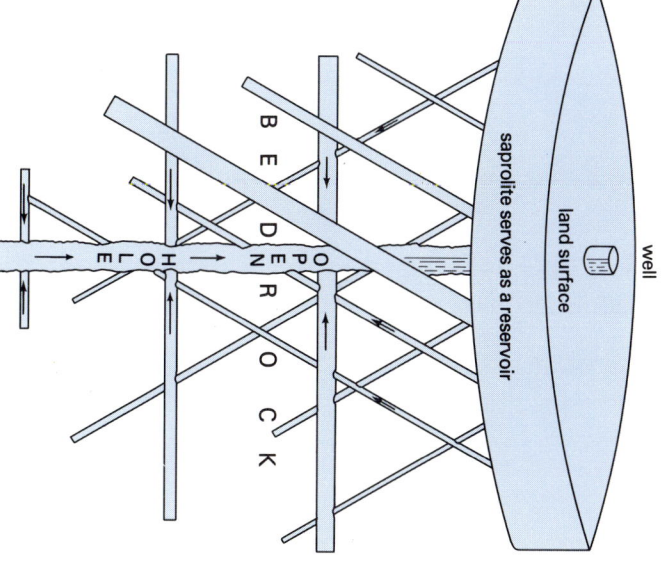

Figure 8.21. Groundwater System in the Mountains and Piedmont of N.C.

Table 8.3. Well Sites and Thickness of Saprolite

Point Value	Thickness of Saprolite
0-2	bare rock–almost no saprolite
2-6	some rock outcrops–very thin saprolite
6-9	a few rock outcrops–thin saprolite
9-12	no fresh outcrops–moderately thick saprolite
12-15	no rock outcrops–thick saprolite

Source: H. E. LeGrand, *Ground Water of the Piedmont and Blue Ridge Provinces in the Southeastern States*, Geological Survey Circular 538 (Washington, D.C.: U.S. Department of the Interior, 1967).

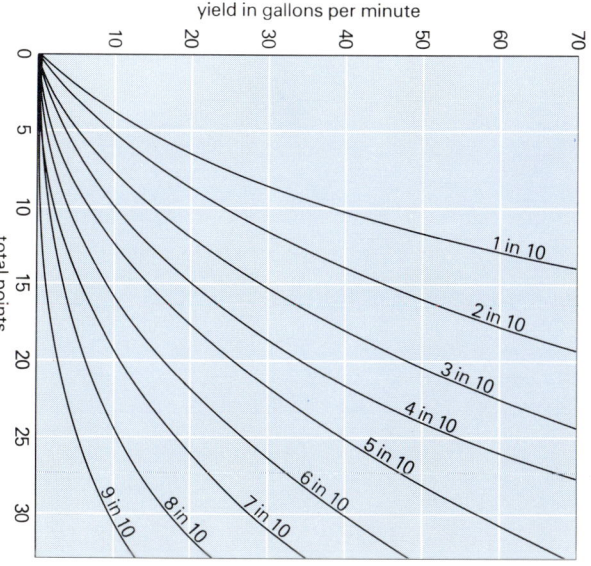

Figure 8.22. Relationship of Well Yields to Points Assigned Proposed Well Locations in the Mountains and Piedmont of N.C.

Note: For example, a site with 16 points has 3 chances in 10 of yielding at least 30 gallons per minute and 6 chances in 10 of yielding 10 gallons per minute.

161

Figure 8.23. Withdrawal Water Uses in N.C., 1950-1970

The first attempt to obtain comprehensive, nationwide data on water use was made in 1950 by the United States Geological Survey. The data obtained in that survey and in subsequent surveys made at five-year intervals provide information essential to long-range planning and water management. The Planning Division of the North Carolina Office of Water and Air Resources has also started a program to obtain better data on water use in the state. Using these data, trends in withdrawals and consumption can be examined. Nonwithdrawal uses such as navigation, recreation, and the enhancement of wetland environments are discussed in other sections of the atlas.

Withdrawal Uses Withdrawal uses are defined here as those uses that require removal of the water from the source. They include (1) hydroelectric power generation, (2) thermoelectric power and other self-supplied industries, (3) public supplies, (4) rural domestic and livestock uses, and (5) irrigation. In 1970, the total withdrawal use in North Carolina, exclusive of hydroelectric use, was 5,589 mgd or about 16 percent of the state's average runoff. Trends in the utilization of each of these categories are shown in Figure 8.23.

The largest withdrawals are for the generation of hydroelectric power along the lower Roanoke River, the lower Yadkin-Pee Dee River, the Catawba River, and various tributaries of the Tennessee River. This use is classified as a withdrawal use, though the use is "in channel." That is, the withdrawal is cumulative, as water is used or successively reused at plants downstream. In 1970, this reuse accounted for the large total of 88,000 mgd, which is equivalent to an average flow of 136,000 cubic feet per second (cfs)—about two and one-half times the state's average annual runoff.

Self-supplied industries, withdrawing 4,920 mgd, represent the second largest withdrawal use. Thermoelectric power plants accounted for most of these withdrawals, increasing from about 1,400 mgd in 1950 to about 4,300 mgd in 1970. The accelerating increase in withdrawals represents a response to increased power demands in the region.

A third important withdrawal use is public water supplies. Of the 460 mgd withdrawn in 1970, 120 mgd were delivered to industrial and commercial users and 340 mgd were for domestic use. Delivery for domestic use includes losses in distribution systems and water supplied for public services such as fire fighting, street washing, municipal parks, and swimming pools. In 1970, about 82 percent of the total withdrawal was from surface water sources.

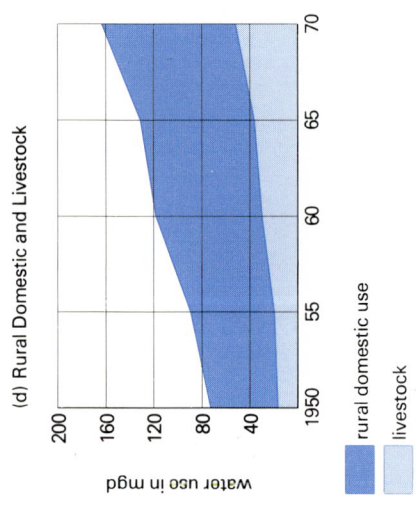

(a) Hydroelectric Power

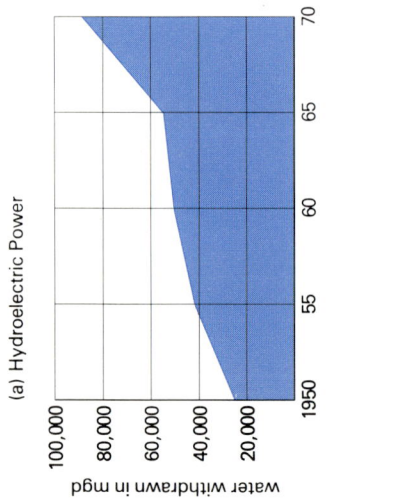

(d) Rural Domestic and Livestock

■ rural domestic use
□ livestock

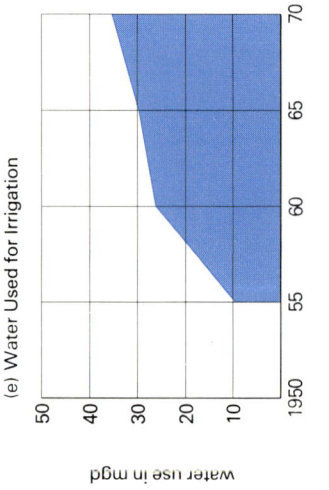

(b) Self-supplied Industries

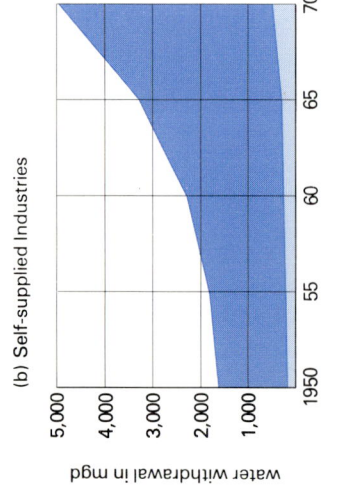

(e) Water Used for Irrigation

Note: Includes golf courses but not lawns and home gardens.

■ thermoelectric
□ other industrial uses

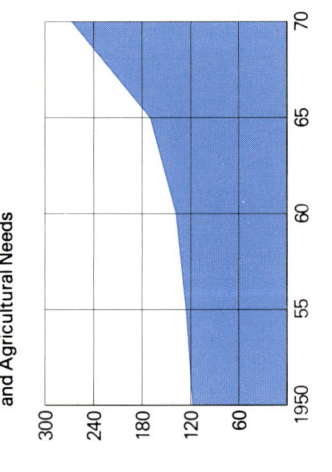

(c) Public Water Use

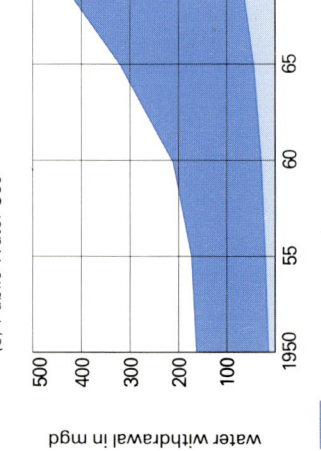

(f) Water Used for Domestic, Manufacturing, and Agricultural Needs

Note: Scales differ.

■ surface water source
□ groundwater source

A fourth category of withdrawal is rural domestic and livestock uses of water. This totaled 164 mgd in 1970. Practically all water withdrawn for domestic use is from groundwater sources.

A fifth major use of water in North Carolina is irrigation, and in 1970, 35 mgd were withdrawn for that purpose. There will normally be large differences in irrigation water use from year to year, as irrigation is used primarily to supplement natural rainfall. However, most farmers having irrigation systems available tend to irrigate sooner during only moderately dry periods, thereby increasing yields.

Perhaps the best summary of use trend is the per capita pattern. Per capita withdrawal uses have steadily increased from slightly less than 120 gallons per day in 1950 to over 250 gallons per day in 1970, for all uses exclusive of hydroelectric and thermoelectric power plants. Thus, from 1950 to 1970 per capita use increased nearly two and one-half times.

As shown by Figure 8.24, in 1970, per capita use for all uses exclusive of hydroelectric and thermoelectric power plants ranged from seventy-five gallons per day in Onslow County to twenty-five hundred gallons per day in Martin County. Counties having the highest per capita uses were the sites of major paper-manufacturing plants or mining operations.

Consumptive Use of Water Withdrawal water may be subdivided into two categories—consumptive and nonconsumptive. After nonconsumptive use, water is immediately available for reuse. It has suffered no appreciable reduction in volume, but the quality may be impaired. On the other hand, water used consumptively is temporarily lost, either by evaporation or by incorporation in a product, and is not immediately available for reuse. A large majority of the water withdrawn is not consumed and is ultimately returned to a nearby stream. In 1970, for example, only slightly more than 7 percent of the 5,589 mgd withdrawn in North Carolina, exclusive of that withdrawn for hydroelectric power uses, was consumed. The comparison of total water quantities withdrawn and consumed by withdrawal uses, other than for hydroelectric power generation, is shown in Figure 8.25. The percentages consumed are as follows: thermoelectric power, 1 percent; other industrial uses, 10 percent; public water supplies, 30 percent; domestic use, 65 percent; livestock use, 90 percent; and irrigation, 100 percent.

The total water consumed, 400 mgd, does not include evaporation losses from reservoirs. Such losses in North Carolina are estimated at 600 mgd. These losses, together with the water consumed, amount to a total loss or depletion of nearly 1,000 mgd. However, with a total state resource of 35,000 mgd, there remains a favorably wide margin for future water development and use—if the resources are properly managed.

Water Quality and Pollution

The most pervasive, destructive, and dangerous water management problem is the deterioration of water quality caused by the addition of dissolved substances, increases in sediment concentrations and temperature, and the reduction in the varieties and numbers of organisms. While pollution is normally thought of as deterioration from adverse effects caused by man, water quality also reflects natural characteristics. The quality of water can be measured by examining a number of characteristics that can be grouped into chemical, physical, and biological categories.

Chemical Quality Because of its ability to dissolve at least small amounts of nearly all substances, water is frequently referred to as the "universal solvent." Precipitation contains both gases and solids dissolved from the atmosphere, and as water flows over the land surface and percolates through underground openings, it dissolves small amounts of the soil, rocks, and other materials it contacts. In addition, much of the domestic, agricultural, and industrial wastes that man generates are soluble. These dissolved substances may include inorganic chemical compounds such as those comprising most soils and rocks; radioactive substances; and complex organic compounds, including pesticides, herbicides, and other compounds contained in domestic and industrial wastes. The kinds and amounts of these substances determine the chemical quality of water.

Most soil and rocks underlying North Carolina are only slightly soluble in water. Consequently, unpolluted water from streams and lakes contains relatively little dissolved mineral matter. Groundwater is similarly low in dissolved solids content, but exceptions are commonly experienced from wells in such rocks as limestone or diorite. The chemical quality of typical streams and wells in each of the three physiographic provinces of the state is shown in Table 8.4.

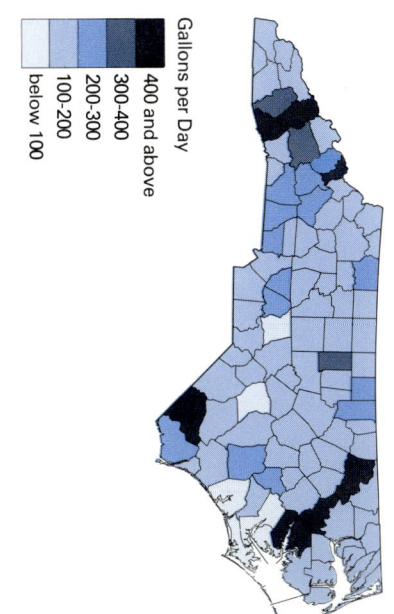

Figure 8.24. Per Capita Use of Water by N.C. Counties

Gallons per Day
- 400 and above
- 300-400
- 200-300
- 100-200
- below 100

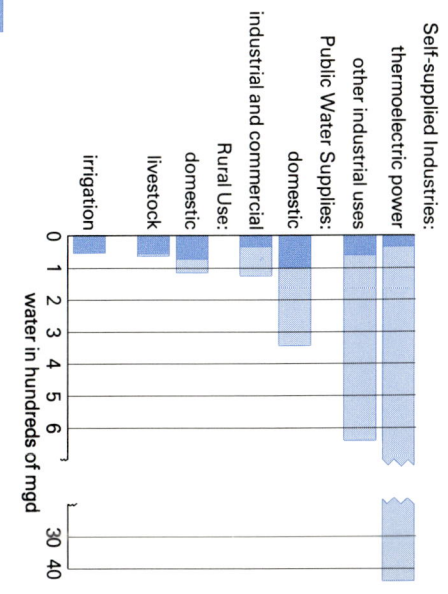

Figure 8.25. Water Consumed by Various Withdrawal Uses in N.C., 1970

Self-supplied Industries:
- thermoelectric power
- other industrial uses

Public Water Supplies:
- industrial and commercial
- domestic

Rural Use:
- domestic
- livestock
- irrigation

water in hundreds of mgd

- water consumed
- water withdrawn

163

The amount of mineral matter dissolved in water, whether from natural sources or pollution, is indicated by the dissolved solids content. The pattern in North Carolina is depicted by Figure 8.26. By comparing these actual levels of dissolved solids with unpolluted overland runoff, shown in Figure 8.17a, and unpolluted groundwater discharge to streams, shown in Figure 8.17b, the extent to which natural levels have been increased by pollution can be determined. The increase in dissolved solids has been especially dramatic in the Piedmont, where levels of many streams are four times as high as the unpolluted waters. These increases result from municipal and industrial wastes that contribute large amounts of dissolved solids.

Because most streams and lakes in the state have low amounts of calcium and magnesium, their waters are generally soft. However, where drainage is from limestone beds—as in a few Coastal Plain streams—the water is moderately hard. The most noteworthy of the streams draining areas underlain by limestone include the Trent River, the New River, and other rivers and creeks draining the coastal zone from the Roanoke River to the Cape Fear River.

Dissolved solids of groundwater from wells (Figure 8.28) tend to be considerably more mineralized than the groundwater inflow to streams (Figure 8.27b). This difference is explained by the fact that whereas most groundwater inflow to streams is derived from shallow aquifers composed mostly of relatively insoluble minerals, most wells draw from deeper aquifers containing more soluble minerals.

Physical Quality Categories of physical pollution usually include color, temperature, and suspended matter. Of greatest interest to water management in North Carolina are suspended sediment and temperature. Suspended matter may settle on a stream bed, smother or burst fish eggs, or create a nuisance with odors of putrefaction. Although domestic and industrial wastes are important sources of suspended matter, the most important source is matter brought into suspension by soil and stream channel erosion. Raindrops falling on bare ground dislodge soil particles, which are then carried in suspension as the water runs over the land surface to stream channels. During the early decades of this century, erosion of cultivated fields was a serious problem. Through the technical assistance of the United States Soil Conservation Service, the damages to farmland caused by this problem have largely been brought under control. However, erosion and the resulting sediment problems have in recent years become a serious problem in urban areas and in highway construction.

Table 8.4. Chemical Analyses of Water from N.C. Streams and Wells

Chemical Constituent or Property	Streams			Coastal Plain Wells			Piedmont and Mountain Wells		
	Mountain Stream Pigeon R. at Canton (D.A. 133 mi²)	Piedmont Stream South Yadkin R. at Cooleemee (D.A. 569 mi²)	Coastal Plain Stream Black R. near Tomahawk (D.A. 680 mi²)	Surficial Deposits Weeksville, Pasquotank Co. (14 ft. deep)	Castle Hayne Limestone Jacksonville, Onslow Co. (200 ft. deep)	Cretaceous Deposits Jacksonville, Onslow Co. (398 ft. deep)	Granite Median of 29 analyses	Granite and Diorite Median of 10 analyses	Diorite Median of 23 analyses
Silica (SiO_2)	7.0	13	7.2	9.4	32	11	30	30	32
Iron (Fe)	.02	.04	.21	.99	.06	.05	.2	.1	.2
Calcium (Ca)	1.8	3.6	3.1	5.0	64	6.6	5	20	38
Magnesium (Mg)	.5	1.5	.9	3.3	4.8	4.0	2	4	12
Sodium (Na)	1.3	3.2	4.4	7.8	6.6	103	7	9	11
Potassium (K)	.6	1.3	1.1	3.6	4.7	13			
Bicarbonate (HCO_3)	9	22	7.7	27	231	316	34	74	127
Sulfate (SO_4)	1.6	4.1	5.4	7.0	.8	1.4	2	3	17
Chloride (Cl)	1.1	2.3	6.2	11	4.6	7.1	2	2	14
Fluoride (F)	.0	.1	.7	.0	.2	1.4	.1	.1	.1
Nitrate (NO_3)	.4	.6	.6	.7	.1	.4	.9	.5	1.3
Phosphate (PO_4)	.01	.02	.03	.1	.0	.1			
Total dissolved solids	21	40	56	62	237	304	71	120	233
Total hardness	6	15	11	26	181	33	23	63	145
Specific conductance	21	65	53	115	385	450			
pH	(5.7–7.0)	(6.4–9.9)	(5.1–7.0)	6.7	8.0	8.3	6.5	6.9	7.1
Color	9	9	74	(0–20)	8	4			

Note: Values in parentheses are ranges. Values for streams are averages or ranges. All values are in milligrams per liter except those for specific conductance, pH, and color.

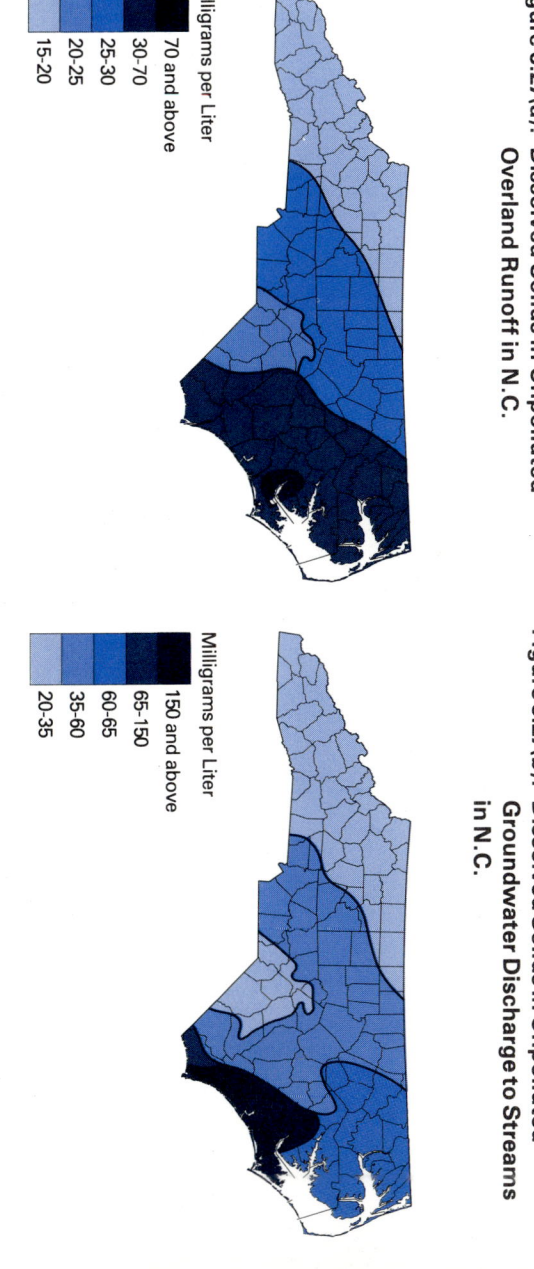

Figure 8.26. Average Dissolved Solids Content of Streams in N.C.

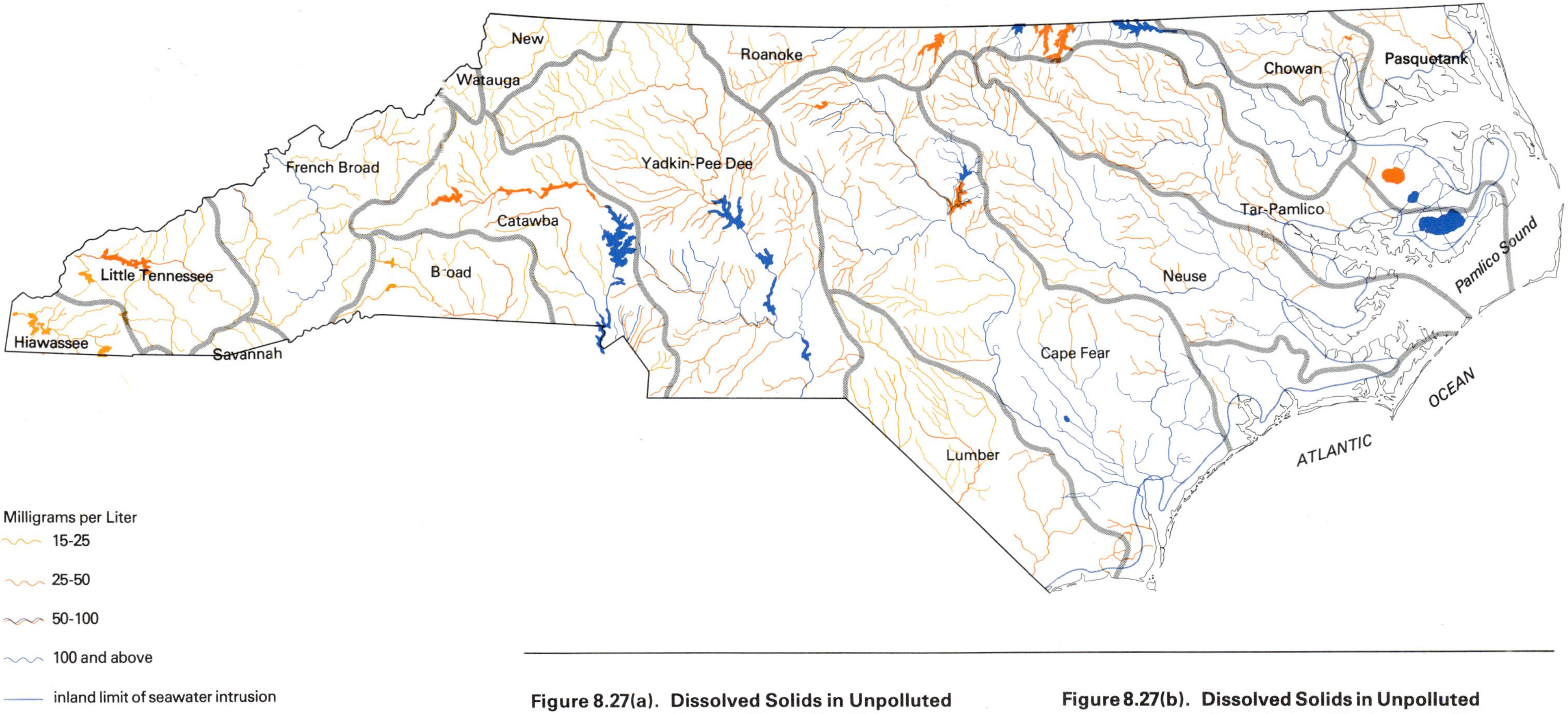

Figure 8.27(a). Dissolved Solids in Unpolluted Overland Runoff in N.C.

Figure 8.27(b). Dissolved Solids in Unpolluted Groundwater Discharge to Streams in N.C.

In order to hold down construction costs of highways and major urban building projects, large tracts of land are sometimes cleared and left exposed for two or three years. Overland runoff from these areas carries large amounts of sediment to be deposited in nearby stream channels and lakes. Deposition of sediment in the channels of urban streams compounds the flood problem discussed earlier, and higher rates of runoff cause erosion, resulting in enlargement of stream channels. Therefore, lakes downstream from urban areas are quickly filled with sediment eroded from construction sites and stream channels.

As illustrated in Figure 8.29, sediment discharge varies considerably, as it depends upon the degree of surface exposure. Four degrees of surface exposure are examined: (1) a severely exposed area—one in which major construction activities are underway, (2) urban areas—those in which development is essentially complete and relatively little construction is in progress, (3) rural areas—extensive cultivated tracts interspersed with small forested areas and with little or no urban development, and (4) wooded areas—largely of forests with few roads and few cultivated fields. Sediment discharge increases about ten times when an area is converted from forest to rural or farmland. When farmland is being rapidly converted into an urban area, the sediment discharge increases about fifty times. In severely exposed areas, where major construction activities are underway, sediment discharge may increase a hundred times or more.

Recognizing the seriousness of sedimentation and of urban flood problems, the General Assembly of North Carolina adopted in its 1973 session Senate Bill 244, "an act to establish a program for the control of pollution from sedimentation." The bill grants local governments the authority to enact local sedimentation control legislation.

For a number of reasons, temperature is considered one of the most important physical characteristics of water. Warm water not only contains less dissolved oxygen than cooler water but biochemical actions proceed more rapidly in warm water, resulting in faster depletion of dissolved oxygen. The temperature of lakes and streams is one of the factors that determines the kinds of fish and other organisms that inhabit them. For example, trout prefer water having a temperature below 70° F. and thus thrive only in streams in the Mountains and upper Piedmont, where temperatures seldom exceed this level. The temperature of water is also important to man in cooling electric power plants, in industrial cooling, and in air conditioning.

Figure 8.28. Dissolved Solids Content of Groundwater in N.C.

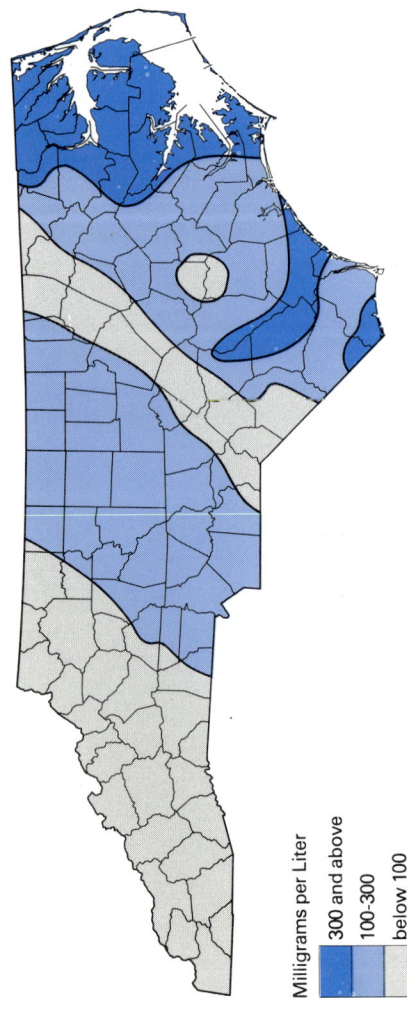

Milligrams per Liter
- 300 and above
- 100-300
- below 100

Source: N.C. Department of Natural and Economic Resources, Groundwater Section.

Figure 8.29. Sediment Discharge and Degree of Surface Exposure

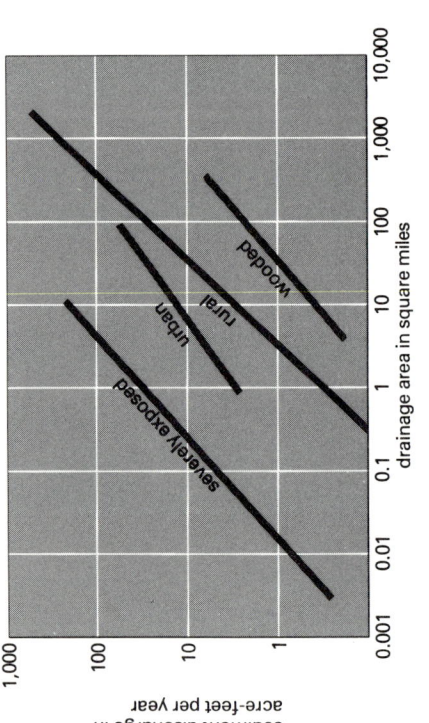

Source: H.R. Malcom, Jr., "Economic Incentives in Urban Sediment Control" (Ph.D. diss., N.C. State University, 1973).

The natural temperature of streams and lakes fluctuates in response to changes in air temperature. In localized areas, temperatures are increased by wastes from manufacturing establishments and by electric power plants that use water for cooling purposes. As shown in Figure 8.30, average temperatures of streams in January range from slightly above freezing in the Mountains to the high forties in the Coastal Plain. Figure 8.31 shows July temperatures ranging from more than 80° F. in the Inner Coastal Plain to the high sixties in the Mountains.

The temperature of groundwater is much more constant than that of surface water and, therefore, groundwater is preferred for air conditioning and other heat exchange uses. At a depth of about fifty feet the temperature of groundwater is essentially constant and within a degree or two of the mean annual air temperature. Below depths of about fifty feet the temperature of groundwater increases about 1° F. per hundred feet-increase in depth.

Biological Quality Streams and lakes generally contain viruses, bacteria, fungi, fish, and other living organisms, the variety and number of which determine the biological quality of the water. Because living things are bacteria and fungi. Even the purest stream has bacteria and fungi, and they have the capacity to multiply rapidly as increasing amounts of nutrients become available. As the free oxygen content decreases, fish die, pathogens (micro-organisms) increase, and the productivity and utility of the stream or lake is decreased. If all the oxygen is used, an anaerobic decomposition process—a process without air—results. Rather than releasing carbon dioxide, the decomposition process releases methane or hydrogen sulfide. In these polluted situations, the river turns dark and gives off unpleasant odors. The amount of oxygen in a water body is therefore one of the best measures of its ecological health.

Pollution of rivers and lakes by excess nutrients occurs from four principal sources in North Carolina: (1) untreated or inadequately treated municipal and industrial wastes, (2) drainage from farms with stock, (3) agricultural fertilizers, and (4) overland urban runoff.

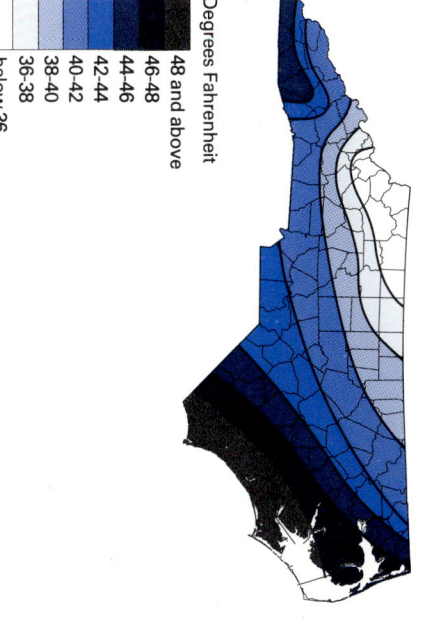

Figure 8.30. Average January Temperature of N.C. Streams

Degrees Fahrenheit
- 48 and above
- 46-48
- 44-46
- 42-44
- 40-42
- 38-40
- 36-38
- below 36

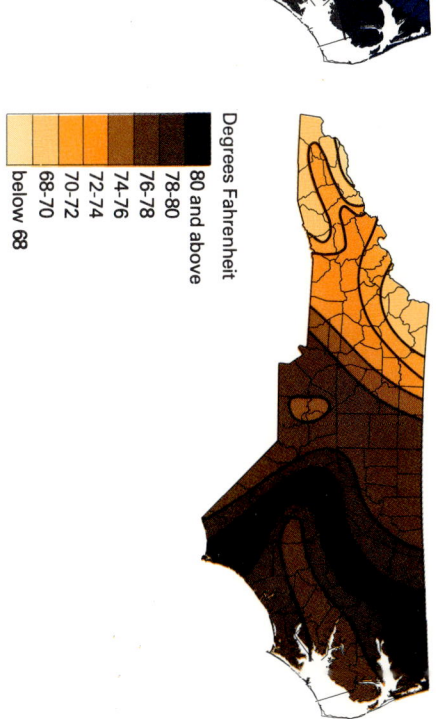

Figure 8.31. Average July Temperature of N.C. Streams

Degrees Fahrenheit
- 80 and above
- 78-80
- 76-78
- 74-76
- 72-74
- 70-72
- 68-70
- below 68

One of the most striking patterns illustrated in Figure 8.33 is the large number of streams in the Piedmont that are classified either A or D. Most of the Class A streams serve as sources of public water supplies and the Class D streams receive the wastes from municipalities and industries. One of the principal efforts of the state's present water pollution control program is to improve the quality of Class D streams as a prelude to upgrading their classification.

Violations of water quality standards occur from time to time on segments of some streams. Such violations result from several causes including exceptionally low streamflows, accidental release of impounded wastes, accidental discharge of toxic substances, and heavy runoff on urban areas during storms. Figure 8.34 shows stream segments for which water quality standards are known to have been violated in 1972.

Pollution of groundwater, a problem of long standing, has only recently attracted widespread attention. Until recently, most groundwater pollution occurred in small amounts at widely separated points and thus did not overload the natural filtration and purification properties of the underground environment. In fact, most pollution consisted of domestic wastes disposed of through cesspools and septic tanks in rural and in unsewered urban areas. Sewering of urban areas in recent years and the decrease in rural population have resulted in a reduction of underground pollution from domestic wastes. Simultaneously, efforts to eliminate stream pollution have, in many instances, resulted in the disposal of industrial wastes on the ground surface or in ponds from which seepage occurs into underlying aquifers. Other examples of groundwater pollution that are receiving increasing attention include pollution resulting from solid waste disposal sites and from animal feed lots. Studies of the amount and extent of the pollution caused by these factors are only in the early stages, and effective and practical control methods must still be developed.

In an effort to assure the development of safe groundwater supplies, the North Carolina Board of Water and Air Resources adopted comprehensive well construction regulations and standards in 1971. To avoid further degradation in the quality of groundwater supplies, the Division of Groundwater of the Office of Water and Air Resources is developing a classification of groundwater supplies similar in concept to that of surface water supplies.

As the treatment of municipal and industrial wastes has become more widespread and effective in recent years, the problem of "nonpoint" sources or diffused pollution has assumed greater importance. Such pollution occurs in overland runoff from urban areas and in seepage from waste-holding ponds, sanitary landfills, and unsewered urban areas. Studies indicate that the pollution in runoff from densely populated urban areas is similar in concentration to that reaching treatment plants through sanitary sewers. Two other nonpoint sources—fertilizers and animal waste—are of special concern. Fertilizers contain nitrogen and phosphorus, two primary nutrients that nourish algae in water. Of nitrates and phosphates, the former pose the greater problem. Whereas phosphates stick to soil, nitrates are very susceptible to runoff from rain and also leach into groundwater. Efforts are now being made to gain a better understanding of this problem in the state. The increasing numbers of animals and modern methods of raising them contribute to the trend of increasing pollution of water. Considerably more information is needed on the origin and amount of diffused pollution before methods for controlling it can be developed. However, animals are pollution sources that cannot be ignored and should command increasing attention in the state.

Classification of Streams and Groundwater

Pollution of the state's waters with municipal, industrial, and farm wastes has long been of concern to citizens and public officials. Among the earliest efforts in North Carolina to control this problem was the passage of the 1893 law providing for protection of public water supplies. Increasing pollution resulting from population and industrial growth led to the passage in 1951 of the Stream Sanitation Law which was designed to protect the quality of streams and lakes for all uses.

Central to the state's pollution control program is the classification of streams in terms of best usage. The different classes are shown in Table 8.5 together with information on the best usage and selected water quality standards applicable to each class. Figure 8.33 shows the four principal classifications of freshwater streams. It is not practical on this small-scale map to differentiate Class A-I and Class A-II waters, to indicate those streams in the Coastal Plain designated as swamp waters, and to show those mountain streams designated as natural trout waters.

Figure 8.32. Expenditures for Waste-Treatment Facilities and Sewer-System Extensions in N.C., 1961-1970

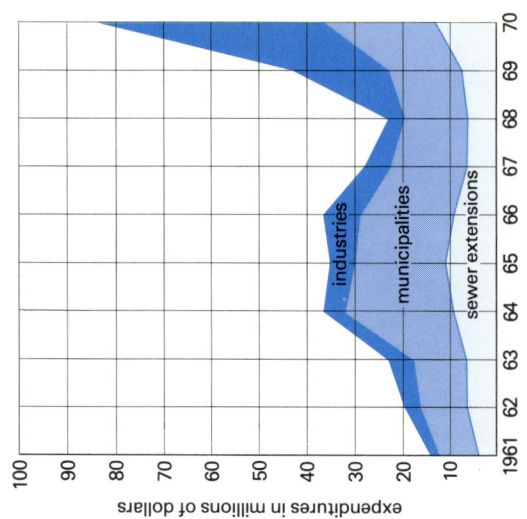

Source: N.C. Department of Natural and Economic Resources.

Progress in the state's efforts to minimize the problem of municipal and industrial wastes is indicated by increasing expenditures from 1961 to 1970 for waste treatment facilities and sewer system extensions (Figure 8.32). In 1972 the state's voters approved by a 2 to 1 margin a $150 million bond issue, half of the money of which is to be used to supplement local and federal funds in the construction of waste treatment plants. It is hoped that this will result in a considerable reduction in stream pollution caused by inadequately treated sewage.

Figure 8.33. Classification of Streams in N.C., 1972

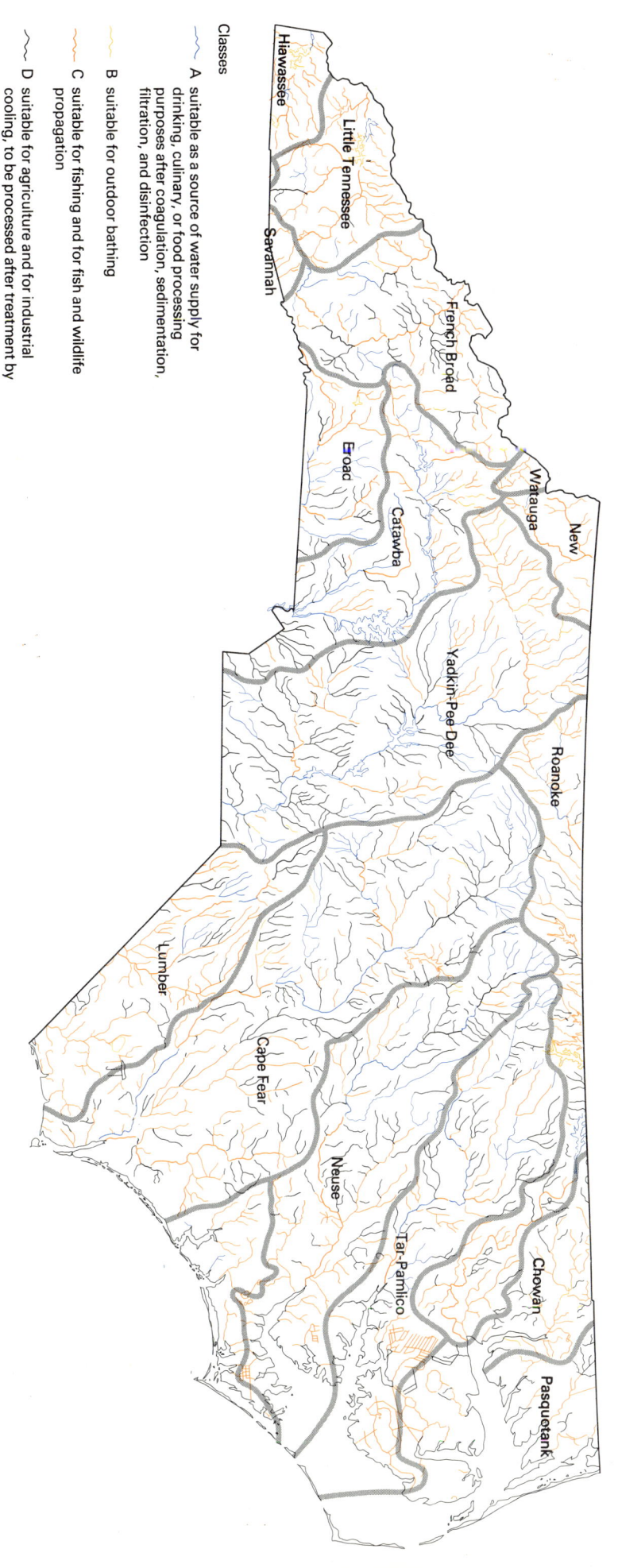

Classes

∿ A suitable as a source of water supply for drinking, culinary, or food processing purposes after coagulation, sedimentation, filtration, and disinfection

∿ B suitable for outdoor bathing

∿ C suitable for fishing and for fish and wildlife propagation

∿ D suitable for agriculture and for industrial cooling, to be processed after treatment by the user as may be required

Source: N.C. Office of Water and Air Resources.

Figure 8.34. N.C Stream Segments in Which Violations of Water-Quality Standards Occurred in 1972

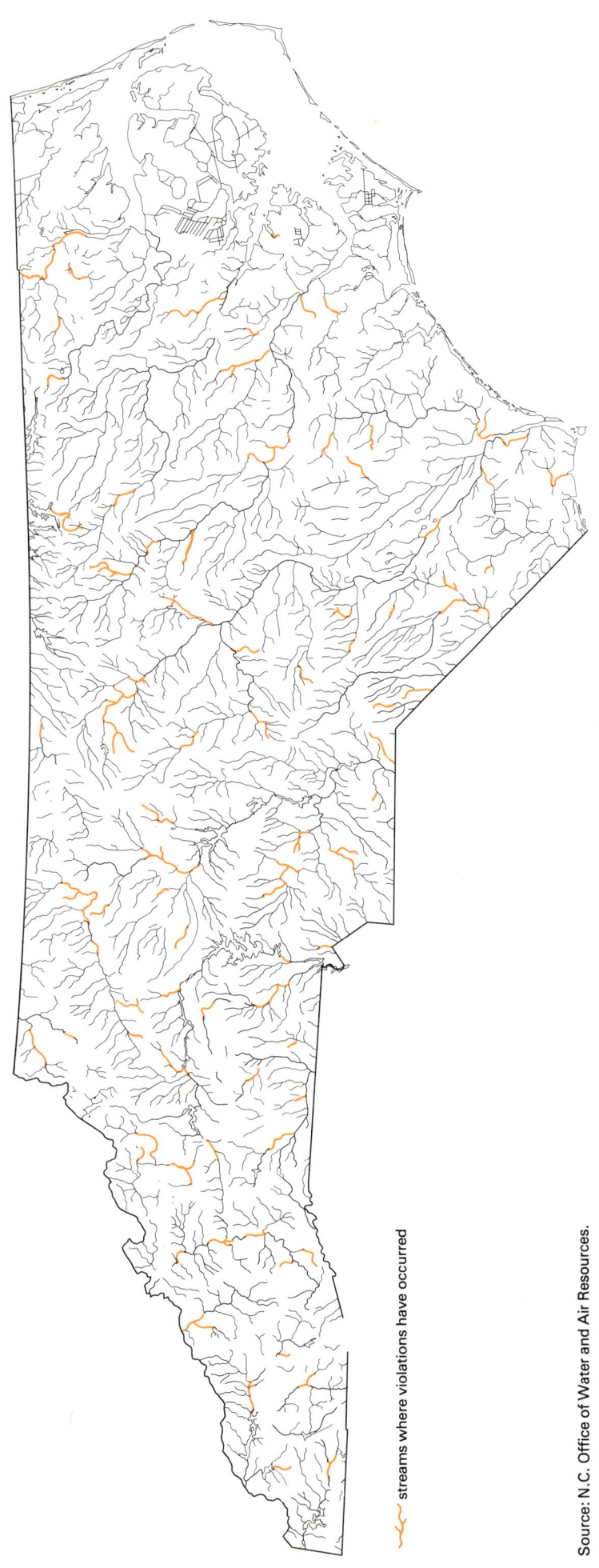

— streams where violations have occurred

Source: N.C. Office of Water and Air Resources.

Table 8.5. Selected Water-Quality Standards Applicable to Surface Waters of N.C.

Class	Best Usage	pH	Dissolved Oxygen (milligrams per liter)	Fecal Coliforms (monthly average of MPN per 100 ml.)	Temperature (maximum increase in °F. above natural temperature)
A-I	Drinking, culinary, and food processing (water from uninhabited and protected watersheds)	—	—	50[1]	—
A-II	Drinking, culinary, and food processing	6.0–8.5[2]	4.0–6.0	1,000	Natural trout waters 0°; "Put and take" trout waters 3°; Others 5°
B	Swimming	6.0–8.5[2]	4.0–6.0	200[3]	Same as A-II
C	Fishing, boating, wading	6.0–8.5[2]	4.0–6.0	1,000	Same as A-II
D	Irrigation, industrial uses	6.0–8.5[2]	3.0+	1,000	5°
SA	Shellfish propagation for market (tidal salt waters)	6.8–8.5	5.0+[4]	70[1]	June–August 1.5°; Remainder of year 4°
SB	Swimming	6.0–8.5[2]	5.0+[4]	1,000	Same as SA

Source: Adapted from rules and regulations of the N.C. Board of Water and Air Resources.

[1]Total coliforms. [2]May be as low as 4.3 in swamp water. [3]Applicable only during months of May through September. [4]Minimum in swamps may be 4.0.

MARINE RESOURCES

The history of North Carolina is deeply rooted in the coastal region. As discussed in the chapter on history, it was in 1587 on the shores of Roanoke Island that the first attempt was made by the English to colonize America. This settlement, however, disappeared and became known as "The Lost Colony." In the 1650s permanent settlers established themselves in that section, and it came to be known as Albemarle. In 1665 a charter delineating the geographic boundaries of "Carolina" was granted. Thus much of the early history of the state was to unfold with an eye toward the sea. In more recent times, however, the mainstream of activity has shifted inland, and the coastal region has declined in relative importance. However, marine resources continue to provide a basis for important commercial and recreational activities in the state.

Figure 8.35. Coastline of the States

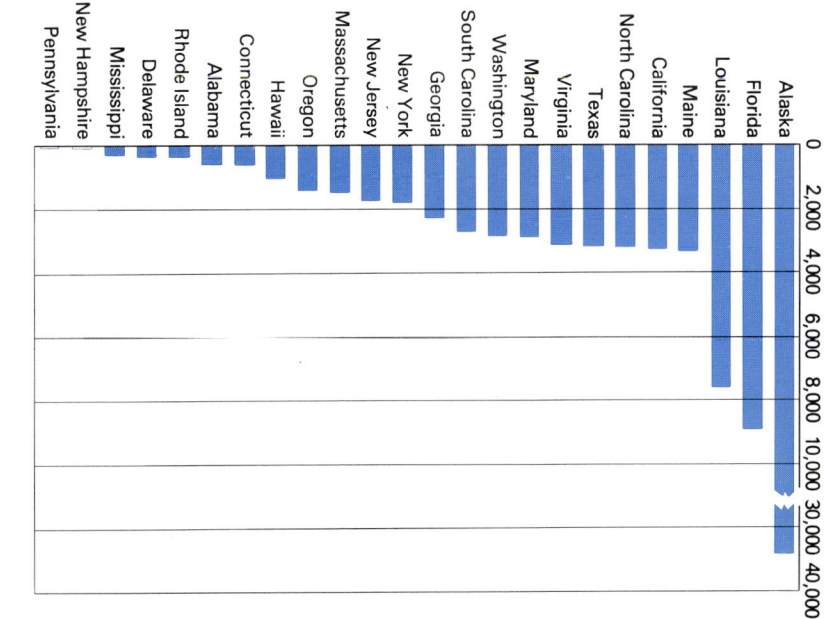

Source: U.S. Department of Commerce, *The Coastline of the United States*, 1968.

Note: Includes the shorelines of estuaries, sounds, and embayments.

Coastline and Estuarine Zone

North Carolina's tidal shoreline and *estuarine zone* (coastal wetlands and shoal water) rank among the largest of those of the Atlantic coastal states. As shown in Figure 8.35, North Carolina's tidal shoreline ranks sixth in the nation and fourth among the Atlantic coastal states in size. The state's long shoreline adjoins an extensive acreage of coastal wetlands and shoal waters. In fact, as depicted in Figure 8.36, North Carolina ranks first in estuarine marsh area among the Atlantic coastal states.

Figure 8.36. Extent of Important Estuarine Zone in Atlantic Coastal States

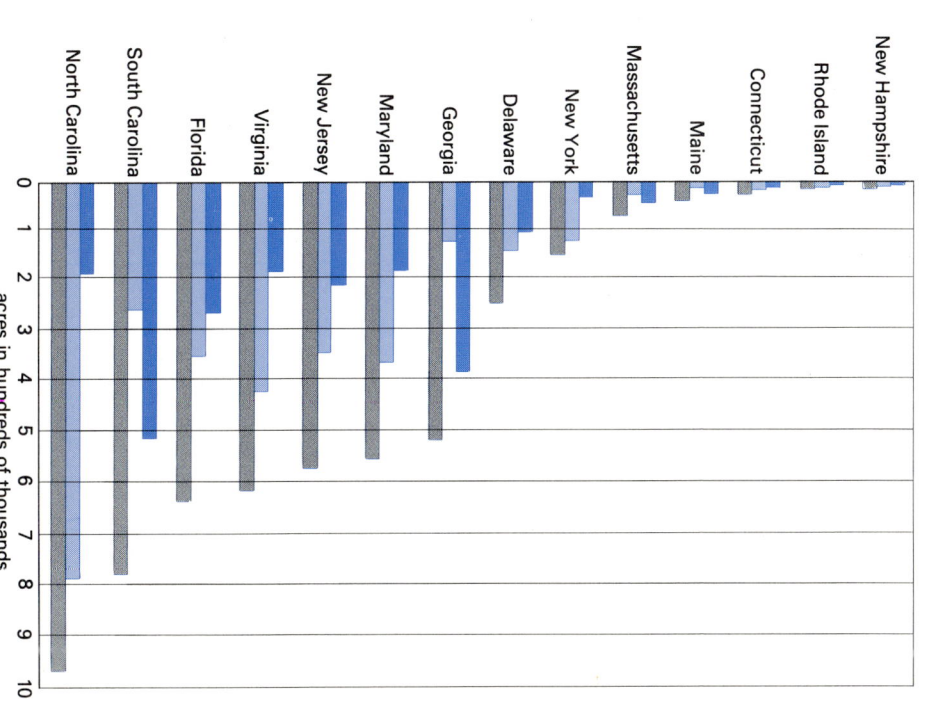

Source: George P. Spinner, ed., *Serial Atlas of the Marine Environment* (New York: American Geographical Society, 1969).

171

This estuarine zone, or marshland, may be a more valuable resource to the state than its sandy beaches. The marshes are the nurseries and feeding grounds for many juvenile finfish, shellfish, and other commercially important marine life forms.

The Continental Shelf

The continental shelf is defined as a platform area extending from the shore of a continent to a point where there is a marked downward steepening of the slope. The continental shelf, in terms of marine resources, is extremely important to North Carolina. It is here that marine productivity is highest, mineral resource potential is greatest, and recreational activities are most common. The federal and state governments have jurisdiction over this shelf area—the state government, from the beach to three miles offshore; the federal government, from three miles offshore to the edge of the shelf.

The edge of the North Carolina continental shelf is fairly easy to recognize from the bathymetric chart shown in Figure 8.37. This broad terrace varies in width from sixteen miles at Cape Hatteras to over sixty-five miles at Long Bay, near Cape Fear. The shelf slopes gently from the coast, decreasing at the rate of approximately 6 feet per mile. The continental shelf is everywhere less than 300 feet below sea level, and south of Cape Lookout terminates at depths of 120 to 240 feet.

Bottom Sediments

The texture and composition of bottom sediments along the North Carolina coast vary widely. In Figure 8.38, the bottom sediments are categorized into four classes and shown spatially. Sediment distribution is very patchy over the entire shelf. However, some general trends can be characterized. The amount of shell material generally increases toward the outer portion of the continental shelf. Along the inner margins of the northern shelf sediments are characteristically fine-texture sands while in the south they change to very shelly, coarse sands.

Underlying the bottom sediments are limestones, sandstones, and shales that extend seaward from the continent. In fact, the shelf is geologically an extension of the continent. It is in these offshore sediments that the greatest potential for commercial oil and gas deposits exists. Several major oil companies have purchased leases in this continental shelf area, but to date, only a few exploratory wells have been drilled and all have proven unproductive.

Figure 8.37. Bathymetry of the N.C. Coastline in Feet

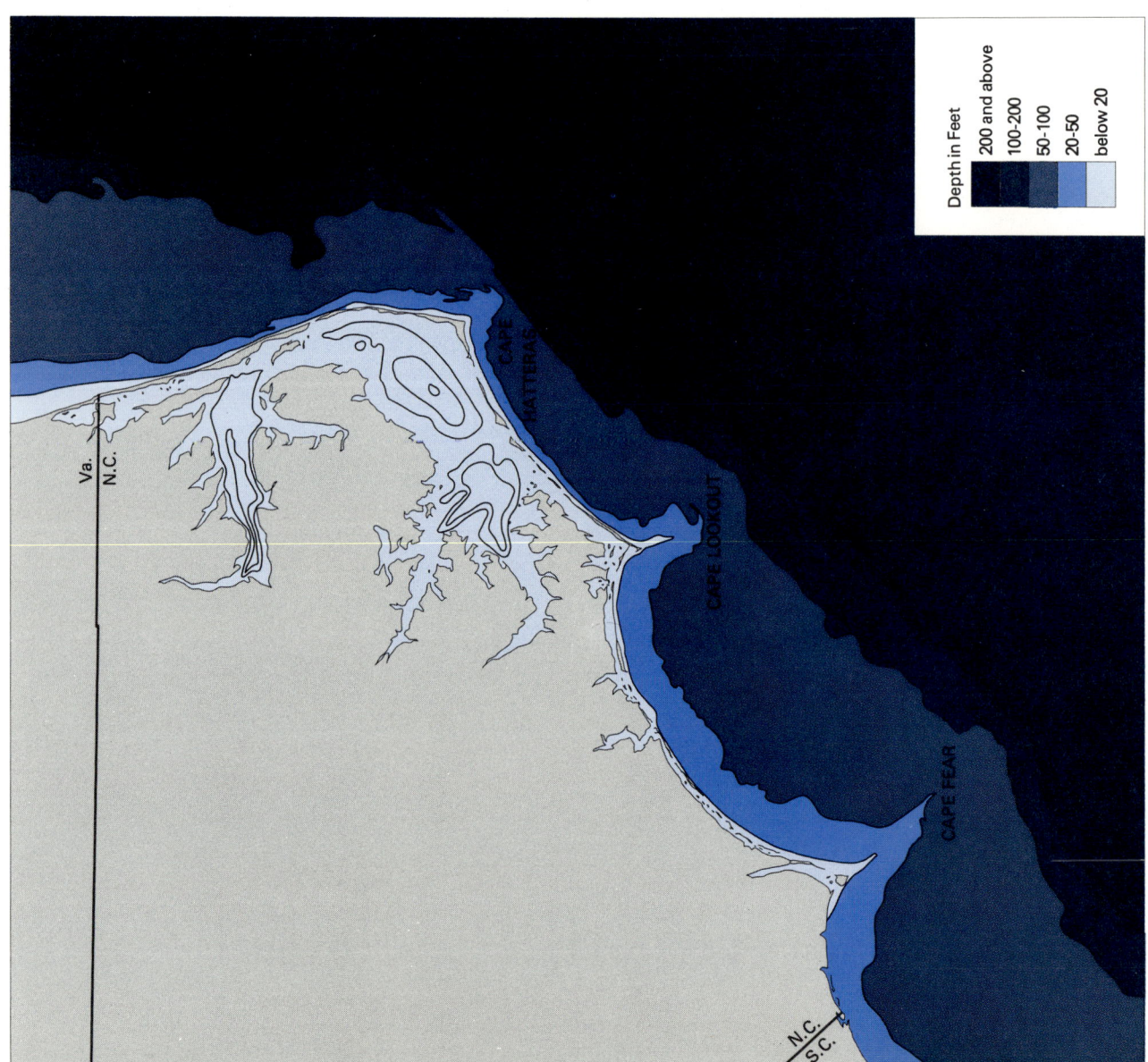

Source: H. F. Belding and W. C. Holland, eds. *Bathymetric Maps, Eastern Continental Margin, U.S.A.* (Tulsa: American Association of Petroleum Geologists, 1970).

Figure 8.38. Bottom Sediments along N.C.'s Continental Shelf

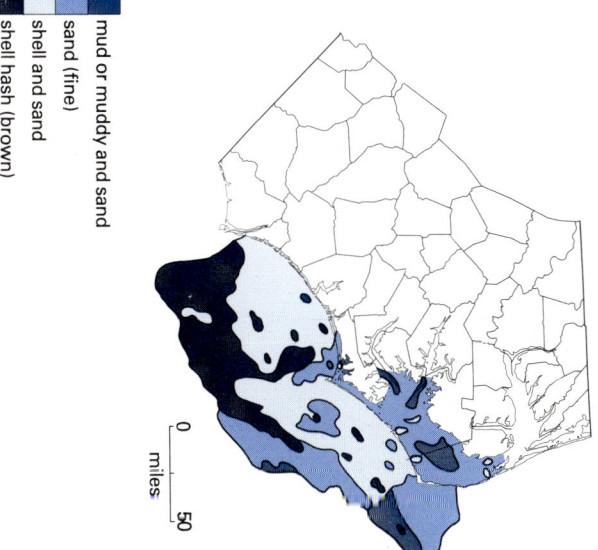

- mud or muddy and sand
- sand (fine)
- shell and sand
- shell hash (brown)

Source: U.S. Department of the Interior, *Characteristics of Estuarine Sediments of the United States*, 1972.

Water Characteristics

Most oceanographic research studies are concerned in some degree with temperature, salinity, and ocean currents. Each of these is important in terms of the biota (the animal and plant life of a region), man's relationship with the ocean, and the influences of each on the other. The water off the shore of North Carolina is a unique region where three distinct "water masses" meet: the Caribbean (Gulf Stream) water, the Labrador (current) water, and the coastal water of North Carolina and Virginia. Thus, considerable variation in water characteristics from place to place is to be expected. Furthermore, these characteristics are not static, but are constantly changing and causing corresponding changes in the life support system. Changes in the salinity and the temperature of seawater induce the fish and other mobile organisms to migrate unexpectedly from one area to another. The most obvious and noticeable changes are in surface water temperatures.

Figure 8.39. Surface Temperature of Ocean Water off the N.C. Coast

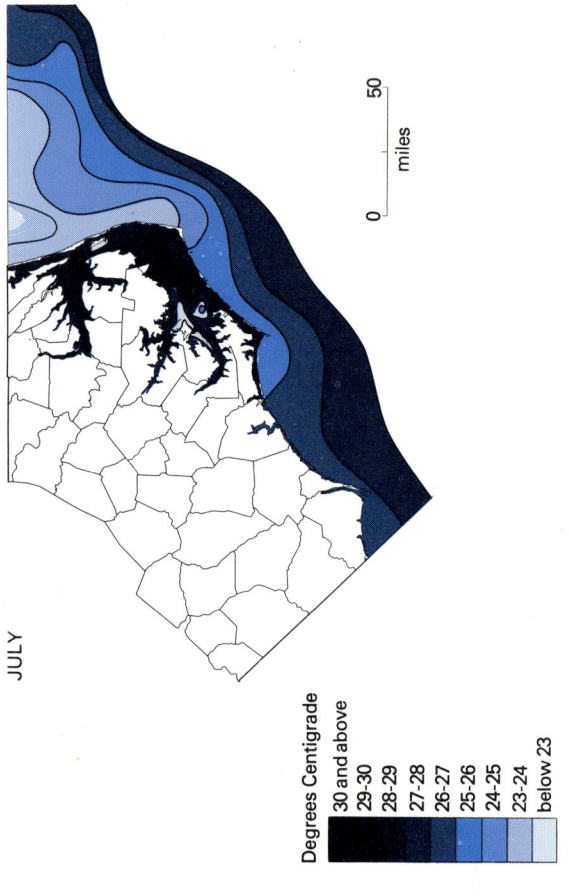

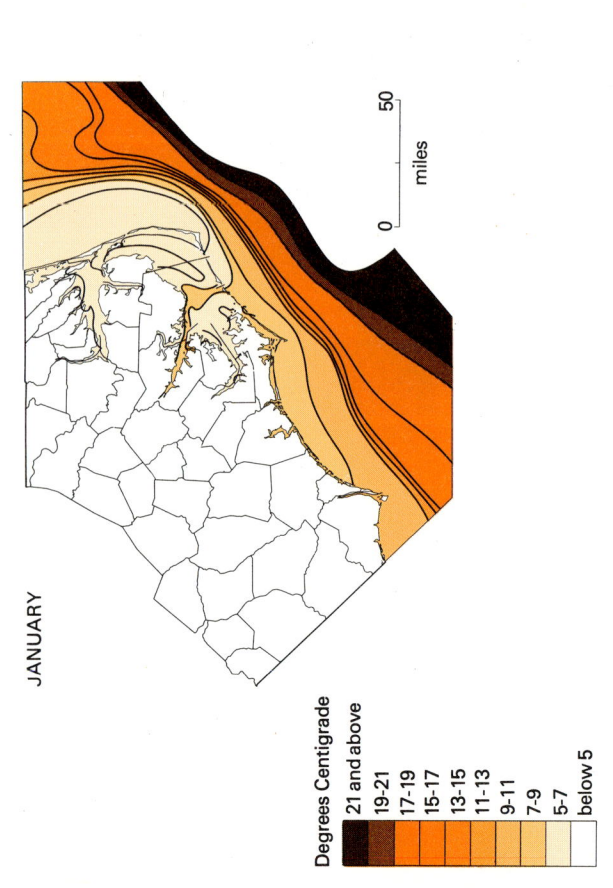

Figure 8.40. Surface Circulation of Water off N.C.'s Coast

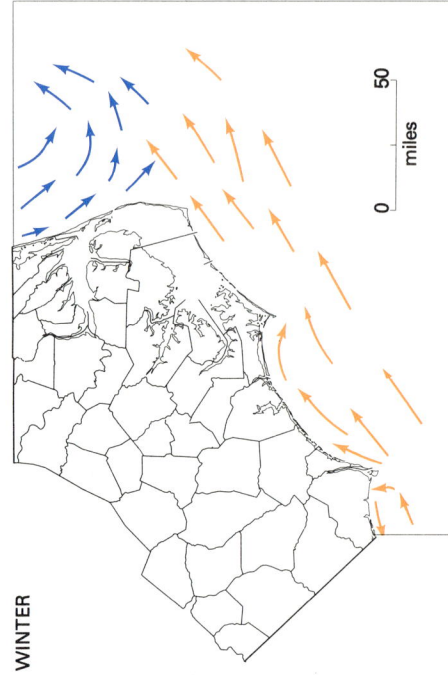

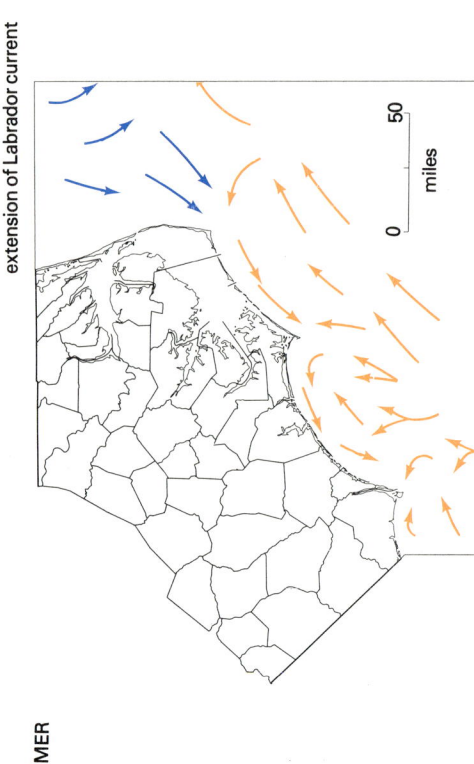

Source: N.C. Department of Conservation and Development, *An Oceanographic Atlas of the Carolina Continental Margin*, 1971. U.S. Department of Transportation, *Surface Isotherms °C Monthly Charts, 1969-72*. Austin B. Williams, Gerald S. Posner, William J. Woods, and Earl E. Deubler, eds., *A Hydrographic Atlas of Larger North Carolina Sounds*, Sea Grant Pub. UNC-SG-73-02, 1973.

Surface water temperatures off the North Carolina coast are depicted in Figure 8.39. In winter, water temperatures generally increase rapidly seaward. Consequently, winter temperatures of surface waters thirty or so miles from the coast are only a few degrees colder than summer temperatures. Strongly related to this pattern are the ocean currents, the most important of which is the Gulf Stream, a large warm ocean current flowing northward from the tropical zone. The Gulf Stream generally parallels the coast at an average distance of about thirty miles from shore (Figure 8.40). The stream follows the outer edge of the continental shelf until it turns eastward off Cape Hatteras. However, there can be substantial day-to-day or week-to-week deviations as the Gulf Stream meanders and shifts under the influence of wind and other factors, developing eddies or creating pockets of warmer and more saline water.

During the summer, temperatures are highest in bays, estuaries, and sounds where the shallow waters are heated by the direct rays of the sun. Along the northern shores are found the coolest waters, for here southward-flowing currents bring in cooler offshore waters. Water characteristics in sounds, bays, and estuaries fluctuate with tides as with the seasons.

Unlike temperature changes, which show the greatest changes seasonally, salinity changes are usually largest with the change in tide. Indeed, as shown in Figure 8.41, there is little seasonal variation in surface salinity. In both summer and winter the lowest salinities occur in the sounds and estuaries; the highest are in the Gulf Stream water near the outer edge of the continental shelf. The Gulf Stream surface salinities are usually in excess of thirty-six parts per thousand. Another consistent pattern of lower salinity water occurs off the northern coast. This is generally explained as resulting from the runoff of fresh water from the Chesapeake Bay region in Virginia.

Commercial Fishing

Fishing is one of North Carolina's oldest economic pursuits. However, it continues to decline in importance. In the relatively warm Atlantic and on the narrower part of the continental shelf, surface (pelagic) rather than bottom (demersal) fishing is characteristic. As shown in Figure 8.42, fourteen types of finfish and five types of shellfish are commercially significant.

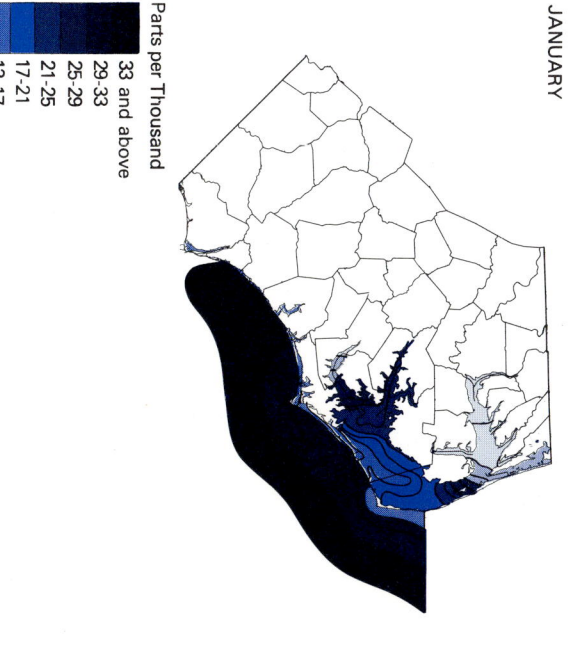

Figure 8.41. Surface Salinity of Ocean Water off the N.C. Coast

JULY

JANUARY

Parts per Thousand
- 33 and above
- 29-33
- 25-29
- 21-25
- 17-21
- 13-17
- 9-13
- 5-9
- below 5

Parts per Thousand
- 33 and above
- 29-33
- 25-29
- 21-25
- 17-21
- 13-17
- 9-13
- 5-9
- below 5

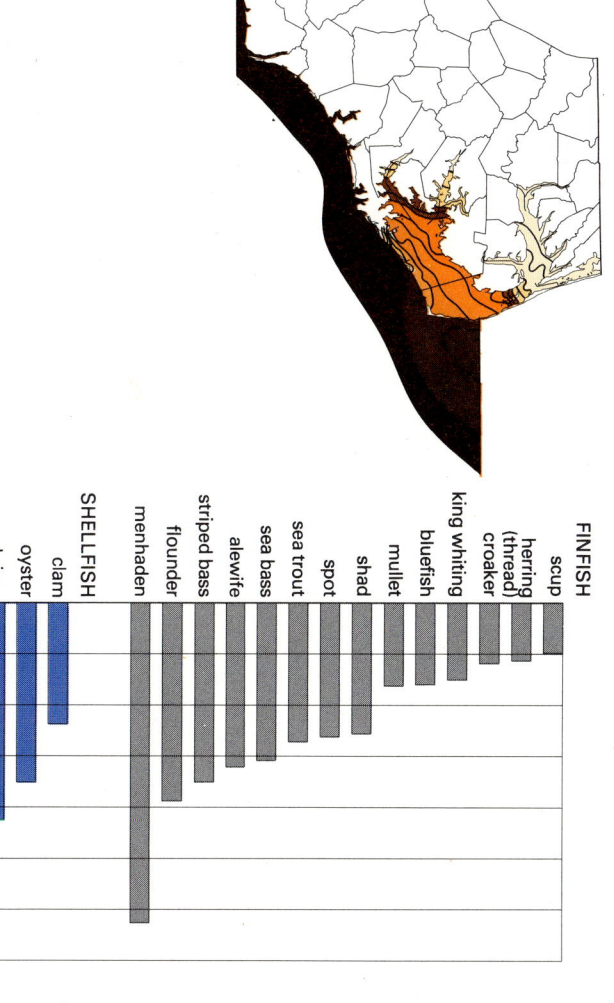

Figure 8.42. Principal Marine Fisheries in N.C., 1966-1970

FINFISH: scup, herring (thread), croaker, king whiting, bluefish, mullet, shad, spot, sea trout, sea bass, alewife, striped bass, flounder, menhaden

SHELLFISH: clam, oyster, shrimp, scallop, crab

thousands of dollars

Source: National Marine Fisheries Service

Source: N.C. Department of Conservation and Development, *An Oceanographic Atlas of the Carolina Continental Margin,* 1971.

Figure 8.43. Total Catch Value of Finfish and Shellfish in N.C., 1956-1970

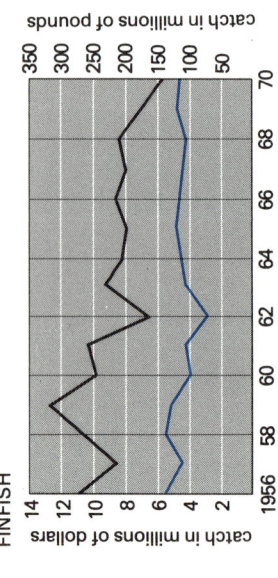

FINFISH

— finfish catch in dollars
— finfish catch in pounds

SHELLFISH

— shellfish catch in dollars
— shellfish catch in pounds

Source: National Marine Fisheries Service.

In Figure 8.43, one observes a substantial increase in the relative economic importance of shellfish during the past fifteen years. This has resulted mainly from the combined effect of a gradual decline in finfish catch and an increase in shellfish prices rather than from an increase in the shellfish catch. The value of the shellfish catch exceeded $6 million in 1971 in comparison to slightly more than $4 million for finfish in the same year. The reverse condition existed in 1956 when the value of the finfish catch exceeded that of the shellfish by a similar margin.

The principal finfish caught has traditionally been the menhaden—a species similar to the herring. Vast catches are possible because the surface schooling habits of the fish make it easy prey. They can be located by air search or by fish-finders. The menhaden's principal uses are as fish meal, oil, and fertilizer. North Carolina's menhaden catch value, as depicted in Figure 8.44, has steadily declined from more than $3 million in 1959 to less than $1 million in 1971.

While the menhaden catch has declined steadily, the flounder and striped bass catches have gradually increased and are now more important commercially than menhaden. As illustrated in Figure 8.45, in 1971 the flounder catch was valued at approximately $4 million, and the striped bass at about $1.5 million. The principal use of both flounder and striped bass is as food.

Among the valuable fisheries of North Carolina are those concerned with shellfish—clams, crabs, oysters, shrimp, and scallops. Of these five, the shrimp is the most important commercially, followed by the crab and the oyster. The relative importance of these three fisheries is shown in Figure 8.46. In 1971, the value of the shrimp

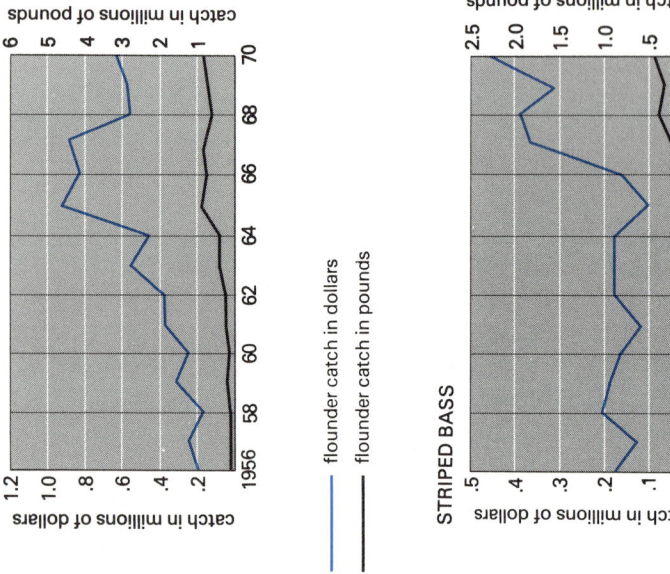

Figure 8.45. Total Catch Value of Flounder and Striped Bass in N.C., 1956-1970

FLOUNDER

— flounder catch in dollars
— flounder catch in pounds

STRIPED BASS

— striped bass catch in dollars
— striped bass catch in pounds

Source: National Marine Fisheries Service.

catch totaled almost $5 million, making it the single most important fishery in North Carolina. Figure 8.47 depicts the principal geographic habitats of individual species of shellfish.

Pollution is an increasing threat to shellfish fisheries. There is a considerable portion of the coastal waters where pollution has advanced to such a degree that harvested shellfish may be unsafe to eat. Consequently, it has become illegal to sell oysters or clams from these areas. The prohibited area is shown by Figure 8.48.

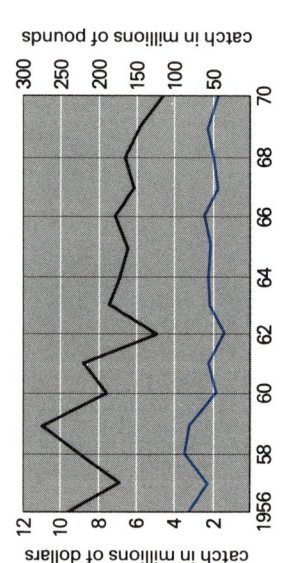

Figure 8.44. Total Catch Value of Menhaden in N.C., 1956-1970

— menhaden catch in dollars
— menhaden catch in pounds

Source: National Marine Fisheries Service.

Figure 8.46. Value of Catch of Principal Shellfish in N.C., 1956-1971

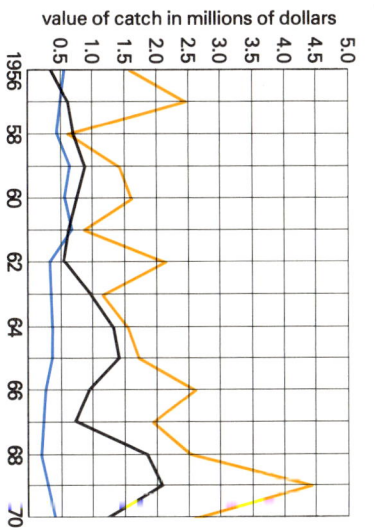

— shrimp
— oyster
— crab

Source: National Marine Fisheries Service.

Figure 8.47. Habitat of Principal Shellfish in N.C.

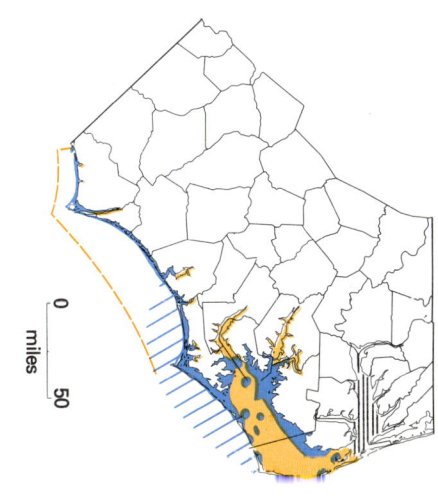

- oyster, hard clam, bay scallop
- shrimp, blue crab
- crab only
- calico scallop taken offshore
- shrimp taken offshore

Source: N.C. Department of Natural and Economic Development, unpublished data, 1973.

Figure 8.48. Prohibited Shellfish Areas in N.C., 1973

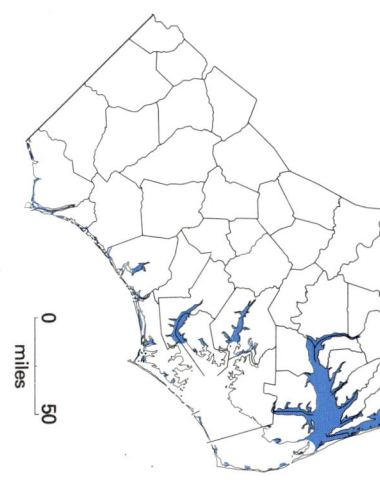

Source: N.C. Department of Natural and Economic Development, unpublished data, 1973.

Coastal Erosion

Along the coast there are many miles of accessible public beaches in addition to those of the National Seashore Parks at Cape Hatteras and Cape Lookout. Erosion along these beaches is a continuous process and developed properties are endangered by loss or damage. The beach itself may sometimes be so severely affected by erosion that guests defect to other locations—thus reducing the summer income of the resort community. Erosion can be a serious economic factor when resort communities depend on tourism as their major income resource. Many geologists feel that this erosion is a natural nonreversible process, and suggest that greater care and planning are required for coastal development.

Water Resources of the Land—Ralph C. Heath and Nathan O. Thomas
Marine Resources—Harold Dubach

SELECTED REFERENCES

Goddard, G. C. *Water Supply Characteristics of North Carolina Streams.* Geological Survey Water-Supply Paper 1761. Washington, D.C.: U.S. Department of the Interior, 1963.

Hinson, H. G. *Floods on Small Streams in North Carolina, Probable Magnitude and Frequency.* Geological Survey Water-Supply Circular 517. Washington, D.C.: U.S. Department of the Interior, 1965.

Jackson, N. M. *Public Water Supplies of North Carolina: Part 1, Northern Piedmont.* Raleigh: Office of Water and Air Resources, N.C. Department of Natural and Economic Resources, 1972.

LeGrand, H. E. *Ground Water of the Piedmont and Blue Ridge Provinces in the Southeastern States.* Geological Survey Circular 538. Washington, D.C.: U.S. Department of the Interior, 1967.

LeGrand, H. E. *Ground-Water Resources of North Carolina.* Division of Mineral Resources Bulletin 69. Raleigh: N.C. Department of Conservation and Development, 1956.

McMaster, W. M., and Hubbard, E. F. *Water Resources of the Great Smoky Mountains National Park, Tennessee and North Carolina.* Geological Survey Hydrologic Investigations Atlas HA-420. Washington, D.C.: U.S. Department of the Interior, 1970.

Malcom, H. R., Jr. "Economic Incentives in Urban Sediment Control." Ph.D dissertation, North Carolina State University, 1973.

Peek, H. M. "The Ground Water Situation in North Carolina." In *Planning for Progress,* vol. 5, no. 3, pp. 8-9, 14-16. Raleigh: Office of State Planning, 1972.

Putnam, A. L. *Effects of Urban Development on Floods in the Piedmont Province of North Carolina.* Geological Survey Open-File Report. Washington, D.C.: U.S. Department of the Interior, 1972.

Thomas, N. O. *Summaries of Streamflow Records in North Carolina.* Raleigh: Office of Water and Air Resources, N.C. Department of Natural and Economic Resources, 1973.

Wilder, H. B., and Slack, L. J. *Summary of Data on Chemical Quality of Streams in North Carolina, 1943-67.* Geological Survey Water-Supply Paper 1895-B. Washington, D.C.: U.S. Department of the Interior, 1971.

With incomes still trailing national norms, economic development is still a critical matter for North Carolina. Energy problems that emerged in the 1970s may retard such development, especially since economic activity has tended to be relatively dispersed throughout the state and rural industrialization has become an important goal of state policy.

The consideration of the economy begins with the state's primary resource—its labor force. From there each sector of the economy is viewed separately. The overall picture is of an economy in transition, with the future outcome of this transition being of vital significance to every North Carolinian.

The dream that Governor Luther Hodges had for North Carolina in 1957 has not been realized but definite improvements in the quality and geographic distribution of economic activities have occurred. The following chapters chronicle those changes and consider the opportunities and challenges that the future may hold.

Perhaps the best measure of the effectiveness of the economy of an area is the income level of its residents. Historically, North Carolinians have had substandard personal incomes, reflecting a heavy emphasis on agriculture. In the twentieth century the state developed a major industrial base that caused income levels to increase substantially and provided a timely alternative to an agricultural system that was rapidly declining as an employer. More recently, diversification of the industrial base led to improvements in the wage-level quality of manufacturing. However, the state's economy remains dominated by low-wage manufacturing and agriculture. Farming is rapidly modernizing and may enjoy a revival in response to global food shortages.

Trade and finance have changed also, with a growing concentration of such activities in the state's urban areas. This is happening at a time when large urban counties are becoming less dependent on manufacturing.

A well-developed transportation network connects the residents of the state with one another and with the world at large. It is a heavily motor vehicle-oriented system although the state is well served by railroads. The Piedmont Urban Crescent has the best-developed transportation facilities, and, generally, north-south movement is easier than is going in east-west directions.

PART IV
THE ECONOMY

[I have] a vision which I believe can be the North Carolina of the future.... I see a land of thriving industry of many kinds—manufacturing, agriculture, research.... This is a land where all citizens have sufficient economic opportunity, spare time, and education to enjoy the best there is in life....

—*Luther H. Hodges*

9. Income and Labor

EDWIN L. ROGERS

Income is a primary measure of the effectiveness of an economy and labor is an essential requirement for any economy. The two are considered in the same chapter because of the close relationship between them.

The particular focus of this chapter is on the level of income in North Carolina, its geographic distribution within the state, and the challenge that its low level poses for the state. Low income levels are both a problem and a cause. Upgrading wage levels is apt to require an upgrading of skills but low-wage labor forces tend to lack those very skills. Thus it seems appropriate to review the interlocking questions of income and labor prior to the discussions of specific economic activities that comprise the remainder of this part of the book.

INCOME

The personal income level of North Carolina has improved dramatically in recent decades. Between 1930 and 1970 the average income available to every individual (per capita income) in North Carolina multiplied fifteen times compared with the tenfold increase experienced by the nation as a whole.* Even though the state level was only 83 percent of the national average in 1972, this was a far cry from the 47 percent of 1930. Another way of comparing income levels is by contrasting the proportions of families with incomes in various ranges. Table 9.1 shows that in 1969 North Carolina families had incomes that clustered strongly in the $3,000 to $7,000 range but were significantly below both the South and the nation in family incomes above $15,000.

Table 9.2 summarizes income sources for North Carolina. While the distribution by type of source for North Carolina resembles that of the South and the United States, relatively more is earned from farming and manufacturing in North Carolina than is the case for the nation or the region.

The steady gain of North Carolina personal income levels on the national average is shown in Figure 9.1. The relative improvement of income levels in the state is explained by a sharp drop in low-wage agricultural employment, rapid expansion of the industrial and service sectors of the economy, and by a higher rate of participation in the labor force by the adult population. Participation rates cannot go much higher and most of the agricultural reductions are over. Further relative gains will come only from improvements in the wage quality of employment opportunities.

That this will be difficult to achieve is shown by projections of the North Carolina Office of State Planning. The projections indicate that gains on the national average are apt to be small throughout the remainder of the present century; the state average is expected to reach only 85.5 percent of the national mean by the year 2000.

Just as the North Carolina average varies from the national mean, so do the counties within the state have varying levels of per capita income. In 1969, the extremes ranged from $4,326 in Mecklenburg County to $1,610 in Washington County. As Figure 9.2 shows, the state's high income counties are mostly urban and in the Piedmont. However, three-quarters of all counties have per capita income levels below the state average—those counties are mostly in the Mountains and the Coastal Plain. These differentials relate primarily to the nature of economic activity in the counties. Those with significant manufacturing or urban concentrations of industry, trade, and other services tend to be high while the largely agricultural and rural counties have low income levels. The urban-rural income gap may not be quite as severe.

---

*Per capita income is one of the most widely used measures of income. It is calculated by dividing total income earned in an area by total population. Its level is influenced not only by wage levels but also by the proportion of the population that is employed. It also includes income earned from nonwage or nonsalary sources. Therefore, it should not be confused with wage levels, even though they are an important determinant of per capita income.

Table 9.2. Personal Income by Source, 1973

	Percentage of Total		
	N.C.	South	U.S.
By Type			
Wage and Salary	82.6	82.8	83.0
Other labor	4.7	5.1	5.1
Proprietors	12.7	12.1	11.5
Total (millions of dollars)	18,965	156,135	836,438
By Industry			
Farm	6.6	5.6	5.1
Manufacturing	32.7	24.0	26.5
Trade	15.1	16.2	16.1
Services	11.6	13.9	15.0
Government	17.0	18.9	17.3
Others	17.0	21.4	20.1
Total (millions of dollars)	18,965	156,135	836,438

Source: Derived from data in *Survey of Current Business* 54, pt. 1 (August 1974): 34, 39-40.

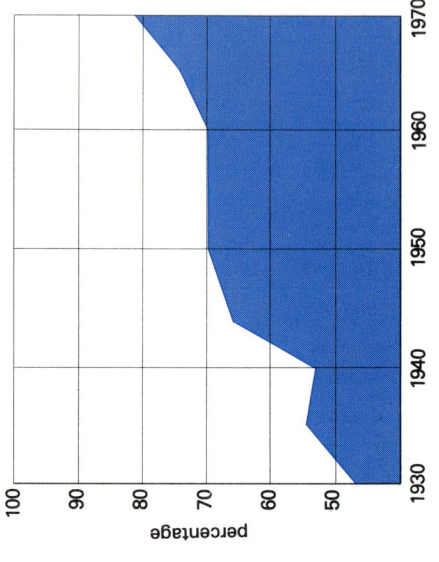

Figure 9.1. N.C. Per Capita Income as a Percentage of U.S. Average, 1930-1970

Source: N.C. Department of Administration, *North Carolina State Government Statistical Abstract*, 1973.

Table 9.1. Family Income Level in the U.S., the South, and N.C., 1969

Family Income Category	Percentage of Total		
	U.S.	South	N.C.
Below $3,000	10.3	14.9	14.6
$3,000-5,000	10.0	13.1	13.7
$5,000-7,000	11.9	14.3	15.8
$7,000-10,000	30.6	20.7	22.2
$10,000-15,000	26.6	22.1	22.2
$15,000-25,000	16.0	11.5	9.0
Over $25,000	4.6	3.4	2.5

Source: U.S. Department of Commerce, *1970 Census of Population and Housing*, 1970.

as the data indicate, however, because the cost of living is probably higher in cities and in rural areas cash incomes can be augmented more readily by part-time farming.

One of the most encouraging developments in the North Carolina income situation is a significant trend toward equalization of the distribution of income over the state.* In 1929 the urban-rural contrast was very pronounced but since then many of the rural counties have experienced higher income gains than have the larger urban areas. Between 1929 and 1970 inflation contributed greatly to a general increase in the dollar level of incomes throughout the state. The decline of low-wage agriculture and the spread of industry helped three-quarters of the state's counties to actually gain on the state average (Figure 9.3).

The populous metropolitan counties still have the highest levels of income in the state but their gains were slow in relation to the state average during the period 1929 to 1970. Cabarrus County, which early developed a major specialization in low-wage textile manufacturing, had the highest per capita income level of any nonmetropolitan county in the state in 1929 but continued reliance on that one industry has caused its average to fall behind that of the state by 1970.

The improvement was not unanimous, however, since seventeen of the state's low income counties experienced a deterioration of per capita income levels compared with the state average between 1929 and 1970. These counties are sprinkled over the state with some concentration in the northern half of the Coastal Plain and along the border with Virginia. Washington County is the most unfortunate member of this group, with its per capita income average dropping from 73 to only 50 percent of the state average during the period.

*Economic inflation has been responsible for a large part of the increase in the dollar level of per capita incomes over this long time period. Relating changes to the state average is probably the best means of showing whether or not a county really improved its income level.

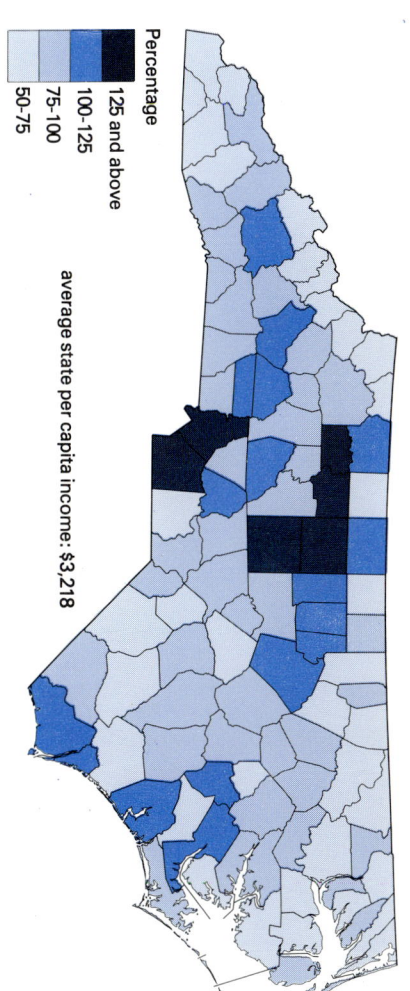

Figure 9.2. Per Capita Income of N.C. Counties and SMSAs as a Proportion of the State Average, 1970

Percentage
- 125 and above
- 100-125
- 75-100
- 50-75

average state per capita income: $3,218

Source: N.C. Department of Administration, *North Carolina State Government Statistical Abstract*, 1973.

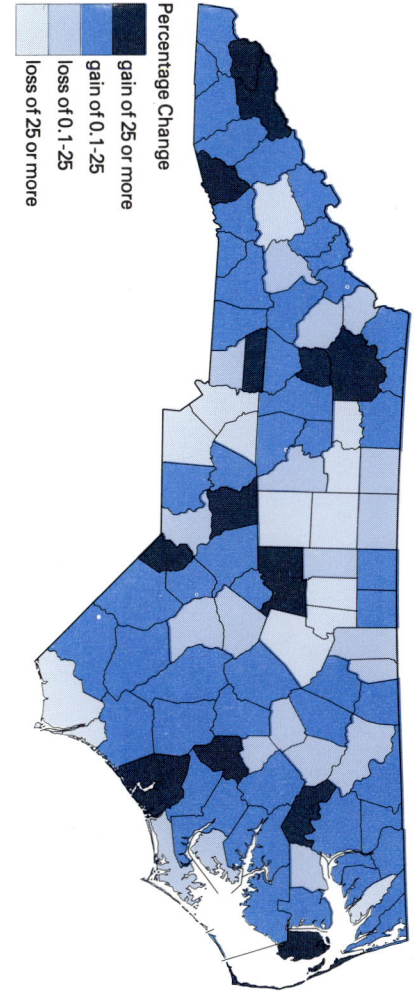

Figure 9.3. Change in Relative Level of Per Capita Income for N.C. Counties and SMSAs, 1929-1970

Percentage Change
- gain of 25 or more
- gain of 0.1-25
- loss of 0.1-25
- loss of 25 or more

Source: N.C. Department of Administration, *North Carolina State Government Statistical Abstract*, 1973.

Averages tend to obscure the fact that, while both the level and the geographic distribution of incomes have improved in the state, many people remain poor. Even though Mecklenburg County had the highest per capita income level in the state, for example, there were still over 44,000 people living there on incomes below the poverty level. Overall, 16 percent of the families in the state had incomes below the official poverty level, according to the census of population for 1970.* The proportion that were poor among families with a female head and with children under eighteen years of age was an incredible 78.1 percent.

The two goals of equalizing North Carolina income levels with those of the nation and equalizing income distribution throughout the state are possibly contradictory. The highest state average can be achieved by emphasizing growth in urban areas that have the economic climate and amenities to attract and support more in the way of high-wage, high-skill activities. Such an approach would increase the gap in income level between large urban areas and the rest of the state since similar growth would not occur in rural areas. Alternatively, growth in rural counties is apt to concentrate on low-wage, labor-intensive activities because, in the main, the principal economic attraction of such areas is the labor supply. The supporting facilities and services of cities that are so important to many economic activities are missing.

Concurrent high-wage city development and low-wage rural development has been the recent trend and it could continue into the future. Relative increases in per capita personal income levels in rural/small-town areas have been accomplished primarily through industrial growth, which has replaced agricultural and related employment. Industry is attracted to rural areas chiefly for their surplus labor supply, since rural areas lack the array of services and amenities that are characteristic of urban areas. The labor-intensive industries that are attracted to rural areas pay relatively low wages—higher than wages in agriculture but otherwise low. The initial result, therefore, has been a dramatic increase in relative income levels in rural areas that have experienced industrialization. However, continued reliance on low-wage industries—the primary kinds that can be attracted to areas that have only labor to offer industry—will act to hold down the state per capita personal income level. Massing growth in cities would produce a higher state average and would require rural residents who wanted employment alternatives to agriculture to migrate to the cities. Thus it seems that the spread of industry to rural areas tends to lower the state average; on the other hand,

concentrating industry in cities will undermine the economic base of rural/small-town areas. Analysts of the Research Triangle Institute have proposed a compromise in the deliberate massing of supporting services and facilities in key locations in rural areas as an inducement to higher wage-quality industry. This would require bold decisions on the part of the state and a modification of past "laissez-faire" approaches to economic development. Such a strategy would be intended to permit growth of high-wage industry, thus increasing relative per capita personal income levels while continuing to disperse growth throughout the state to some degree.

LABOR

The composition of North Carolina's labor force has undergone a dramatic change in recent decades. Following a strong national trend, agricultural employment has declined while both the service and the goods-producing sectors increased in about equal proportions between 1962 and 1970 (Table 9.3). This trend is projected to continue through at least 1980.

A comparison of North Carolina's occupational structure with that of the nation is given in Table 9.4. A combined decline in agricultural workers and increase in the proportion of both white-collar and service workers is a feature of both structures. The major difference is that while the nation shows a drop in the blue-collar category, North Carolina shows a slight increase, in a proportion that is already substantially higher than for the nation as a whole.

Table 9.3. Distribution of Employment in N.C. by Sector

	Percentage of Total		
	1962	1970	1980
Agricultural employment	15	8	3
Goods-producing employment	35	38	41
Service-producing employment	50	54	56

Source: Research Triangle Institute, *North Carolina Employment and Income Projection: 1980*, 1971.

*The official poverty level used in the census for 1970 was established at $3,388 for an average family.

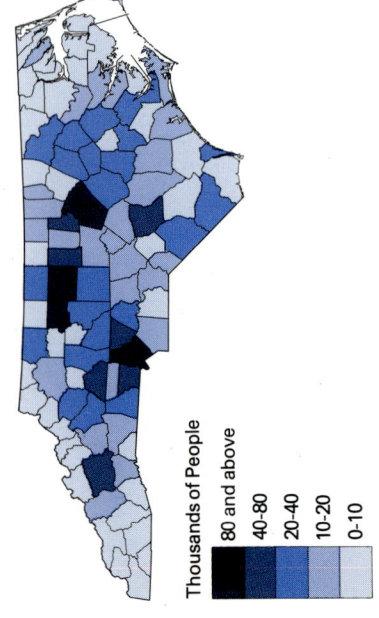

Figure 9.4. Civilian Work Force in N.C., 1971

Thousands of People
- 80 and above
- 40–80
- 20–40
- 10–20
- 0–10

Source: N.C. Department of Administration, *North Carolina State Government Statistical Abstract*, 1973.

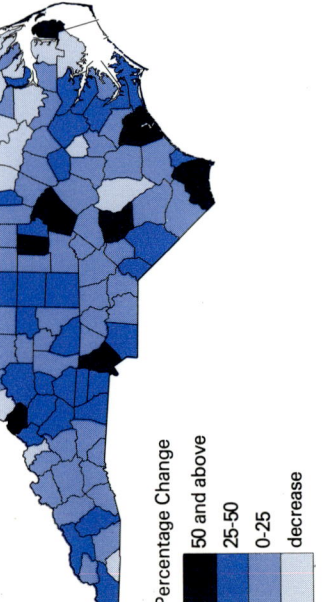

Figure 9.5. Change in Civilian Work Force in N.C., 1962–1971

Percentage Change
- 50 and above
- 25–50
- 0–25
- decrease

Source: N.C. Department of Administration, *North Carolina State Government Statistical Abstract*, 1973.

Between 1962 and 1971 total employment in the state increased from 1.7 to 2.2 million and by 1980 another increase of about 500,000 jobs is projected. Replacements needed due to death, retirement, and other separations will generate another 600,000 jobs during the 1970s. This means that more than one million new jobs will be available to North Carolinians during the decade. Employment opportunities are expected to grow fast enough to support a substantial increase in population. The question is whether or not the labor force can meet the skill requirements that are expected.

The greatest numbers will be needed in categories such as semiskilled machine operators, clerical workers, and service workers. Professional and technical workers, craftsmen, and foremen are expected to be in great demand. This projection is based on the assumption that the state will experience a continued development of high-skill, high-wage industries.

By contrast, jobs for unskilled workers will not expand. By 1980 there will be over 13,000 fewer jobs for unskilled farm workers as agriculture continues to become more efficient, and employment opportunities for unskilled nonfarm workers will develop only through replacements.

The geographic distribution of the civilian work force, shown in Figure 9.4, parallels the distribution of population rather closely, with a substantial concentration in the Piedmont and a few other, largely urban, counties. Figure 9.5, which shows changes in the distribution of the work force between 1962 and 1971, reflects the combined decline of agricultural employment and the related migration of people to urban areas and nonagricultural jobs. Slightly over 40 percent of the total North Carolina increase between 1962 and 1971 occurred in the state's four largest and most urban counties (Forsyth, Guilford, Mecklenburg, and Wake) even though they contained just 21 percent of the state's 1970 population.

Wage Rates

One of the most significant facts about the economic situation of North Carolina is that its workers on the average earn less than their counterparts elsewhere. For example, factory production workers in March 1973 had average hourly earnings of $2.92, only two cents an hour more than in Mississippi and four cents less than in South Carolina (Figure 9.6). Even though the North Carolina rate increased by nineteen cents between March 1972 and March 1973, it stood at only 73.4 percent of the national average and 93.0 percent of the rate prevailing throughout the southeastern states.

To a great extent, low factory wages are attributable to the state's concentration of labor-intensive, low-skill types of manufacturing and a low level of unionization. However, union hourly rates paid to building craftsmen suggest that type of job and union participation do not explain all of the difference.

Table 9.5 summarizes prevailing union rates for four groups of workers for all United States cities and selected southern cities. Charlotte was the only North Carolina example reported. Charlotte's rate in these categories was not only below the national city average, but below the rates established in the other southern cities. Only local truck drivers were paid above the average.

Table 9.6 presents a broad view of income distribution by occupational groups. Even though the data are for 1969, they show a general pattern that probably has not changed much since then.

In every case, males earned less in the same occupation in North Carolina than in the nation. Negro males earned less than white males, and females earned more than Negro males only when working as farmers and farm managers. These differentials persist for more specific occupation groups. For example, North Carolina engineers made about $1,300 less than the national average and accountants earned more than $1,000 below the national average; male bakers earned only 76 percent of the amount paid to their counterparts across the nation. In fact, the differentials became proportionately stronger from the professional level to the craftsman, operative, and laborer levels, as is emphasized in the data for the Charlotte SMSA. At the professional, managerial, and sales levels, Charlotte workers come close to or exceed the national average. Beginning with clerical workers and extending through craftsmen, operatives, nonfarm laborers, and service workers, a significantly lower level appears in Charlotte. Chemists averaged $1,400 more in Charlotte and college teachers were $400 higher but construction workers made $1,800 less than their counterparts in the nation and bakers fell $800 short of the national average.

The inescapable conclusion is that earnings gaps are greatest for the lowest-wage categories and in rural areas. In cities, as represented by Charlotte, the better-paid occupations earn at levels comparable with the national average but there is still a gap with the national average for the lower-wage occupations.

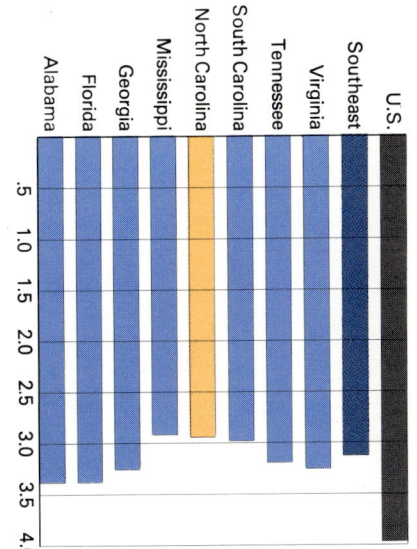

Figure 9.6. Average Hourly Earnings of Factory Production Workers in Eight Southeastern States and in the U.S. in March 1973

Source: N.C. Department of Labor, Bureau of Labor Statistics, 1973, and U.S. Department of Labor, Bureau of Labor Statistics, 1973.

Note: The Southeast consists of selected southern states.

Table 9.4. Distribution of Employment by Type of Worker

	Percentage of Total							
	U.S.				N.C.			
	1960	1970	1980		1960	1970	1980	
White-collar workers	43.1	48.3	50.6		32.0	36.5	39.3	
Blue-collar workers	36.3	35.3	33.0		43.5	45.8	45.7	
Service workers	12.5	12.4	13.7		11.5	11.8	12.1	
Farm workers	8.1	4.0	2.7		13.0	5.9	2.9	

Source: Employment Security Commission of N.C., *North Carolina Manpower Projections to 1980*, 1972.

The earnings gap between North Carolina and the nation has been a major concern of state officials for some years. Many explanations have been offered but perhaps the most thorough is contained in a study by the North Carolina Office of State Planning. The study revealed that the gap between earnings in North Carolina and the nation in 1971 was attributable to two effects. One was the mix of industry, a tendency to concentrate on labor-intensive, low-wage types of employment. This is shown in Chapter 11 (Manufacturing), a significant improvement in the industrial mix within manufacturing has occurred in recent years and relative gains on national averages have resulted. However, the study by the State Planning Office demonstrated that the concentration in the state of low-wage industries accounts for only about one-third of the total earnings gap.

The second factor is referred to as a local effect, the tendency for workers in a given industry to be paid less in North Carolina than their counterparts in the rest of the country. Employers pay less for the same job. This tendency has a strong historical basis. Low earnings have characterized the state for decades and a new employer could cull the labor market by paying wages that were attractive locally but which were below the national average. The local effect is very pronounced in the construction trades.

Table 9.5. Average Hourly Union Rates for Selected Trades in All U.S. and Selected Southern Cities, 1972

City	Journeymen Construction Workers	Newspaper Workers	Local Truck Drivers	Local Transit Workers
All cities	$7.69	$6.09	$5.49	$4.68
Atlanta	7.43	5.45	5.48	3.97
Birmingham	6.76	5.37	5.36	3.62
Charlotte	**5.87**	**4.72**	**5.57**	**3.03**
Knoxville	6.55	4.79	5.25	3.14
Memphis	6.65	5.54	5.49	3.97
Norfolk	6.10	4.98	5.26	3.58
Richmond	6.32	5.08	5.48	3.61

Source: U.S. Department of Labor, Bureau of Labor Statistics, 1972.

The result of these effects is to diminish the impact of growth in high-wage industries. Continual improvements in the industrial mix will be required, but closing the earnings gap will come about largely by bringing wage levels in all industries up to the national average. This will be difficult for those industries that came to the state primarily to take advantage of a relatively inexpensive labor supply. There are even suspicions that in some areas locally dominant employers have discouraged industrial development because of their inability to compete with the wages that a new entrant might offer.

In addition to a low average for the state as a whole, there is a great differential in wage levels throughout the state (Figure 9.7). Weekly wages earned by insured employees (about two-thirds of total employment) averaged $120.36 for the state in 1971, but they ranged from a low of $72.94 in Tyrrell County up to a high of $146.61 in Mecklenburg. The differential would be even greater if most agricultural workers had been included in the data.

Labor Force Participation

The total income of an area's population is influenced strongly not only by what individuals are paid for their work but also by the proportion of the population that chooses to work. Between 1960 and 1970 the proportion of the state's adult population that was employed rose from 42 to 50 percent. This compared with a 60 percent participation rate for the nation as a whole. The apparently low participation rate is explained partly by a large military contingent that is counted in population but not in the labor force. Another factor is the low level of nonagricultural employment alternatives for people in many Coastal Plain and Mountain counties, where unemployment rates are also high (Figure 9.8).

An interesting difference between the state and the nation is that a higher proportion of women are employed in North Carolina. Over 46 percent of all females, sixteen years old or over, were employed in the state in 1970. This probably reflects the availability of jobs for women in the textile and furniture industries and, because of low wages in those industries, the necessity for several members of a family to work. This is supported by the fact that nearly 60 percent of the women with children aged six to seventeen years were employed. In Cabarrus County, highly specialized in textiles, over 72 percent of the mothers of school-age children were employed.

Figure 9.7. Average Weekly Wages for Insured N.C. Employees, 1971

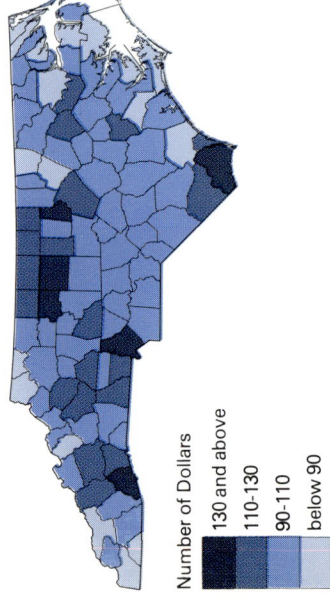

Number of Dollars
- 130 and above
- 110–130
- 90–110
- below 90

Source: N.C. Department of Administration, *North Carolina State Government Statistical Abstract*, 1973.

Figure 9.8. Unemployment Rates in N.C., 1971

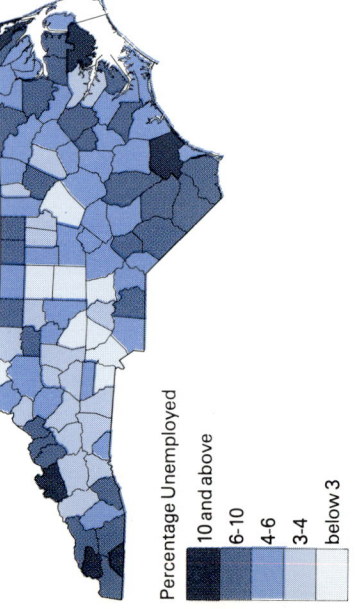

Percentage Unemployed
- 10 and above
- 6–10
- 4–6
- 3–4
- below 3

Source: N.C. Department of Administration, *North Carolina State Government Statistical Abstract*, 1973.

High female participation rates have been a major reason why the state's per capita income has managed to gain on the national average over the last several decades despite generally low wages. Future relative gains will be more difficult because it will not be possible to increase participation rates much further. That is, improvements will have to come from increases in the wage quality of employment opportunities rather than from increases in the proportion of the population that is employed.

Blacks in the Labor Force

Blacks represent one segment of the labor force that still has the potential for higher rates of employment. Only 32.5 percent of the state's black population was employed in 1970, compared with 40.9 percent of all whites. Blacks constituted 18.4 percent of employment and 22.1 percent of total population.

The distribution of black employment among industries is similar to that for whites except that blacks are more heavily concentrated in the primary industries and personal services (Table 9.7). They are markedly less well represented in trade and in the finance and business services group. The largest employer for both races is manufacturing. The textile industry was once noted for its "lily white" hiring practices but in 1970 blacks made up 13.7 percent of the employment in that industry. No doubt pressure from federal agencies has been responsible for some of this change. Additionally, however, blacks constitute a relatively underdeveloped labor source for that industry, which is finding it difficult to compete with other manufacturers for labor. However, even though blacks have gained substantial access to industrial jobs they tend to be concentrated very heavily in the lower-skilled occupations. For example, blacks represent 18.5 percent of all manufacturing operatives but only 8.6 percent of the higher-skilled craftsmen.

Table 9.6. Median Annual Earning for Those Employed 50-52 Weeks, by Occupation, 1969

Occupational Group	U.S. Males	N.C. All Males	N.C. Negro Males	N.C. All Females	Charlotte SMSA Males
All	$ 8,517	$6,387	$4,258	$4,101	$ 7,933
Professional and technical	11,752	9,648	6,593	5,991	11,016
Managers and administrators	11,747	9,478	6,165	5,282	11,940
Sales workers	9,454	7,820	5,156	3,394	10,195
Clerical	7,973	6,747	5,112	4,533	7,397
Craftsmen	8,730	6,649	4,756	4,486	7,466
Operatives, except transportation	7,439	5,340	4,481	4,004	5,749
Transportation operatives	7,583	5,763	4,407	4,423	6,598
Nonfarm laborers	6,135	4,379	3,851	3,704	4,966
Farmers and farm managers	5,122	3,597	2,124	2,502	5,364
Farm laborers	3,628	2,724	2,009	1,887	3,626
Service workers	6,381	4,872	4,756	3,845	3,170	5,485
Private household workers	3,118	1,786	1,726	1,313	—

Source: U.S. Department of Commerce, 1970 Census of Population, 1970.

Table 9.7. Employment of Negroes and Whites in N.C., 1970

Industry	Total Employment	Percentage Negro	Distribution of Negro Employees (percentage)	Distribution of White Employees (percentage)
Agriculture, forestry, fishing, mining	108,421	28.4	8.5	4.8
Construction	133,545	17.3	6.3	6.8
Manufacturing	704,306	16.3	31.3	36.4
Transportation, communications, utilities	109,063	15.5	4.6	5.7
Trade	347,589	12.1	11.5	18.9
Finance, real estate, business services	110,390	8.8	2.7	6.2
Personal and entertainment services	118,622	49.0	15.9	3.7
Professional and related services	282,636	21.6	16.7	13.7
Public administration	69,830	12.8	2.5	3.8
Total	1,984,402	18.4	100.0	100.0

Source: U.S. Department of Commerce, 1970 Census of Population, 1970.

Figure 9.9. Unemployment Rates of Major Labor Markets in N.C. Regions, 1962-1971

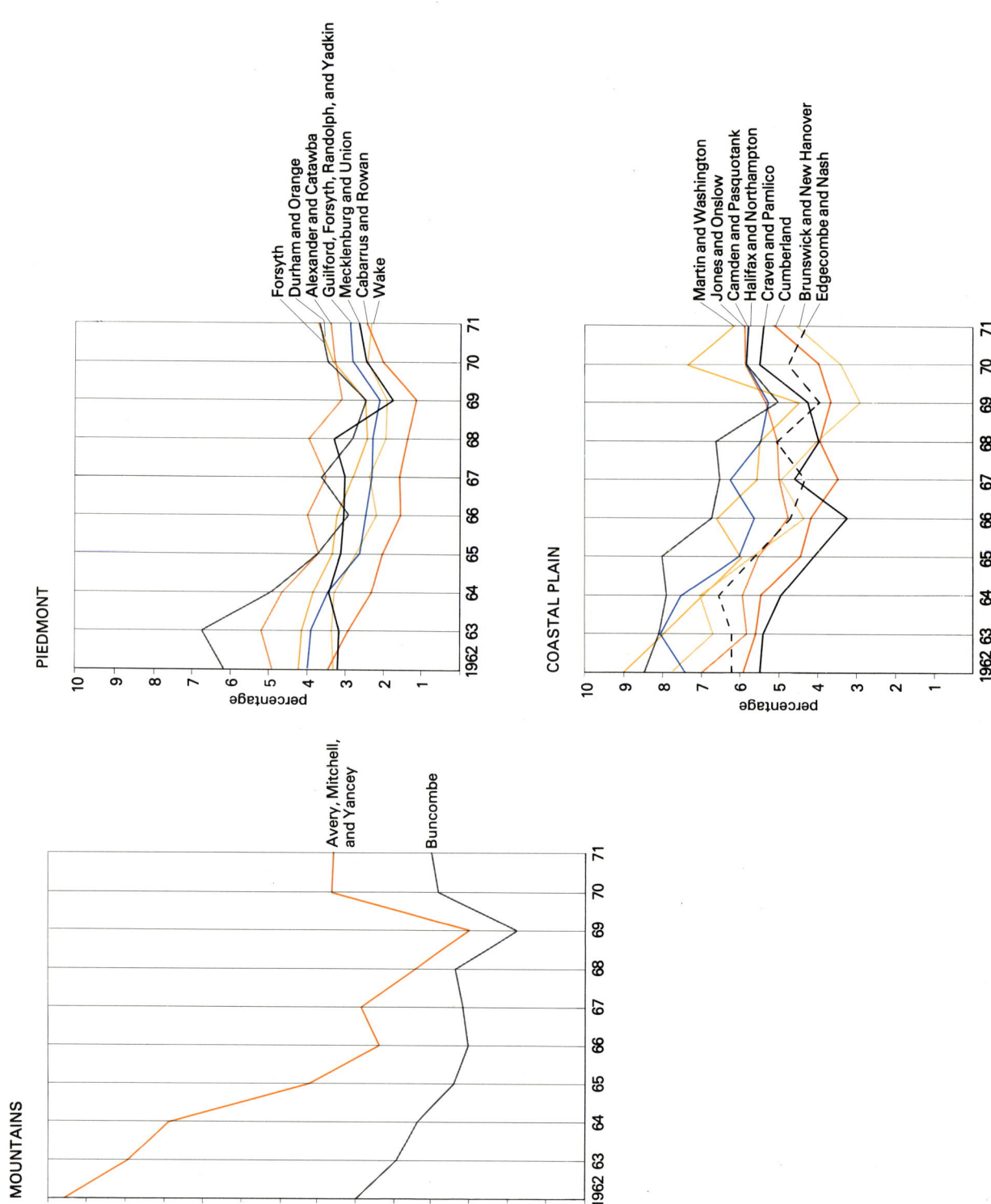

Source: U.S. Department of Commerce, *North Carolina Work Estimates by County, Area, and State,* 1968, 1969, 1970, and 1971.

Unemployment

North Carolina has tended to enjoy relatively full employment. Throughout the 1960s unemployment rates were in the 4 to 5 percent range and since 1970 they have tended to fall below 4 percent (Figure 9.9). By 1972 the North Carolina rate was 3.2 percent, in contrast with a national average of 5.6 percent.* There are important differentials within the general level, however. One is the tendency for unemployment to fall heavily on teenagers and blacks. In 1971 white teenagers in the South experienced a 12.9 percent unemployment rate while nonwhite teenagers suffered a staggering 30 percent rate of unemployment. This was part of a national trend, and the North Carolina situation was typical.

Another important differential is the geographic distribution of unemployment (Figure 9.9). The Piedmont and eastern Mountain counties generally show low unemployment, or relatively full employment, while high unemployment rates characterize most of the Coastal Plain counties and some in the far west.

Labor Supply

The availability of suitable labor is an important ingredient in economic development. The creation of jobs may induce people to move into an area, but the business that locates in an area must have a more immediate supply of adequate workers upon which to draw. Suitable labor as defined by the North Carolina Employment Security Office refers to experienced workers who are seeking employment, inexperienced but trainable workers, and high school graduates entering the labor market for the first time. The estimated supply of workers available for industrial opportunities in March 1973 is portrayed in Figure 9.10. While it is true that the state's largely rural counties in the Mountains and on the Coastal Plain show fewer surpluses, especially on the Inner Coastal Plain, the greatest supplies of workers tend to be in a mix of the state's large urban counties together with several rural counties. Cumberland County has the greatest supply in the state, followed by adjacent Harnett County and by Pitt, Durham, Mecklenburg, Forsyth, Wake, Hoke, and Moore. The labor force available in the urban counties is dominated by inexperienced, recent high school graduates. Cumberland and the rural counties are characterized by supplies of both inexperienced but trainable labor and those with nonindustrial, presumably

*This analysis of unemployment was prepared before the severe national recession that began in 1974. By early 1975 the North Carolina rate of unemployment exceeded 11 percent, above the national average. It remains to be seen what the long-term effects of the recession will be on the geographic distribution of unemployment within the state.

agricultural, experience. Among those that had supplies of fifteen hundred or more potential workers, only in Cabarrus County was the bulk of that supply composed of experienced industrial workers, presumably textile employees interested in higher-paying jobs. Ironically, many of the large labor-potential counties are those with low unemployment rates while most of the high unemployment counties had small labor pools. In the first case workers are staying in an unsatisfactory job until a better alternative becomes available. In the latter case there is little hope of a job and people are more likely to migrate to another area.

Trade Unions

North Carolina labor is the least unionized of any in the nation. In 1970 only 8 percent of the state's nonagricultural workers belonged to trade unions compared with 28 percent for the nation. Despite the state's very low wages, the North Carolina proportion of unionized workers has increased little in recent years. This paradoxical situation is difficult to explain. Perhaps earlier violent and unsuccessful strikes and organization attempts left bitter memories. Even a low-paying mill job can seem uncommonly attractive to an unemployed (or underemployed) farm worker. The strong rural heritage of North Carolinians may also have inculcated a general distaste for any form of regimentation. The successful union effort at organizing the J. P. Stevens plants at Roanoke Rapids in 1974 and the relatively close union defeat at Cannon Mills in 1975 may be an indication that this lack of interest in unionization is changing.

North Carolina's employers have tended to experience a low rate of labor stoppages. Only 0.1 percent of total work time was lost to labor stoppages in 1970, compared with 0.44 percent for the nation. There were 45 labor stoppages in North Carolina that year, compared with 572 in New York, 633 in Ohio, and 635 in Pennsylvania. Neighboring Virginia and Tennessee each experienced more than 100.

Vocational Training

In order to increase the material well-being of its citizens and to encourage economic development in the state, North Carolina began to create a system of industrial education centers in 1959. By 1974 there were fifty-six technical/vocational institutes operating in the state. These schools make available direct occupational training and remedial adult education. These and other programs are coordinated by the North Carolina Manpower Council. That these programs are needed is supported by a report of the North Carolina State Board of Education, which states that in 1972 "approximately 31.8 percent of all North Carolinians over fifteen years of

age were functionally illiterate." Only 53.2 percent of all North Carolina workers in 1970 had completed between one and four years of high school compared with a national average of 58.1 percent.

Occupational training, reinforcing the state's system of general education, will play a crucial role in the effort to move North Carolina workers out of low-wage, low-skill agricultural and manufacturing jobs into higher-skill and better-paying types of industrial and service occupations. This will be especially true for the state's blacks who tend to be employed relatively heavily in low-skill jobs. Yet, as noted earlier, the number of jobs of this kind will increase only slightly in the years to come. Only through a continual upgrading of general and specific skills will North Carolina workers be able to enjoy access to high-wage industries.

SELECTED REFERENCES

N.C. Department of Administration. *North Carolina Manpower Council: Biennial Report, 1971-1973.* Raleigh: The Commission, 1972.

N.C. Employment Security Commission. *North Carolina Manpower Projections to 1980.* Raleigh: The Commission, 1972.

Survey of Current Business 53 (August 1973): 47.

U.S. Department of Labor, Bureau of Labor Statistics. *Geographic Profile of Employment and Unemployment, 1971; Report 402.* Washington, D.C.: The Department, 1972.

Figure 9.10. Recruitable Labor for Industrial Development by N.C. County, March 1973

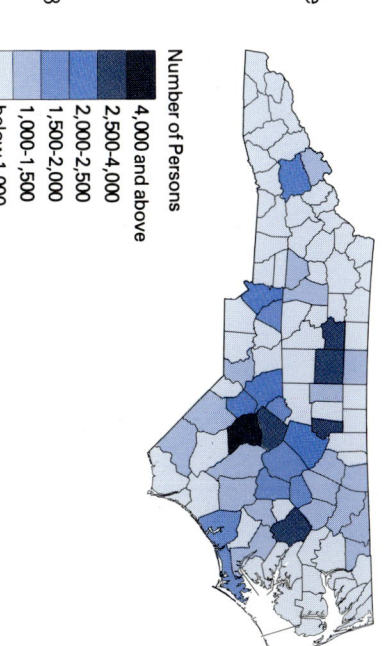

Number of Persons
- 4,000 and above
- 2,500-4,000
- 2,000-2,500
- 1,500-2,000
- 1,000-1,500
- below 1,000

Source: U.S. Department of Commerce, *Estimated Recruitable Labor for Industrial Development in North Carolina, 1973.*

10. Agriculture

CHARLES R. PUGH
JAMES G. MADDOX

North Carolina has long been a major agricultural state and farming is a direct source of livelihood for a relatively large proportion of its population. In turn, farm products provide raw materials for processing, manufacturing, and marketing businesses within and outside the state.

Tobacco has traditionally been a major source of the state's farm income. Rapid expansion has occurred in recent years in the production of various classes of poultry. However, the diversity of farming systems across the state provides for a "variety agriculture," in the same sense that the differences in climate and scenic attractions within the state have spawned the slogan "variety vacationland."

Flue-cured tobacco is produced from the eastern to midsections of the state, while Burley leaf is grown in the Mountains. The state's peanut production, concentrated in only a few counties, ranks third in the nation. A wide variety of fruits and vegetables for fresh market and for processing is grown in many parts of the state. Corn occupies a larger acreage than any other single crop. An eastern "corn belt" has developed in the Tidewater counties with their specialized corn-soybean operations.

The dynamic agricultural industry periodically adopts new enterprises and new production systems. Trellised tomatoes have been introduced in the Mountain region. Soybean production has expanded dramatically, providing a protein-rich crop for domestic and export uses.

Dairy production is being concentrated on larger farm units. Close coordination has developed between producers, feed suppliers, processors, and other sectors of the expanding poultry industry. Today, many hog farmers specialize in producing feeder pigs, while others may concentrate on feeding hogs to market weight.

The importance of North Carolina agriculture is shown by its high rank among the states of the South and nation. As shown in Table 10.1, the state leads in sales of tobacco and sweet potatoes, is among the top three or four states in sales from various classes of poultry, and ranks high in the sale of many other commodities. In total cash receipts from farm marketings in 1971, North Carolina was second in the South and eleventh in the nation. A relatively large proportion of the state's population is engaged in agriculture. In 1970, North Carolina ranked second in the nation in rural farm population and had been first a decade earlier. With consolidation of farm operating units, the number of farms has declined, but still the state ranked fourth in the South and seventh in the nation.

Agriculture in North Carolina is intertwined with the total economy and many of the national trends affect or characterize North Carolina agriculture:

1. Agriculture is an economically competitive industry because of the relatively large number of farms in the state.

2. Total farm output is increasing, but the gains in productivity present problems to farmers. When food supplies expand faster than population growth, farm prices are depressed. Consequently, most of the benefits of increased farm efficiency are passed on to consumers. More recently, sharp increases in retail food prices have not always been shared by the farmer.

3. Farmers purchase goods and services from the non-farm economy for use in farm production and for direct consumption by the farm family. Therefore, agriculture is directly affected by conditions in the overall economy.

4. Since agriculture is a biological industry, economic instabilities are created by variations in weather or infestations of diseases or pests.

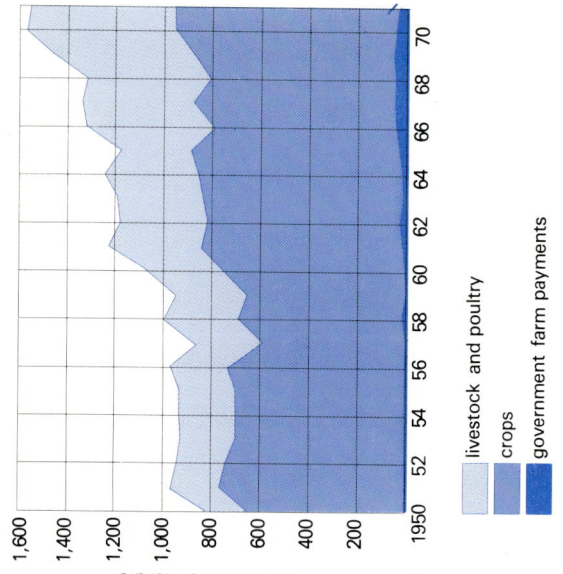

Figure 10.1. N.C. Farm Income, 1950–1971

- livestock and poultry
- crops
- government farm payments

Source: U.S. Department of Agriculture, *Farm Income Situation*, supplements, August 1969 and August 1972.

Table 10.1. Rank of N.C. Agriculture within the South and U.S.

Farm Sales and Other Characteristics	South	U.S.
Flue-cured tobacco	1	1
All tobacco	1	1
Sweet potatoes	1	1
Rural farm population	1	2
Eggs	2	3
Turkeys	1	3
Peanuts	3	3
Broilers	4	4
All crops	3	6
Number of farms	4	7
Apples	3	9
Corn	1	10
Grapes	3	10
Peaches	4	10
All farm sales	2	11
Hogs	1	11
Soybeans	6	12
Livestock and poultry	4	18

Sources: All farm sales pertain to 1971 data from the U.S. Department of Agriculture; rural farm population data are from the *1970 Census of Population*, and number of farms is from the *1969 Census of Agriculture*.

Size of the Agricultural Industry

Gross Farm Income As shown in Figure 10.1, gross farm income in North Carolina has almost doubled in the last twenty years, growing from $838 million in 1950 to $1,567 million in 1971. North Carolina accounted for 2.8 percent of the nation's total farm income in 1971, and ranked second to Texas in the South in gross farm income in 1971, followed closely by Florida, Georgia, Arkansas, Oklahoma, and Mississippi. Between 1961 and 1971 the increase in gross farm income was 36 percent for North Carolina, 52 percent for the South, and 54 percent for the United States.

In addition to increases in the overall level of farm income, the commodity-mix on farms has changed over time (Figure 10.2). Although North Carolina showed a 36 percent gain in gross farm income from 1961 to 1971, sales increased by a larger percentage for soybeans, hogs, horticultural crops, poultry, cattle, grains, dairy, and peanuts, and income from tobacco maintained about the same absolute level, while income from cotton declined.

Farm income varies widely from county to county within North Carolina. This variation is often related to the amount of land devoted to farming, the suitability of soils, climate, and other resources for agricultural production, and the types of commodities produced. Estimates developed jointly by the North Carolina Agricultural Extension Service and the Federal-State Crop Reporting Service show that gross farm income in 1971 ranged from $76,713,000 in Duplin County and $59,530,000 in Sampson County to $689,000 in Graham County and $67,000 in Dare County (Figure 10.3). Generally, farm income is greater in the central and southern counties of the Coastal Plain than in other parts of the state (Table 10.2).

Resources Used in Farming North Carolina agriculture is characterized by relatively small farms. The data in Table 10.3 illustrate some of the resources devoted to farming.

In adapting to the small farm situation, North Carolina farmers have invested more capital per acre in land and buildings than the national average. In effect, the farming system utilized within the state involves more labor and capital relative to land acreage than many other parts of the nation.

Figure 10.2. Source of Farm Income in N.C., 1961 and 1971

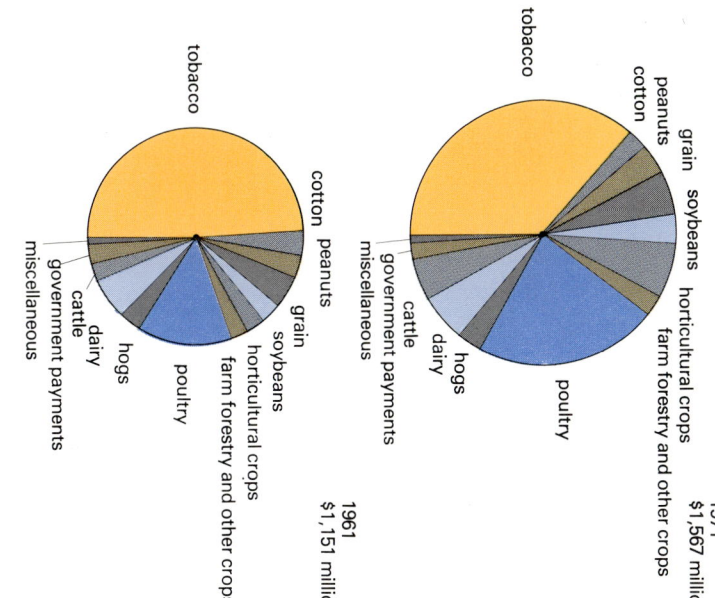

1971 $1,567 million

1961 $1,151 million

Source: U.S. Department of Agriculture, *Farm Income Situation*, 1962 and 1972.

Table 10.3. Agriculture in the U.S. and N.C., 1969

	N.C.	U.S.
Number of farms	119,386	2,730,250
Percentage of land in farms	40.8	47.0
Average acreage per farm	106.6	389.5
Cropland harvested per farm	29.1	100.0
Value of land and buildings:		
Per farm	$35,551	$75,725
Per acre	333	194

Source: U. S. Department of Commerce, 1969 Census of Agriculture, 1969.

Table 10.2. Leading N.C. Counties in Cash Farm Receipts from Crops, 1971

All Farm Marketings	All Crops	Flue-cured Tobacco	Burley Tobacco	Corn	Soybeans	Peanuts	Vegetables, Fruits, Nuts, and Berries	Cotton and Cottonseed
1. Duplin	1. Robeson	1. Pitt	1. Madison	1. Wayne	1. Robeson	1. Northampton	1. Sampson	1. Robeson
2. Sampson	2. Pitt	2. Johnston	2. Buncombe	2. Robeson	2. Beaufort	2. Halifax	2. Henderson	2. Scotland
3. Robeson	3. Sampson	3. Johnston	3. Yancey	3. Pitt	3. Union	3. Bertie	3. Johnston	3. Northampton
4. Johnston	4. Sampson	4. Columbus	4. Ashe	4. Duplin	4. Johnston	4. Martin	4. Duplin	4. Halifax
5. Pitt	5. Columbus	5. Wake	5. Haywood	5. Greene	5. Sampson	5. Hertford	5. Wilson	5. Cleveland
6. Wayne	6. Nash	6. Nash	6. Watauga	6. Lenoir	6. Harnett	6. Edgecombe	6. Nash	6. Sampson
7. Wilkes	7. Wayne	7. Wilson	7. Mitchell	7. Wilson	7. Washington	7. Chowan	7. Haywood	7. Hoke
8. Columbus	8. Wilson	8. Sampson	8. Beaufort	8. Washington	8. Columbus	8. Gates	8. Columbus	8. Edgecombe
9. Wake	9. Duplin	9. Wayne	9. Alleghany	9. Columbus	9. Duplin	9. Pitt	9. Pasquotank	9. Nash
10. Nash	10. Wake	10. Harnett	10. Avery	10. Sampson	10. Perquimans	10. Bladen	10. Wayne	10. Anson

Source: N.C. Department of Agriculture, *North Carolina Farm Income, 1970–71*, 1971.

189

Agriculture and the closely related industries of forestry and fisheries provide the major source of employment for about 100,000 North Carolinians (Table 10.4). This figure amounted to about 5 percent of the employed labor force in the state in 1970 compared to only 3.7 percent in the nation. However the labor force data include only paid workers. The North Carolina Department of Agriculture estimates that in 1972 the average number of farm workers was 210,000, of whom 52,000 were paid a cash wage and 158,000 were nonsalaried family workers. This employment was seasonal and reached a high of 375,000 persons in July. The annual average has dropped steadily over the years, from 676,000 in 1940 to 418,000 in 1960. The labor force employed in agriculture in North Carolina (1) is predominantly male, (2) consists of a larger number of whites than blacks, although a higher percentage of the employed blacks work in agriculture, and (3) generally lives on farms although some rural nonfarm and urban residents work on farms.

Crop Production

A wide variety of crops is produced in the Tar Heel state. Tobacco generates the largest cash farm income among the crops. Soybeans, peanuts, and cotton are other crops produced primarily as a source of cash farm income. Other than farmland devoted to woods, corn occupies more land than any other single crop. Since some of the corn and other grains are fed directly to livestock and poultry, all feed grains that are produced do not enter the cash market.

In 1971 cash receipts from crops sold from North Carolina farms totaled almost $925 million. Table 10.5 indicates the acreage harvested, the quantity produced, and the value of sales of selected crops in North Carolina in 1971. Table 10.2 indicates the leading counties in cash receipts from certain crops.

The maps in Figure 10.4 show production patterns for the most important crops in North Carolina. Figure 10.4a illustrates production in terms of value while Figure 10.4b shows the number of acres in production. The two maps for tobacco are visible evidence of that crop's significance to North Carolina farmers. The number of acres devoted to tobacco is not unusually high, but in value the crop stands alone. Corn, on the other hand, shows a wide dispersion over the state, and many acres are devoted to it. It is the leading crop by a wide margin in terms of acreage but falls to a very distant second to tobacco in value of harvested crop (Table 10.5).

Tobacco Both flue-cured and Burley tobaccos are produced in North Carolina. The state has for many years led the nation in the total value of tobacco sold and it has the largest production of flue-cured tobacco. Cultivation of the crop was introduced into North Carolina from colonial Virginia even though low-quality grades were found growing in the area in the 1580s. Additional states now producing flue-cured tobacco are South Carolina, Georgia, Florida, and Alabama.

Fully sixty-four counties in the eastern two-thirds of the state produce some flue-cured tobacco (Figure 10.4). The sales of flue-cured tobacco in North Carolina in 1972 amounted to more than $566 million.

Tobacco is a labor-intensive crop but technological innovations adopted since the 1950s have substantially reduced labor requirements. Mechanical transplanters, improved insecticides, and even mechanical harvesters are among recent technological improvements.

Flue-cured tobacco is produced under a government-authorized quota system. Each quota holder is allowed to produce up to a designated poundage without penalty. Recent developments tend to encourage larger volumes per farm in order to justify mechanization. Consequently, there is some consolidation of operating units through more cash rental or leasing of allotments under the lease-and-transfer program.

Under the tobacco program that assures that national production will not exceed the designated quota, a minimum price per pound is assured to growers. A farmer-owned cooperative holds leaf for resale when no more than the support price is bid for the designated grade at the auction market.

In 1971, around 339,000 acres of flue-cured tobacco were produced in North Carolina with an average yield of 2,102 pounds per acre. The 1971 total production of 712 million pounds in North Carolina was 66 percent of the national flue-cured production. The average national price on the 1972 flue-cured market was 85.3 cents per pound compared with an average of 68.4 cents for the previous five years.

Burley tobacco is produced in nineteen counties in western North Carolina (Figure 10.4). Kentucky and Tennessee are the leading states in production of Burley tobacco. Burley is grown under authority of government program that provides a system of price supports and poundage quotas for each farm. The average quota per Burley farm in North Carolina is much smaller than the typical flue-cured farm's quota.

Table 10.4. Characteristics of Employed Labor Force Engaged in Agriculture, Forestry, and Fisheries in N.C., 1970

Labor Force	Number Employed in Agriculture, Forestry, and Fisheries	Total Employment	Percentage of Total
Sex			
Male	89,092	1,176,912	7.6
Female	14,713	807,490	1.8
Race			
White	71,410	1,604,630	4.5
Black	30,052	364,673	8.2
Residence			
Rural farm	54,892	199,018	27.6
Rural nonfarm	40,303	882,244	4.6
Urban	8,610	903,140	1.0
Total	103,805	1,984,402	5.2

Source: U.S. Department of Commerce, *1970 Census of Population, 1970.*

Table 10.5. Acreage, Production, and Sales of Major Crops in N.C., 1971

Crop	Harvested Acres (×1,000)	Production (×1,000 units)	Cash Receipts from Farm Marketing (×1,000)
Tobacco:			
Flue-cured	339	712,690 lbs.	$549,921
Burley	7	14,455 lbs.	11,726
Corn for grain	1,520	86,640 bus.	72,885
Soybeans for beans	936	22,464 bus.	61,067
Wheat	270	11,610 bus.	11,058
Peanuts	155	325,500 lbs.	49,468
Cotton	175	135 bales	29,765
Vegetables			53,061
Fruits, nuts			18,812
Greenhouse and nursery			22,000
Farm forestry			33,501
Other crops			11,712
Total crops			924,976

Sources: Preliminary data on acreage and production from N.C. Crop Reporting Service for 1971 crop year. Cash receipts during calendar year of 1971 from U.S. Department of Agriculture, *Supplement to the Farm Income Situation*, August 1971.

Figure 10.3. Gross Farm Income of N.C. Counties, 1971

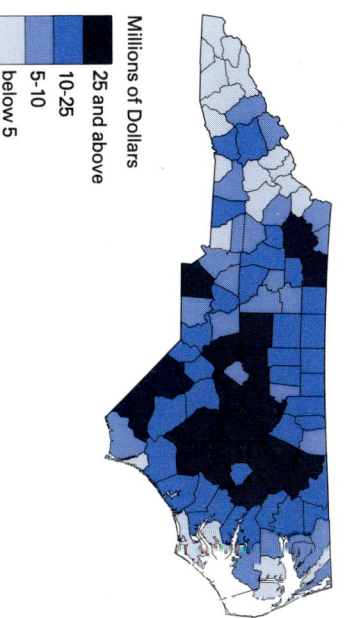

Millions of Dollars
- 25 and above
- 10-25
- 5-10
- below 5

Source: N.C. Department of Agriculture, North Carolina Farm Income, 1970-71, 1971.

North Carolina's Burley crop in 1971 was estimated at 14,455,000 pounds. Yields averaged about 2,065 pounds per acre. North Carolina's Burley production is 3.0 percent of the national total.

Corn While corn is produced in most areas of the state, the largest acreages are in counties of the Coastal Plain and Tidewater regions (Figure 10.4b). A substantial part of the state's corn production is fed to livestock and poultry on the state's farms.

Yields of corn have tended to increase both in the state and the nation. Adoption of hybrid varieties in the 1940s and 1950s resulted in higher levels of production. Larger equipment and use of herbicides for weed control have reduced labor requirements for production. Some new farming lands are being cleared, drained, and put into cultivation in some of the Tidewater counties. These high-organic soils appear to be well suited for corn and soybean production.

Figure 10.4(a). N.C. Farm Income from Selected Crops by County, 1971

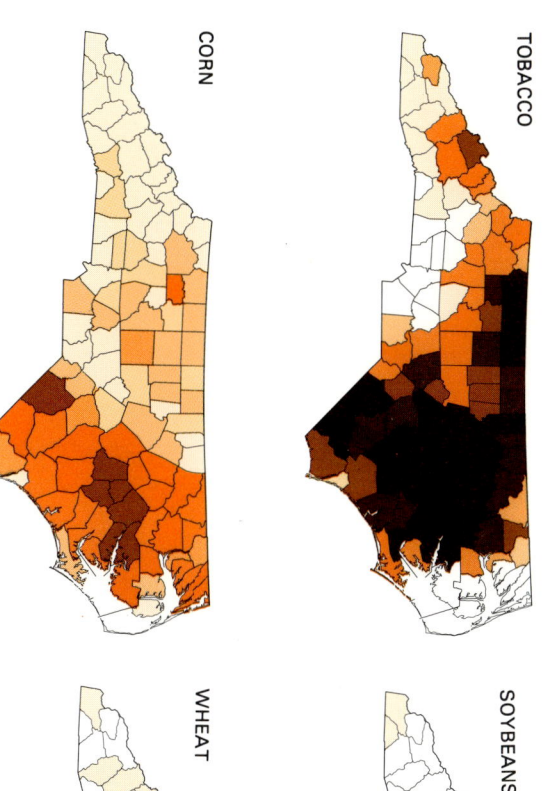

TOBACCO

CORN

Value in Thousands of Dollars
- 1,280 and above
- 640-1,280
- 320-640
- 160-320
- 80-160
- 40-80
- 20-40
- 10-20
- below 10
- no production

Source: N.C. Department of Agriculture, North Carolina Crop Reporting Service Reports, 1972.

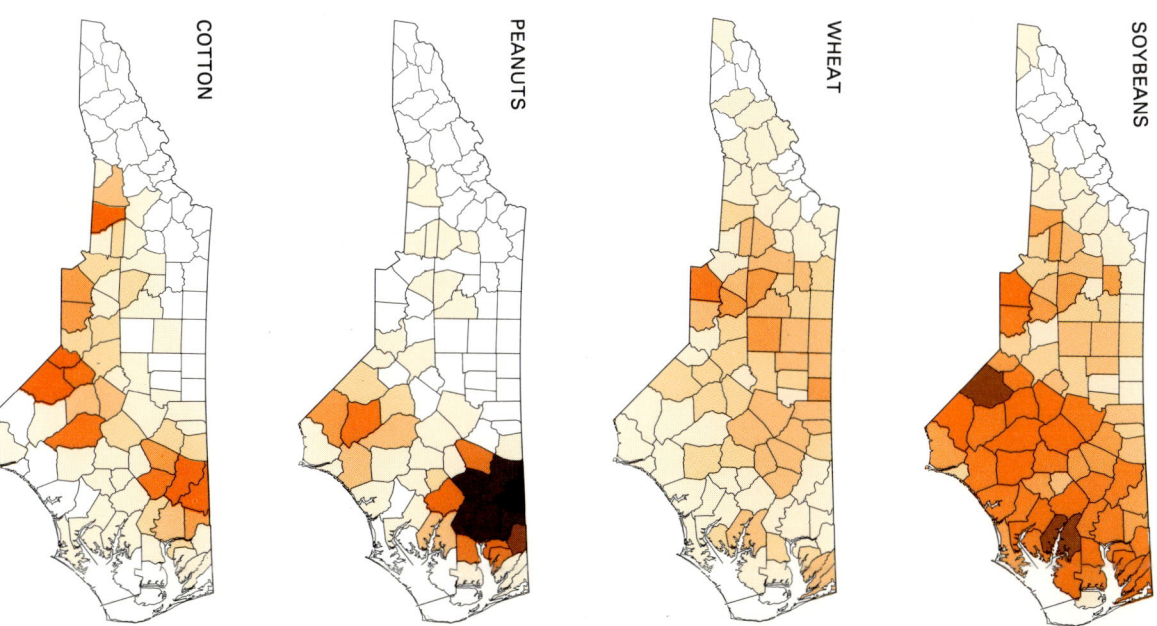

SOYBEANS

WHEAT

PEANUTS

COTTON

Figure 10.4(b). Number of Harvested Acres of Selected Farm Products in N.C. by County, 1971

Soybeans This source of plant protein has been described as the "wonder crop." It has long been valued as a protein supplement in livestock and poultry feedstuffs and many new uses have recently been developed for it. Exports of soybeans to other nations for feed and direct food uses have expanded. Soybean oil is used widely for margarine and cooking oil. Research has developed soy protein for "simulated meat products" and soy ingredients for bakery flours, macaroni and spaghetti, beverages and dessert toppings, and pet foods. Industry uses the soybean in resins, coating materials, and as a component in the manufacturing of paints, varnishes, plastics, and adhesives.

Acreage of soybeans has expanded in most producing areas (Figure 10.4). From 1962 to 1972 North Carolina's crop increased from 558,000 to 1,100,000 harvested acres. Increasing demand for soybeans has meant substantially expanded acreage in the South, especially in the delta states. The United States crop increased from 27,608,000 in 1962 to 42,701,000 acres in 1971. Impetus for expanded acreage of soybeans has been provided by the demand for protein feedstuffs for meat animals and by increased exports. Income from soybeans in North Carolina more than doubled between 1965 and 1972.

Wheat This crop is relatively less important in North Carolina's agriculture than in major producing regions such as the Great Plains states. Food uses from the soft, red winter type of wheat produced in North Carolina are primarily for cakes, pastries, and home-baked products. The amount used for livestock feeding purposes tends to vary according to market prices in the competing uses. Wheat and other grains such as oats, barley, rye, and grain sorghum are often used in systems of double-cropping and crop rotations.

Peanuts This crop is a vital source of farm income in about ten counties in northeastern North Carolina (Figure 10.4). It is a relatively high value crop with yields that typically range from two thousand to four thousand pounds per acre. In 1971 peanuts accounted for over 40 percent of the gross farm income of Northampton County. The leading peanut counties in North Carolina, along with neighboring counties in Virginia, produce the large type of peanuts, which is popular for roasting. Mechanization of peanut harvesting occurred in the 1950s and early 1960s and replaced manual techniques of digging, shaking, and stacking peanuts for field drying.

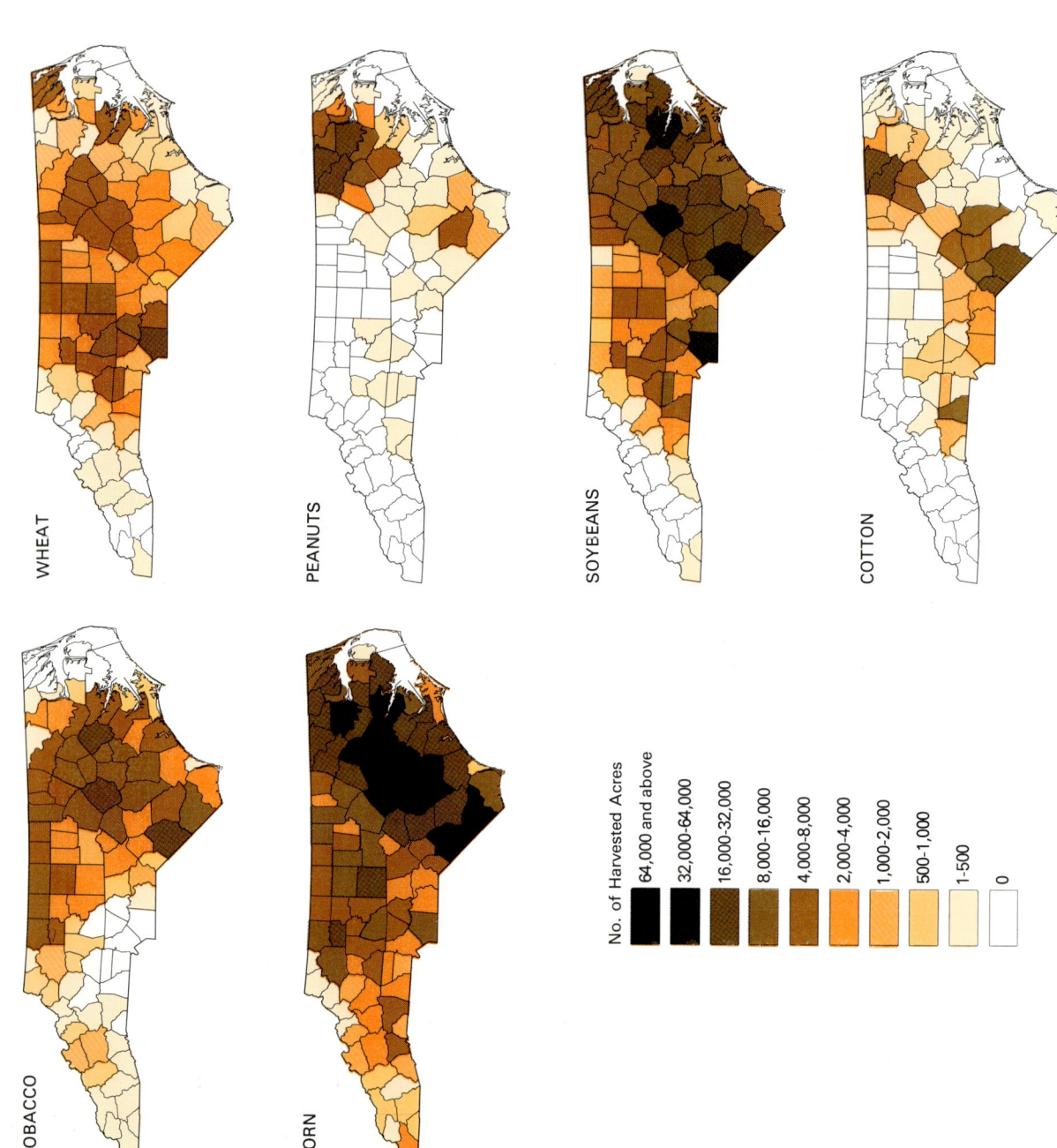

Source: N.C. Department of Agriculture, *North Carolina Crop Reporting Service Reports,* 1972.

Cotton

This crop was historically more important in the Deep South states than in North Carolina. In the last several decades, the state's cotton acreage has declined. About 175,000 acres were harvested in 1971 and this acreage was concentrated in a few counties (Figure 10.4b). This contrasts with the 829,000 acres harvested in 1940.

Fruits and Vegetables

A wide variety of horticultural crops is grown in North Carolina. The location of the state places much of its production midway between the early harvests of fruits and vegetables in Florida and the late season production in more northern states. The variation in soils and climatic conditions within the state results in a concentration of particular fruit and vegetable crops in certain areas.

Sweet potatoes, for which North Carolina is the leading producer in the nation, are grown in many of the same Coastal Plain areas as flue-cured tobacco. Sandy loam soils suit both crops. Sweet potatoes are harvested after the peak labor requirement for tobacco harvest. In 1972 the value of the sweet potato crop exceeded that of the cotton crop. Irish potatoes, a prominent crop in many home gardens, are produced commercially in two areas, the northern Tidewater counties and some northern Mountain counties.

Snap beans are grown in Coastal Plain counties such as Sampson County as well as in Mountain areas such as Henderson County. Those utilized in processing are often grown under contractual arrangements with processors. Coastal Plain counties are major producers of cucumbers for fresh market and pickling. Field tomatoes are grown in some eastern counties. Trellised tomatoes, attractively packed as "vine-ripe," are a major crop in several western counties. Interest is increasing in year-round production of tomatoes in plastic greenhouses.

Apples are an important enterprise on some specialized farms in western counties. Peaches and some small fruits are produced commercially in the sandhills area. Commercial strawberry production is concentrated in two areas, the southern Coastal Plain and certain Mountain counties. Fields where customers may "pick their own" are becoming increasingly popular for strawberries and some other fruits and vegetables. Blueberries are important in some Coastal Plain counties.

Forestry

North Carolina is a well-forested state. In contrast to regions such as the Great Plains where trees serve only as windbreaks or for decorative purposes, forests in North Carolina provide the base for a significant part of the economy. Pulpwood logs undergird the pulp and paper industry, and pine and hardwood lumber are used for construction and furniture manufacturing.

Forestry is significant to the agricultural economy because it provides an additional source of income to farm owners. Almost 40 percent of the state's farmland is in woods. Sales of forest products from farms in 1971 surpassed $33 million. Additional acreages of woodlands are owned by pulpwood and lumber companies, the state and federal governments, and individuals in nonfarm tracts. County extension agents estimate that these additional sources add another $31 million in income from forests in the state.

Livestock and Poultry Production

Cash receipts from various classes of livestock and poultry in North Carolina totaled over $600 million in 1971. This represented a gain of about 87 percent from a decade earlier. Livestock and poultry, especially hogs, beef, dairy, broilers, eggs, and turkeys represent a growing share of the state's agricultural economy. Livestock and poultry receipts were 38.4 percent of the gross farm income of North Carolina in 1971 as compared with only 28.0 percent a decade earlier. Leading counties in sales of various classes of livestock and poultry in 1971 are shown in Table 10.6.

Hogs

North Carolina ranked eleventh in the nation and first in the South in cash receipts from hogs in 1971. The $117 million income from hogs represented a 125 percent increase from a decade earlier. States that continue to lead North Carolina in hog income are located in the Midwest, where large acreages of corn and soybeans are produced.

The leading counties in hog production are in the eastern part of the state (Figure 10.5). However, there are some hogs produced in every county in the state.

North Carolina hog producers may ship hogs to any of the eighty-four commercial hog-slaughter plants in the state or they may ship them out of the state. The processing and marketing of about one million country-cured hams annually, representing over $50 million in retail sales, is a relatively new commercial industry that has developed from hog production in North Carolina.

Beef

Beef is produced in North Carolina principally by the cow-calf herd that produces feeder calves. Small herds of brood cows fit the conditions on many North Carolina farms, especially as a source of supplementary income. Figure 10.5 shows the distribution among counties of beef cows and dairy cows. The gross farm income from cattle and calves in North Carolina totaled about $62 million in 1971.

Figure 10.5. Livestock in N.C. by County, 1971

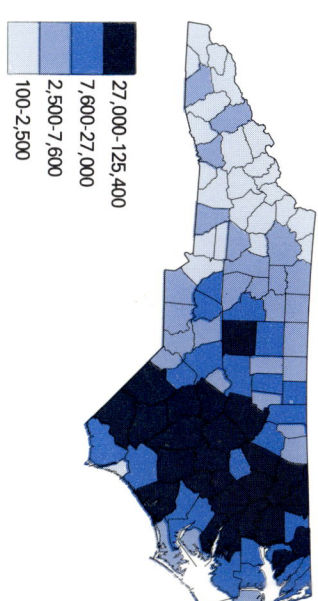

HOGS

27,000–125,400
7,600–27,000
2,500–7,600
100–2,500

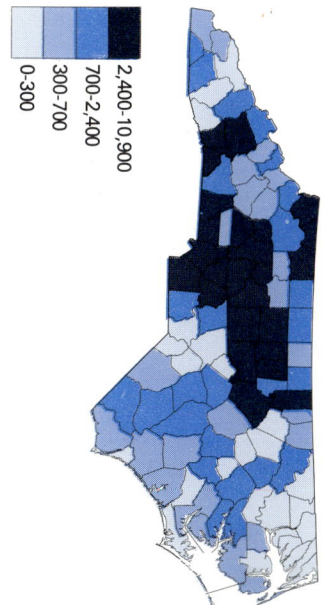

MILK COWS AND HEIFERS THAT HAVE CALVED

2,400–10,900
700–2,400
300–700
0–300

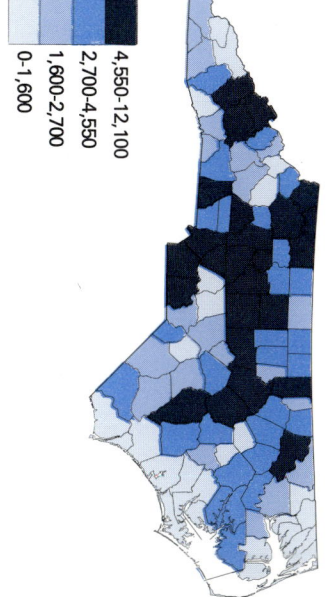

BEEF COWS AND HEIFERS THAT HAVE CALVED

4,550–12,100
2,700–4,550
1,600–2,700
0–1,600

Source: N.C. Department of Agriculture, *North Carolina Agricultural Statistics*, 1971.

Dairy North Carolina, like most of the states in the South, is not one of the nation's major dairy areas. However, production of milk within the state equals milk usage in most seasons. Milk contributed around $101 million to North Carolina farm income in 1971.

The milk marketing structure has evolved from small dairies, serving nearby towns and cities, to larger private and cooperative processing plants and even to regional marketing organizations that coordinate the flow of milk throughout multistate territories. In 1973 there were 26 dairy processing plants selling fluid milk in the state compared with 120 plants in 1955.

Broilers The increase in broiler production in the state and the nation has been phenomenal. In 1951 some 788 million broilers were produced in the United States and in 1971, 2,945 million. North Carolina's share of the national output rose from 4.1 percent to 9.8 percent during the two decades. By 1971 North Carolina ranked fourth in the nation in broiler income, with broiler output valued, at the farm level, at $147.6 million.

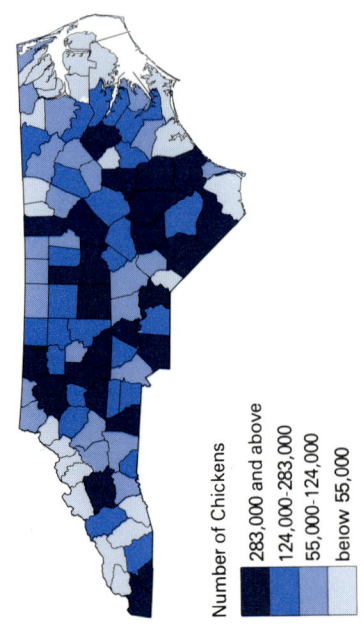

Figure 10.6. Number of Chickens Other than Commercial Broilers on N.C. Farms by County, 1971

Number of Chickens
- 283,000 and above
- 124,000-283,000
- 55,000-124,000
- below 55,000

Source: N.C. Department of Agriculture, *North Carolina Agricultural Statistics*, 1971.

Per capita consumption of broilers and other poultry meats increased by 50 percent in the United States between 1960 and 1972 compared to a 25 percent increase in beef and relatively little change in the amount of pork, eggs, and dairy products consumed. Much of the increased consumption of broilers can be traced to favorable prices in relation to other meats and to the development of a highly standardized product. Another distinguishing characteristic of the broiler industry is its high degree of vertical integration, a production system through which farmers growing broilers operate production contracts with feed companies, broiler processors, and hatcheries.

The principal broiler-producing counties, based on farm level value of production in 1971, are shown in Table 10.6. Many of these are in the Piedmont area where the amount of farmland suitable for row-cropping is relatively limited. Furthermore, broiler production fits well into the part-time farming prevalent in that section of the state.

Eggs North Carolina is a net exporter of commercial eggs. The degree of vertical integration is less pronounced in egg production than with broilers, but, like broilers, much of the cost is for feed.

North Carolina ranked third in the nation, after California and Georgia, in value of eggs sold in 1971. The $113.7 million cash farm receipts from eggs in North Carolina was over 6 percent of the national total. Leading North Carolina counties in egg sales are shown in Table 10.6. Figure 10.6 shows the number of chickens other than commercial broilers in various North Carolina counties.

Turkeys North Carolina ranked third in the nation in cash farm receipts from turkeys in 1971. Only California and Minnesota produced more turkeys. The value of turkeys sold in North Carolina increased about fourfold in the decade ending in 1971. While consumption of turkey meat is still highest in the holiday season, the year-round market is expanding. Unlike some farm commodities that are dispersed widely over the state, turkey production is concentrated in the southeastern Coastal Plain and the southern Piedmont (Table 10.6). The top five counties accounted for two-thirds of the total turkey sales in 1971.

Structure of Farms

The story of how North Carolina farms are now organized reveals the nature of the change in the state's agricultural structure. Fewer and fewer farms have been able to expand total farm production, in terms of both physical output and value of sales. As a result, there have been obvious increases in acreage, investment, and sales per operating unit. Farm consolidation is the product of many

Table 10.6. Leading N.C. Counties in Cash Farm Receipts from Livestock and Poultry, 1971

All Livestock and Poultry	Hogs	Cattle and Calves	Milk	Broilers	Eggs	Turkeys
1. Duplin	1. Sampson	1. Iredell	1. Iredell	1. Wilkes	1. Wilkes	1. Duplin
2. Wilkes	2. Johnston	2. Ashe	2. Rowan	2. Surry	2. Surry	2. Union
3. Chatham	3. Duplin	3. Union	3. Randolph	3. Moore	3. Duplin	3. Sampson
4. Union	4. Wayne	4. Buncombe	4. Orange	4. Chatham	4. Stanly	4. Wayne
5. Moore	5. Robeson	5. Haywood	5. Alamance	5. Randolph	5. Pitt	5. Robeson
6. Sampson	6. Columbus	6. Cleveland	6. Buncombe	6. Union	6. Sampson	6. Anson
7. Randolph	7. Greene	7. Surry	7. Wake	7. Alexander	7. Iredell	7. Lenoir
8. Wayne	8. Pitt	8. Wilkes	8. Davie	8. Montgomery	8. Robeson	8. Richmond
9. Surry	9. Martin	9. Guilford	9. Guilford	9. Richmond	9. Cherokee	9. Richmond
10. Iredell	10. Edgecombe	10. Stanly	10. Henderson	10. Caldwell	10. Cleveland	10. Pender

Source: N.C. Department of Agriculture, *North Carolina Farm Income, 1970-71*, 1971.

technical and economic forces. Mechanization, chemicals, and other labor-saving innovations have permitted a single farmer to conduct a much larger scale of business. Farm operators purchase many of their production items such as fertilizer, supplies, and equipment from other economic sectors and produce food, fiber, and tobacco for cash sale. The availability of nonfarm jobs within and outside the state has permitted mobility for the population that did not need to remain in agriculture.

North Carolina ranked seventh in the nation in number of farms in 1969. However, in line with the national trend, farm numbers have fallen rapidly in North Carolina, from over 190,000 in 1959 to around 148,000 in 1964 and down to 119,386 in 1969 (Table 10.7). In that last year, North Carolina accounted for 4.4 percent of the nation's 2.7 million farm units.*

There is a wide divergence in the number of farms among counties (Figure 10.7). In 1969 Johnston County had the largest number of operator units with a total of 3,894. Although 10.4 percent of the state's population was classified as living on farms, each of the counties had a rural farm population of more than 15 percent. While agriculture may be a smaller proportion of the total economic activity in some populous counties, there is still a significant number of farms in such urban areas as Buncombe, Guilford, and Wake counties.

One of the manifestations of a changing agricultural structure is seen in farm tenure patterns (Figure 10.8). Tenants, including sharecroppers, accounted for 30 percent of the state's farm operators in 1959, but for only

15 percent a decade later. Some explanations for the reduction in the number of tenants include (1) better job opportunities in the nonfarm economy, (2) a progression of some tenants into farm-owner status, (3) a substitution of hired workers and mechanization for tenant labor, and (4) a change in the commodity-mix that placed less dependence upon cash crops like tobacco and cotton. The 1969 Census of Agriculture indicates that 63 percent of the North Carolina farm operators were full owners and almost 22 percent were part owners who rent some land to supplement their acreage.

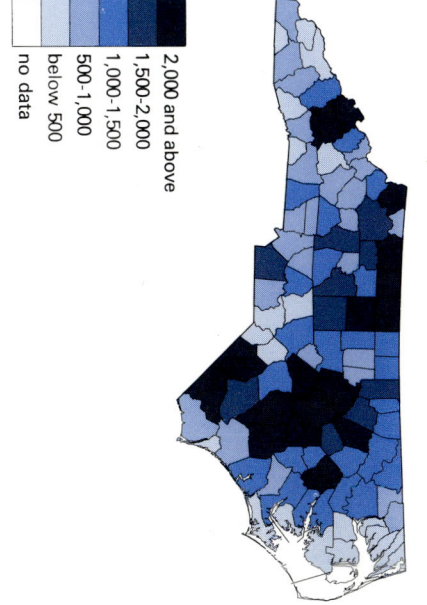

Figure 10.7. Number of Farms by N.C. County, 1969

- 2,000 and above
- 1,500-2,000
- 1,000-1,500
- 500-1,000
- below 500
- no data

Source: U.S. Department of Commerce, *U.S. Census of Agriculture*, 1969.

*The United States Census of Agriculture is taken every five years. Data from the census for 1974 were not available at the time this book was written.

Many of North Carolina's major industries are closely related to agriculture. An examination of employment data by industry (Figure 10.9) reveals that over one-third of the state's workers are employed in agribusiness industries. The basic production industries of agriculture, forestry, and fisheries were the principal sources of employment for about 5 percent of the employed labor force in 1970. But, employment in many additional industries is closely related to agriculture.

Retail Value of North Carolina Farm Products The state's farms provide the source of raw products for many consumer items. When the various manufacturing and marketing services are added to farm products produced in North Carolina, it is estimated that one dollar of product sold by North Carolina farmers has a final retail value of about five dollars. Thus the raw products produced by farmers provide a base for a fourfold increase in value between the farmer and consumer.

Figure 10.10 indicates the estimated final retail value of farm commodities initially produced on North Carolina farms in 1971. The products valued at $1.5 billion at the farm level in North Carolina eventually were sold to consumers for more than $7.4 billion. These estimates were developed by dividing the cash receipts at the farm level for a particular commodity by data from the United States Department of Agriculture on the farmer's share of retail cost. The increase in volume from farm to retail level represents the addition of many services by the marketing sector. The final retail value involves consumer expenditures wherever the North Carolina-grown products were finally consumed. In marketing and manufacturing terms, much transfer between states is likely. For example, North Carolina textile mills use far more cotton than is produced in the state, while some of the tobacco and peanuts produced on North Carolina farms is manufactured and sold in other states.

The multiplication in value from the farm through the marketing sector to the retail level is greater for the agriculture of North Carolina than for that of the nation as a whole because of differences in the commodity-mix. For example, the final retail value of tobacco is about nine times greater than the farm value, but for most classes of livestock and poultry the value roughly doubles between farmer and consumer. The intervening industries that use agricultural raw materials have substantial costs and employ significant numbers of workers in the process of adding services to the farm product. Furthermore, the final retail cost includes taxes, about three-fourths the level of the value added by the marketing sector in the case of tobacco. Table 10.8 itemizes the differences in value added to farm value of various commodities.

Other structural changes on North Carolina farms are related to farm consolidation. As shown in Table 10.7 average farm acreage and investment per farm is increasing, and a larger proportion of farms sell more than $10,000 of farm products per year.

Some other characteristics of North Carolina farm operators in 1969 were as follows:

1. More than 46,000 farm operators, or 38.7 percent of the total, worked off the farm for one hundred days or more.

2. The average age of farm operators was 52.4 years with only 9.5 percent under 35 and 18 percent 65 years and over.

3. About 89 percent of the farms were operated by whites and most of the rest by blacks.

4. Most North Carolina farms are operated as proprietorships or partnerships. Despite substantial national publicity to the effect that business conglomerates were entering agricultural production, only 1,031 incorporated commercial farms were reported in North Carolina in 1969. Since 961 had ten or less shareholders, it is likely that most of these farms simply represented the corporate form of business organization chosen by most farm families.

Agriculture in the Overall Economy

As one major industry within the total economy, agriculture has many types of linkages with other economic sectors. First, the farm producer is linked to the supplier of various items and services used in farm production, and he sells his farm commodities to others who process and market goods to consumers. Many North Carolina industries directly utilize agricultural products. These industries employ a significant proportion of the state's labor force. Second, North Carolina farmers and service-adding industries provide food, fiber, and tobacco to millions of consumers. Third, relatively large proportions of the types of commodities produced on North Carolina farms enter international trade. A final type of linkage between agriculture and the rest of the economy is related to rural manpower resources. Many of the people who live on farms in the state occupy full-time or part-time jobs in other industries.

Agribusiness in North Carolina The farmer may be viewed, in diagrammatic fashion, as a link in the agribusiness chain:

Farm supplier→Farmer producer→Marketing→Consumer

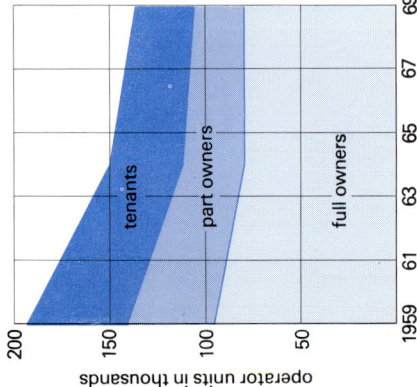

Figure 10.8. Number of Farms by Type of Operator in N.C., 1959-1969

Source: U.S. Department of Commerce, *U.S. Census of Agriculture,* 1969.

Table 10.7. Changes in Number, Size, Value, and Sales Categories of N.C. Farms

	1959	1964	1969
Number of farms	190,567	148,205	119,386
Average acreage per farm	83.4	97.0	106.6
Value of land and buildings per farm	$15,475	$24,442	$35,551
Percentage of farms with sales:			
Less than $2,500	51.1	43.9	45.0
$2,500-5,000	22.7	16.1	15.6
$5,000-10,000	17.6	19.5	15.7
$10,000 or more	8.6	20.5	23.7

Source: U.S. Department of Commerce, *Census of Agriculture* for year cited.

Figure 10.9. Proportion of Employment Related to Agriculture in N.C., 1970

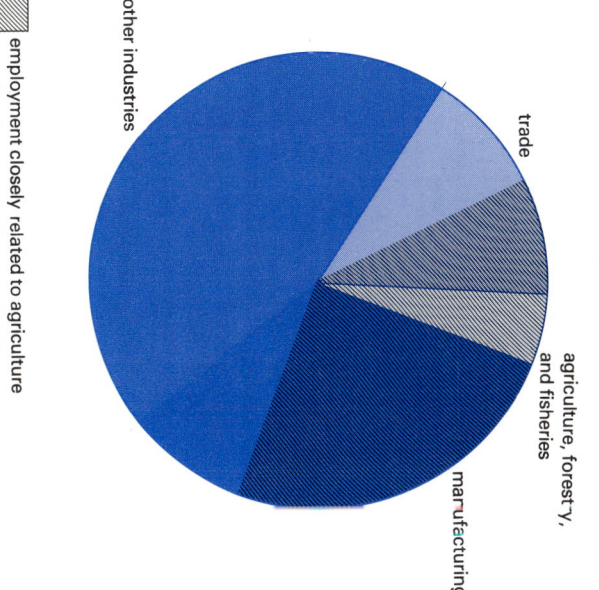

Figure 10.10. Multiplication in Value of N.C. Farm Products from Farm Level to Final Retail Value, 1971

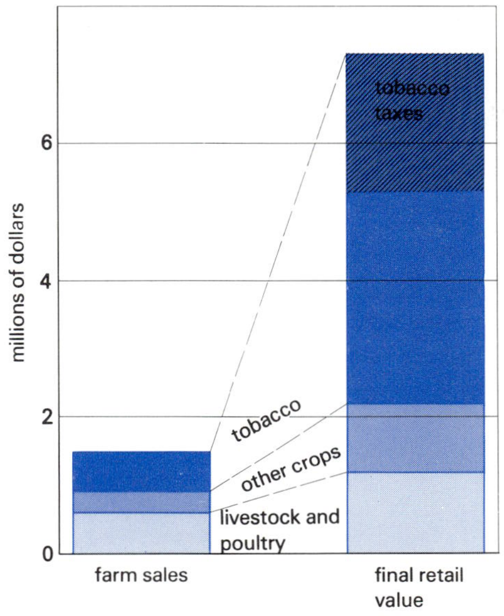

Note: The final retail value is estimated for 1971 by dividing N.C. cash farm receipts by national data on farmers' share of retail sales of selected items.

Figure 10.11. Selected Agricultural Exports as a Percentage of N.C. Total Farm Sales, 1972

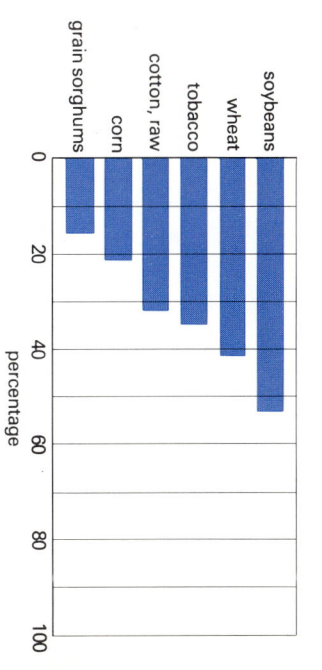

Source: U.S. Department of Agriculture, *Farm Income Situation*, August 1969 and August 1972.

Exports of Agricultural Products

Figure 10.11 shows the proportion of various commodities exported from the United States. It can be seen that foreign markets are extremely important for the tobacco, soybeans, and grain produced in North Carolina. Although about 35 percent of all United States–produced tobacco was exported in 1971-72, North Carolina's share in foreign trade is probably greater than that of other states because of the predominance of flue-cured leaf. In 1971-72, 43 percent of flue-cured tobacco was exported compared to less than 10 percent of Burley leaf.

Foreign trade involving farm products serves several purposes:

1. Agricultural trade has moderated the problem of balance-of-payments for the United States. In 1972, our agricultural exports of $7.7 billion exceeded agricultural imports of $5.8 billion. A positive agricultural trade balance has persisted for at least a decade. However, this may change in the face of rising prices and food shortages.

2. Maintaining access to foreign markets is vital to agriculture in North Carolina. Nationally, exported crops accounted for about 21 percent of the acreage of crops harvested. As noted earlier, a large share of key crops produced in North Carolina is exported.

3. Exports of North Carolina farm products generate business for ports in Wilmington and Morehead City as well as for Norfolk and Charleston in adjacent states.

Nonfarm Work by Farm People

Part-time work in nonagricultural jobs is commonplace with many farm operators and other members of rural-farm households. About 53 percent of the state's 119,386 farm operators reported some days of work off the farm, according to the 1969 Census of Agriculture. A total of 35,741 worked off the farm two hundred days or more. This work period indicated that 30 percent of all farm operators essentially had a full-time, off-farm job, so agricultural work was conducted "after hours" and on weekends.

The principal occupation of the majority of employed persons living on farms was not in agriculture. Only 27 percent of the employed rural farm labor force was engaged primarily in farm work. This does not rule out the possibility that some farm workers combine farm work with a nonfarm job. However, the leading occupations of the remaining 73 percent of employed rural-farm people were in "blue-collar," off-farm jobs.

There are no fully adequate measures of differences in the quality of life between geographic areas. Nevertheless, it is possible to make comparisons of such items as levels of income and conditions of housing in rural versus urban counties of the state. Practically all such comparisons show that most predominantly rural counties rank lower than highly urbanized counties with respect to these indicators of the quality of life.

The most rural class is defined for purposes of this analysis as those counties having more than 20 percent rural farm population. Most of the other counties were classified in descending order, according to the percentage of population living on farms. However, a separate classification is established for those counties containing a city with a population of 50,000 or more. Such urban centers provide employment opportunities for farm as well as nonfarm people in the respective counties. Figure 10.12 illustrates the classification of counties according to degree of rurality.

Family Incomes and Degree of Rurality The average family income for 1969 for each of the five groups of counties is shown in Table 10.9. The average family income for the state as a whole was $8,872. In the more rural groups of counties, the average family income was below the average for the state. Moreover, there was a steady rise in average family incomes from the most rural counties to the most urbanized. Most of the counties having average family income above the state average contained a town or city of some size or a military reservation, or they were relatively near urban centers in the Piedmont region. Figure 10.13 shows the pattern of income of families by county.

The family income of rural farm families tended to be (1) lower than that for all families in the same group of counties and (2) lower in the most rural counties than in the more urbanized areas. In only seventeen of the state's one hundred counties was the average income of rural farm families greater than the average for all families.

A similar pattern prevailed with respect to the percentage of families with incomes below the poverty level. In 1969 it was higher in the more rural groups of counties than in the urban groups (Figure 10.14).

Based on the lower average family income and the higher proportion of rural farm families with incomes below the poverty level, there is a strong presumption that the quality of living in rural areas of North Carolina is lower than that in urban areas.

Figure 10.12. Percentage of Rural Farm Population in N.C. by County, 1970

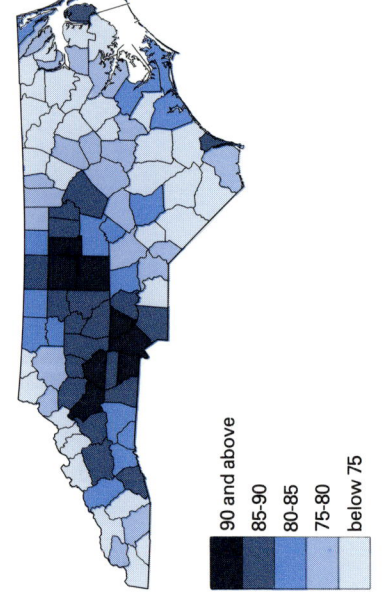

Rural Farm Population
- cities above 50,000
- 0–5
- 5–12.5
- 12.5–20
- 20 and above

Source: U.S. Department of Commerce, *1970 Census of Population and Housing*, 1970.

Figure 10.13. Median Family Income in N.C. by County, 1970

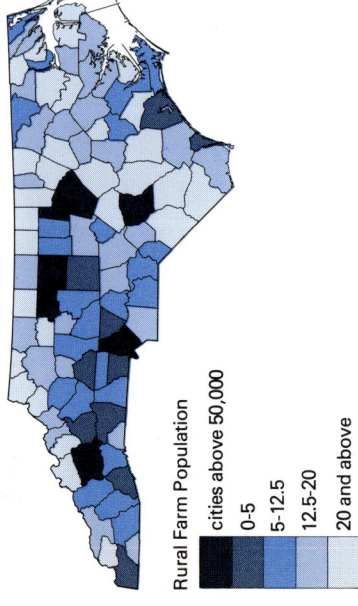

Dollars
- 9,000 and above
- 8,000–9,000
- 7,000–8,000
- 6,000–7,000
- below 6,000

Source: U.S. Department of Commerce, *1970 Census of Population and Housing*, 1970.

Figure 10.14. Percentage of Families with Incomes Above Poverty Level in N.C. by County, 1970

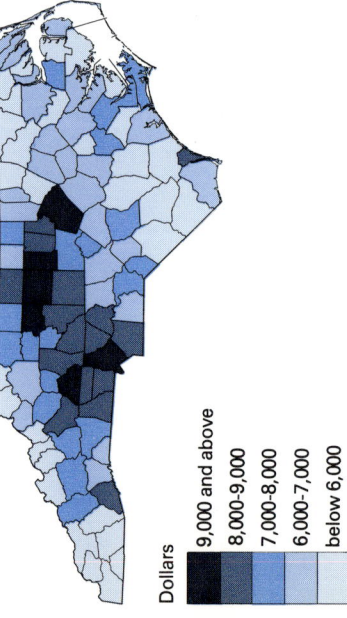

- 90 and above
- 85–90
- 80–85
- 75–80
- below 75

Source: U.S. Department of Commerce, *1970 Census of Population and Housing*, 1970.

The mixture of farm and nonfarm work by people living on farms has several advantages in North Carolina. The combination of jobs may help to boost the net income of many families who work the small average farms of the state. Multiple opportunities for employment also compensate for the state's relatively low rank in the average factory wage rate. Many people find living in a rural area to be personally satisfying. Social problems associated with congested central cities may have been reduced by part-time farming. North Carolina's agricultural industry is dispersed over the state and among more towns than is the case with many other states, where most nonfarm jobs are concentrated in a few major cities. Therefore, commuting from rural homes to nonfarm jobs is more feasible for many North Carolinians.

The Quality of Life in Rural Areas

The past two decades have been a period in which there were rapid increases in farm family incomes and significant gains in agricultural efficiency. However, the level of living in the rural areas of North Carolina is still below that in urbanized areas of the state. During periods of rapid economic growth and great changes in the structure of society, it is quite common for the development of rural areas to lag behind that of urban areas. This appears to have been the case in North Carolina in recent years.

Table 10.8. Estimated Final Retail Value of Farm Commodities Produced and Sold by Farmers in N.C., 1971

Commodity	Farmer's Share of Retail Cost (percentage)	Cash Farm Receipts (×1,000)	Estimated Retail Value (×1,000)
Tobacco	11[1]	$ 561,647	$5,105,882
Cotton	40[2]	29,765	74,412
Peanuts	32[3]	49,468	154,588
Soybeans	32[3]	61,067	190,834
Wheat	12[4]	11,058	92,150
Feed grains	75[5]	80,223	106,964
Fresh fruits and vegetables	31[6]	44,304[10]	142,916
Processed fruits and vegetables	18[7]	27,570[11]	153,167
Other crops	38[8]	59,874	157,563
(total crops)		(865,102)	(6,178,476)
Dairy	47[9]	101,258	215,443
Meat (beef, pork)	55[9]	178,935	325,336
Poultry	47[9]	199,397	424,249
Eggs	57[9]	113,678	199,435
Other livestock products	38[8]	8,236	21,674
(total livestock)		(601,504)	(1,186,137)
Total commodities	20.7	1,526,480	7,364,613

Sources: U.S. Department of Agriculture, *Tobacco Situation*, September 1972, tables 23-25; U.S. Department of Agriculture, *Cotton Situation*, February 1972, table 7; U.S. Department of Agriculture, *Marketing and Transportation Situation*, February 1972, table 11.

[1] Based on implied farmer's share of retail cost, with $12,323 million expenditure for tobacco products, U.S., 1971. Instead of 10.8 percent when tobacco taxes are included, share would be 17.8 percent when $4,673 million in taxes are excluded from retail cost.
[2] Based on implied farmer's share of value of unfinished cloth obtainable from a pound of cotton fiber, U.S., 1971. Fiber value is 73.42 cents compared to 29.02 cents per pound of raw cotton.
[3] Based on 1971 farmer's share for fats and oils.
[4] Based on 1971 farmer's share for bakery and cereal.
[5] Estimated.
[6] Based on 1971 farmer's share for fresh fruits and vegetables.
[7] Based on 1971 farmer's share for processed fruits and vegetables.
[8] Based on 1971 farmer's share for market basket.
[9] Based on 1971 farmer's share for specific livestock and poultry products.
[10] Fresh fruits and vegetables are defined to include sweet potatoes, potatoes, tomatoes, cabbage, sweet corn, watermelons, lettuce, apples, peaches, pecans, and strawberries.
[11] Processed fruits and vegetables are defined to include cucumbers, snap beans, peppers, grapes, and miscellaneous fruits and vegetables.

Table 10.9. Family Income Status by Degree of Rurality of County, N.C., 1969

	Average Family Income			Percentage of Families below the Poverty Level		
	All Families	Rural Families	Rural Farm Families	All Families	Rural Families	Rural Farm Families
Counties with more than 20% rural farm population (29)	$ 6,932	$6,137	26.9	29.7		
Counties with 12.6-20.0% rural farm population (28)	7,651	6,880	21.7	24.5		
Counties with 5.2-12.5% rural farm population (28)	8,728	8,112	14.5	15.7		
Counties with 5% or less rural farm population (7)	9,090	8,234	11.7	13.4		
Counties with a city of over 50,000 population (8)	10,446	8,603	11.6	12.7		
Total N.C. counties	8,872	7,152	16.3	22.5		

Source: U.S. Department of Commerce, *1970 Census of Population*, 1970.

Rural versus Urban Housing Rural housing in North Carolina is generally of lower quality than is that occupied by urban residents. Four characteristics of year-round housing units were selected to show differences in the quality of housing between rural and urban residents. They were the proportion of housing units (1) with hot and cold water piped into the house, (2) with flush toilets, (3) with complete kitchen facilities, and (4) occupied by more than 1.01 persons per room. As measured by each of the four characteristics, the quality of rural housing was lower than that of urban housing (Figure 10.15). Based on these characteristics, rural farm housing is more deficient than either the rural nonfarm or urban areas.

There are, of course, thousands of homes in both rural and urban areas of North Carolina that fall far below adequate standards. From many points of view, housing conditions in some of the crowded slum areas of large cities may be less healthful and otherwise less desirable places to live than equally poor housing in rural areas. City slum areas are commonly more highly visible than the poor housing found in rural areas. There can be little doubt that there is a higher proportion of rural people than of urban people who are poorly housed. Some rural housing, much of which is not readily seen from highways, is far below commonly accepted standards.

A Summary View of the Quality of Life in Rural Areas

The preceding review of family incomes, the percentage of poverty, and housing conditions point toward the general conclusion that the level of living in rural areas of North Carolina is below that in urban areas. In addition, in Chapter 15 (Health Care Resources), it is shown that rural areas are served by fewer physicians and have access to smaller hospitals than do their urban counterparts. Other differences are difficult to measure. It is probable, however, that the quality of primary and secondary schooling in most rural areas is below that in cities because the variety of course offerings is more limited, library and laboratory facilities are not as adequate, and specialized teaching for either handicapped or especially talented children is less likely to be available in rural schools than in large urban school systems. Likewise, public libraries, art museums, theaters, musical concerts, and similar cultural amenities are more readily accessible in cities than in rural areas.

There are, of course, offsetting factors. Traffic jams, air pollution, and congested living conditions are more prevalent in cities than in rural areas. Whether there is an acceptable net balance between the totality of advantages and disadvantages of living in rural versus urban areas often depends on each individual's values and preferences. Nevertheless, many conditions of life in rural areas need to be improved if rural people are to live at levels generally comparable to those of urban residents and if the flood of people to the cities is to be diminished.

Future Challenges for North Carolina Agriculture

A two-pronged effort can provide a brighter future for the agricultural industry and for rural North Carolina. Both public bodies and private initiative are challenged (1) to increase the efficiency of commercial agriculture and (2) to promote economic, social, and cultural development in rural areas.

Efficiency in Commercial Agriculture Gross and net income for North Carolina farm families lag far behind the national average. Among the various techniques that can help the farmers and agribusiness firms of North Carolina become more competitive are the following:

Increase in size of farm operating units. Further consolidation of operating units is needed if the volume of business on the typical North Carolina farm is to reach the national average. Purchases of additional farmland may be possible by many operators. Rental may provide a good alternative for those who can obtain higher returns for their capital in other ways. Estate planning and family farming agreements can be utilized to reduce fragmentation of farm operating units when transferred from one generation to another. An adequate farm credit system can assist in increasing the productivity of many livestock and poultry farms.

Changes in the farm enterprise-mix. Most of the expansion in agricultural production will likely occur in enterprises other than tobacco. In fact, it is likely that tobacco will be produced on fewer farms in the future because of the adoption of mechanical harvesting and especially if legislative changes are made to allow lease-and-transfer of tobacco quotas across county lines.

Adoption of new technology. Innovations in production techniques are developed by land-grant universities, various public agencies, and private industry. North Carolina farmers need to search continually for improved technology to raise crop yields to the national average and to offset the experience of the livestock industries in some other regions of the country.

Improved business management practices. Entrepreneurs on farms and in agribusiness need to sharpen their business skills in order to increase volumes of business, utilize credit and hired labor more effectively, and adjust to changing conditions of production and market demand.

Search for new agricultural opportunities. Specialized operations can occasionally capitalize on particular resource situations. For example, horticultural specialties may fit small farms near urban centers if quality products are grown and appropriate marketing methods are used. Fish farms and improved utilization of small woodland holdings may offer added opportunities.

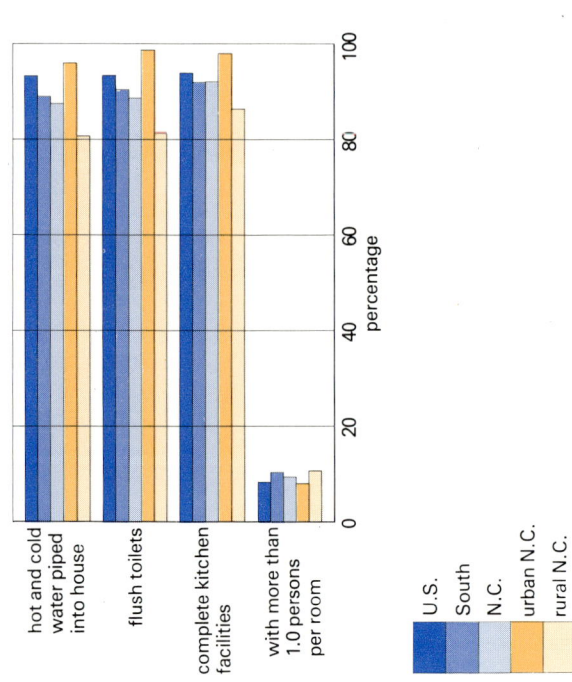

Figure 10.15. Percentage of Year-Round Housing Units in N.C. with Specific Characteristics by Residence, 1970

Source: U.S. Department of Commerce, *1970 Census of Housing*, 1970.

Competitive markets. With the size and diversity of the state's farm production, adequate attention must be given to marketing. Coordination between farmers and agribusiness helps to provide a flow of products of acceptable quantity and quality. The entire marketing sector needs to keep alert to changing patterns of demand at the national and international levels. Efforts should be made continually to improve the efficiency of agribusiness.

Positive public programs affecting agriculture. Commercial farmers, like other businessmen, operate within an environment affected by policies developed at local, state, and federal governmental levels. North Carolina farmers have historically been affected by federal programs related to tobacco, peanuts, cotton, and feed grains. The nature of future commodity programs will have a substantial influence on the level of farm income, the structure of farms, and the quantity of agricultural products available to consumers. In addition, the welfare of farmers and others in agribusiness depends upon general economic policies that affect the business climate. Public officials shape the future of agriculture when actions are taken on such matters as labor, credit, land use, taxation, environmental quality, industrial location, and international trade. Public investment in agricultural research and education adds to the productivity of agriculture, increases the base of raw materials available to industries, and provides consumer benefits through more economical food supplies. The number of commercial farmers may decline further in the future. But the need remains for positive public programs to keep a viable agricultural industry that will supply the basic food requirements of urban and rural citizens.

Development of Rural Areas

All of North Carolina's rural population is not now, and will not likely in the future be, involved in the mainstream of commercial agriculture. About one-third of the state's farms were classified in 1970 as other than commercial farms because of the low value of their farm sales and their dependence upon nonfarm work. Traditional agricultural programs are of little consequence in improving their well-being. Further, about 45 percent of the state's population lives outside urban areas but not on farms. This large rural, nonfarm population is vitally concerned with public programs to create a better community life in rural areas.

In order to enrich life in rural areas, efforts are warranted to create job opportunities and to provide community facilities.

Job opportunities for rural people. The dispersion of North Carolina's population over the landscape has permitted, to date, the avoidance of many social problems. While some states have a stark contrast between depopulated rural areas and congested cities, North Carolina still has an opportunity to preserve much of its small town-rural character but efforts are needed from the public and private sectors to provide nonfarm job opportunities within commuting distance of rural residents.

Community facilities in rural areas. The development of adequate facilities and services may require attention to two types of problems:

1. With a dispersed population in rural areas, the costs of providing public services such as water, sewer, and health care may be high in relation to the costs in dense urban areas. Therefore, information needs to be readily available on assistance from public programs for such services.

2. There may be a lack of organized structures for mobilizing and operating facilities in rural areas. There are generally agencies of city government directly charged with such responsibilities. Extra attention may be required to effect the delivery of comparable public services in rural areas.

The solution of both types of problems calls for more cooperation among rural political units. Multicounty facilities and service centers would be more efficient for sparsely populated counties than the individual facility in each and every county that has traditionally served rural areas. Success in these ventures would greatly enhance the quality of life for all rural residents, farmers and nonfarmers alike.

SELECTED REFERENCES

N.C. Agricultural Extension Service. *Agricultural Opportunities in North Carolina.* Extension Circular no. 355. Rev. Raleigh: The Service, 1972.

N.C. Agricultural Extension Service. *Impact '76, 5-Year Program.* Raleigh: The Service, 1972.

N.C. Crop Reporting Service. *North Carolina Agricultural Statistics.* Raleigh: The Service, published annually.

N.C. Crop Reporting Service and N.C. Agricultural Extension Service. *North Carolina Farm Income—Cash Receipts from Farm Marketings and Government Payments by Counties.* Raleigh: The Services, 1972.

N.C. State University, Agricultural Policy Institute. *The Structure of Southern Farms of the Future.* A.P.I. Series 30. Raleigh: The University, 1968.

Tar Heel Economist, published monthly.

U.S. Department of Agriculture, Economic Research Service. *Farm Income Situation.* Washington, D.C.: The Department, published annually.

U.S. Department of Agriculture. *1972 Handbook of Agricultural Charts.* Agricultural Handbook no. 439. Washington, D.C.: The Department, 1972.

U.S. Department of Agriculture. *The Yearbook of Agriculture.* Washington, D.C.: The Department, published annually.

U.S. Department of Commerce, Bureau of the Census. *Census of Agriculture.* Washington, D.C.: The Department, published every five years.

U.S. Department of Commerce, Bureau of the Census. *Census of Population.* Washington, D.C.: The Department, published every ten years.

11. Manufacturing

ALFRED W. STUART
WAYNE A. WALCOTT

North Carolina is one of the leading industrial states in the nation and ranks behind only Texas among southern states. In 1972 it ranked ninth in the United States in number of manufacturing employees and tenth in value added by manufacturing.* About 14.2 percent of the state's population worked in factories in 1970, a higher participation rate than that of any of the other twelve leading industrial states.

Manufacturing is North Carolina's largest employer and its leading source of personal income. It is also important because factories are highly concentrated employment units and their locations strongly influence an area's tax base, service needs, transportation flows, and even the distribution of population. Manufacturing has a special meaning because it has been the principal means by which regions have changed from subsistence agriculture to modern economies. It continues to be an agent of economic development throughout North Carolina.

There are many ways of analyzing an area's industrial activities. In this chapter the role of manufacturing as an employer and source of income is emphasized. The other principal emphasis is on the geography of manufacturing—where industry is located and how this spatial pattern has changed in recent decades. This analysis indicates that the income quality of manufacturing in North Carolina shows strong possibilities of improving after decades of being near the bottom of the national list.

There is much that makes North Carolina manufacturing unusual or even unique. The most striking feature is that despite its high degree of industrialization North Carolina has a low degree of urbanization. This unusual occurrence is due to the fact that North Carolina industry is not concentrated in a few large cities but rather is dispersed over the state. In 1967 there were eighty-nine cities and towns that had at least 450 employees in manufacturing. The sixty-five for which the actual employment was reported, which included all of the larger cities, contained only 53 percent of the state's total.

Another significant feature of the state's industrial base is that it has experienced a period of sustained growth since the early 1960s that has resulted in a major change in the location and composition of manufacturing industries. Between 1947 and 1960 manufacturing employment increased by about 85,000 but employment in factories increased nearly a quarter of a million between 1960 and 1972. This rapid growth caused North Carolina to gain or even the rapidly developing South, increasing its share of the region's manufacturing employment from 13.7 to 14.3 percent between 1963 and 1971. During the same time the proportion of the national total increased from 3.2 to 3.8 percent.

Growth occurred throughout most of the state, spreading the economic benefits of industrialization to other than just those counties in the already heavily industrialized Piedmont. These changes have produced industrial regions that are more complex than the traditional Coastal Plain–Piedmont–Mountain groupings. It will be shown that new regions do exist and that they differ from each other in important social and economic characteristics.

INDUSTRIAL COMPOSITION

Table 11.1 summarizes the composition of manufacturing in North Carolina. Traditionally the "Big Three" of industrial activity in the state have been textiles, tobacco, and furniture. However, while textiles still dominate in both employment and value added, its share has decreased steadily over the years. Tobacco's share has also decreased and, even though furniture experienced substantial growth, the "Big Three" share of employment dropped from 63.1 percent of employment in 1956 to 50.7 percent in 1972. While it is true that textiles and furniture were leaders in total increase in employment, the apparel industry had the largest gain of all and a wide variety of industry groups had higher rates of gain. The result of the surge in manufacturing that occurred in the 1960s was a very substantial diversification of the state's industrial base.

One of the effects of this diversification was the improvement of the wage quality of industrial employment in the state. The twelve industry groups that had average annual earnings per employee above the state average of $6,105 in 1971 increased in employment by 114 percent between 1956 and 1972 while those below the state average increased only 39 percent. The twelve higher-wage industries added almost 111,000 jobs during the period. Average annual earnings per employee in North Carolina increased from 66.1 percent of the national average in 1958 to 71.8 percent in 1971, an impressive relative increase.

Another consequence of diversification was an increase in the capital intensity of manufacturing.* Traditionally a state with a labor-intensive industrial base, North Carolina's value added per employee was still substantially below the national average in 1971. High value added per employee to some degree indicates high labor productivity but mainly it means that the industry is relatively mechanized and automated. Therefore, low value added per employee signals a labor-intensive industry while high value added per employee identifies a capital-intensive activity. The distinction is important because capital-intensive industries tend to be products of modern technology and pay higher wages to a more skilled labor force. Conversely, the state's long-standing concentration of labor-intensive industries has led to a chronic inability to increase wages in the face of competition for labor. The apparel and textile industries must pay low wages because wages have a strong effect on prices. A textile company that pays high wages risks pricing its product out of the market. Either it must have low-wage labor or it must significantly increase its mechanization in order to improve productivity.

The twelve industry groups that had higher earning levels than the state average in 1971 had an average value added per employee of $22,865, well above the national figure. The six lower-wage industries, by contrast, averaged only $10,227 per employee. Between 1963 and 1971 North Carolina's share of total value added by manufacturing in the United States increased faster than did its

---

*The term "value added" is a statistic that measures the increase in worth that is attributable to labor and capital at the point of manufacture. Excluded from the final price of a product are such things as the cost of raw materials, purchased power, and subcontracted labor. It is generally considered to be the truest measure of economic output at a factory or from an area.

*The term "capital intensive" refers to industries that use machinery and other capital goods to a relatively great extent. "Labor-intensive" industries use less machinery and more labor. For the capital-intensive industry payrolls make up a small part of total value added (less than 13 percent in the North Carolina cigarette industry in 1971) but a large part for the labor-intensive type (51 percent for the North Carolina apparel industry in 1971).

share of employment, further evidence of the increasing sophistication of the state's industrial base.

Geographic Distribution

Manufacturing is remarkably dispersed throughout the state and dispersion is increasing. While it is true that 31.1 percent of total employment in manufacturing occurred in only five counties in 1956, that proportion had decreased to 26.7 percent by 1972, despite the fact that all five counties experienced substantial increases.

Figure 11.1 portrays the geographic pattern of manufacturing employment in 1972. Historically, in North Carolina manufacturing has been a Piedmont business. In 1972 eight counties had at least 20,000 manufacturing employees and of those only Buncombe County was not in the Piedmont. Another thirteen counties had between 10,000 and 20,000 manufacturing employees and all were in the Piedmont except Robeson and Cumberland. However, counties in the 5,000 to 10,000-employee range are found in all parts of the state, with a particularly notable concentration in the Coastal Plain east of Raleigh.

Figure 11.2 portrays the changes in employment that occurred between 1956 and 1972. Predictably, the greatest gains were experienced in the Piedmont. Only seven counties gained more than 8,000 employees each and all but Buncombe were in the Piedmont. However, the changes were not entirely a duplication of the pattern in Figure 11.1. In the northern Piedmont, for example, Guilford County had a very large gain, to maintain its position as the state's leading manufacturing county and Wake County had one of the largest gains in the state, almost tripling its employment during the period. Otherwise, the large industrial counties of the northern Piedmont did not record impressive gains. Forsyth County recorded less than a 2,000-employee increase and fell into fourth place in the state, behind Mecklenburg County. Durham, Orange, and Stokes counties suffered a net loss in industrial jobs during the period. Some of the counties that surround Forsyth and Guilford showed gains, suggesting a move toward the periphery of the metropolitan areas.

In the southern Piedmont growth was more consistent. Catawba County was the strongest gainer in the state and adjacent Burke County also recorded impressive gains. Mecklenburg and Gaston counties each added over 10,000 industrial jobs. To the west, the gains continued strong all the way into Buncombe but trailed off around that metropolitan county, with Polk County showing a loss. Of the other counties that are mostly in the Mountain region only McDowell and Cherokee reported increases of at least 2,000.

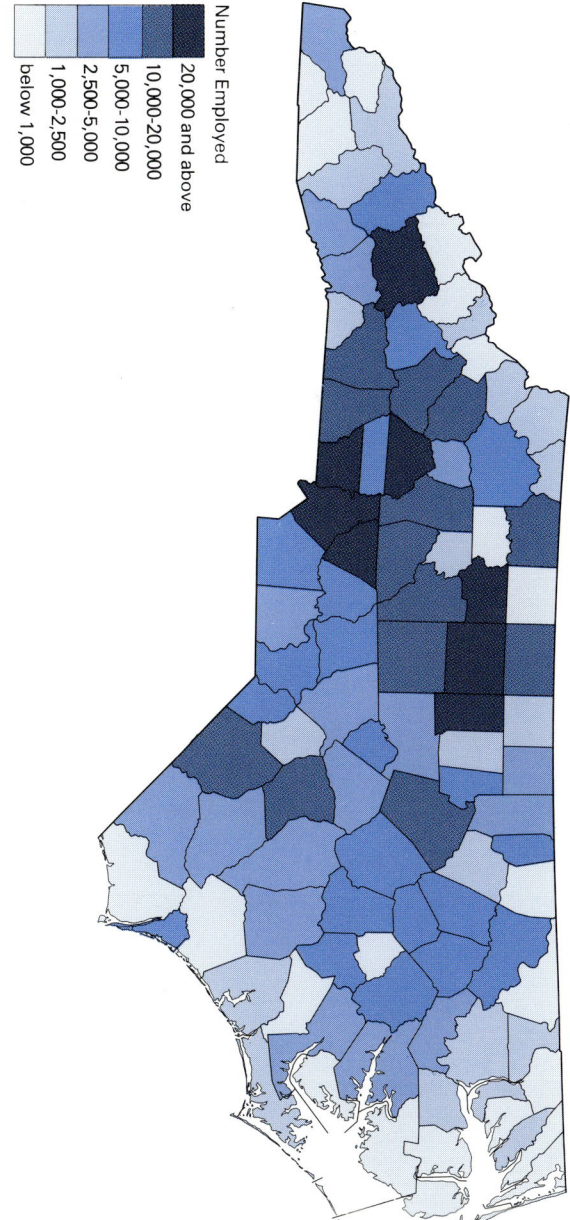

Figure 11.1. Total Manufacturing Employment in N.C., 1972

Number Employed
- 20,000 and above
- 10,000–20,000
- 5,000–10,000
- 2,500–5,000
- 1,000–2,500
- below 1,000

Source: U.S. Department of Commerce, *County Business Patterns, 1972*, and various supplemental sources.

East of Charlotte an almost continuous string of counties along the South Carolina border to Wilmington showed increases. Cumberland more than doubled its industrial employment while Robeson's jumped almost fivefold. Only the counties in the backyard of Wilmington seem to be relatively unattractive to manufacturers.

To the north the spectacular increases in Wake County continued eastward into a cluster of Coastal Plain counties. Duplin, Edgecombe, Johnston, Lenoir, Martin, Nash, and Wilson counties each more than doubled their employment during the period, while Pitt nearly quadrupled its industrial base.

Otherwise, gains occurred generally but at very modest levels, especially in the northeastern corner of the state where four counties had fewer employees in manufacturing in 1972 than they did in 1956.

As revealing as Figure 11.2 is, the data on changes in the number of jobs tend to emphasize the large industrial counties and to obscure high growth rates in small counties. Figure 11.3 attempts to rectify this by showing the net changes in each county's proportion of the state total. Those that are portrayed as having slow growth gained at a rate less than the state average and their share of the total decreased. The average group paralleled the state rate, while the above average and fast groups managed to increase their share of the total. As the employment base becomes large it also becomes difficult to sustain high growth rates as opposed to large absolute gains. Of the four largest manufacturing counties only Mecklenburg was able to meet the state increase rate. Gaston and Guilford slipped back in their proportions despite strong absolute increases and the slight increase reported by Forsyth caused it to slip from 7.1 to 4.8 percent of the state total.

The growth rates shown in Figure 11.3 bring out even more strongly the apparent sluggishness of the northern Piedmont industrial counties and the vigorous growth in the southern Piedmont, especially in Burke, Catawba, and Lincoln counties. Catawba increased its share from 3.9 to 4.6 percent of the state's total and moved into fifth place among the state's industrial counties. However, the poorest relative performance was also in the southern Piedmont, where Cabarrus County dropped from 4.9 to only 3.5 percent of the state.

203

In the Mountains, outside of Buncombe County, rapid growth was confined to the extreme west and was even more pronounced in the northwest corner of the state. Watauga County seems to be the center of significant growth in the northwestern mountains.

In the Coastal Plain the dramatic growth revealed by Figure 11.2 is even more striking in Figure 11.3. With a few exceptions the northeastern counties still tended to lag behind, but otherwise rapid increases were the rule. Almost every county at least met the state average and most exceeded it.

INDIVIDUAL INDUSTRY PATTERNS

With so much change occurring in both the composition of manufacturing in North Carolina and its distribution throughout the state, it is useful to examine the changes that have occurred within the component industry groups (Figure 11.4).

Textiles

The backbone of manufacturing in North Carolina has long been the textile industry. It was among the first major industries to develop in the state and the state's economy is still very much tied to it. It has had such a strong effect on development patterns in North Carolina that it is useful to review briefly its history.

There were a few cotton textile mills operating in the state as early as 1813 but most production was for strictly local consumption until about 1880. That year marked the beginning of the "Cotton Mill Campaign" in which the central notion was that the economic salvation of the war-ravaged South lay with converting the staple into cloth rather than depending on the exportation of the raw material.

Community after community, most very small, began campaigns to finance a mill in the town. Local capital and local leadership were typical. Northern machinery makers would sell the necessary machinery for stock while commission houses advanced operating capital against the anticipated output of the mills. Originally intended to provide jobs for surplus labor, the mills eventually had to reach out into the Mountain region for workers. The mills found it necessary to provide housing and other facilities for their employees, giving rise to the company town. Growth continued steadily into the twentieth century until the South surpassed New England to become the leading textile-producing region in the United States. During this century the family-owned company tended to be replaced by multiplant corporations, such as North Carolina-based Burlington Industries, the largest textile concern in the nation.

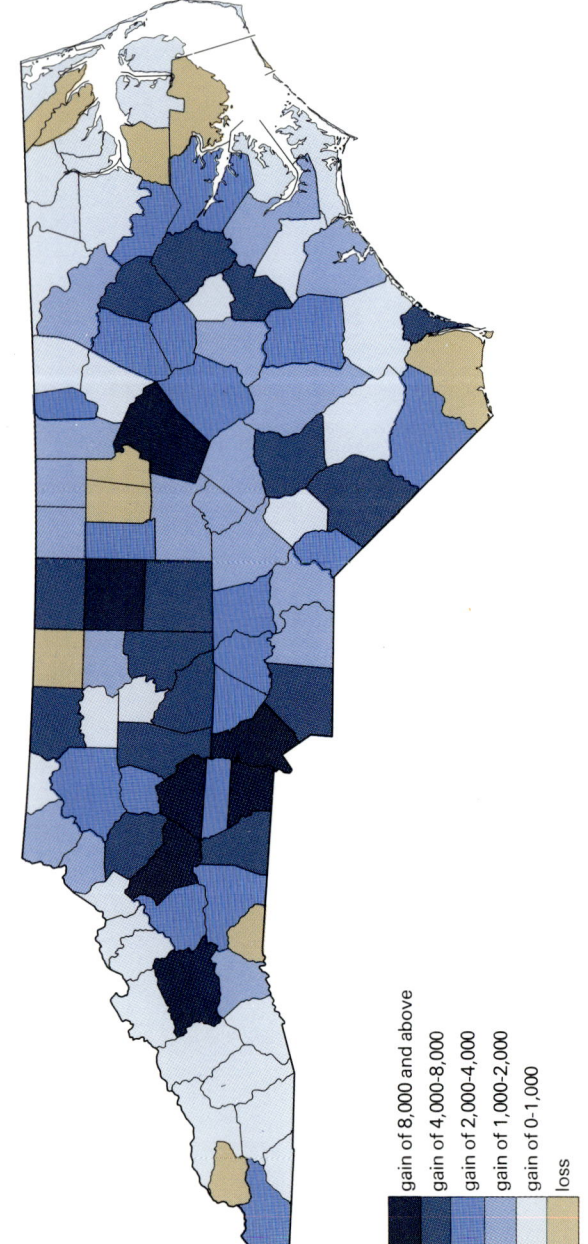

Figure 11.2. Change in Total Number of Manufacturing Employees in N.C., 1956-1972

gain of 8,000 and above
gain of 4,000-8,000
gain of 2,000-4,000
gain of 1,000-2,000
gain of 0-1,000
loss

Source: U.S. Department of Commerce, *County Business Patterns*, 1956 and 1972, and various supplemental sources.

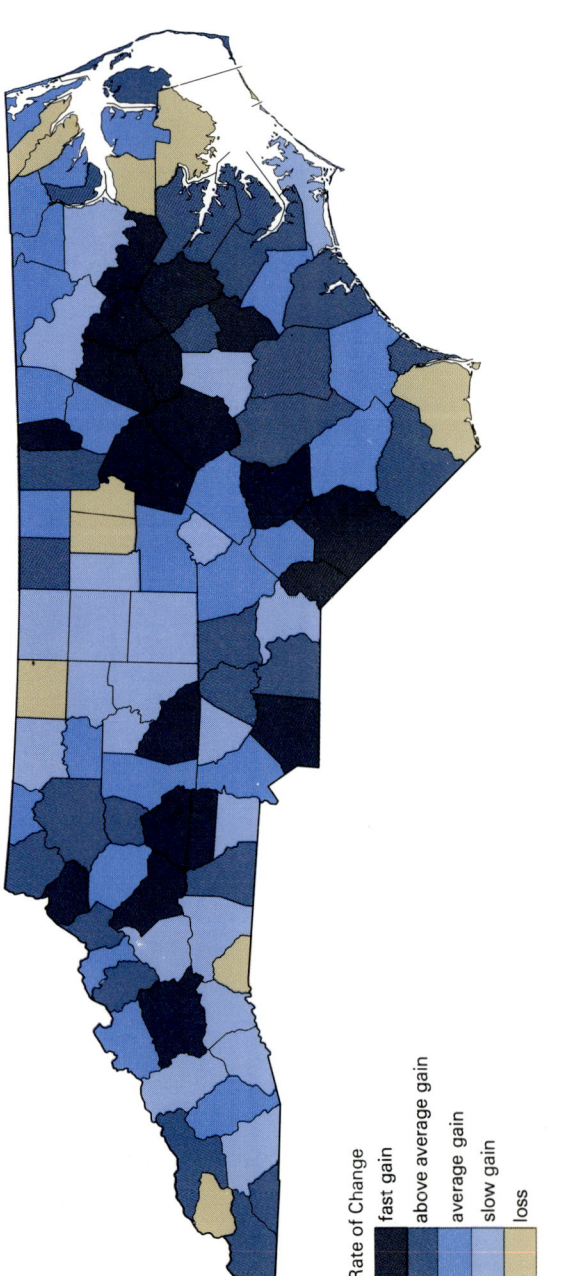

Figure 11.3. Relative Change in Manufacturing Employment in N.C., 1956-1972

Rate of Change
fast gain
above average gain
average gain
slow gain
loss

Source: U.S. Department of Commerce, *County Business Patterns*, 1956 and 1972, and various supplemental sources.

While favorable labor-supply conditions helped textile production grow throughout the South, the industry concentrated heavily in the Piedmont areas, and North Carolina emerged as the ranking southern state. The concentration in the Piedmont (Figure 11.4) has been attributed to the settlement there of more mechanically minded people, the early development of a middle-class population group, more towns, water power provided by rapidly flowing Piedmont streams, and the completion in 1870 of a rail line that connected the Piedmont with northern markets.

The practice of building a mill in virtually every town in the Piedmont tended to stabilize population in and around the towns, in contrast to the tendency in other industrializing areas for rural populations to empty into a few large cities. The dispersion of industry led to the dispersed population and relative lack of large cities that is such a striking characteristic of the region today.

In the early days the North Carolina mills produced mostly rough-quality cotton cloth. Since then the industry has broadened to include woolen and synthetic fibers and a great variety of product types and qualities. Table 11.2 summarizes the current diversity of the state's textile industry.

There is a modest degree of geographic specialization in the component industries of textiles. The Piedmont metropolitan counties tend to concentrate on knitting mills, despite the fact that they are the lowest-wage component of the textile industry. Knitting mills are small and staffed largely by women, to a greater extent than are other types of textile operations, and in urban areas there exists a substantial pool of female workers who are secondary income providers for the family. Knitting mills are also the leading textile type in Catawba and Burke counties where the heavily male-dominated furniture industry also generates a "by-product" supply of female labor.

Gaston County, the leading textile employer in the state, is specialized in yarn and thread mills and this type of textile production is also common in many of the more rural southern Piedmont counties. The second leading employer of textile workers, Cabarrus County, emphasizes the production of broad woven fabrics, both cotton and synthetic, and knit products.

Figure 11.5 shows that recent growth in textile employment has not been in the heavily industrialized Piedmont counties but more in the previously less industrial Piedmont and, even more markedly, in the Coastal Plain. Many of the Piedmont counties either experienced a decrease in textile employment or had growth at rates below the state average. Among the metropolitan coun-

Table 11.1. Major Manufacturing Industries in N.C.

Industry		Employment 1972	Value Added 1971 (×1,000)	Value Added per Employee 1971	Per Employee Average Annual Earnings 1971	Employment Change, 1956-1972 Total	Percent
20	Food products	35,767	$ 638,600	$17,306	$ 6,084	14,842	71.0
21	Tobacco	22,139	1,264,700	54,513	7,905	2,210	11.1
22	Textiles	275,549	2,769,500	10,373	5,436	46,243	20.2
23	Apparel	73,230	594,100	8,206	4,185	49,284	205.9
24	Wood	26,987	246,300	9,365	4,681	-10,787	-28.5
25	Furniture	71,077	686,100	10,588	5,511	33,423	88.8
26	Paper	16,149	278,400	17,961	8,645	7,178	80.1
27	Printing-publishing	13,138	186,900	11,681	6,238	7,022	114.9
28	Chemicals	27,497	744,900	30,280	8,415	15,486	129.0
30	Rubber and plastics	13,357	197,200	15,287	6,104	11,375	574.0
31	Leather	3,344	35,200	11,000	5,094	2,594	345.9
32	Stone, clay, glass	13,276	206,900	16,291	6,850	5,908	80.2
33	Primary metals	6,064	121,700	20,983	7,690	5,234	630.6
34	Fabricated metals	15,567	484,100	29,699	7,724	9,233	145.8
35	Nonelectrical machinery	28,393	432,400	16,657	8,437	20,044	240.1
36	Electrical equipment	35,998	629,500	18,735	7,095	18,084	101.0
37	Transportation equipment	11,737	116,400	13,379	6,402	6,126	109.2
38	Instruments	5,333	107,700	20,712	7,096	3,039	132.5
	Administrative-auxiliary	25,499			11,075	20,617	422.3
	Others	7,965	83,600	15,333	5,729	6,385	404.2
	N.C.	727,349	9,824,200	14,055	6,105	272,498	59.9
	U.S.		314,138,000	17,107	8,506		

Sources: *Annual Survey of Manufacturers*, 1971, N.C. Employment Security Commission, U.S. Department of Commerce, *County Business Patterns*, 1972, and various supplemental sources.

Note: Numbers before the industry name are those of the Standard Industrial Classification (SIC) that is used in major statistical sources.

Table 11.2. N.C. Textile Industry

Industry		Employment 1972	Average Annual Earnings per Employee 1971	Value Added 1971 (×1,000)	1972 Number of Units	1972 Average Number of Employees per Unit
221	Weaving mills, cotton	42,845	$5,522	$ 300,000	93	461
222	Weaving mills, synthetics	40,627	5,957	459,000	93	437
223	Weaving and finishing, wool	2,560	6,192	14,100	14	183
225	Knitting mills	85,249	4,942	939,000	702	121
2251	Women's hosiery	30,405	4,639	289,500	187	163
2252	Hosiery, other	18,366	4,445	159,600	258	71
2256	Knit fabrics	22,538	6,209	385,900	165	137
226	Textile finishing, except wool	16,789	6,214	203,600	86	195
228	Yarn and thread mills	73,761	5,471	671,100	303	243
2281	Yarn, except wool	51,383	5,340	405,200	213	241
2282	Throwing and winding	13,737	5,824	186,600	52	264
	Total	275,549	5,436	2,769,500	1,444	191

Sources: *Annual Survey of Manufactures*, 1971, N.C. Employment Security Commission, U.S. Department of Commerce, *County Business Patterns*, 1972, and various supplemental sources.

Note: Numbers before the industry name are those of the Standard Industrial Classification (SIC) that is used in major statistical sources.

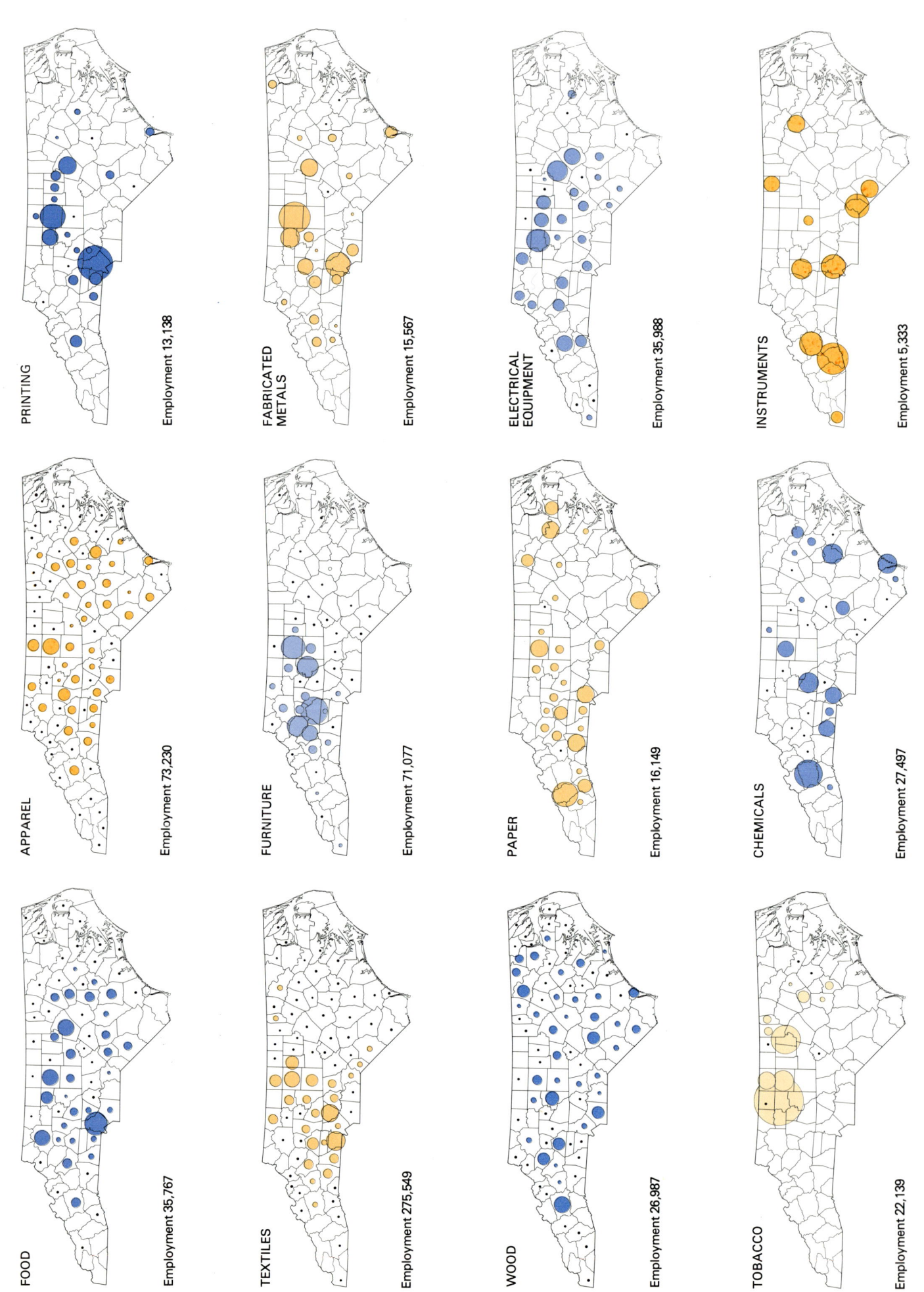

Figure 11.4. Distribution of Manufacturing Employment in N.C. by Industry, 1972

NONELECTRICAL MACHINERY

Employment 28,393

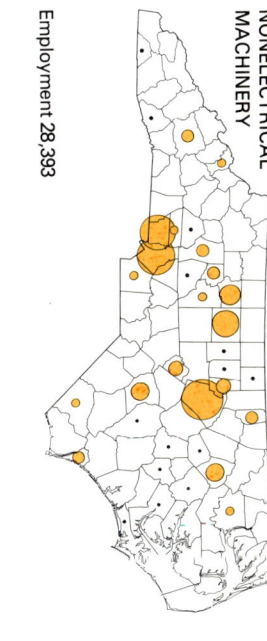

TRANSPORT EQUIPMENT

Employment 11,737

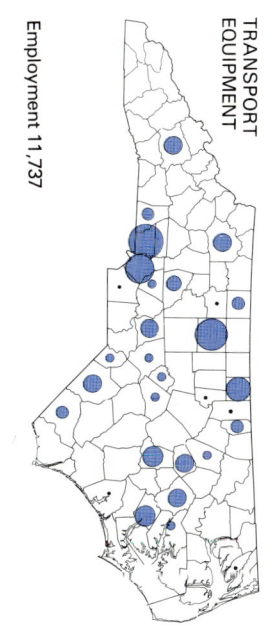

STONE, CLAY, GLASS

Employment 25,499

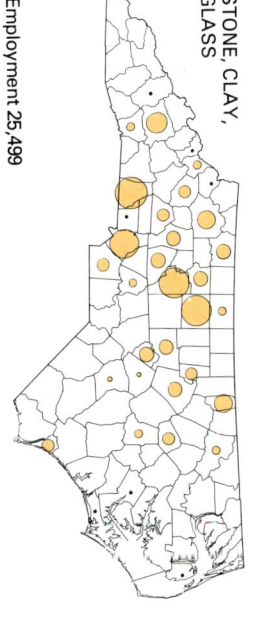

Source: U.S. Department of Commerce, *County Business Patterns,* 1972, and various supplemental sources.

RUBBER, PLASTICS, LEATHER

Employment 16,701

PRIMARY METALS

Employment 6,064

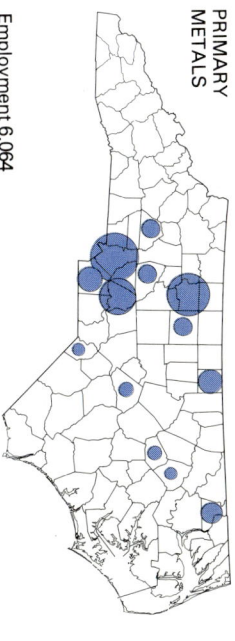

ADMINISTRATIVE-AUXILIARY

Employment 13,276

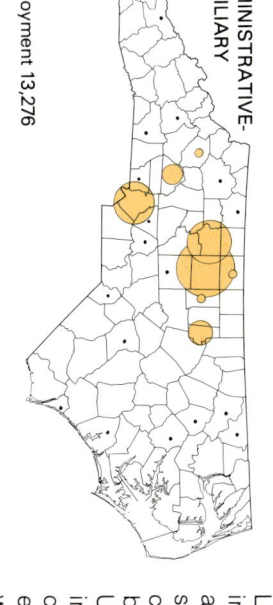

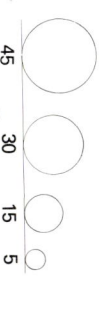

County's Share of State Total Employment in Each Industry

45
30
15
5
Percentage

competitive disadvantage with imports. If tariffs are used to protect the American industry, the consumer will have to bear higher costs for cloth and clothing. If neither is done, the industry will lose its labor to other higher-wage industries that are growing rapidly in the state or it will lose much of its market to foreign competitors. A dramatic increase in the capital intensity of the industry that would substantially increase labor productivity would solve the problem but this would require a major research effort by the industry.

Whatever the outcome may be, it is of vital significance to North Carolina. There is an ominous analogy with the Lancashire district of England, the world's first great industrial area. Its spectacular growth in the eighteenth and nineteenth centuries was followed by an equally spectacular decline after World War I. Hundreds of mills closed, thousands of jobs vanished, and the area became a major economically depressed region in the United Kingdom. Only strong and direct government intervention has begun to bring the area out of this catastrophe. In a thorough study of the region's economic history, Lars Sandberg concluded that decline was due not to poor management but to the decline of export markets. There was some slowness in adopting new technology but the main problem was the rise of more efficient foreign competition. He concluded by saying that "it might be claimed that the story of Lancashire's decline has a lesson for all industrialized countries. That is, as industrialization spreads, the more advanced countries will tend to lose their comparative advantage in those industries that can be operated efficiently with a relatively unskilled work force using relatively little capital equipment. Thus, if free competition is maintained, the advanced countries will have to shift out of such industries."[*]

The more orderly transition of New England's reduction of its specialization in textiles suggests that since the American industry is less dependent on exports a Lancashire-type catastrophe is not in store for North Carolina. Nonetheless, it seems inevitable that a major readjustment is in prospect for the state's economy and that diversification of the industrial base should be a matter of crucial concern for all those interested in the future of the state.

Apparel

The manufacture of clothing from the products of the textile mill suggests an obvious relationship with the textile industry. However, for a long time the fashion-sensitive nature of the apparel industry kept it highly

ties, only Wake had growth in textiles employment at a rate higher than the state average. Apparently the labor-intensive textile industry is having to move out into less urbanized areas to avoid competition for labor with higher wage-paying employers in the larger cities. Textile employment is still heavy in the Piedmont counties, but most of the workers are employed in related fields such as the manufacturing of textile machinery and chemicals, or in nonmanufacturing activities such as banking, wholesaling, research, and administration.

The future of the textile industry is clouded by the severe competition for labor that it faces within the state and the equally severe competition for markets it faces from foreign producers. If the industry increases wages substantially, it will be at an increasingly greater

[*]*Lancashire in Decline* (Columbus: Ohio State University Press, 1974), p. 223.

207

Table 11.3. N.C. Apparel Industry

Industry	Employment 1972	Average Annual Earnings per Employee, 1971	Value Added 1971 (×1,000)	Number of Units 1972	Number of Employees per Unit 1972
232 Men and boys' suits and coats	21,397	$3,859	$140,100	106	202
233 Women's and misses' outwear	14,998	4,076	109,100	118	127
234 Women's and children's undergarments	11,358	4,174	128,000	63	180
236 Children's outwear	8,036	4,049	52,300	48	167
238 Miscellaneous apparel and accessories	3,859	5,086	29,000	22	175
239 Miscellaneous fabricated textile products	11,755	4,603	117,500	124	95
Total	73,230	4,185	594,100	510	144

Source: U.S. Department of Commerce, *County Business Patterns*, 1972, and various supplemental sources.

Note: Numbers before the industry name are those of the Standard Industrial Classification (SIC) that is used in major statistical sources.

Table 11.4. N.C. Furniture Industry

Industry	Employment 1972	Average Annual Earnings per Employee, 1971	Value Added 1971 (×1,000)	Number of Units 1972	Number of Employees per Unit 1972
251 Household furniture	64,911	$5,480	$622,600	518	125
2511 Wood household furniture	36,287	5,308	335,400	170	213
2512 Upholstered household furniture	24,853	5,816	251,200	286	87
252 Office furniture	3,251	5,909	43,300	16	203
Total	71,077	5,511	686,100	612	116

Source: U.S. Department of Commerce, *County Business Patterns*, 1972, and various supplemental sources.

Note: Numbers before the industry name are those of the Standard Industrial Classification (SIC) that is used in major statistical sources.

Table 11.5. N.C. Food Products Manufacturing Industry

Industry	Employment 1972	Average Annual Earnings per Employee, 1971	Value Added 1971 (×1,000)	Number of Units 1972	Number of Employees per Unit 1972
201 Meat products	10,813	$5,119	$118,700	156	69
2015 Poultry dressing	7,165	4,395	68,000	39	184
202 Dairy products	3,772	6,800	64,100	56	67
2026 Fluid milk	3,327	6,806	52,400	40	83
204 Grain mill products	2,174	5,440	61,200	116	18
205 Bakery products	7,667	6,956	133,500	68	113
208 Beverages	5,340	6,755	161,500	109	49
2086 Soft drinks	5,216	6,064	63,700	103	51
Total	35,767	6,084	638,600	672	53

Source: U.S. Department of Commerce, *County Business Patterns*, 1972, and various supplemental sources.

Note: Numbers before the industry name are those of the Standard Industrial Classification (SIC) that is used in major statistical sources.

Table 11.6. N.C. Electrical Equipment Manufacturing Industry

Industry	Employment 1972	Average Annual Earnings per Employee, 1971	Value Added 1971 (×1,000)	Number of Units 1972	Number of Employees per Unit 1972
361 Electrical test and distributing equipment	4,740	$7,154	$80,600	15	316
362 Electrical industrial apparatus	3,777	6,786	42,800	13	291
363 Household appliances	4,493	5,702	81,800	11	408
364 Electrical lighting and wiring equipment	3,845	7,303	66,300	22	175
366 Communications equipment	8,933	—	—	12	744
367 Electronic components	5,399	5,156	54,900	29	186
Total	35,998	7,095	629,500	124	290

Source: U.S. Department of Commerce, *County Business Patterns*, 1972, and various supplemental sources.

Note: Numbers before the industry name are those of the Standard Industrial Classification (SIC) that is used in major statistical sources.

concentrated in New York City. In recent decades it has become possible to separate the production of clothing from its design and sales, at least for mass market lines, and to locate where labor and other costs are lower than in Manhattan's garment district. As North Carolina came within overnight trucking distance of the garment district, the state's surplus of female labor and other attractions triggered a dramatic surge in this low-wage and labor-intensive industry after World War II. As Table 11.1 indicates, apparel manufacturing added more employees than any other industry between 1956 and 1972, causing its share of total manufacturing employment in North Carolina to rise from 5 to 10 percent.

Figure 11.4 shows that there is some degree of concentration of apparel manufacturing in the Piedmont but a large share occurs in other areas, especially in the Coastal Plain. Figure 11.6 demonstrates that the recent expansion of the industry has focused in the Coastal Plain as well as in some of the Mountain counties. Growth also occurred in most of the Piedmont but generally at a rate below the overall rate of expansion for the state. Apparel plants, which in 1970 employed over 83 percent females and paid the lowest wage of any industry in the state, seem to seek primarily surplus female labor in rural areas but also tap the "by-product" female labor market generated by strong employment of males in the cities. Table 11.3 summarizes employment in the various subgroups of the apparel industry. Only higher fashion items such as millinery and fur items are not well represented. The North Carolina apparel mill averaged 144 employees, in marked contrast to those in the Manhattan garment district where the average is closer to 20.

The vigorous growth of the apparel industry in the state has been a mixed blessing. It has provided new jobs for many, particularly in rural areas, and this has perhaps helped stem the flow of migrants from rural to urban regions. On the other hand, it is the lowest-wage major industry in the nation and its expansion has no doubt helped perpetuate North Carolina's low standing in industrial wage levels. Yet it may be just an early stage in the economic development of many formerly agricultural areas, just as textiles laid the basis for further economic sophistication of the Piedmont urban counties. The apparel plants are providing a first taste of industrial employment for many and the creation of an industrially experienced labor force may attract other, higher-wage industries to the same areas. The apparel industry will then be obliged to seek other labor supplies or to increase productivity and thus become more competitive in wages.

Tobacco

Tobacco is the highest-value agricultural commodity produced in North Carolina, the nation's leader in the production of tobacco. The state also dominates the manufacturing of tobacco products, especially of cigarettes. In recent years North Carolina has averaged about one-third of the nation's employment in the manufacture of tobacco products and nearly half of the value added by the industry. About 55 percent of the 583 billion cigarettes produced in the United States in 1970 came from North Carolina plants.

Because of a very high level of automation, the cigarette industry ranks behind only textiles in total value added among the state's industries, even though it ranked ninth in employment. Its very capital-intensive nature is indicated by the incredibly high $54,513 value added per employee in 1971. Steady increases in automation have allowed the industry to rid itself of an earlier low-wage, labor-intensive character.

The tobacco-manufacturing industry is highly concentrated in a few northern Piedmont counties, especially in Forsyth and Durham, and in a few others nearer the tobacco-growing areas (Figure 11.4). Forsyth and Durham are the sites of cigarette factories whereas the plants in the tobacco-growing areas are specialized in tobacco stemming and redrying. The cigarette factories are large, averaging 1,738 employees each in 1972.

The tobacco-manufacturing industry is highly concentrated in a few northern Piedmont counties, especially in Forsyth and Durham, and in a few others nearer the tobacco-growing areas (Figure 11.4). Forsyth and Durham are the sites of cigarette factories whereas the cigarette factories are specialized in the tobacco-growing areas are specialized in tobacco stemming and redrying. The cigarette factories are large, averaging 1,738 employees each in 1972.

While proximity to high-quality production of tobacco—particularly of the bright leaf varieties used in cigarettes—has been significant in the localization of tobacco

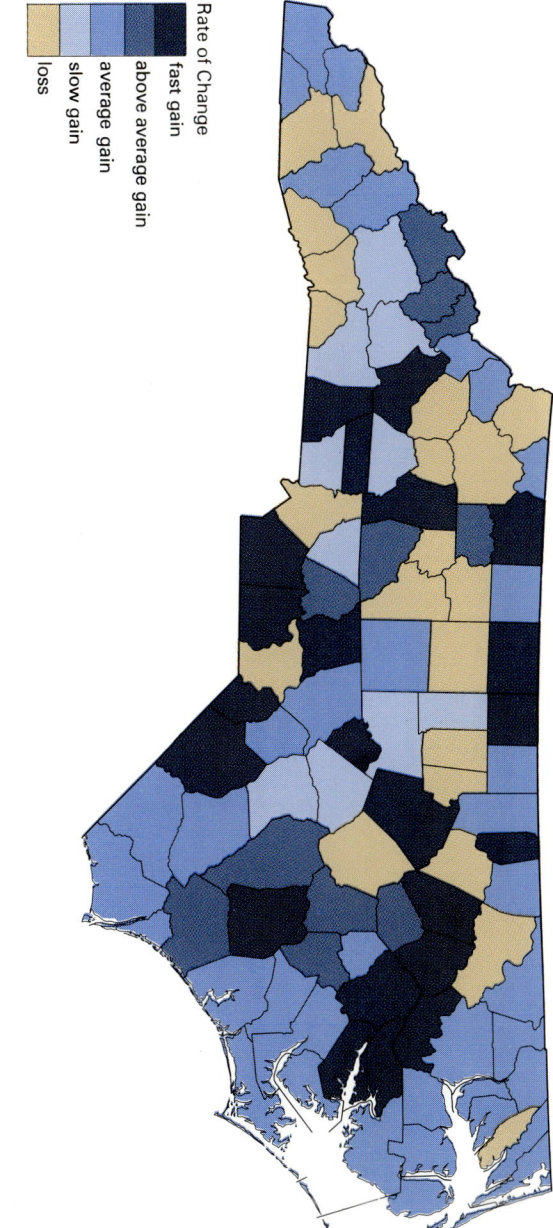

Figure 11.5. Growth in Share of Textiles Employment in N.C., 1956-1972

Rate of Change
- fast gain
- above average gain
- average gain
- slow gain
- loss

Source: U.S. Department of Commerce, *County Business Patterns*, 1956 and 1972, and various supplemental sources.

factories in North Carolina, the emergence of forceful industrialists was probably even more decisive. Men such as J. K. Green, W. T. Blackwell, Washington Duke and sons, and Richard J. Reynolds proved to be imaginative and capable entrepreneurs who created giant corporations that came to dominate the industry. Through production efficiencies and aggressive marketing the "Big Four" of North Carolina tobacco—American Tobacco, Liggett and Myers, P. Lorillard, and R. J. Reynolds—were able to capture great shares of the national market. Steady investment in improved production processes has allowed these companies to continue their leadership. They have now realized the great economies of scale available to cigarette manufacturers and only a collapse in the demand for cigarettes could cause North Carolina to lose its top position in tobacco manufacturing. However, continued automation, which has caused employment to increase far slower than production, is apt to mean that tobacco manufacturing has only limited potential for future employment increases.

Furniture

Another industry in which North Carolina is a national leader and one of several which has traditionally characterized the state's economy is furniture. Like textiles, it is labor intensive and has an earnings level below that of the state average. Unlike textiles, it has undergone strong growth in recent years and is concentrated in a relatively few counties.

Table 11.4 indicates that the North Carolina furniture industry specializes in wood furniture, a large part of which is upholstered. Very little metal furniture is produced. Apparently a good supply of hardwood, proximity to urban markets in the northeast, and a supply of ready labor induced the emergence of the industry in the northern Piedmont during the late nineteenth century. Since then High Point has become the site of one of the nation's top furniture markets for buyers, and with the development there of a number of national brand-name furniture products, it has helped secure the state's position as a furniture producer even though the local supply of virgin hardwood is no longer abundant. The furniture manufacturers also benefit from the existence of a complex of other manufacturers that specialize in supplying the industry with glue, lacquer, paint, foam rubber, spring, plastics, veneers, plywood, wood-turning products, furniture parts, mirrors, and bedding. Proximity to textile products is also an advantage for the makers of upholstered furniture.

209

and the Schlitz brewery in Winston-Salem. The strong urban orientation of the industry in Figure 11.4 is an outgrowth of the orientation to consumer areas. Exceptions to this are the livestock feed producers, canneries, and other processors of perishable foods that tend to locate closer to agricultural areas. The high level of activity in Wilkes County is a reflection of the large broiler production that occurs there.

There is a tendency for the more farm-oriented food processors such as poultry dressers and feed producers to pay substandard wages while the more urban market-oriented producers such as bakers and beverage handlers pay wages above the state average.

The future of the food industry as an employer is clouded by the fact that, while the production of processed food has increased faster than has population, the industry has been subject to considerable technological innovation. Increasing productivity has been achieved nationwide with fewer workers. On the bright side, this increasing productivity has improved the wage quality of the industry.

Lumber and Wood Products

The lumber and wood products industry is the only major industry group in the state to decline in employment between 1956 and 1972. The decline has been concentrated primarily in the sawmills and planing mills category where modernization apparently has resulted in more product with fewer employees. In the category of millwork, plywood, and related products, there has been a sharp increase in employment.

Despite the drop in employment this industry remains a nationally important producer of softwood lumber and of plywood and veneers for furniture making, and a variety of nonfurniture wood products.

The state's forest resources have actually increased over the last several decades, indicating an effective forest management system. It should continue to be a significant industry for the state although its low value added per employee implies that opportunities for further modernization exist and, consequently, employment may continue its decline.

The wood products facilities are widely distributed throughout the state, reflecting a need to be close to the source of the raw material (Figure 11.4). This industry is particularly widespread in the Coastal Plain but it is also important in several Piedmont and Mountain counties.

Paper Products

The paper industry in North Carolina is concentrated primarily into two components: the production of paper

Figure 11.6. Growth in Share of Apparel Employment in N.C., 1956-1972

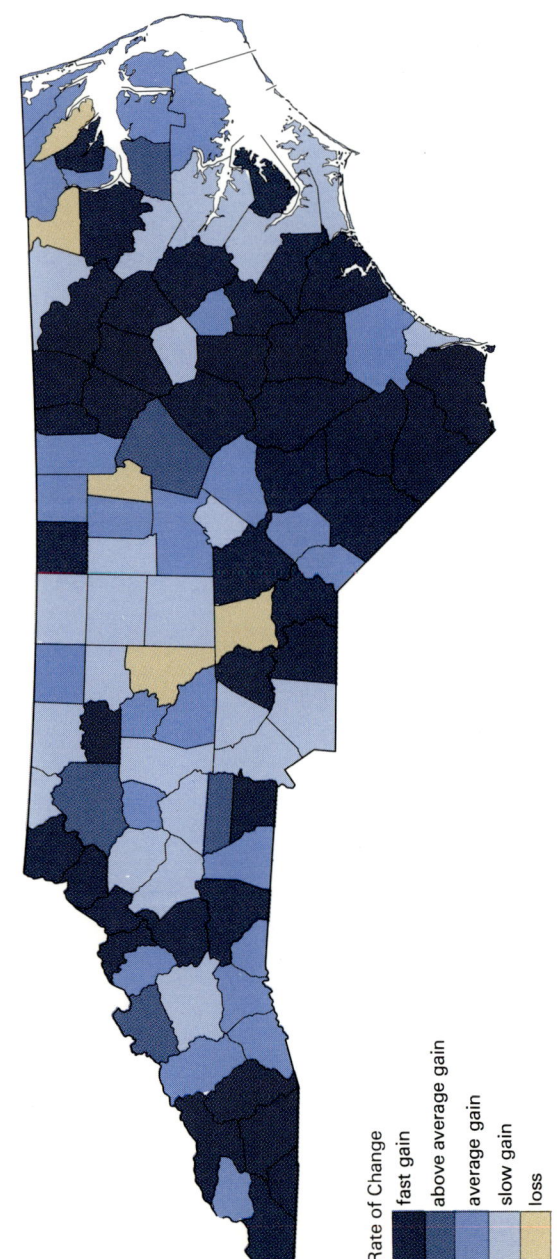

Rate of Change
- fast gain
- above average gain
- average gain
- slow gain
- loss

Source: U.S. Department of Commerce, *County Business Patterns*, 1956 and 1972, and various supplemental sources.

Furniture manufacturing is concentrated in five counties—Guilford, Davidson, Catawba, Burke, and Caldwell. Together they contained nearly two-thirds of the state's 1972 employment in the industry. Growth has been most rapid in Catawba County, especially in Hickory and Newton, and it has now become the top furniture-producing county in North Carolina.

The furniture industry is apt to remain an important one in the state. The high costs of transporting it protects the industry from the foreign competition that has been such a problem for the textile industry and the domestic market should continue to grow. The industry is important also because of its linkages with other industries. Increases in furniture production will create further demands for the products of the supplying industries as well.

Unlike the tobacco industry, both the furniture and textile industries have not been able to automate and thus remain low wage-paying and labor intensive. As shown earlier, recent growth in manufacturing has been greatest in those industries that can pay better wages than do furniture and textiles. This situation poses a long-term threat to the furniture industry which stands to face severe competition for its labor unless it is able to

increase productivity through automation or other means and thus be able to pay substantially higher wages. Recent strong growth in Catawba, Burke, and adjacent counties to the north and west suggest that the industry in the western Piedmont has been able to tap a labor surplus in the nearby Mountain counties. Unlike the state's other large labor-intensive industries, textiles and apparel, the majority (72 percent) of employees in the furniture industry are males, lessening the possibility of finding "by-product" labor supplies within high-wage urban labor markets.

Food Products

As befits a major agricultural state, North Carolina has an important and rapidly growing food industry. While a great many commodities are processed, the industry is dominated by only a few kinds of activities: the dressing and packaging of poultry; the processing and packaging of fluid milk; the preparing of feed for animals; the baking of bread, cookies, and cakes; and the bottling and canning of soft drinks (Table 11.5). Most of this production is oriented to a local consumer market although some of it is also intended for regional markets such as the chicken processors, some potato chip producers, and paperboard and the fabrication of various paper products, especially paperboard containers and boxes. The state's employment in the paper industry is almost evenly divided between these two components.

The paper and paperboard mills tend to be large (with an average of 455 employees), capital intensive ($22,765 value added per employee), and high wage-paying (with an average of $10,000 annual earnings per employee). They are located in the Mountains in Haywood and Transylvania counties, and in both the northeastern and southeastern corners of the Coastal Plain. The paper products plants are smaller (with an average of 73 employees), are less capital intensive (with an average added per employee), pay less high wages ($13,100 value average of $7,692 annual earnings per employee), and are found in and around the Piedmont urban counties, where the market for paper and cardboard containers is strong. This kind of product is often bulky and, in relation to its value, expensive to transport. It, therefore, tends to associate strongly with its market. The paper mills, or the other hand, tend to be near raw materials, water, and large sites in rural areas. They are particularly important because of their high-wage levels which are in marked contrast to the wage levels of the more typical type of manufacturing to be found in rural areas.

Printing and Publishing

The printing and publishing industry is almost exclusively an urban activity (Figure 11.4). Better than 45 percent of total employment in 1972 was in Mecklenburg and Guilford counties alone. It is also a relatively labor-intensive industry but the skills required by it have led to earnings levels that exceed the state average. The units are small, also, averaging only twenty-four employees each. About half of all employment is in newspapers, while much of the rest is in commercial printing and business forms.

Chemicals

One of the most important growth industries in North Carolina involves the production of various chemicals. While total employment is modest, only 3.8 percent of the state's total, it has more than doubled between 1956 and 1972. However, since the chemicals industry is second only to the tobacco industry in value added per employee, it ranks third in the state in value added, with 7.6 percent of the state's total. Because of this great capital intensity, the chemicals industry is one of the highest-wage industries in the state.

The single most important component of the chemicals group is the manufacture of noncellulosic organic fibers, a raw material for the textile industry. Over half of the

industry's employees and value added are in this one sector. It is a highly localized activity, its thirteen plants averaging 1,147 employees each. In this it symbolizes the rapid-growth, high-wage industries of the state in that this growth tends to be in a very few large plants.

The big fiber plants tend to be scattered in small cities, such as the DuPont facility in Kinston, American Enka in Enka, and Fiber Industries plants in Shelby and Salisbury. These four plants almost alone cause their respective counties to rank among the top six employers in chemicals in the state (Figure 11.4).

The remainder of the chemicals industry is divided among a number of product types including industrial chemicals, mainly for the textile industry, pharmaceutical preparations, paints, and agricultural chemicals. Unlike the fiber plants, these chemical producers are characterized by small facilities. Agricultural chemical plants, for example, average only fifty-nine employees apiece. Agricultural chemicals, mainly fertilizers, tend to occupy Coastal Plain locations, near both raw materials and markets, while the metropolitan counties have a wide range of chemicals facilities. Mecklenburg County has one-fifth of all chemical plants in the state but only about 8.0 percent of state employment in chemicals. Included in the products of the county are various industrial chemicals, soaps and cleaners, gum and wood chemicals, adhesives and gelatins, printing ink, and many others.

The chemicals industry is an important component of the North Carolina industrial base in that it has provided a significant number of high-wage jobs away from the major urban centers and because it produces a range of products for other industries, especially for the textiles industry. The evolution of sets of such interdependent activities is one of the best indications that the North Carolina industrial base is moving away from the potentially dangerous specialization of the past.

Rubber, Plastic, and Leather Products

The making of rubber, plastic, and leather products has undergone a dramatic expansion in North Carolina between 1956 and 1972. Some of the growth has come through the addition of single large plants, such as the Kelly-Springfield tire plant at Fayetteville, while another large component has been through the addition or expansion of many relatively small plastics manufacturers who employ an average of seventy-one persons. Rubber and leather footwear and miscellaneous leather products are also among the products made in small plants. Shoe factories have come into mountainous Alleghany, Jackson, Watauga, and Wilkes counties and into Burke, Randolph, and Wayne counties. With average

annual earnings per employee of only $4,815 in 1971 and a value added figure of only $10,481 per employee, this is obviously a labor-intensive industry that has moved into areas of surplus rural labor. In 1970 about 71 percent of all employees in shoe factories were female.

By contrast, the rubber and plastics fabricators are somewhat more urban-oriented (Figure 11.4) and more capital intensive, and they pay higher wages (Table 11.1).

Stone, Clay, and Glass

The structural products industry covers a great range of products made directly from earth materials, including glass, cement, structural clay products, concrete, cut stone, abrasives, and asbestos. For the most part, the structural products are heavy and tend to be produced near the market. As a result much of the industry is found in the Piedmont (Figure 11.4). Various concrete products, especially ready-mixed concrete for construction, represent the largest single component of the industry group in terms of employment (36 percent). Another 17 percent is employed in the making of clay bricks, an industry in which North Carolina leads the nation. In 1971 the state's plants produced over one billion bricks, 13 percent of the national output. Virtually all of this production is located in the Piedmont where fine clays combine with proximity to markets to make it a particularly attractive area for brick making.

Primary and Fabricated Metals

The making of raw metal shapes or their fabrication into basic metal forms tend to be concentrated heavily in the Piedmont (Figure 11.4). Much of the primary metals activity is in ferrous and nonferrous metals foundries that are common to most industrial areas, with a major exception being the Alcoa aluminum refinery in Stanly County.

The fabricated metals industry produces a variety of items, including hardware, machine screws, metal stampings, plating and polishing products, wire, pipe valves, and fittings. However, the largest single component is in structural metal products, such as structural steel, sheet metal work and doors, and sash and trim. Most of this activity is directly related to the construction industry so its concentration in and around the urban Piedmont is to be expected.

Both the primary and fabricated metals industries are notable for high value added per employee and high-wage levels. Notable, too, is that fully two-thirds of the 1972 employees in these industries have been added since 1956, with the highest growth rate being in the primary metals component of the industry (Table 11.1).

The largest concentrations of the industry are in Guilford, Gaston, and Mecklenburg counties, but otherwise it is not a Piedmont-dominated industry (Figure 11.4). The plants are mostly small, averaging eighty-four employees each, and those that are scattered in the Coastal Plain include shipbuilding and repairing facilities on the coast.

Instruments

The instruments industry is rather small but it is significant because of its rapid growth, high capital intensity, and high wages. It includes the making of mechanical measuring devices, surgical and dental equipment and supplies, photographic equipment, and watches and clocks. The plants average 124 employees each and they are rather evenly distributed across the state (Figure 11.4).

Research and Administrative Offices

An important characteristic of an industrially advanced area is the existence of a significant "headquarters function," where major policy decisions are made, research is conducted, new products are designed, and sales efforts are directed. North Carolina suffers what is sometimes referred to as "branch plantitis" in that it tends to receive only the production function, or part of it, for a company that has its headquarters function elsewhere. In such a situation most of the jobs are for production workers rather than for white-collar office workers, engineers, scientists, and managerial personnel, which implies that only the repetitive, low-skill kinds of jobs are developing. Although production workers make up only 70 percent of all manufacturing employees in the nation, in North Carolina the proportion of production workers exceeds 81 percent. Another measure of the prevalence of branch plants in North Carolina is that in 1972, 225 of the nation's 500 largest firms operated 895 manufacturing plants in the state and only 8 of those companies were actually domiciled in the state.

On the other hand, there is one statistic that suggests that the headquarters function is developing rapidly in the state even if branch plants are rather common. A category that federal statistical sources label "administrative and auxiliary" includes separate administrative, research, and similar facilities that are an integral part of manufacturing companies but that do not carry out actual production. In many cases, of course, these operations are housed within the plant and are not counted separately. The administrative and auxiliary category includes only such office and laboratory functions as are conducted in completely separate facilities.

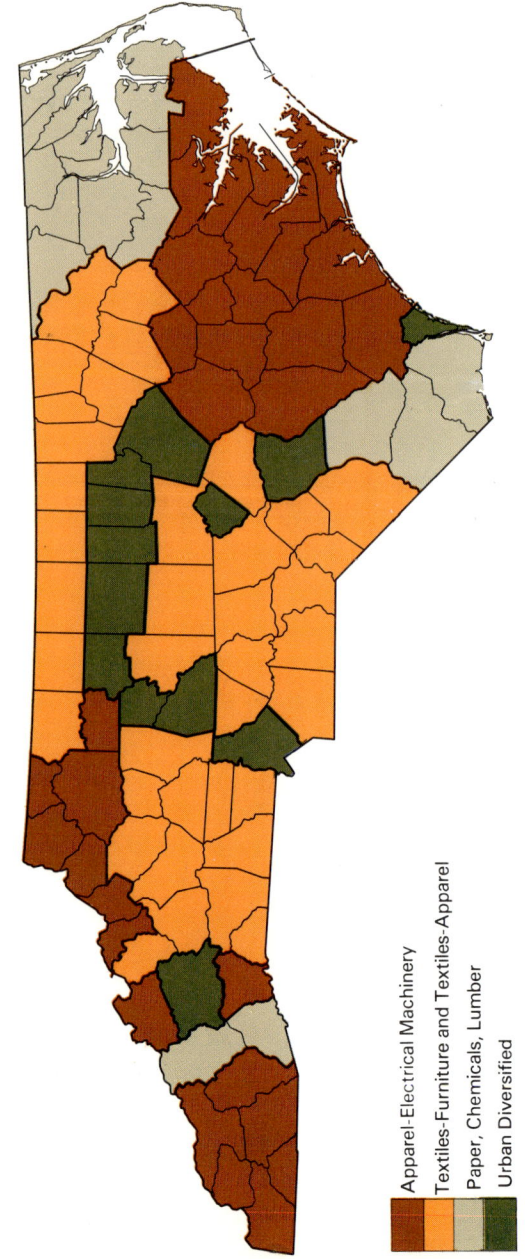

Figure 11.7. N.C. Industrial Regions, 1972

- Apparel-Electrical Machinery
- Textiles-Furniture and Textiles-Apparel
- Paper, Chemicals, Lumber
- Urban Diversified

Nonelectrical Machinery

Another rapid-growth, high-wage, and capital-intensive industry that has emerged principally in the urban Piedmont (Figure 11.4) is the nonelectrical machinery industry. Most of the plants are small, averaging only forty-eight employees and only 9 of the 579 plants have as many as five hundred employees. Major items range from steam turbines for nuclear power plants turned out by Westinghouse in a Charlotte plant to farm machinery, metalworking machinery, general industrial machinery, computing machines, and refrigeration machinery. Largest and perhaps most significant of the subgroups is the special-industry machinery, which employs about one-third of the total number of employees in the industry. Within this category is machinery for textile industries, primarily for the textile industry. The establishment of textile machinery plants in the state by old New England and European firms, as well as the emergence of native factories, is strong evidence of the leadership role of the North Carolina textile industry.

Electrical Equipment

The manufacture of various items of electrical appliances and devices is now the fourth largest employer among North Carolina industries, having doubled its employment between 1956 and 1972. It is a capital-intensive activity and wages are well above the state average.

Probably the most noted factory in this category is the large Western Electric facility near Winston-Salem. The communications equipment component of the industry, which includes Western Electric, uses about one-quarter of the industry's total employment (Table 11.6).

Like most of the rapid-growth, capital-intensive, and high-wage industries, the electrical equipment industry is well represented in the Piedmont (Figure 11.4). However, the greater part of the industry is in a northern tier of Piedmont counties, from Forsyth to Wake and extending eastward into the Coastal Plain in Johnston County. Otherwise, the industry, characterized by generally large plants, is scattered among a number of Mountain, western Piedmont, and Coastal Plain counties.

Transport Equipment

The transport equipment industry is characterized by the manufacture of special purpose vehicles, truck bodies, school buses, and various accessories such as the oil, air, and gasoline filters made by the Wix Corporation in Gaston County. Although it is not an especially capital-intensive industry, its wage levels are above average and its employment more than doubled between 1956 and 1972.

The administrative and auxiliary category grew fivefold in employment in North Carolina between 1956 and 1972. This growth not only signifies a considerable sophistication in the state's industrial system, but the $11,075 paid to the average employee in 1971 was quite a boost to the state's income picture.

In 1967 administrative and auxiliary units constituted 4.3 percent of all manufacturing employment in the United States. The North Carolina proportion in 1972 was 3.5 percent, suggesting that "branch plantitis" may be only slightly worse in North Carolina than it is in most places.

The bulk of employment in the administrative and auxiliary category is associated with three industry groups: textiles (32.8 percent), electrical equipment (23.8 percent), and tobacco (13.0 percent). Nearly 72 percent of this employment is found in only four counties: Guilford, Forsyth, Mecklenburg, and Durham (Figure 11.4). Guilford has major research and administrative offices for communications equipment, furniture, textiles, and tobacco. Forsyth's share of employment is mainly in tobacco, as is Durham's. Mecklenburg's employment is primarily in chemicals and textiles but most of the chemicals category is concerned with the textiles end of the chemicals business.

INDUSTRIAL REGIONS

Manufacturing continues to be a leading element of economic development in North Carolina. If this development is to be guided more effectively in the future, it is essential to recognize the existence of groups of counties that have similar mixtures of industries. It was shown throughout the foregoing discussion that many of the industrial groups did not neatly fit into the traditional Coastal Plain–Piedmont–Mountain regions pattern.

A powerful statistical technique, factor analysis, was used to help identify industrial regions.* Data on employment by each group in every county were analyzed and counties were grouped according to similarities in industrial mix. No matter how small or how large a county was, it was grouped with other counties that had approximately the same proportions of the various industry types. In the final industrial regions each county had an industrial mix that was more like those of others in the same region than that of any in different regions.

The analysis revealed four major industrial regions in North Carolina (Figure 11.7). Further analysis was made of the industry mix of the counties in each region to determine what the characteristic industries were. It is important to emphasize that even though a region might be characterized by a particular industry, that does not necessarily mean that a large part of the industry is found there.

For example, one region is referred to as the *Urban Diversified* region. The counties in it are noted for diversification rather than specialization, yet those thirteen counties contain large shares of most types of manufacturing.

The second region is characterized by employment in *apparel*, with a secondary specialization in *electrical machinery*. A third type is specialization in *textiles*, with secondary specialization in apparel in the Coastal Plain and furniture in the Piedmont. The fourth region is characterized by specialization in *chemicals, paper products,* and *lumber and wood products*.

Figure 11.7 shows that the regions are not all contiguous and even where they are they sometimes cut across traditional areas. The Urban Diversified region traces the core of the Piedmont but the apparel region occurs in both the Mountains and Coastal Plain, as does the chemicals, paper, and lumber and wood types.

Table 11.7 summarizes some of the more salient characteristics of the four regions. The most striking contrast is between the Urban Diversified region and the other three. Unemployment is lower, and incomes, wages, and educational levels are higher. The Urban Diversified region experienced net in-migration of population during the 1960s while the other three had migration losses.

The most heavily industrialized regions are the Urban Diversified region and the one characterized by heavy employment in textiles, especially the latter. However, in terms of educational levels, earnings, and income, the people in the heavily industrialized textiles region do not enjoy a substantially better situation than do those in either of the two more lightly industrialized regions. That this is recognized within the textiles region is indicated by the negative population migration rate, one that was stronger than for the apparel region.

Industrialization alone is not responsible for the characteristics of each region. No doubt the nature of the region has influenced the kind of manufacturing as much as the kind of manufacturing has influenced the character of the region. It does seem that the virtues of diversification are well demonstrated. They imply that future industrial development policy should focus primarily on diversification in the three specialized regions. Continued industrial growth in only a few industries, particularly in textiles and apparel, will tend to be counterproductive to the goal of improving economic opportunity and its related benefits in all parts of the state.

Table 11.7. Selected Characteristics of N.C. Industrial Regions

Characteristic (1970)	I. Urban Diversified	II. Apparel (Electrical Machinery)	III. Textiles (Apparel or Furniture)	IV. Paper, Chemicals–Lumber and Wood
Percent state population	38.4	19.2	35.6	6.8
Percent county employment in manufacturing	28.9	22.8	40.3	20.4
Unemployment rate	3.5	7.0	4.7	6.8
Percent urban	58.8	16.1	25.0	14.3
Number school years completed	11.4	9.7	9.6	9.6
Net migration	3.0	-1.2	-2.6	-4.0
Per capita income	$3,533	$2,495	$2,878	$2,413

Sources: U.S. Department of Commerce, *1970 Census of Population and Housing*, 1970, and N.C. State Employment Security Commission.

SELECTED REFERENCES

Gilman, Glenn. *Human Relations in the Industrial Southeast.* Chapel Hill: University of North Carolina Press, 1956. Reprint. Gloucester, Mass.: Peter Smith, 1966.

Mitchell, Broadus. *The Rise of Cotton Mills in the South.* 1921.

N.C. Division of Commerce and Industry. *North Carolina Industrial Directory.* Raleigh: The Division, 1972.

Stuart, Alfred W. "Manufacturing." In *Metrolina Atlas,* ed. James W. Clay and Douglas M. Orr, Jr., pp. 87–105. Chapel Hill: University of North Carolina Press, 1972.

U.S. Department of Commerce. *County Business Patterns.* Washington, D.C.: The Department, published annually.

U.S. Department of Commerce, Bureau of the Census. *Annual Survey of Manufactures.* Washington, D.C.: The Department, published annually except during those years in which *Census of Manufacturers* is published.

U.S. Department of Commerce, Bureau of the Census. *1967 Census of Manufactures.* Washington, D.C.: The Department, 1967.

---

*To arrive at the grouping of counties suggested in this chapter, factor analysis was used to determine the underlying structure of several variables used to describe manufacturing characteristics of the one hundred counties. Five such structures or factors were found to explain 82 percent of the variation in the original data set. The score patterns for each factor were compared with one another, using a grouping algorithm, and counties that tended to be similar to one another were placed into the groups as indicated in the text.

12. Trade, Finance, and Communications

D. GORDON BENNETT
CHARLES R. HAYES
JOSEPH E. JOHNSON

In this chapter many economic activities are discussed. Retail and wholesale trade, banking, radio, television, newspapers, and telephones seem to have little in common. Yet they all depend upon interpersonal relationships. The consumer has direct contact with the business world and the communications media are important in linking the store with the customer. Partly in order to carry on trade more conveniently people have developed cities and the communications systems to connect them. Transportation is obviously a part of that system but it requires separate treatment in another chapter. The emphasis in this chapter, as in this book, is on the forces of change that are modifying the landscape of North Carolina.

RETAIL TRADE

Trade Centers

Total retail sales in North Carolina approached $14.5 billion in the fiscal year ending in 1972. This represented an increase of 70 percent over the $8.5 billion recorded in 1966. The statewide pattern of gross retail sales is portrayed in Figure 12.1. Predictably, the pattern is dominated by the state's populous urban counties. Mecklenburg and Guilford counties each exceeded $1 billion while Wake and Forsyth were the only other counties to exceed $500 million in gross retail sales in 1972. Seven other of the state's most populous and urban counties recorded levels between $250 and $500 million. The primary concentration of retail sales is in the tier of counties between Winston-Salem and Raleigh, around Charlotte and, to a lesser degree, in the three smaller metropolitan areas, Asheville, Fayetteville, and Wilmington. The eleven leading counties accounted for just over half of all retail sales in North Carolina. However, since these eleven counties also contained 39.2 percent of the state's population in 1970, it is not so surprising that they dominated the retail trade picture (Table 12.1). Also, as retail trade centers become larger, they tend to support stores that carry more specialized goods and services that are not found in smaller trade centers. High-fashion specialty shops and highly specialized medical services are among the attributes of a large city that distinguish it from a smaller place. Since these specialty activities are in addition to the more mundane activities such as supermarkets, barber shops, and service stations that are found almost everywhere in proportion to population, the large trade center tends to have a disproportionately large share of retail activities.

Over time the dominance of large retail centers has tended to increase. As transportation has become easier and more accessible, the village general store, with its low volume, limited selection, and high prices has been bypassed in favor of more distant centers where comparison shopping is made possible by a greater range of stores and where higher volumes of sales and competition produce lower prices. This trend is reflected in Census of Business data which show that while total retail sales increased by one-third between 1963 and 1967, the number of stores increased by only 6 percent. Obviously, the average size of each store increased dramatically. The tendency of large trade centers to increasingly dominate retail sales is further reflected in the relative decline of small towns as shown in the chapter on urbanization. Small towns historically have existed primarily as trade centers for surrounding rural areas and when the trade function diminishes so does the town. Boarded-up or dilapidated stores are a common sight in most small towns in North Carolina and they stand in marked contrast to the glossy new shopping centers of the larger urban areas.

The steady shift of more and more of the state's retailing to large cities is both a cause and a result of the equally steady urbanization of the state. The decline of the rural population caused by the decline of agriculture as an employer has undercut the retail market for small trade centers. Conversely, as the town becomes less competitive with the city as a retail trade center, it becomes less attractive as a place to live and work. Thus retailing is revealed as not just another economic activity but also as a major centralizing force that is part of the basis for urbanization. That is, it is far more convenient to have stores concentrated at a central location than it is to have them scattered over the landscape, and as roads focus on these centers they become highly accessible. Because retail trade is a major urbanizing force, it is instructive to distinguish the retail trade that a community maintains to serve its own population from its role as a trade center for an external area.

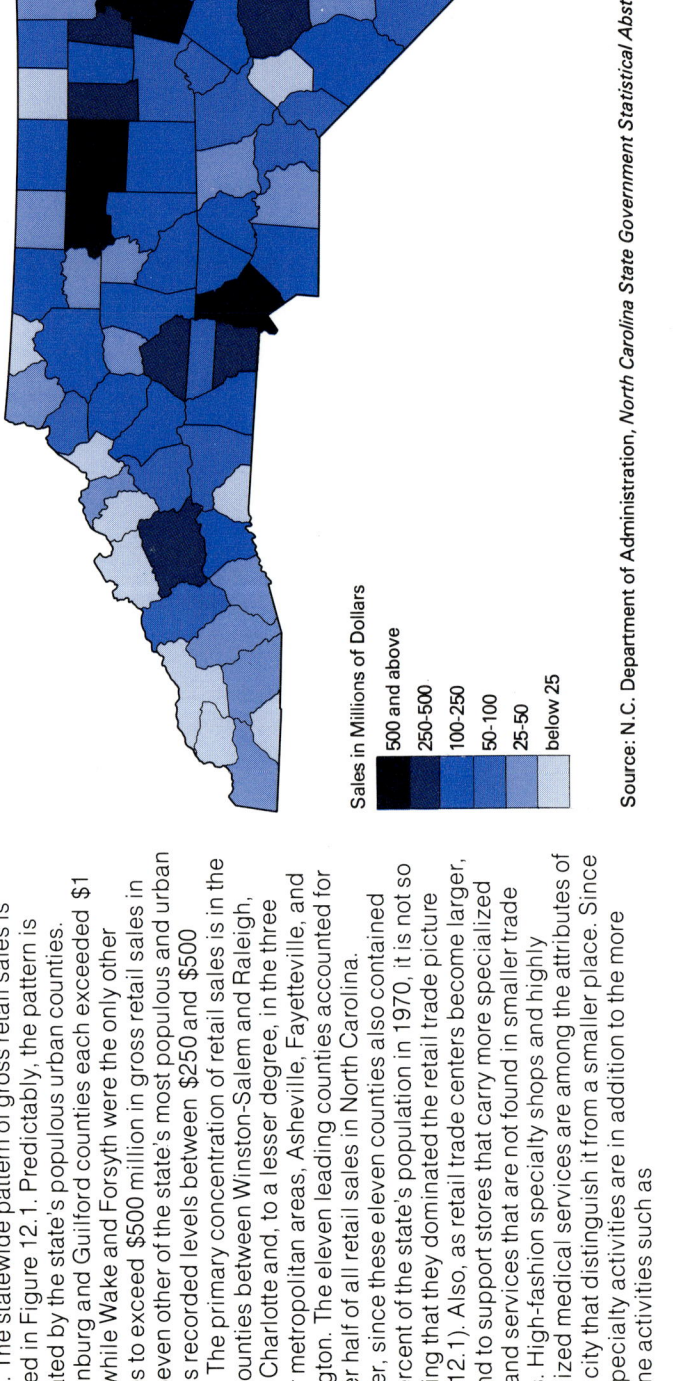

Figure 12.1. Gross Retail Sales in N.C., 1971-1972

Sales in Millions of Dollars
- 500 and above
- 250-500
- 100-250
- 50-100
- 25-50
- below 25

Source: N.C. Department of Administration, *North Carolina State Government Statistical Abstract,* 1972.

The external trade function in North Carolina seems to fall into three categories:

1. The large urban center that, in addition to supplying the day-to-day retail goods and services of its large population, also supplies more specialized goods and services to a broad, sometimes interstate, region.

2. A smaller city that acts as an intermediate trade center for a surrounding, several-county, agricultural area. In North Carolina, tobacco markets, implement dealers, and fertilizer dealers join a significant array of shops and services that serve both the farmers of the area and the population of the town itself.

3. The sparsely to moderately populated county that contains a scenic or recreational attraction. Travelers to these attractions inject a significant amount of money into the local trade system.

The existence of these three types of trade functions is revealed more clearly by displaying gross retail sales on a per capita, rather than on a total basis (Figure 12.2). The high status of Mecklenburg, Guilford, and Wake counties is reaffirmed, but the other northern Piedmont counties, most notably Forsyth County, drop back a bit. The other populous urban counties maintain a high ranking except for Cumberland County. These exceptions are examined below, but basically, the large urban counties seem to fit the first type of trade center. The most interesting result of the per capita map is the appearance of sparsely populated Dare County as a top retailing area. In fact, this county had the fourth highest per capita level of retail sales among all North Carolina counties (Table 12.2). It is an example of the recreation-type trade center. Nash County also shows a per capita ranking as a retail trade center that exceeds its ranking in total sales. It presumably illustrates the type of county that has a small city (Rocky Mount) that has emerged as a major trade center for a surrounding rural population.

Table 12.1. Leading N.C. Counties in Gross Retail Sales, 1970

County	Gross Retail Sales (×1,000)	Per Capita	Population	Per Capita Income
Mecklenburg	$ 1,435,075	$4,046	354,656	$3,323
Guilford	990,056	3,430	288,590	3,185
Wake	774,446	3,390	228,453	3,007
Forsyth	603,464	2,815	214,348	3,109
Buncombe	384,907	2,654	145,056	2,671
Cumberland	376,353	1,774	212,042	2,340
Durham	311,220	2,345	132,681	2,900
Gaston	306,106	2,062	148,415	2,748
Catawba	266,709	2,935	90,873	2,910
New Hanover	246,721	2,973	82,996	2,761
Alamance	219,311	2,349	93,362	2,936
N.C.	11,731,451	2,308	5,082,059	2,492

Source: N.C. Department of Administration, *North Carolina State Government Statistical Abstract*, 1973.

Note: Retail sales levels for 1970 are used in this table to allow computation of per capita values with 1970 population data. Retail sales for 1972 are shown in Figure 12.1.

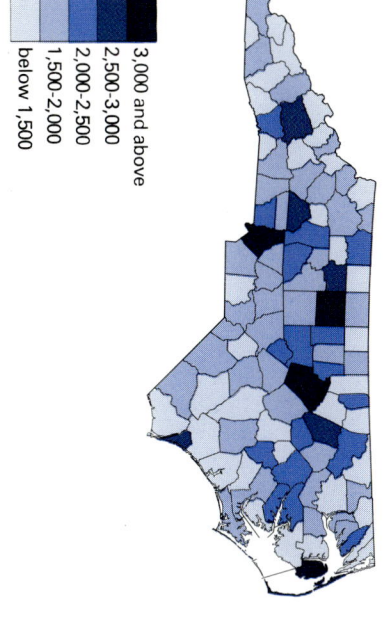

Figure 12.2. Gross Retail Sales per Capita in N.C., 1970

- 3,000 and above
- 2,500–3,000
- 2,000–2,500
- 1,500–2,000
- below 1,500

Source: N.C. Department of Administration, *North Carolina State Government Statistical Abstract*, 1970, and U.S. Department of Commerce, *1970 Census of Population and Housing*, 1970.

Table 12.2. Leading N.C. Counties in Per Capita Retail Sales, 1970

County	Per Capita Retail Sales	Population
Mecklenburg	$4,046	354,656
Guilford	3,430	288,590
Wake	3,390	228,453
Dare	3,358	6,995
New Hanover	2,973	82,996
Catawba	2,935	90,873
Forsyth	2,815	214,348
Buncombe	2,654	145,056
Nash	2,607	59,122
Lee	2,490	30,467
Lenoir	2,422	55,204
Durham	2,346	132,681
N.C. average	2,308	

Source: N.C. Department of Administration, *North Carolina State Government Statistical Abstract*, 1973.

Figure 12.3. Per Capita Surplus or Deficit Retail Sales in N.C., 1970

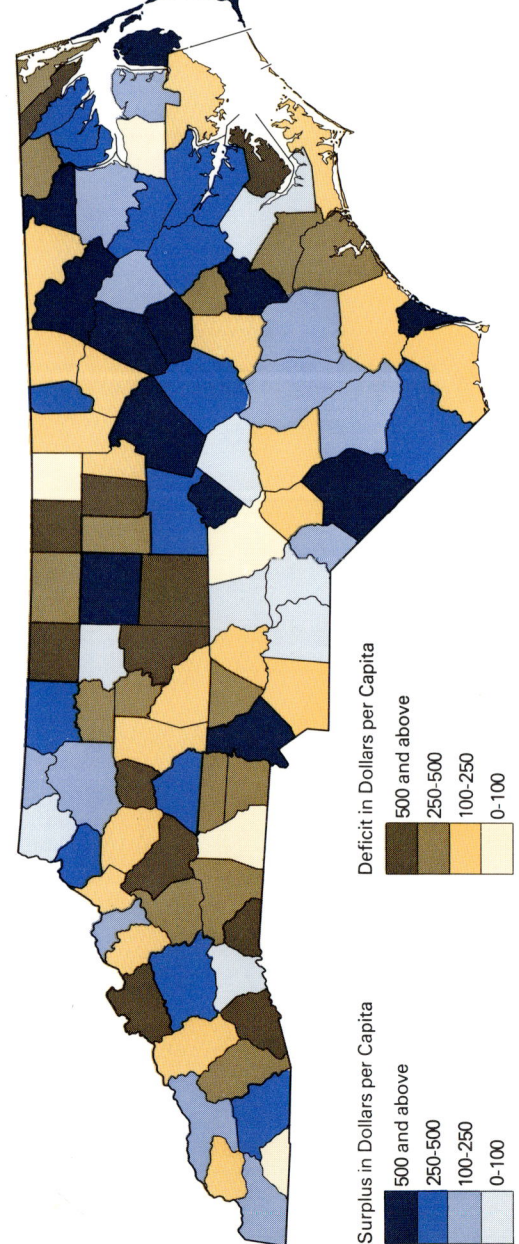

Surplus in Dollars per Capita
- 500 and above
- 250-500
- 100-250
- 0-100

Deficit in Dollars per Capita
- 500 and above
- 250-500
- 100-250
- 0-100

Source: U.S. Department of Commerce, *1970 Census of Population and Housing*, 1970, and N.C. Department of Administration, *North Carolina State Government Statistical Abstract*, 1970.

Figure 12.4. Per Capita Expenditures by Travelers in N.C., 1972

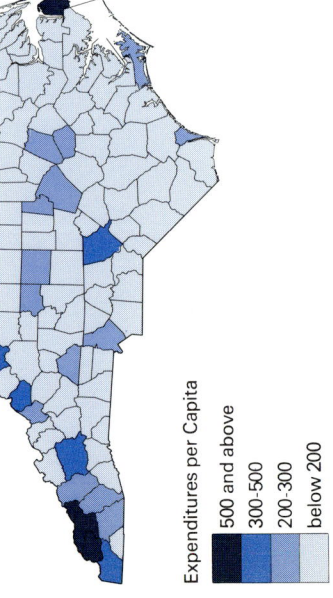

Expenditures per Capita
- 500 and above
- 300-500
- 200-300
- below 200

Source: N.C. Department of Administration, *North Carolina State Government Statistical Abstract*, 1972.

A factor, other than population, that caused the major urban counties to dominate the statewide pattern of total retail sales is the relatively high income levels of urban residents. Forsyth, Guilford, Mecklenburg, and Wake were the only North Carolina counties to report per capita incomes of at least $3,000 in the 1970 Census of Population, for example. It is reasonably accurate to assume that the amount of retail sales that occur solely to serve the needs of the resident population of a place is determined primarily by the two factors of population and income. Based on this assumption, a statistical routine was applied to income data for North Carolina counties.* The result was an estimation of per capita retail sales by the residents of each county. When compared with the actual level of sales as estimated surplus or deficit results. A surplus would indicate that actual sales exceeded those necessary to supply the resident population. That is, a proportion of net sales is made to nonresidents of the county. Therefore, the magnitude of the surplus gives an approximation of the extent to which the county draws sales from outside populations. On the other hand, some counties show a deficit, indicating a net flow of shopping dollars out of the county. The greater the deficit the weaker is the retail attraction of the county. These patterns are shown in Figure 12.3.

Among the main metropolitan counties, Guilford, Mecklenburg, New Hanover, and Wake still appear to be strong retail centers. Buncombe shows somewhat less strength and Forsyth is barely on the surplus side. Durham and Cumberland counties actually show deficits. Apparently Wake County draws a significant amount of business away from adjacent Durham County, and a large volume of sales takes place at the commissary and post exchange at Fort Bragg in Cumberland County. These sales are not included in the data.

The most surprising result of this analysis is the emergence in the top surplus category of eight counties in or near the Coastal Plain, in addition to metropolitan New Hanover County. All are between 25 and 50 percent urban, except for entirely rural Dare County and Wilson County, which is barely more than 50 percent urban. In 1970 all had populations ranging between 20,000 and 85,000, except for sparsely populated Dare County.

Each of the six most populous of these counties contained a small city, the smallest being Sanford in Lee County (11,716), the largest being Rocky Mount (34,284) in Nash and Edgecombe counties. Interestingly, population growth in the 1960s in these cities was below the state average and in two (Kinston and Sanford) actual decreases occurred. This slow growth or loss is reflected in the population decrease that occurred in most of these counties, and apparently reflects the direct dependency of the town on its immediate region.

Clearly, the six counties with small cities, plus Hertford County with a retail center in Ahoskie, form primary examples of the rural market center type of retail focus. The somewhat more modestly positive per capita surpluses in other counties suggest that the rural service center is also an important feature in the rest of the Coastal Plain and in the eastern edge of the Piedmont. Only along the actual coast and along the Virginia border are deficits the general rule.

In the rest of the Piedmont the powerful attraction of retailing in the large metropolitan counties produces a retail shadow of deficits throughout the remaining counties with the exception of rapidly urbanizing Catawba County. To some degree this drawing power is a tribute to the good accessibility enjoyed by the Piedmont, which makes it feasible for its residents to shop conveniently in Charlotte, Greensboro, Hickory, Raleigh, and Winston-Salem.

*Predictions of per capita retail sales were made through a regression analysis. A least-squares line was fitted to the data by solving the simple regression equation $Y = a + bx$. Differences between actual and predicted sales (residuals) form the basis for estimates of surplus and deficit.

In the Mountain region the pattern found in the Coastal Plain is repeated but at lower levels, reflecting the sparser population of most of the Mountain counties. About half of the Mountain counties had surpluses, while the others, mainly those adjacent either to the Piedmont or to Asheville, showed deficits. The surplus recorded in metropolitan Buncombe County has been noted earlier, reinforcing the view that Asheville is the regional trade center for the western part of the state. However, other counties with a surplus are largely rural with 1970 populations of less than 10,000. Half the Mountain counties with estimated trade surpluses had total populations of less than 20,000 and the most populous barely exceeded 50,000 in 1970. Places such as Mount Airy, Wilkesboro, Boone, Murphy, and Franklin are locally important retail centers, but the areas they serve are too sparsely populated to generate much growth for the towns themselves.

The surpluses shown in the Mountain counties, along with the very high level of surpluses in Dare County, suggest that recreational travel to these areas has an important impact on trade surpluses. Figure 12.4 shows 1970 per capita expenditures by travelers (noncommuters) in the state. This value, which averaged $182 per person, indicates the relative impact of both tourist and cross-county shopping expenditures.

The highest levels of per capita expenditures by travelers are recorded in a number of Mountain counties, in Moore County (Pinehurst–Southern Pines) and, highest of all, in Dare County. These expenditures represent outdoor, recreationally oriented tourist travel. The modest, above-average levels in most of the metropolitan counties probably result from cross-county trips to urban stores and indoor recreational facilities.

In not every case does an above-average expenditure by travelers offset the flow of shopping dollars out of a county. Those counties that had both high per capita travel expenditures (above $300) and per capita retail sales surpluses can lay claim to a relatively strong recreationally oriented trade function. Three areas stand out: (1) the Coastal Plain, centering on Dare County, of which Manteo is the "urban" center, (2) the western Mountain region, centering on Asheville, and (3) the northwestern Mountain region, centering on Blowing Rock and Boone (Table 12.4).

Figure 12.5 maps the total surplus or deficit of retail sales for each county rather than the per capita values shown earlier. The total surplus for the strongest trade centers is given in Table 12.3 and the counties are divided into three orders on the basis of the magnitude of the estimated surplus. Nash County ranks in the first

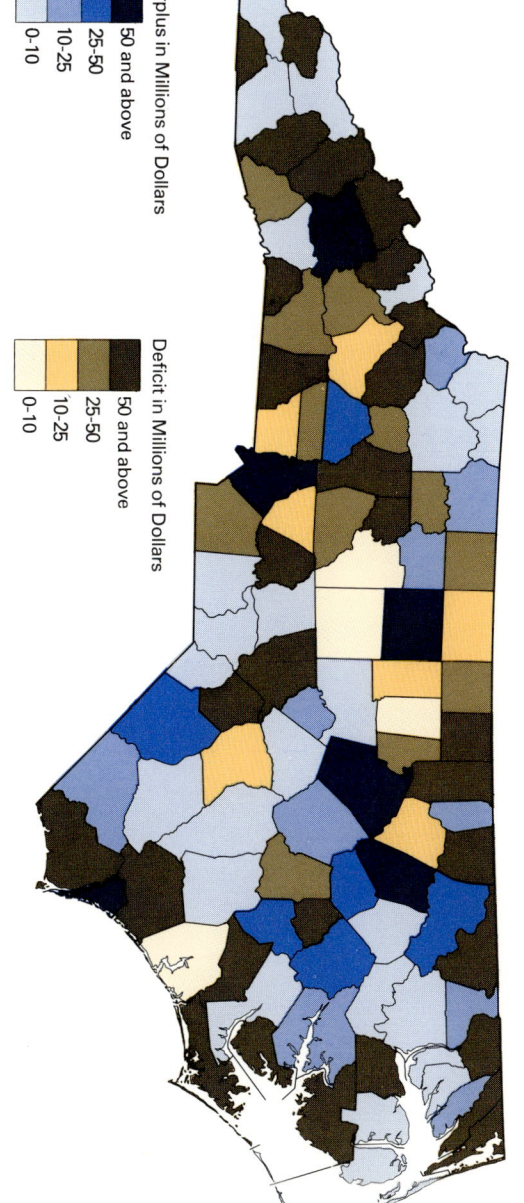

Figure 12.5. Total Surplus and Deficit Retail Sales in N.C., 1970

Surplus in Millions of Dollars
50 and above
25–50
10–25
0–10

Deficit in Millions of Dollars
50 and above
25–50
10–25
0–10

Source: U.S. Department of Commerce, *1970 Census of Population and Housing, 1970*, and N.C. Department of Administration, *North Carolina State Government Statistical Abstract, 1970*.

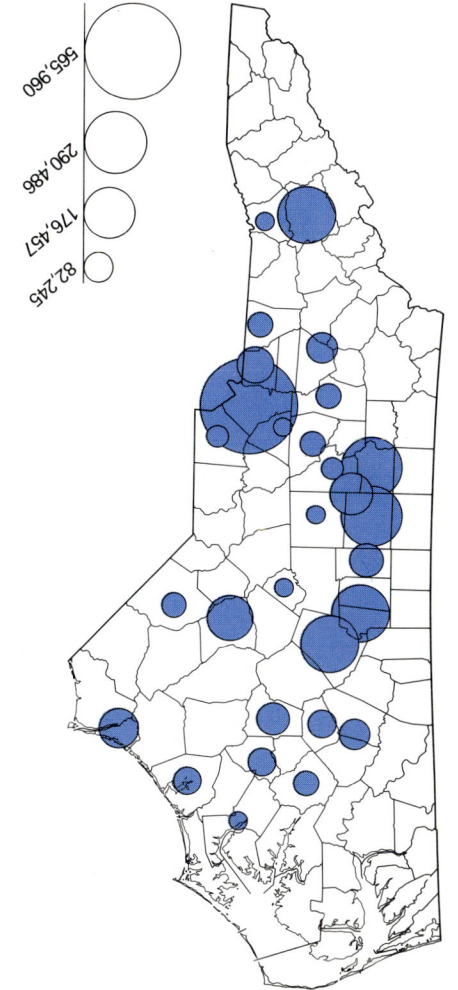

Figure 12.6. Retail Sales by N.C. Cities, 1967

565,960
290,486
176,457
82,245

Source: U.S. Department of Commerce, *1967 Census of Business, 1967*.

217

Table 12.3. Leading N.C. Counties in Estimated Surplus Retail Sales, 1970

County	Gross Retail Sales (×1,000)	Per Capita	Estimated Surplus Retail Sales (×1,000)	Per Capita	Surplus as % of Total Gross Sales
First Order			($50,000+)		
Mecklenburg	$1,435,075	$4,046	385,188	$1,086	26.8
Guilford	990,056	3,430	178,210	618	17.9
Wake	774,446	3,390	175,379	768	22.6
Buncombe	384,907	2,654	56,664	391	14.7
Nash	154,183	2,607	55,371	937	35.9
New Hanover	246,721	2,973	50,917	613	20.6
Second Order			($25,000-49,999)		
Halifax	119,186	2,212	46,912	871	39.3
Robeson	142,936	1,685	44,651	526	31.2
Wilson	132,237	2,300	39,998	696	30.2
Catawba	266,709	2,935	37,831	416	14.1
Pitt	157,086	2,126	34,297	464	21.8
Lenoir	133,679	2,422	31,463	570	23.5
Third Order			($10,000-24,999)		
Johnston	111,627	1,808	18,254	296	16.3
Forsyth	603,464	2,815	17,943	84	2.9
Lee	75,876	2,490	16,637	546	21.9
Beaufort	73,138	2,033	15,774	438	21.5
Vance	69,374	2,122	14,937	457	21.5
Columbus	78,158	1,665	14,437	308	18.4
Surry	110,909	2,157	13,317	259	12.0
Pasquotank	59,567	2,221	13,049	486	21.9
Hertford	43,303	1,840	12,637	537	29.1
Watauga	46,117	1,971	10,710	458	23.2

Source: N.C. Department of Administration, *North Carolina State Government Statistical Abstract*, 1973. Surplus retail sales estimated in a statistical analysis prepared by J. Dennis Lord at The University of North Carolina at Charlotte.

order despite an intermediate level of total sales and Forsyth ranks only in the third order despite a high total level of sales.

Figure 12.6 confirms the idea of a strong city focus for retailing. It portrays the level of retailing in the state's twenty-nine largest cities, rather than counties, for 1967, the latest year for which such information is available.* Although the pattern is not remarkably different from the county level data shown in Figure 12.1, the map is still revealing. For example, it shows that Guilford County's high rank can be ascribed to the presence of both Greensboro and High Point. In fact, Greensboro is apparently no stronger a trade center than is Winston-Salem. On the other hand, the top position of Mecklenburg County is attributable almost entirely to the city of Charlotte.

Trade Areas

As the range and variety of goods increase in a trade center, there is a tendency for people to travel farther in order to shop there. The great reach of Charlotte, for example, is approximated in Figure 12.7. That map shows the distance traveled by 95 percent of the people who shopped in each of the major cities. The size of each retail trade area takes into account not only the drawing power of each center and competition with other centers but also such things as ease of travel and population density. The Coastal Plain cities must have relatively large trade areas since the population is more dispersed around them. Greensboro, however, can still have a large amount of sales within a small area simply because a great many people live in that area. The great size of the Charlotte trade area occurs despite the proximity of a number of other smaller retail centers. This is a valid reflection of Charlotte's drawing power as a high-level retail concentration. The large trade area for Raleigh reflects that city's sophistication as a retail center and also less competition toward the east.

*Comparable data from the 1972 *Census of Business* were not yet available when this book was written.

Figure 12.8 presents an interesting way to generalize about trade areas. In it, counties are grouped in most cases as they fall into the trade area of a core city. This is particularly the case with Charlotte, Raleigh-Durham, Asheville, and Wilmington, along with several smaller centers. In two cases large trade areas are not clearly dominated by a core city. In the Piedmont Dispersed City, Greensboro, Winston-Salem, and other cities have strongly overlapping trade areas. The term "dispersed city" suggests that to some extent the area functions as a single mass, even allowing some specialization to occur at various places in the area. This may explain the smallness of the estimated trade surplus that was shown earlier for Forsyth County. Winston-Salem apparently is more specialized in manufacturing activities for the area, while Greensboro, although an important industrial city, too, has captured a substantial share of the region's trade.

The strongly overlapping trade areas of Rocky Mount, Wilson, Greenville, Goldsboro, and Kinston suggest that their counties together form a Coastal Plain Dispersed City. In this area many residents fall into broad zones of indifference, in which it is just as convenient to go to one city as to another. The very strong surplus shown earlier in Figure 12.5 for Nash County suggests that Rocky Mount is beginning to emerge as this region's dominant trade center and the strong deficit estimated for Wayne County implies that Goldsboro is slipping in its status as a trade center.

Retailing within Cities

The largest single concentration of retail outlets in urban areas traditionally has been in the Central Business District (CBD), the "downtown" of every community. However, this has been changing rapidly and by 1967 only 30 percent of all retail goods sold in each city was sold within the CBD. The rest was sold in scattered individual stores, small clusters of stores, in stores strung along major thoroughfares, or in large planned shopping centers. For many Americans, the CBD as the principal shopping area is no longer relevant in practice, but it persists in many minds. The large planned shopping center has replaced the CBD as the focus of many shopping trips. Like everything else, it seems, retailing has suburbanized throughout the urban area.

Nonetheless, retailing remains as a strongly centralizing activity, benefiting as it does from the advantages of clustering. Even though stores may be more dispersed throughout individual cities, the tendency for stores to concentrate in cities is stronger than ever. The tendency for retailing to concentrate in large cities will continue to reinforce other factors that are leading North Carolina to an increasing level of urbanization.

Table 12.4. N.C. Counties Specializing in Recreational Trade

County	Gross Retail Sales (×1,000)	Per Capita	Estimated Surplus (×1,000)	Per Capita	Surplus as % of Total Gross Sales
Coastal Plain					
Dare	$23,490	$3,358	$8,330	$1,191	35.5
Western Mountain					
Buncombe	384,907	2,654	56,664	391	14.7
Macon	28,611	1,812	6,418	407	22.4
Cherokee	26,640	1,631	3,194	196	12.0
Swain	11,252	1,431	1,091	139	9.7
Northwestern Mountain					
Alleghany	14,360	1,765	1,673	206	11.7
Watauga	46,118	1,971	10,710	458	23.2

Source: N.C. Department of Administration, *North Carolina State Government Statistical Abstract*, 1973. Surplus retail sales estimated in a statistical analysis prepared by J. Dennis Lord at The University of North Carolina at Charlotte.

Note: Specialization in recreational trade is defined for those counties that had 1972 per capita travelers' expenditures in excess of $300 and estimated retail trade surpluses. Many other counties enjoyed a brisk business serving the needs of recreational visitors but they were not as clearly specialized in that activity as were the listed counties.

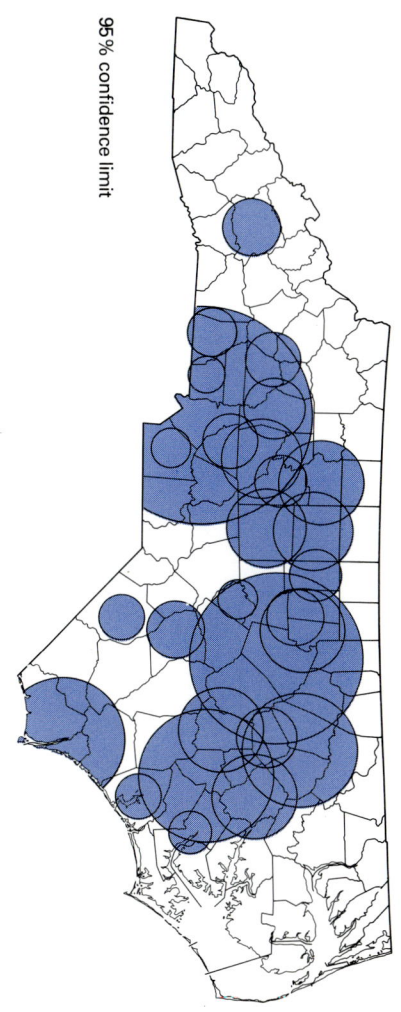

Figure 12.7. Retail Trade Areas of N.C. Cities, 1971

95% confidence limit

Source: N.C. Department of Administration, *Factors of Spatial Interaction*, 1971.

WHOLESALE TRADE

Wholesale trade is only indirectly related to the consumer's purchases of goods. It is generally hidden from the view of the general public even though wholesalers perform the essential service of distributing goods from the producer to the retailer. Without an effective system of wholesaling, the retail sector would be crippled. Even though less visible, the typical wholesale establishment averages ten times the volume of sales of a retailer.

United States Department of Commerce data indicate that in 1972 there were 8,509 wholesale establishments in North Carolina and their sales exceeded $14.3 billion, an increase of 50 percent over 1967. This made North Carolina one of the leading wholesalers in the South, trailing only Texas, Florida, and Georgia.

Wholesale trade focuses even more strongly on urban areas than does retail trade (Figures 12.9 and 12.10). In fact, Mecklenburg, Guilford, and Wake counties accounted for 59 percent of the state's total wholesale trade in 1967. Put another way, seventy-seven counties accounted for only 23 percent of total wholesale sales.

Charlotte is one of the leading wholesale trade centers in the United States, comparable in annual volume to Baltimore, Seattle, Denver, and New Orleans. In 1967 it ranked first in wholesale sales per capita among cities with wholesale volumes of over $1 billion.* Further, Charlotte was the number one wholesale trade area in North Carolina and showed an increase in wholesale activity of 38 percent between 1963 and 1967, slightly higher than the state's rate of increase. The growth in wholesale trade in North Carolina is indicative of the state's expanding economy. During the period from 1958 to 1967 only four states experienced more rapid growth in this category. Employment and income data indicate that a similar growth rate has continued to the present.

*The U.S. Census Bureau's 1967 *Census of Business* was the latest source of detailed information about wholesaling that was available at the time this book was written.

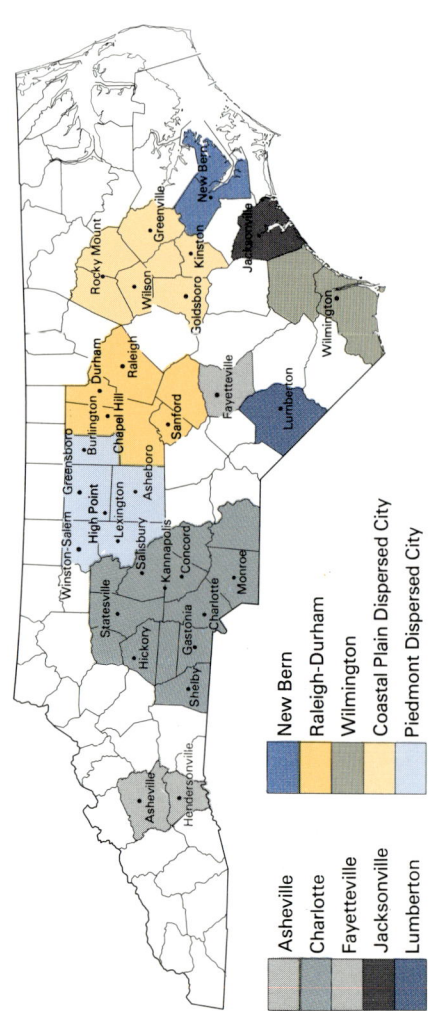

Figure 12.8. Major Trade Centers and Trade Areas in N.C., 1971

Source: N.C. Department of Administration, *Factors of Spatial Interaction*, 1971.

Note: Major trade areas have been adjusted to county boundaries.

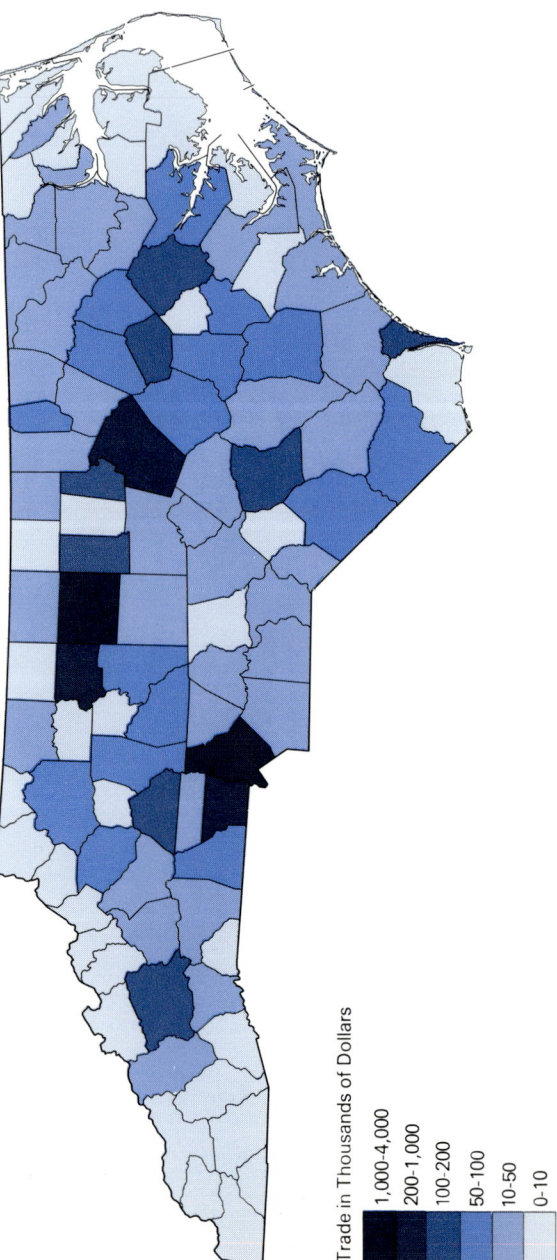

Figure 12.9. Wholesale Trade in N.C. by County in 1967

Source: U.S. Department of Commerce, *1967 Census of Business*, 1967.

Wholesale trade in North Carolina is characterized by a high percentage of national firms. The 1967 Census of Business provides data on the volume of sales by "Merchant Wholesalers" and "Other Operating Types." Merchant Wholesalers are generally considered to be businesses that purchase and resell items. The "Other Operating Types" encompass manufacture representatives, including factory sales forces and branch sales offices.

During 1967 some 4,462 merchant wholesalers had sales of $3.4 billion in North Carolina. Other operating types had sales of $6.1 billion, or 62.2 percent of all wholesale trade in North Carolina. This compares with New York where merchant wholesalers accounted for 47.5 percent and other operating types for 52.5 percent of total wholesale sales. The bulk of wholesale trade in North Carolina is generated by the transfer of newly manufactured goods from within the state, and the movement of goods through the state by way of branch sales offices.

The major flow of wholesale trade is centered in the Charlotte and Greensboro areas, the only North Carolina cities for which information on the composition of wholesale trade is available. Wholesale trade in these two areas is indicative of wholesale business the Charlotte SMSA ranked twenty-fifth in sales among the seventy-seven largest SMSAs in the United States, and the Greensboro SMSA ranked fifty-second.

The Charlotte SMSA ranked sixth among the nation's SMSAs in sales of drugs and chemicals, but twenty-fifth in number of firms, showing that a relatively few firms were doing a disproportionately large volume of business. The Greensboro SMSA ranked forty-ninth in drugs and chemical sales in the United States. In the chemicals and allied products portion, Charlotte ranked third but only eighteenth in the rest of the sector—drugs, proprietaries, and sundries. Greensboro was considerably less important in both areas.

However, in piece goods, notions, and apparel, Greensboro held the leadership role in the state by being the SMSA with the eighth largest volume of sales in the nation, but Charlotte followed closely, holding tenth position. A more detailed breakdown shows that Greensboro was the SMSA with the sixth largest volume of sales in notions and other dry goods, and in the area of woven fabrics it had the eighth largest volume of sales in 1967. In the area of cotton products, Charlotte ranked third nationally in volume of sales in 1967. Other areas of importance were electrical goods (Charlotte, eighteenth; Greensboro, fifty-fifth), machinery equipment and sup-

plies (Charlotte, twenty-sixth; Greensboro, forty-seventh), and furniture (Greensboro, twenty-sixth; Charlotte, thirty-first).

From this list it is apparent that North Carolina's status in wholesaling stems from its industrial specialization in textiles, furniture, and related items rather than from its activity as a distributor of general consumer goods. The great concentration of wholesaling in urban areas indicates that, as is shown elsewhere, even though manufacturing is relatively dispersed in North Carolina, it supports another economic sector that adds to the increasing concentration of activities in large cities.

FINANCE AND INSURANCE

The fields of finance and insurance are vital components of a modern economy. Their growth has been an important factor in the development of North Carolina's economy. Through them the capital necessary for developing the state's economy has been collected and invested.

Banking

Banking in North Carolina is distinguished by its competitive nature and the existence of statewide branching. Many observers have noted recently that banking in North Carolina may be more highly competitive than anywhere else in the country. This type of competition is thought to lead to good service for the consumer whether he is an individual or a large industrial firm.

At the end of 1972 North Carolina listed two banks among the fifty largest banking institutions in the nation. These two institutions were far ahead of other southeastern banks in capital and services. In addition, there were five other North Carolina banks with regional and perhaps national recognition. The significance of having such large banking corporations lies in the fact that they enjoy economies of scale that allow them to assemble highly specialized financial experts in the corporate headquarters. Their high level of sophistication in financial service to clients cannot possibly be matched by the small independent bank even though the small bank may have access to large capital resources through corres-

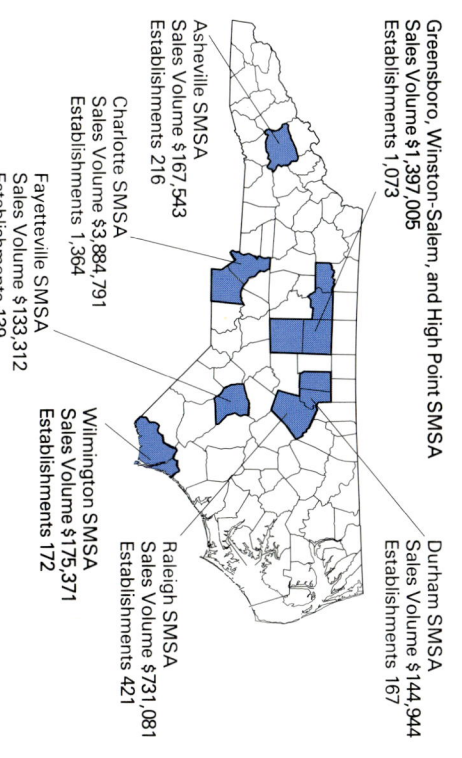

Figure 12.10. North Carolina's Standard Metropolitan Statistical Areas with Sales Volume and Number of Establishments, 1967

Greensboro, Winston-Salem, and High Point SMSA
Sales Volume $1,397,005
Establishments 1,073

Asheville SMSA
Sales Volume $167,543
Establishments 216

Charlotte SMSA
Sales Volume $3,884,791
Establishments 1,364

Fayetteville SMSA
Sales Volume $133,312
Establishments 139

Durham SMSA
Sales Volume $144,944
Establishments 167

Raleigh SMSA
Sales Volume $731,081
Establishments 421

Wilmington SMSA
Sales Volume $175,371
Establishments 172

Source: U.S. Department of Commerce, *1967 Census of Business*, 1967.

221

Figure 12.11. Commercial Bank Deposits in N.C. by County, 1972

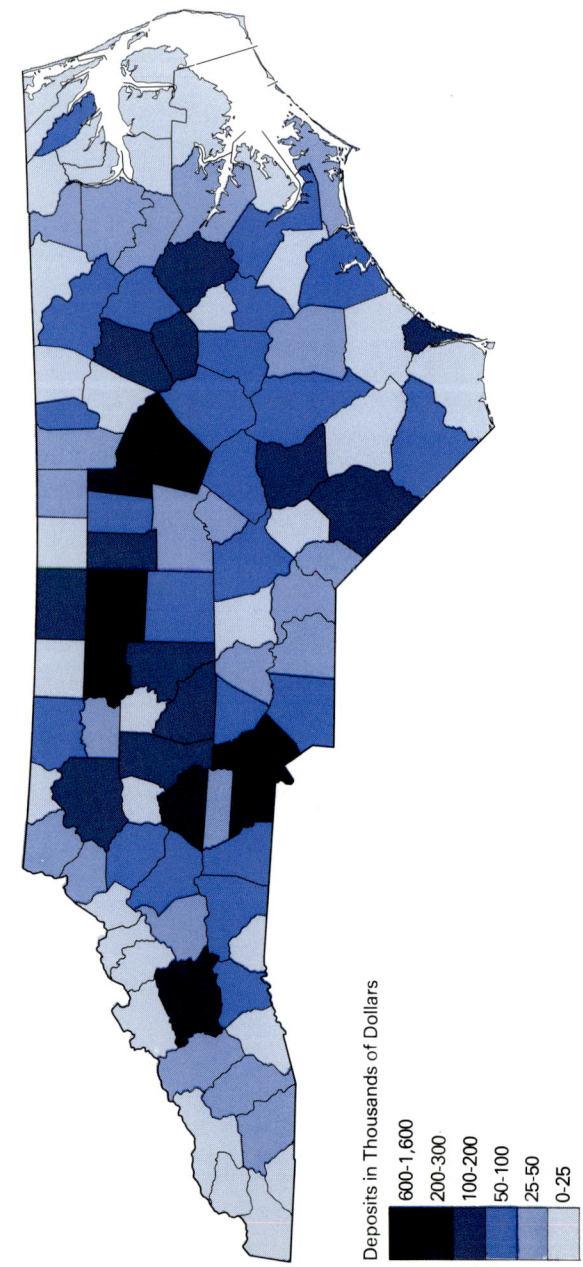

Deposits in Thousands of Dollars

- 600–1,600
- 200–300
- 100–200
- 50–100
- 25–50
- 0–25

Source: N.C. Department of Administration, *North Carolina State Government Statistical Abstract*, 1972.

Banking is another activity that is dominated by the state's metropolitan areas (Figure 12.11). Four counties had deposits of more than $500 million each and together accounted for 40 percent of the state's total. Mecklenburg County recorded deposits of more than $1.5 billion. The leadership of Charlotte is symbolized by the presence there of a branch of the Richmond district office of the Federal Reserve Bank. Charlotte is also headquarters for two of the state's three largest banks, North Carolina National Bank and First Union National Bank, and the Winston-Salem-based Wachovia Bank and Trust Company has a very large office there. Trailing Mecklenburg County as banking leaders are the metropolitan counties of Forsyth, Guilford, and Wake.

Savings and Loan Associations

The second ranking group of financial institutions in North Carolina is the savings and loan associations. These organizations provide North Carolinians with construction and mortgage loans. They have contributed heavily to North Carolina's exceeding the national average in the percentage of families who own their own homes.

At the end of 1972 there were 140 savings and loan associations spread across the state with assets of over $3 billion. Unlike commercial banks, these associations are restricted to operating in their home areas. Most are locally owned and are relatively small in the amount of total assets. This characteristic of local control and local lending to home buyers makes mortgage loans available to most North Carolinians. Many associations have built new branches in recent years to reflect the spread of North Carolina's metropolitan areas.

Insurance Companies

The extent of its operations in insurance makes North Carolina one of the key states in the Union in that service business. In 1971 there were 750 insurance companies operating in the state. Of these, 73 were domestic corporations (companies organized and based in North Carolina), and included 22 life insurers, 20 property-liability insurers, 30 assessment mutuals, and 7 hospital service associations. The various insurers operating in North Carolina owned better than 90 percent of all assets of United States insurers.

pondent relationships with other banks. That is, the advantage of large banks is not necessarily the amount of capital to which they have access but more the quality of the financial service they can provide prospective business clients. An example of this advantage has been the entry of the large North Carolina banks into international finance. Several operating offices now represent North Carolina banks in the Caribbean, Europe, and Asia.

The relative size of banks in the state is due primarily to statewide branching, which allows a single corporate entity to operate with offices in many cities and towns throughout the state. Banks in North Carolina have grown both internally, as a result of the state's economic boom, and externally through merger.

Between 1960 and 1970 the number of insured banking firms in North Carolina decreased from 183 to 97. Most of this decrease is attributable to mergers of small one-city banks into statewide banks. By 1972 there were 92 banks with over 1,100 branches in the state. This ranked North Carolina sixth in the nation in number of bank branches, while it was thirty-fifth in number of banking corporations.

First Union National Bank, North Carolina National Bank, and Wachovia Bank and Trust Company have led the rise of North Carolina banks to prominent positions in national as well as instate banking. During the 1960s North Carolina National Bank was the fastest-growing large bank in the nation, for example.

The total assets of North Carolina banks amounted to nearly $8.5 billion in 1972, reflecting $3.7 billion in demand deposits and $3.5 billion in time deposits, and enabling North Carolina to rank sixteenth among all states. In 1972 total deposits in North Carolina banks were almost $9 billion, including almost $3.3 billion in demand deposits and nearly $4 billion in time deposits.

Insurers operating in North Carolina reported premiums written in the state of $1,581.6 million in 1971, a 13.7 percent increase over 1970. This amount was 2.06 percent of all premiums written in the United States, ranking the state sixteenth among all states.

Insurance, like banking, is a service business that expands or contracts with general economic activity. For the decade 1961 to 1971 insurance in North Carolina kept pace with the economic boom, increasing by 53 percent in premiums written.

These premiums provided protection of all kinds for North Carolina's businesses and citizens. In 1971 the average amount of life insurance in force per family in North Carolina was $19,600 and 3,937,000 North Carolinians had basic hospitalization coverage.

North Carolina has for many years been one of the few states that has required that all motor vehicles be covered by automobile liability insurance. This requirement led to increased premium volume in the property-liability category and the highest percentage in the nation of drivers in the assigned risk pool or involuntary market. It also means that proportionately more North Carolina drivers are covered by liability insurance than are drivers in other states. A new development in automobile insurance in 1973 was the establishment of the first Reinsurance Facility in the United States for automobile liability insurance. This action abolished the assigned risk pool. However, the substandard market for collision and comprehensive coverage on automobiles still flourishes in North Carolina. It is expected that these lines of insurance will be added to the Reinsurance Facility in 1975.

In 1971 the insurance business paid benefits to North Carolinians amounting to $920.5 million. It contributed additional dollars to the state through direct investment and mortgage financing.

COMMUNICATIONS

Television

Figure 12.12 portrays the areas that include 95 percent of the viewers of each city's commercial television stations. While the central part of the state has a high density of coverage, the Mountains and parts of the Coastal Plain have rather poor coverage. The overlapping coverages in the Piedmont probably greatly reduce the advertising pull of those stations except in the immediate area of the station. Adding to the problems of overlapping coverage is the increasing availability of cable television, which gives viewers a choice from stations in a range of cities. In Charlotte, for example, viewers can select stations

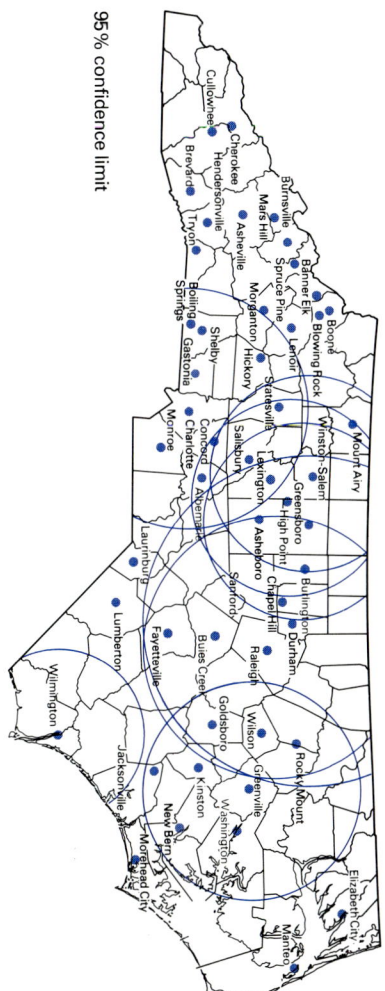

Figure 12.12. Television Service Areas in N.C., 1971

95% confidence limit

Source: N.C. Department of Administration, *Factors of Spatial Interaction*, 1971.

from Greensboro–High Point–Winston-Salem, from Columbia, South Carolina, and from Spartanburg, South Carolina, as well as from six local commercial and educational television channels.

The reception in the state of out-of-state stations and the use of rooftop antennas make it certain that every corner of North Carolina can be reached by television. In addition to commercial stations, the state is served by the multiple unit system of The University of North Carolina's educational network. Additional educational broadcasting is provided in the Charlotte area by a station operated by the Charlotte-Mecklenburg school system.

Although the coverage areas of television stations are not easy to define, it is clear that most North Carolinians watch television. A recent survey in the state indicated that 85 percent of the respondents watched television at least two hours a day. About 12 percent of the same survey group had visited a specific store or shopping center in response to television advertising.

Radio

Radio coverage is more widespread than is television coverage (Figure 12.13). The map shows the areas covered by 95 percent of the listeners of the stations in the state's largest cities. The smaller listening areas suggest that radio stations have a less regional and more local viewer identification. In fact radio service areas correlate closely with trade areas.

Newspapers

Apparently the daily newspaper is the most popular form of public communication in North Carolina. Ninety-seven percent of the people in a survey group indicated that they read a newspaper every day. The advertising appeal of the newspaper is impressive, with 40 percent of the survey group claiming to have shopped in a particular store or shopping center in response to a newspaper advertisement.

The circulation areas of the state's daily newspapers are shown in Figure 12.14. The great reach of the Charlotte and Raleigh dailies probably reflects the influence of the former in business and the latter in state politics. Otherwise, newspaper circulation areas tend to extend only slightly beyond a city's trade area, especially in the case of smaller cities.

Telephone

The telephone has become possibly the most widely used medium of communication aside from face-to-face conversation. In 1972 North Carolinians made 5.6 billion telephone calls, an average of nearly 1,000 calls per person. This approximates the national average. However, since there were only 48.9 telephones per hundred people in the state in 1971, compared with 60.4 in the nation, North Carolinians must make more use of each telephone. It is evident that although North Carolina has fewer telephones than the national average, the gap is being closed. Between 1960 and 1972 the number of telephones in service increased 157 percent in the state while the nation as a whole experienced an increase of 78 percent.

Twenty-four companies offer telephone service in the state but only two, Southern Bell and Carolina Telephone and Telegraph accounted for the great majority of all calls, 54.8 percent and 20.8 percent, respectively. Southern Bell offers service in the state's larger cities and Carolina Telephone and Telegraph operates in the eastern part of the state.

Trade and Communications—D. Gordon Bennett and Charles R. Hayes
Finance—Joseph E. Johnson

SELECTED REFERENCES

Bennett, D. Gordon, and Hayes, Charles R. *Downtown Shopper Characteristics and Media Coverage in North Carolina.* State Planning Report no. 112.08. Raleigh: State Planning Division, N.C. Department of Administration, 1970.
Berry, Brian J. L. *Geography of Market Centers and Retail Distribution.* Englewood Cliffs, N.J.: Prentice-Hall, 1967.
Hayes, Charles R., and Bennett, D. Gordon. *Factors of Spatial Interaction in North Carolina.* State Planning Report no. 64.13. Raleigh: State Planning Task Force, N.C. Department of Administration, 1969.
N.C. Department of Administration. *North Carolina State Government Statistical Abstract.* 2d ed. Raleigh: The Department, 1973.
N.C. Department of Revenue. *Statistics of Taxation.* Raleigh: The Department, 1973.
Sales Management. *1971 Survey of Buying Power.* New York: Sales Management, 1971.
U.S. Department of Commerce, Bureau of the Census. *1967 Census of Business.* Washington, D.C.: The Department, 1967.

Figure 12.13. Radio Service Areas in N.C., 1971

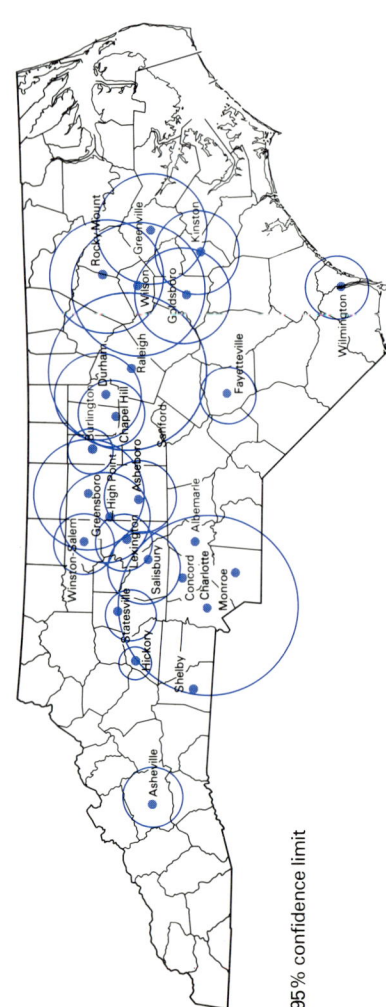

95% confidence limit

Source: N.C. Department of Administration, *Factors of Spatial Interaction*, 1971.

Figure 12.14. Newspaper Service Areas and Trade Areas in N.C., 1971

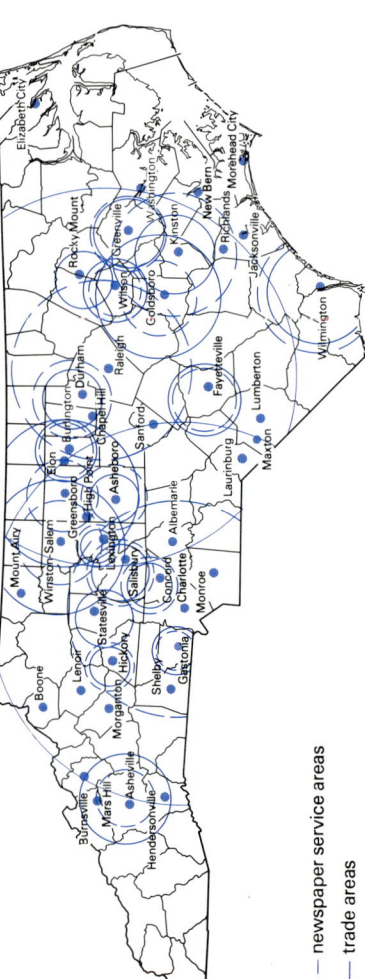

- - - newspaper service areas
——— trade areas

Source: N.C. Department of Administration, *Factors of Spatial Interaction*, 1971.

13. Transportation and Energy Utilities

W. JOHN CAMERON
GEORGE T. LATHROP
C. E. VICK, JR.

TRANSPORTATION

North Carolina has been recognized as a state with a large and generally good transportation system that provides the foundation for the commerce, the recreation, and the other varied activities of its citizens. The land and buildings in which people go about their daily activities and the transportation system are but two sides of a coin that includes all activity in the state.

Historical Development of Transportation

Figure 13.1 illustrates the dramatic changes that have taken place in North Carolina's transportation facilities during the long history of the state. The background of the map illustrates North Carolina's railroad system just prior to the Civil War. Superimposed over the railroad system are three lines that illustrate the distance that could be traveled from the center of the city of Raleigh in one hour. Prior to the advent of the railroad, when overland travel speed was limited to the human walk or to the horse, the one-hour travel distance was only three to five miles from the point of origin. With the railroad, the distance covered in one hour increased to about ten to twelve miles. Given the speed on the interstate highway system, the average distance traveled in an hour has increased to something on the order of fifty-five miles.

Prior to the railroad, the time for a trip from Raleigh to Asheville was sixty hours, assuming no stops, over six, ten-hour days of continuous travel. With rail, nonstop travel became possible, and the time involved decreased to forty-eight hours. The travel time now, by automobile, from Raleigh to Asheville, again assuming no stops, is about four hours.

Today's transportation system in North Carolina is, in many ways, a function of geography and the historical application of new technologies. First, in the waterways and streams of the eastern part of the state, navigation was possible only to the point of the "fall line," commonly thought of as the inland boundary of the Coastal Plain where navigation was forced to stop. It marked the westward limit of settlement along navigable rivers. To the west of the head of navigation, "roads" were often little more than trails—and developed—they were often little more than trails—and in the early part of the nineteenth century some of the longest plank roads in the nation were built to connect rural settlements in North Carolina and to lead to the head of navigable streams.

The first railroads in North Carolina were built to connect the head of navigation with the interior. By the 1850s, railroads centered on ports, but they had begun to penetrate to the larger settlements in the Piedmont area of the state. The coincidence of the original rail lines (Figure 13.1) with the interstate highway system in North Carolina is more than a matter of chance. Along the railroads, the early settlements in the state began to grow into towns and cities, and it was natural, one hundred years later, to define the interstate system along the same corridors of high activity.

Transportation has traditionally been a major factor in determining the pattern of human settlement as it relates to the location of amenities and services that are part of the daily lives of North Carolina citizens. It also provides access to and utilization of the physical resources of the state. The dramatic changes that have occurred in transportation in North Carolina and the nation over the last twenty-five years have permitted an increase in specialization on the part of individuals, greater concentration of industrial, commercial, and service locations, and a complete change in the daily living patterns of the people of this state.

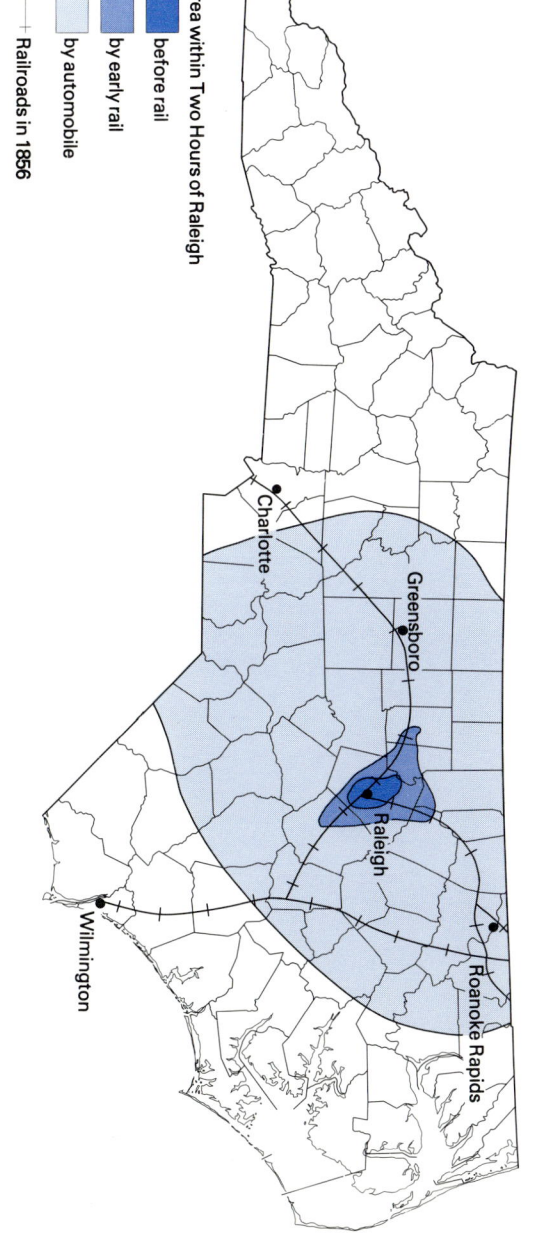

Figure 13.1. Historical Changes in Travel Time in N.C.

Area within Two Hours of Raleigh
- before rail
- by early rail
- by automobile

—+— Railroads in 1856

225

Figure 13.2. Passenger Enplanements on Commercial Air Carriers for 1972

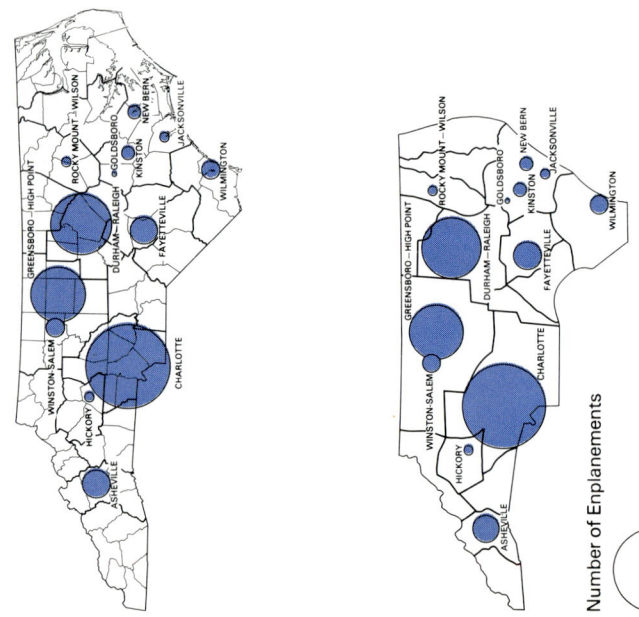

Source: U.S. Department of Transportation, *Airport Statistics, C.A.B., Certificated Air Carriers, Calendar Year 1973.*

Note: Cartogram of Multicounty Planning Regions determined by population density.

One hundred years ago North Carolina was characterized by self-sufficient small farms and a predominantly rural economy. Today there is an interdependence of work place, shopping, residence, recreational locations, and other activity sites, all of which are more concentrated and completely different because of the economies inherent in larger scale. The modern medical center within an hour's drive of many of the residents of the state has replaced the lone country doctor of a century ago. The country store with its limited stock, located at nearly every crossroads in the state, has given way to the modern supermarket with its thousands of items available for comparison and selection. The one-room schoolhouse, with its single teacher attempting to educate children from six to seventeen years of age, is gone and in its place is the large consolidated school with a wide variety of educational opportunities. Subsistence farming, and all the misery that that meant to the citizens of the state, has been supplanted by jobs in more productive and higher-wage retail, industrial, and service industries. As a result, North Carolina is becoming increasingly urban and suburban. There is much interaction in the state between formerly rural areas and emerging cities.

Most important in understanding the role of transportation in daily activities is a recognition of the amount of resources that is devoted to moving people and things from one place to another. One hundred years ago every citizen in the state devoted a large amount of time to the simple task of moving about. Today a greater and greater share of our resources is devoted to transportation, but in return, there is an enormous gain in mobility and accessibility. As transportation facilities have become more complex, they have required greater and greater capital investment from both the public and the private sectors. Increasingly, it is recognized that investments in transportation facilities must be made to serve population growth in the state, to meet the increasing demand for the services that transportation fills, and to insure that transportation can be used as a tool for the physical and economic development of the state.

The Present Transportation System

It is difficult to assess the relationship of transportation facilities with the physical area that they serve and with the people who use the transportation system. This can be seen better on maps that show areas proportional to the population that lives within each of the planning regions of the state, and not to the land area, as is the usual case. A populous area is indicated as being large regardless of the number of square miles it contains, and a sparsely populated area is shown as small, even though it contains many square miles. Figure 13.2 illustrates the two kinds of maps. The top figures show airline enplanements on a traditional land area map. The bottom figures show airline enplanements on a base that is proportional to population rather than to land area. The population base map shows more clearly than does the land area one the close correlation between population and the utilization of facilities. The population base map highlights the Piedmont portion of the state.

Five or six modes of transportation are available in North Carolina. Some are very slow and inexpensive and others are fast but very costly. Each has its place in the total transportation picture of the state and has grown to satisfy demand evidenced by the citizens of this state.

Each mode of transportation has its own network, facilities, and services, and each has its separate use characteristics that distinguish it from other modes and describe a particular mode's contribution to the total transportation spectrum. The following sections present an analysis of each of the major transportation modes.

Aviation and Airports

According to the records of the Federal Aviation Administration, North Carolina has approximately 200 airports. Of these, 110 airports accommodate 80 to 90 percent of the state's aviation activity. Thirteen have scheduled air carrier service, as is shown in Figure 13.3. Several other airports, not shown, have commuter (third-level carrier) service. Currently, there are five commuter airlines operating in the state. They provide vital connections between several commercial airports and between smaller points. Douglas Airport at Charlotte is the most active in the state. It ranks eleventh in annual enplanements among the 49 hub air terminals in the sixteen southeastern states.

North Carolina's three largest commercial airports are located in the Piedmont: the Raleigh-Durham Airport, the Greensboro-High Point Airport, and Douglas Airport at Charlotte. These facilities serve most of the air carrier needs of the Piedmont Crescent as well as a large number of contiguous counties. About 10 percent of the enplanements at Raleigh-Durham Airport originate in the twenty counties lying to the east of Raleigh, for example.

Over one hundred thousand scheduled service aircraft departures occur annually from the thirteen commercial airports (Figure 13.3). Two-thirds of these departures and 80 percent of the passenger enplanements occur at the four Piedmont Crescent air carrier airports (Figure 13.2). Between 80 and 90 percent of the freight, express, and mail carried in scheduled service in the state originates at these same four facilities. Nearly 99 percent of all enplanements occur at the thirteen largest airports.

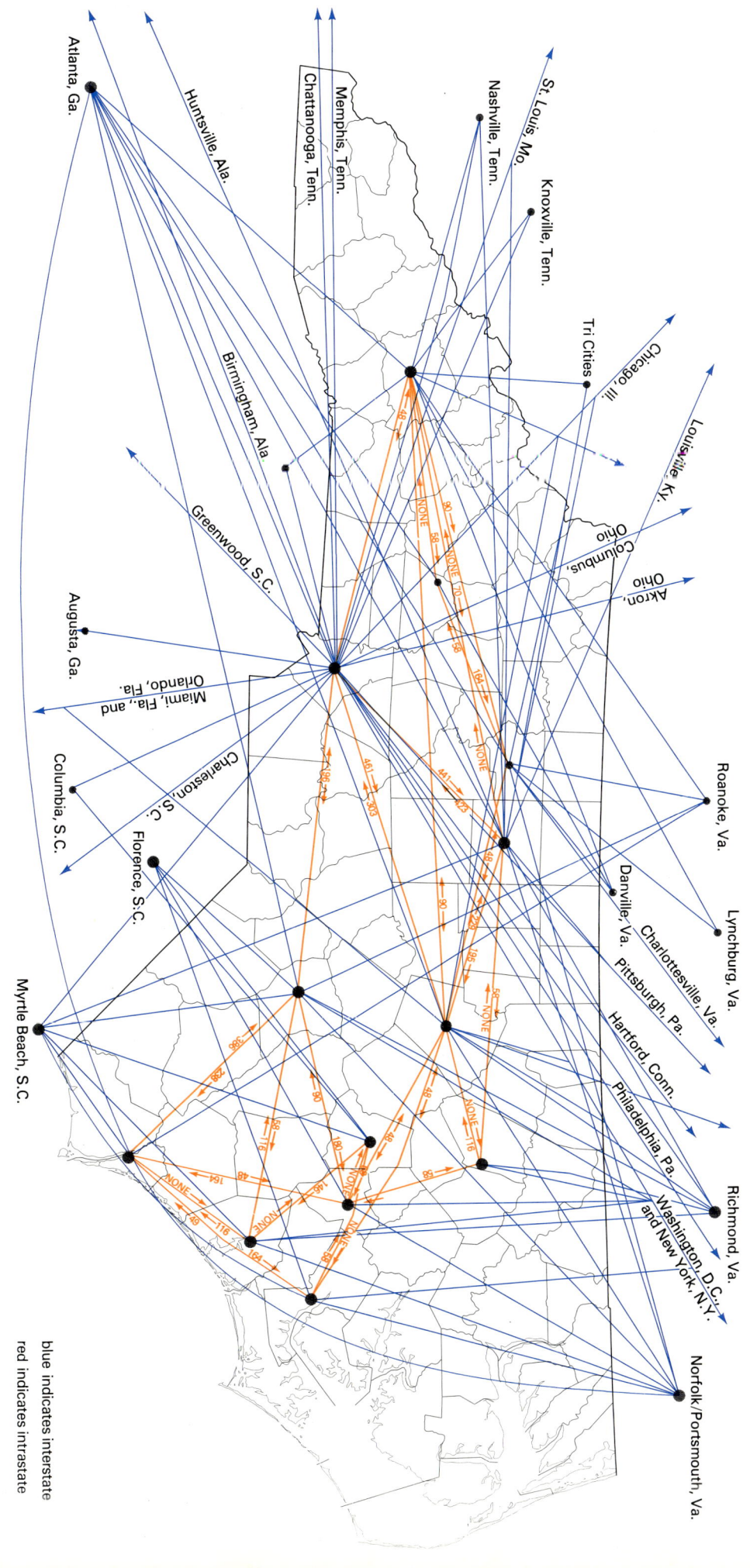

Figure 13.3. Daily Intrastate Seat Capacity and Interstate Air Routes, 1972

Source: *Official Airline Guide* (New York: R. H. Donnelley Corporation, 1974).

blue indicates interstate
red indicates intrastate

Scheduled air service at North Carolina's commercial airports functions not only to tie North Carolina together, but also to tie it to the nation and to the world. Scheduled air carrier service is accessible to most of North Carolina's residents. But, for many, access to a commercial airport involves travel time often in excess of an hour. (Even then, schedules at many of the air carrier airports, particularly in the east, are infrequent.)

Scheduled commercial air service is available between most major cities in North Carolina. Airport routes are oriented north-south for the most part, and as a result, east-west service in North Carolina is noticeably deficient. North Carolina lies across major north-south travel routes on the East Coast. East-west interstate routes have tended to skirt the Appalachian mountain barrier to the south, to follow the southern edge of the Great Lakes to the north, or to pass through the few river valleys that penetrate the Appalachians. This historic pattern has been perpetuated in modern airline routes. Thus much of the space available between North Carolina cities is not used for intrastate travel. Commercial airlines provide about five hundred one-way seats every day between Charlotte and Raleigh, but typically only sixty to seventy are used by travelers going from one city to the other. A greater number are transients who are collected at the two airports for trips to Chicago, Atlanta, Washington, and other more distant points.

Figure 13.2 shows the proliferation of small airports east of Raleigh, which, in most cases, has resulted in inadequate service for each community. Since 1972 scheduled commercial services from airports at Elizabeth City and Southern Pines-Pinehurst have been discontinued because of insufficient traffic. Increasing aircraft size and cost, requiring higher levels of traffic, indicate that residents of eastern North Carolina (and, similarly, western North Carolina) may face extended ground time in order to gain better air carrier service, that is, more frequent flights to more important destinations and more safety on more comfortable equipment.

Alternatives exist: commuter airlines could act as feeder lines; service could be concentrated in a single, existing airport; one or more regional facilities could be constructed at new, more central locations. Communities must be willing to give up close proximity to poor air carrier service in order to gain much improved service at more distant airports. Existing airport facilities should be retained and improved for general aviation use (including corporate aircraft) and commuter airlines, if appropriate. This reorganization may be forced on these communities because current trends in the commercial air industry point to a reduction in the number of airports with scheduled air carrier service over the next decade, with an overall improvement in service for the air traveler from that smaller number of airports.

No multimodal terminal facilities exist at any airport, even though all major air carrier airports in North Carolina are within reasonable distance of interstate highway facilities and all have adequate highway access, given current enplanement statistics. In practically every case, neither inter- nor intracity buses serve airports. The automobile (private, rental, taxi, or limousine) is the only form of passenger access to the air terminals. Trucks serve as an intermediate (or final) mode for freight. Wilmington is the only point in the state that has regularly scheduled air service as well as rail and water facilities. But air service is limited at Wilmington, and little interchange occurs between the several transportation modes.

Military aviation in North Carolina is extensive. Camp Lejeune is the largest Marine air station in the world in terms of both size and operations. Fort Bragg and adjacent Pope Air Force Base, Seymour Johnson Air Force Base, Cherry Point, the Elizabeth City Coast Guard station, and other military airports create in North Carolina one of the largest proportions of restricted air space areas in the nation. This fact has been a source of inconvenience to general aviation and recreation flier's in the coastal section of the state, particularly during times of intense airborne military operations. It is impossible to fly the length of North Carolina's coastline without receiving permission to penetrate a restricted air space.

Three state-owned general aviation airports on the Outer Banks of North Carolina (with others in the planning stages) provide air access to the recreation opportunities in the area for private craft. It is possible to land on a three thousand-foot paved airstrip within a few hundred yards of the point where the Wright brothers began modern aviation. Farther south, the general aviation pilot or passenger may fish in the surf only a few hundred feet from the airstrips at Ocracoke or Cape Hatteras. Other airstrips that provide recreational access to the mountains of North Carolina enable people to hike, camp, and fish in the summer and to ski in the winter.

Leadership in aviation development in North Carolina has traditionally come at the local level. Master planning and layout for public airport facilities have been accomplished generally by local governments with local funds and federal assistance. Until recently, the state government's participation in aviation development was limited to approximately $125,000 per year and that was for general aviation airports. Since 1973 the Airport Development Aid Program has grown to $2 million annually and is available for airport development for all publicly owned facilities. Funds may be used for airport runway, taxiway, and apron expansion and strengthening, navigational facilities, security items, fire-fighting equipment, and terminal building construction. In addi-

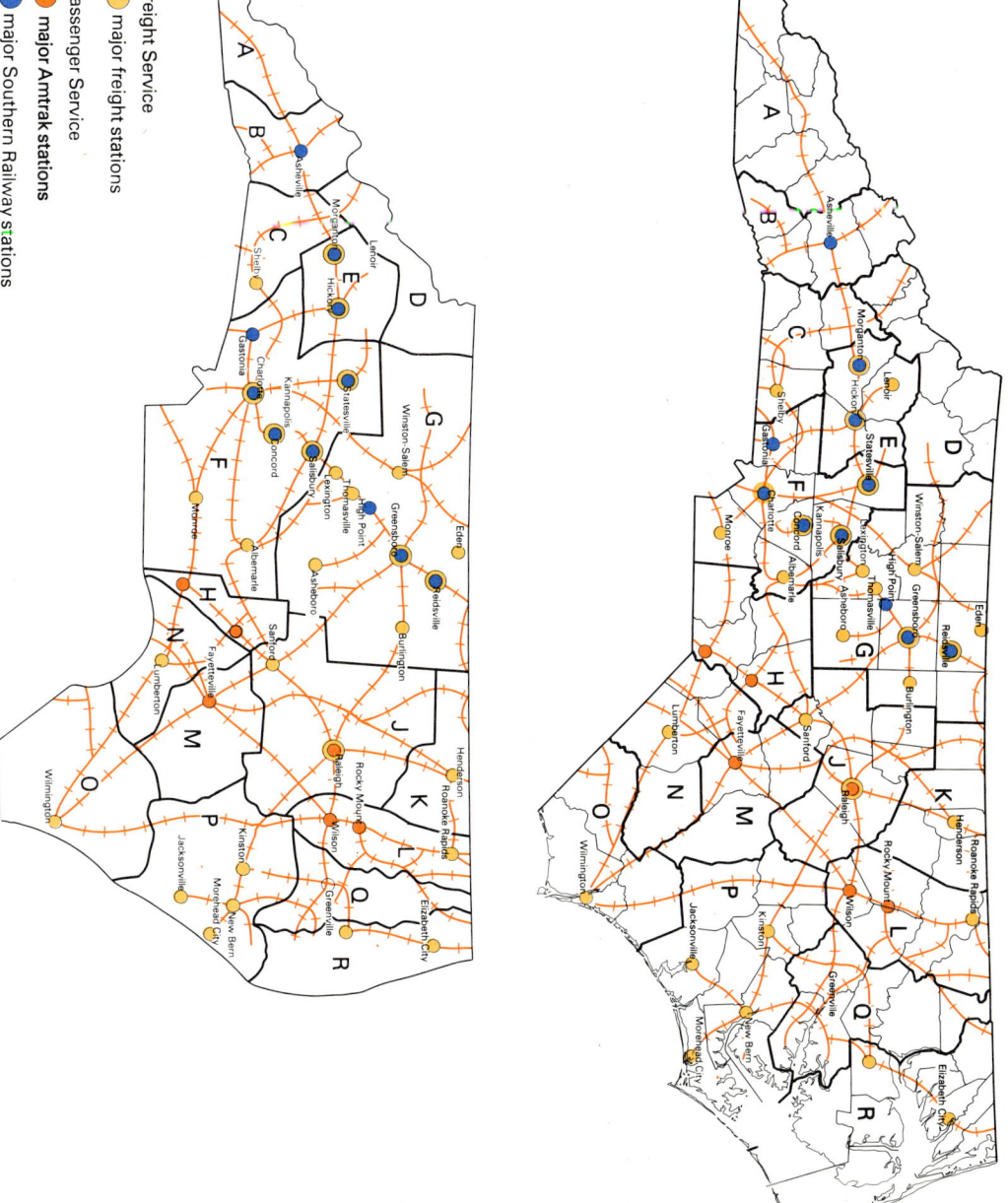

Figure 13.4. Railways in N.C.

Freight Service
○ major freight stations
Passenger Service
● major Amtrak stations
● major Southern Railway stations

Source: Compiled from information provided by operating companies.

229

tion, the state is promoting aviation safety by sponsoring an airport licensing act that will require annual inspection of all publicly owned facilities to assure compliance with minimum safety standards.

Railroads

The contrast between North Carolina's limited rail network of 1856 and the present extensive network shown in Figure 13.4 is dramatic. Today, a large proportion of the state and its population are served by the railroads, including all the major cities. However, several of these are served only by spur lines and only those on the Seaboard Coast Line and Southern Railway mail lines have passenger service. Eight counties are completely without railroad service, as are a number of areas of the state.

North Carolina has a history of rail planning. Unknown to most citizens is the fact that the state of North Carolina owns the right-of-way for the railroad between Goldsboro and Charlotte through Raleigh and Greensboro. Although this facility is leased for private operation, its ownership underlines the foresight of North Carolina's leaders in recognizing the need for developing a major transportation system in the state.

The fact that rail services are available to a community no longer means that transportation service is adequate. Sixty or seventy years ago the local railroad station was the major focus of public transportation. The state was dotted with rail stations and every city had a major terminal served by frequent passenger trains and freight service. Today, rail service has been reduced in many instances to freight movement with limited passenger service.

Passenger service is now provided north and south by the National Passenger Rail Corporation (Amtrak) and by Southern Railway. Southern operates intrastate passenger service between Asheville and Salisbury. North Carolina has had a major role in promoting north-south rail service. Stops are made by Amtrak and Southern at Rocky Mount, Wilson, Fayetteville, Raleigh, Hamlet, Greensboro, High Point, Salisbury, Charlotte, and Gastonia for north-south runs. For east-west runs, however, Southern Railway provides service only at Asheville, Morganton, Hickory, Statesville, and Salisbury.

As Figure 13.5 shows, frequent freight service is available in most major cities in the state, but the dominance of north-south movement is obvious even across the western part of the state. East-west intrastate freight service is relatively poor. Although the rail facilities are available, relatively few trains are operated on them and great dependence is placed on highways. Particularly graphic examples of poor service are seen at the state ports of North Carolina. Relatively infrequent freight service is offered to Wilmington and Morehead City, while the Norfolk Southern Railway connects the central part of North Carolina to the port of Norfolk in southeastern Virginia.

Passenger trains that pass through North Carolina are oriented to departure and arrival times on the northeastern seaboard and in the Deep South. Consequently, most trains arrive and depart at hours that are inconvenient for state travelers. Note, too, Southern Railway's lines enter North Carolina north of Greensboro and exit into South Carolina west of Gastonia, while the Seaboard Coast Line runs roughly parallel to the edge of the Coastal Plain.

Statistics describing the extent of railroads in the state of North Carolina are summarized in Table 13.1. Of the twenty-three companies operating, 25 percent were Class I companies that occupied 85 percent of the track and carried 92 percent of the freight and all of the railway passengers in North Carolina. Only three companies —Seaboard Coast Line, Southern Railway, and Norfolk Southern—occupied more than five hundred miles of track each in North Carolina, and together occupied 80 percent of the total track in the state.

Of major importance, in addition to the location of rail lines in the state, are the major terminals and classification yards that provide interchange for freight. Every major city has rail yard facilities, but there are eight major terminals and classification yards located at Charlotte, Winston-Salem, Greensboro, Hamlet, Wilmington, Morehead City, Raleigh, and Edenton. Most of the interconnection between rail service and other modes of transportation is provided by highways and trucks. The only true multimodal freight terminals are located at Wilmington and Morehead City.

Figure 13.5. Daily Train Movements in N.C., 1973

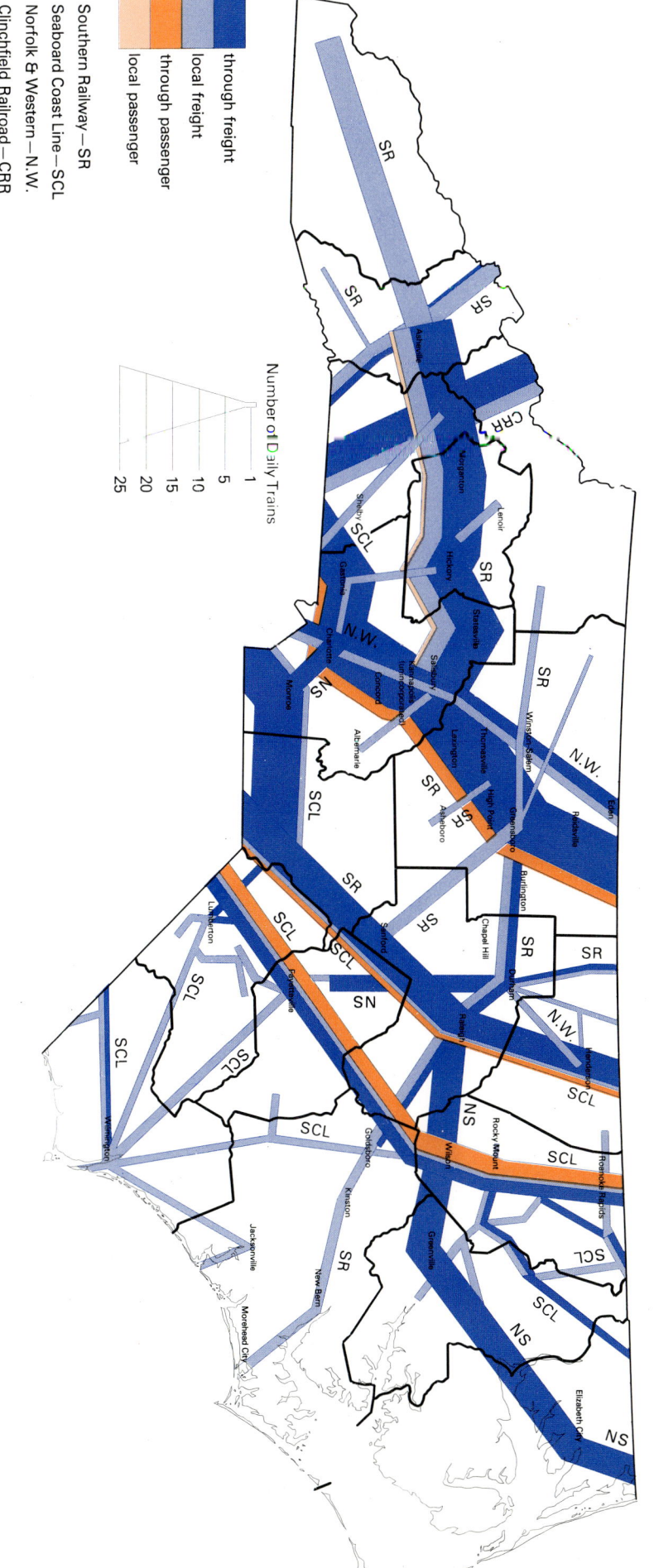

Southern Railway—SR
Seaboard Coast Line—SCL
Norfolk & Western—N.W.
Clinchfield Railroad—CRR
Norfolk Southern—NS

Table 13.1. N.C. Railroads, 1972

	Class I[1]	Class II[2]	Total	Change from 1969 Percent
Number of companies	6	17	23	−4.2
Mileage in N.C.	3,656	635	4,291	−1.2
Tons of revenue freight				
Hauled in N.C.	108,689,000	12,002,000	120,691,000	+8.1
Originating in N.C.	24,652,222		24,652,222	
Passengers hauled in N.C.	164,668	0	164,668	−85.8
Passenger revenue in N.C.	$814,260	0	$814,260	−86.1
Freight revenue in N.C.	$206,452,000	$13,654,000	$200,406,000	+24.8

Source: N.C. Utilities Commission, Eighth Statistical and Analytical Report, 1974.

[1] Annual revenues of $5,000,000 or more.
[2] Annual revenues of less than $5,000,000.

231

Water Transportation

Water transportation has historically served a vital role in the economy of the state, particularly in the eastern part of North Carolina. Figure 13.6 shows the two major state ports and the navigable waterways parallel to the coast and penetrating the Coastal Plain along the major rivers. Shipping activity occurs at the mouth of each of the rivers and at many points upstream.

The North Carolina State Ports Authority is charged by statute with the responsibility for developing, improving, operating, and maintaining seaports and harbors within the state's jurisdiction. Funds come from three sources: operating revenues generated by port charges, appropriations from the North Carolina General Assembly, and revenue bonds issued on bank loans secured in the name of the State Ports Authority.

Shipping statistics for North Carolina's state-operated ports, Wilmington and Morehead City, illustrate the kinds of activities that occur. The principal commodities that flow through the state's public and private shipping facilities consist of tobacco, phosphates, lumber, logs, and plywood. Other leading commodities include steel, fiber, urea, scrap metal, wood pulp, paperboard, chemicals, concrete products, petroleums, asphalt, and fish meal. Other products are iron (both ore and concentrates), crude petroleum, crude tar, oil and gas products, alcohols, chemical fertilizers, gasoline, jet fuel, kerosene, distillate fuel oil, and building cement. The commodities composition has changed little in the last one hundred years and reflects North Carolina's economy.

The combined tonnage passing through North Carolina ports has grown from less than a half million tons in 1952 to 2.75 million tons in 1972 (Table 13.2). By 1990 it is expected to reach 7.5 million tons per year. The Wilmington state port serves primarily for imports and Morehead City's primary activity is handling exports. Considering the larger volume of traffic through Wilmington, the state ports together handle more imports than exports. The origin and destination of international shipments are shown in Figure 13.7.

Users of the state port in Wilmington are heavily concentrated in and around Charlotte and Wilmington, but other regions use the port quite often. The state port of Morehead City is frequently used by industries in or near Henderson, Rocky Mount, Wilson, New Bern, and Greenville.

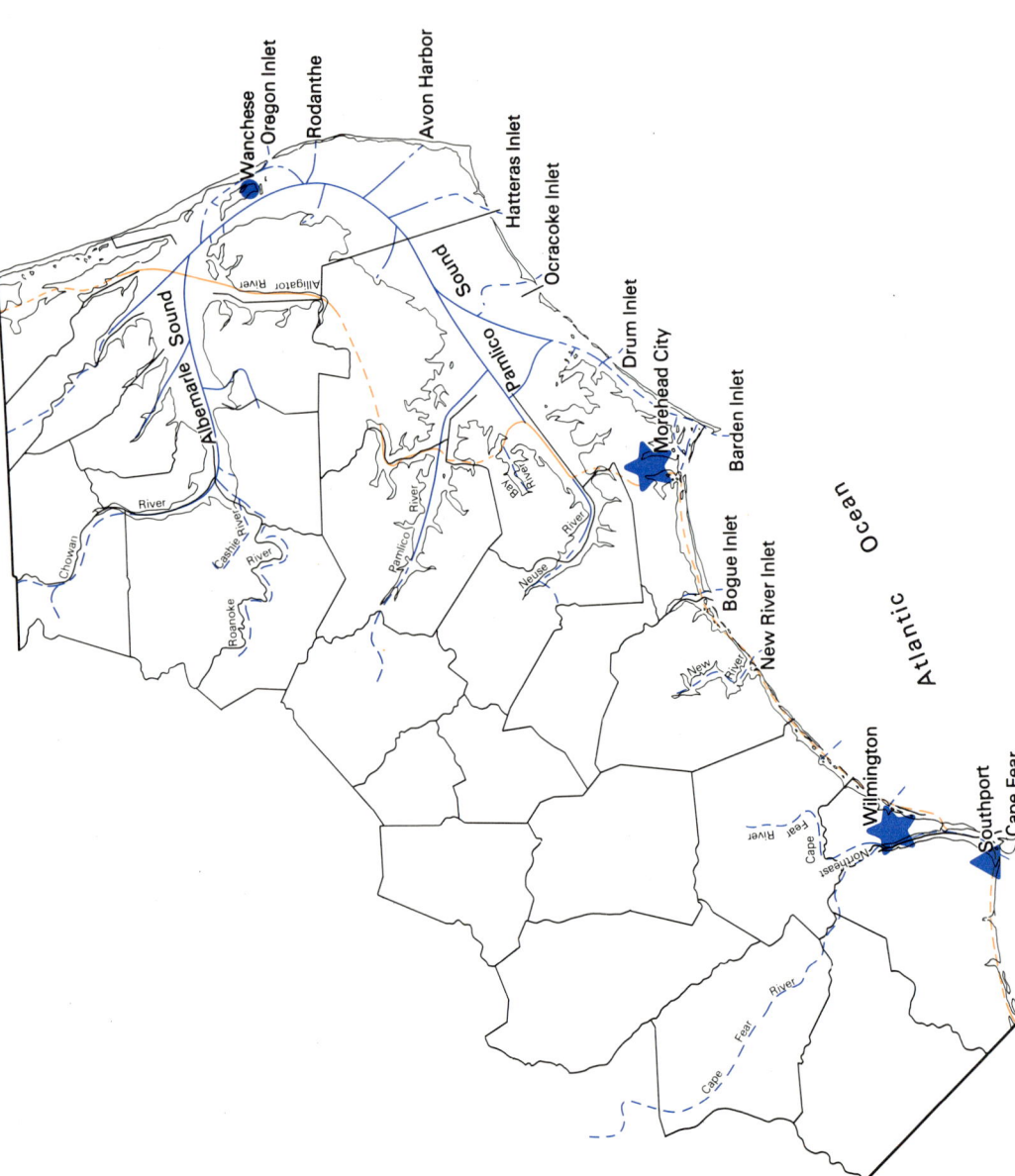

Figure 13.6. Navigable Waters and State Ports in N.C.

—— navigable rivers and channels (depths are generally between 6' and 12')
—— Atlantic Intracoastal Waterway (controlling depth is 12')
★ state ports—freight
▲ Southport Boat Harbor—recreation
● Wanchese Harbor (proposed)—freight

Source: U.S. Corps of Engineers.

Note: Natural deep waters are indicated by a solid line. Improved channels are indicated by a dashed line.

The state ports are important to the economic well-being of the coastal regions of the state. Over twenty-five hundred people are employed in direct port-related activities in the two counties that include Wilmington and Morehead City, and they represent between 5 and 5 percent of the total employment of those areas. In a survey of manufacturers using the state ports who located in North Carolina in the period between 1950 and 1974, 64 percent (270) indicated that ocean transportation was "very significant" or "critically significant" in their locational decision. North Carolina state ports have grown at an annual rate slightly greater than 20 percent during the last decade and are among the fastest growing on the eastern seaboard, but they tend to handle only North Carolina traffic. These ports are at a competitive disadvantage because of the lack of four-lane interstate-standard highways and good rail service connecting them with inland market areas. By comparison, both Charleston and Norfolk are served by the interstate highway systems and they consider Piedmont North Carolina as a major part of their hinterland. Even though port charges at the State Ports Authority facility at Morehead City compare favorably with competitive ports, inland freight rates to Piedmont North Carolina are not competitive.

Table 13.2. Traffic Activities at N.C. Ports

Port	1960	1972
Wilmington total tonnage		
Foreign		
Import	118,510	723,995
Export	226,995	143,613
Coastwise		
Inbound	2,566	442,957
Outbound	4,200	283,635
Total	352,271	1,594,213
Morehead City total tonnage		
Foreign		
Import	281,713	261,688
Export	100,668	462,766
Military	125,223	8,159
Coastwise		
Inbound	—	382,128
Outbound	—	49,956
Total	507,604	1,164,697

Source: N.C. State Ports Authority.

Textiles, agricultural products such as soybeans and grain, and processed food products are examples of locally produced commodities that North Carolina ports lose to neighboring ports. However, North Carolina ports are the principal eastern outlets for lumber and veneer products. This market continues to increase at both Wilmington and Morehead City. More captive industry within the service area of Morehead City is needed to make that port a viable and profitable facility for the state.

Highway Transportation

Streets and highways, in combination with bus passenger terminals, motor freight terminals, automobile rental agencies, and other facilities supply the physical attributes of the most extensive and most used transportation system in the state. Services provided by the highway transportation system include common carriers (passenger bus and motor freight operators), but the facilities themselves also serve the private user. The highway system accounts for about 95 percent of passenger transportation in the state, and over 80 percent of freight transportation.

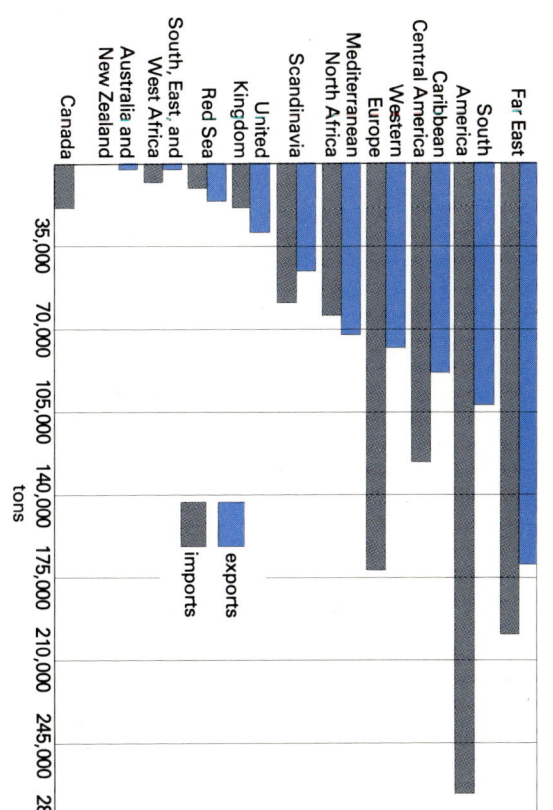

Figure 13.7. Export and Import Totals for N.C. Ports, 1972

Source: U.S. Department of Commerce, Social and Economic Statistics Administration, Foreign Trade Division, 1972.

Note: Coastwise (within the U.S.): exports = 333,590; imports = 833,519.

The private automobile is a major part of the highway transportation system. It is privately owned, allows for personal, individualized transportation, and is paid for over a period of time rather than on a per ride basis as with common carriers. The private automobile/private driver combination provides an enormous, yet casually accepted, share of transportation service.

Trucks connect rail terminals, deliver the goods to final destinations, provide the connection between ports and other industries, and complete the eventual delivery of air freight. Rental cars, taxicabs, and limousines provide the large majority of connections for the passenger between the terminal of one mode and final destination or terminal of a second mode. Emphasis on the use of the private or rental automobile for interconnection is overwhelming. Only rarely are intermodal connections facilitated by the provision of good public transportation service in North Carolina.

The highway system in North Carolina is made up of over fifty thousand miles of interstate, primary, and secondary roads. North Carolina's Department of Transportation controls more road mileage than does any other state transportation department. The system has been maintained entirely by state funds, except within municipalities, since the depression of the 1930s when the state assumed responsibility for county road systems. Funding for construction of highways (with the exception of those within municipalities) is almost entirely from the state and federal levels. The state motor fuel tax, fees received for licenses and registrations, and other miscellaneous fees support the system with assistance from the federal government in an amount approximately 20 percent of the annual $500 million highway budget. No local revenues are used for highway construction or maintenance in North Carolina, except within municipalities, a situation shared by only a few states throughout the country.

Responsibility for planning the state's highway system has long rested with the State Department of Transportation and its predecessor agency, the State Highway Commission. As with funding, a major exception to this policy has been within urban areas and municipalities of the state. However, increasingly, local governments are participating in the planning of road systems to serve their physical areas.

Highway Facilities

The interstate principal and minor arterial systems in place and planned for the state of North Carolina for 1990 are shown in Figure 13.8. Many of these highways already exist or are in advanced stages of construction. More importantly, when contrasted with the physical and population distribution of the state, it is clear that the state is adequately provided with highways in the Mountains, in the Coastal Plain, and in the more populous Piedmont region. The map of highway traffic volumes (Figure 13.9) also illustrates the heavy traffic that is characteristic of the populous Piedmont.

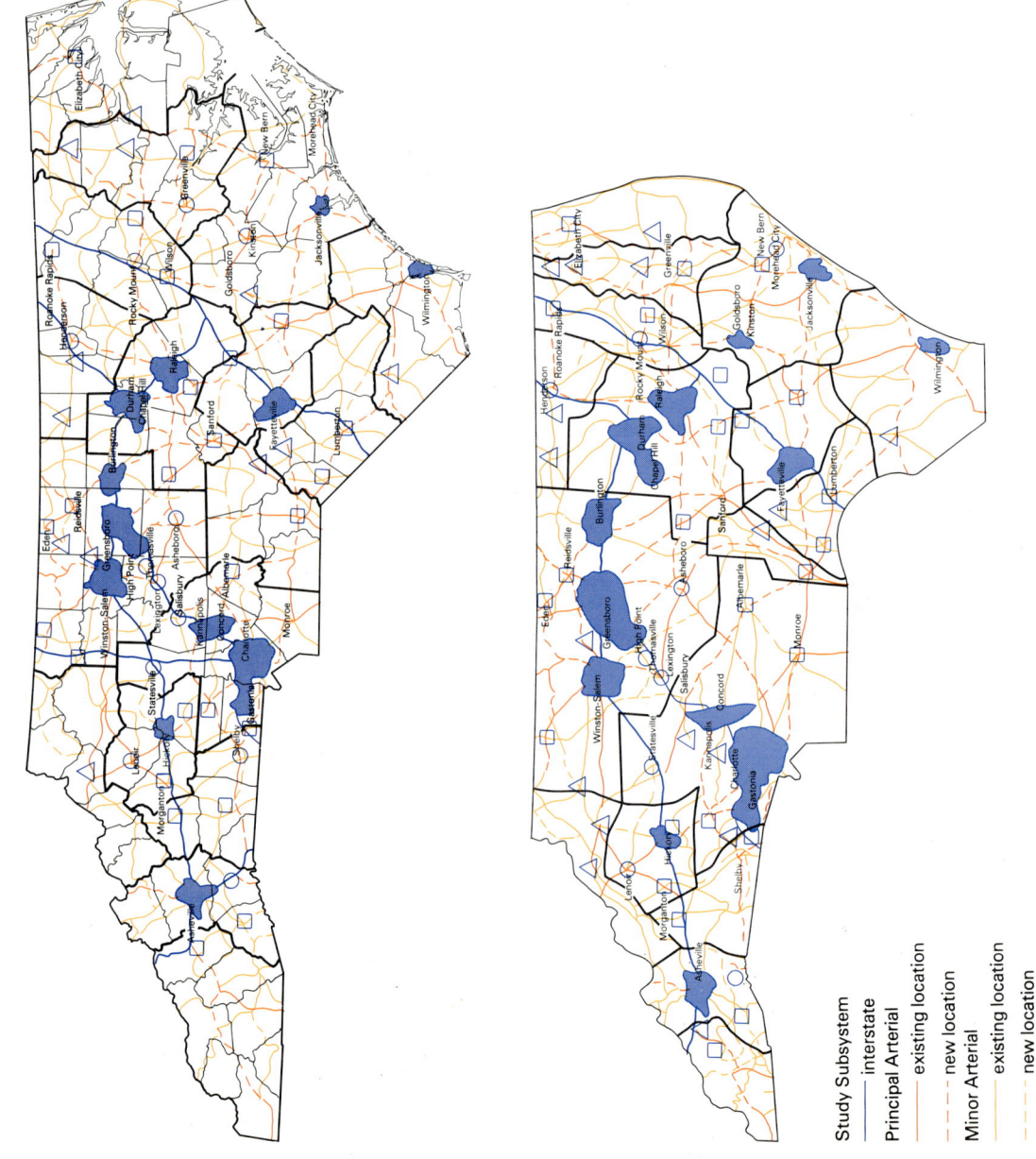

Figure 13.8. N.C. Rural Arterial Highway System Existing and Projected to 1990

Study Subsystem
— interstate
Principal Arterial
— existing location
--- new location
Minor Arterial
— existing location
--- new location

Projected 1990 Population
■ 50,000 and above
○ 25,000–50,000
□ 10,000–25,000
△ 5,000–10,000

Source: N.C. Department of Transportation and Highway Safety, modified from *1990 National Highway Functional Classification Study*, 1972.

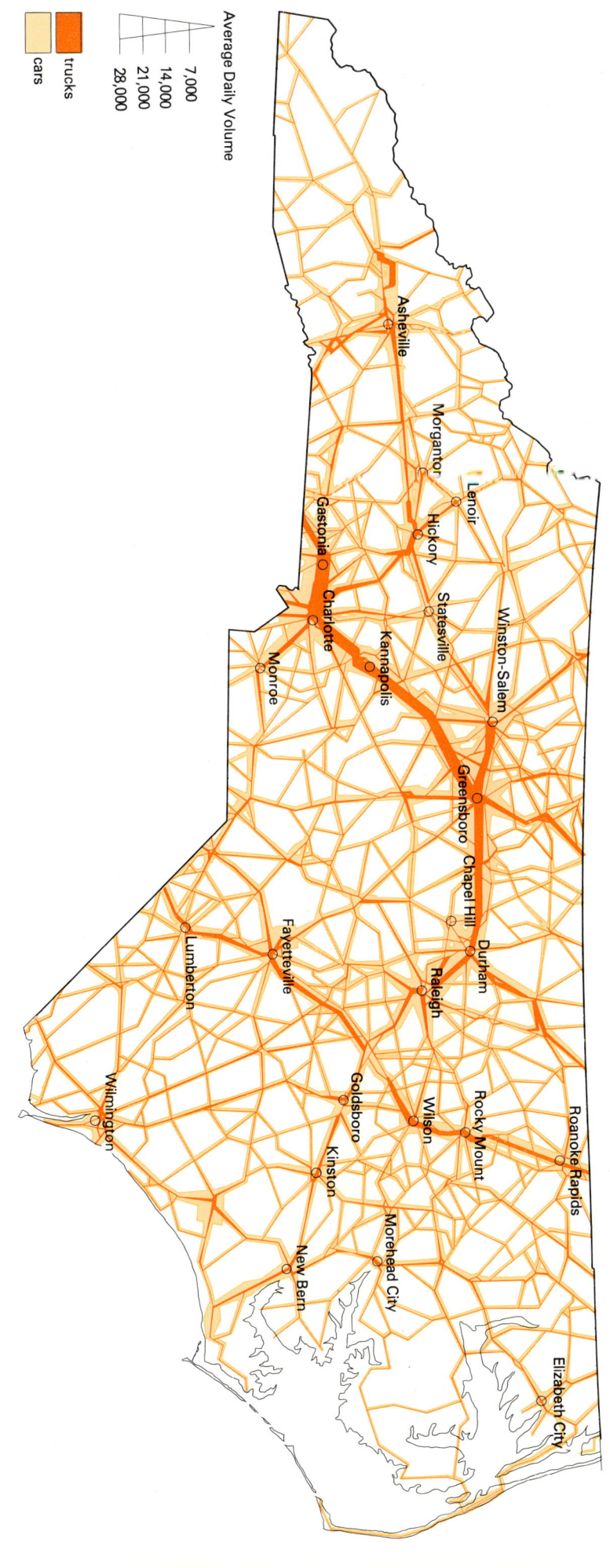

Figure 13.9. Vehicle and Truck Traffic Volume in N.C., 1972

Source: N.C. Department of Transportation and Highway Safety, 1972

Figure 13.10. Typical County Road System, County Road Map for Harnett County

The principal and minor arterials shown in Figures 13.8 and 13.9 are actually part of the primary highway system of the state. Figure 13.10 illustrates the extensiveness of the highway system in the state by showing as a representative example Harnett County's secondary road system as well as its primary system. The primary system consists of the interstate, United States, and North Carolina numbered highways. Although interstate and United States numbered highways are probably most familiar to the majority of drivers, it is the secondary road system that provides access to the houses, shopping locations, and industries that are primary activity centers for many citizens of the state. The density of the highway network in Harnett County exemplifies the fact that North Carolina's state-maintained road system is the largest in the United States.

The other major physical aspects of the state's highway system are the terminal facilities to which the various motor transport services are directed. Figure 13.11 shows the locations of motor freight terminals, interline gateway terminals, and auto rental terminals.

There are sixty-six cities in North Carolina with motor freight terminals: Charlotte has the most with fifty-two, with others ranging down to one. Greensboro, Asheville, and Hickory show twenty or more. Raleigh, Winston-Salem, Wilmington, and Durham have more than ten, and all the rest have less than ten within their urban areas. The physical map of the state shows a rather even distribution, but the map altered to reflect population size shows a more irregular distribution. The difference points up the relationship between the provision of terminal facilities for motor freight carriers and the demand for those facilities. Where population and activity are greatest, motor freight carriers have responded with the construction of terminals.

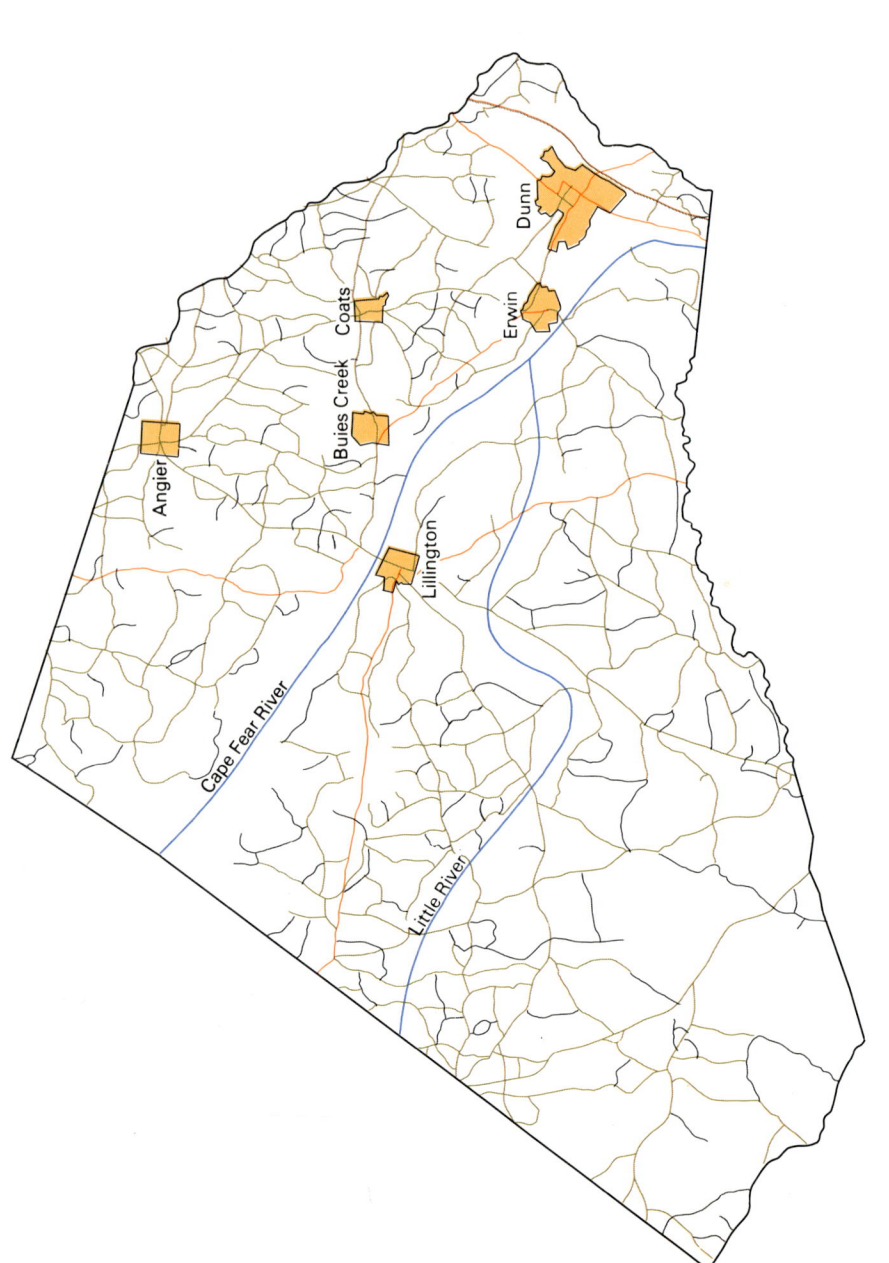

— interstate highways
— U.S. numbered highways
— N.C. numbered highways
— secondary roads
— rivers

Source: N.C. Department of Transportation and Highway Safety, 1972.

There are seventy-two company-owned intercity bus stations throughout the state and local stops are provided in many towns that lack central terminals for intercity bus service. Typically, bus terminals are located in deteriorated areas. Local government and the State Utilities Commission have not encouraged the revitalization or reconstruction of many bus stations, and in some cases, companies have been allowed to construct separate terminal buildings, making connections more difficult for the traveler.

In 1971, 640 freight carriers were registered with and regulated by the State Utilities Commission to engage in intrastate commerce. In addition, approximately thirty thousand tractors and trailers were registered in the state.

In the same year, forty common carriers providing passenger service were registered with the state's Utility Commission. Figure 13.12 shows intercity passenger service for the state and illustrates clearly that intercity bus service is widely available to citizens of the state, particularly in the Coastal Plain and Piedmont regions. Total route mileage, one way, is in excess of nine thousand miles. Although carriers attempt to establish schedules for the convenience of potential users, many are controlled by out-of-state or by large-city destinations, and arrive or depart at inconvenient hours from the point of view of the local intercity traveler.

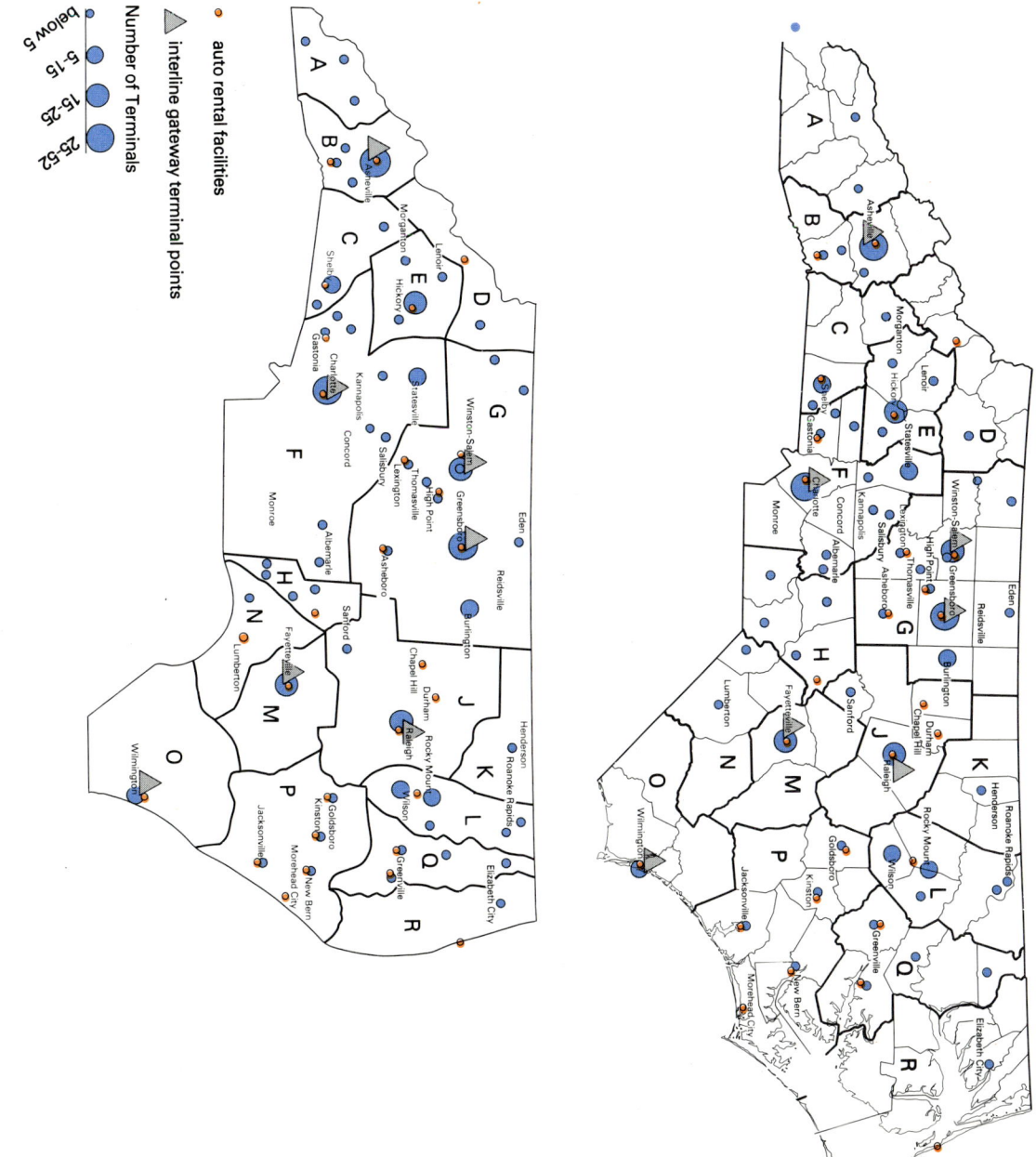

Figure 13.11. Motor Freight Terminals, Interline Gateway Terminals, and Auto Rental Terminals in N.C., 1972

Source: Compiled from information provided by operating companies.

237

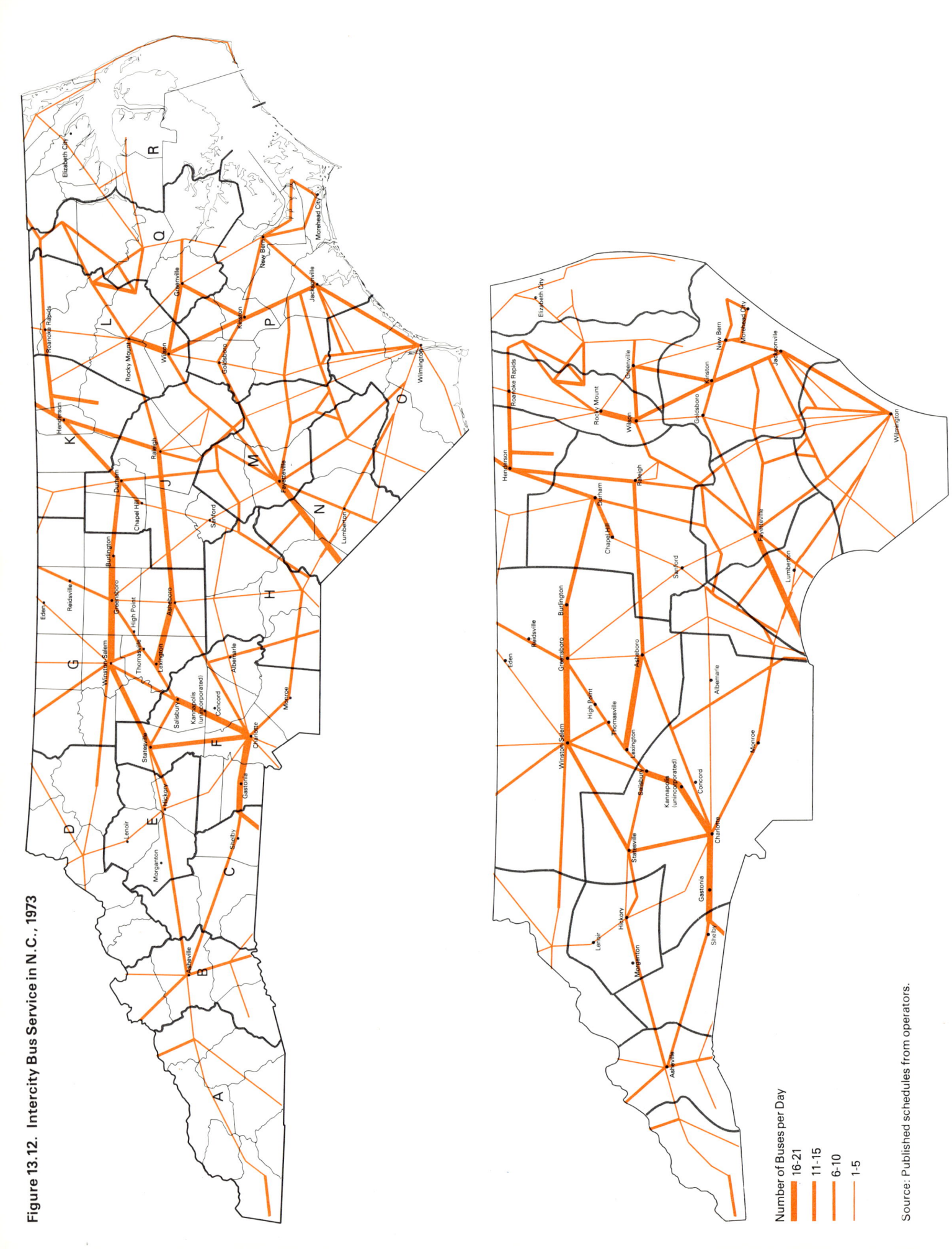

Figure 13.12. Intercity Bus Service in N.C., 1973

Number of Buses per Day
- 16-21
- 11-15
- 6-10
- 1-5

Source: Published schedules from operators.

Class 1 and Class 2 common carriers of motor freight, those with average annual gross operating revenues of at least $300,000, showed an increase in vehicle miles of operation in North Carolina of 5.8 percent from 1970 to 1971. This continues a linear trend that reflects an increase from about 140 million vehicle miles in 1960 to over 300 million miles in 1971. At the same time, operating revenues from North Carolina portions of the carriers' systems increased 20 percent from 1970 to 1971 and from about $70 million in 1960 to over $240 million in 1971.

Accurate figures on truck movements within the state and on the movement of intercity or intrastate freight are not available. A general idea of the movement of motor freight may be obtained from the map of overall highway volumes in Figure 13.9.

Passengers carried on intercity common carriers in North Carolina continue to decrease, although there are some indications of a reversal of the trend in 1972 and 1973. Of the forty-one carriers under regulation by the State Utilities Commission, the eight Class 1 carriers, each of which have an annual revenue of $1 million or more, accounted for over 95 percent of the gross operating revenues, over 95 percent of operating expenses, and over 95 percent of the revenue passengers hauled. Revenue among the Class 1 carriers has maintained a general increase of 4 to 5 percent for a number of years, which reflects a steady increase in fares and a decrease in the number of revenue passengers at about the same rate.

Other publicly available highway transportation services include urban taxis and limousines and auto rental facilities for both intra- and intercity use. Auto rental facilities are found primarily at the major scheduled air carrier airports and in most cities and towns of ten thousand population and above. Although uneven distribution is noted on the physical map of the state, a rather uniform distribution appears on the map altered to reflect population density. Many counties and several regions of the state are without auto rental facilities. Even though the facility and service maps indicate uniform availability of public transportation service and facilities in the state of North Carolina, many citizens are completely dependent on the use of the private automobile for their transportation needs.

Figure 13.13. Automobile Ownership by Race and Poverty Status in N.C., 1970

(a) Percentage of All Households in N.C. with No Automobile

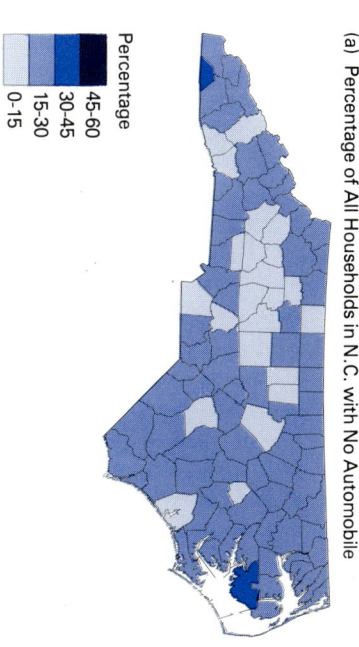

Percentage
45-60
30-45
15-30
0-15

(b) Percentage of Nonwhite Population in N.C. without an Automobile

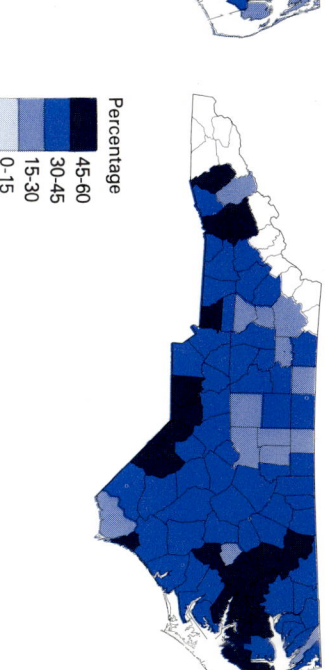

Percentage
45-60
30-45
15-30
0-15

(c) Total Percentage of All Households in N.C. with Income below Poverty Level

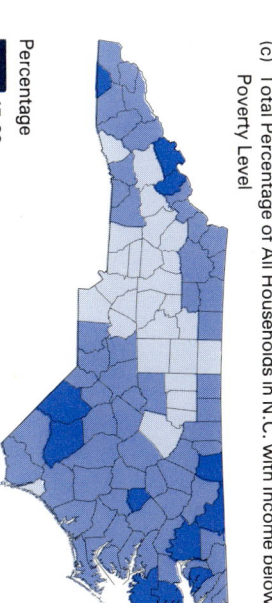

Percentage
45-60
30-45
15-30
0-15

(d) Total Percentage of Nonwhite Households in N.C. with Income below Poverty Level

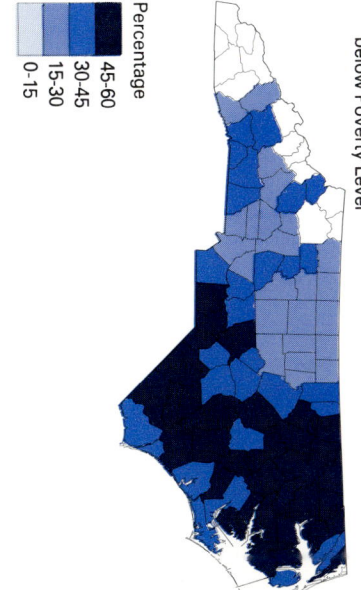

Percentage
45-60
30-45
15-30
0-15

(e) Percentage of Total N.C. Households that are Nonwhite

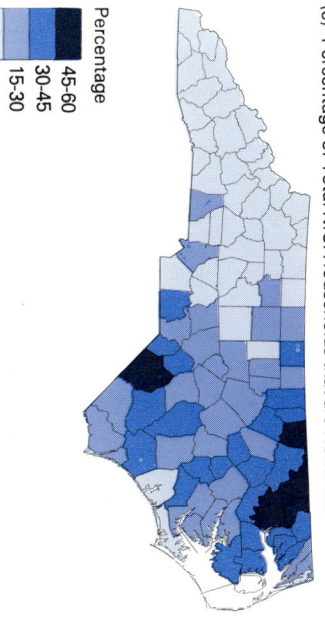

Percentage
45-60
30-45
15-30
0-15

Note: White counties indicate no data.

Source: U.S. Department of Commerce, *1970 Census of Population*, 1970.

Figure 13.14. Intercounty Journey-to-Work Patterns in N.C., 1970

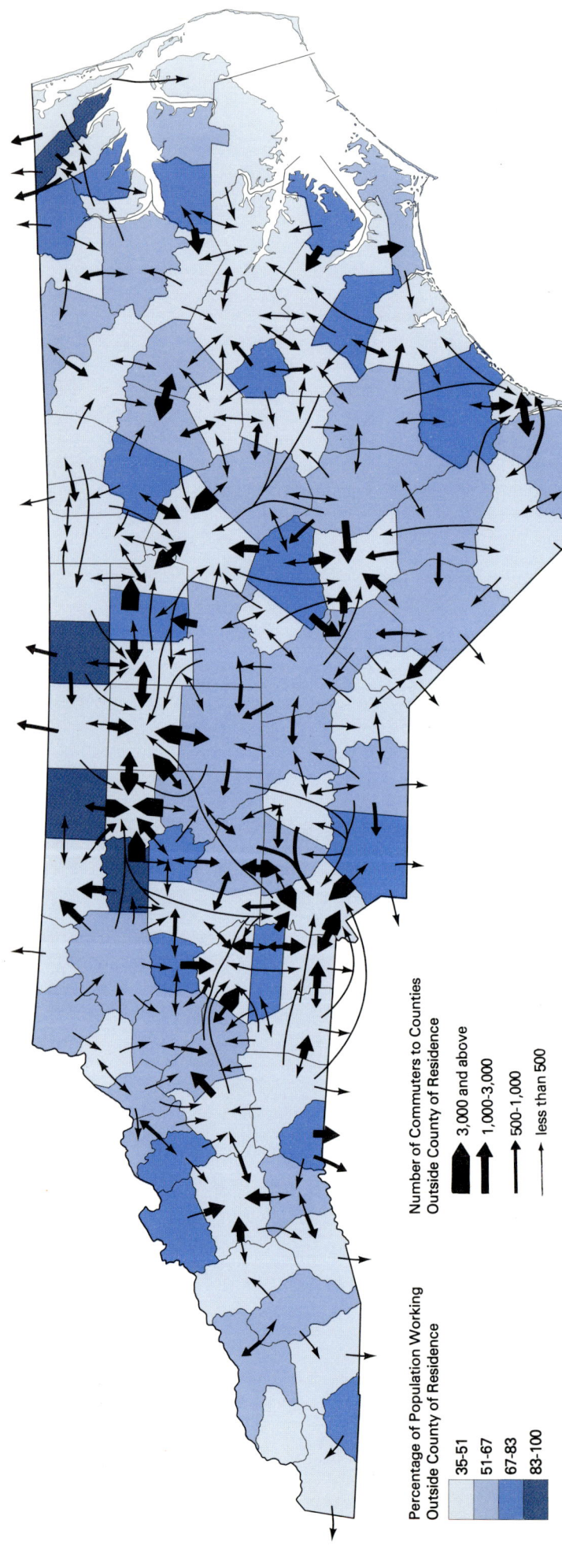

Percentage of Population Working Outside County of Residence
- 35-51
- 51-67
- 67-83
- 83-100

Number of Commuters to Counties Outside County of Residence
- 3,000 and above
- 1,000-3,000
- 500-1,000
- less than 500

Source: U.S. Department of Commerce, *1970 Census of Population*, 1970.

The maps in Figure 13.13 illustrate deficiencies in the availability of private automobiles in contrast to the availability of public transportation services. The first pair of figures indicates the percentage of households with no automobile available for use by the occupants, within each county in the state. One map illustrates that percentage for all households and the other shows that percentage for nonwhite households. The second pair of maps shows those households for which household income is below the defined poverty level. Again, the first map shows the percentage of all households; the second, the percentage of nonwhite households below the poverty level. Finally, the third pair of maps shows the percentage of population that is nonwhite, by county. The coincidence of nonwhite population percentages, low income households, and low automobile availability are more than coincidental. In many cases, the lack of transportation, illustrated by low automobile availability for households, is not only a function of poverty but also a cause. The great distances involved and the lack of either public or private transportation make travel to work difficult for those who most need to work.

Figure 13.9 shows the volume of trucks and automobiles that use the highways of the state of North Carolina. Heavy volumes of vehicles use the interstate highways that pass through North Carolina: Interstate 95, north and south along the Coastal Plain; Interstate 85, through the Piedmont; and Interstate 40, from Greensboro west to Asheville. Heavy use of interstate highways is notable near major urban areas. In other parts of the state, the highway system is characterized by its evenness of use. With isolated exceptions, volumes of vehicle use tend to be even on the majority of both primary and secondary roads included on the map.

The presentation of the same information on the map that has been altered to reflect regional population size graphically illustrates the effect of large population and intense activity in the three Piedmont regions. Figure 13.14 shows major commuting connections between counties throughout the state, which explains in large part the reasons for the concentration of high volumes of highway traffic near urban areas.

Urban Transportation Systems

A series of six maps focusing on the major urban regions of the state (Figure 13.15) illustrates a number of points concerning the state's transportation system and the subsystems within the individual areas. Major terminal facilities and highway, rail, and passenger common carrier routes are shown on these maps. The maps of the entire state tend to create the impression that each city in which these facilities are located is a very specific point. Yet it is clear from examination of the maps of the urban areas that many of the terminal facilities for the various modes of travel are dispersed throughout major cities.

The primary means of intermodal connections for freight at these large-city terminal points is by truck, and only in the case of bulk commodities does the product reach its recipient by rail facilities. For less than carload freight, for all air freight, and for the majority of freight carried by truck, transfer is necessary to local delivery vehicles within the urban area.

Passengers arriving at major intercity terminals throughout the urban area have little choice but to use a private automobile, taxi, or limousine to reach their eventual destination. Although these urban areas are served by public transit systems, they do not provide connections between major intercity passenger transportation terminals. They serve primarily the central area of the city, a majority of their patrons being local residents who are not able to afford an automobile.

Public policy in the state has not encouraged interconnection and organization of service for the convenience of the user, intracity or intercity. Although it's true that North Carolina is served by an extensive, and in many ways, notable transportation system, it is also true that many problems remain to be solved by both public action and private industry.

The recent energy crisis in this country underlined the fact that North Carolina can no longer continue to rely upon the private automobile or the laissez-faire, privately owned "public" common carrier to provide the majority of its transportation services.

ENERGY UTILITIES

Pipelines and Natural Gas

Figure 13.16 shows the major pipelines that bring natural gas and petroleum products into and through the state. The more populous areas of the state are served by a dense network of pipes.

Liquid petroleum products also move into the state, which has no production of its own, by means other than pipelines. The entire supply of natural gas is shipped from Texas and Louisiana on the line of the Transcontinental Gas Pipeline Corporation. This gas is in turn distributed to consumers by five gas utility companies and eight municipal gas systems.

Although industrial customers constituted only about 1 percent of the total number of customers in 1972, they consumed two-thirds of the natural gas used in North Carolina. Consumption by all classes of customers increased two and a half times between 1963 and 1972. Industrial customers paid an average of 62.47 cents per million cubic feet. Residential users in North Carolina paid $1.50 per million cubic feet, compared with a national average of $1.09.

The rapid growth of North Carolina industry, much of which uses natural gas, and the inability of the Transcontinental Gas Pipeline Company to purchase additional supplies of gas, led to a reduction of industrial gas supplies in North Carolina in 1971. More companies were shifted to an interruptible gas service schedule, under which service could be discontinued during periods of high demand. Restrictions were placed on the attachment of new customers and restrictive-load growth programs were initiated. Suddenly, industrial firms could no longer assume that unlimited quantities of this energy source would be available. Many firms installed standby petroleum-fired energy units and the utilities invested over $18 million in plant facilities in 1972, most of it for peaking facilities that store propane or liquified natural gas for release during short periods when pipeline supplies are inadequate.

The storage of available natural gas is only part of the national energy crisis that emerged in the 1970s. It remains to be seen what effects it may yet have on the economic development of the state.

Figure 13.15. Modes and Locations of Transportation Facilities in Eleven N.C. Cities, 1974

Source: Published schedules of bus companies, Federal Aviation Administration, U.S. Department of Transportation, Federal Highway Administration, and N.C. Department of Transportation and Highway Safety, 1974.

Electricity

Commercial electricity for North Carolina is provided by four major utilities and nine small electric companies. The service areas of the four large companies are shown in Figure 13.17. The large companies sell directly to consumers or on a wholesale basis to twenty-nine electric membership corporations, seven independently owned distributing companies, three publicly owned distributing companies, and seventy-two municipalities operating electric distribution systems in the state.

Figure 13.18 shows the dramatic increase in electric power consumption that has occurred since 1960. Part of the threefold increase has resulted from the doubling of per capita consumption by the average residential customer. The 10,253 kilowatt hours consumed per customer in North Carolina in 1972 was 49 percent greater than the United States average. One explanation for this high rate of usage is that the average charge per kilowatt hour in 1972 was only 70.7 percent of the national average. Industrial usage also tripled between 1960 and 1972.

As Table 13.3 indicates, the four Class A utilities owned or purchased generating capacity that exceeded 19.3 million kilowatts in 1972. Of that amount, 11.1 million kilowatts of capacity was located in North Carolina.

Since it would take only about 10.3 million kilowatts of capacity to equal the share of the sales of each company that occurs in North Carolina, apparently total generating capacity now located within the state is adequate to meet present demands. With consumption increasing rapidly, the utilities are planning or building for greater capacities that will be needed soon. Seven nuclear-powered generating plants had been announced or were under construction in the state in 1974 (Figure 13.17). However, poor economic conditions in the nation during that year caused the reduction of plans for expansion.

Energy in North Carolina

The emergence of a national energy shortage in the 1970s ended decades of energy surpluses. North Carolinians, like other Americans, were used to having enormous quantities of energy made available on demand. An era of plentiful, low-cost energy did not require planning on the part of the state. Even now it is difficult to develop a comprehensive understanding of North Carolina's total energy situation. In January 1974 the report of the Energy Crisis Study Commission of the North Carolina General Assembly stated that "the energy accounting and monitoring of energy flow necessary to permit detailed analysis was not necessary when the nation operated from an energy surplus."

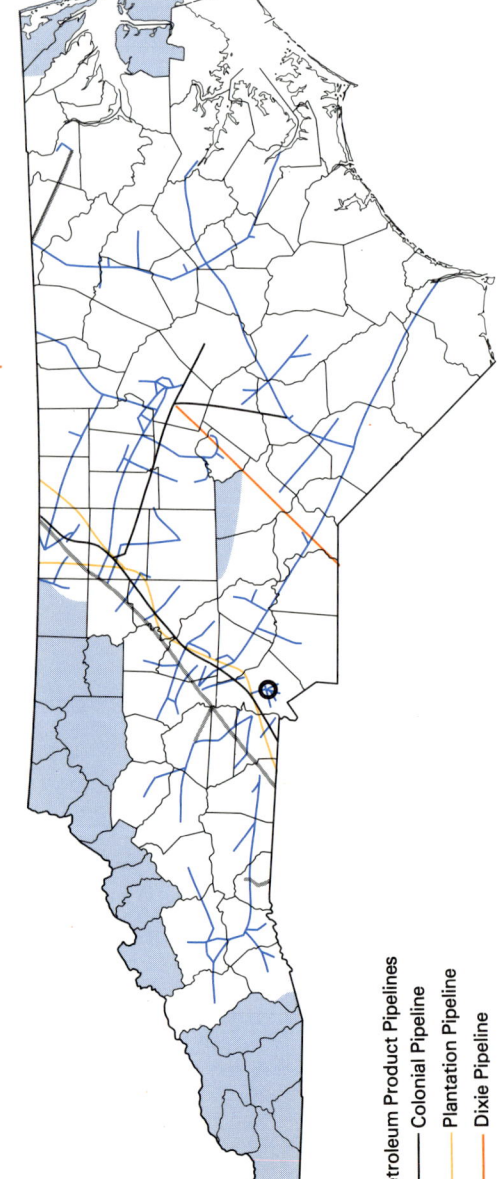

Figure 13.16. Pipelines in N.C., 1973

Petroleum Product Pipelines
— Colonial Pipeline
— Plantation Pipeline
— Dixie Pipeline

Natural Gas Pipelines
— Transcontinental Gas Pipeline Corp.
— other gas lines

○ major terminal

▒ areas without gas service

Source: Compiled from information provided by operating companies.

Table 13.3. Electrical Generating Capacity Owned and Purchased by Class A Power Companies Operating in N.C., 1972

	Percent of Sales in N.C.	Capacity in Kilowatts				
		Steam	Gas Turbine	Hydroelectric	Purchase	Total
Carolina Power & Light	85	4,117,342	565,142	219,600	455,000	5,357,084
Duke Power	67	5,937,125	425,000	1,007,875	186,460	7,556,460
Nantahala Power & Light	100	0	0	99,460	0	99,460
Virginia Electric & Power	9	5,444,860	563,308	288,240	0	6,296,408
Total generated in N.C.		8,652,626	695,422	1,124,635		11,113,543
Total		15,499,327	1,553,450	1,615,175	641,460	19,309,412
Percent generated in N.C.		55.8	44.8	69.6	—	57.6

Source: N.C. Utilities Commission, *Eighth Statistical and Analytical Report*, 1974.

Figure 13.17. Private Class A Power Company Service Areas and Generating Points in N.C., 1973

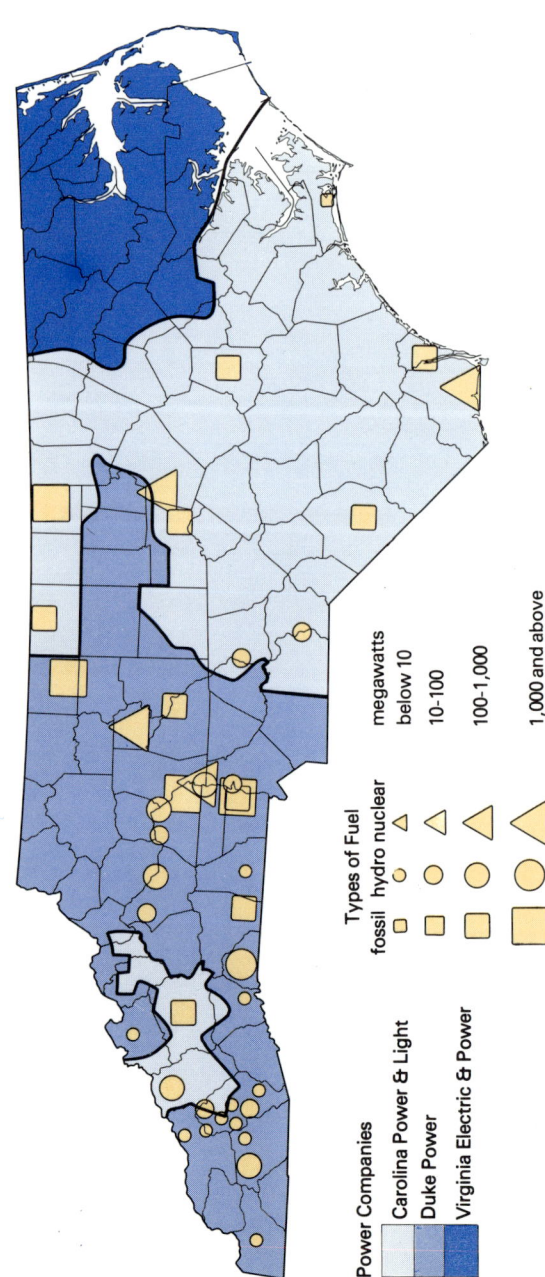

Power Companies
- Carolina Power & Light
- Duke Power
- Virginia Electric & Power

Types of Fuel: fossil, hydro, nuclear

megawatts: below 10, 10–100, 100–1,000, 1,000 and above

Source: N.C. Utilities Commission, *Eighth Statistical and Analytical Report*, 1974.

Note: Nantahala serves portions of the following counties: Cherokee, Clay, Graham, Jackson, Macon, and Swain.

Three characteristics of North Carolina make it particularly vulnerable to a national energy shortage. One is that the state is entirely dependent on external sources of energy, except for the 1 percent supplied by hydropower generating units. Data on the consumption patterns of these major sources are summarized in Tables 13.4a, b, and c. The second is that population and activities are relatively dispersed in this state, tending to require more energy per capita to overcome the distances between residences and jobs. Third, the state economy needs to develop further in order to complete the transition from an agricultural to an industrial economy and to allow the present emphasis on low-wage industry to be replaced by higher-wage industry. It takes great quantities of energy to keep the present economy operating; it will take a substantial additional amount to accommodate economic expansion. And without economic expansion the prospects for achieving substantial net increases in income levels will become poor.

The magnitude of the problem was dramatized by the acute shortage of gasoline that developed in February 1974. In order to determine the impact of a possible curtailment of natural gas supplies in late 1973, a survey of 235 industrial plants and institutions was conducted by the governor's office. A majority (143) indicated that they would have to cease operating entirely and another 26 said they would have to reduce their operations. Over 93,000 persons were employed in those plants and institutions that faced a complete or partial reduction in operations. Fortunately, such a curtailment was not required and the mild winter of 1973–74 allowed natural gas supplies to be maintained almost without interruption.

Many industrial concerns shifted to liquid petroleum fuels, as indicated by U.S. Bureau of Mines data showing a 134 percent increase in the consumption of number 2 oil and diesel oil between 1971 and 1972 and a 40.9 percent increase in the use of nonheating number 5 and 6 oils by industry during the same time. Apparently a shortage of one energy source causes pressure to shift to other sources. The legislature's Energy Crisis Study Commission recognized the urgent necessity for a comprehensive study of the total energy situation and the need for plans to deal with an era in which energy use will have to be much more carefully managed.

SELECTED REFERENCES

N.C. Department of Administration. *North Carolina State Government Statistical Abstract*. 2d ed. Raleigh: The Department, 1973.

N.C. Department of Administration, Office of State Planning. *A Report on Transportation Needs in North Carolina*. Raleigh: The Department, 1973.

N.C. General Assembly, Energy Crisis Study Commission. *Report*. Raleigh: The Commission, 1974.

N.C. Utilities Commission. *Eighth Statistical and Analytical Report*. Raleigh: The Commission, 1974.

Table 13.4(a). Consumption of Liquid Petroleum in N.C., Selected Items, 1971 and 1972 (in thousands of gallons)

	1971	1972	Percent Change
Total petroleum products consumed	3,099,118[1]	3,294,382[1]	+6.3
Gasoline	2,572,506	2,793,722	+8.6
Nonheating no. 5 & 6 oils			
Electric utilities	55,062	170,016	+208.7
Industrial	284,172	400,428	+40.9
No. 2 oil & diesel			
On highway	173,040	183,414	+6.0
Railroads	70,644	66,360	−6.0

Source: Report of the Energy Crisis Study Commission to the General Assembly of N.C., 1974.

[1]Fiscal year ending June 30 of year reported; other items for calendar year.

Table 13.4(b). Energy Sources Used by Major Electrical Utilities in N.C., 1972

Type	Carolina Power & Light[1]	Duke Power[1]
Hydropower	3.92%	4.86%
Nuclear power	21.44	—
Fossil steam		
Coal	63.94	87.97
Residual oil	7.07	
Light oil	0.24	2.00
Gas	2.47	3.02
Internal combustion peaking units		
Gas	0.10	1.22
Oil	0.83	0.92
Total	100.00	100.00
	(22,525,023 MWH)	(40,340,621 MWH)

Source: Report of the Energy Crisis Study Commission to the General Assembly of N.C., 1974.

[1]Total system.

Table 13.4(c). Consumption of Natural Gas in N.C., 1963 and 1972

	Million Cubic Feet		
Distributor	1963	1972	Percent Change
N.C. Natural Gas	16,316,603	45,735,009	180.3
N.C. Gas Service	1,553,304	3,241,111	108.7
Piedmont Natural Gas	22,630,460	52,045,689	130.0
Public Service Co.	18,368,678	43,502,276	136.8
Other regulated utilities	331,980	1,470,351	342.9
Municipals	5,604,001	11,101,329	98.1
Total	64,805,026	157,095,765	142.4

Source: N.C. Utilities Commission, *Eighth Statistical and Analytical Report*, 1974.

National statistics give a clear indication of these trends. According to the American Music Conference, there were 43.9 million amateur musicians in 1974, about twice as many as in 1950. The number of "Sunday painters" is estimated at 40 million, according to one study, and there are also a million "art" photographers and a half million amateur actors. The utilization of public park and wilderness areas has been increasing at an annual rate of over 10 percent, and the Outdoor Recreation Resources Review Commission has predicted a tripling in the overall demand for recreation by the year 2000. Educational programs for lifelong learning are abounding as courses are made available for enrichment as well as for the retraining of people of all ages. Finally, millions now have greater accessibility to health care through more public health departments and national programs such as Medicare, Medicaid, and the new Health Maintenance Organization (HMO), thereby providing the opportunity for far more individuals to enjoy society's amenities. What are the discernible developments and trends in the service and amenity sector of North Carolina's lifestyle? The following chapters portray a variety of patterns.

A telling measure of the quality of life in any society is the accessibility to and quality of its services and amenities. This last group of chapter topics—Education, Health Care Resources, Outdoor Recreation, and Cultural Arts—in a sense comprises the capstone in the *Atlas*'s sequence of themes and reaches to the core of the state's system of values.

As North Carolina addresses its future in the last quarter of the twentieth century, it will doubtless be greatly concerned about its services and amenities—given impetus by a steadily rising material well-being. An increasingly affluent society each year spawns more hours of leisure time that demand fulfillment. The forces responsible for leisure time are familiar ones, whether on the national or local scene. The longer life span because of better health care resources, the retirement years, a shorter work week and longer vacations have given today's average worker twenty-two years more leisure during his lifetime than his father had. And, of course, he has considerably more means and mobility with which to enjoy it. The average housewife now has an increasing opportunity as well as inclination for leisure time pursuits. The overall result is a significant challenge as to how this time will be utilized; some suggest a substantial reorientation of human society may be necessary.

PART V

SERVICES AND AMENITIES

In the cities, the towns and the country may the multiplication and acceleration of the mechanical contacts of civilization increasingly mean the enjoyment of leisure and recreation, the widening of information and sympathies, and the deepening of the cultural and spiritual content of the lives of the people.

—*Frank Porter Graham*

14. Education

RICHARD C. PHILLIPS
BENJAMIN H. ROMINE, JR.

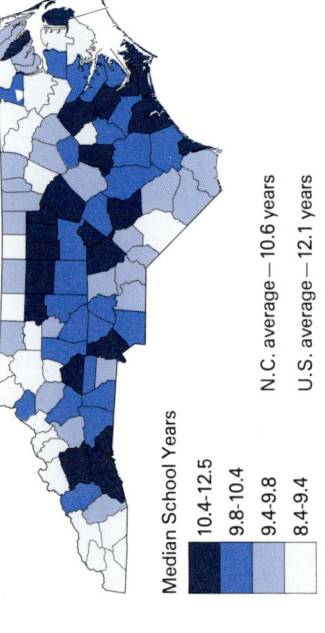

PUBLIC SCHOOL EDUCATION

Public school education has long commanded a position of great importance to the people of North Carolina as demonstrated by the fact that there are few states in which a higher percentage of family income is allocated for the support of public education than in North Carolina. Unfortunately, however, the state ranks forty-fourth in per family income, and both absolute per pupil expenditures on public education and teachers' salaries are below the national average. North Carolina ranks forty-second among the states in total educational expenditures per pupil, including state, federal, and local funds. In 1970 North Carolina ranked forty-eighth among the states in the percentage of the population twenty-five years old and older who had completed four years of high school or more. Similarly, the median numbers of years of schooling completed by persons twenty-five years old or older in 1970 was 10.6 compared with 12.1 nationally. Figure 14.1 shows the county pattern of median school years completed in North Carolina. Many factors account for the relatively poor ranking of North Carolina on the more basic educational indexes, including average per pupil expenditures, teacher salaries and qualifications, low median educational attainment by the population, lack of adequate preschool and kindergarten programs, the high degree of rurality characterizing the state, and a nonwhite population approximately twice as large as the national average in proportion to total population.

Public School Expenditures

Although the capital cost of providing school buildings must be borne by the local government, the major source of public school current operating expenses is the state of North Carolina. In addition to providing for buildings, local funds are utilized to supplement teacher salaries, purchase supplementary materials, and generally enhance instructional program quality. Federal monies have been used largely to provide vocational education, support for school lunch programs, funds for textbooks and library materials, aid to the disadvantaged, and support to school districts in which large numbers of military or other federal personnel are concentrated.

State funds are allocated on a formula based on average daily attendance for a portion of the preceding school year. The proportion of total public school expenditures for current operations provided by the state in 1971-72 was 66.8 percent statewide. North Carolina is truly a "state system" in its provision for public schooling as indicated by the fact that the state ranks fourth in the nation in the proportion of state expenditures. The proportion of total expenditures provided by the state varied from 79.6 percent in Davidson County to a low 57 percent in Mecklenburg County. Federal support, 15.2 percent statewide, ranged from 6.5 percent in Catawba County to 33.7 percent in Halifax County. Local support, 18.0 percent statewide, varied from 3.5 percent in Wayne County to 36.3 percent in Mecklenburg County. Figure 14.2 indicates the sources of school funds in North Carolina. Except for Charlotte, Winston-Salem, Wilmington, and some smaller communities, most cities are in special school-tax districts that provide more school support than does the county as a whole. Figure 14.3 therefore portrays the average for the school administrative unit rather than for the county to avoid distortion.

According to the North Carolina State Department of Public Instruction, the average per pupil expenditure for public education in North Carolina in 1971-72 was $784, including state, federal, and local funds. The average per pupil expenditure ranged from $568 in Randolph County to $966 in Hyde County. The estimated national average per pupil expenditure for public education in 1971-72, according to the National Education Association's research division, was $929; North Carolina ranked forty-fourth among the fifty states in this respect. Although the absolute figures for North Carolina depicted in Figure 14.4 do not coincide exactly with the figures from the State Department of Public Instruction, the state's ranking of forty-fourth was unchanged by the discrepancy.

Figure 14.1. Median School Years Completed in N.C., 1970

Source: U.S. Department of Commerce, *1970 Census of Population and Housing,* 1970.

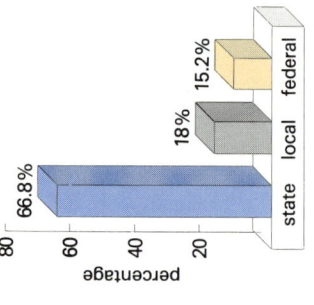

Figure 14.2. Source of N.C. School Funds, 1971-1972

Source: N.C. Department of Public Instruction, *North Carolina Public Schools: Biennial Report of the State Superintendent, 1971-1972,* 1972.

Figure 14.3. Average per Pupil Expenditure for Public Education in N.C., 1971-1972

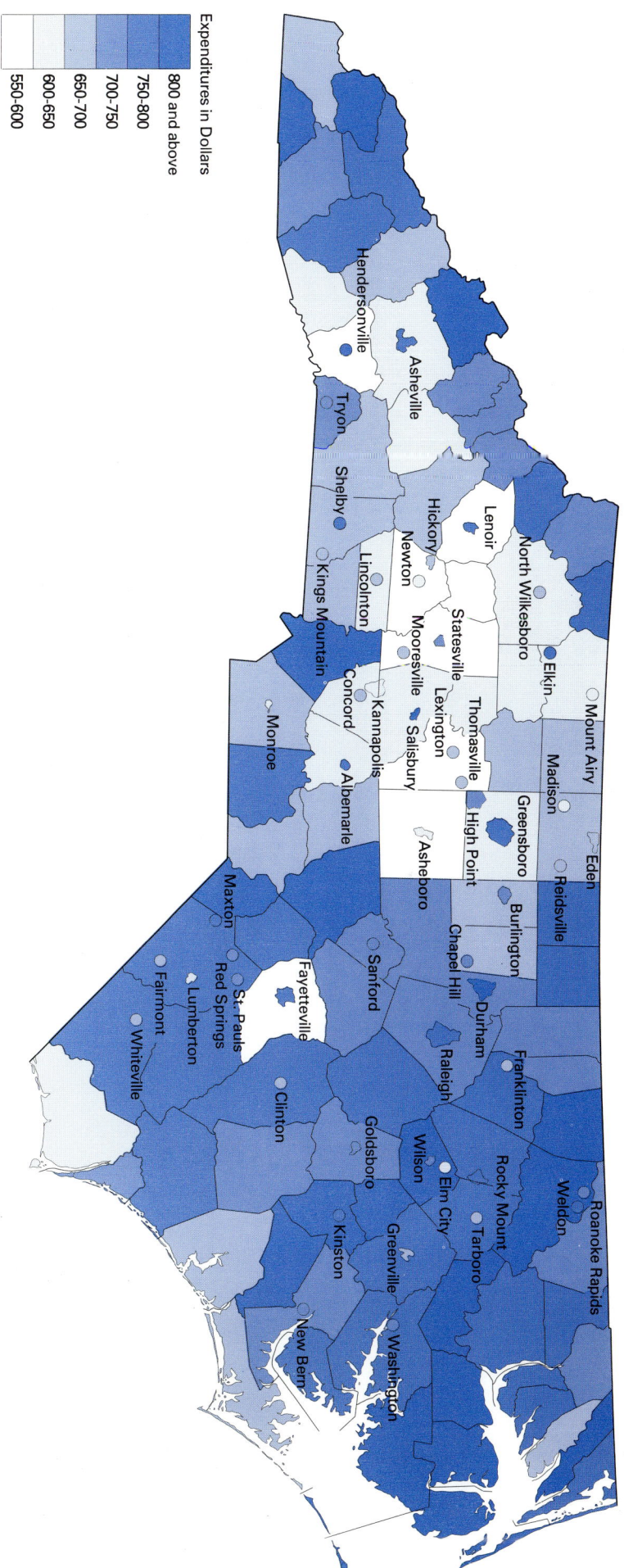

Source: N.C. Department of Public Instruction, *North Carolina Public Schools: Biennial Report of the State Superintendent, 1971-1972,* 1972.

North Carolina's estimated average per pupil expenditure of $802 in 1972-73, compared with the national average of $1,034, enabled the state to improve its ranking significantly over 1971-72 to thirty-seventh as shown in Figure 14.4. It is important to note that the estimated $802 average per pupil expenditure in North Carolina in 1972-73 was less than 80 percent of the national average. However, North Carolina had managed to improve its ranking among the states from forty-fifth in 1968-69 to thirty-seventh by 1972-73.

North Carolina ranks fourth among the twelve southeastern states depicted in Figure 14.4 in estimated average per pupil expenditures for 1972-73. This represents a major improvement over the ranking of eighth in 1968-69 or five years earlier.

The average per pupil expenditure for public education in any state is closely related to per capita personal income. North Carolina lags far behind the national average in per capita personal income, and its rank has remained rather constant in recent years. Its per capita personal income in 1971 was $3,424 compared with the southeast region's $3,825 and with the nation's $4,156 for a national ranking of thirty-ninth. Such a large disparity of income takes on increased significance when the public school revenue from state and local sources as a percent of personal income is examined. In 1970 North Carolina ranked a poor thirty-fifth in the nation with its allocation to public education of 4.5 percent of personal income compared with the national average of 5 percent.

An important index of a state's financial support of its public school system is its teachers' salaries. North Carolina pays the base salary of most teachers and other professional personnel, though upward of two-thirds of them receive supplements to their base salaries from local taxes. Although these local supplements create major disparities from one local system to another, the average salary for teachers in 1971-72 was $8,051 compared with the national average of $9,690. North Carolina ranked thirty-seventh among the states in average salaries for teachers.

proportion of high school graduates is typically greater in the more urbanized and industrialized counties and in the counties with large military bases.

Counties with large percentages of blacks tend to have fewer high school graduates in the population twenty-five years of age and older. Comparison should be made between Figure 14.5 and Figure 14.3, which depicts per pupil expenditures on education. In general, the percentage of high school graduates in the adult population is smallest in those counties expending the least in state and local funds per pupil.

Percentage of High School Graduates Compared to Fifth-Grade Enrollment Seven Years Earlier

Per pupil expenditures, the quality of teaching, and the variety of courses are among the many factors that determine the quality of a school. But perhaps the most telling index of school quality is the dropout rate, or the "holding power." Holding power may be defined as the percentage relationship between the size of the high school graduating class and the size of the fifth-grade class seven years earlier. Since the ultimate destination of transient students is not systematically "tracked" from school system to school system, inferences derived from such statistics must be very tentative. For example, inferences drawn from such statistics are questionable for counties characterized by a high net loss or gain of population as well as for small counties in which school enrollments may fluctuate dramatically from school year to school year.

A multiplicity of cultural factors determines to a large extent the proportion of the population that completes high school. Rural youth in general are less likely to complete high school than urban youth. Rural youth living on farms are less likely to graduate than rural youth whose parents work in factories or at other nonfarm jobs. Black youth are less likely to graduate than white youth. Youth generally remain in school longer than either of their parents. Youth attending larger high schools with considerable variety in curricular offerings are more likely to graduate than those attending smaller ones whose curricular offerings tend to be largely college preparatory.

The average percentage of the state's 1964-65 fifth-grade enrollment that completed high school in 1972 was 66.3 percent (Figure 14.6). The national average was approximately 78 percent. The ten North Carolina counties with the highest percentages of high school graduates were Wake (84.7), Watauga (81.9), Clay (80.6), Forsyth (76.5), Davie (76.2), New Hanover (74.9), Haywood (74.3), Cumberland (74.0), Polk (73.9), and Chowan (73.1). Chowan, Clay, Davie, Polk, and Watauga had small total populations and chance variations tend

Qualifications of Teachers

In 1971-72 the North Carolina public schools had a professional staff of 56,729, of whom 54,091 were classroom teachers. Of the latter group 95.2 percent held certificates based on at least the bachelor's degree compared with a nationwide average of 97 percent. In 1969-70, only 92.9 percent of North Carolina's teachers held at least a bachelor's degree.

One important indicator of the quality of a state's public school teachers is the percentage possessing at least the master's degree. North Carolina lags far behind the national average in this regard. Among the teachers employed in North Carolina public schools in 1971-72, only 15 percent held the master's degree compared with the national average of more than 27 percent.

For the first time since the 1930s teacher supply in North Carolina and in the nation has caught up with demand—except in the areas of early childhood education, science, and mathematics. An important consequence of the essential equilibrium achieved between supply and demand has been that school systems can be more selective in their employment policies and can upgrade the quality of their faculties. Teacher candidates deficient in bachelor's degree credits have increasingly over the past decade been eliminated from public school faculties. Nationwide, the percentage of public school teachers in the classroom with less than a bachelor's degree has dropped dramatically from 15 percent in 1961 to 3 percent in 1971.

High School Graduates

The proportion of the North Carolina population that has graduated from high school has increased significantly in recent years, though the state has slipped in comparison with other states in the percentage of its adult population who have completed at least four years of high school. In 1950 North Carolina ranked a very poor forty-eighth with its 20.5 percent of those twenty-five years of age and over who had completed at least four years of high school compared with the national average of 33.3 percent. By 1960 North Carolina closed the gap considerably to rank forty-second with 32.3 percent compared with the national average of 41.1 percent. By 1970 the state had fallen in ranking to forty-eighth based on its 38.5 percent as compared with the national average of 52.3 percent on this index.

The geographic patterns in Figure 14.5 that depict the percentage of North Carolina population twenty-five years of age and over who have completed four years of high school are indicative of both the quality of high schools in each county and the economic opportunities the counties offer their high school graduates. The

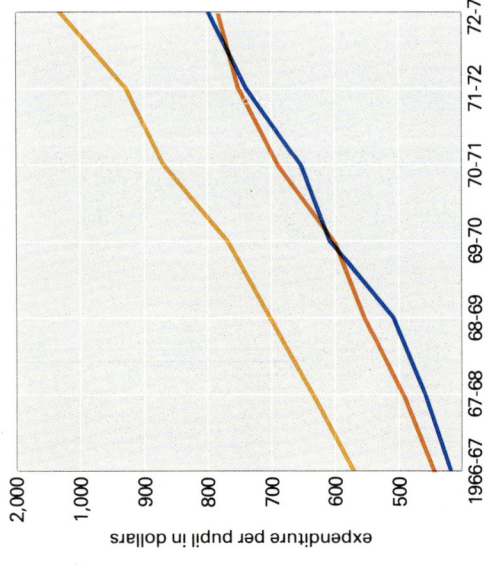

Figure 14.4. Trends in Average per Pupil Expenditures in N.C., the Southeast, and the U.S., 1966-1973

Source: The National Education Association (based on average daily attendance).

to make their ranking misleading. Forsyth, New Hanover, and Wake were in the top twelve in locally provided per pupil expenditures, which educational authorities agree constitutes a rather reliable index of the quality of schools.

Percentage of High School Graduates Who Continued with Higher Education

An important index of the quality of high schools is the percentage of students who pursue some form of higher education. The average percentage of North Carolina high school graduates who went on to higher education in 1972 was 58.1. Of this percentage 30.9 enrolled in senior colleges, 22.7 percent enrolled in junior colleges, community colleges, and technical institutes, and 4.6 percent entered private trade, business, and nursing schools. Of those not pursuing higher education, 3.9 percent went into military service, 28.1 percent became gainfully employed, and insufficient information was available on 9.8 percent.

North Carolina lags well behind the nation in the average percentage of high school graduates who continue with higher education. Even with the inclusion of students entering certificate-granting technical institutes in the group pursuing programs in degree-granting colleges and universities, the state's 53.6 percent was far below the national average of 62 percent.

The Kindergarten Program

Most educational authorities agree that the availability of kindergarten programs for five-year-old youngsters greatly enhances their chances for academic success in later years. Benjamin Bloom of the University of Chicago has advanced rather strong evidence that more than half of the child's intelligence develops prior to his enrollment in the first grade. Bloom estimated that 50 percent of measurable intelligence develops by age four, another 30 percent between ages four and eight, and about 20 percent between ages eight and seventeen. Although Bloom is not suggesting that these estimates are infallible or irreversible, he is emphasizing the crucial importance of each child's having the most intellectually stimulating environment possible as a means of maximizing his chances for academic success in later school years.

North Carolina made a very belated entry into kindergarten education in 1969 when the legislature allocated $1 million for the planning and implementation of eight public kindergarten centers, one in each educational district, to serve as model projects for curriculum planning and teacher education. Later, $4.3 million was appropriated by the state legislature for 1971-73 to study these centers and to expand the program by increasing

the number to seventy-four. The seventy-four centers operating during 1972-73 accommodated approximately 3,400 five-year-olds.

The 1973 General Assembly took a truly dramatic step toward providing adequate kindergarten education in North Carolina for all five-year-olds. It appropriated some $12.3 million to maintain the 149 classes operating in seventy-four centers during 1972-73 and to provide for the opening of 522 new kindergarten classes by the beginning of the 1973-74 school year. The proposed number of five-year-olds that was to be served in 1973-74 was 15,433. The legislation provided that each school district in the state operate a minimum of two kindergarten classes beginning in September 1973. The remaining funds were to be divided among the school districts on a formula basis, which takes into account the average daily attendance of children enrolled in the first grade. The legislation also provided that kindergartens will be available for all five-year-olds

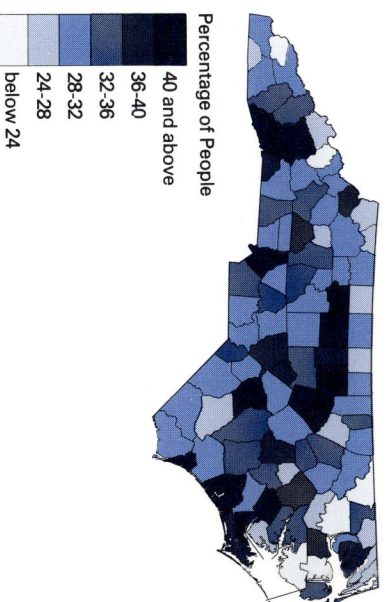

Figure 14.5. Percentage of N.C. Population 25 Years of Age and Over with High School Degrees, 1970

Source: U.S. Department of Commerce, *1970 Census of Population and Housing*, 1970.

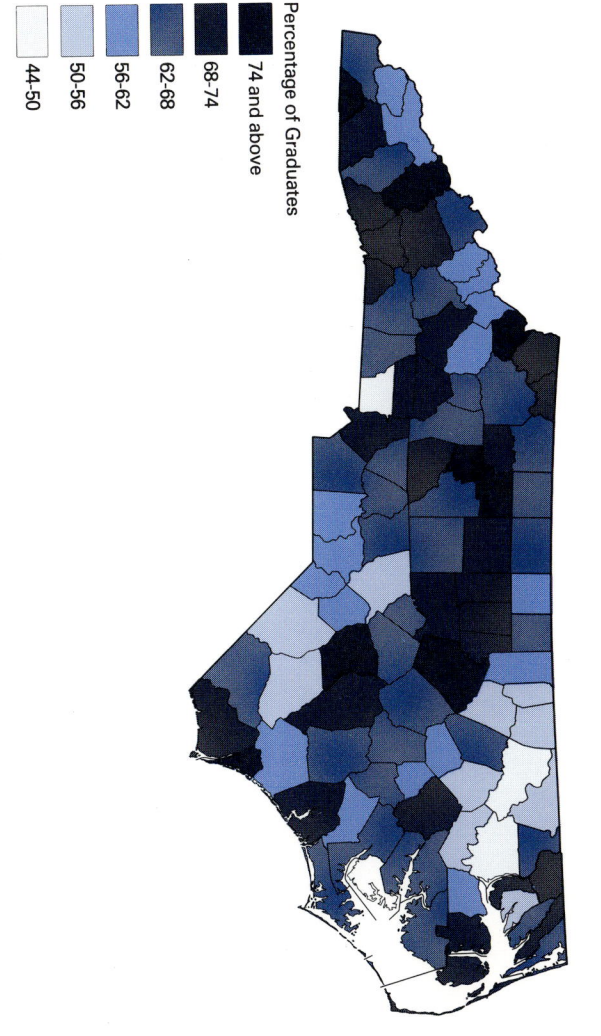

Figure 14.6. N.C. High School Graduates, 1972, Relative to Fifth-Grade Enrollment Seven Years Earlier

Source: N.C. Department of Public Instruction, *Survey of 1972 High School Graduates*, 1972.

by September 1978. The five-year growth trends in kindergarten classes and numbers of youngsters accommodated are depicted in Figure 14.7. These data can be compared with data presented in Figure 14.8 to determine North Carolina's position in relation to the Southeast and the nation.

It should be noted that beginning with the school year 1966-67 the federal government began supporting kindergarten programs in North Carolina at an accelerated rate that reached its peak in 1970-71 when 12,362 youngsters were provided kindergarten programs in seventy-nine school systems. But like many other federally funded programs, the amount of support was curtailed substantially in 1971-72. Although such federal funding provides initial impetus to educational programs, it is very undependable. The state and local governments must assume the basic responsibility for funding kindergarten programs if all five-year-olds are to be accommodated consistently with high quality education.

The low standing of North Carolina among the states on all too many indexes of educational achievement is due in considerable measure to the relative absence of public kindergarten programs for its five-year-olds. The state ranks near the bottom in number of five-year-olds enrolled in public kindergartens in comparison with other states in the southern region and across the nation as is readily apparent from examination of the data in Figure 14.8. According to the United States census for 1970, North Carolina's 18.6 percent of five-year-olds in public kindergartens placed it ahead of only Kentucky (16 percent), West Virginia (14.5 percent), and Arkansas (13 percent). The national range in percentage of five-year-olds in public kindergartens in 1970 was from 13 percent in Arkansas to 97.9 percent in Iowa. Thirty-one states and the District of Columbia in 1970 enrolled at least half of their five-year-olds in public kindergartens; and most of these states enrolled percentages closer to 80 percent than 50 percent.

The critical importance of public kindergarten programs is perhaps best illustrated in terms of the extent to which they facilitate learner advancement through the public school program, thereby reducing the retention or failure rate and ultimately the dropout rate. According to the North Carolina State Department of Public Instruction, each year more than 18,000 youngsters in the state's first three grades fail and are retained in the same grade.

Systematic evaluation of the 1969-71 state-supported kindergarten program in North Carolina revealed that students advanced from approximately the thirty-fifth percentile at the beginning of the school year to the sixty-fifth percentile at the end of the school year on two basic tests of knowledge in the areas of mathematics and language arts. In other words, at the beginning of the kindergarten experience, the North Carolina students' average on the tests scored in the bottom third of the national five-year-olds' sample; at the end of the school year the North Carolina youngsters' average had improved to rank in the top third of the national sample. On another test the results revealed that the average mental age of North Carolina preschoolers increased approximately two months for each month they had been enrolled in the kindergarten program.

Another important finding of the study was that North Carolina six-year-olds who have attended kindergarten are better prepared for school. This was found by comparing the performance on the nationally standardized Stanford Achievement Test of first-grade students who had attended kindergarten with those who had not. Data also reveal that fewer six-year-olds are being retained in the first grade in areas with kindergarten centers. For example, a December 1972 sampling of schools with state-supported kindergarten programs was surveyed to determine the effect kindergarten had upon the retention rate. The survey yielded the following results:

	Retention Percentage among Children Not Attending State-supported Kindergartens	Retention Percentage among Kindergarten Children
First grade (1970-71)	8.77%	1.34%
Second grade (1971-72)	3.27%	only one retained
First grade (1971-72)	7.45%	less than ¼%

The brief experience North Carolina has had with state-supported kindergartens shows rich promise. The foregoing research results strongly suggest that kindergartens build readiness for reading, mathematics, and other basic academic subjects. They dramatically reduce the retention rate in the primary grades and greatly diminish retardation among North Carolina youth in comparison with the national average.

It is worthy of special note that the 1969-71 evaluation of the performance of youngsters in North Carolina kindergarten programs revealed that learners who gained the most in academic achievement were the ones who needed to gain the most. This was evident in the finding that the center with the lowest averages at the beginning made the largest gains on four of the basic tests. In the absence of such public kindergarten programs it is reasonable to predict that these deprived five-year-olds would be poor performers in school. Public kindergarten programs represent the best in compensatory education for the deprived or disadvantaged and further stimulate other types of students.

The Sixth-Grade Assessment Study

The evaluation of North Carolina's state kindergarten program was paralleled by a statewide assessment of the educational progress of sixth-grade students. Initiated by the State Superintendent of Public Instruction, the study was provided for by action of the State Board of Education in 1970. It was conducted by the Research Triangle Institute with a sample of 11,283 randomly selected youngsters from the total of 101,549 sixth-grade students enrolled in North Carolina public schools during the 1971-72 school year. The goal was to determine reliable estimates of average achievement for the entire state as well as for certain particular groups, namely, the educationally disadvantaged receiving federal educational aid under Title I law, three types of North Carolina communities, and the three major geographical regions of the state.

The results of this study, coupled with the emerging results of studies of youngsters exposed to public school kindergarten programs, provide an increasingly clear indication of the current status of public education in North Carolina for the youngsters concerned, along with strong suggestions as to their likelihood of success in later schooling. Assessment results, however, should be interpreted cautiously in terms of comparisons with the Southeast region and the nation for reasons to be discussed later.

In a single day of testing each sixth-grader in the sample completed among other things an academic ability test called the Lorge-Thorndike Test and an achievement test concerning reading, mathematics, and language arts called the Iowa Test of Basic Skills. Both of these tests have been standardized according to sound scientific principles and yield reliable results.

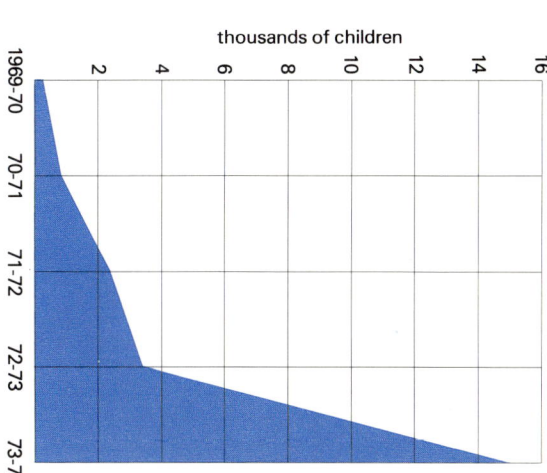

Figure 14.7. Enrollment of Five-Year-Olds in N.C. Kindergartens

Source: N.C. Department of Public Instruction, unpublished data.

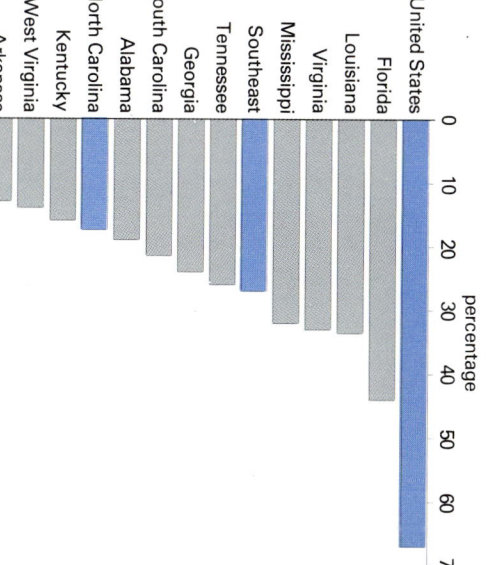

Figure 14.8. Percentage of Five-Year-Olds in Public Kindergartens in N.C., the Southeast, and the U.S., 1970

Source: N.C. Department of Public Instruction, unpublished data.

The Lorge-Thorndike Test measures the student's ability to deal with abstract ideas that are basic to success in further schooling as well as in the adult world of work. It includes both verbal and nonverbal sections to maximize fairness to all learners. In interpreting the results one should be mindful that the scores reflect present academic ability that is closely correlated with success in learning the concepts emphasized in school; test results do not represent permanent general learning ability.

Statewide results on the Lorge-Thorndike Test on academic ability reveal that North Carolina sixth-graders taking the test averaged slightly below the average of the sample of students in the nation used in standardizing the test. The six point difference in average scores means that, according to the measurement procedure of this test, the sixth-graders tested in the process of standardizing it have slightly more academic ability than North Carolina sixth-graders sampled.

Further analysis of test results reveals that, in terms of regions in North Carolina, the scores of Mountain students were highest, the scores of Piedmont students followed closely, and the scores of Coastal Plain students were exceeded by those of both other regions. It was found that there was almost no difference between large-city and large-city-fringe/medium-city groups. Both of these groups scored slightly higher than rural/small-town students, however. Non-Title I students scored substantially higher than the educationally disadvantaged Title I students; and white students' scores exceeded the nonwhites' scores by a similar though not identical margin.

The foregoing comparative results on academic ability are similar to those reported on academic achievement measures (Iowa Test of Basic Skills). Assessment of sixth-graders' reading skills focused on vocabulary and comprehension. In general, the vocabulary performance of sixth-graders in North Carolina and the Southeast region was exceeded by that of sixth-graders in the nation taking the test. Whereas the Southeast lagged 6 to 10 percent behind the nation, North Carolina was 9 to 20 percent behind the national average. Students taking the test in North Carolina were nine months behind those taking it in the nation. Differences in reading comprehension were less pronounced, though North Carolina lagged about seven months (or 7 to 15 percent) behind the nation. It also lagged behind the Southeast.

Comparison of measures of both vocabulary and comprehension skills in reading shows that Mountain students exceeded Piedmont students; both of those groups exceeded the Coastal Plain average. Large-city students were slightly ahead of medium-city/large-city-fringe students, and both of those groups exceeded the rural/small-town student average.

The language skills questions of the Iowa Test of Basic Skills deal with spelling, capitalization, punctuation, and usage. Considered as a whole, the Southeast region sixth-graders were slightly ahead of the sixth-graders in North Carolina in language skills. The national group was 4 to 10 percent ahead of the Southeast and 11 to 16 percent ahead of North Carolina. North Carolina sixth-graders lagged behind the national average seven to ten months.

Regional comparisons reveal that the Mountain sixth-graders averaged higher than those of the Piedmont, and both averaged higher than the Coastal Plain students. However, the only statistically significant difference in scores was that between Mountain and Coastal Plain students, and the difference disappeared when other factors such as type of community and sex were held constant. Statistically significant differences were found, however, in the average scores in terms of Title I eligibility, sex, and race. Non-Title I students scored higher than Title I students, females higher than males, and white students higher than nonwhite students.

In mathematics skills, North Carolina students lagged 6 to 12 percent behind Southeast sixth-graders and 14 to 20 percent below the national sample. North Carolina youth were behind the nation approximately seven to nine months. Analysis by region shows that Mountain student scores exceeded those of Piedmont students, but only slightly; both sets of scores exceeded those of Coastal Plain students. Large-city-fringe/medium-city students scored slightly higher than the students in the other two groups. Comparison in terms of Title I eligibility and race reveals that non-Title I students scored higher than Title I students, and whites averaged higher than nonwhites.

Environmental factors are known to be closely associated with educational achievement. Thus the results described above concerning the assessment of the academic ability and achievement of North Carolina sixth-graders should be interpreted within the total context of this book.

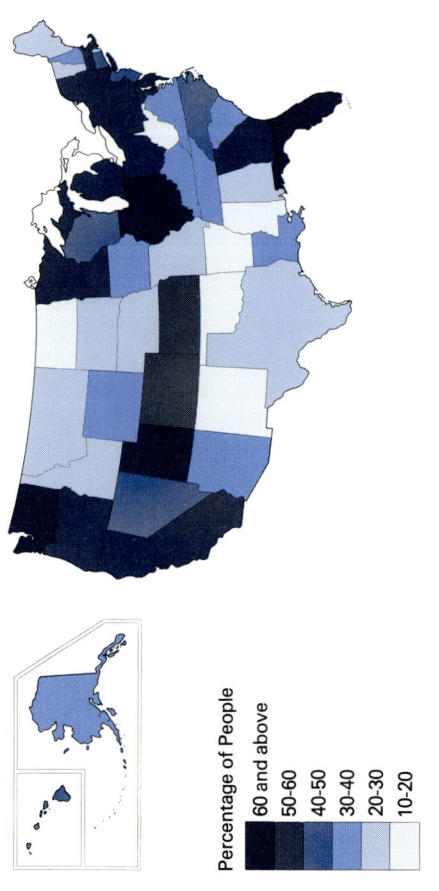

Figure 14.9. Percentage of Handicapped, Age 21 and Under, Accommodated Educationally, 1973

Percentage of People
- 60 and above
- 50-60
- 40-50
- 30-40
- 20-30
- 10-20

Source: N.C. Department of Public Instruction, unpublished data.

The amount and availability of revenue, coupled with factors associated with income, race, and degree of rurality largely account for North Carolina's low ranking in educational achievement. With the nation's eleventh largest public school enrollment (1970-71) and the forty-fourth lowest per family income, North Carolina bears an especially heavy burden in trying to improve the average educational achievement level of its population. Per pupil expenditures, average salaries for teachers, and expenditures for special education and guidance have been well below the national average because of the state's comparatively weak revenue base. The fact that North Carolina's percentage of nonwhites is twice that of the nation has worked against rapid improvement in its rankings in educational attainment, probably because nonwhites have been taught in traditionally inferior schools. Although the nation is approximately 11 percent nonwhite, North Carolina and the Southeast is 20 percent nonwhite. More than 95 percent of the nonwhites reside in the Coastal Plain and Piedmont regions. Regional differences reveal that the Coastal Plain is 31.6 percent nonwhite and the Piedmont is 21.1 percent nonwhite. Only 5.7 percent of the people in the Mountains are nonwhite. In terms of degree of rurality, North Carolina ranks ahead of the nation and Southeast. For example, 55 percent of the state's population is classified as rural compared with 41.5 percent for the Southeast.

Special Services

The lag in expenditures for education in North Carolina is perhaps most apparent in what until recently were looked upon as frill areas—preschool education, special services, and special education. Although the ratio of professional personnel (which includes all certificated staff) to students in 1971-72 in North Carolina of 1 to 20.9 approximated the national average, the state's ranking of forty-seventh in kindergarten education underscores the low priority accorded so-called special areas.

North Carolina's deficiencies in professional personnel for dealing effectively with educational problems largely beyond the purview of the classroom teacher or administrator are easily documented. For example, the 870 full-time and 125 part-time guidance counselors employed in elementary and secondary schools of the state in 1972-73 could accommodate only an estimated 25 percent of the student enrollment. Moreover, despite the fact that the number of school psychologists working in the schools has increased by a substantial percentage since 1968, they numbered a mere thirty-six in 1971-72. This paltry number could accommodate barely 10 percent of the school population. According to the State Department of Public Instruction, only two part-time psychiatrists were employed in the state's schools.

Provision for the handicapped in the public schools in North Carolina falls short of meeting its many needs (Figure 14.9). Although a limited amount of institutional care is available for some youngsters, too little is available in the public schools where most of them should be enrolled. The state makes educational provision for an estimated 43 percent of its handicapped youth through age twenty-one, which places it near the top among southern states, but only slightly above the national average of 41 percent. The percentage of handicapped youth between ages 0 and 21 accommodated by the state ranges from 10 percent in Arkansas to 81 percent in Washington.

Instructional programs for specific types of exceptional children in the public schools (including the gifted) are summarized in Table 14.1. It is apparent from examination of these data that a wide gap exists between the high and low percentages of students accommodated by special instructional programs. The highest percentages are for the educable mentally retarded (86 percent), the trainable retarded (67 percent), and the speech impaired (41 percent); the lowest percentages are for the hearing impaired (2.6 percent), the emotionally disturbed (4.2 percent), and the crippled (8.8 percent).

Outlook

In conclusion, it is apparent from the foregoing evidence that North Carolina's low ranking among the states in important educational indexes demands dramatic change and improvement. Population trends and school enrollment projections for the next decade suggest that North Carolina will have an unusual opportunity to improve the quality of public education. Data from the National Center for Health Statistics of the United States Public Health Service indicate that the number of live births in this nation reached an all-time high of 4.3 million in 1961 and then declined each year until it reached 3.5 million and in 1968. In 1969 the number rose to almost 3.6 million and in 1970 to 3.7 million; the number again fell to 3.6 million in 1971. Based on continually falling birthrates, the center's projections show that there will be small annual reductions in elementary school enrollment for the next five years. Beginning in 1977 and continuing for several years thereafter we can expect a tapering off of enrollment at the high school level. The elementary school enrollment decline has already begun as evidenced by the fact that enrollment between 1971-72 and 1972-73 dropped from 36.4 million students in grades kindergarten-8 to 35.9 million—a decrease of approximately 1 percent.

North Carolina school enrollment patterns are currently consistent with national trends. At the elementary level, enrollment reached 872,758 youngsters in 1967-68 and has declined each year since to the current enrollment of 833,261 in 1971-72. High school enrollment is still on the increase; it has risen from 345,430 in 1967-68 to 364,536 in 1971-72. Illustrative of the declining trend in enrollments are the data presented in Figure 14.10 showing decreases in the numbers of youngsters attending the primary grades in North Carolina schools. As the full effects of declining enrollments are felt, North Carolina will be able to address itself to heretofore mind-boggling problems in improving educational quality. Increased revenues should enhance the quality of education for the smaller numbers of youngsters in school.

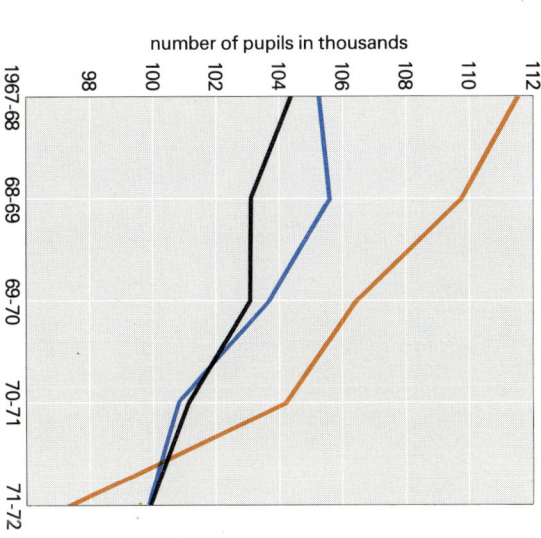

Figure 14.10. Declining Enrollment Trends in Primary Grades in N.C. Schools, 1967-1972

Source: N.C. Department of Public Instruction, unpublished data.

Actions by the 1973 General Assembly exemplify the type of efforts necessary for improving the quality of public elementary and secondary education in North Carolina. For example, it increased the appropriation for the 1973-74 school budget almost 22 percent over the previous year. This included more than $123 million for new and improved educational services. In addition to providing for a major expansion of the public kindergarten program, the money will be used in many other ways. For example, some $33.4 million will be used to extend the ten-month term and thus increase teachers' salaries. The ten-month term includes provision for significantly more instructional planning time for teachers—a fact that promises to improve student educational achievement.

The 1973 budget also provided for some $26 million to reduce class size. With these funds, classes for grades 1-3 are to be limited to twenty-six students; grades 4-8 to thirty-three students; and high school grades to thirty-five students per class or 150 students per day. The reduction in class size should enable teachers more adequately to meet the individual instructional needs of learners.

The 1973 state school budget also provided some $5.8 million to improve occupational education. The money provides for 446 teachers to expand courses in such occupations as seafood industries, environmental control occupations, construction trades, and so on.

Other major budget increases included approximately $865,000 to assist students with learning disabilities. The budget also provided for two hundred additional teachers to work with the gifted and talented, the mentally retarded, the speech and hearing impaired, and other youngsters with physical problems.

In addition to lengthening the school year and thereby increasing the average salary for teachers by 6.7 percent, the General Assembly provided a 5 percent cost-of-living increase for all teachers for 1973-74. Many teachers also received an average 5 percent increase in salary as a result of increments in the revised salary scale. Thus many teachers received salary increases of almost 17 percent.

These financial appropriations by the 1973 General Assembly should very significantly address and eventually materially alleviate many of the deficiencies in North Carolina public education. The long-term trend appears to be improved quality public education, particularly if the General Assembly continues its enlightened leadership in this very basic social priority.

HIGHER EDUCATION

Of the many important resources of a state, perhaps the most vital is a well-trained and well-educated citizenry, for without that element, natural abundance may be squandered or left to waste.

This section examines those institutions whose purpose it is to develop leaders, train technicians, and inform laymen for their roles in defining and pursuing progress in North Carolina. As if that task were not large enough, these institutions and their people are daily involved in such issues of statewide concern as providing medical service, improving agricultural production, conducting and applying research in fields as varied as nuclear physics and gerontology, and enriching the lives of tens of thousands through cultural and athletic events.

In surveying the contributions, conditions, and challenges of higher education in the state, attention is directed to its history and resources and to the types and magnitude of the services provided. Moreover, an attempt is made to suggest some of the problems and opportunities that will in all likelihood confront higher education during the remainder of the twentieth century.

History

When, in 1795, the University of North Carolina first opened its doors in Chapel Hill, the institution afforded the ultimate in one-to-one instruction. The professor doubled as president; the student was Hinton James.

James was not the first North Carolinian to engage in higher learning. Prior to 1795, the state was represented by at least two students at Yale, one at William and Mary, another at Brown, five at Harvard, about twenty-five at Princeton, plus, of course, the handful who attended Oxford or Cambridge.

Closer home, young people were enrolled in the Reverend David Caldwell's "Log College" near Greensboro, which was established in 1766 or 1767. An institution called Queens College had opened in Charlotte, moved to Salisbury, changed its name twice, and closed its doors all between 1767 and 1791. Salem Female Academy began in 1772 as a school for the daughters of the Salem community and exists today as

Table 14.1. Instructional Programs for Exceptional Children, N.C. Public Schools, 1971-1972

	CR	MH (DB)	ED	ER	GT	HH	HI	LD	SI	TR	VI	Total
Est. total no. of exceptional children[1]	5,989	125	35,934	41,923	107,802	1,797	5,989	35,934	71,868	4,791	2,396	314,548
Est. % of school population	0.5%	0.01% (0.0001)	3%	3.5%	9%	0.15%	0.5%	3%	6%	0.4%	0.2%	26.26%
No. of pupils served	475	20[2]	1,499[5]	36,190	22,657	710	154	7,525[5]	29,613	3,228	750[5]	102,821
Est. % of pupils served	8.8%	16%	4.2%	86%	20%	39%	2.6%	21%	41%	67%	33%	33%
Est. no. and % of pupils not served	5,514 (91.2%)	105 (84%)	34,435 (95.8%)	5,733 (14%)	85,145 (80%)	1,087 (61%)	5,835 (97.4%)	28,409 (79%)	42,255 (59%)	1,563 (33%)	1,646 (67%)	211,727 (67%)
No. of teachers	31	9[3]	24 ½	1,859 ½	256 ⅓[4]	68 ½	22	80 ⅙	305 ⅙	269	14	2,939 ⅙

Source: N.C. Department of Public Instruction, unpublished data, 1973.

Note: CR=Crippled; MH=Multiple-Handicapped (deaf-blind only); ED=Emotionally Disturbed; ER=Educable Mentally Retarded; GT=Gifted and Talented; HH=Homebound and/or Hospitalized; HI=Hearing Impaired; LD=Learning Disabled; SI=Speech Impaired; TR=Trainable Mentally Retarded; VI=Visually Impaired. Figures showing "number of pupils served" are from principals' year-end reports, except figures for HI, SI, and TR, which are from special local unit reports directly to Division for Exceptional Children, Department of Public Instruction.

[1] Based on total 1971-72 enrollment of 1,197,797.
[2] Plus 16 in summer program.
[3] Plus 4 in summer program.
[4] Plus at least 446 regular teachers.
[5] Figures too high; possible error in reporting.

Salem College. Franklin Academy, from which Louisburg College traces its development, was chartered in 1787.

These early attempts to provide higher learning, i.e., formal instruction beyond that deemed essential, are especially noteworthy, for the conditions of the period did not foster the development of nonessential institutions. In retrospect, the establishment of the University of North Carolina must be considered the first major benchmark in higher education. The 1789 Chartering Act and the arrival of the first student in 1795 presented the newborn nation with its first operating, state-supported institution of higher education. (The University of Georgia was chartered in 1785 and offered instruction first in 1801.)

The next one hundred years witnessed dramatic changes in higher education in North Carolina. The state's first constitution, which had provided for a state-maintained university, was amended in 1835 and the reforms created a more favorable political climate for the fledgling institution. But a generation later, the Civil War took most of its faculty and students; and Reconstruction had a devastating effect. Indeed, from 1870 to 1875, the university was forced to close its doors. There were sectarian and political attacks, public apathy, and little money. But there were successes, and building upon them, the university came to prosper.

There was also movement on the other fronts, slow at first and uneven, but during the last two-thirds of the nineteenth century, no fewer than sixty-two institutions of higher education were chartered in North Carolina. Of those, thirty-nine have survived, including such outstanding private institutions as Wake Forest University (1834), Davidson College (1837), and Duke University (1838), and the state's two land-grant institutions: North Carolina State University at Raleigh (1887) and North Carolina Agricultural and Technical State University (1891). The institutions were small and would remain so for three more decades but the foundation had been laid. Figure 14.11 depicts the growth in enrollment in all North Carolina colleges and universities from 1900 to 1970.

Through the early 1900s the institutions operated almost totally independently of one another, competing for scarce public and private monies, duplicating programs, and variously defining what higher education should be about. In 1931, however, the General Assembly passed legislation designed to consolidate the three largest state-supported institutions. Thus the University of North Carolina at Chapel Hill, the North Carolina State College of Agriculture and Engineering at Raleigh, and the North Carolina College for Women at Greensboro were brought together under a single Board of Trustees, and Dr. Frank Porter Graham was appointed first president of the "Consolidated University." This arrangement remained essentially unchanged until the late 1950s when the General Assembly (1) established the North Carolina Board of Higher Education (BHE) to coordinate higher education in the state, (2) provided for the development of "community colleges" under this new board, and (3) created a system of industrial education centers under the State Board of Education.

Meanwhile, the private institutions of North Carolina prospered, claiming almost half of all students enrolled in higher education in the state. And the several public institutions increased in political strength and educational aspirations. By the early 1960s, there was evidence of what might be termed "academic sprawl."

Thus Governor Terry Sanford appointed the Commission on Education Beyond the High School, chaired by Senator Irving Carlyle (the Carlyle Commission), and in 1963 it made its recommendations to the General Assembly. In response to the commission's report, legislation was passed that (1) explicitly restricted authority to offer doctoral programs in the public institutions to the campuses of The University of North Carolina, (2) established procedures whereby additional campuses might be added to the university, and (3) combined the community colleges and industrial education centers into a new community college system.

The Department of Community Colleges was established under the State Board of Education to administer the new community college system. The role of the new system was to fill the gap between high school and the senior colleges and universities by providing comprehensive programs in occupational education, college transfer and general education, adult basic and adult high school education, and community-related extension education. The system was designed to serve adults eighteen years of age and older, whether high school graduates or not, who could benefit from the instruction offered. Moreover, the offerings were to be provided at minimum cost and maximum convenience both in terms of times and places of instruction.

In theory, then, the state was to have private higher education at both two-year and senior college levels, and a public system that could be conceived of as a pyramid: community colleges and technical institutes (offering certificates and associate degrees) would comprise the first tier; general purpose senior institutions (offering baccalaureate and, in some cases, master's degrees) would comprise the second tier; and The University of North Carolina (offering baccalaureate, master's, first-professional, and doctoral degrees) would form the apex.

The coordination and governance of the system was neither as clear nor as logical as the model. The university was governed by a one hundred-member board of trustees and was presided over by a chancellor. Each of the three existing campuses had a president. The general purpose senior institutions each had its own twelve-member board of trustees and, of course, local administrators (presidents), as did the private institutions. The community colleges, attached to the Department of Community Colleges, each had its own board of trustees and president.

Finally, there was the Board of Higher Education whose responsibility it was "to plan and promote the development of a ... coordinated system of higher education." Theoretically, prior approval of all new programs proposed by the public senior institutions was a responsibility of the BHE, which also made recommendations to the legislature concerning budgets and other matters affecting the development of higher education in the state. If, however, its recommendations were negative, an institution could bypass the board and appeal to the legislature directly. This happened on a number of occasions, and the BHE's power to coordinate was seriously undermined.

Furthermore, misunderstandings and disputes developed from time to time between the BHE and the boards of trustees of the several institutions. Many of these differences grew out of conflicts between various legal instruments fixing responsibility and granting authority, and on several occasions legislation was proposed to strengthen the BHE. The opposition to such measures was formidable, however, and the political might to accomplish the task could not be mustered.

Then the General Assembly in 1965 reconstituted the Board of Higher Education to include trustees of public institutions among its members and authorized creation of the fourth campus of The University of North Carolina at Charlotte, designating Charlotte College as its base. Thus the apex of the pyramid included four campuses. During the following General Assembly (1967), a bill was passed that bestowed "regional university" status on four of the general purpose institutions and extended to them authority to offer programs at the doctoral level. Furthermore, the 1969 General Assembly, in an attempt to bolster the power of the BHE, made the governor chairman of that board and provided for the appointment of key legislators to its membership. The 1969 General Assembly also added five more general purpose colleges to the list of regional universities and converted Asheville-Biltmore College and Wilmington College into the fifth and sixth campuses of The University of North Carolina. Higher education had truly become a political football, and the logic of the pyramid model had been crushed in the pileup.

While these steps were being taken by the state legislature in the sixties, the number of students accommodated by public institutions alone was more than doubling. State appropriations for higher education increased from $29.9 million in 1960 to $144.5 million in 1970, and no effective means seemed available to promote the equitable, nonpolitical distribution of these funds. By the end of the decade, higher education clearly represented a major commitment of the state; and, ironically, the words of the 1963 Carlyle Commission Report seemed to fit exactly:

Figure 14.11. Enrollment in N.C. Colleges and Universities, 1900-1970

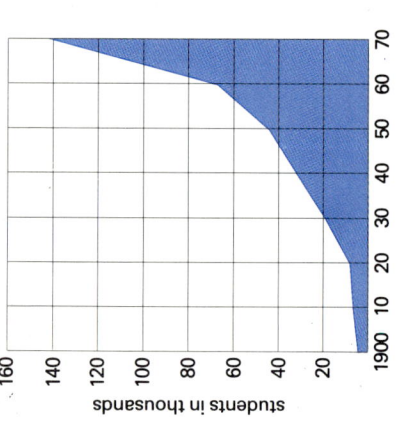

Source: N.C. Department of Public Instruction, unpublished data.

The public system of post-high school education is going to grow. The times demand it. It is essential that such growth be well planned and coordinated if the public's investment of money and energy is to produce maximum returns in terms of educational services to the people of the state. The state must have, in short, a functioning system of public higher education and not a mere aggregation of independent institutions, each pursuing its own conception of public interest.

So in January 1971, Governor Robert Scott appointed a twenty-three member Study Committee on Structure and Organization of Higher Education and named Senator Lindsay C. Warren as its chairman. The committee included trustee representatives from The University of North Carolina and each of the ten other public sen or institutions as well as members from the Board of Higher Education. The basic charge to the committee was to study and make recommendations to the governor concerning the structure and organization of the system of public higher education. The report was submitted to the governor on 17 May 1971.

After much debate, the General Assembly, meeting in special session in October 1971, adopted legislation that:

1. Combined the functions of the Board of Higher Education with those of the Board of Trustees of The University of North Carolina and merged ten senior institutions into The University of North Carolina which became a multicampus university of sixteen constituent institutions governed by a 32-member Board of Governors elected by the General Assembly for 8-year terms;

2. Established for each of the sixteen campuses of the University of North Carolina a thirteen-member board of trustees whose functions are delegated by the Board of Governors;

3. Authorized the Board of Governors to present to the legislature a consolidated budget representing all public senior institutions in the state;

4. Empowered the Board of Governors to make certain transfers within the budget once state funds are appropriated; and,

5. Vested in the Board of Governors full authority to govern the constituent institutions.

The Board of Governors came into being officially on 1 July 1972. Both before and since that time a great amount of energy and effort has been devoted to assure the success of the system. Within the first year of its existence, the board organized itself into committees, appointed an administrative staff for the university with William C. Friday as its president, devoted careful attention to the development of a code for the university, delegated certain functions to the boards of trustees, and presented to the Advisory Budget Commission of the legislature a historic, consolidated budget for consideration by the General Assembly.

Types and Locations of Institutions

In 1974, North Carolina had 115 nonproprietary, post-secondary educational institutions operating within its boundaries. Of these, forty were technical institutes that do not feature college-transfer curricula. The remaining seventy-five institutions included seventeen public community colleges, ten private junior colleges, sixteen public senior universities, and twenty-nine private senior colleges or universities. There were also two Bible colleges and one autonomous theological seminary. By action of the 1973 General Assembly, one private junior college (Mitchell College) and one of the technical institutes (Craven Technical Institute) were converted to community colleges.

The senior colleges and the universities, of course, feature baccalaureate and the higher-degree programs, though not all of the institutions offer work beyond the bachelor's level. The private junior colleges and community colleges offer two-year college-transfer programs leading to associate degrees. In addition, the fifty-seven community colleges and technical institutes provide a variety of technical and vocational programs and occupational extension courses, offering instruction in over 160 occupational fields. Technical institutes and community colleges award associate in applied science degrees, diplomas, and certificates.

Figure 14.12 presents the locations of the senior institutions and the two-year institutions, respectively. The institutions are distributed in a pattern that generally follows the scatter of the state's population, with the senior institutions noticeably clustering in the Piedmont section. Excluding the technical institutes, twenty-four of the remaining seventy-five institutions are located in the four most populous counties (Forsyth, Guilford, Mecklenburg, and Wake). On the other hand, a total of only four of the seventy-five institutions is to be found among the forty-two counties whose populations were less than twenty-five thousand in 1970.

Further analysis of the location of the state's college-transfer and college-level programs reveals that eighty-nine of the one hundred North Carolina counties either contain an institution offering some college-level instruction or border a county that does. The eleven counties not so situated had a combined population of 117,292 in 1970, representing only 2 percent of the citizenry of the state. Viewed in this light, it may be said that the vast majority of North Carolinians live within reasonable commuting range of some type of institution offering college-level work.

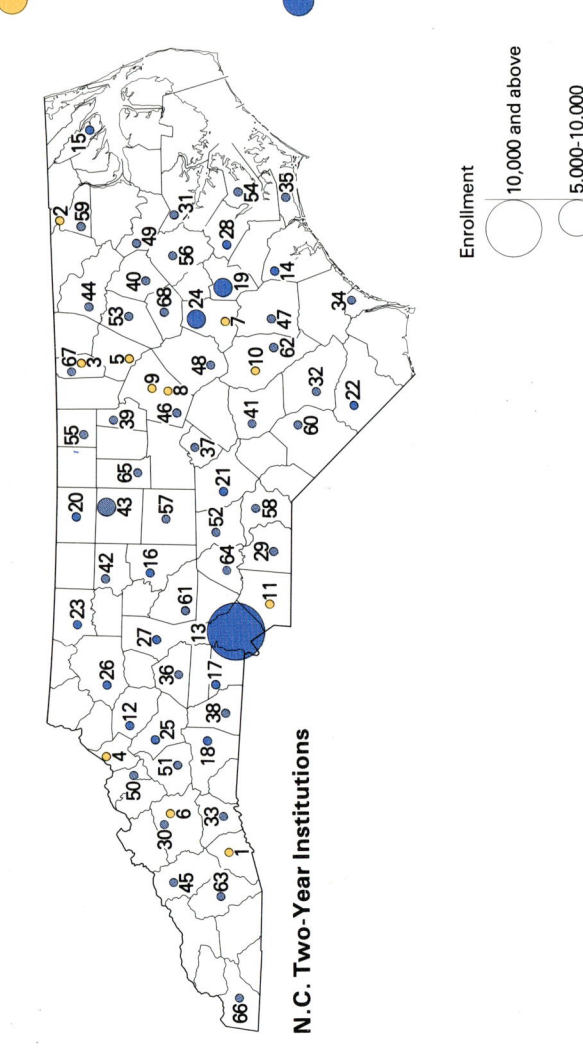

Figure 14.12. Type and Location of Post-Secondary Educational Institutions in N.C., 1973

The data presented in Figure 14.13 suggest that many students, especially those attending community colleges, take advantage of this situation. In the fall of 1972, 86 percent of those enrolled in community colleges crossed no more than one county line in traveling from home to college. The public senior institutions likewise enrolled large numbers of students who lived within commuting range, but the majority were drawn from areas of the state beyond the immediate vicinity of the institution. The private institutions, as would be expected, tended to draw relatively larger proportions of their students from out-of-state, but their student bodies, too, were composed largely of North Carolinians.

It would not be surprising to witness an increase in the proportion of instate students attending private institutions within the foreseeable future. The 1973 General Assembly appropriated funds to provide these institutions $200 for student financial aid for each North Carolina resident enrolled. In addition to contributing to the solution of financial problems among some private institutions, this move may encourage these colleges and universities to seek and admit larger numbers of North Carolina students.

Enrollment

Current attendance patterns and recent trends in the state's postsecondary institutions may best be presented in terms of enrollments in college or college-transfer programs and noncollege-transfer programs.

Figure 14.14 presents the fall enrollments in college-level (including two-year college-transfer) and graduate programs in North Carolina from 1962 through 1972. Some institutions that were two-year colleges in the early 1960s have since become senior institutions. The data for a given year reflect the enrollment by type of institution as the institutions were classified in fall 1972.

Nationwide, the 1960s was a period of rapid growth for higher education. At the beginning of the decade, 3.6 million students were enrolled in degree programs. By 1970, that number had increased to 7.9 million for a 121 percent gain. Enrollments in public institutions rose 174 percent during the period, while private colleges and universities grew at a rate of 145 percent.

North Carolina did not match these percentages, but the pattern in the state reflected the national trends. The total enrollment in the state's college-level programs increased by 108 percent during the decade. Public institutions increased by 158 percent and the private institutions by 51 percent.

Figure 14.13. Geographical Origin of Students by Type of Institution in N.C., Fall 1972

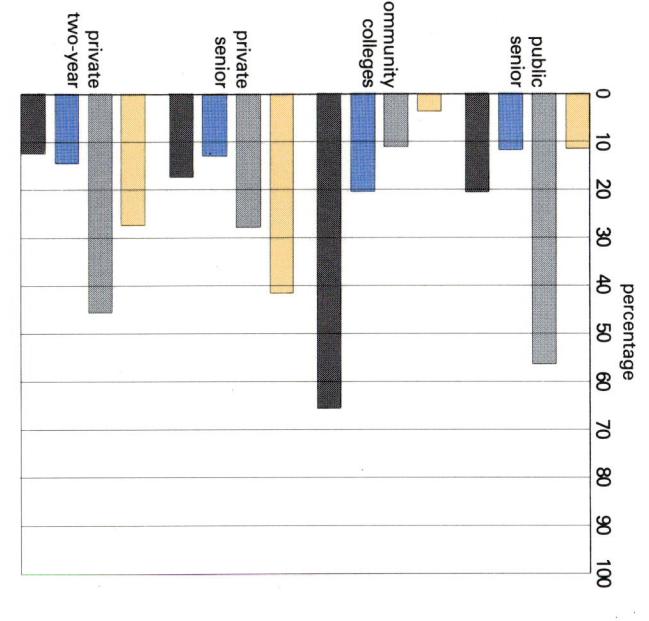

Source: University of N.C., *Statistical Abstract of Higher Education,* 1972-1973, 1973.

Figure 14.14. Fall Headcount Enrollment in Academic Programs in N.C. Colleges and Universities, 1962-1972

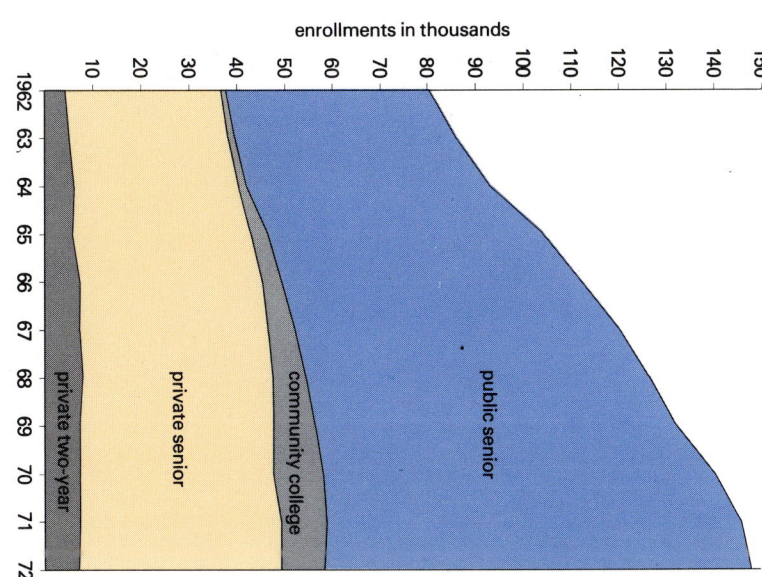

Sources: N.C. Board of Higher Education, *Statistical Abstract(s) of Higher Education,* by year, 1962-72. University of N.C., *Statistical Abstract of Higher Education,* 1972-1973, 1973.

263

Enrollment in the nation's two-year institutions virtually exploded during the 1960s. While senior institutions approximately doubled their enrollment during the decade, the junior and community colleges increased by 261 percent. Again the same pattern was visible in North Carolina.

In addition to illustrating the trends cited above, Figure 14.14 reflects that the private institutions claimed almost half of all students enrolled in the state's colleges and universities in the early 1960s; but by 1972, that proportion had dropped to one-third (33.5 percent). This relative decline is probably due primarily to the increasing costs of private higher education.

Figure 14.14 also reveals a leveling off of higher educational enrollments from 1971 to 1972. A number of factors, no doubt, contributed to this development. The reorganization of the military draft removed one motive for college attendance. Publicity concerning poor job prospects for college graduates may also have caused many to postpone or forego college. Some students in 1972 were turning to occupational training rather than to college work. Moreover, economic factors no doubt interfered with the educational plans of many as the cost of living increased. For whatever the reasons, 1972 was not a boom year for college attendance in North Carolina; nor was the national picture much different. From 9.0 million in 1971 to 9.2 million in 1972, enrollment in the nation's higher education institutions increased by only 2 percent. With the decrease in the birthrate that has already begun, it is safe to conclude that the dramatic enrollment increases of the 1960s will not characterize the 1970s and early 1980s except in the cases of institutions whose circumstances are so unusual as to offset the general cooling-off period that seems on its way.

Enrollment in advanced-degree programs has been watched carefully during the last half decade because of the declining demand for individuals with graduate degrees, especially Ph.D.'s in certain fields. Figure 14.15 presents enrollments in first-professional (e.g., D.D.S., M.D., J.D.) and graduate (e.g., M.A., Ed.D., Ph.D.) programs in North Carolina institutions from 1962 to 1972.

These data reveal that enrollment in these programs has increased at a fairly steady rate during the decade. From 1963 to 1964 the gain was only 2 percent, but the following year enrollment jumped 13 percent and the total gain during the ten-year period was 109 percent. This figure actually exceeds the rate of increase in undergraduate enrollment (83 percent) in the same institutions for the same period.

The data presented in Figure 14.16 allow a comparison of the number of earned doctorates awarded by field in North Carolina in 1967-68 and the number awarded in 1971-72. The number of such degrees awarded increased during the five-year period in all comparable areas except two, foreign languages and health professions. Of the six fields that awarded thirty-five or more degrees in both 1967-68 and 1971-72, four (biological sciences, education, engineering, and letters) increased their output by 75 percent or more.

Overall, the productivity of graduate programs in North Carolina is encouraging. However, some programs—the foreign languages program, for example—did not fare well during the half decade under consideration. Educators must look carefully at the possible causes of what may, in given instances, develop as permanent enrollment declines. In such instances, compelling arguments for continuation of programs should be forthcoming or, in fairness to the state, the programs should be phased out.

At the beginning of the 1970s, North Carolina's senior institutions had almost thirty-five thousand graduate and undergraduate registrations in extension courses creditable toward a degree. These registrations were in addition to the students registered in regular-degree programs discussed above. The contribution made to the citizens of the state through extension courses offered by senior institutions is often overlooked. It is clear, however, from this data that direct educational benefits accrue to a substantial number of North Carolinians who are not counted among the so-called college student population.

Attendance at public two-year institutions increased by 105 percent between 1967 and 1971. This rapid growth in community college and technical institute enrollment may be attributed, in part, to the establishment of seven new two-year institutions during the period under consideration, but to a large extent the gains must be recognized as an expression of the postsecondary educational needs and desires of many of the state's citizens.

Figure 14.17 presents the unduplicated headcount enrollment by type of program in North Carolina's public, two-year institutions from 1967 to 1972. The programs of the two-year institutions may be treated under two broad categories: curriculum programs and extension courses. The former category includes vocational, technical, college-transfer, and general education programs and courses. The extension category includes adult education, occupational extension, and general adult education courses.

Figure 14.15. Fall Enrollments in First Professional (D.D.S., J.D., M.D.) and Graduate (M.A., Ed.D., Ph.D.) Programs in N.C. Universities, 1962-1972

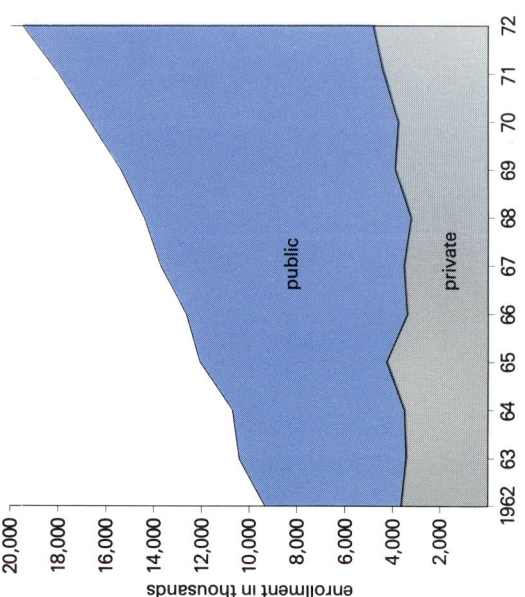

Sources: N.C. Board of Higher Education, *Statistical Abstract(s) of Higher Education,* by year, 1962-72. University of N.C., *Statistical Abstract of Higher Education, 1972-1973,* 1973.

As can be seen in Figure 14.17, extension courses in 1971 accounted for well over three-quarters of the total enrollment of the public two-year institutions. Within the extension category, occupational courses accounted for almost half the registrations. In terms of increase since 1967, enrollment in occupational courses grew by approximately 119 percent. College-transfer enrollment increased by 52 percent during the period, but there was a net loss of students in these programs from 1970 to 1971.

In interpreting the data in Figure 14.17, it is important to note that the data are presented in unduplicated headcount. This means that every individual enrolled in a course during any term is counted once but not more than once. The extension category includes many students who took only one course, whereas those enrolled in curriculum programs were likely to take several courses. Therefore, inferences such as the number of hours of instruction offered in curriculum programs versus the number of hours of instruction offered in extension courses cannot be drawn from these data. What can be concluded is that the public two-year institutions alone directly touched the lives of approximately seven out of every one hundred North Carolinians in 1971. This record of service to the state is remarkable, and the trend in the aggregated enrollment of these institutions seems to be solid indeed. This fact, coupled with the commitment the state has made to its two-year institutions, promises a bright future for the community colleges and technical institutes of North Carolina.

Financial Considerations

In the discussion of the distribution of the various types of institutions, it was pointed out that location has a bearing on attendance patterns, especially among the community colleges. Geography, of course, is not the only consideration in a student's choice of an institution. The availability and reputation of specific programs, the fame of athletic teams, the recommendation of friends, and other such factors must also be taken into account. Even then, a major determinant has yet to be considered: student cost.

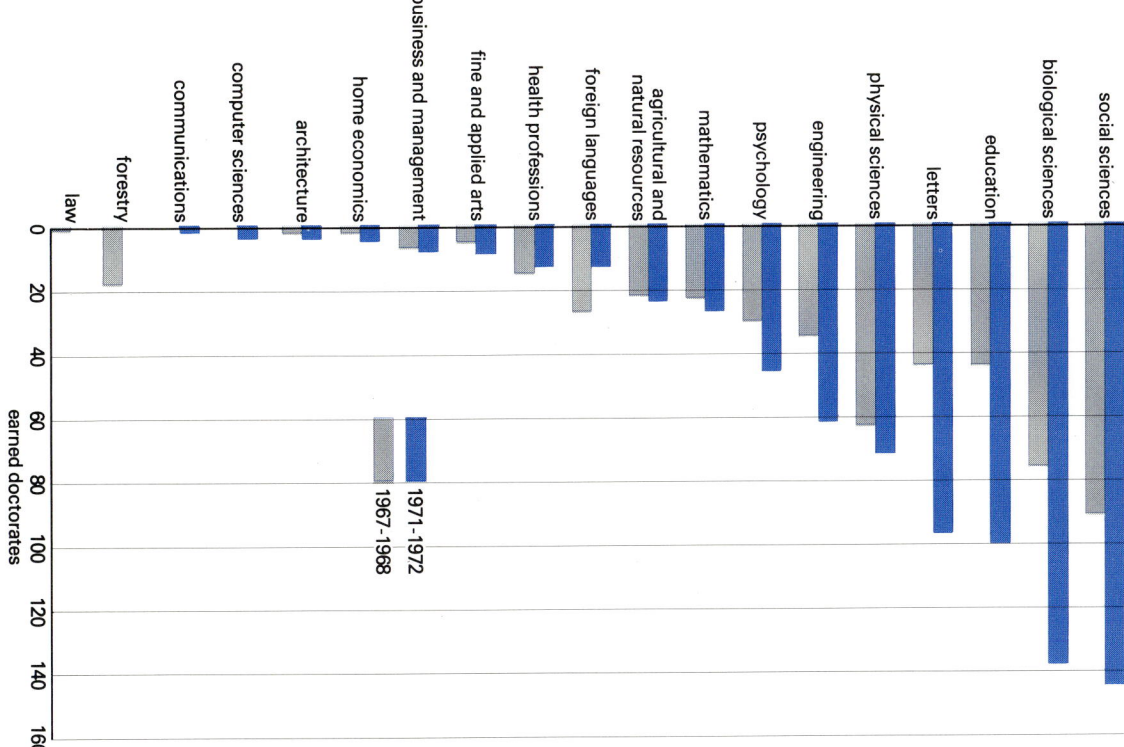

Figure 14.16. Earned Doctorates Awarded by N.C. Universities by Field, 1967-1968 and 1971-1972

Sources: N.C. Board of Higher Education, *Statistical Abstract of Higher Education, 1968-1969*, 1969. University of N.C., *Statistical Abstract of Higher Education, 1972-1973*, 1973.

Note: No Ph.D's awarded in law in 1972. Graduate degrees in forestry were reported under agricultural and natural resources in 1972.

Figure 14.17. Unduplicated Headcount Enrollment by Type of Program in N.C. Public Two-Year Institutions, 1967-1972

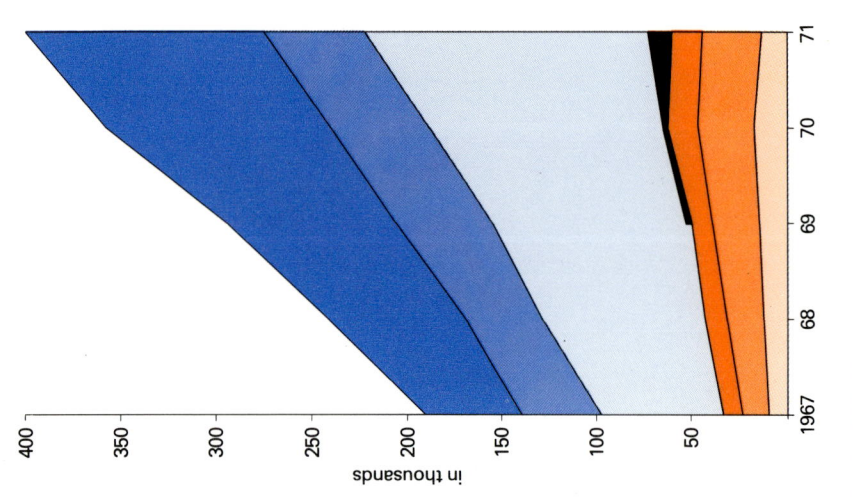

Figure 14.18. Average Cost for Undergraduate Tuition and Required Fees per Academic Year, 1968-1972

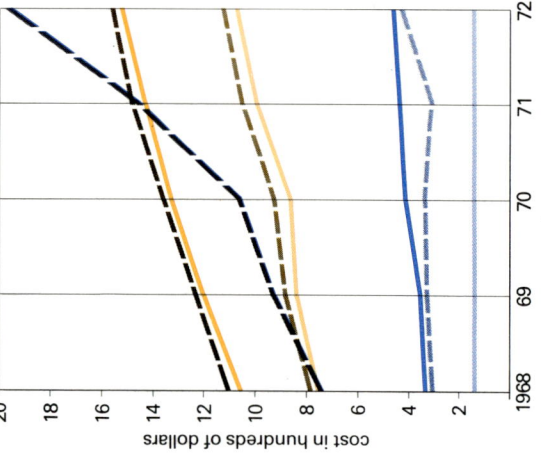

— — public senior out-of-state
– – private senior out-of-state
—— private senior in-state
—— public senior in-state
– – private two-year out-of-state
– – private two-year in-state
– – community colleges out-of-state
—— community colleges in-state

Sources: N.C. Board of Higher Education, *Statistical Abstract(s) of Higher Education*, by year, 1968-72. University of N.C., *Statistical Abstract of Higher Education, 1972-1973*, 1973.

Figure 14.18 presents the average cost for undergraduate tuition and required fees per academic year at North Carolina institutions from 1968 through 1972. With the exception of the community colleges, all types of institutions have found it necessary to increase the basic academic charges made to in-state students by substantial amounts. The major change, however, has been in the amount charged to out-of-state students by public senior institutions. This figure increased 164 percent between 1968 and 1972, nearly doubling (84 percent increase) between 1970 and 1972. This phenomenal rate hike causes the in-state increases to appear modest by comparison.

The increase grew out of the position taken by the 1971 General Assembly that out-of-state students should pay an amount approximating the cost of their education when they attend a tax-supported institution in this state. The higher charge has discouraged many out-of-state students from attending North Carolina institutions, and as a result there has been some loss of income to the public universities. The rate hike has also created an unusual condition, in that it may be less expensive for an out-of-state student to attend a given private institution than a public university in North Carolina.

Of course, tuition and fees are not the only costs involved in attending college. To those figures must be added travel, room, and board that might amount to another $1,000 to $1,500; books, clothes, and other personal items; and, indirectly, the loss of private income.

Figure 14.18 also suggests a basis for the relative decline observed in enrollment among private institutions. Inflation in the general economy has forced tuition rates up among these institutions during a time when many individuals have had to cut back on personal spending. This combination of factors has caught many private institutions in a serious situation. When one considers that the private institutions drew well over half of their students from North Carolina in 1972 (Figure 14.13) and that in-state students pay over three times as much tuition and fees to attend a private senior institution rather than a public institution, it is by no means surprising that private enrollments are actually declining in some instances. It is too soon to predict the outcome, but it is probably safe to say that North Carolina will have fewer private, postsecondary institutions in 1980 than at the present.

general adult education
occupational
adult education
general education
college transfer
technical
vocational

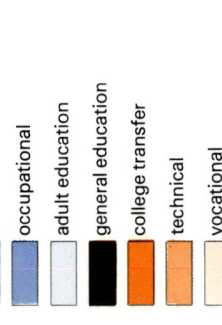

Source: N.C. Department of Community Colleges, *Annual Enrollment Reports*, by year, 1967-72.

Note: The blue spectrum indicates extension programs, and the red spectrum indicates curriculum programs.

This eventuality becomes even more likely when one examines the data presented in Figure 14.19. These data reveal the extent to which private institutions, especially the junior colleges, depend upon tuition and fees for educational and general operating expenses. (The data presented in Figure 14.19 do not include current fund revenues earmarked for student aid grants or funds collected through auxiliary enterprises.)

In spite of this rather bleak picture, the trend in total current fund revenues for the state's higher education institutions appears solid. Figure 14.20 reveals that in 1971–72 income generated by all North Carolina colleges and universities had increased by 54 percent over the 1968–69 figure. The percent increase was greatest among the community colleges (124 percent) and least among the private junior colleges (36 percent). This latter fact, coupled with the data referred to above, suggests that as a "type" the private, two-year college is a troubled institution.

The other side of the financial profile of higher education in North Carolina is equally revealing. Together the two-year and senior institutions of the state spent $632.3 million dollars during 1971–72 in current funds alone. Of this amount, $396.7 million (63 percent) was spent by public institutions. The private institutions did exceed the public institutions in the amount spent for student aid grants. This is not surprising since, as has been pointed out, the cost of attendance is so much greater in the private colleges and universities.

These data also suggest the extent to which higher educational institutions contribute to the state's economy. Statewide expenditures for such things as capital improvements, utilities, and salaries run into eight figures on a monthly basis. Indeed, higher education's contribution to local economies is essential in the cases of some communities.

Apart from this direct, monetary benefit, colleges and universities attract highly trained and educated citizens, provide jobs for local residents, sponsor athletic and cultural events, and, in many cases, bring substantial amounts of governmental and private capital into the region. Perhaps the most tangible example of the attracting power of outstanding institutions of higher education is the Research Triangle Park, located between Duke University, The University of North Carolina at Chapel Hill, and North Carolina State University. There is little likelihood that this multimillion-dollar complex of research organizations and light industrial installations would have developed had it not been for the university resources in the immediate vicinity.

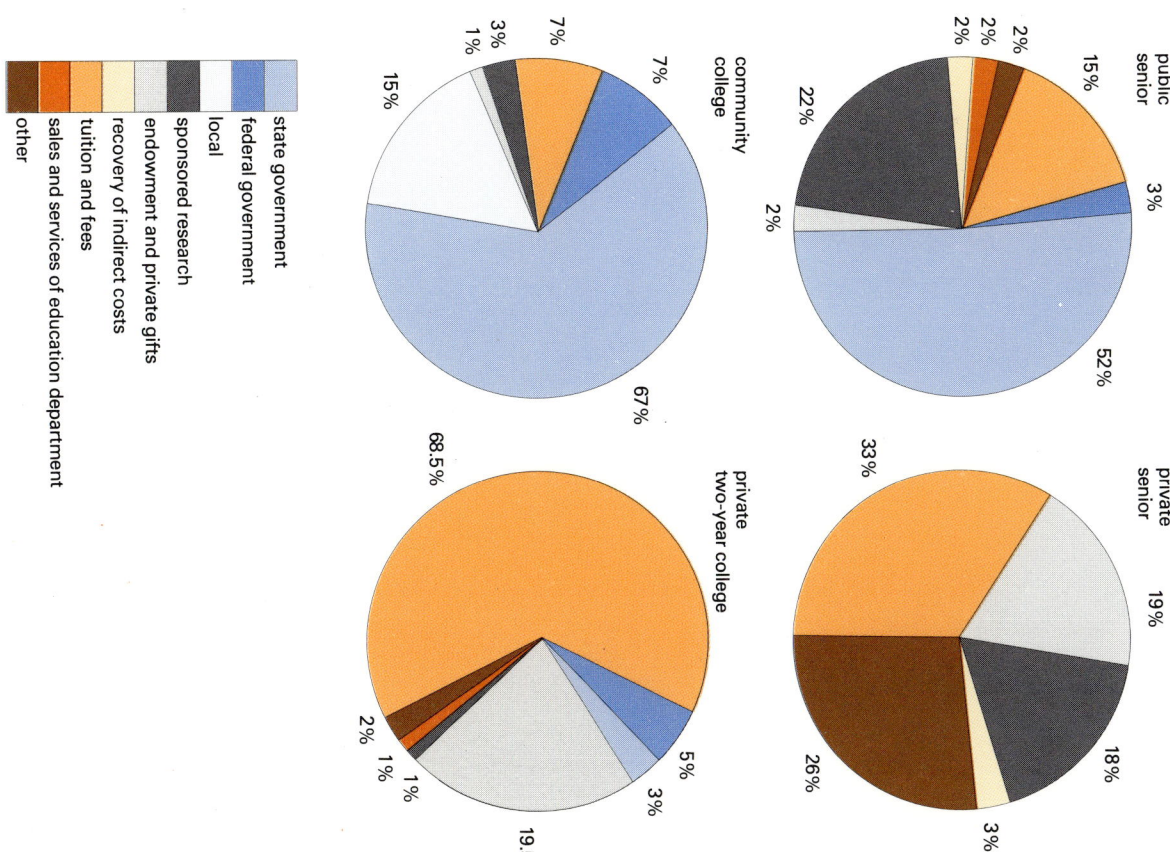

Figure 14.19. Sources of Funds for N.C. Colleges and Universities, 1971-1972

Legend:
- state government
- federal government
- local
- sponsored research
- endowment and private gifts
- recovery of indirect costs
- tuition and fees
- sales and services of education department
- other

Local appropriations, recovery of indirect costs, and sales and services of education departments contribute less than 1% to the total current funds revenue and are not shown.

Source: University of N.C., *Statistical Abstract of Higher Education, 1972-1973*, 1973.

267

Figure 14.20. Total Funds for Operating N.C. Colleges and Universities, 1968-1972

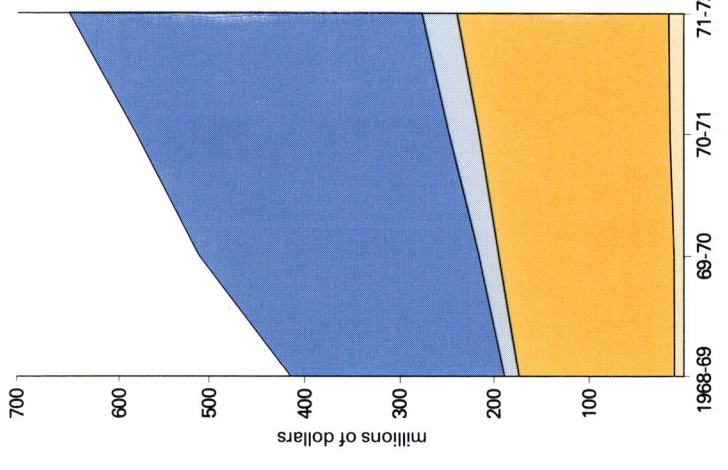

public senior
community college
private senior
private two-year

Sources: N.C. Board of Higher Education, *Statistical Abstract(s) of Higher Education*, by year, 1968-72. University of N.C., *Statistical Abstract of Higher Education, 1972-1973*, 1973.

Figure 14.21. Professional Employees in N.C. Senior Institutions, 1972

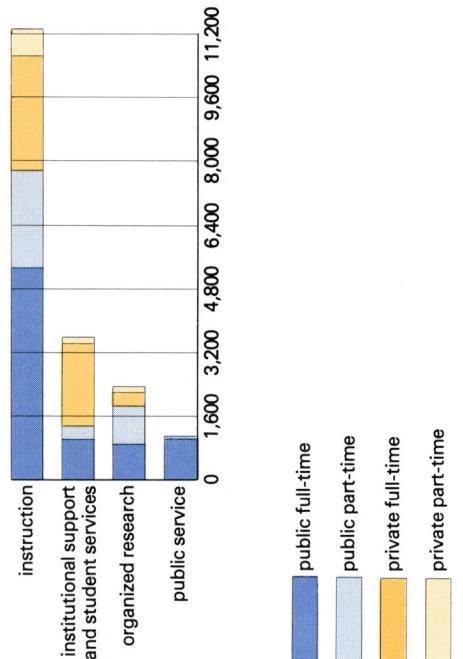

public full-time
public part-time
private full-time
private part-time

Source: University of N.C., *Statistical Abstract of Higher Education, 1972-1973*, 1973.

Faculty

Of all the instructional resources of a higher education institution, none is more important or valuable than its faculty and other professional employees. Figure 14.21 presents the number of professionals employed in the state's forty-five senior colleges and universities in the fall of 1972.

Of the 18,323 professional employees, by far the largest proportion (11,344 or 62 percent) were involved in instructional programs. The sixteen public institutions employed 68 percent of all the instructional staff but claimed only 39 percent of the 3,566 professionals serving in institutional support and student services positions.

Figure 14.21 also reveals the extent to which professional service is rendered on a part-time basis. Such arrangements are especially common in the area of organized research, and 32 percent of the instructional staff in the public institutions teach less than full time. The vast majority of these part-time staff members hold advanced degrees in their field, and many are distinguished scholars and/or researchers.

Figure 14.22 presents the ranges of institutional averages and averages of salaries paid to full-time faculty members. The data do not include salaries paid to the faculty of the three medical schools in the state nor does it include salaries of those employed by the Agriculture Experiment Station at North Carolina State University.

Perhaps the most striking feature of the data is the difference between the lowest and the highest institutional average salaries within a given rank, especially among the higher ranks in the private institutions. For example, the average salary paid to full professors at the highest-paying private institution is slightly more than two and one-half times greater than the comparable figure at the lowest-paying private institution. The ranges among the public institutions are relatively much more restricted.

Figure 14.22 further reveals that the average of salaries paid by public institutions is greater than that in private colleges and universities for all ranks, but the top of the range is higher in the private sector than in the public. Again, this is true for all ranks.

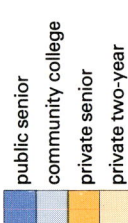

Although it is not reflected in Figures 14.21 or 14.22, it is interesting to note that slightly more than half of the full-time faculty members employed by the state's colleges and universities have doctoral degrees. Another 43 percent hold first-professional or master's degrees.

Libraries

As a higher education resource, libraries run a close second to faculty members in terms of importance. Figure 14.23 presents the total number of bound volumes included in the state's college and university libraries from 1967 to 1972. The data presented in Figure 14.23 reveal a steady increase during the six-year span in the number of bound volumes in the state's college and university libraries. The holdings in public institutions increased by 44 percent while those in private institutions grew by 32 percent during the period.

Both the public and private higher education libraries are greatly bolstered by two truly outstanding university collections: the Duke University library, with 2.3 million bound volumes in 1972, and the library of The University of North Carolina at Chapel Hill, with 1.9 million bound volumes in that year. These two libraries are respectively second and fourth among southeastern universities and together account for 43 percent of all bound volumes in senior institutions throughout the state.

Although the total number of bound volumes held by a library is an important variable, it is not the only factor to be considered in judging its adequacy. Perhaps a more penetrating statistic is the number of volumes it possesses in relation to the size of its constituency. Thus Figure 14.24 presents the bound volumes per full-time equivalent student. (The term "full-time equivalent student" refers to a derived figure calculated by adding the full-time student population to the quotient that results from dividing the total number of credit hours taken by part-time students by the number of credit hours considered to constitute a full load. Also note that neither Figure 14.23 nor 14.24 includes data on the number of periodicals, unbound documents, and items of microform.)

As can be seen, the private institutions taken in aggregate are able to afford almost twice as many books for each of their students as the public institutions. The range for this statistic is enormous: from 30 volumes per student in some public institutions to 287 at Duke. Of course, these figures must be interpreted in terms of the types and levels of instruction that are offered. For example, an institution deeply committed to graduate education would be expected to feature more extensive library holdings than one that concentrates on undergraduate programs.

Figure 14.22. Averages and Ranges of Average Salaries Paid Full-Time Faculty Members in N.C. Senior Institutions, 1972

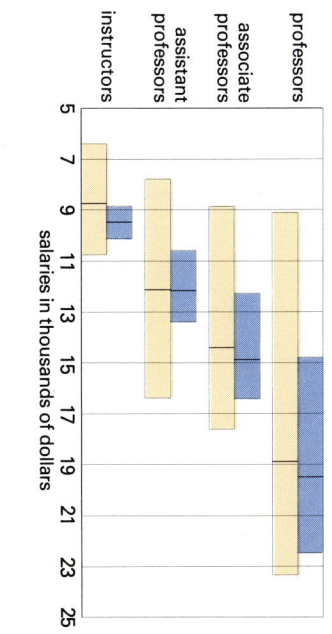

Source: University of N.C., *Statistical Abstract of Higher Education, 1972-1973*, 1973.

In addition to the 9.7 million bound volumes contained in the state's senior institutions in 1972, the community colleges held another 363,000 volumes and the junior colleges 360,000 more.

From the data presented in this section, it should come as no surprise that the postsecondary educational institutions of the state expended nearly $19 million in operating funds on libraries alone in 1971-72.

North Carolina Higher Education in Context

North Carolina can take pride in the support it has given to its postsecondary educational institutions and in their achievements. Consider, for example, the comparisons presented below between North Carolina, thirteen other southeastern states (Alabama, Arkansas, Florida, Georgia, Kentucky, Louisiana, Maryland, Mississippi, South Carolina, Tennessee, Texas, Virginia, and West Virginia), and the nation as a whole.

North Carolina ranked first among the southeastern states in:

—State appropriations for higher education per $1,000 of personal income, 1970 ($10.77 in North Carolina versus a southeastern average of $8.18 and a national average of $7.76);

—Per student expenditures, 1968-69 ($2,036 in North Carolina versus a southeastern average of $1,587 and a national average of $1,647);

—Net migration (in-state/out-of-state) in public higher education institutions at both the undergraduate and graduate levels, 1968;

—Two-year college enrollment in nondegree-credit programs, 1970.

North Carolina ranked second among the southeastern states in:

—Federal funds available for vocational education, 1972;

—State appropriations as a percent of taxes, 1971-72 (17.2 percent in North Carolina versus a southeastern average of 15.8 percent and a national average of 15.0 percent);

college-age population (18-21), 1970 (41.0 percent in North Carolina versus a southeastern average of 46.0 percent and a national average of 60.6 percent);

—Ninth in black undergraduate enrollment as a percent of the black college-age population (18-21), 1970 (19.9 percent in North Carolina versus a southeastern average of 20.0 percent and a national average of 21.0 percent).

To explore thoroughly the reasons behind these facts would require a more extended analysis than is intended here. The facts themselves, however, suggest that North Carolina should examine its system of access to higher education with a view toward eliminating all barriers that are economically and educationally feasible to remove. Clearly, the state cannot afford to remain almost twenty percentage points behind the national average in "college enrollment as a percent of the college-age population" without addressing the issues behind the statistics. Such an undertaking should direct attention to the counseling programs in postsecondary institutions to name but one of the important variables.

A second issue that deserves attention is the mechanisms for movement within the higher education system once access has been gained. Figure 14.25 presents graphically the extent to which students move from one institution to another. The data reveal that nearly 10,000 undergraduates transferred into a North Carolina college or university in the fall of 1972. Of this number, over 2,500 transferred from out of state, almost 5,800 transferred from one category of institution to another category of institution (e.g., from a community college to a public university), and approximately 1,500 students moved from one school to another school of the same category.

The data allow a variety of comparisons and yield several striking observations. For example, as a category, the public senior institutions experienced a net gain of 2,129 students through transfers. On the other hand, private junior colleges as a category experienced a net loss of 1,599 students. Another type of comparison reveals that community colleges (usually considered to be a transfer-producing category) received 1,142 transfer students in the fall of 1972.

These and other comparisons that might be made from the data in Figure 14.25 reflect the degree to which the transfer phenomenon must be considered a major factor in planning for postsecondary education in the state. It is likely that the movement reflected in the figure will increase with the continued development of the community college system, with increased mobility in the general society, and with the development of more cooperative programs among the various types of institutions.

Figure 14.23. Number of Bound Volumes In Libraries of N.C. Senior Institutions, 1967-1972

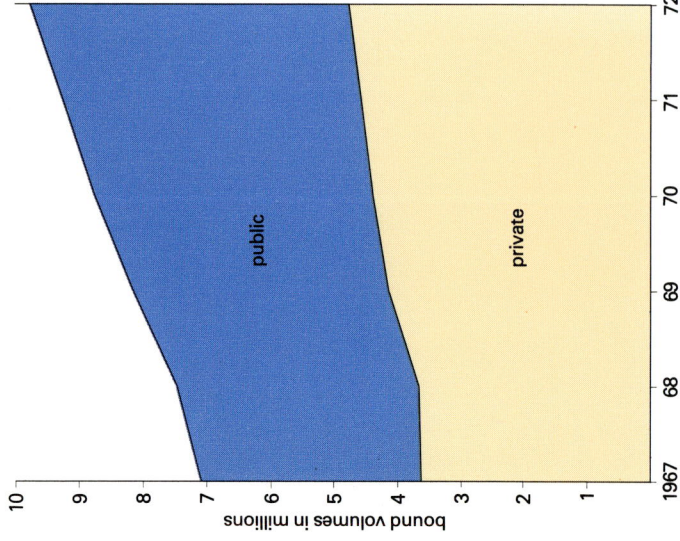

Sources: N.C. Board of Higher Education, *Statistical Abstract(s) of Higher Education*, by year, 1967-72. University of N.C., *Statistical Abstract of Higher Education, 1972-1973*, 1973.

Figure 14.24. Number of Bound Volumes per Full-Time Equivalent Student in Senior Institutions, 1967-1972

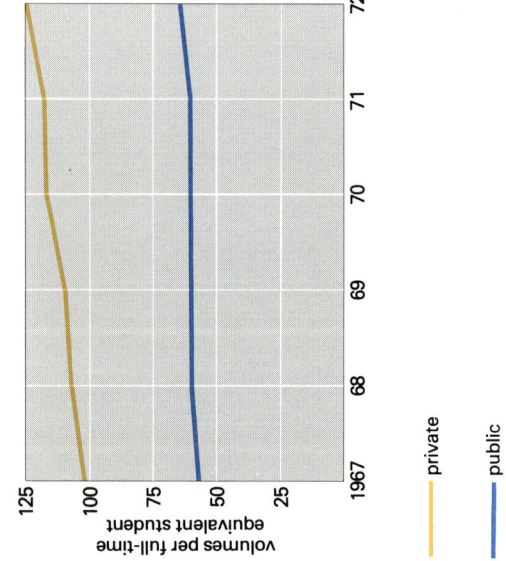

Sources: N.C. Board of Higher Education, *Statistical Abstract(s) of Higher Education*, by year, 1967-72. University of N.C., *Statistical Abstract of Higher Education, 1972-1973*, 1973.

On the other hand, there are areas in which North Carolina's rank in the higher education hierarchy should be a cause for concern. Using the fourteen southeastern states listed above for comparative purposes, North Carolina ranks:

—Ninth among the fourteen states in percent of population twenty-five years old or over with education beyond high school, 1970 (16.8 percent for North Carolina versus a southeastern average of 19.1 percent and a national average of 21.2 percent);

—Twelfth in percent of high school graduates entering college, 1968 (40.7 percent for North Carolina versus a southeastern average of 51.1 percent and a national average of 58.3 percent);

—Tenth in college enrollment as a percent of the

—Total federal obligations and expenditures for higher education, 1970;

—Percent increase in state operational appropriations for higher education, 1963-73 (507.1 percent in North Carolina versus a southeastern average of 403.8 percent and a national average of 350.7 percent);

—Formal awards (certificate and diplomas) conferred in occupational, technical, and/or vocational programs, 1969-70;

—Number of higher education institutions, 1973.

Other items and other types of variables could be cited as evidence of accomplishment: outstanding graduates of the state's educational institutions; innovative instructional programs; major university research projects; and, of course, topflight athletic teams.

There are many positive results of such movement, but the careful planning and coordination are needed to make the process smooth and educationally beneficial. For example, compatibility of programs and the transferability of credit among the major transferring and receiving institutions need to be considered.

On a different plane, the issue of program duplication becomes important. If movement among institutions could be optimized, would the state need to support the same specialized programs in a number of institutions? There are increasing educational as well as economic forces that mitigate against such a practice, and already firm steps are being taken to reduce the amount of unnecessary program duplication among the state-supported schools. There is, however, a thin line between desirable duplication and unnecessary duplication, and decisions in these areas should be based on the soundest educational experience and thinking available.

Such considerations lead naturally to the question of comprehensive coordination of postsecondary education. There are many advantages in preserving the organizational boundaries that define the various types of institutions. On the other hand, it seems increasingly important to discover the means by which the total educational resources of the state can be brought to bear on these considerations in a concerted manner. This issue is one that will, no doubt, be the center of much discussion during the remainder of the 1970s and will likely demand attention well beyond that time.

Yet another matter that will warrant attention is that of the relationship between state politics and higher education. The Board of Governors of The University of North Carolina has demonstrated through its actions and achievements to date that it can work effectively in governing the public senior education system, but it is, and will continue to be, entirely possible for that body to be seriously weakened by political activity. If such development were to occur, the state would suffer as educational issues once again were debated and settled in the political arena. The best that one can expect under such conditions is short-term gains for individual institutions. In the long run, the results are surely to be a system in shambles and an organization in disarray.

Finally, the statistics presented in this chapter raise an issue that has been the topic of debate in higher education circles for a number of years, i.e., the relationship between the state and its private education institutions. The questions are complex: Is it economically more feasible to subsidize private education than to provide more student openings in public institutions? Is it to the citizens' advantage to have available to them institutions relatively free from governmental constraints and controls? How is autonomy to be maintained if state funds carry with them (as they surely will) a mandate to be accountable for them? Is it constitutionally sound to allocate state funds for the support of private higher education?

Most would agree that strong private colleges and universities are an important resource for a state and that the private institutions present alternatives that are deemed desirable in a pluralistic society. There would be further agreement that many, if not most, private institutions are undergoing a period of serious belt-tightening and that some will not survive.

As mentioned previously, the 1973 General Assembly partially addressed the problem by appropriating funds to private institutions for student aid purposes according to a formula based on the school's enrollment of North Carolina students. Many have voiced objections to this plan for a variety of reasons. Some suggest that this move invites a tuition hike among private colleges. Others claim that it is inappropriate to offer private institutions inducements to enroll more North Carolina students at a time when some tax-supported institutions have empty dormitory beds. Still others question the wisdom of temporarily sustaining through state aid some institutions that may—and perhaps should—cease to exist.

The problems of private colleges and universities will not disappear overnight, nor could these institutions be replaced if they were suddenly removed. The challenge to the state and to these institutions is to discover means by which the most promising of the private institutions can survive and be strengthened without sacrificing the autonomy that is part and parcel of their uniqueness. At the same time the continued development of the public institutions must not be neglected. The solution is not readily apparent, but the issue is important enough to merit the best thinking and judgment the state can bring to it.

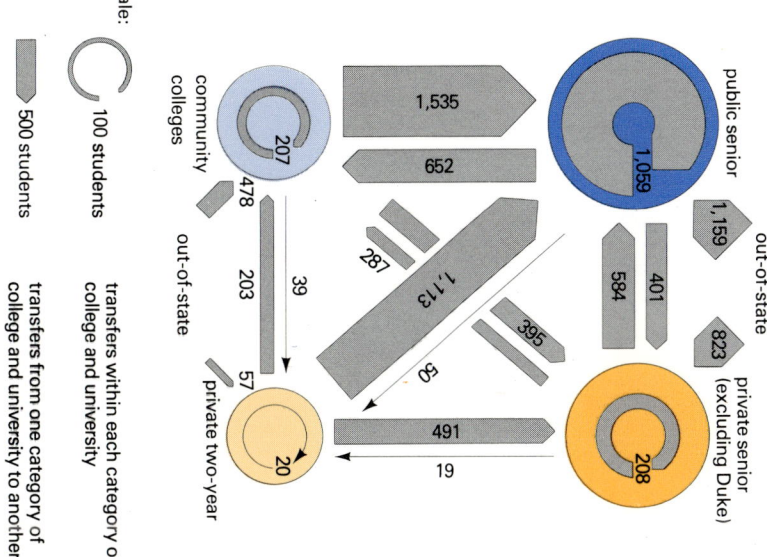

Figure 14.25. Flow of Undergraduate Transfers among N.C. Colleges and Universities, Fall 1972

Source: University of N.C. *Statistical Abstract of Higher Education, 1972-1973,* 1973.

It is neither trite nor exaggerated to suggest that North Carolina is in a position again to lead the way in postsecondary education. Other states are watching closely the new governance structure. The community college system seems only to have found its legs. The state can boast with justification of the grand accomplishments of many of its institutions, both public and private. The higher education leadership in North Carolina is hardly to be surpassed anywhere. But it is the considered judgment of many that the continued success of higher education in this state will be dependent, more than on any other single variable, upon an informed citizenry, capable of playing the fair-minded critic and the loyal supporter.

Public School Education—Richard C. Phillips
Higher Education—Benjamin H. Romine, Jr.

SELECTED REFERENCES

Governor's Study Committee on Structure and Organization of Higher Education. *Report of the Governor's Study Committee on Structure and Organization of Higher Education.* Raleigh: The Committee, 1971.

Grant, W. Vance. "Education's New Scorecard." *American Education* 8 (October 1970): 4-7.

Holton, Samuel M. "Education in the Changing South." *High School Journal* 54 (October 1970): 41-54.

N.C. Board of Higher Education. *Planning for Higher Education in North Carolina.* Special Report 2-68. Raleigh: The Board, 1968.

N.C. Board of Higher Education. *Private Higher Education in North Carolina: Conditions and Prospects.* Special Report 2-71. Raleigh: The Board, 1971.

N.C. Board of Higher Education. *Statistical Abstract of Higher Education.* Research Reports. Raleigh: The Board, 1966-72.

N.C. Department of Administration. *North Carolina State Government Statistical Abstract.* Raleigh: The Department, 1971.

N.C. Department of Community Colleges. *Annual Enrollment Report.* Raleigh: N.C. State Board of Education, 1966-73.

N.C. Department of Public Instruction. "Comparison of High School Graduates with 1964-65 Fifth-Grade Enrollment." Raleigh: The Department, 1972.

N.C. Department of Public Instruction. *How North Carolina Ranks Educationally among the Fifty States.* Raleigh: The Department, 1972.

N.C. Department of Public Instruction. *The 1971-72 Assessment of Educational Progress in North Carolina.* Raleigh: The Department, 1972.

N.C. Department of Public Instruction. *North Carolina Public Schools, 1970-72: Biennial Report of the State Superintendent.* Raleigh: The Department, 1972.

N.C. Department of Public Instruction. *Survey of 1972 High School Graduates.* Raleigh: The Department, 1972.

Powell, William S. *Higher Education in North Carolina.* Raleigh: State Department of Archives and History, 1970.

Southern Regional Education Board. *Fact Book on Higher Education in the South, 1971 and 1972.* Atlanta: The Board, 1972.

U.S. Department of Commerce, Bureau of the Census. *Statistical Abstract of the United States.* Washington, D.C.: U.S. Government Printing Office, 1970.

U.S. Office of Education. *Digest of Educational Statistics.* Washington, D.C.: U.S. Government Printing Office, 1962-72.

University of North Carolina. *Statistical Abstract of Higher Education, 1972-1973.* Research Report 1-73. Chapel Hill: University of North Carolina, 1973.

15. Health Care Resources

HARVEY L. SMITH
SHANNON P. HALLMAN

Health care can be defined as organized attention to the problems of illness—its treatment, prevention, and the reduction of disability—and to the maintenance of health.

The distinction between focusing efforts toward the treatment of illness on one hand and the maintenance of health on the other is crucial. Until the recent past most care has been directed toward acute sickness and has dealt with patients so disabled that they had to seek professional help, often while bedridden. Such care was functional enough when most illness was caused by infectious diseases. That kind of illness usually began abruptly with symptoms all too apparent to the patient, ran a fairly severe course and, more frequently as science progressed, was successfully terminated by medical treatment.

Today the treatment of most infectious diseases and other acute illness is a relatively minor problem for the health care professions. Although these conditions still occur and still account for the majority of all hospital admissions and physician visits, their duration is relatively brief and there is normally no residual disability to the patient. Their prevention, however, is a major problem and requires intervention at pre-illness levels lightly touched upon until now except in the field of public health.

The other major problem today is the care of people with chronic diseases. Figures 15.1 and 15.2 indicate the growing importance of these diseases as causes of death. Their importance as cripplers has increased even more. Unlike acute illnesses, these illnesses frequently have an onset insignificant in terms of discomfort and may advance to a life-threatening stage before becoming apparent to the victim. In addition, many of these diseases are never "cured"; once identified they require continued surveillance and treatment.

Thus developing patterns of care enlarge the scope of health care to include prevention, early diagnosis, continuous care, and rehabilitation. Such care aims to maintain health or arrest illness in its earliest stages. It seeks to do so with outreach efforts that carry health care to the settings in which people live in intimate contact with their families and communities.

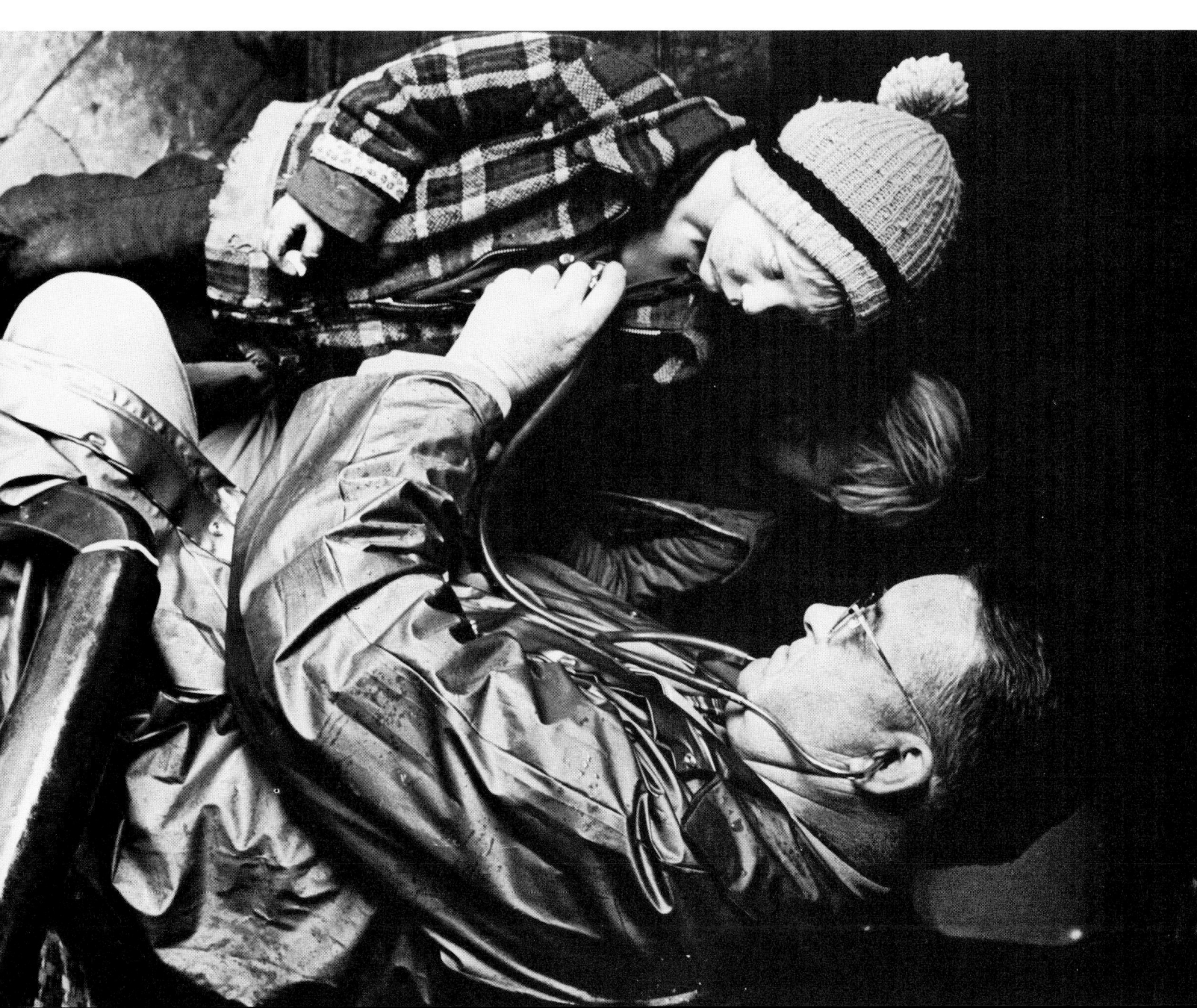

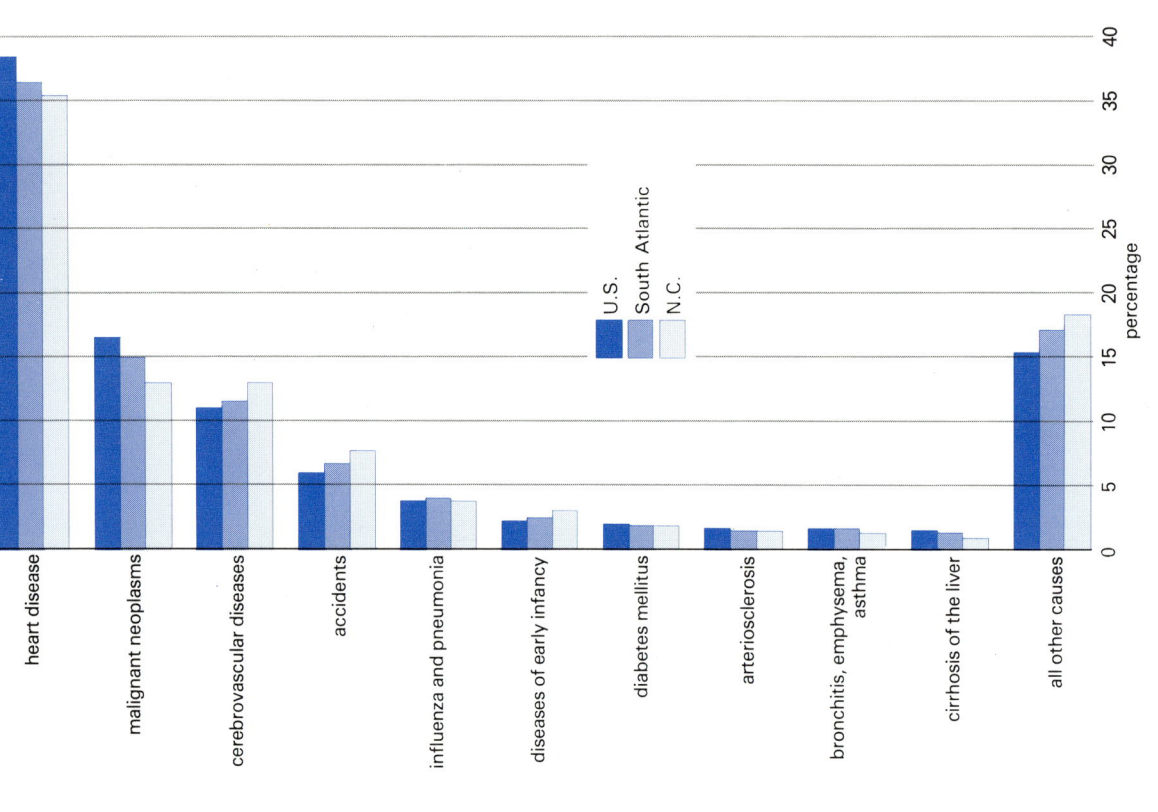

Figure 15.2. Leading Causes of Death as a Percentage of All Causes for N.C., the South Atlantic, and the U.S., 1968

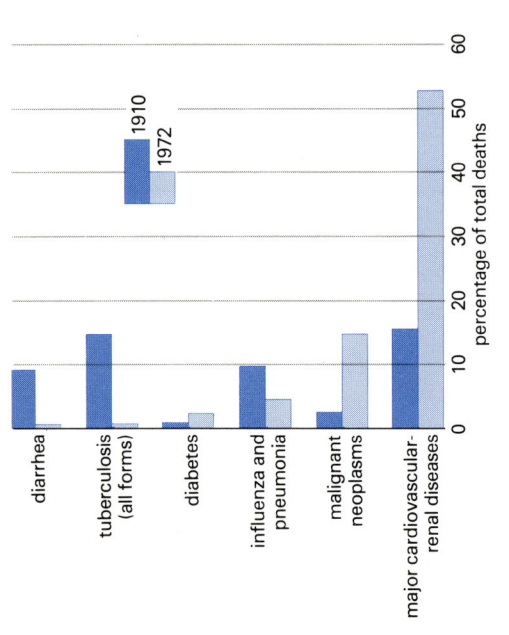

Figure 15.1. Selected Causes of Death as a Percentage of All Causes in N.C., 1910 and 1972

Note: 1910 deaths represent only those municipalities of 1,000 or more population. 1972 deaths are for first six calendar months.

This chapter reviews the major present components of health care in North Carolina, including the needs of its people and the resources mobilized to meet them, the major problems encountered by current procedures, and the growing edge of change pointing toward the future.

Hospitals

As of April 1972 there were 165 hospitals in North Carolina containing some 38,000 beds. Of these, 32 hospitals are "special care" institutions in the sense that they admit only certain groups of people such as veterans or Cherokee Indians or in that they serve only persons with certain diseases or stages of affliction such as tuberculosis or disabilities that require rehabilitation. Neither the number of these special hospitals nor their bed capacity is changing significantly, yet as general hospitals come more to deal with chronic conditions, the efficient division of labor between the two hospital types will require careful planning.

The state has been the beneficiary of an excellent program for construction of general hospitals under the guidance of its Medical Care Commission. The commission's program of financial and consultative assistance greatly aided the development and distribution of this prime health care resource for the people of North Carolina. But as is so often the case, the solutions of the past may not be adequate to the problems of the present and the future. Historically, North Carolina has been a state of small hospitals, widely distributed. Now the sophistication of equipment and personnel needed to provide good hospital care, and the cost of providing it, demand that hospitals be larger and fewer. Thus the trend has been toward consolidation (Figure 15.3).

Where consolidation has taken place, problems of accessibility are aggravated, especially those involving emergency care. Also complicated is the already difficult task of providing continuity of care once the patient returns to his community. Where consolidation has not taken place, most hospitals are too small to afford and supply a broad range of hospital care.

The accompanying map (Figure 15.4) shows the bed complement and distribution of hospitals in North Carolina. Many health care experts are convinced that only hospitals with two hundred beds or more can supply the mix of manpower specialties and technical equipment required to provide the forms of care of which modern medicine is capable. The great majority of the state's hospitals have fewer than two hundred beds (Figure 15.5).

It is of interest to note that a significant number of patients travel to neighboring counties for hospital zation. Thus hospitals in certain counties tend to serve local regional needs even though they may be relatively small facilities. Furthermore, based upon a study of deaths in hospitals by county of origin of patients, it was found that six distinct areas of the state could be delineated in which patients moved about for hospitalization but which few patients left. These areas and the relationships among counties within them are shown in Figure 15.6. Both these findings, the extension of hospital service to neighboring counties, and the tendency of hospital use patterns to cluster in six distinct areas, are forms of spontaneous regionalization of North Carolina's hospital resources. Such regionalization could form the basis for further planning for the future of the state's hospital system.

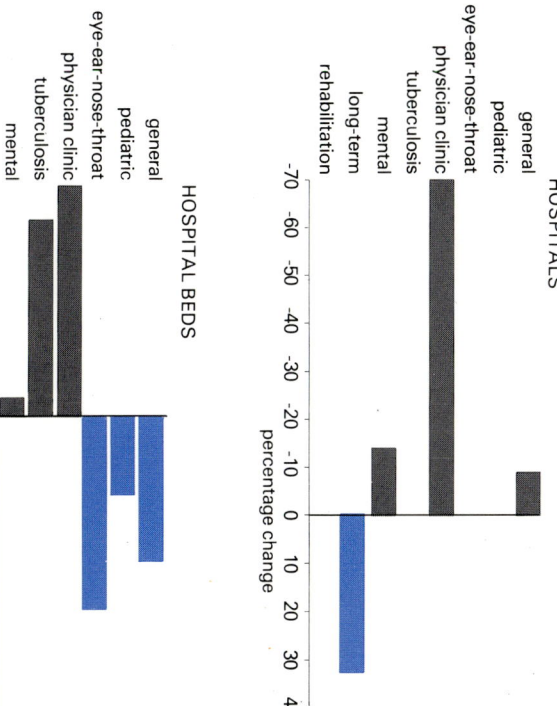

Figure 15.3. Change in Existing and Planned Nonfederal Hospitals and Number of Hospital Beds in N.C. by Type of Care Provided, 1964-1972

Source: N.C. Medical Care Commisson, *A Complete Listing of North Carolina Hospitals (Nonfederal)*, 1 February 1964, 1 April 1972.

Figure 15.4. N.C. Hospitals Existing and under Construction, 1971

Note: Map does not include military or V.A. hospitals.

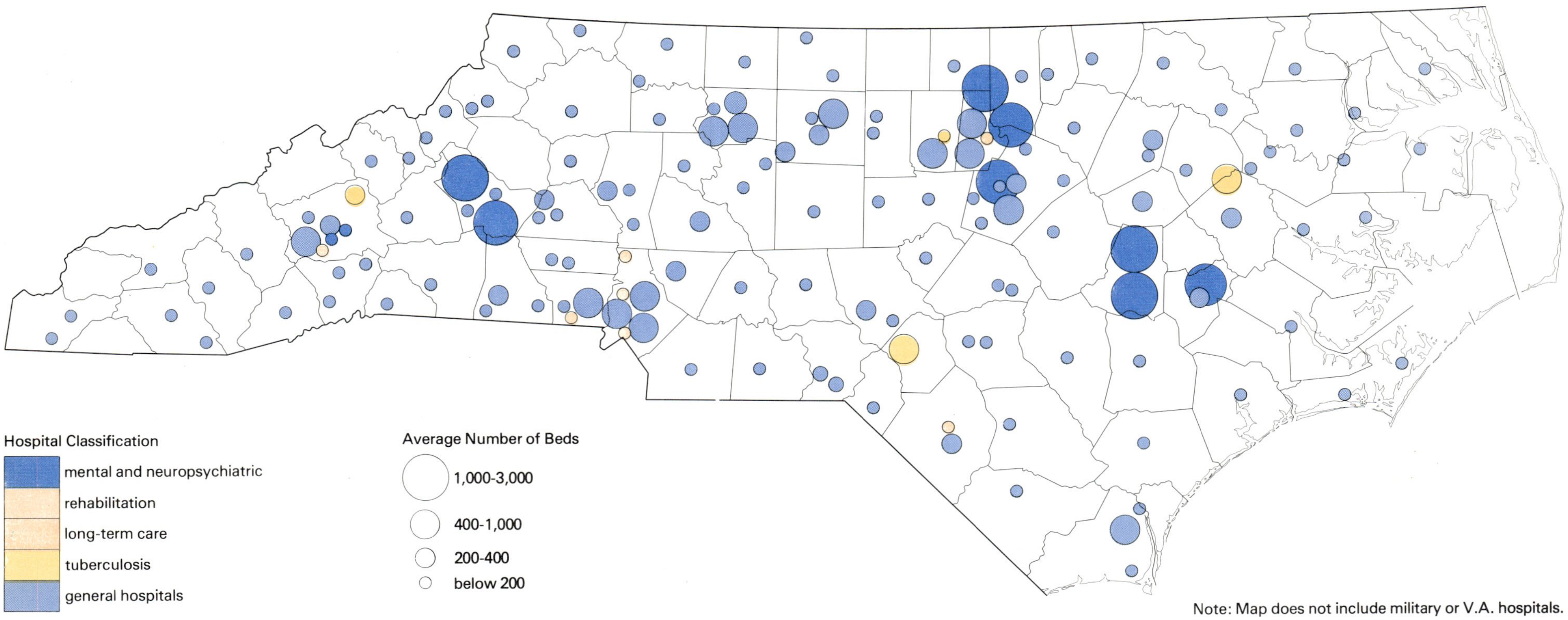

Figure 15.5. Size of N.C. Hospitals as of 1971 and Change, 1947-1971

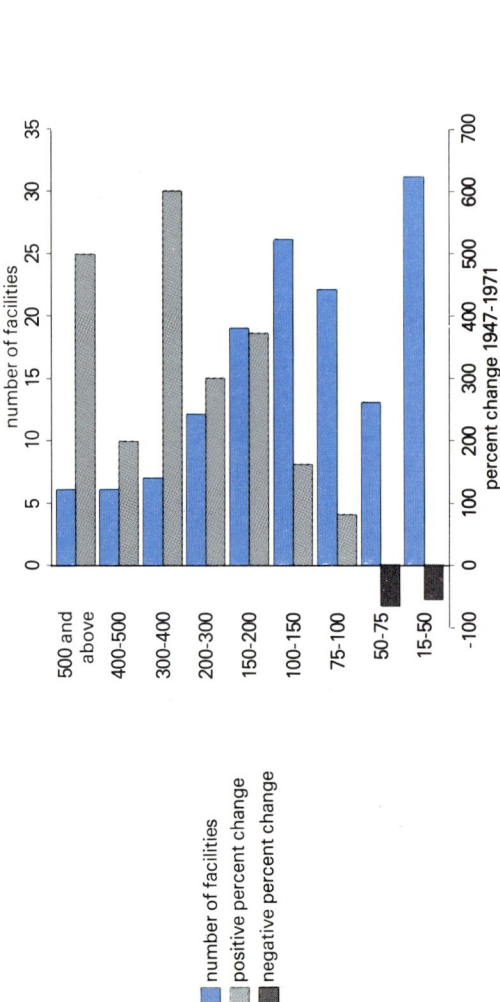

Figure 15.6. General Hospital Admissions by Six Distinct N.C. Service Areas, 1969

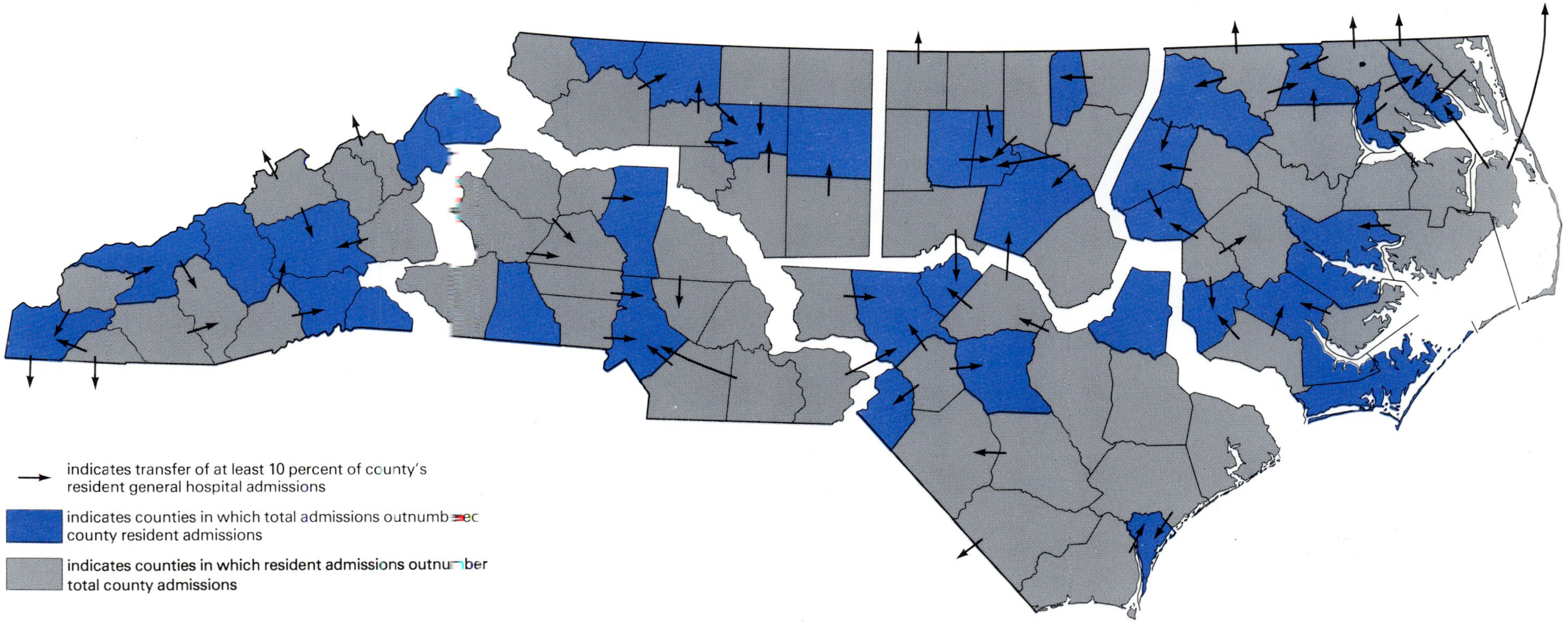

↓ indicates transfer of at least 10 percent of county's resident general hospital admissions

■ indicates counties in which total admissions outnumber county resident admissions

■ indicates counties in which resident admissions outnumber total county admissions

Hospitals show considerable variation in the services they are capable of supplying to the people in their localities. Important differences may be noted in the presence or absence of critical types of health specialties and in the varieties of therapeutic equipment and laboratory services available to patients. Although such differences are ultimately the result of variations in hospital size, the uneven distribution of large and small hospitals results in areal differences as well (Figure 15.7).

There are some one hundred other facilities in the state with real but tangential health care functions. These include four schools for the deaf and blind, two homes for unwed mothers, twelve facilities for mentally retarded or emotionally disturbed children, and thirty homes or schools for orphaned or dependent children. Their roles and special problems must be considered in a truly comprehensive health plan.

Health Manpower

Along with most of the United States, North Carolina suffers from a chronic shortage of many kinds of health care personnel. But North Carolina's particular problem is one of distribution of services, and it reflects the rurality of the state and its pockets of poverty. The needs for health care blanket the state but the manpower resources for providing health care cluster significantly in the socioeconomically more advantaged areas. The presentation of the patterns of location of selected types of critically important health professionals highlights this problem.

Physicians Physicians form the linchpin of health care manpower resources. Their presence and the type of practice they develop determine the availability of most other health services. Their absence at the very least suggests difficult problems of accessibility to care.

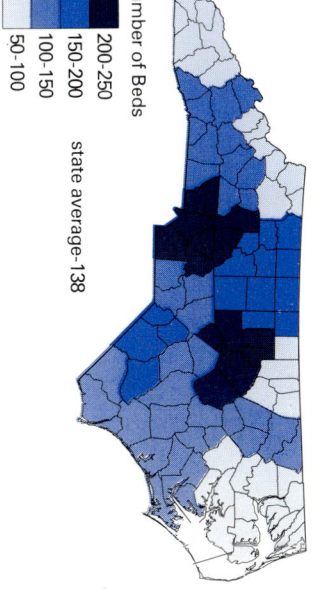

Figure 15.7. Average Number of Beds in General Hospitals by N.C. Administrative Planning Region, 1970

Number of Beds
- 200-250
- 150-200
- 100-150
- 50-100

state average-138

277

At the end of 1971 there were 6,255 physicians in the state. Eighty-two percent of them were in active, nonfederal practice. Figure 15.9 shows the distribution of these physicians by county and the number of people per physician for each of the administrative planning regions of the state. In general, the urbanized Piedmont possesses a relative concentration of physicians, with much thinner distribution in the Coastal Plain and Mountain portions of the state. Although all counties have at least one physician, seven counties have only one.

The physicians in the more rural portions of the state tend to cluster in the urban centers that do exist. People adjacent to these centers can be assumed to utilize the physicians there, but as their distance increases so must their unwillingness to seek help for all but the most pressing medical problems. In addition, the physicians in these centers have only limited capacity for extension of services to surrounding areas, so the population to be served soon becomes too great. As a result, there are many counties in the state that are doubly deprived of sufficient medical resources, having too few of their own and being beyond the outreach of those adjoining them (Figure 15.10).

Another aspect of maldistribution is the lack of young physicians in rural areas. The majority of physicians newly in practice seek economic, cultural, and professional opportunities that are more readily available in urban areas. Thus the average age of those practicing in rural counties tends to be higher. At the end of 1970 twelve counties were served by physicians of whom at least a quarter were sixty-five years of age or older; in four of these counties at least half the physicians were sixty-five or older (Figure 15.11).

As for type of practice, 87 percent of the active physicians in North Carolina were engaged in direct patient care in 1971. Another 7 percent served full time in teaching or research, a vital component of the state's health care resources. The remaining 6 percent were in administration.

In recent years there have been important changes in the composition of medical practice. Between 1950 and the end of 1971, the total number of practicing physicians increased 82 percent. This included a 113 percent increase in specialists and a 21 percent decrease in general practitioners. More specifically, in North Carolina in 1950 general practitioners comprised 47 percent of all practicing physicians. This figure had dropped to 20 percent by the end of 1971.

This shift is an alarming one, and some of the steps being taken to redress the balance toward general practice will be noted later. North Carolina's situation follows a national pattern. For the United States in 1971 general practitioners comprised 18 percent of all practicing physicians.

The number of physicians tells only part of the story. Not all are in private practice, and many practice specialties that do not meet the patient's general medical needs. The cardinal problem, as noted, is one of distribution. Here the disparity between specialties and general practice is great.

Figures 15.12 and 15.13 show the population per active general or family practitioner by county and the number of these professionals by planning regions.Clearly such ratios are poorest in the Coastal Plain and Mountain counties. In six counties there is a lone general practitioner. But even in ten counties with general practitioners no medical or surgical specialists are located. In six other counties having general practitioners there is one specialist, in each case a general surgeon.

Such "front-line" specialties as internal medicine (Figure 15.14), pediatrics, obstetrics, gynecology, cardiology, neurology, and pathology all reveal a sharply limited distribution in North Carolina, tending to cluster in the more urban and advantaged areas of the state. These include the areas where medical training centers are located. Other specialties, such as psychiatry, are even more tightly clustered.

Further analysis of the state's physician distribution by urban-rural county types indicates that the seven metropolitan statistical areas defined by the census for 1970, which have 37 percent of all practicing physicians, possess 62 percent of all practicing physicians. The thirty-two most rural counties, with 9 percent of the total population, have only 3 percent of the state's active practicing physicians. For specialists, such differences in location are even sharper, as Figure 15.15 indicates.

Metropolitan counties, with 37 percent of the population, have 72 percent of the total specialists. Rural counties, with 9 percent of the population, have 1 percent of the specialists.

The implication of such medical manpower distribution for health care is clear. For example, 34 percent of all the state's births occur in the fifty-nine rural and semirural counties. Yet these counties contain less than 19 percent of all practicing obstetrics and gynecology specialists; indeed, the strictly rural counties contain none at all. Seventy-four percent of all the births in the state attended by midwives occur in these fifty-nine counties.

Figure 15.8. Hospitals and Hospital Beds Existing and Planned in N.C. by Type of Ownership, 1972

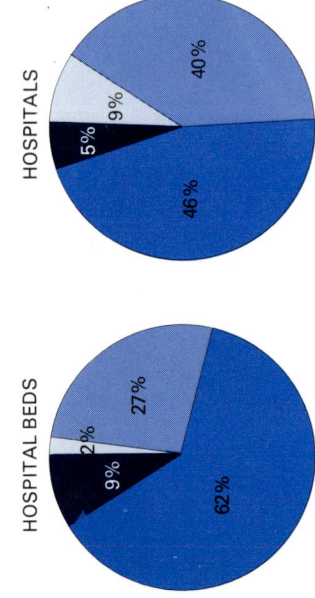

HOSPITAL BEDS
9%
2%
62%
27%

HOSPITALS
40%
5%
9%
46%

Hospital and Hospital Bed Construction

federal government
other government
other nonprofit
profit

Source: N.C. Medical Care Commission, *A Complete Listing of North Carolina Hospitals (Nonfederal)*, 1 April 1972.

Figure 15.9. Population per Active Nonfederal Physician in N.C., 1971

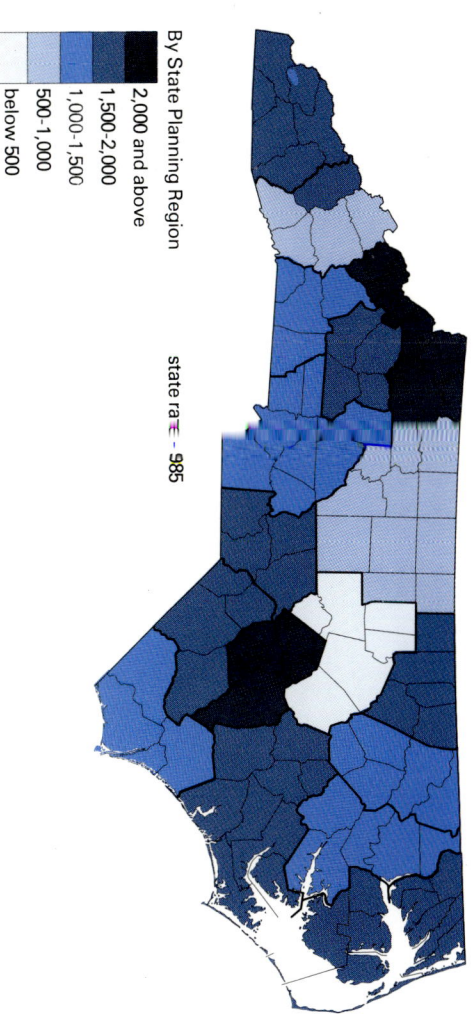
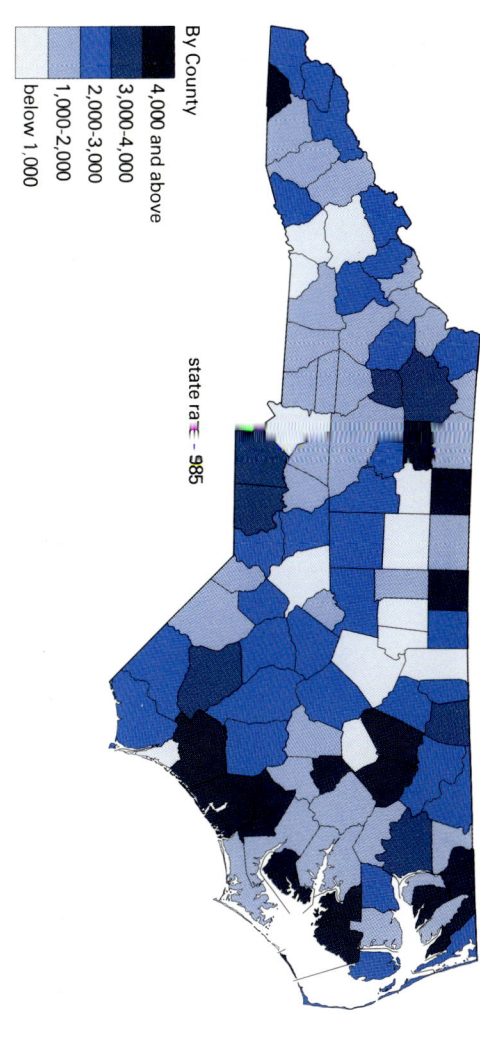

By County
- 4,000 and above
- 3,000–4,000
- 2,000–3,000
- 1,000–2,000
- below 1,000

state rate = 985

By State Planning Region
- 2,000 and above
- 1,500–2,000
- 1,000–1,500
- 500–1,000
- below 500

state rate = 985

Figure 15.10. N.C. Counties Deficient in Patient-Care Physicians, 1971

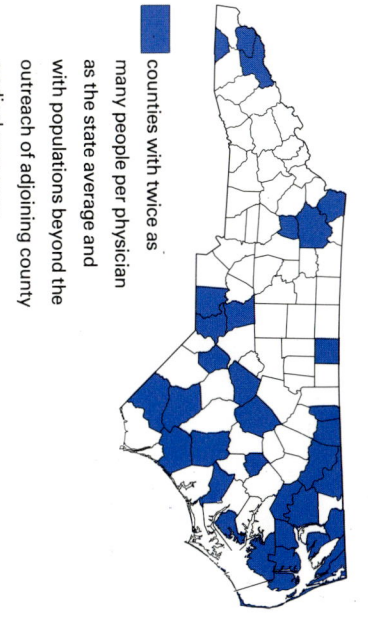

■ counties with twice as many people per physician as the state average and with populations beyond the outreach of adjoining county medical resources

Source: Josef Perry, Social Research Section, University of N.C. at Chapel Hill, unpublished data, 1973.

Figure 15.11. N.C. Counties with High Proportions of Physicians 65 Years of Age or Older, 1970

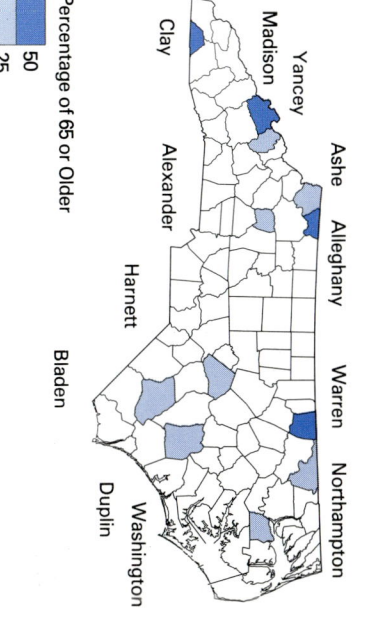

Percentage of 65 or Older
- 50
- 25

Ashe, Alleghany, Warren, Northampton, Yancey, Madison, Alexander, Harnett, Clay, Bladen, Duplin, Washington

279

Figure 15.12. Population per Active General or Family Practitioner in N.C. by County, 1971

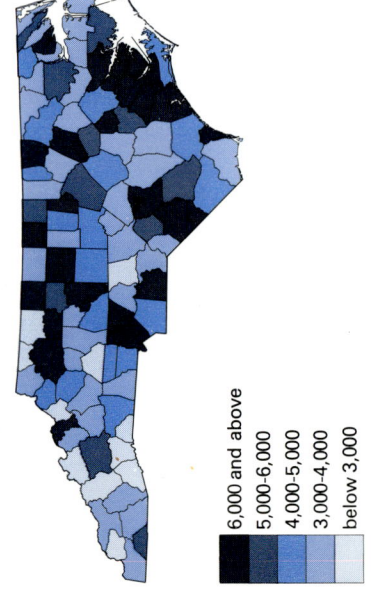

Figure 15.14. Physicians Specializing in Internal Medicine in N.C. by County, 1971

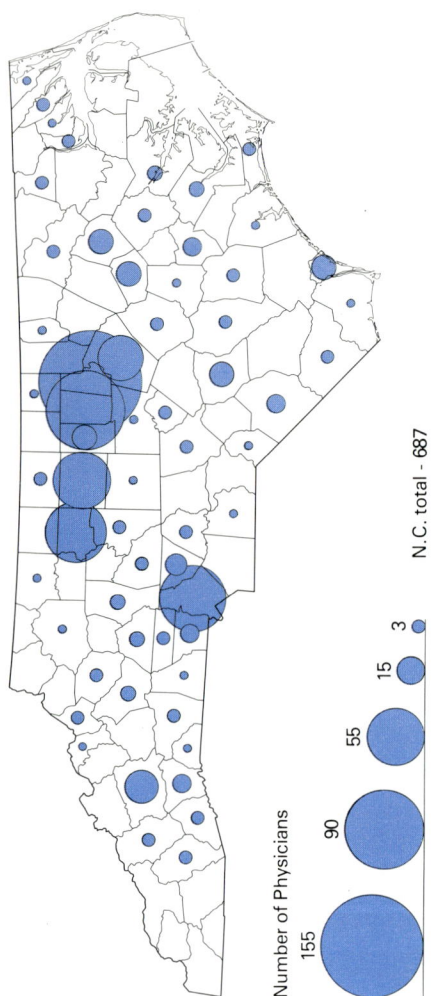

Note: Does not include specialists in cardiology, pediatric cardiology, allergy, pediatric allergy, pulmonary disease, or gastroenterology.

Figure 15.13. Population per Active General or Family Practitioners in N.C. by Planning Region, 1971

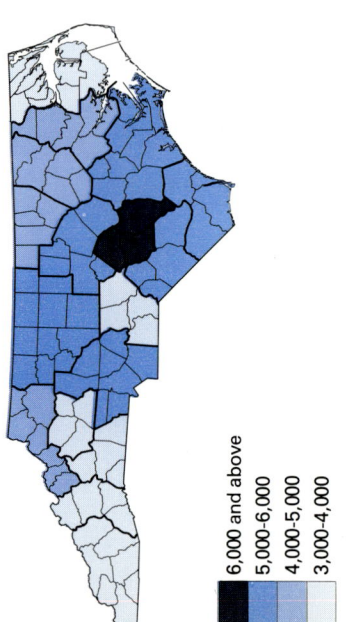

Having examined the current status, it may be meaningful to see the directions in which the state is moving. A comparison of North Carolina with the South and with the United States from 1942 to 1971 shows that the state, fortunately enough, has had the largest reduction (31 percent) in the number of people per physician (Figure 15.16), even though it still lags considerably behind the South and even more so behind the United States. During this period of time the number of physicians in North Carolina increased from 2,808 to 5,694.

Closer analysis reveals that the state's progress, too, has been differentially made for different regions of the state. Metropolitan areas have shown more than twice the percentage growth in practicing physicians than has the rest of the state. There has been also twice the percentage drop in general practitioners in the metropolitan areas.

Dentists The distributional patterns of most types of health manpower are similar to that of hospital beds and that of physicians; so, selected highlights of such distribution should suffice. The general geographic pattern of dentists, and the population per active dentist, is shown in Figure 15.17. The state population per dentist of 3,159 is relatively high, with only thirty counties achieving a lower figure. The eight counties that have no dentists are all rural counties and tend to cluster in the eastern part of the state.

The metropolitan counties of North Carolina contain 26 percent of the state's population and 37 percent of its active dentists; rural and semirural counties, with 33 percent of the population, have 21 percent of the dentists.

For dental specialties the distributional skew is even more marked. Figure 15.18 shows the number and locations of oral surgeons, clearly an urban area clustering. For all other types of dental specialists (Figure 15.19) the same urban clustering predominates. Moreover, 13 percent of all active practicing dentists are dental specialists.

North Carolina has improved little over the past decade and still lags considerably behind the nation in population per dentist. For example, in 1965 the population per dentist for North Carolina was 3,176, fourth from the bottom and twenty-six states below the national level. In 1970 the state was tied with Alabama and Arkansas for forty-seventh place, twenty-four states below the national level. Along with the geographic maldistribution, the rate of progress is uneven. Rural and urban counties and those adjacent to metropolitan counties have been improving slightly, while metropolitan and semirural counties have fallen back somewhat. Thus North Carolina remains far from having achieved satisfactory dental resources for all parts of the state.

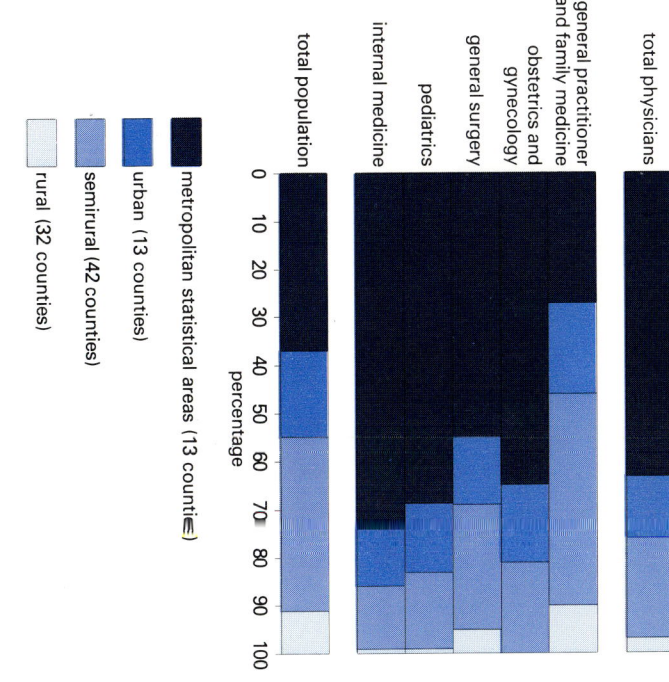

Figure 15.15. Urban-Rural Distribution of Active Nonfederal Physicians in N.C. by Selected Specialties, 1971

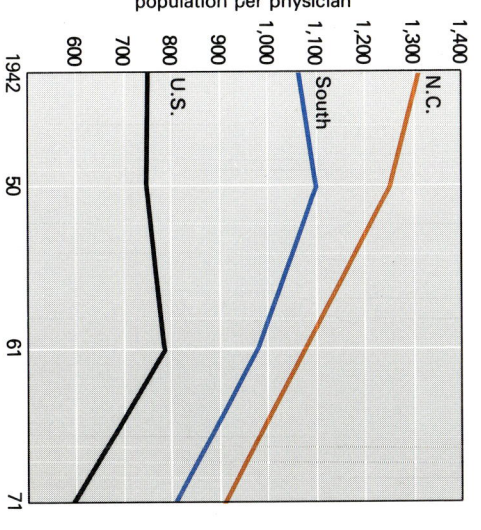

Figure 15.16. Population per Nonfederal Physician for the U.S., South, and N.C., 1942-1971

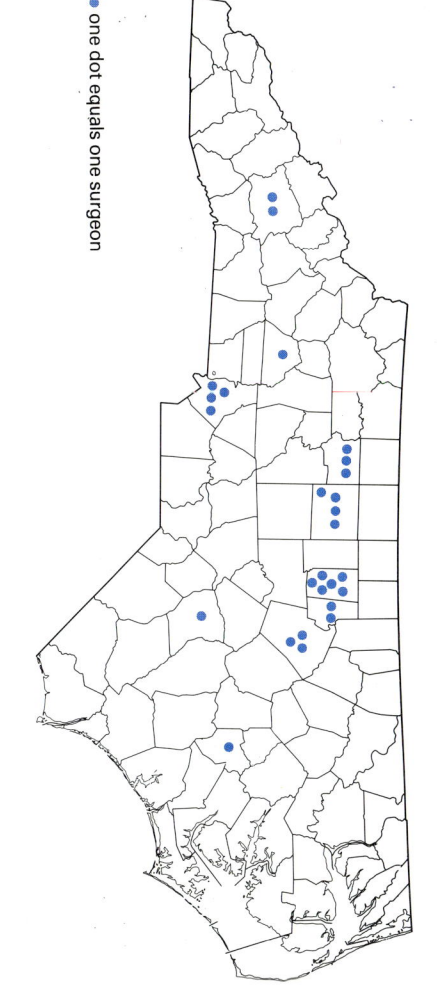

Figure 15.18. Oral Surgeons in N.C., 1969

Figure 15.17. Population per Active Dentist in N.C., Excluding Oral Surgeons, 1969

281

Figure 15.19. Dental Specialists in N.C., Excluding Oral Surgeons, 1969

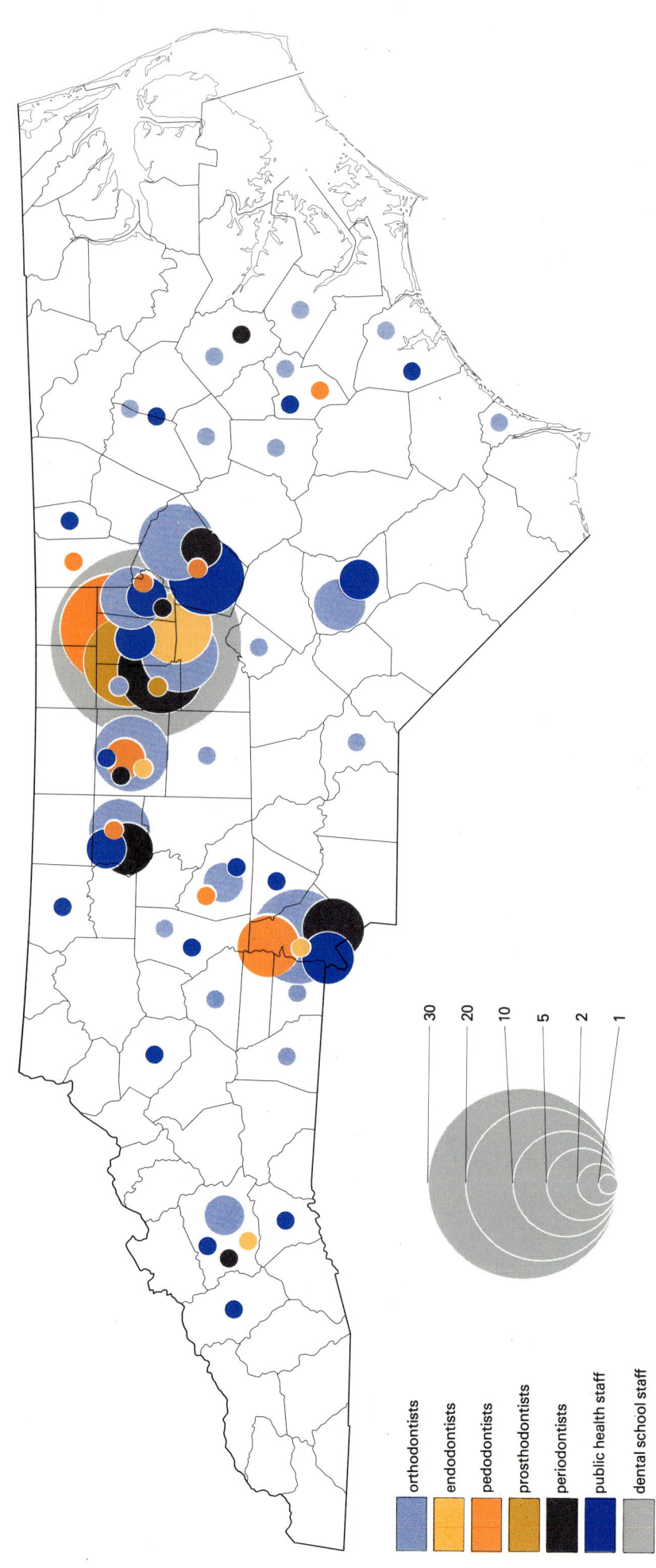

Nurses Figures 15.20 and 15.21 show the general distribution of active registered nurses and active practical nurses in North Carolina. The range for both is enormous. If public health nurses are excluded, Orange and Durham counties, with teaching-medical centers, have ratios of 152 persons per registered nurse and 164 persons per practical nurses respectively, while Pamlico and Greene counties have no nurses.

It is important to note that in 1971 there were 3,306 inactive registered nurses living in the state. Energetic but sporadic efforts to recruit these nurses to active practice have met with little success. They represent 17 percent of the total registered nurses. In similar fashion, 16 percent of the total of licensed practical nurses are reported inactive.

Because of their special potential for "casefinding" and for contact with people outside the traditional doctor-hospital care system, public health nurses represent a prime resource at the community level. Their distribution is shown in Figure 15.22. Although they too are overrepresented in urban and metropolitan areas, they are broadly distributed across the state, more so than any other health worker.

Pharmacists In 1970 there were 2,183 pharmacists in North Carolina. Of these, approximately 191 were not professionally active. Their distribution by county type is shown in Figure 15.23, which also notes the population per pharmacist. Once again, the metropolitan counties have the most favorable ratios, the rural counties the least favorable.

In comparison with the national pattern for pharmacists, North Carolina comes off badly. Federal statistics of 1971 show that the United States had a ratio of 63.2 pharmacists per 100,000 population. The figure reported for North Carolina is 41.1 pharmacists per 100,000 people. According to this report, only Alaska and Hawaii fare as badly as North Carolina in this respect. In recent years there has been a leveling-off in the state's ratio of pharmacists to population at a level substantially below that for the nation as a whole.

North Carolina pharmacists may be compared with their national counterparts along several dimensions: there are fewer pharmacists under age thirty (18.99 percent in the United States, 15.29 in North Carolina); more phar-

282

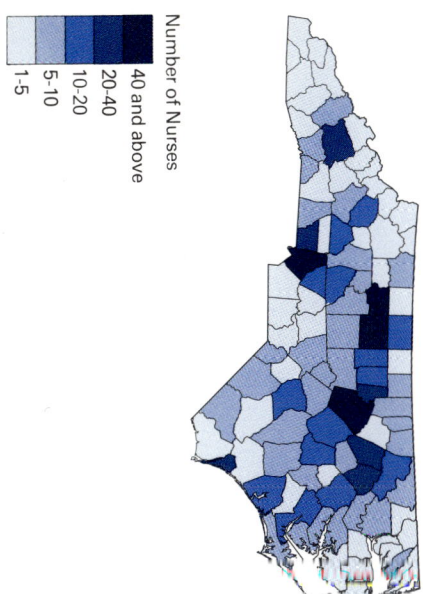

Figure 15.20. Population per Active Registered Nurse in N.C., Excluding Public Health Nurses, 1970

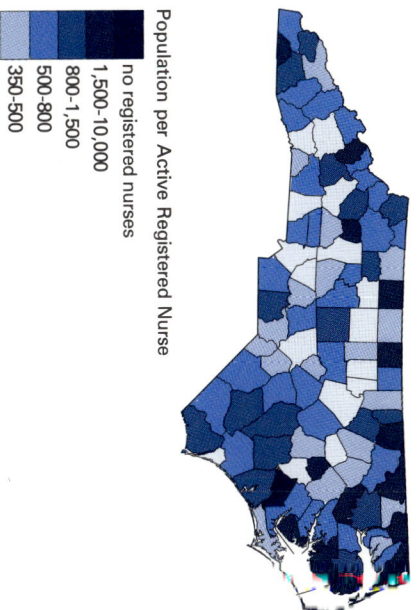

Figure 15.21. Population per Active Licensed Practical Nurse in N.C., 1970

macists aged sixty-five and over (11.1 percent in North Carolina, 8.4 percent in the United States); more of the state's pharmacists actively dispense prescriptions and other health care items (95.7 percent in North Carolina, 89 percent in the United States); fewer pharmacists are engaged in teaching and research (1.4 percent in North Carolina, 0.61 percent in North Carolina); more pharmacists are in community pharmacy (91.5 percent in North Carolina, 84.5 percent in the United States); and fewer pharmacists are in hospital or clinic pharmacy (7.5 percent in the United States, 5.84 percent in North Carolina).

Pharmacy leaders of the state, aware of the relatively poor numerical showing, assert that this is more than offset by the superior productivity of North Carolina's pharmacists. They also feel that pharmacists of the future, because of their special training and general distribution, may play important new roles in emerging patterns of health care.

Allied Health Professions

There are personnel in some fifty traditional and newly emerging allied health professions practicing and being trained in the state. The following list is representative of the range of these professions: Dental Assistant, Dental Hygienist, Dietitian, Family Nurse Practitioner, Hospital Administrator, Medical Laboratory Assistant, Medical Technologist, Medical Office Assistant, Medical Records Technician, Psychiatric Aide, Clinical Psychologist, Occupational Therapist, Optometrist, Physical Therapist, Physicians' Assistant, Radiologic Technician.

These people provide technical skills and therapeutic services to patients and improve the effectiveness of services provided by the health professionals mentioned earlier. But here too problems of shortage and maldistribution exist. Indeed, a special sort of shortage exists in many of these fields: an unusually high turnover rate causes great inefficiency in time spent in on-the-job training and plays havoc with the smooth running of facilities. The problem is due in many instances to the responsibilities of marriage and motherhood that fall on the many women in these jobs.

In general, workers in the older occupations are as broadly distributed as the facilities that employ them. That distribution reflects the more established role assigned to them in the traditional model of health care delivery. The newer fields tend currently to cluster in those localities that have the more complex mixes of service, teaching, and research resources. This cluster-

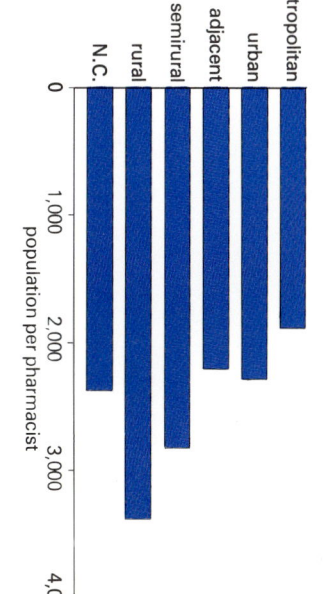

Figure 15.22. Public Health Nurses in N.C., 1970

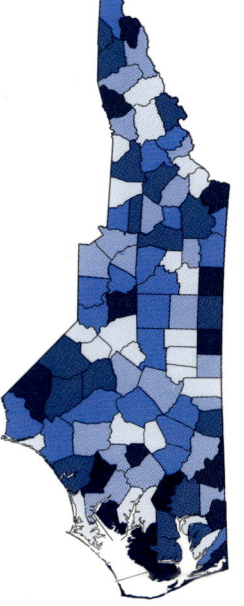

Figure 15.23. Population per Pharmacist in N.C. by Type of County, August 1970

283

However, since 1 January 1970, the department's participation has increased enormously through the state's participation in the federal Medicaid program. Indeed, in the decade since 1961 the department's expenditures for medical assistance increased from $5.9 million to $90.7 million.

Medicaid provides payments for medical services rendered to persons receiving general assistance under four programs: Aid to the Aged, Aid to the Disabled, Aid to Families with Dependent Children, and Aid to the Blind. In addition, medical payments are provided for those who, while earning too much to qualify for the above four general assistance programs, otherwise qualify for participation and are deemed to have insufficient income for medical expenses.

Under Medicaid the department may provide payment to providers of any of the following services: inpatient hospital care, outpatient care, dental services, prescribed drugs, physician services, chiropractic services, optometric care, home health services, nursing home care, or mental hospital care in one of the state's four mental hospitals for those over sixty-five and medically needy.

In addition, the department pays the monthly premium for physician services under Medicare for those medically needy persons sixty-five or older. The department employs some 370 persons at both the state and county levels solely to determine eligibility for medical assistance. The State Board of Health provides for the detection, reporting, prevention, and control of infectious, communicable, occupational, and any other diseases or hazards that may endanger the public health. The following selection of problems dealt with by the board's divisions indicate the breadth of its concerns.

—Epidemiology Division: communicable disease control, accident prevention, and occupational health hazards.

—Laboratory Divison: cancer detection through cytological examination.

—Community Health Division: health education, nutrition, administration of local health programs, migrant health, and emergency and disaster services to local hospitals.

—Dental Health Division: prevention of dental problems, education, and diagnosis and treatment.

—Personal Health Division: crippled children, chronic disease, Medicare-Medicaid standards, nursing home standards, mental retardation, and maternal health.

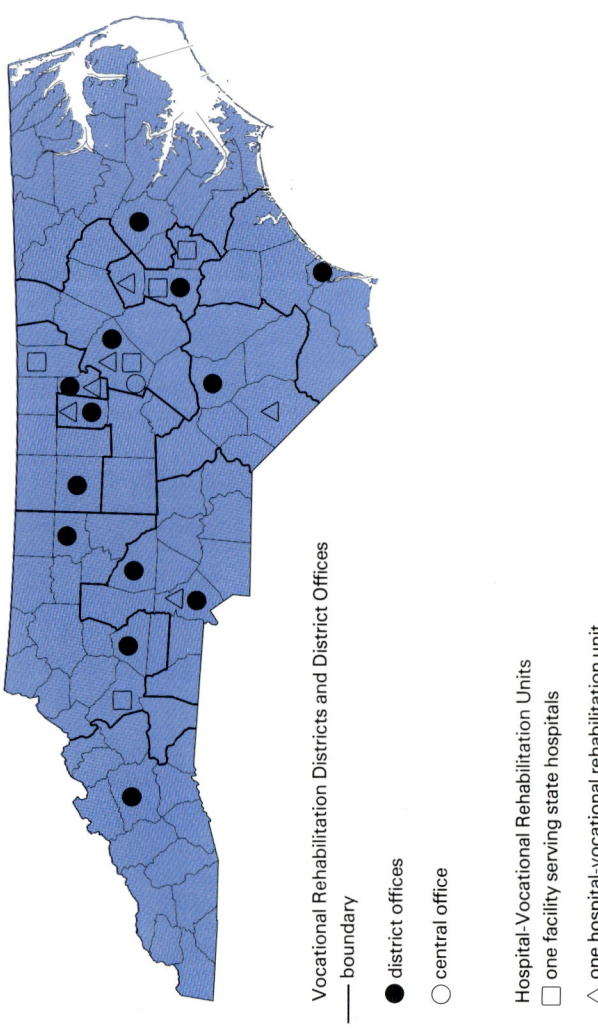

Figure 15.24. Vocational Rehabilitation Districts, District Offices, and Hospital-Vocational Rehabilitation Units in N.C., 1973

Vocational Rehabilitation Districts and District Offices
— boundary
● district offices
○ central office

Hospital-Vocational Rehabilitation Units
□ one facility serving state hospitals
△ one hospital-vocational rehabilitation unit

ing is probably as it should be for the more exotic occupations; but for the others, vital for the provision of the continuous, high-quality local care possible today, a more even distribution is needed.

Special Care Systems

The public sector of the health care network provides a variety of important services—direct care services, and preventive, diagnostic, aftercare, and rehabilitative services. In addition, public agencies may provide the indigent and medically indigent with the financial means of securing medical and related services.

Division of Vocational Rehabilitation The Division of Vocational Rehabilitation of the Department of Human Resources functions to preserve or restore the capacity of physically or mentally disabled persons to engage in productive employment. Special services are offered for the deaf, the alcoholic, and for juvenile and adult offenders. In addition to its central office, services are provided through thirteen district offices, in facilities serving the state mental hospitals and centers for the retarded, and in special units within hospitals (Figure 15.24). In the typical year 1969-70, the agency worked with some 42,000 applicants, 29,000 of whom were judged eligible for rehabilitation services. In the course of serving these people the division spent some $3 million for diagnostic procedures and physical restoration. Current agency planning would provide for the development of a major comprehensive rehabilitation center linked to statewide services through the establishment of a series of regional centers.

Department of Social Services Since 1961 the Department of Social Services, formerly the Department of Public Welfare, has provided payment to providers or "vendors" of medical care for certain types of health services offered to eligible persons.

Figure 15.25. Regional, District, and City Administrative Units for N.C. Public Health Programs, 1973

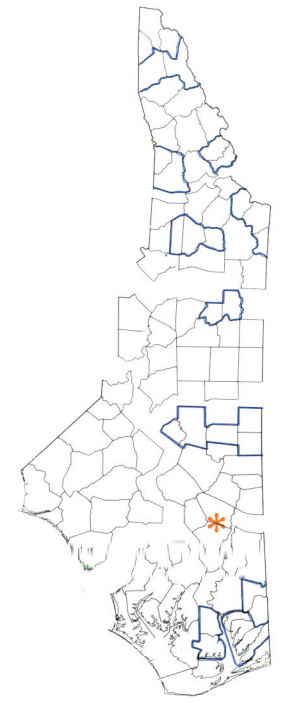

▭ delineates regional public health offices

✶ city board of health (Rocky Mount)

— multicounty board of health districts

Note: All other counties have their own boards of health.

—Sanitary Engineering Division: radiological hazards and control of disease-carrying organisms and substances.

The board's programs are supervised and consultation is provided through six regional offices. The programs are administered in the one hundred counties by one city, sixty-nine single-county, and eleven multicounty boards of health (Figure 15.25). For the biennium 1969–70 there were 2,200 persons employed at state and local levels. The total budget for those years was over $55 million.

The majority of the local jurisdictions is served by full-time medical directors; a smaller proportion is served by physicians in part-time private practice or—in line with a recent innovation—by nonphysician directors trained in public health administration. Each of the local units has a large measure of autonomy in program development, and thus the programs that are offered will vary from county to county.

Department of Mental Health The North Carolina Department of Mental Health has responsibility for a broad range of problems and disorders including mental illness, mental retardation, and alcoholism. It also has special programs for problems of drug abuse. Three related systems have been established to deal with these problems: mental hospitals and community mental

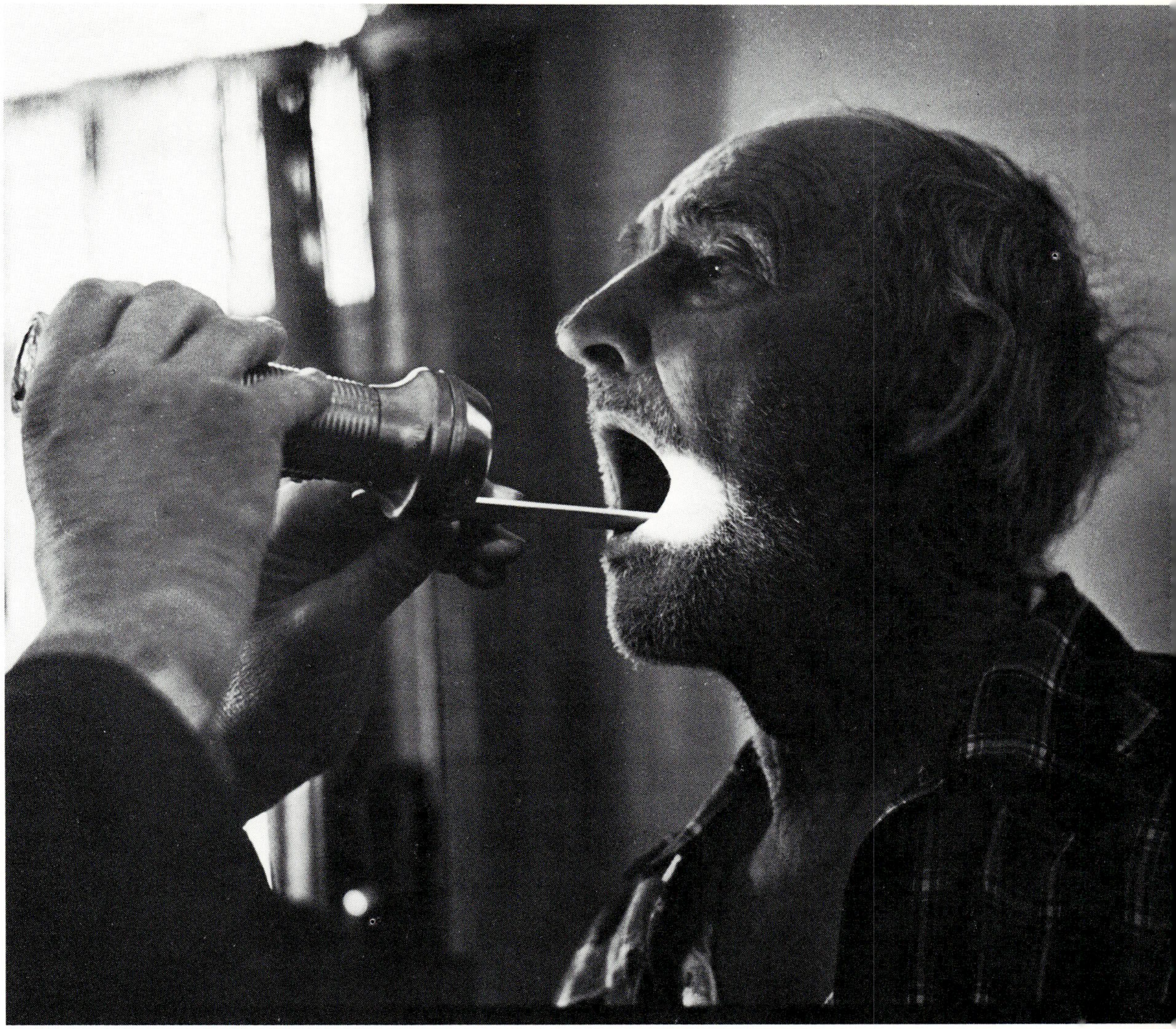

The rate of growth of community clinic services is demonstrated in Figure 15.27. Still a new development, it is clear that their operation in the future will further meet mental health problems at the local level by helping families to avoid the traumas of separation and hospitalization.

State centers for the mentally retarded have recently begun to redirect their efforts from custodial care toward community treatment and the development of programs for returning patients to the community. For those who must remain in the institutions, various modes of care and treatment have been developed to achieve their maximal personal and social development. There are four such centers in the state and during 1972 they served 4,842 patients.

North Carolina also has three alcoholic rehabilitation centers. These offer short-term intensive treatment. The first of these centers, at Butner, served some five hundred persons in fiscal year 1967. Since then increases in Butner's case load and the development in 1969 and 1970 of the two other centers at Black Mountain and at Greenville have caused a sharp and rapid rise in persons served (Figure 15.28). During 1972 the three centers served approximately 3,100 patients. Here again, every effort is made to maintain contact between the patient and his family and community during the course of treatment.

health centers, alcoholic rehabilitation centers, and centers for mental retardation. All of these centers are coordinated on a four-region basis through the cooperation of central office staff and staff at the local level. Every effort is made to deal with problems at the local level. If they cannot be resolved locally, the efforts are backstopped by the system of hospitals.

North Carolina has four mental hospitals. Each serves an assigned area of the state. The "unit system" is in effect; that is, patients from specified clusters of counties are housed and treated together to facilitate communication between hospital and community resources in the interests of continuity of care.

Sixty-four community clinics and mental health centers are in operation. All provide diagnostic, treatment, and consultative services. The more developed centers provide twenty-four-hour service, partial hospitalization (day or night care), and beds sited in the locality. The development of community clinics and recent advances in therapy for the mentally ill have drastically changed the functions of the state hospitals. Formerly, they were essentially "storage-bins," accumulating a growing population. Now, although they serve many more patients, the total patient load continues to decline (Figure 15.26).

Voluntary Associations In addition to the health practitioners and agencies, both public and private, there is a third component of North Carolina's health care network—voluntary associations. Such associations are organized citizen efforts, coordinated through centralized administrative cores, and supported through voluntary contributions. They work toward the cure of disease and the promotion of health. They are therefore a major component of the state's health care resources.

There are about fifteen such agencies in North Carolina. The following list indicates the wide variety of programs they sponsor: continuing education for health professionals, public education, purchase of diagnostic and therapeutic equipment, training fellowships, research, operation of diagnostic clinics, support for free clinics, support for registries, provision for nursing services and related home care needs, rehabilitation, provision for drugs and medication, counseling, liaison with professional organizations, training of volunteers, meetings and conferences, short courses and seminars (including some trainee support), maintenance of community health care informational services, preparation and distribution of literature, school health programs, promotion of health careers, and training for emergency services.

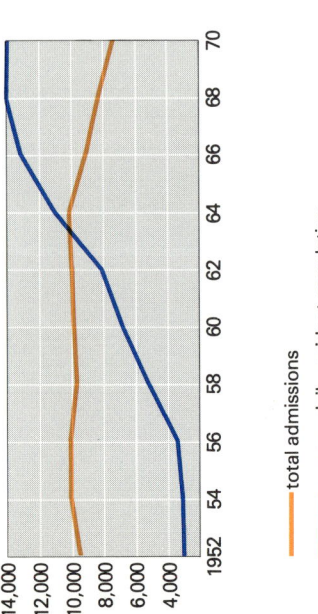

Figure 15.26. Use Rate for N.C. Mental Hospitals, 1952-1970

Source: N.C. Department of Mental Health, *Annual Report ARR-15*, 11 September 1972.

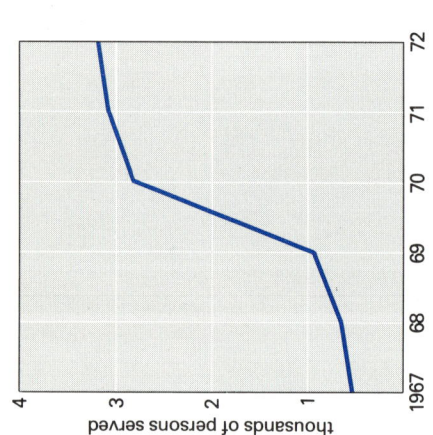

Figure 15.28. Persons Served by N.C. Alcoholic Rehabilitation Centers, 1967-1972

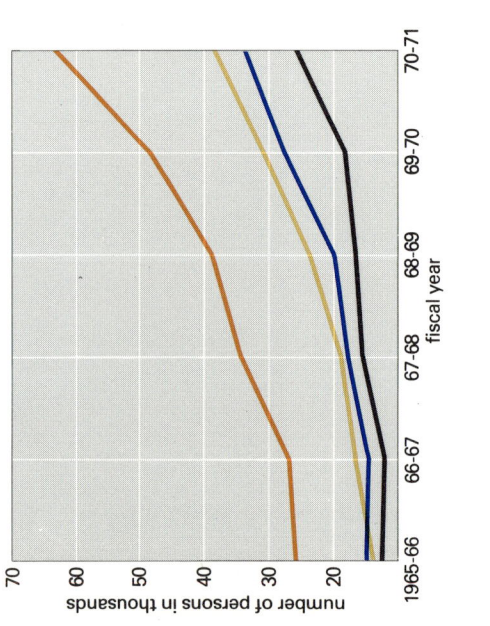

Figure 15.27. Use Rate for N.C. Mental Health Clinics and Centers, 1965-1971

Source: N.C. Department of Mental Health, *Annual Report ARR-17*, 8 October 1971.

Health Care Training Resources

North Carolina has a relatively wide array of educational resources to provide trained personnel for its health care professions and agencies. The state has three four-year Schools of Medicine and a newly established one-year school. It also has a School of Pharmacy, a School of Dentistry, and a School of Public Health. Nursing education leading to a bachelor's degree is offered in twelve institutions and there is one graduate-degree program. In addition, there are twenty-one associate and fourteen diploma programs for the teaching of registered nurses. These programs provide the core professionals of health care. Closely related professional programs are also offered: two in medical social work and four in clinical aspects of psychology.

The allied medical and health professions are at the forefront of health care improvement in North Carolina as well as nationally. They provide for the expansion of the activities of the core professions and for the modes of care that require their own special skills. Educational programs are offered in the state's universities, community colleges, technical institutes, and hospitals for more than fifty allied health occupational categories. The recency of the development of this field is seen in the fact that, of fifteen programs for which the American Medical Association has outlined essentials, nine were developed within the past ten years.

The following 1972-73 figures indicate the order of magnitude of North Carolina's educational commitment in the field of health care: the entering classes of the medical schools represent a combined total of 334 students; the School of Dentistry had over 240 students; the School of Pharmacy had 419 students; the combined total for nursing was 853 students (diploma: 429; associate degree: 158; baccalaureate programs: 263). The community colleges and technical institutes offer eleven types of programs that serve a total of 1,992 students.

For medical training it is of particular interest to note that North Carolina ranks twenty-eighth in the nation in the number of students entering medical schools per 100,000 population although it ranks fortieth in per capita income and thirty-second in entering students per one thousand bachelor's degrees awarded.

Many of the state's health care problems require research and practice skills directed toward communities rather than individual patient care. These problems are in the public health domain. Environmental pollution, nutritional deficits, and the control of epidemics are public health problems that press for solution with the greatest urgency. Similarly, a community focus is involved in the organization of health care delivery systems and in programs of health education. Nurses are called upon for home and family visits rather than for clinical care.

Training for public health careers centers mainly in the School of Public Health, with programs of more limited scope offered for undergraduates at five other universities. There are 456 students currently enrolled in the School of Public Health, in fields such as environmental sciences and engineering, biostatistics, epidemiology, health administration, maternal and child health, health education, community nursing, nutrition, and parasitology.

The pressures of the state's cities and expanding population's have made the public care professions an increasingly important component of North Carolina's health apparatus.

Selected Problems

Some important problems of the health care network in North Carolina have already been noted: shortages of some types of health manpower and maldistribution of most; and the great number of small hospitals that are hard pressed to deliver the complex and expensive modes of care that recent advances have made available.

Areas of poverty and rural areas, which are likely to be poor, can neither support nor attract health care resources. Too many parts of the state are rural, and poor. These difficulties are shared with other parts of the nation where similar conditions prevail. Such resource and support problems are not without their consequences. It was noted earlier that where obstetrical-gynecological specialties are not present the use of midwives is most frequent, an archaic practice that is being abandoned in more advantaged areas.

The draft rejection rates for the state are a sad commentary on its general health. During the years 1970-71, 51 percent of the youth examined for the military draft were rejected. In one county the rejection rate ranged as high as 60.1 percent (Figure 15.29). Of those rejected, 69 percent were rejected for physical disabilities (including some with psychiatric and mental disabilities as well). The remainder were rejected primarily for substandard mental functioning.

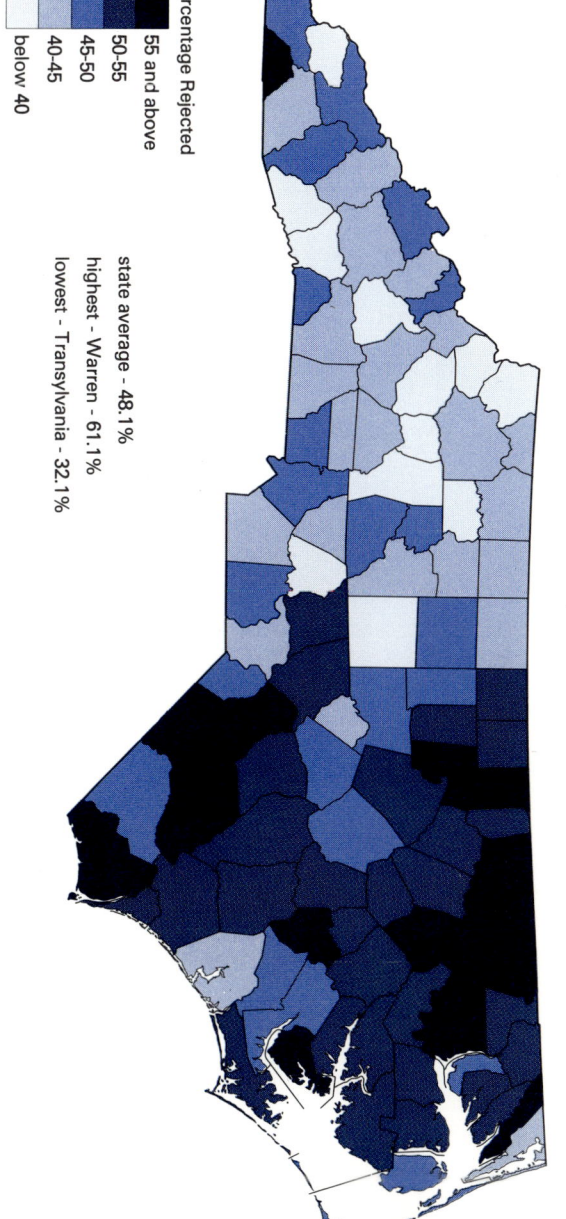

Figure 15.29. N.C. Military Draft Rejection Rate, 1970-1971

Percentage Rejected
- 55 and above
- 50-55
- 45-50
- 40-45
- below 40

state average - 48.1%
highest - Warren - 61.1%
lowest - Transylvania - 32.1%

Source: Josef Perry, Social Research Section, University of N.C. at Chapel Hill, unpublished data, 1973.

Infant mortality figures highlight the extent to which nonwhites may be especially vulnerable to poor health. Table 15.1 shows the differences in rates for whites and nonwhites. The problems for nonwhites are, in general, an exaggeration of the problems of people who are rural and poor since the nonwhites in North Carolina are more rural and poorer than the whites. Although the higher risk mortality rate for nonwhites is clearly evident in both populations, and North Carolina still lags behind the nation as a whole, the state's rate of improvement is considerably faster. In 1960 the United States nonwhite infant mortality rate was 1.9 times higher than the white rate, and in 1968 it was 1.8 times greater. North Carolina, however, progressed from a nonwhite rate in 1960 at 2.3 times the white rate to one that was 1.8 times as great in 1968.

The effect of racial risk differences is revealed vividly by comparing combined racial rates with those viewed separately. In 1968 the total infant mortality rate per one thousand live births was 21.8 for the United States and 26.3 for North Carolina. However, a breakdown by race reveals that North Carolina's rate of 20.8 for whites was quite close to the United States rate of 19.2. The nonwhite rate for North Carolina, on the other hand, was 39.1 compared with 34.5 for the United States. Figure 15.30 shows those counties with infant mortality rates at least 50 percent above that for the state as a whole.

It is clear that the presence or absence of a physician is critical if health care needs are to be met. Equally critical is the presence or absence of specialists qualified to deal with the disorders that require their particular competence. The limited distribution of physician specialists was noted earlier, and it highlights here another facet of that problem: the distribution of categories of people likely to require specialized care with note taken of the presence or absence of such care. Figure 15.31 shows the population likely to need the services of a pediatrician, along with the numbers and distribution of pediatricians. Figure 15.32 does the same for obstetricians and gynecologists and the numbers and location of women likely to need their services. Such analysis illustrates a way of studying the particular kinds of physicians likely to be needed, and where they will be needed, rather than an undifferentiated physician shortage.

Another critical problem is that portions of North Carolina's health care network are close to, or at, a situation of dangerous overload. Many front-line physicians are so hard pressed by patients' demands that the stability of their personal and family lives is threatened. The development of private and federal health insurance (Medicare and Medicaid) has made for additional

Table 15.1. Fetal and Infant Mortality by Race in N.C., 1972

	Total		White		Nonwhite	
	Number	Rate	Number	Rate	Number	Rate
Perinatal deaths	2,790	30.9	1,648	26.4	1,142	40.9
Fetal deaths	1,338	14.8	773	12.4	565	20.3
Physician in hospital	1,282	95.8	760	98.3	522	92.4
Physician not in hospital	34	2.5	10	1.3	24	4.2
Midwife and other	22	1.6	3	0.4	19	3.4
Out of wedlock	275	20.6	38	4.9	237	41.9
Neonatal deaths (under 28 days)	1,452	16.3	875	14.2	577	21.1
Postneonatal deaths (28 days-1 year)	555	6.3	247	4.1	308	11.5
Infant deaths (under 1 year)	2,007	22.6	1,122	18.2	885	32.4

Source: N.C. Sate Board of Health, *North Carolina Vital Statistics, 1972,* vol. 1, *Population, Births, Deaths, Marriages, Divorces* (Raleigh: The Board, 1972).

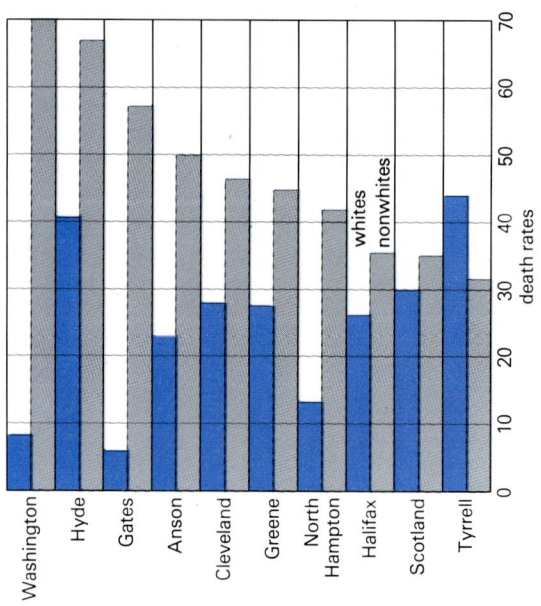

Figure 15.30. Infant Death Rates by Race for N.C. Counties Having Highest Total Rates, 1970-1972

Note: Rates are number of deaths of infants less than one year of age per 1,000 births.

pressure by enabling the public to increase its demand and for health services without providing additional care resources. It has been said that we really have no health care system (some have even called it a nonsystem), but are approaching the complexities of contemporary health care with the apparatus of a cottage industry.

The Developing Future

The developing future is with us now. The entire health care apparatus is in ferment. Hospitals, the health professions, the government, and the public are all involved in many changes.

The relative decline of the general practitioner and the escalation of the specialist was noted earlier. This trend has left parts of North Carolina unserved, or underserved, by locally available physicians. In this state as elsewhere, serious efforts are underway to fill the resultant health care gaps and bring better and more accessible health care resources to the population.

The state's schools of medicine have assumed the important responsibility for the training of front-line physicians by developing units of family and community medical care. Such programs include periods of training in community hospitals and in the offices of practicing front-line physicians in all parts of the state. Their aim is to produce physicians who are prepared for front-line medicine and attracted to its challenges and opportunities.

The all-purpose general practitioner has also undergone change, emerging as a specialist in his own right, in family practice. The Academy of General Practice has accordingly been renamed the Academy of Family Practice.

Although many front-line physicians practice alone, as "solo" practitioners, the development of group practice has proceeded rapidly, from 100 groups in North Carolina in 1965, involving 738 physicians, to 155 groups, involving 1,087 physicians in 1969. Such groups permit more effective referrals, the purchase of more sophisticated equipment, more varied technical staff assistance, and a continuing colleague availability for patients. Group practice frees the individual physician from what often becomes the unrelenting tyranny of patients' demands.

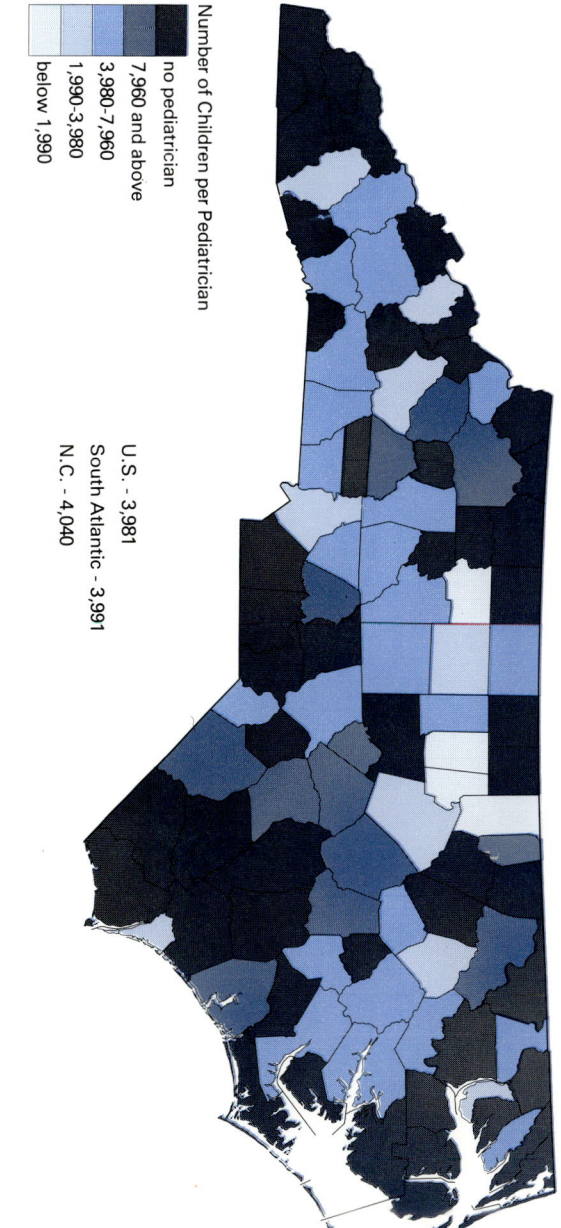

Figure 15.31. Number of Children per Pediatrician in N.C., 1971

Number of Children per Pediatrician
- no pediatrician
- 7,960 and above
- 3,980-7,960
- 1,990-3,980
- below 1,990

U.S. - 3,981
South Atlantic - 3,991
N.C. - 4,040

Note: Children are categorized here as being less than 15 years of age.

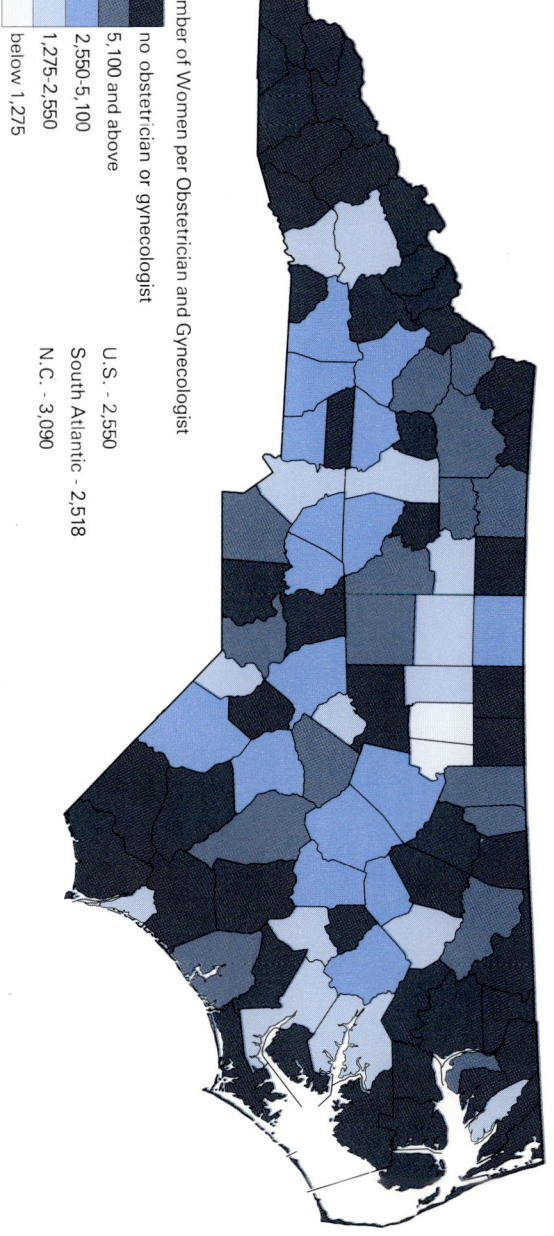

Figure 15.32. Number of Women per Obstetrician and Gynecologist in N.C., 1971

Number of Women per Obstetrician and Gynecologist
- no obstetrician or gynecologist
- 5,100 and above
- 2,550-5,100
- 1,275-2,550
- below 1,275

U.S. - 2,550
South Atlantic - 2,518
N.C. - 3,090

Note: Women included are 15 through 44 years of age.

There is a sharp awareness of health manpower shortages. Efforts at remediation have taken two directions: the numbers of professionals being trained in the core health professions are increasing and the numbers and types of allied health professionals are increasing. These latter, often referred to as "physician expanders," may be trained more quickly and in a greater variety of settings than the core professionals. Virtually all health professional schools are increasing the numbers of students admitted.

Planning efforts, initiated over the past several years with federal funding, have begun to have important impacts. The North Carolina Regional Medical Program has provided significant support for linking the resources of the health professions training centers to community hospitals and local health professionals. Comprehensive and area health planning have begun to assure that health care developments are feasible and effectively linked with existing resources. All such planning efforts have begun to amass data on the health care needs and resources of the state to undergird informed response. They are a primary component in shifting the development of the health care network from a political process to a planning process.

The federal government over the past several years has directed its funding priorities somewhat away from basic research toward applied programs in health care. The changing pattern of federal support has had direct impact upon the state. A variety of innovations has been catalyzed by this support. Neighborhood health centers have been developed in poverty areas. Such centers, with control often in the hands of the consumers, are attempting to devise modes of health care best suited to meet the needs of the urban poor. Health maintenance organizations are being developed to provide comprehensive health service to clients enrolled through prepaid health insurance. Health service organizations are a similar development designed to serve rural areas. Area health education centers are an important move toward the regionalization of health care and training, linking together educational institutions, community hospitals, and varieties of practicing health professionals. The Health Service Corps seeks to locate physicians in underserved areas.

National health insurance seems so inevitable that even its former opponents are now presenting plans for its implementation. Perhaps a dozen such alternate plans are being readied by health care lobbyists and congressional committees for consideration by Congress. It is clear that a growing sentiment exists among the public that there is a right to health care, whether at public expense or not, similar to the right to an education. There is also increasing feeling that the providers of health care should receive counsel and direction from the recipients of health care. Consumer participation has become a reality of health care planning and program implementation.

Many of these developments call for a new focus on community-based health care and a new orientation for many biologically oriented and hospital-trained health professionals. The traditional professions are forming relationships with representatives from public health and the behavioral sciences to enlarge the scope of their research and to develop programs of service. Health care teams, which bring together a broad spectrum of specialized competence, are now required to meet the tasks of these newer modes of care. If the specialists are to work effectively together, at least some of their training must involve shared experience. This new kind of training is a frontier venture for most of the health professions' educational institutions.

In these new settings a gray zone of the division of labor among health professionals may develop. Specific functions and the allocation of tasks become unclear. New working arrangements are being forged, no longer in terms of professional fiat but in terms of the health needs that must be met. Enlarged professional horizons and more effective care could well be a result of these new arrangements. Thus we find nurse practitioners insisting upon independent practice and colleagueship with physicians and not accepting a traditionally subordinate role. Physicians' assistants and associates work directly with patients in doing their assigned part of the doctor's work.

There are other innovations that strive for more effective linkages between resources and needs. Hospitals send out mobile teams to underserved areas, or establish satellite clinics, or provide transportation to their clinics; health services research centers explore innovative health care staffing patterns and evaluate their effects.

In a time of crisis, accustomed habits must give way to the exploration of new solutions. The many developments cited here are examples of the search for such solutions to a variety of pressing problems. Their outcome may well be a greatly changed health care network, one more responsive to the needs of the people and more effective in meeting them. The present travail of change would be well worth such an outcome.

North Carolina's citizens would also be better served if another result of change is the development of a continuing organized planning effort, working from basic data to the setting of priorities, the formulation of policy, and the delineation of needed programs. Meeting health care needs is too important a problem to be left to sporadic and random efforts.

Health care must increasingly come to mean more than battling illness. It must be further directed toward the maintenance of health. The task of providing the conditions of life that are conducive to good health is one in which the health professionals may play an important role, but it is a task toward which all the resources of society must be mobilized.

SELECTED REFERENCES

American Medical Association, Center for Health Services. *Profile of Medical Practice.* Chicago: The Association, published annually.

American Medical Association, Center for Health Services. *Reference Data on Socioeconomic Issues of Health.* Chicago: The Association, published annually.

American Medical Association, Center for Health Services Research and Development. *Distribution of Physicians in the U.S., 1971.* Chicago: The Association, 1971.

American Medical Association, Council on Medical Education. *Allied Medical Education Directory.* Chicago: The Association, published annually.

"Life and Death and Medicine." *Scientific American,* September 1973.

Medical Care Review, published monthly.

N.C. Department of Administration. *North Carolina State Government Statistical Abstract.* Raleigh: The Department, 1971.

N.C. Department of Human Resources. *North Carolina Hospitals (Non-Federal).* Raleigh: North Carolina Medical Care Commission, 1972.

N.C. Department of Human Resources, Division of Health Services. *North Carolina Communicable Disease Morbidity Statistics, 1972.* Raleigh: The Department, 1972.

N.C. Hospital Association, Health Careers Program. *Education Programs for Health Careers in North Carolina.* Raleigh: The Association, 1969.

N.C. Regional Medical Program, Research and Evaluation Division. *Data and Procedures: First Biennial Report, 1968.* Chapel Hill: Social Research Section, University of North Carolina, 1968.

N.C. State Board of Health. *North Carolina Vital Statistics, 1972,* vol. 1, *Population, Births, Deaths, Marriages, Divorces.* Raleigh: The Board, 1972.

Social Research Section. *A Decade of Change in North Carolina, 1960-1970: Selected Measures Relative to Mental Health.* Chapel Hill: University of North Carolina, 1972.

Social Research Section. *Education for Family Practice: Views of Front Line Physicians.* Chapel Hill: University of North Carolina, 1972.

U.S. Department of Health, Education, and Welfare. *Health Resources Statistics: Health Manpower and Health Facilities, 1971.* Rockville, Md.: National Center for Health Statistics, 1972.

16. OUTDOOR RECREATION

LELAND L. NICHOLLS
H. DANIEL STILLWELL

North Carolina has been endowed with a natural setting that affords a wide variety of outdoor recreation opportunities. The state has the highest mountains in the eastern United States and a complex tidal shoreline of nearly 3,500 miles. Within and between these two natural features are found national parks, forests, and reservoirs, and many state, local, and private outdoor recreation facilities (Figure 16.1).

Total recreation area in the state approximates four and one-half million acres or about 13 percent of the total state area. Although this might appear at first glance to be an ample amount of space for recreational needs, the many forces causing increasing numbers of people to seek outdoor recreational experiences are placing unprecedented pressures on such resources. It is important to examine the characteristics of North Carolina's outdoor recreation base, and the pressures upon its utilization, in order to gain some insight into what the future holds for the state's recreational lands and waters.

These resources break down into six classes of recreation areas identified by the Bureau of Outdoor Recreation and are shown in Figure 16.2 by location and acreage. Natural Environment Areas, occurring mainly in the Appalachian mountain range, account for more than half of the recreation acreage. High Density Recreation Areas are located mostly in the urbanized Piedmont and resource-oriented and private recreation sites are more typical of the Coastal Plain and Mountain regions. The general pattern of recreation site ownership in North Carolina shows a dominance of federal control over most recreation land area, and of local or private ownership—rather than state control—over most of the other recreation sites, especially the lakes and campgrounds.

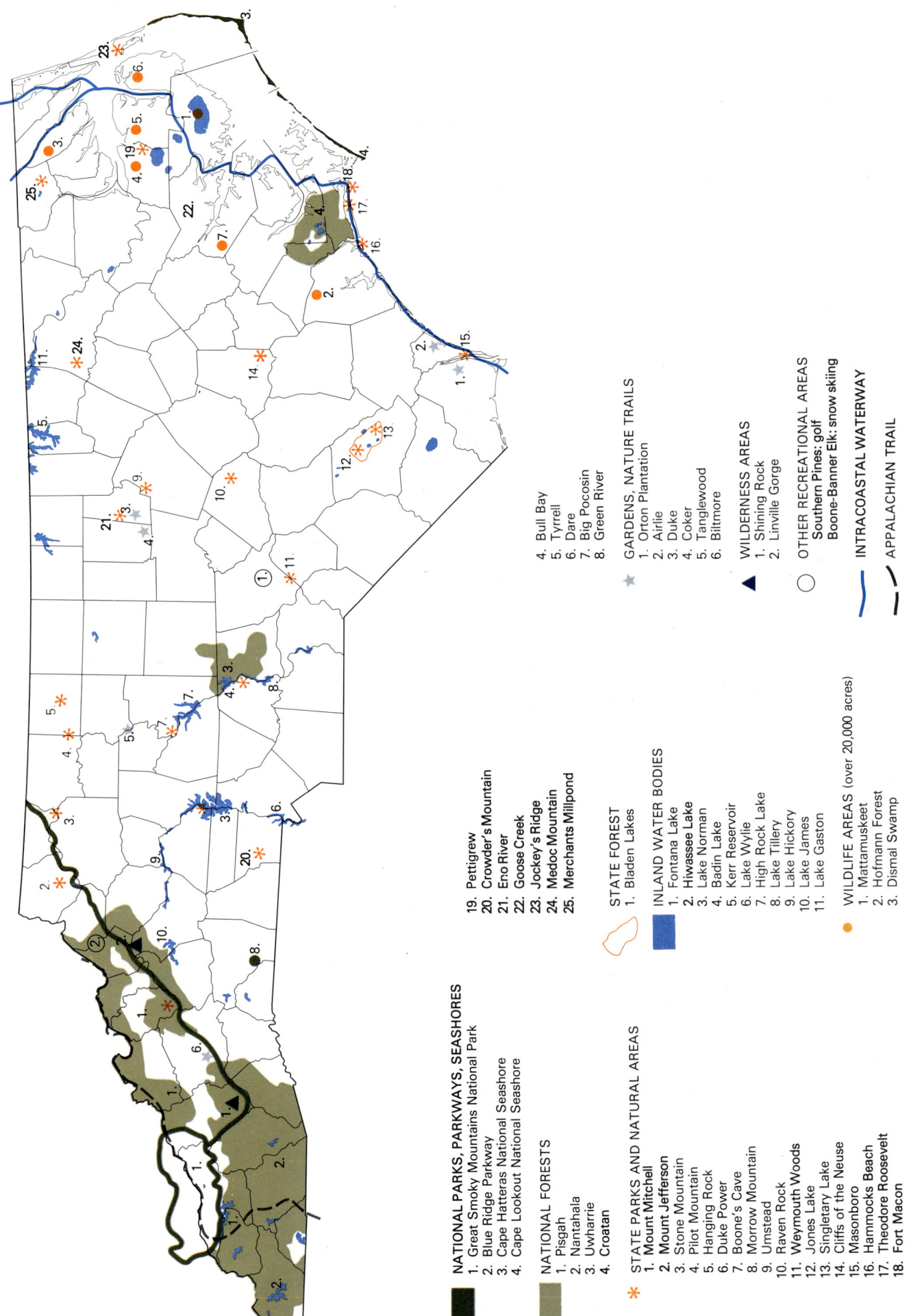

Figure 16.1. Selected Outdoor Recreation Areas in N.C.

Selected Government-Owned Outdoor Recreation Facilities

Federal and state recreation lands in North Carolina approximate one and two-thirds million acres, of which two-thirds are national forests lying predominantly in the Mountain section. The following table summarizes area coverage:

Recreation Lands	Acres
National forests	1,123,600
National park and parkway	309,300
National wildlife areas	71,600
National reservoirs	69,800
National seashores	40,500
State forests	38,900
State parks	30,735
Total	1,682,935

The national forests of North Carolina provide varied and superb recreation areas. Outstanding among these are two wilderness areas in Pisgah National Forest: Linville Gorge and Shining Rock. Nantahala National Forest contains the Joyce Kilmer Memorial Forest, one of the few primitive wilderness areas left in the eastern United States.

The Great Smoky Mountains National Park straddles the border of North Carolina and Tennessee with the famed Appalachian Trail running along the mountain crest for 170 of its 2,000 miles. Over eight million people visited this park in 1972, making it the most used one in the United States. Its popularity has increased so rapidly that, beginning in 1972, the number of hikers and campers in the backcountry has had to be limited to a specific quota based on the capacity of the area to absorb visitors without serious ecological or aesthetic harm. Adjacent to the park lies the Blue Ridge Parkway, which had nearly fourteen million travelers in 1972. A large portion of the 469-mile parkway—254 miles—lies within North Carolina.

Of the eighty-nine wildlife areas in North Carolina, twelve are part of the national system. Probably the best known of these is Lake Mattamuskeet in the Coastal Plain. It is the largest natural lake in the state, about 30,000 acres, and an important link in the Atlantic waterfowl flyway.

Reservoirs have enhanced the recreational facilities of the state. Kerr Reservoir, developed by the United States Army Corps of Engineers, overlaps the Virginia-North Carolina line and has a shoreline of eight hundred miles. The Tennessee Valley Authority is responsible for Fontana Lake, impounded by the highest dam in the entire TVA system. It is located at the southern boundary of the Great Smoky Mountains National Park.

The nation's first national seashore was established at North Carolina's Cape Hatteras and includes some 28,000 acres of land on Bodie, Hatteras, and Ocracoke islands, stretching along seventy miles of open beach. Cape Lookout National Seashore, recently established, adds another fifty-eight miles of shoreline to this unique Outer Banks recreation area. Another noteworthy feature of this area is the Intracoastal Waterway extending the length of the North Carolina coast on its Atlantic Coast route. This waterway provides an outstanding source of major commercial and recreational boating.

North Carolina's state parks system includes nineteen sites (Figures 16.1 and 16.3) from the highest point east of the Rocky Mountains at Mount Mitchell to the Atlantic Coast. The total attendance at state parks has been growing rapidly from slightly over one million visits in 1950 to almost three million in 1972 (Figure 16.4) and is presently increasing at about 5 percent per year. The most popular area is Fort Macon with its beach location. Morrow Mountain and Umstead parks are also visited heavily due to nearby population centers. Four parks have shown a consistent decline in visits in the past ten years: Cliffs of the Neuse, Hanging Rock, Mount Mitchell, and Singletary Lake. There is no obvious reason to explain this decline. On the other hand, visits to Mount Jefferson have quadrupled and those to Fort Macon and Umstead have doubled in the past ten years. Over one-fourth of the visits to state parks are for picnicking, the most popular activity, followed by swimming, hiking, fishing, and camping.

State forests of North Carolina are limited. Bladen Lakes State Forest consists of over 37,000 acres of the Coastal Plain and includes the state parks of Jones Lake and Singletary Lake. In addition, there are five new small state forests of 300 acres each, mainly in the Mountain section of the state. These will no doubt increase in recreational importance.

Private recreation areas are scattered throughout North Carolina and total acreage is difficult to ascertain. Probably the most significant areas lie in the Piedmont within the Catawba River and Yadkin River basins. An example is Tanglewood Park, an 1,100-acre estate donated to Forsyth County by William and Kate B. Reynolds.

The use of private land and water areas for recreation also defies statistical analysis; however, of the most popular areas for boating, fishing, and hunting, nearly two million acres are open to limited public use—chiefly hunting—under the Wildlife Commission's Game Lands Program.

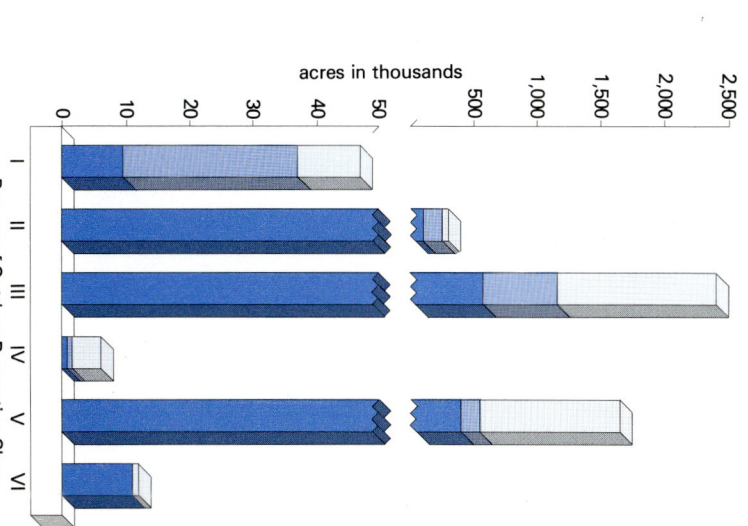

Figure 16.2. Distribution of Recreation Lands in N.C.

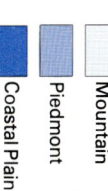

Bureau of Outdoor Recreation Class

	Acreage
I. High Density Recreation Areas	47,000
II. General Outdoor Recreation Areas	300,000
III. Natural Environment Areas	2,250,000
IV. Outstanding (unique) Natural Areas	6,000
V. Primitive Areas	1,650,000
VI. Historical and Cultural Sites	12,000
Total	4,265,000

293

Outdoor Recreation Activity

Of land-based recreational activities in North Carolina, hunting, golf, tennis, camping, skiing, and viewing outdoor events are especially popular.

Hunting Bears, white-tailed deer, raccoon, squirrels, rabbits, quail, wild turkey, fox, dove, and waterfowl offer sport to North Carolina hunters, who purchased more than four hundred thousand licenses in 1970. Although nearly two million acres of land are open to public hunting in North Carolina, specific geographic patterns of wildlife abundance can be detected.

For example, black bear hunting is primarily concentrated in the Mountain areas of North Carolina with the major portion of the 150 to 200 annual harvest by hunting coming from a one hundred-mile radius of Asheville. The Coastal Plain, however, does have nearly twenty bear sanctuaries evenly distributed from Brunswick to Currituck counties, where hunting is occasionally permitted.

The white-tailed deer is North Carolina's primary big game species, producing an annual harvest of about forty thousand head. Of the four species of big game in the state, the white-tailed deer is the most responsive to management, and its population has apparently quadrupled in the past twenty-five years. Although they are found in all regions, major deer concentrations are located in Transylvania, Montgomery, Granville, Hertford, Bertie, Perquimans, Hyde, Pamlico, and Pender counties. With continued favorable conditions, annual harvests of more than fifty thousand head are projected by state game officials by 1980.

Raccoon and opossum hunting have many adherents in North Carolina. Hounds are almost always employed in this sport, and in both the Coastal Plain and the Mountains, field trials and other canine contests are important ancillary activities of the sports. Many of these events are highly organized and involve interstate competition.

Rabbits, quail, and squirrels absorb 75 percent of the hunting pressure on resident game species. Squirrels are found in every county, but are especially numerous in mature hardwood oak forests, along cornfields and stream courses. Studies indicate that hunting pressure seldom removes more than 15 percent of the population, although in some years well over two million squirrels are taken by hunters. Rabbits are found in every county of the state, and while there are several species, the cottontail is by far the most common. Approximately two million rabbits are taken by hunters each year. Quail are also found throughout the state, with population densities highest in the Coastal Plain, moderate in the Piedmont, and scattered throughout the Mountain region.

Surveys indicate that the largest kills are made in the counties with the highest human population rather than the highest quail population. Even without hunting, natural mortality factors would take a toll of 80 percent of the previous autumn's quail population by the spring nesting season. Thus the number of birds taken by hunters (about two million) has little impact on year-to-year population trends. Because of their versatility and adaptability as well as their responsiveness to management, quail should hold their own for future generations of Tar Heel hunters.

The wild turkey is the largest of the state's game birds. In the early days when there were fewer hunters and more extensive wilderness areas, the birds were able to maintain their numbers. But with inroads of civilization and the increase in hunting pressure during the past twenty years, the turkey population has been reduced to remnant flocks at widely scattered locations. Field investigations indicate that most of the state's wild turkey concentrations are located in the central portions of the state between Montgomery and Caswell counties.

Both red and gray foxes are found in North Carolina. The reds are usually associated with farm habitat and the more common grays with timberlands.

Figure 16.3. N.C. State Park Acreage, 1916-1973

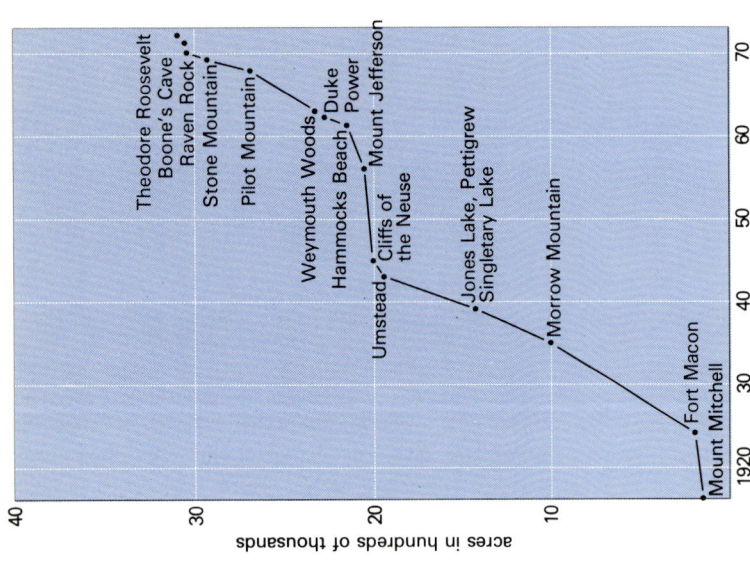

Source: N.C. Department of Natural and Economic Resources, *North Carolina State Parks, Now or Never*, 1973.

Figure 16.4. N.C. State Park Attendance by Region, 1950-1972

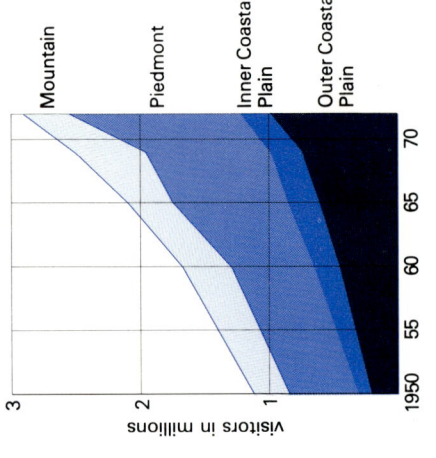

Source: N.C. Department of Natural and Economic Resources, *North Carolina State Parks, Now or Never*, 1973.

The mourning dove is North Carolina's most popular—and most hunted—game bird. Some years over three million doves are brought to bag throughout the state. Scattered concentrations of woodcock and Wilson's snipe are also found in the state, but are seldom noticed by local hunters.

Nearly forty species of waterfowl are available to Tar Heel hunters, most of them in coastal waters. Currituck Sound and Lake Mattamuskeet host the largest numbers of the state's half million duck and geese. Roanoke, Croatan, Pamlico, and Core-Bogue sounds also have good waterfowl locations. Good waterfowl hunting is also available along the state's many miles of streams and rivers.

Golf Golf has been a favorite form of recreation in North Carolina since the 1890s, but its increase in popularity during the last few decades has been astounding. In 1940 there were three major national tournaments held in North Carolina. By 1973 there were ten major tournaments in which golfers from all over the world played for more than $1.1 million in prize money at the leading courses in Pinehurst, Greensboro, Charlotte, Wilmington, and Raleigh. In 1973, the state ranked first nationally in professional prize money offerings. It therefore seemed appropriate that in September 1974 the World Golf Hall of Fame was opened at Pinehurst. The president of the United States participated in the opening ceremonies for this $2.5 million facility overlooking the famous number two course at Pinehurst Country Club.

Tens of thousands of both North Carolinians and out-of-state visitors enjoy the sport at more than 350 public and private golf courses in the state, and golfing vacations are a prime source of tourist income. Golf is money for North Carolina in other ways. According to the National Golf Foundation, a standard golf course, excluding land costs, utilities, roads, equipment, and clubhouse, rarely costs less than $500,000, or $28,000 a hole.

Tennis As is the case with golf, a moderate climate permits practically year-round participation in tennis. The recent nationwide boom in tennis popularity has been particularly in evidence throughout the state. For example, of all the states in the southern region of the United States Lawn Tennis Association, North Carolina has the most registered tournament players, the largest number of registered tennis clubs and parks, and the most sanctioned tennis tournaments each year. The establishment in the early 1960s of the North Carolina Tennis Foundation to support and promote tennis throughout the state was a forerunner of its kind in the South. The North Carolina Tennis Association estimates that as many as two hundred thousand people are actively playing tennis in the state. New tennis

295

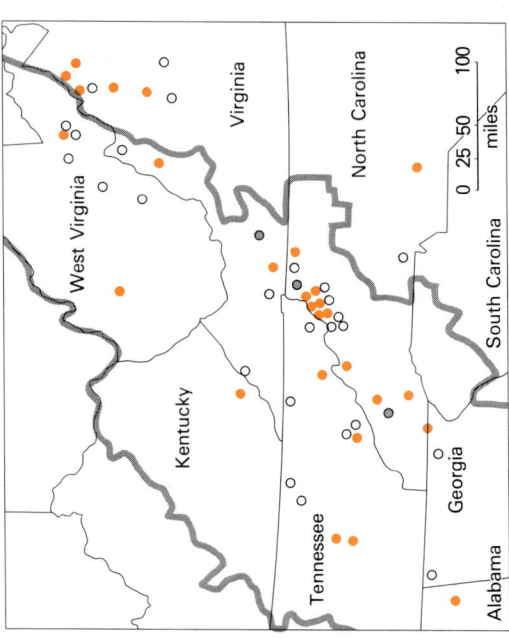

Figure 16.5. Ski Centers in the Southeastern U.S., 1972

- ● active ski center
- ◐ under construction
- ○ proposed
- ━ Appalachian region boundary

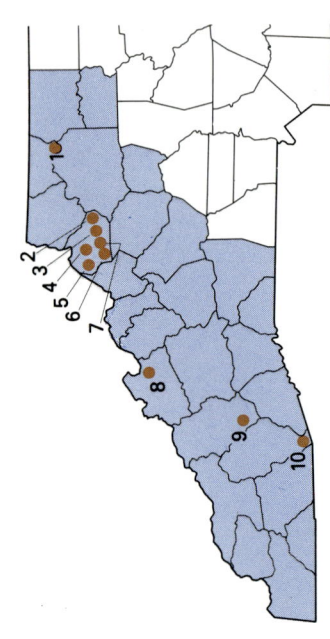

Figure 16.6. Ski Centers in Western N.C., 1972

1. High Meadows
2. Appalachian Ski Mountain
3. Hound Ears
4. Seven Devils
5. Beech Mountain
6. Sugar Mountain
7. Mill Ridge
8. Wolfe Laurel
9. Cataloochee
10. Sapphire Valley

Source: Field Surveys and Appalachian Regional Commission.

clubs—often including indoor facilities—have become a focal attraction for many new subdivisions and resort developments. In addition, top international tennis events are frequently hosted in North Carolina. Of particular note is the 6,500-seat tennis stadium at Olde Providence Racquet Club in Charlotte, which has been the site of a number of men's and women's professional tour events and of the prestigious Challenge Round of the Davis Cup Competition.

Camping Environmental awareness became a national phenomenon in the early 1970s. One of the easiest ways to appreciate nature is by camping, and by 1972 there were three hundred private campgrounds in North Carolina with more than fifteen thousand campsites. Three of the four national forests in the state accommodate campers as do nine of the nineteen state parks. The Great Smoky Mountains National Park, the Blue Ridge Parkway, and the Cape Hatteras National Seashore also offer outstanding camping facilities.

Skiing Until 1959 skiing in the South had not been recognized as a major outdoor recreation activity. Since that time, however, over forty-six areas have been proposed, developed, or are presently under construction as far south as Georgia and Alabama (Figures 16.5 and 16.6).

During the 1960s land speculation became widespread within the highland areas of the South. Much of the speculation was accompanied by development of many seasonal recreational-real estate complexes. Most of these highland developments were backed by capital from Florida, New York, and other populous states. Initially, they provided recreational activities in the summer, fall, and spring. Skiing was introduced to offer winter recreation. Although the inclusion of skiing at most developments led to increased employment for the local population, a more important service was to stimulate the sales of mountain lands for year-round recreational use. In the South, ski developments generally followed or developed concurrently with real estate endeavors, in contrast to the West and New England where ski resort development usually preceded large-scale real estate activities.

The steady increase in personal disposable income, coupled with the decline in the average work week, has produced a dramatic increase in the demand for resort homes and recreation. Skiing offers a somewhat novel recreational activity to many southerners since the region has traditionally been associated with warm-weather recreation.

Thus in the space of a decade, skiing in North Carolina has become a major form of winter recreation, stimulating travel and generating expenditures and employment, and benefiting the state in general and the affected local economies in particular. For example, a recent survey indicated that skier expenditures over all five Boone area resorts averaged $28.66 for a weekday of skiing, $74.15 for a weekend, and $279.28 for a typical vacation. (These figures represent averages of total spending and do not necessarily represent spending at a single resort.)

Based upon the reported average per capita expenditures, it was estimated that the 160,000 visitors to the Boone area resorts spent about $5.3 million for skiing in 1970-71. It was figured that approximately $1.8 million of the $5.3 million was earned by the five resorts near Boone. By the time the initial $5.3 million expenditure has worked its way through the whole economy, it was estimated that a total spending of $8 to $11 million may have been generated.

The Boone resort complex is located within one of the twenty-three terminal recreational complexes analyzed by the Appalachian Regional Commission (ARC). This particular terminal or destination recreational complex is referred to as the Boone-Linville-Roan Mountain Complex by the ARC and includes Watauga, Avery, Mitchell, and parts of Caldwell and Burke counties. Considerable growth for this area is anticipated over the next decade. For instance, the ARC estimates that by 1985 skiing will account for between 441,000 and 518,000 activity days for the Boone-Linville-Roan Mountain Complex, and that expenditures by skiers there will range from $8.3 million to $9.8 million. These projections amount to a 75 percent increase in demand and between a 72 and 75 percent increase in skier expenditures above 1970 levels.

In spite of the fact that many of the present resorts report underutilization of ski capacities, several additional ski facilities in North Carolina have been recently completed or proposed. Mill Ridge, near Boone, operated during the 1972-73 season. Sky High ski area, near Pinehurst, opened in 1972 as the state's first year-round synthetic turf ski area. And new ski areas near Boone, West Jefferson, and Waynesville are presently under construction.

Recent new resorts, plus planned additions, are likely to meet the future demand for skiing as projected by the ARC. Most of the skiing facilities, including those under construction and proposed, will be part of year-round recreation-real estate development.

Spectator Activities Regionally publicized and highly organized events in 1972 were viewed by more than an estimated three million people in North Carolina. Spectators traveled from within and from outside the state to witness more than five hundred performances in auditoriums, coliseums, stadiums, and speedways. Admission fees to these events alone generated more than $10 million.

Outdoor events such as football, tennis, baseball, and outdoor dramatic presentations attracted a large percentage of the more than three million spectators in 1972. Of the nearly 600,000 spectator seats available, approximately 400,000 are accounted for by major open-air stadiums in the state. The largest stadium in North Carolina is Wallace Wade Stadium in Durham with a seating capacity of 57,000. The Charlotte Motor Speedway, however, can accommodate 50,000 spectators in seats and 30,000 spectators in the infield of the track. A stadium of 50,000 or more seats for professional football is being discussed as a future possibility for the Charlotte area, and a World Football League franchise was awarded recently to the city.

North Carolina has seventeen outstanding botanical gardens and nature trails that offer pleasure to thousands of visitors annually. A state zoo—the first of its kind nationally—is currently being developed at Purgatory Mountain near Asheboro.

Finally, at a site ten miles south of Charlotte and located astride the North Carolina-South Carolina state line is Carowinds, the only "theme" park ever built in the two states. The park features a wide variety of "magic kingdom" rides and emphasizes the history and culture of the Carolinas in seven theme areas. During its 1973 season, in the first year of operation, almost 1.5 million people came to Carowinds. With seventy-six acres, it is one of the nation's largest entertainment parks and it forms the nucleus of an eventual $250 million resort and development complex adjacent to Lake Wylie.

Water-Based Outdoor Recreation In 1970, 46 percent, 29 percent, and 24 percent of the nation's population nine years of age and older participated in swimming, fishing, and boating, respectively. These statistics attest that water is a key element in the total outdoor recreation spectrum.

The Water Resources Council recognized recently that about one-fourth of all outdoor recreation nationwide—boating, ice skating, and water skiing—accounted for over 3 billion activity days in one year and is projected to increase to 7.7 billion by the end of the century. Further, the juxtaposition of water and land enhances the recreation experience afforded by such outdoor activities

297

Figure 16.7. N.C. Coastal Water Recreation Features

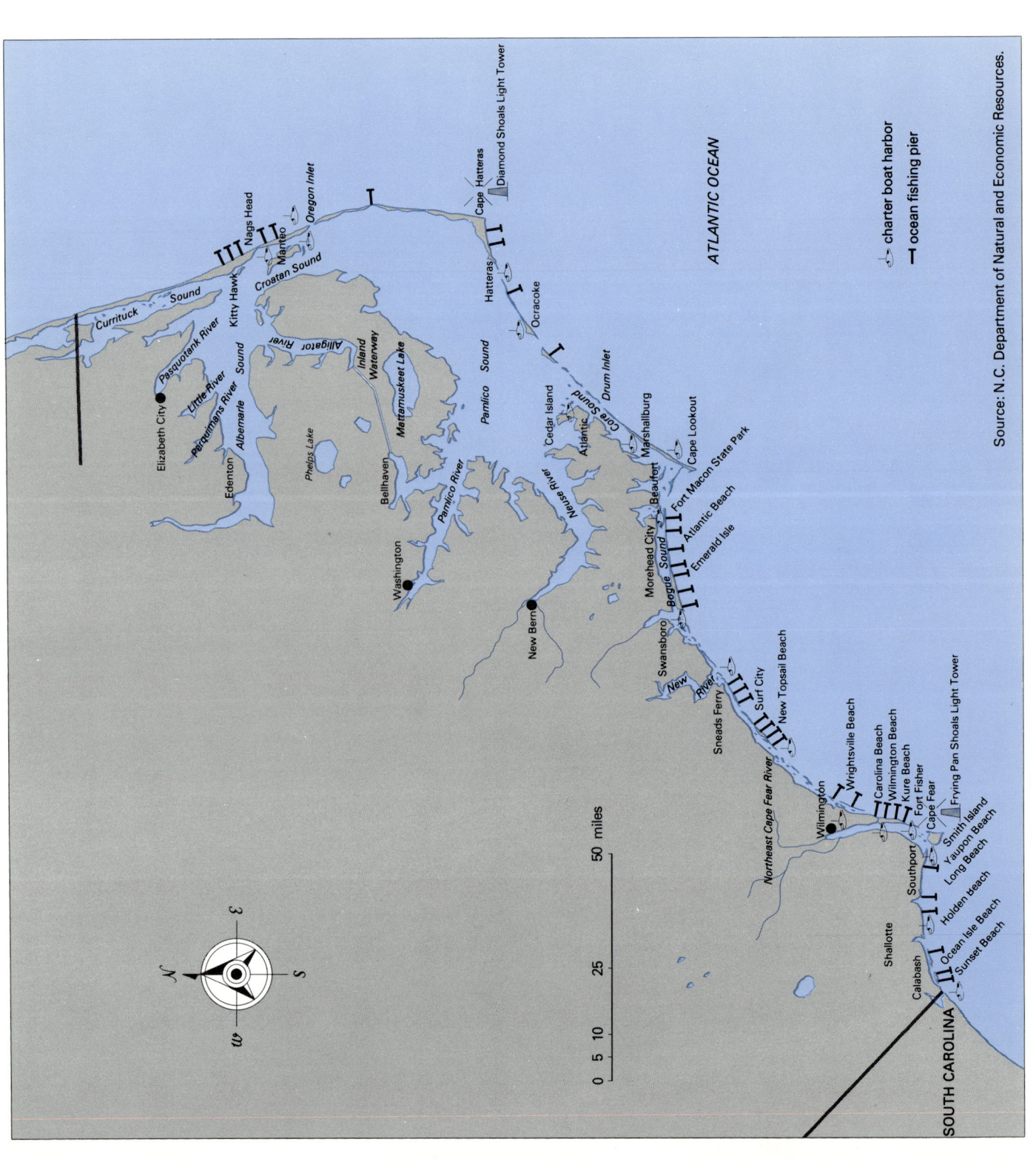

as camping, picnicking, and hiking. The council further noted that there has been a remarkable increase in the amount of surface water in reservoirs in recent years—much of it available for outdoor recreation use. This increase has been greatest in the South. The upward trend in the number of reservoirs and in reservoir surface area, and the concurrent decline in the miles of free-flowing streams, is expected to continue.

The phenomenal increase in lake-oriented recreation has led to (1) problems of determining the recreation needs and judging the feasibility of project proposals based upon those needs; (2) a heightening of the conflicts in project purposes (power, water supply, flood control, recreation); (3) conflicts in recreation uses of reservoirs (i.e., boating vs. swimming vs. fishing); and (4) problems of safety, access, crowding, littering, sanitation, environmental quality control, and other actors in the planning, development, and management of reservoirs.

The increasing recreational use of water resources is particularly evident in North Carolina, with its physical location and its natural and man-made water resources, which include rivers, ponds, streams, sounds, marshes, oceans, and natural and man-made lakes.

There are two and one-third million acres of surface water within the state, of which 269,000 acres are lakes and reservoirs. North Carolina has 135 lakes and reservoirs of 100 acres or more of surface area in or partially within its borders. More than half this total water acreage (150,000 acres) is privately owned. 80,000 acres are under federal ownership, 30,000 acres are owned by the state, and 17,000 acres are local government-owned.

From Nags Head to Sunset Beach, hundreds of thousands of people annually visit the state's popular beaches. Thousands of others swim in the state's outdoor public and private pools, lakes, and reservoirs.

Salt- and freshwater sport fishing in North Carolina ranks among the nation's best. In the highlands of western North Carolina clean and cold streams support several varieties of trout and small-mouth bass. The Piedmont has many streams, farm ponds, and nearly twenty power reservoirs containing catfish, large-mouth bass, pickerel, perch, and black crappie, and several species of panfish.

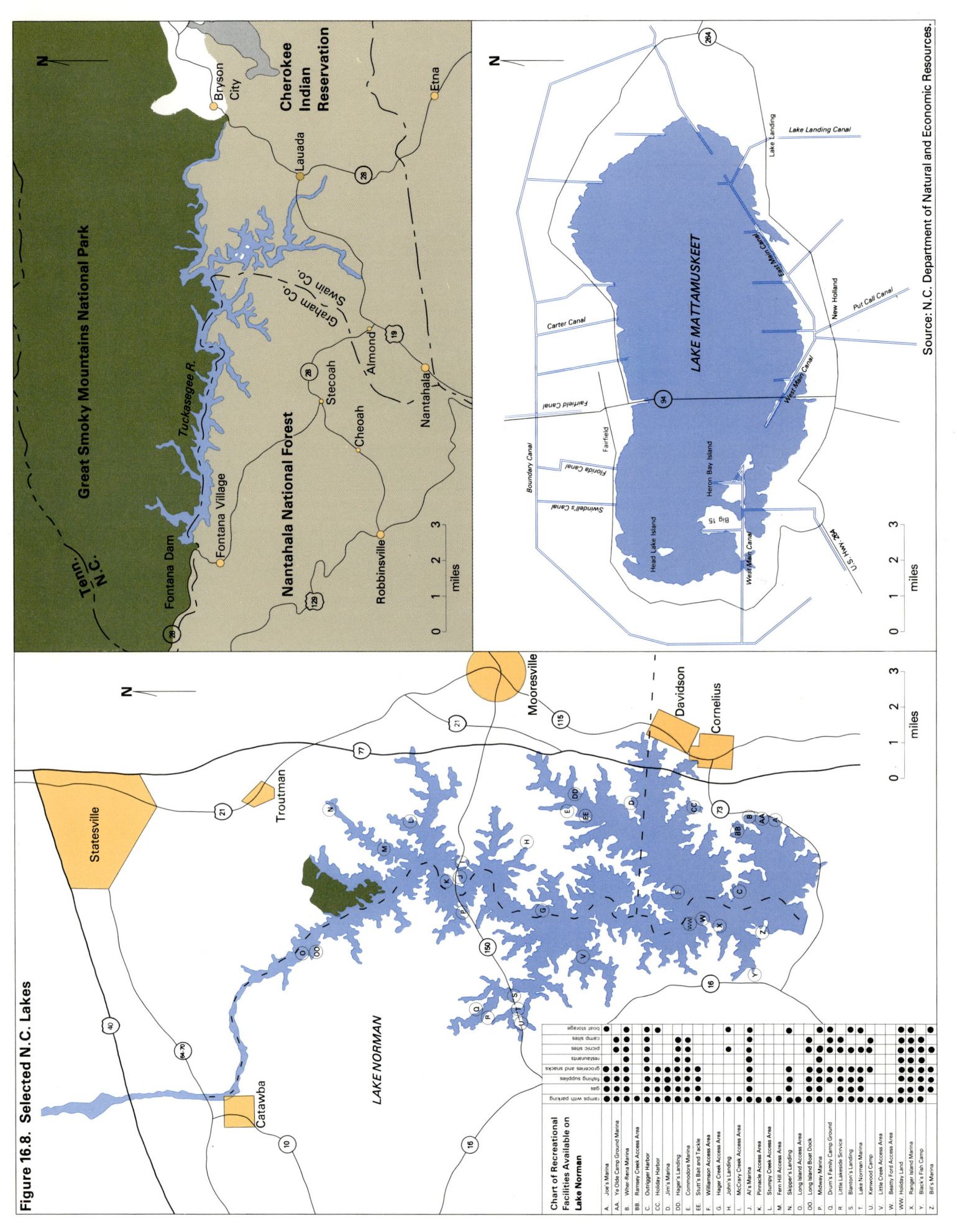

Figure 16.8. Selected N.C. Lakes

Source: N.C. Department of Natural and Economic Resources.

The Outer Banks, a barrier reef of open beach and sound-side woods, extends from the Virginia line to Cape Lookout and then curves back to the mainland. The five major sounds of Currituck, Albemarle, Pamlico, Core, and Bogue support sport fish suited to both fresh and salt water. The seashore and inlets of the Outer Banks provide unsurpassed surf fishing for channel bass, bluefish, and striped bass. Adjacent to the sounds at Oregon Inlet, Hatteras, Ocracoke, and Beaufort are offshore marine environments supporting king mackerel and blue marlin. Hatteras, located only twelve miles from the Gulf Stream, is considered to be "Gamefish Junction," since it is here that northern and southern species of gamefish meet.

The value of fishing licenses and permits was nearly $1 million in 1970, or an increase of nearly $100,000 since 1968. Approximately 430,000 licenses and permits were issued in 1970. Trends in the usage of lake and reservoir facilities are indicated in the steady increase in boat registrations. In 1969, more than 37,500 boats were registered in North Carolina. By 1970, 76,000 boats were registered, and nearly 93,000 boats were registered in 1972. Most of the state's boating is centered around areas such as the Atlantic Coast and lakes (Figures 16.7 and 16.8).

Travel

Most people take vacation trips simply to sightsee and thus places of scenic interest are the most visited. According to a recent study, historic places rank second in interest, and places of educational interest rank third in attracting visitors. North Carolina, again, is well endowed with a variety of vacation and travel attractions.

In 1972 an estimated forty-five million out-of-state people visited North Carolina. Travel expenditures by these tourists were nearly $600 million in 1972, more than double the $245 million expenditures in 1960. Out-of-state travel expenditures are projected to reach $730 million during 1975 and over $1 billion by 1980. During a two-day stay in North Carolina, the average tourist party of two spends $5.50 at inns and lodging places, $7.50 in cafes and for food services, $5.00 at tourist attractions, $2.75 at gas stations and garages, $3.75 in retail stores, and $2.50 for miscellaneous items, totaling $27.00.

In-state tourists spent an estimated $328 million in 1972, an increase of more than $165 million since 1970. Annual in-state tourist expenditures are projected to reach $380 million in 1975.

All sections of North Carolina share in the travel industry. Although the Mountains and the Coastal Plain each receive more vacation travelers than the Piedmont, the Piedmont does experience the bulk of through traffic and has more inns, convention facilities, and auto services. Increases in travel expenditures have approximately doubled in the ten leading North Carolina counties between 1964 and 1972 (Figure 16.9).

Much of North Carolina's tourist trade derives from the mobile tourist market flowing along the middle Atlantic Coast. Destinations throughout the Atlantic and Gulf coasts and in Florida and the Appalachians are major attractions for interregional journeys. An analysis of Figure 16.10 reveals the origin of visitors coming to North Carolina. Forty percent of North Carolina's visitors come from the border states of Virginia, Tennessee, Georgia, and South Carolina. However, a substantial number of visitors is drawn from the Northeast and North Central regions—approximately one-third of the total.

Future Outdoor Recreation Needs

Great strides have been made during the last decade toward providing North Carolina with better recreational opportunities. All but five of the state's cities of five thousand or more people have year-round recreational departments. Yet state leaders in the field of recreation cite the pressing needs of the cities, the disadvantaged, the handicapped, and the military. Access to recreational opportunities is also a continuing concern.

Although North Carolina is still a state of medium-sized cities and small towns, it is following the national trend of increasing urbanization. By 1980 more than half of the population is expected to live in cities. Now is the time to plan programs for open spaces in these areas, to guarantee that the city dweller—the person least likely to have immediate access to outdoor facilities—has an opportunity to enjoy the outdoor environment. Open land on the fringes of the state's urban areas needs to be set aside now for future recreational use. Land must also be acquired for inner city areas.

Many disadvantaged persons who live in urban areas do not have the means and opportunity to relax in leisure activity. It is vital that special consideration be given to planning and acquiring outdoor recreation facilities for such persons. This means increased emphasis upon ways of providing persons with readily accessible, high-quality recreation in areas where transportation services are poor.

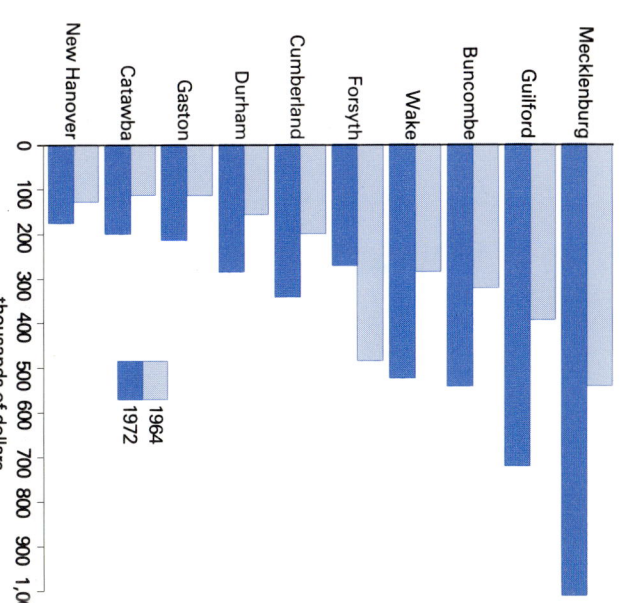

Figure 16.9. Leading N.C. Counties for All Travel Expenditures, 1964 and 1972

Source: N.C. Department of Natural and Economic Resources.

Figure 16.11. State Park Acreage per 1,000 Population for States in the Southeastern U.S., 1970

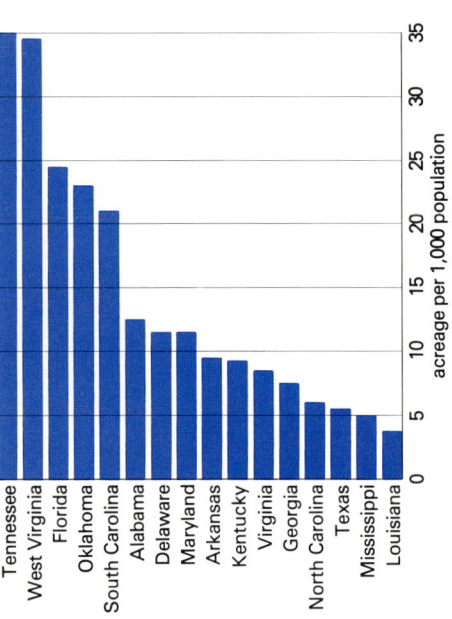

Source: National Conference on State Parks, *State Park Statistics*, 1970.

Figure 16.12. Total State Park Funding by N.C. and Adjoining Southern States, 1973

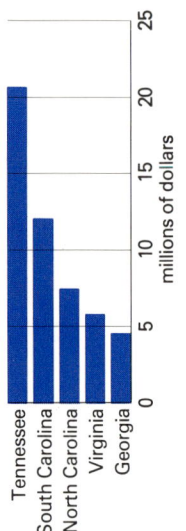

Source: N.C. Department of Natural and Economic Resources, *North Carolina State Parks, Now or Never*, 1973.

Figure 16.10. Origins of N.C. Visitors, 1972

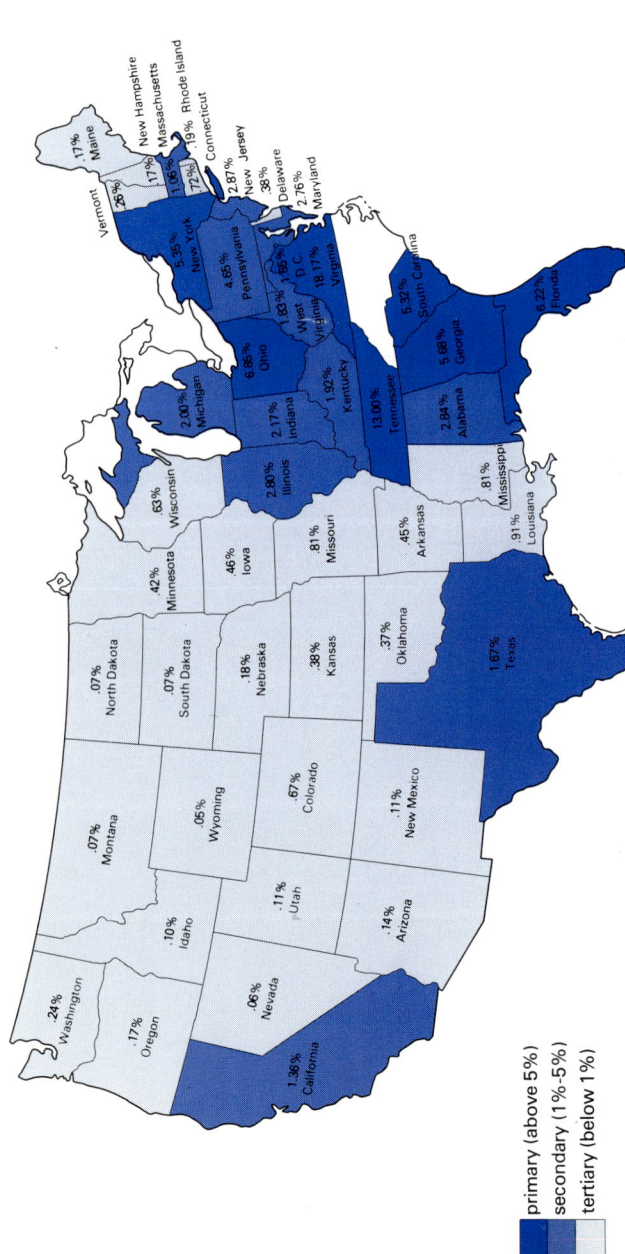

Source: N.C. Department of Natural and Economic Resources.

Too often, planners of recreational areas pay attention only to the facilities and their site characteristics. A high priority should also be given to the accessibility to these areas. Roads and highways, bridges, airports, scenic drives, parking areas, and complete coordination for access development must be evaluated and improved by local, state, federal, and private organizations.

The disabled are frequently prevented from participating in recreational activities because of physical, emotional, or mental handicaps. Facilities within and around each community must be made accessible and available to the handicapped. There is also a great need for outdoor recreational opportunities for persons in institutions such as prisons, detention houses, mental hospitals, and homes for the elderly.

North Carolina has five major military bases and military personnel and their families make up an important part of the population of the state, especially in the Coastal Plain. Outdoor recreation planners must consider the needs of these population concentrations and develop programs in coordination with those already being offered by the military establishment.

Since the passage of the Land and Water Conservation Act of 1965, North Carolina has received more than $6 million from the fund and has contributed an equal amount from state and local sources for planning, acquisition, and development of recreational resources. More than one hundred state and local projects and land acquisitions have been made by the state. Additional funding will be needed, however, to satisfy project demands for outdoor recreation. Increasingly it has become difficult for the state to compete for valuable real estate. The rise in prices of real estate can be seen in the example of mountainous Avery County, where land values in 1963 were at an average of $50 per acre and now sell for over $2,000 per acre. Another example is Smith (Bald Head) Island, which in 1938 the state had an opportunity to acquire for only $5,000. By 1955, its value had increased to approximately one-third of a million dollars. Today its estimated value is many millions of dollars and it is being privately developed.

The accelerating cost of land dramatizes the sense of urgency in acquiring additional state park acreage, especially when North Carolina's very low ranking in amount of state park acreage is considered. The state's 1973 total park acreage ranked only thirty-sixth in the nation and last in acres per person. The national average for state park space per one thousand persons is 42 acres; North Carolina maintains only 5.9 acres per one thousand persons. A 1969 commission appointed by the state legislature recommended that ten new parks be established so as to have one park within fifty miles of every North Carolina resident. In addition, ten existing parks would be enlarged and all parks would receive improvements. The Department of Natural and Economic Resources indicates a need for at least 100,000 more acres of state park land by 1980. This would bring the park total up to almost thirty acres per one thousand people, a substantial improvement, but still under the national average. Figures 16.11 through 16.13 emphasize the need and potential for expanding state park acreage, as well as other types of outdoor recreational areas, in order to preserve North Carolina's richly diverse recreational lands for the enjoyment of all its citizens.

SELECTED REFERENCES

Appalachian Regional Commission. *Appalachian Highlands Recreation Study, Phase I: Inventory and Analysis.* Washington, D.C.: The Commission, 1968.

Appalachian Regional Commission. *Recreation Potentia. in the Appalachian Highlands: A Market Analysis.* Washington, D.C.: URS Research Company, 1971.

Lee, Robert. *Religion and Leisure in America.* Nashville: Abingdon Press, 1964.

Nicholls, Leland L. "A Geographical Analysis of Selected Ski Resorts in the South." Ph.D. dissertation, University of Tennessee, 1972.

N.C. Department of Conservation and Development. *North Carolina Travel Survey 1971: An Economic Analysis of North Carolina's Travel Industry.* Raleigh: Travel and Promotion Division, 1972.

N.C. Department of Local Affairs. *Summary of the N.C. Outdoor Recreation Plan.* Raleigh: Division of Recreation, 1971.

N.C. Department of Natural and Economic Resources. *Camping in North Carolina.* Raleigh: Travel and Promotion Division, n.d.

N.C. Department of Natural and Economic Resources. *Fishing in North Carolina.* Raleigh: Travel and Promotion Division, n.d.

N.C. Department of Natural and Economic Resources. *North Carolina Golf State, U.S.A.* Raleigh: Travel and Promotion Division, n.d.

N.C. Department of Natural and Economic Resources. *North Carolina State Parks, Now or Never.* Raleigh: Division of State Parks, 1973.

N.C. Wildlife Resources Commission. *Hunting in North Carolina.* Raleigh: The Commission, 1972.

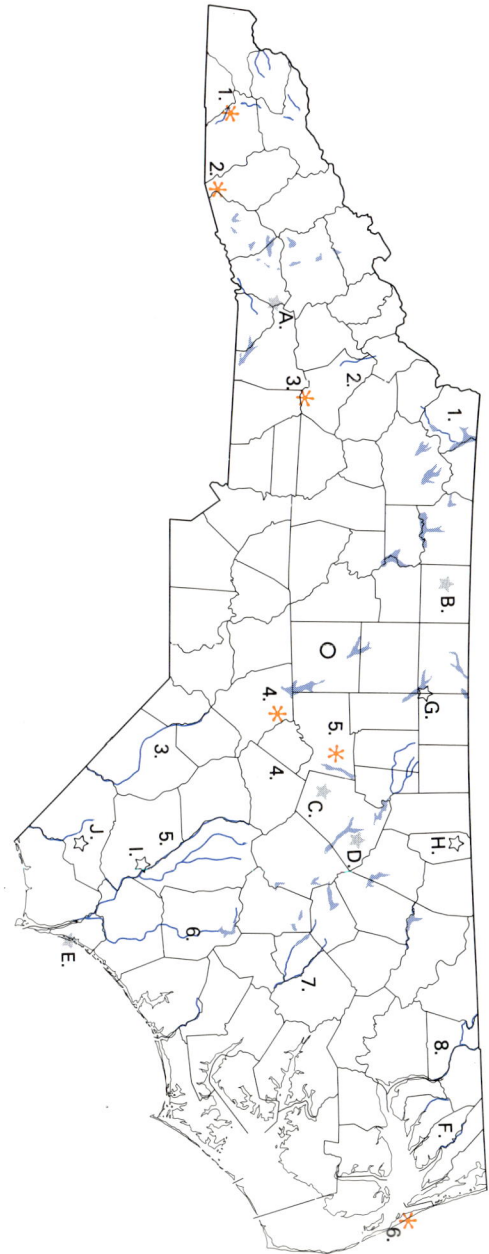

Figure 16.13. Proposed N.C. Outdoor Recreation Areas

MAJOR WILD AND SCENIC RIVERS
1. South Fork of New
2. Yadkin
3. Lumber
4. Cape Fear
5. South
6. Northeast Cape Fear
7. Neuse
8. Chowan

MAJOR RESERVOIRS (over 10,000 acres)
A. Clinchfield
B. Upper Donnaha
C. Styers
D. New Hope
E. Falls
F. Spring Hope

STATE PARKS (west to east)
1. Nantahala
2. Whiteside Mountain
3. South Mountains
4. Deep River Bend
5. Haw River, South
6. Nags Head—Jockey's Ridge

NATURAL AREAS
A. Bat Cave
B. Lower Cascade Falls
C. Hemlock Bluff
D. Mitchell Mill
E. Masonboro Island
F. Dismal Swamp

STATE RECREATION AREAS
G. Haw River, North
H. Kerr Reservoir
I. Bay Tree Lake
J. Lake Waccamaw

O STATE ZOO SITE

Please Be Seated North Carolina, Inc. *Please Be Seated North Carolina.* Charlotte: Please Be Seated North Carolina, Inc., 1972.

Stillwell, H. D.. "The Geography of Recreation in North Carolina." *North Carolina Geographer* 2 (Winter 1966): 2-7.

U.S. Department of the Interior, Outdoor Recreation Resources Review Commission. *Outdoor Recreation for America: A Report to the President and to Congress by the Outdoor Recreation Resources Review Commission.* Vols. 1-27. Washington, D.C.: Government Printing Office, 1962.

17. Cultural Arts

MORTON SHAPIRO

The state of the arts in any region is a significant measure of the spiritual and intellectual health of its people. In North Carolina the past has joined with the present to promote a fortunate cultural situation.

Architectural Diversity

Many architectural styles may be found in North Carolina, dating from the seventeenth century on. These styles reflect, of course, the changing artistic and cultural milieu that the state has experienced through three centuries of growth and development.

After a period of neglect, many of the older, historical buildings have been restored to a condition approximating their original condition. The climate of opinion is moving in the direction of preservation, restoration, and maintenance—undoubtedly as a part of the present national concern with environmental reform and conservation.

In this context, the North Carolina Division of Archives and History has a substantial program of restoration under way, and administers twenty historic sites (see endpapers). In addition, the division has participated in various restoration projects. In rural Bertie County, Hope Plantation (1808-10) has been restored to its early nineteenth-century beauty. Thalian Hall (1855) in Wilmington is an urban building carefully restored inside and out. At Murfreesboro, the entire town is quietly undergoing restoration.

This recent concern for the architectural heritage of North Carolina has served to balance the great advancement that modern architectural methods and technology have made in the past three decades. Many buildings combining beauty and function have been designed and built throughout North Carolina—in small towns as well as in the larger cities—reflecting the generally progressive climate among the business, educational, religious, health care, and cultural leadership in the state. The School of Design at North Carolina State University has played a significant role since its establishment in 1948 in shaping the contemporary architectural environment of the state.

A number of old towns in North Carolina have notable historical features.

Bath, in Beaufort County: This first town in the state is the home of St. Thomas Episcopal Church (1734), the oldest extant church in North Carolina. The Palmer-Marsh House (1734) is the oldest residence in the town.

Halifax, in Halifax County: In a region settled as early as 1723, this town contains a few small clapboard buildings of the colonial period. Also of interest are the Old Gaol (1764) and Constitution House (before 1776). Like Murfreesboro, the entire town is slowly undergoing restoration.

Williamsboro, in Vance County: St. John's Church (1757) is a lovely old building here.

Edenton, in Chowan County: The Cupola House (1758) is an American variation of the Jacobean architecture. The Chowan County Courthouse (1767) has been called "perhaps the finest Georgian courthouse in the South." St. Paul's Church (completed 1774) could be mistaken for an English parish church of the period. The Barker House, now located on the waterfront, dates from about 1782.

New Bern, in Craven County: The Masonic Temple (1808) and the many early nineteenth-century homes are background to one of the most elaborate restorations in the United States. Built between 1767 and 1770, Tryon Palace served as the earliest state capitol and the residence of the governor.

Beaufort, in Carteret County: Eight houses date from the eighteenth century, and many times that number from the period 1800 to 1860.

Hillsborough, in Orange County: Early residences from the 1700s on are being restored. The old Orange Courthouse (1845) is of particular architectural significance.

Salem, in Forsyth County: Established in 1766, the Moravian community contains some excellent examples of early buildings in good repair—the Brothers' House (1769), the Lick-Boner House (1785), the Sisters' House (1786), and the John Vogler House (1819).

From the seventeenth century through the nineteenth, a variety of architectural influences reached North Carolina.

Southern plantation architecture: the House in the Horseshoe (ca. 1770) in Moore County, Fairntosh (1802) in Durham County, Sommerset Place (ca. 1830) in Washington County, Orton (additions, 1840) in Brunswick County, and Cooleemee (1850), a handsome example in Davie County of the romantic revival.

The classic revival: A few of the outstanding structures are Ingleside (1817) in Lincoln County, the state capitol (1840) in Raleigh, Eaton Place (1843) in Warren County, the Mint Museum (1845) in Charlotte, the old Gaston County Courthouse (1846) in Dallas, the Eumanean Hall (1848) and the Philanthropic Hall (1850) at Davidson College, the Playmakers Theatre (1849) in Chapel Hill, the old Rowan County Courthouse (1857) in Salisbury, and the old Davidson County Courthouse (1858) in Lexington.

The gothic revival: The old Market House (remodeled, 1837) in Fayetteville, St. James Church (1839) in Wilmington, the Chapel of the Cross (1842-46) in Chapel Hill, Christ Church (1848-53) in Raleigh, and Grace Church (1859-60) in Plymouth.

Victorian architecture: the Heck-Andrews House (1870), the Dodd-Hinsdale House (1873), the Briggs Building (1874), and the Executive Mansion (1883), all in Raleigh.

The church of St. John in the Wilderness (1833-54) at Flat Rock in Henderson County is a representative example of the Italian Renaissance style, and the impressive Biltmore House (1890-95) near Asheville is an extravagant replica of a French chateau.

Contemporary architecture in North Carolina has kept pace with that of other sections of the country. Most of the larger towns and cities in the state support architectural firms that not only design modern public and private structures, but also plan environmental projects such as parks, playgrounds, and industrial complexes. Many such buildings and projects in North Carolina have won awards and citations for excellence of design. A representative sampling of notable contemporary architecture throughout the state might include: the Legislative Building, Raleigh; the Arthur Cogswell residence, Chapel Hill; Warren Wilson College Chapel, Swannanoa; the James B. Duke Memorial Library, Charlotte; Sandhills Community College, Moore County; The Bank of Asheville, Asheville; Branch Banking and Trust Company, Fayetteville; the Randolph Medical Center, Charlotte; the Dorton Arena, Raleigh; the George Matsumoto home, Raleigh; the Eduardo Catalano home, Raleigh; St. Giles Presbyterian Church, Raleigh; St. Martin's Lutheran Church, Albemarle; Woodlawn Middle School, Mebane; Hamlet Hospital School of Nursing, Hamlet; North Carolina National Bank, the Beatties Ford Branch and Park Road Branch, Charlotte; North Carolina Blue Cross and Blue Shield, Chapel Hill; and the Burlington Industries Executive Office Building, Greensboro.

Visual Arts

Both handicrafts and the graphic arts in North Carolina evince vitality, but the former is in the more flourishing condition at present. Many talented artists reside in and exhibit throughout the state. Craft guilds and schools in North Carolina employ and train prospective craftsmen and artisans, performing a valuable function, particularly in rural areas. The three major craft guilds are the Carolina Designer Craftsmen, the Piedmont Craftsmen, and the Southern Highland Handicraft Guild. Most craftsmen belong to the American Craftsman's Council.

A number of North Carolina artists have received national and international attention; among them are Elliot Dangerfield, Romare Bearden, Mabel Pugh, Frank London, Francis Speight, Charles Baskerville, Hobson Pittman, Henry Jay MacMillan, William C. Fields, Claude Howell, Joseph W. King, Kenneth Nolan, Kenneth Ness, George Kachergis, Robert Howard, Duncan Stuart, George Bireline, and Joe Cox. Other North Carolina artists who have received recognition are Warren Brandt, Henry C. Pearson, Thomas Sills, Ruth Clarke, Bob Timberlake, Maud Gatewood, Lloyd Oxendine, and Doris Leeper.

Display of Visual Arts

Most of North Carolina's urban centers or towns maintain adequate facilities for the display of art and crafts, although its finest museums and galleries are found in the larger cities of the state. Small towns and rural communities display art in banks, libraries, schools, and other facilities available to the general public.

The outstanding art museum in the state, the North Carolina Museum of Art in Raleigh, is unique in that $1 million was appropriated in 1948 by the state for the establishment of an art collection, making North Carolina the first state in the nation to use public funds to establish an art collection for all its people. Works of art that were made possible by the Phifer Bequest and the Kress Foundation were on display when the museum opened in 1956. The present value of art by old and new masters is estimated at over $20 million. The museum's Mary Duke Biddle Gallery for the Blind, the first such museum of its kind, is world renowned. Other significant functions of the museum include its sponsorship of an annual show by native and resident North Carolinians. Its traveling exhibitions reach several dozen communities each year.

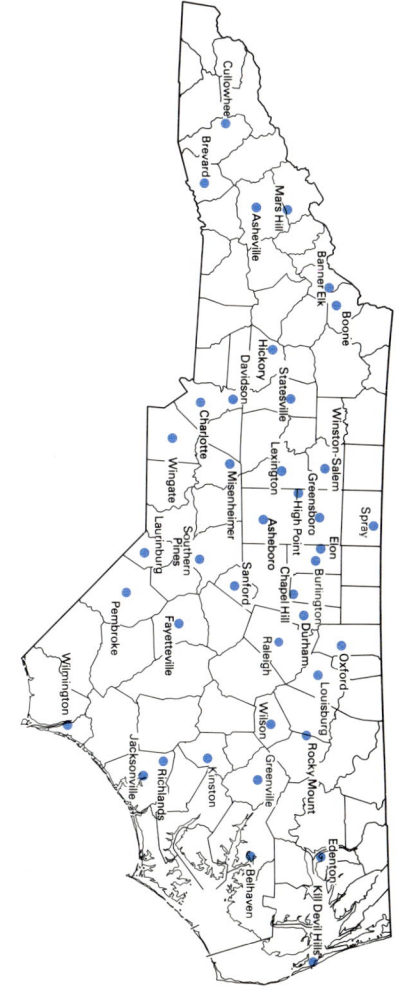

Figure 17.1. Art Display Centers in N.C.

Other established art museums in the state with their dates of dedication are the Mint Museum in Charlotte (1936), the Hickory Museum of Art (1944), the Asheville Art Museum (1948), the Statesville Arts and Science Museum (1956), and the Ackland Art Center in Chapel Hill (1958). There are also a number of noteworthy art galleries, among which are the Weatherspoon Gallery in Greensboro (1942), the Genevieve B. Morehead Memorial Gallery in Chapel Hill (1949), the Gallery of Contemporary Art in Winston-Salem (1956), the Greenville Art Center (1960), the St. John's Art Gallery in Wilmington (1962), and the Rocky Mount Arts Center (1963).

Crafts in North Carolina are prominently displayed and exhibited at many museums and galleries, but there are a number of centers and annual fairs that specialize in the creation and display of pottery and other crafts. These include the Craftsman's Fair in Asheville, the Penland School of Crafts near Spruce Pine, the Crafts Center at Jugtown, and the Craft Fair in Winston-Salem.

Finally, corporate support and display of art should be noted. The North Carolina National Bank has for several years given purchase awards to the Piedmont Painting and Sculpture Annual sponsored by the Mint Museum of Art as well as to other art competitions around the state. Central Carolina, Wachovia, and other banks as well as industry also collect the works of local artists and sponsor local exhibitors and exhibitions.

Literary Activity

The cultural climate of North Carolina has always been amenable to the good health of writers. Judging from the number of them, either native or resident, the state has had its fair share of literary talent.

North Carolina has either given birth to or provided haven for many notable literary figures. Some eminent writers of the past are Albion W. Tourgee, Walter Hines Page, Charles W. Chesnutt, Thomas Dixon, O. Henry, John Charles McNeill, Josephus Daniels, James Boyd, W. J. Cash, Wilbur Daniel Steele, Olive Tilford Dargan, Hatcher Hughes, Carl Sandburg, James Street, Betty Smith, Inglis Fletcher, Bernice Kelly Harris, Randall Jarrell, and Robert Ruark. Thomas Wolfe, native of Asheville, has had the widest national and international impact, and is generally regarded as one of the great American novelists.

So many first-rate writers live and work in North Carolina today that it is quite impossible to survey the field. However, a few of the most prominent of these should be mentioned. Paul Green, a Pulitzer Prize winner, with many successful Broadway plays, is most famous for his outdoor historical dramas. James Larkin Pearson, poet laureate of North Carolina, lives in North Wilkesboro. Other active writers in the state are Glenn Tucker, LeGette Blythe, Harry Golden, Glen Rounds, Frances Gray Patton, Manly Wade Wellman, Helen Bevington, Ovid Williams Pierce, Daphne Athas, Guy Owen, John Ehle, Max Steele, Doris Betts, Reynolds Price, Fred Chappell, Ben Haas, and Heather Miller. Native Tar Heel writers living outside the state are Gerald Johnson, A. R. Ammons, Jonathan Daniels, Burke Davis, Charles Edward Eaton, and Tom Wicker.

Many of these writers have won the National Book Award, the Newbery Medal, the Caldecott Medal, the John Masefield Award of the Poetry Society of America, and the O. Henry Award for short stories. North Carolina organizations also encourage and reward literary effort by conferring annual awards for outstanding work. These include the Mayflower Cup for nonfiction, the Sir Walter Raleigh Award for fiction, and the Roanoke-Chowan Cup for juvenile literature.

Forums and conferences are held annually in North Carolina for the purpose of encouraging and publicizing writers. These are the annual North Carolina Writers Conference, the Town Meeting on Books in Greensboro, the North Carolina Literary Forum in Raleigh, and the North Carolina Writers Forum in Charlotte.

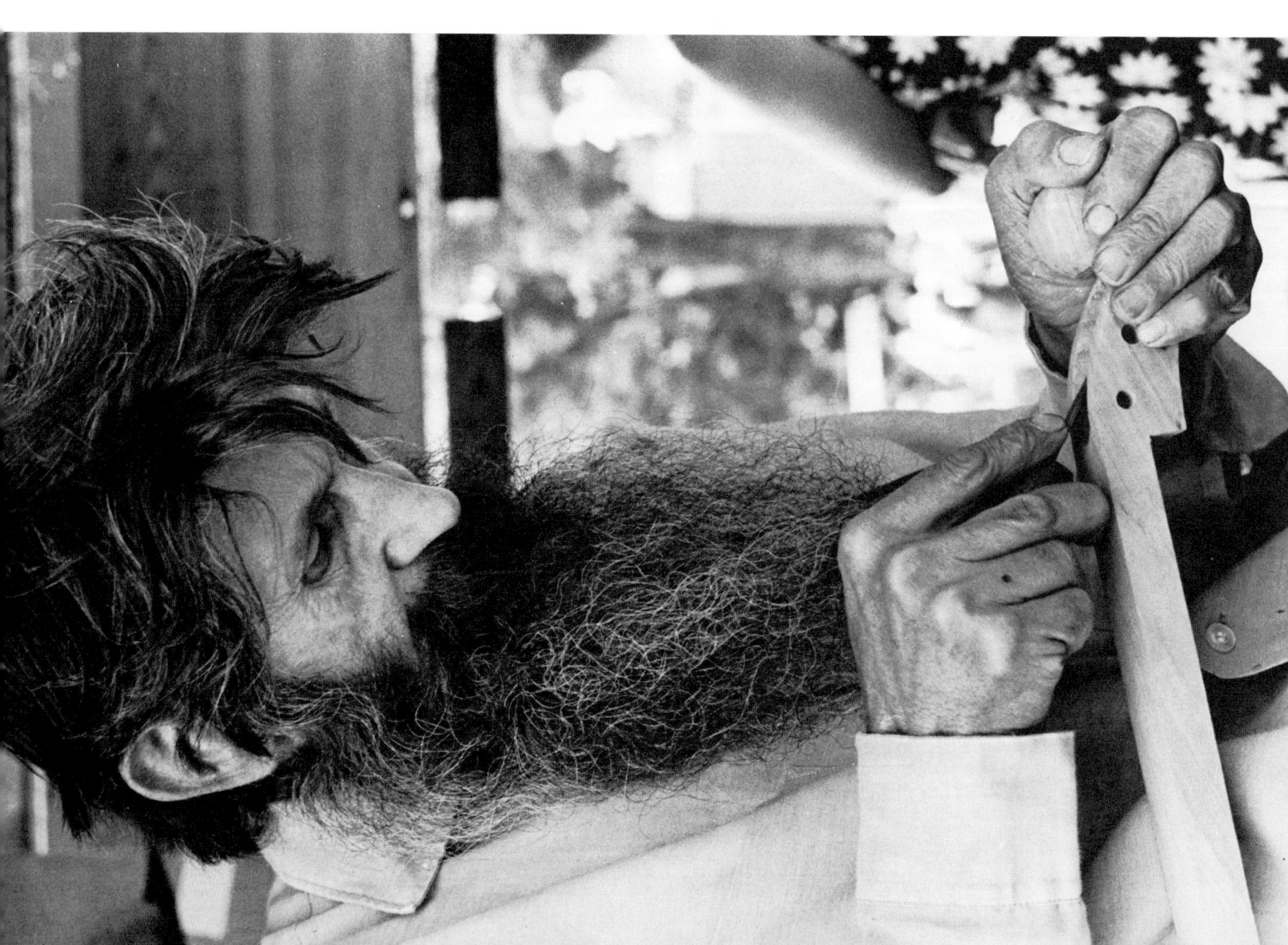

Many "little" magazines in North Carolina help foster and disseminate the art of writing. Among the better known of these are *The Rebel, Crucible, Southern Poetry Review, Greensboro Review, Pembroke Magazine,* and *Miscellany.*

Black Mountain, North Carolina, was the site of a renowned experimental school, Black Mountain College (1933–56), devoted to fostering the innovative in the arts. It was the refuge and, in some cases, the proving ground of many well-known literary figures and artists: Robert Creeley, Merce Cunningham, Charles Olson, John Cage, Paul Goodman, Robert Rauschenberg, William de Kooning, Buckminster Fuller, and others. The *Black Mountain Review* (1954–57), edited by poet Robert Creeley, included among its contributors, Denise Levertov, Allen Ginsberg, Jack Kerouac, William Carlos Williams, Charles Olson, and Robert Duncan.

The North Carolina Poetry Circuit, formed in 1961 and at that time one of two such circuits in the nation, and the Poetry in the Schools Program are two successful attempts to bring published and recognized poets into closer contact with college and public school students for the mutual benefit of all concerned. The North Carolina Arts Council has aided and encouraged this program and other literary programs in the state.

The state library system, in which all libraries—local, state, university, private college, community college, and technical institute—are linked in an interchange program under which any citizen anywhere can borrow books or obtain answers to questions almost immediately, is of tremendous significance in any report on the cultural arts. The North Carolina Union Catalogue at the University Library at Chapel Hill has teletype service throughout the nation, and the State Library in Raleigh can make telephone connections with almost all libraries in North Carolina. Through these agencies, a needy researcher can have an obscure book delivered into his hands within a few days.

Moreover, in almost every county in the state the public libraries are becoming the true cultural centers of their communities. Scores could be named—Lumberton, Laurinburg, Whiteville, Raleigh, Carthage, Southern Pines, Asheboro, Albemarle, Wadesboro, and others—in which there are regular programs of art exhibitions, sculpture showings, music concerts, poetry readings, dramatic productions, and humanities forums.

Finally, mention should be made of two of the most dynamic literary and scholarly forces in the South. The University of North Carolina Press, established in 1922, is the fourth oldest American university press sponsored by a state university. For more than fifty years, the University Press has published outstanding scholarly and literary books. Some of the Press's most significant recent titles include *The Papers of George Mason, 1725-1792*, edited by Robert A. Rutland; *North Carolina: The History of a Southern State*, by Hugh T. Lefler and Albert R. Newsome; *The Notebooks of Thomas Wolfe*, edited by Richard S. Kennedy and Paschal Reeves; and *The American Drawings of John White, 1577-1590*, edited by Paul Hulton and David B. Quinn.

The Duke University Press, established in 1921, publishes some of the most important scholarly journals in the country, and its books include a number of important works in literature and in other disciplines. It has published the following invaluable literary studies: Lewis Leary's *Articles on American Literature, 1900-1950* and *Articles on American Literature, 1950-1967*, Clarence Gohdes's *Bibliographical Guide to the Study of the Literature of the U.S.A.*, and Jay B. Hubbell's *The South in American Literature, 1607-1900*.

Three smaller publishers with emphasis on regional material are John F. Blair in Winston-Salem, McNally and Loftin in Charlotte, and Moore Publishing Company in Durham.

Musical Activity

Extensive and varied musical activity has long been a trademark of North Carolina. Opera companies, symphony orchestras, chamber groups, folk and country music conventions—all have their supporters in the state. In the public schools, education and training in music fare better perhaps than do the other arts. As usual, it is mainly in the schools of the larger towns and cities where musical education, training, and appreciation are inculcated in young people.

Symphony orchestras are located in various cities of the state. Asheville, Charlotte, Chapel Hill, Durham, Greensboro, Winston-Salem, Salisbury, and Fayetteville boast symphonies either semiprofessional or amateur. Occasionally, original compositions by North Carolina composers are performed by the state's orchestras. One example of such innovative programming, Wilmer Welsh's Symphony No. 1 in E Flat, was given its premiere performance in a March 1973 concert by the Charlotte Symphony. Several North Carolinians—including Lamar Stringfield, Walter Golde, Hunter Johnson, and Robert Ward—have won national acclaim as composers.

Founded in 1933 and given a grant by the General Assembly in 1943, the North Carolina Symphony was the first state symphony orchestra in the nation. It serves the people of North Carolina as well as those of surrounding states during its annual tours. In its concerts in the public schools, the symphony has brought music to more children than any other symphony orchestra in the nation. More than 60 percent of the symphony's budget is subsidized by the state and the balance comes from more than sixteen thousand memberships and from fees for performances.

Opera, with its multiple requirements of singers, dancers, stage settings, and orchestras has not fared quite so well in North Carolina as has symphonic music. Yet Winston-Salem, Greensboro, Greenville, Charlotte, and the Brevard Music Center all have been active in producing and promoting opera, each with its own company. For years, however, the single most important opera in the state has been the National Opera Company of Raleigh. This touring group has given thousands of performances in many states throughout the nation since its first in 1948. It has played to more than a million listeners in schools and small communities during the past twenty-five years. Many of its trainees have moved on to careers in opera companies in Europe and America.

Figure 17.2. Symphony Orchestras and Opera Groups in N.C.

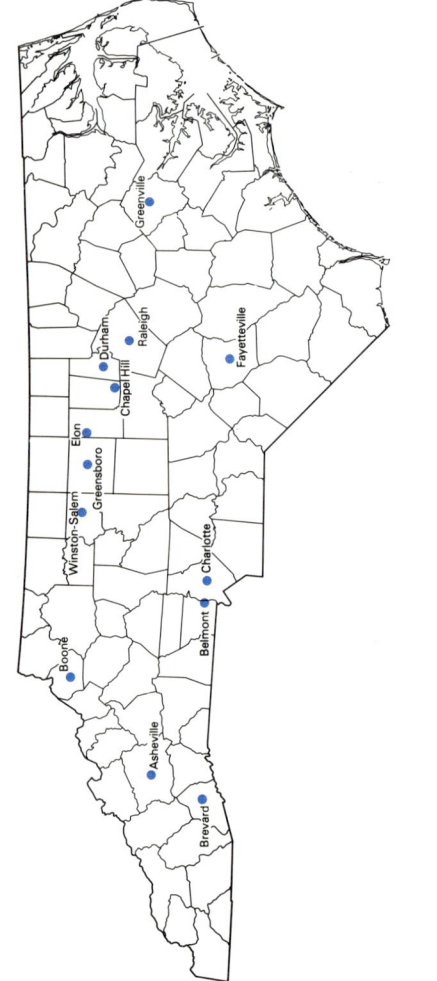

Figure 17.3. Concert Series in N.C.

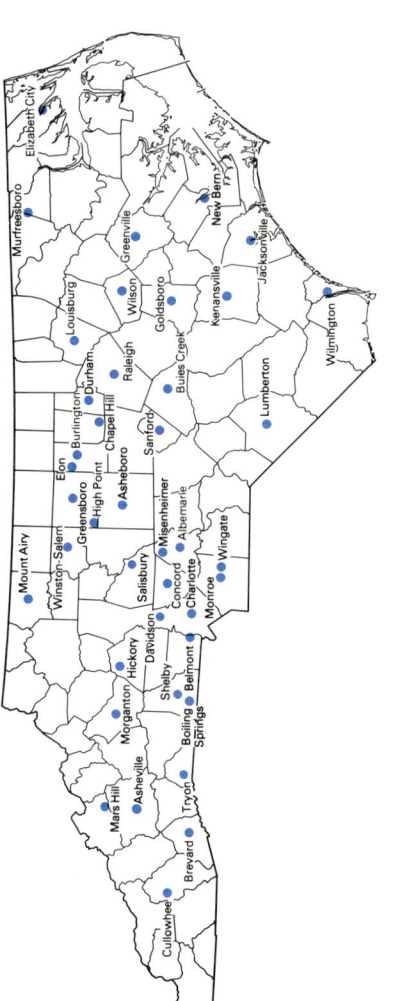

Famous national and international artists have performed in North Carolina under the auspices of various concert series such as those at Charlotte, Greensboro, Raleigh, Durham, Fayetteville, Asheville, Wilmington, and the forty-year-old Winston-Salem Civic Music Association. The larger cities, and even some of the smaller ones, have brought in the world's foremost soloists and symphony orchestras as part of their concert series. These series appear to be mushrooming all over the state. The Friends of the College at North Carolina State University in Raleigh, with twenty thousand members, is the largest such group in the country today, attracting patronage from both the Piedmont and Coastal Plain.

Folk and country music indigenous to North Carolina has always played a large role in the lives of the state's people. This type of music, with a history stretching back over hundreds of years, is still very much alive today. Folk music gatherings and conventions, including "fiddlers' conventions" such as those at Union Grove and Fiddler's Grove, attract thousands of adherents from North Carolina and other states every year. Although it is basically a music of and by country people, many city dwellers sometimes travel long distances for the opportunity to hear it performed.

A fascinating but little-known form of old music is that composed by the Moravians at Salem between 1700 and 1860. Most of the Moravians' original music was religious in nature, but in the 1780s John Frecerik Peter composed six string quintets, the earliest-known chamber music written in America. The Moravian Music Foundation, Inc., was established in 1956 to continue the research into its musical history, to serve as custodian of the music of the Moravians, and to make this early music available for performance and study. A number of recordings have been issued.

For smaller communities, a salutary innovation has been the cooperative effort of the North Carolina Arts Council and the Department of Community Colleges in administering and financing a musician-in-residence program throughout the state. The program started with five musicians, and an increasing number have taken up residence in various community colleges, such as Coastal Carolina Community College in Jacksonville and Randolph Technical Institute in Asheboro, for the purpose of developing musical programs, giving concerts and lectures, and introducing music generally into community life. A somewhat similar program—the Affiliate Artists Program—financed by the National Endowment for the Arts, Sears Roebuck, and The University of North Carolina at Charlotte was highly successful.

To enable drama students to witness superior professional performances, The University of North Carolina at Greensboro was the first university in the nation to have an Equity Association production company—the National Repertory Company—in residence. Professional directors are utilized frequently by the North Carolina School of the Arts, the Carolina Playmakers, the Winston-Salem Little Theater, and the East Carolina Theater at Greenville.

Regional workshops and conferences allow theater people to come together in order to discuss and view new techniques and developments in their field. The Southeastern Theater Conference, the largest regional theater conference in the nation, was set up primarily by the Carolina Playmakers, which also helped originate the Carolina Dramatic Association, a state drama conference.

Civic theaters are organized by citizen groups as nonprofit, tax-exempt entities with boards of directors elected by the membership to set policy. The amateur civic theaters produce children's plays, adult dramas, comedies, and musicals. The quality of productions by such civic groups varies greatly, as does the physical condition of their theaters. The skill, training, and experience of the directors of civic theaters are often the determining factors in the quality of productions. Charlotte, Raleigh, Greensboro, Asheville, Hendersonville, Fort Bragg, Winston-Salem, Mooresville, Wilmington, Southern Pines, Rocky Mount, Salisbury, Wilson, and a number of other communities have active civic theaters.

Commercial theaters are those organizations that employ paid performers and staff, produce plays that approach or attain professional quality, and are supported primarily from paid admissions. The actors and directors of such theaters most often come from out of state, many from the New York City area. Dinner theaters and summer theaters, especially in or around the cities, employ professional personnel to stage successful Broadway hits. Charlotte, Winston-Salem, Raleigh, and Greensboro have profitable dinner theaters.

From its inception in North Carolina, outdoor drama has attracted much attention from both within and outside the state. People from every section of the country as well as from other countries have traveled to see such productions as "The Lost Colony" at Manteo, "Unto These Hills" at Cherokee, and "Horn in the West" at Boone. For the most part, professional standards have been maintained in these productions, accounting for the excellent financial rewards of the tourist trade. The Institute of Outdoor Drama, based at Chapel Hill, has proved a great boon to the maintenance of high standards in such productions.

Figure 17.4. Theaters in N.C.

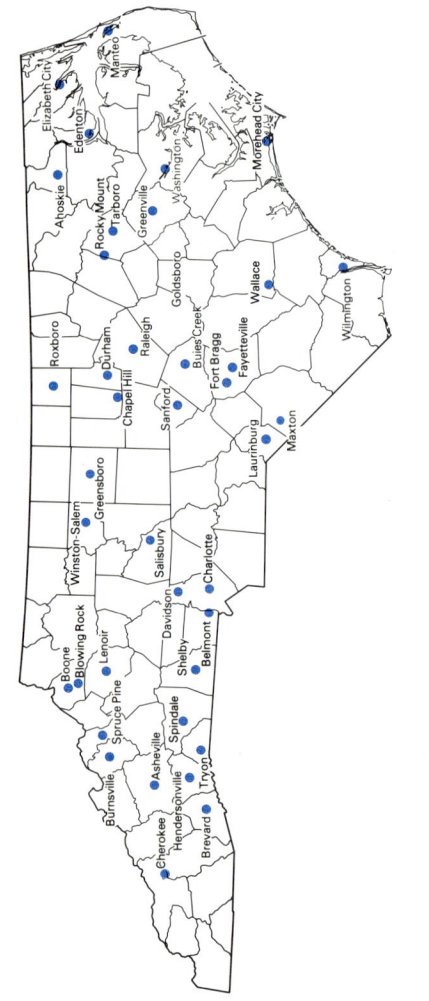

Serious effort has been made to build strong music programs in the state's system of higher education. One such example is the School of Music at the North Carolina School of the Arts in Winston-Salem. Less than a decade old, NCSA is dedicated to the training of performing artists who enroll at the high school or college level in the first state-supported school of its kind in the country. In a few short years, the school attracted many young performers who study in a unique and specialized arts environment. Many of the noted faculty spend time outside of their instructional duties as members of the Piedmont Chamber Orchestra, a professional affiliate of NCSA that has become known as an excellent ensemble of its kind.

The highly innovative Creative Arts Department at The University of North Carolina at Charlotte is also building a strong music program under the leadership of Luca DiCecco. The newly formed Rowe String Quartet is in residence there.

Finally, mention should be made of some of the musical artists who were born in or are now citizens of the state, such as William Welsh, Nicholas Harsanyi, Lou Mennini, Luca DiCecco, Robert Ward, Elaine Richey, and Giorgio Ciompi.

The North Carolina School of the Arts, the National Opera Company, the North Carolina Symphony, and the Musicians-in-Residence program will eventually reach larger numbers of people in the state and will enrich many more thousands of lives in the future.

Drama

There are four basic types of dramatic groups in North Carolina: college and university theaters, civic theaters (amateur or semiprofessional personnel), commercial theaters (professional personnel), and outdoor theaters. Only the first- and last-named categories appear to be flourishing at present, but each maintains a reasonable level of interest and competency.

College and university theaters have burgeoned in the past two decades. As interest in teaching students the fundamentals of drama has increased, so more and better departments have developed. Even the smaller colleges have evinced renewed interest in drama, thus ensuring that a great variety of plays is produced every year throughout the state. Although original plays are infrequent, the Blue Masque at Catawba College, the Carolina Playmakers at Chapel Hill, and the Frank Thompson Theater at North Carolina State University annually produce one or more. The North Carolina School of the Arts is also hospitable to original material because of its theater arts program. Attempting to expose students to varying conditions, a few college groups have toured widely: the Carolina Playmakers have toured the South and East; the Blue Masque has toured Europe; the Theater of The University of North Carolina at Greensboro has toured the Far East; and the School of the Arts annually tours elementary and high schools throughout the state.

It is worth noting that North Carolina was the first state to provide support for outdoor dramas and the first to produce the symphonic drama—"The Lost Colony" was first performed in 1937. Other outdoor historical dramas have been successful in Asheville, Lincolnton, Bath, Winston-Salem, Waxhaw, Valdese, Charlotte, and Snow Camp.

Dance

In the last decade an increased interest in dance has been evident in North Carolina. Few but significant resident companies have been formed in various cities, and many out-of-state and nationally known dance companies have performed and held demonstrator-lectures in the state.

As an indication of the growth of interest in dance in the South, the formation and success of the North Carolina Dance Theater, a professional affiliate of the North Carolina School of the Arts, should be noted. This company was established in 1970 by a grant from the Rockefeller Foundation, which has continued to provide financial assistance. Assistance is also provided by the National Endowment for the Arts, the North Carolina Arts Council, and the School of the Arts Foundation, of which the Dance Theater is a part. In the first three years of its professional existence, the Dance Theater performed in over fifty communities in the South, and was soon able to meet approximately 50 percent of its expenses through booking income. The company is now able to support fifteen dancers and a staff of six on a year-round basis.

As with most other art forms, dance has received the largest part of its support in the state's urban centers: Greensboro, Winston-Salem, Asheville, Wilmington, Raleigh, and most recently, Salisbury, have formed their own civic ballets. Furthermore, for many years, first-rate modern dance groups have come to North Carolina, sponsored and financed in large part by the North Carolina Arts Council and the National Endowment for the Arts.

Summary

In examining the state of the arts in North Carolina at the present time, a few significant facts stand out. A great deal of activity and variety in the arts is evident in North Carolina and much of it is in and immediately contiguous to the state's urban centers. The small towns and communities receive support from the North Carolina Arts Council with its diversified programs and grants-in-aid.

The first arts council in the United States, the North Carolina Arts Council, was organized at Winston-Salem in 1949 and established by executive order in 1964. The movement subsequently spread all over the country and it is perhaps the most significant movement in the arts in past decades. The North Carolina Arts Council has assisted in the organization of local arts councils, which are always growing in number. These local councils have undertaken a great variety of arts programs—in drama, in dance, in music, in literature, and in crafts—and they have involved entire communities in these programs. Through grants, salary assistance, and technical assistance, the North Carolina Arts Council has channeled funds from the National Endowment for the Arts into hundreds of communities in the past several years, and the results have been of great importance in raising the level of the cultural arts in North Carolina.

"Culture Week," a unique occasion peculiar to North Carolina, is held annually in Raleigh each autumn. Under the aegis of the parent North Carolina Literary and Historical Association, members of the various cultural societies gather for a spate of meetings. Music, art, preservation, local history, poetry, museums, genealogy, and folklore are among the subjects discussed at sessions sponsored by organizations whose special province they are. In between the meetings are dinners, exhibitions, and receptions. Though one wag facetiously suggested that "Culture Week" was a clever method North Carolinians had devised to dispose of their cultural responsibilities in a few days and then, for the other fifty-one weeks of the year, got on with everyday business, such of course is not quite the case.

For North Carolina is, day in and day out, one of the nation's leaders in the support of the arts, and in her participation in them. She was the first state to have a state symphony, the first to purchase an art collection for her people (at the North Carolina Museum of Art), the first to support outdoor dramas, the first to support a school for the performing arts (the North Carolina School of the Arts in Winston-Salem), the first to establish a Cabinet-level department devoted to the arts (the Department of Cultural Resources, established by the General Assembly in 1971), the first to institute a state agency by executive order whose sole purpose is to promote "all of the arts throughout all of the state" (the North Carolina Arts Council, in 1964, by Governor Terry Sanford). Though less than 1 percent of the state's total expenditures was in support of the arts in 1972, North Carolina is certainly progressive in her attention to the arts and their role in the future of the state.

SELECTED REFERENCES

Allcott, John V. *Colonial Homes in North Carolina*. Raleigh: Carolina Charter Tercentenary Commission, 1963.

Hoyle, Bernadette. *Tar Heel Writers I Know*. Winston-Salem: John F. Blair, 1956.

Johnson, F. B., and Waterman, T. T. *The Early Architecture of North Carolina*. Chapel Hill: University of North Carolina Press, 1947.

N.C. Arts Council. *The Arts in North Carolina*. Raleigh: The Council, 1967.

N.C. Arts Council. *The Second Biennium, July 1969-June 1971*. Raleigh: The Council, 1971.

N.C. Department of Conservation and Development. *Historic North Carolina*. Raleigh: Travel Information Division, 1964.

Robinson, B. P., ed. *The North Carolina Guide*. Chapel Hill: University of North Carolina Press, 1955.

"The State of the Arts." *Quarterly Newsletter of the North Carolina Arts Council*, 1968-73.

Walser, Richard. *Literary North Carolina*. Raleigh: State Department of Archives and History, 1970.

Wodehouse, Lawrence. "Architecture in North Carolina, 1700-1900." *North Carolina Architect* (November-December 1969): 9-28, and (January-February 1970): 9-33.

PART VI
RETROSPECT AND PROSPECT

> We have traditions which are precious to us—and a destiny worthy of the best in our powers as in our past. We shall not find the way into the future easily—I find no easy roads for most people running through the past.
>
> —Jonathan Daniels

Retrospect and Prospect

JAMES W. CLAY
DOUGLAS M. ORR, JR.
ALFRED W. STUART

Continued population growth and associated land-use changes promise to be dominant forces in American society for at least the remainder of this century. Birthrates dropped to low levels during the early 1970s but growth will continue so that by the year 2000 the nation's population will probably approach 300 million (Figure G). Even more substantial will be the increase in housing needs; most of the people requiring housing for the remainder of this century are already born and changes in birthrates will have minimal impact on this need. The unevenness of this growth will present a further challenge as most of the population increase will occur in urban areas as a result of strong migration from low income, rural, and economically depressed areas to urban centers. In 1970, 73.5 percent of the United States population was urban; it is expected to be 85 percent by the year 2000 and during this period the nation must build almost as many homes, schools, and hospitals as have been built since the country's birth. Most of the new construction will likely come in suburban areas, unincorporated subdivisions, and in areas now classified as open space.

To accommodate this rapid growth, land, by one estimate, is presently being urbanized in the United States at the rate of three thousand acres per day. This rate can be expected to accelerate for not only will there be more people, but if past trends continue, the people will occupy more land per person. This increased per person requirement relates to increased freedom provided by the automobile, which, in turn, has encouraged a trend toward single-family homes and a desire for larger lots, more outdoor living space, and country living. This trend has ended the popularity of the narrow 25-foot to 60-foot lots found in many older cities.

Urbanization, coupled with increased affluence of the population, also contributes significantly to new demands for transportation, recreation, and service land in and beyond urban areas. Living in the confines of urban places and having more free time, the urban populace is demanding more parks, golf courses, and other user-oriented facilities. To move people in, out, and within urban areas, new demands are being placed on highways, airport facilities, and related service areas.

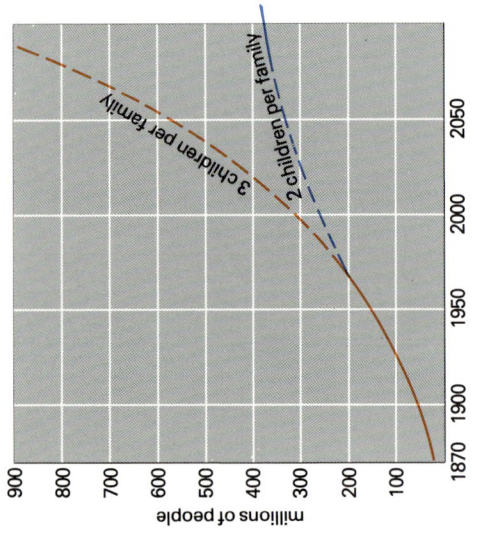

Figure G. U.S. Population Growth

Source: Commission on Population Growth and the American Future, *Population and the American Future*, 1972.

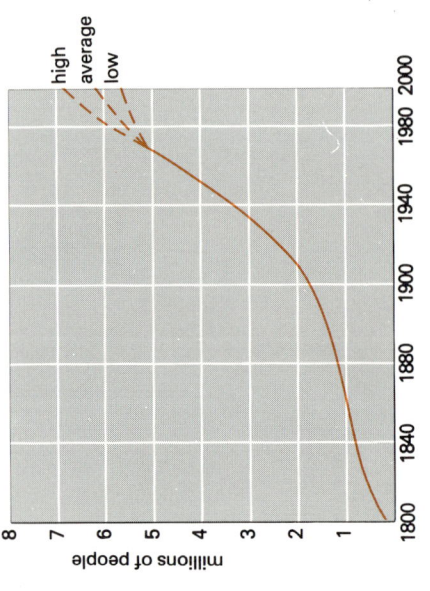

Figure H. N.C. Population Growth

Source: C. Horace Hamilton, *North Carolina Population Trends: A Demographic Sourcebook*, vol. 1 (Chapel Hill: Carolina Population Center, 1974).

The problem is not that the United States or North Carolina is running out of land, but rather that urbanization is sprawling in random fashion over the most accessible and most desired locales. The preponderance of change is occurring on the former farmlands around population centers, and over scenic and resort areas. Here the land is very much limited and often the physical environment is sensitive to high densities. Thus, in countless cases, the land is being abused.

Further complicating the matter is that growth has not been geographically uniform. The older industrial areas of the North were the first to develop a high degree of urban concentration. Recently, however, these areas have lost much of their magnetism. In the immediate past, the most rapid growth has been in the South and West where net in-migration, supplementing growth from natural increase, has produced high urban and regional growth rates with the corresponding threat to a highly prized physical environment. In the South, this urban flow is compounded by a parallel intrastate shift of population from rural areas to urban centers. For the past quarter of a century, the whole rural South has been in the midst of an urban and economic transformation without historical parallel for the region.

As the preceding chapters indicate, North Carolina is a good example of these trends. The state is expected to add more persons during the 1970s than during the previous decade—boosted substantially by increased net in-migration. By the year 2000, North Carolina's population could be as high as 7.3 million—a 43 percent increase over the 5.1 million recorded in the 1970 census (Figure H). But even more notable is the increased use of land for urban uses. In North Carolina, a population increase of 13 percent over a recent ten-year period was accompanied by an 83 percent increase in urban and built-up land, reflecting the high rate of growth in the state's urban centers. This example is typical of national trends.

Such rapid growth often results in a situation in which people respond to growth rather than take a deliberate part in directing it. Without sound planning, land patterns seldom yield optimal benefit to the users. Misuse of the land is of particular concern today because of the pervasive ill effects that carry over to so many facets of society. The high social, economic, and environmental costs that result are endless. Many of the subject areas in this book demonstrate problems—from physical environment deficiencies to maldistribution of health care to transportation network deficiencies—that could be at least partly overcome by a more rational relationship between man and the land. Examples are plentiful throughout the country of the manner in which urban sprawl and overdevelopment of environmentally sensitive areas greatly intensified other societal problems such as air and water pollution, housing, and crime. In planning for the anticipated growth over the next several decades, North Carolina could benefit from an analysis of the mistakes of older developed areas.

Changing Attitudes toward Growth and Land Use

Existing approaches to land use can be traced to the movement and development trends across the continent over the last three centuries. There was always additional frontier land to which the developer could turn. Public ownership of land was looked upon as transitory while unlimited rights of private ownership seemed necessary for productive use of the land. It was also no doubt a reaction on the part of the colonialists against the restrictions on land ownership, use, and transfer they had known in the European countries of their origin. Few value systems have since been more sacrosanct in the American value system than the concept of private property. Although this pioneer ethic of acquiring, using, and selling land in whatever manner the individual wishes is not quite as prevalent today as it once was, the residual effects still remain. These attitudes are probably accountable for the lack of local, state, and national mechanisms for the effective planning and directing of growth and change.

There are increasing signs that the negative side effects of unguided growth and misuse of the land are, at long last, being better understood. Indeed, a ground swell of changing attitudes seems to be taking place. Throughout many parts of the country, social, economic, and environmental pressures have compelled numerous cities and towns to try to limit the size and nature of their populations. These limitations range from explicit population ceilings to moratoriums on building permits. A widely publicized example is the community of Boca Raton, Florida, where the voters approved a "population cap" of forty thousand dwelling units.

Similar movements have been going on at the state level. Beginning with Hawaii over a decade ago, many states have taken a variety of actions to curb the growing despoliation of the landscape and subsequent ills that are created. Delaware has banned industry from its coast. California, Maine, Florida, and other states are regulating developments along their shorelines. Colorado voters vetoed a bid to host the 1976 Winter Olympics because of the possible developmental consequences. And Oregon has declared that it does not want any more residents, period. A recent report to the Council of State Governments indicated that over thirty states were exploring the subject of comprehensive land-use planning; that twenty-one states were trying to formulate long-range goals for their population and

resources; that ten state legislatures had adopted resolutions on stabilizing their populations; and that six states had established population commissions. Although these sentiments have not on the whole been translated into specific actions, they are representative of an unmistakable trend.

Meanwhile, the federal government, while reviewing various proposals for national growth policies and land-use guidelines, has abstained from advancing any coordinated national program. A major limiting factor, of course, is the strong feeling about jurisdictional prerogatives between the federal and state or local levels of government.

The courts are becoming more and more involved in the whole land-use question as a myriad of suits has developed concerning the economically discriminatory features of community and state growth controls. The legal basis for many of these cases is the Constitution's Fifth Amendment provision that "private property" shall not be taken for public purposes "without just compensation." The provision is applicable to the states through the Fourteenth Amendment's provision that property shall not be taken "without due process of law." Courts have traditionally upheld land-use regulations designed to protect the general public interest as long as the property owner was left some reasonable use of the land. The question that has arisen more recently—with enormously critical lands, for example—is what happens when regulations do not leave the owner with any economic use of his land whatsoever.

There are perplexing dilemmas raised by all of these issues. Certainly no community or state can be expected to keep expanding without end. There are limits on accessible space, on population density, and on public utilities. At the same time, how are constraints on expansion to be reconciled with people's rights under the Constitution to travel freely and settle where they please? Is society benefited by the attitude at some locales to "pull up the gangplank" and allow no more people while other areas are much more overpopulated? Clearly a policy of rigid no-growth seems as full of pitfalls as the blind faith in continuous growth. These questions were effectively addressed recently by the highly regarded Task Force on Land Use and Urban Growth, headed by Laurance S. Rockefeller. The Task Force, in its report, suggested that a balance must be found to allow a reasonable level of social and economic opportunity in the context of a more realistic contemporary view of property rights. It rejected no-growth as a viable option in the near future, expressing concern that housing or mobility not be shut off for any segment of the population. At the same time, the Task Force placed particular attention on the need for rethinking some of the long-accepted views on private property rights. It suggested that the time is coming when the ownership of open spaces without urbanization rights will become commonplace. In one notable recommendation, the Task Force urged the United States Supreme Court to reexamine decisions made at an earlier time when land was evaluated for its maximum marketable value rather than for its value as an irreplaceable natural resource.

In the Constitution, authority concerning land use rests with the states, but they have historically delegated this control to local governments. During recent years, however, land use and growth problems have tended to transcend the boundaries of any single municipality and this has led to jurisdictional tangles and a reexamination of the whole question of intergovernmental relationships. More and more the state is being pointed to as the most practical place for development of overall strategies for guiding future growth. The state-level institutions seem best able to combine the metropolitan and regional perspective and they possess the legal powers and controls sufficient for effective action. Many states are consequently moving to recover their original power. A variety of state "tools" for directing growth are, of course, available—taxation policies, utilities and new highway construction, manpower training, tourist and industrial promotion, to name a few. The means of implementation of a statewide land-use and growth policy, with the use of such state powers, is of primary importance. The unmistakable tendency so far has been to adapt a regional approach to many of the decision-making processes. This approach reflects a recognition of the growing interdependence of towns and cities, of rural with urban areas, and of metropolitan centers with their hinterlands. States are moving toward this substate-level regionalism not as a promotion of regional government, but as a common response to common problems—creating mechanisms for responding to their mutual concerns on a regional basis. Only time will tell, of course, how well this readjustment of geographic perspective can be made for a society grown accustomed to only a very localized viewpoint.

Regions and County Types

There are many kinds of regions recognized within North Carolina. Multicounty Planning Regions or health care planning regions, for example, were created for administrative purposes. Administrative or planning regions are designed to implement programs or to develop plans for future action.

A second type of region is one composed of units that are similar to one another. A general region of this nature is designed not for administrative purposes but to provide a broader framework for analysis than do the component units. In North Carolina, the basic informational unit is the county but many trends often transcend the county and need to be viewed on a more extensive scale.

Traditionally, the tendency in North Carolina has been to use for analysis the historical/physiographic regions that divide the state into Coastal Plain, Piedmont, and Mountains. Phrases such as "down east," often used in politics, are but a variation on the historical/physiographic regions. The implicit recognition is that these intrastate regions have a common heritage, environmental setting, and even economic patterns. The three basic historical/physiographic regions represent for North Carolina a means by which they perceive their state. They are not administrative "states within a state." They are not administrative or problem-solving regions but rather groupings of similar counties that are an aid to generalizing about events, problems, trends, and opportunities. A difficulty arises when, over time, the similarities between counties within a grouping changes and certain counties really become more like those in a different region. If this occurs without an appropriate adjustment in the definition of regions, then those who persist in using traditional definitions are in danger of having weak or false perceptions of contemporary realities.

That the historical/physiographic regions are possibly inadequate was suggested in Chapter 11 (Manufacturing), where it appears that, in terms of industrial structure, the Piedmont breaks into several distinct types of counties. In addition, certain Mountain and Coastal Plain counties are more like some Piedmont counties than they are like their neighbors.

Therefore, an effort was made to divide the state's one hundred counties into a few types based on available statistical information. The purpose was to provide a new framework for looking at some of the more important problems and opportunities that emerge from the chapters of this book. That is, these new regions or groupings of counties simply provide an organizational framework for overview purposes and are not necessarily appropriate as administrative units.

To make such an analysis two mathematical techniques, a factor analysis and a grouping analysis, were applied to twenty-six variables that measured important aspects of income, population characteristics, education, economy, land use, and air quality. Not every statistic that one would like to have is available for each of the counties nor are many important characteristics subject to statistical measurement. Common sense and empirical knowledge were added to the computerized results to soften some of the inadequacies of these purely mathematical approaches.

Figure 1 shows the distribution of the four types of counties that resulted from the analysis. There is a tendency for the types to resemble the physiographic regions, especially in the Coastal Plain and the Piedmont, but some Outer Coastal Plain counties are revealed as having more in common with some Mountain counties than with any others. Another group that is dominated by the state's metropolitan counties spreads across the state. Thus, while the traditional physiographic regions are not entirely abrogated, it is clear that they also represent a rather oversimplified view of current North Carolina realities. The map even suggests some evolutionary patterns, such as an apparent spread of Piedmont characteristics into the Mountains. Table A summarizes some of the more important characteristics of each county that went into the analysis. Table B gives important statistics for the individual counties.

Dispersed Urban Type This group is largely urban in nature and is d spersed throughout the state. Population density is high and growth is strong, as is indicated by population in-migration (Table A). Associated with these characteristics are high income and educational attainment levels, which set this region apart from more rural areas. These and other urban-rural contrasts are a persistent theme that appears throughout this book.

Even though manufacturing was shown in Chapter 11 to be spreading across the state, it tends to be rather specialized and of a low-wage quality except in the urban areas. In them is found an increasingly diversified, higher-wage industrial base. Coincident with this is the tendency for retailing to be increasingly concentrated in the urban centers. It was also observed in both Chapter 2 (Population) and Chapter 3 (Urbanization) that an increasing share of the state's population is concentrated in its urban areas.

What seems to be happening is a "snowballing" concentration of people and generally desirable economic activities in the state's larger cities. The implications of this concentration are many. It could mean that North Carolina is on its way to losing its "urban anomaly" character that was noted in Chapter 3. Are Charlotte, Raleigh, and a few other cities becoming major metropolitan centers or, alternatively, growing toward each other to form a giant metropolitan region that will ultimately match Atlanta or others in magnitude? The noted urban analyst, Jerome Pickard, has forecast that the North Carolina Piedmont cities would form the backbone of such a metropolitan region, one of the largest in the country, before the century is over.

The northeastern United States has experienced a coalescence of its large cities. This has not happened in North Carolina because North Carolina lacks the large cities that might act as nuclei for such a pattern. For North Carolina, perhaps a better model than coalescence might be a "federation" of cities in which development is guided in a way such that certain cities specialize in some activities for an entire area and other cities have specialized functions on a smaller scale. Charlotte is already a business center and Raleigh is its equivalent in political administration. A consciously developed system of this sort might make unnecessary the emergence of the "super cities" that some feel will be the logical outcome of contemporary American growth patterns.

Several rural counties are being strongly affected by the urbanization change in the neighboring dispersed urban counties. Nash County, on the Coastal Plain east of Raleigh, is an example of this change. Although the county had strong population out-migration between 1960 and 1970 (estimates for 1970-73, however, indicate net in-migration), it was shown in Chapter 12 to be a powerful retail center, focusing on Rocky Mount. It was also shown in Chapter 11 to be a rapidly developing manufacturing area. Nash County seems to represent the spread of metropolitan growth into formerly rural-agricultural areas. Another example of creeping urbanization that appeared as a surprise in this analysis is Polk County, on the South Carolina line south of Asheville. By Census Bureau definitions, Polk is still entirely rural and it exhibits few of the features of metropolitan areas. It does have relatively high educational standards and a moderately high level of income. Only a small amount of its land is devoted to agriculture. What it also has is a

Table A. Selected Characteristics of N.C. County Types

	County Type			
	Dispersed Urban	Piedmont Industrial	Coastal Plain Agricultural	Recreational Fringe
Per capita income ($) (1969)	2,714	2,487	1,886	1,900
Families below poverty level (%) (1969)	14.3	14.9	26.5	26.4
Unemployment (%) (1971)	3.9	4.2	5.9	8.5
Urban population (%) (1970)	53.0	24.6	23.0	9.3
Population density (persons/square mile) (1970)	2,816	1,085	714	392
Black population (%) (1970)	24.0	11.5	40.5	18.9
Population migration (%) 1960-70	5.2	.07	-15.0	-8.0
Per pupil school expenditure ($) (1971)	1,250	1,166	1,131	791
Median school years completed (1970)	10.9	9.8	9.5	9.5
Nonfederal active physicians (per 1,000 population) (1971)	1.88	.53	.52	.46
Acres harvested (% of total) (1971)	6.6	4.9	18.1	7.3
Manufacturing % of nonagricultural employment (1971)	43	69	58	46
Retail sales per capita ($) (1970)	2,509	1,731	1,526	1,486
Recreation acreage (% of total) (1971)	2.7	6.9	3.6	15.0
Particulates (tons/acre) (1971)	.05	.06	.02	.01
Carbon monoxide (tons/acre) (1971)	.25	.09	.06	.03

Sources: All data were derived from the 1970 U.S. Census of Population or the North Carolina State Government Statistical Abstract, 1973.

Figure I. N.C. County Types

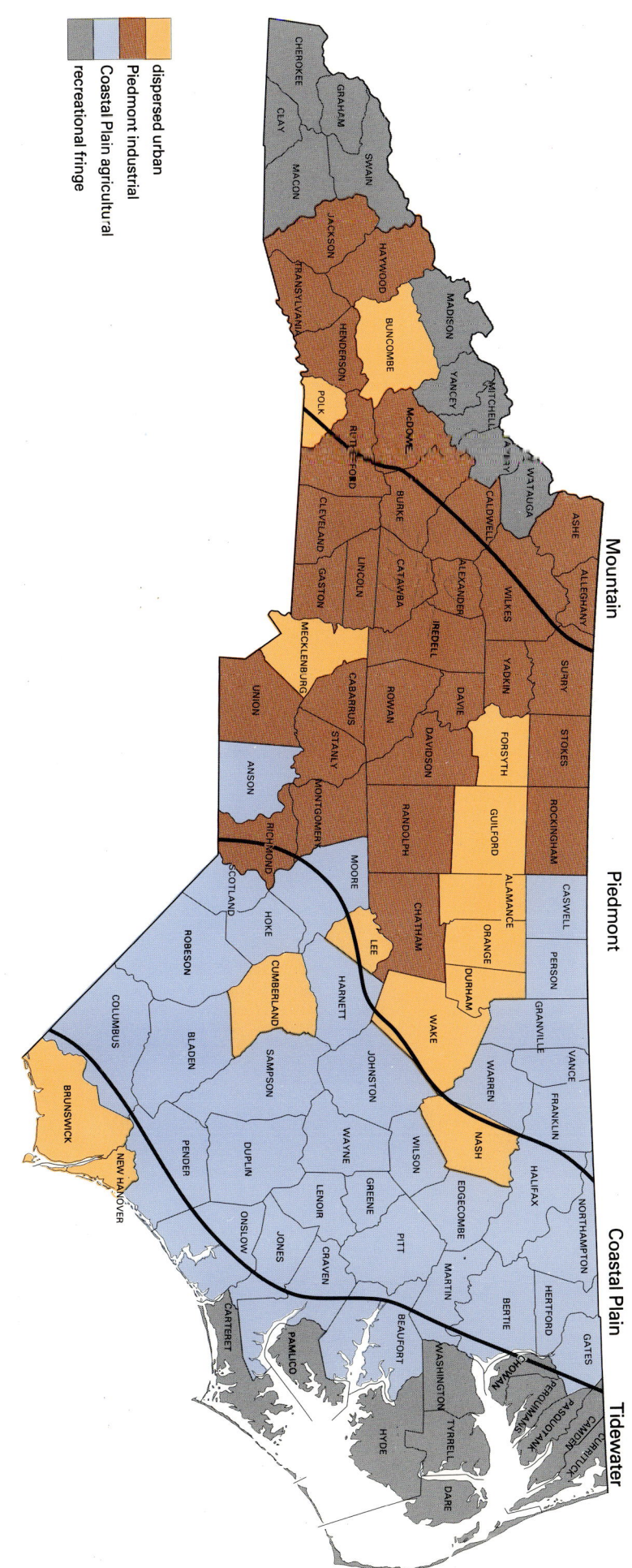

- dispersed urban
- Piedmont industrial
- Coastal Plain agricultural
- recreational fringe

location on Interstate 26 between Asheville and the Greenville-Spartanburg area in South Carolina. While urbanization is not an obvious feature of Polk County at present, it may be that the county is beginning to experience the sprawl of urban growth from the several metropolitan areas.

Some of the data in Table A remind the reader that metropolitan growth is not an unmixed blessing. The several measures of air quality show that the dispersed urban county has high counts of particulates that are emitted into the air. Even more notable in this county is the concentration of carbon monoxide, that sure indicator of great concentrations of cars and trucks. It symbolizes problems not only with air quality but also with traffic and other manifestations of this society's devotion to the automobile.

Piedmont Industrial Type In many respects the counties of this group represent the traditional nonurban, industrialized Piedmont—classic mill-town and furniture-factory county. These counties have relatively small black populations, moderate population densities, and marginal population growth. Actually, population change is uneven. Some counties, such as Alexander and Catawba, showed strong in-migration along with some of the neighboring metropolitan counties, while some of the more established Piedmont Industrial counties, such as Cabarrus and Rowan, experienced a net out-migration of population during the 1960s.

The Piedmont Industrial group represents an important, and perhaps unique, aspect of the North Carolina development experience. It is symbolized by the small-town or rural textile mill that, as early as the 1880s, provided an alternative to farming for a rural population at a time when the national trend was for such a population to shift to cities. The emergence in North Carolina of a small-town-rural industrial base allowed the state to develop its unusual degree of population dispersion that today is so characteristic of it, especially in the Piedmont.

Unlike the metropolitan counties, those in this group have experienced little industrial diversification and enjoyed few of the features of balanced economies. For example, they have limited concentrations of retail and service activities, and they tend to rely on the nearby cities for all but the more day-to-day commodities and services.

At one time this group enjoyed the advantages of an industrial economy dispersed throughout a small-town and rural setting. The present danger is that unless the great dependence on such traditional low-wage industries as textiles and furniture can be reduced, fewer people will find this type of area a suitable environment. They will be attracted in greater numbers to the metropolitan areas. The other danger is, of course, that if the textile industry, in the face of competition from cheaper imports and rising domestic labor costs, were to cut back severely, the people of this group of counties would suffer enormously.

Table B. Selected Statistics on the Counties of N.C.

Counties	(1) Area 1971 Thousand Acres	(2) Total population 1970	(3) percent population Urban 1970	(4) 1973 Population Estimate	(5) percent population Nonwhite 1970	(6) Estimated percent Net Migration 1960-1970	(7) percent population Net Migration 1970-1973	(8) percent population 65 years or Over 1970	(9) Median Number School years Completed, population over 25, 1970	(10) per Capita Income 1969	(11) percent Families with Incomes below poverty Level	(12) Total Employment 1971	(13) percent Total Employment in Manufacturing 1971	(14) Retail Sales per Capita 1970	(15) Total Farm Income 1971 (in thousands)	(16) Active Nonfederal physicians per 1,000 population 1971
Alamance	278	96,362	52.4	100,000	17.9	-0.9	1.2	7.9	10.4	2,936	8.8	48,110	50.2	2,276	$19,268	.84
Alexander	166	19,466	0.0	21,500	7.8	13.2	7.2	8.4	9.1	2,391	11.8	7,430	55.3	1,228	13,554	.31
Alleghany	147	8,134	0.0	8,500	3.0	-1.7	2.6	14.2	8.9	2,012	26.0	3,530	38.2	1,765	4,953	1.00
Anson	343	23,488	16.9	23,900	46.6	-16.1	-0.5	11.6	8.9	1,744	27.2	8,510	33.4	1,318	10,367	.26
Ashe	273	19,571	0.0	19,200	1.1	-9.9	-3.7	12.1	9.2	1,717	27.8	6,830	34.4	1,283	14,479	.35
Avery	158	12,655	0.0	13,200	0.8	-5.1	-1.9	10.4	9.4	1,739	28.9	4,150	20.5	1,153	3,553	.92
Beaufort	613	35,980	24.9	36,100	33.3	-9.5	-1.4	8.9	10.2	2,045	24.9	15,810	26.1	2,033	29,811	.64
Bertie	461	20,528	0.0	20,300	56.6	-25.3	-2.3	8.4	8.7	1,555	36.9	6,820	21.0	1,193	22,978	.29
Bladen	570	26,477	0.0	27,200	39.5	-18.6	0.4	11.8	9.5	1,633	30.5	8,110	29.3	1,401	20,611	.27
Brunswick	581	24,223	0.0	29,800	30.7	6.9	19.3	8.4	9.8	2,010	22.9	8,320	17.8	1,338	9,993	.38
Buncombe	414	145,056	52.2	148,500	9.1	2.4	0.9	11.8	11.3	2,671	13.5	61,830	32.6	2,654	11,857	1.43
Burke	331	60,364	28.5	63,200	7.3	2.1	1.6	8.0	9.6	2,533	10.0	30,410	59.9	1,505	2,759	1.00
Cabarrus	230	74,629	64.0	76,700	16.1	-1.9	0.2	8.6	9.9	2,772	8.9	42,660	61.4	1,988	7,910	.95
Caldwell	307	56,699	30.9	57,700	6.4	-1.9	-2.1	6.9	9.4	2,365	11.9	22,810	57.3	1,772	9,372	.49
Camden	197	5,453	0.0	5,600	37.2	-13.6	2.3	10.7	9.7	1,916	21.5	980	3.1	563	6,106	.20
Carteret	680	31,603	27.2	33,600	11.5	3.4	3.4	9.2	10.8	2,407	16.6	9,590	14.9	1,816	3,906	.72
Caswell	278	19,055	0.0	19,600	48.1	-14.8	0.6	8.9	8.7	1,878	19.1	5,580	21.3	647	12,957	.05
Catawba	264	90,873	42.9	95,700	8.9	8.8	1.8	7.1	10.5	2,910	7.5	57,880	54.3	2,935	7,597	.90
Chatham	453	29,554	15.9	29,300	30.5	0.8	-3.0	9.3	9.8	2,252	16.1	11,750	45.6	2,077	33,165	.37
Cherokee	299	16,330	0.0	16,200	2.7	-9.1	-2.6	11.9	8.8	1,896	25.2	6,590	44.9	1,631	4,867	.50
Chowan	150	10,764	44.3	10,600	42.1	-17.2	-3.5	10.5	8.9	2,040	25.0	4,890	24.1	1,988	10,062	.82
Clay	140	5,180	0.0	5,200	0.9	-12.0	-1.4	13.9	8.8	1,643	37.7	1,300	20.8	1,119	5,771	.20
Cleveland	298	72,556	34.0	74,400	20.6	-4.2	-0.4	8.3	10.2	2,380	13.5	34,360	46.0	1,909	17,480	.79
Columbus	611	46,937	8.9	48,300	31.8	-17.4	0.5	8.1	9.3	1,823	27.7	19,280	27.3	1,665	42,190	.37
Craven	502	62,554	55.2	52,100	26.1	-14.9	1.6	5.9	10.9	2,322	18.7	21,220	13.1	1,989	19,506	.78
Cumberland	424	212,042	72.1	215,300	26.5	13.9	-4.7	3.3	11.2	2,340	17.1	58,060	16.1	1,775	21,201	.39
Currituck	300	6,976	0.0	8,500	26.5	0.9	20.3	11.8	9.6	2,094	19.2	1,400	7.9	1,316	9,431	.43
Dare	797	6,995	0.0	7,800	7.3	10.6	10.1	12.9	10.5	2,581	13.3	3,030	1.7	3,358	28	.43
Davidson	358	95,627	37.1	99,600	10.0	6.2	1.1	7.6	10.0	2,685	10.4	37,440	52.7	1,754	11,015	.45
Davie	169	18,855	23.4	19,700	11.9	2.1	1.5	9.9	9.7	2,379	14.0	6,010	41.9	1,523	12,834	.42
Duplin	527	38,015	14.9	38,500	34.3	-16.6	-1.1	8.7	10.0	1,893	28.9	15,440	25.3	1,580	83,700	.39
Durham	192	132,681	75.9	138,000	32.9	6.9	1.4	8.2	11.8	2,900	12.8	70,600	20.1	2,346	5,957	5.87
Edgecombe	327	52,341	47.1	52,100	47.6	-16.2	-2.8	8.3	8.7	1,899	26.4	21,950	28.1	1,616	32,699	1.29
Forsyth	271	214,348	68.8	224,500	22.5	0.4	1.7	7.9	11.3	3,109	11.0	108,670	34.4	2,815	12,675	2.15
Franklin	316	26,820	11.0	27,800	41.8	-16.3	2.4	10.4	9.1	1,984	27.9	9,020	24.1	1,411	21,819	.33
Gaston	232	148,415	60.3	155,600	12.3	0.2	1.1	7.5	9.5	2,748	9.5	68,400	56.4	2,063	4,832	.59
Gates	223	8,524	0.0	8,200	53.4	-15.3	-4.6	11.4	9.4	1,754	25.5	1,980	11.1	1,012	8,957	.22
Graham	191	6,562	0.0	6,400	4.9	-12.3	-4.5	10.9	8.6	1,753	24.8	1,370	18.2	1,172	686	.43
Granville	347	32,762	32.7	32,900	43.9	-11.5	-1.4	8.7	9.8	1,792	24.1	13,110	25.1	1,110	18,907	1.16
Greene	172	14,967	0.0	15,000	47.0	-23.5	-1.6	6.4	9.6	1,719	32.6	4,700	11.5	905	30,529	.07
Guilford	417	288,590	66.3	298,700	22.5	3.1	0.6	7.7	10.8	3,185	9.4	170,510	35.7	3,430	20,572	.94
Halifax	463	53,884	32.5	53,500	49.4	-21.4	-3.2	9.3	8.3	1,808	29.9	21,680	31.1	2,212	28,575	.46
Harnett	389	49,667	22.5	52,100	25.1	-8.8	2.2	7.9	10.0	1,998	20.5	16,730	25.6	1,636	28,567	.44
Haywood	348	41,710	27.9	42,300	2.0	-6.5	-0.7	10.9	10.2	2,289	15.8	14,040	40.0	1,730	9,612	.71
Henderson	244	42,804	28.0	45,300	4.7	9.3	4.2	13.5	11.0	2,407	19.8	16,410	30.0	2,007	17,355	.99
Hertford	231	23,529	22.6	22,500	55.4	-9.4	-6.3	9.1	8.9	1,772	27.5	8,870	22.7	1,840	12,823	.75
Hoke	213	16,436	19.3	17,100	54.9	-14.1	-0.3	6.8	8.8	1,663	26.2	5,920	40.0	994	12,559	.50
Hyde	873	5,571	0.0	5,600	41.3	-8.5	0.6	12.9	9.2	1,642	33.5	1,530	8.5	968	6,348	.16
Iredell	380	72,197	44.2	75,700	17.2	3.0	2.4	8.9	10.1	2,569	11.3	32,920	47.9	2,020	27,339	.72
Jackson	319	21,593	0.0	23,300	10.6	12.7	5.4	9.8	9.8	1,921	25.3	6,980	19.3	1,164	1,477	.77
Johnston	509	61,737	22.9	62,300	21.3	-10.6	-1.0	8.7	9.4	1,968	24.8	23,550	27.3	1,808	54,616	.45
Jones	300	9,779	0.0	9,700	45.1	-22.1	-2.6	8.2	10.0	1,640	29.8	2,700	8.5	849	11,128	.20
Lee	164	30,467	38.5	32,300	23.1	0.2	3.2	8.2	10.6	2,372	16.3	14,770	36.6	2,490	7,740	.80
Lenoir	250	55,204	45.0	58,100	37.0	-12.7	2.4	7.4	9.9	2,286	23.7	26,250	28.5	2,422	34,007	.82

320

Table B—Continued

Counties	(1) Area 1971 Thousand Acres	(2) Total Population 1970	(3) Percent Population Urban 1970	(4) 1973 Population Estimate	(5) Percent Population Nonwhite 1970	(6) Percent Net Migration 1960-1970	(7) Estimated Percent Net Migration 1970-1973	(8) Percent Population 65 Years or Over 1970	(9) Median Number School Years Completed, Population over 25, 1970	(10) Per Capita Income 1969	(11) Percent Families with Incomes below Poverty Level	(12) Total Employment 1971	(13) Percent Total Employment in Manufacturing 1971	(14) Retail Sales per Capita 1970	(15) Total Farm Income 1971 (in thousands)	(16) Active Nonfederal Physicians per 1,000 Population 1971
Lincoln	198	32,682	16.2	35,600	10.3	5.7	8.3	9.8	8.7	2,576	12.0	12,580	51.7	1,685	9,498	.51
McDowell	286	30,648	30.6	31,800	5.3	1.1	0.6	9.3	8.4	2,196	15.0	11,570	61.0	1,378	1,850	.36
Macon	333	15,788	0.0	16,800	5.5	14.3	5.4	14.3	9.1	1,868	24.9	5,010	20.0	686	5,439	.50
Madison	292	16,003	0.0	16,000	0.7	-0.8	-0.6	13.1	8.2	1,514	31.9	3,850	6.5	8,203		.44
Martin	309	24,730	26.6	24,000	44.9	-21.2	-13.1	10.1	9.1	1,681	29.0	11,740	32.9	1,645	26,249	.36
Mecklenburg	351	354,656	79.6	370,000	24.1	14.0	-0.6	8.2	11.6	3,323	9.4	204,090	18.2	4,046	6,159	1.29
Mitchell	141	13,447	0.0	13,700	0.3	-12.0	-5.5	12.6	9.4	1,922	28.1	4,740	37.8	1,678	5,526	.54
Montgomery	319	19,267	24.9	19,100	24.9	0.2	-3.7	10.4	9.6	2,138	19.6	10,090	55.2	1,790	8,799	.42
Moore	484	39,048	15.2	41,400	25.1	-5.8	4.0	10.8	10.4	2,225	20.3	15,100	27.6	1,776	34,719	1.18
Nash	353	59,122	32.2	61,200	22.9	-14.4	1.2	8.7	10.4	2,116	23.6	30,090	27.3	2,607	36,580	.12
New Hanover	144	82,996	69.5	92,100	59.1	5.6	7.9	8.5	12.1	2,761	14.3	37,120	24.3	2,973	2,558	1.30
Northampton	348	24,009	0.0	23,600	35.8	-21.0	-3.2	9.9	8.5	1,868	37.9	7,420	20.2	872	24,930	.38
Onslow	516	103,126	57.5	94,200	16.1	-9.9	3.2	9.9	12.1	1,514	31.9	19,700	7.9	1,276	13,390	.19
Orange	255	57,707	50.3	65,600	10.2	17.6	10.4	6.6	11.2	2,205	11.1	19,700	6.2	1,669	12,535	8.34
Pamlico	369	9,467	0.0	9,400	33.2	-10.5	-2.5	11.7	9.8	1,882	27.6	2,240	18.3	846	5,669	.11
Pasquotank	186	26,824	52.4	27,100	38.0	-6.8	-1.0	9.7	10.4	2,176	20.3	14,070	15.9	2,221	11,497	.93
Pender	556	18,149	0.0	18,300	43.9	-11.7	1.5	9.9	9.9	1,713	28.8	4,970	10.7	1,050	18,816	.22
Perquimans	207	8,351	0.0	8,300	41.5	-16.4	-0.8	13.2	10.0	1,634	35.0	2,560	11.7	1,637	8,527	.13
Person	256	25,914	20.7	27,100	33.0	-13.9	1.3	8.6	9.3	2,121	20.1	11,490	34.8	1,614	15,192	.39
Pitt	420	73,900	50.0	73,500	34.8	-8.4	-3.2	7.1	9.7	2,108	27.1	31,520	18.1	2,126	57,874	.96
Polk	150	11,735	0.0	12,200	12.3	-2.9	3.8	19.1	10.6	2,336	19.1	2,639	27.0	1,322	2,639	1.25
Randolph	513	76,358	30.2	79,800	7.4	11.1	1.6	7.9	9.2	2,731	9.7	31,700	57.4	1,562	25,571	.42
Richmond	309	39,889	33.4	39,600	29.7	-9.0	-3.2	9.0	9.2	2,180	21.3	15,770	35.7	1,801	12,543	.45
Robeson	607	84,842	27.3	88,300	57.3	-21.2	-1.1	7.3	8.5	1,637	31.6	35,930	27.0	1,685	53,591	.57
Rockingham	366	72,402	44.7	74,900	20.6	-9.0	0.8	9.3	9.8	2,529	12.0	32,850	49.9	1,722	20,142	.61
Rowan	337	90,035	42.1	92,000	16.1	-1.3	0.0	9.9	9.9	2,888	10.3	35,110	41.0	2,039	12,620	.71
Rutherford	364	47,337	30.1	48,800	10.8	-5.0	0.7	10.7	9.6	2,368	15.7	18,630	50.5	1,585	6,279	.57
Sampson	616	44,954	15.9	46,600	36.3	-16.3	1.8	9.1	9.6	1,772	28.8	15,350	23.3	1,488	64,192	.49
Scotland	203	26,929	32.9	28,100	37.8	-7.5	-0.1	6.9	9.4	2,033	23.8	14,140	45.8	1,322	57,874	.82
Stanly	260	42,822	26.0	44,000	11.0	-5.7	0.3	9.0	10.3	2,533	10.1	19,680	52.2	1,965	19,329	.63
Stokes	294	23,782	0.0	26,100	9.2	11.0	6.8	9.8	9.8	2,303	16.3	6,930	16.2	859	15,073	.21
Surry	344	51,415	25.0	53,100	5.0	-5.4	9.5	11.2	9.3	2,329	15.7	28,130	45.9	2,157	33,249	.59
Swain	348	7,861	0.0	9,700	19.8	5.0	0.5	9.5	9.3	1,762	25.8	3,960	26.8	1,431	960	.33
Transylvania	243	19,713	26.6	19,800	15.8	7.2	11.8	9.3	10.8	2,356	13.4	7,550	45.0	1,328	2,437	.45
Tyrrell	373	3,806	0.0	3,700	43.4	-17.8	-1.9	8.0	8.4	1,762	37.9	1,100	15.5	1,231	3,502	.50
Union	412	54,714	25.3	59,800	19.1	-21.2	-1.9	8.0	8.4	1,562	13.2	18,850	39.0	1,841	31,272	.33
Vance	172	32,691	42.5	32,300	42.3	-10.6	-4.3	9.6	9.1	2,111	22.2	17,260	35.4	2,122	12,200	.43
Wake	555	228,453	69.6	250,800	22.6	19.9	6.4	6.7	11.0	3,007	11.2	115,320	13.4	3,390	38,017	1.22
Warren	285	15,810	0.0	17,200	62.5	-27.1	8.1	12.7	9.9	1,730	34.3	4,720	18.9	1,094	9,146	.31
Washington	269	14,038	34.0	13,600	41.5	-10.3	-5.8	7.9	9.5	2,112	23.7	3,200	11.6	1,629	8,147	.36
Watauga	205	23,404	37.4	26,500	1.1	21.7	10.8	8.4	11.1	1,969	22.2	9,520	18.5	1,971	4,751	.61
Wayne	355	85,408	46.7	87,600	33.5	-13.2	-1.2	6.8	10.6	1,998	22.8	33,290	18.7	1,370	52,697	.75
Wilkes	490	49,524	6.8	52,500	5.2	-2.6	2.9	10.8	8.8	2,093	20.1	18,530	40.6	1,764	45,204	.32
Wilson	239	57,486	51.1	58,000	36.9	-13.1	-1.6	9.3	8.8	2,054	22.9	27,480	23.1	2,300	31,400	.99
Yadkin	214	24,599	0.0	26,100	5.2	-2.8	3.5	10.1	9.3	2,303	16.5	6,050	13.6	1,463	19,671	.20
Yancey	199	12,629	0.0	13,100	1.4	-18.9	2.1	11.8	9.0	1,624	30.3	3,350	31.9	978	3,609	.38
N.C.	33,736	5,082,059	45.0	5,273,000	23.2	-2.1	0.7	8.1	10.6	2,492	16.3	2,223,200	32.5	2,308	1,674,014	1.02

Note: Items 2, 3, 5, 6, 8, 9, 10, 11 from U.S. Department of Commerce, *1970 Census of Population, 1970.* Items 4 and 7 from U.S. Department of Commerce, *Current Population Reports,* Series P-26, no. 68, 1974. Item 14 derived from N.C. Department of Administration, *Profile: North Carolina Counties,* 1970, 3d ed., 1973.

Sources: Items 1, 12, 13, 15 from N.C. Department of Administration, *North Carolina State Government Statistical Abstract,* 1973. Item 16 derived from data of the American Medical Association.

In summary, these counties have a rare combination in the distribution of residence and work—a mixture of rural living and industrial employment opportunities—but this situation is threatened by a slow rate of economic diversification.

Coastal Plain Agricultural Type Heavily rural and agricultural, the traditional Coastal Plain counties have a long history of strong out-migration, especially by their large black population. More recently, out-migration of whites has either slowed to a trickle or even stopped, suggesting that the spread of industry to these counties now provides an alternative to agriculture. However, as of 1970 the effects of out-migration of blacks were less apparent. In rapidly industrializing Robeson County net out-migration totaled 18,884 people between 1960 and 1970, but over 15,000 were blacks even though blacks made up only just over half of that county's population. Despite a steady modernization of agriculture through increasing farm size and mechanization (Chapter 10) and often spectacular industrial growth, these counties remain poor with better than one family in four officially classified as living in poverty. And as Chapter 15 (Health Care Resources) and Chapter 17 (Cultural Arts) indicate, the region lacks sufficient medical care and cultural facilities.

There is opportunity in this region, though. In a society that has begun to face the possibility of food shortages, the agricultural capacity of the region takes on new importance. If the trend toward modernization continues and if the recommendations outlined in Chapter 10 (Agriculture) are acted upon, this area could enjoy an agricultural renaissance. And in a rapidly urbanizing society this region's expanses of open fields and forests are a valuable aesthetic resource. The poverty, inadequate health care, and poor educational opportunities suffered by many residents of this region are a high price to pay for these opportunities, however. Perhaps the day has arrived when multicounty cooperation in the development of public facilities can be taken more seriously. If the services base can be improved and better employment opportunities can be provided perhaps this kind of region will provide an attractive alternative to the thousands who now must seek their fortunes in the cities.

Recreational Fringe Type This widely separated group of counties on the eastern and western fringes of the state represents North Carolina's great scenic and recreational resources, both the sandy beaches of the Outer Banks and the forested slopes of the western mountains. These counties have in common a highly rural population that is less black than is the Coastal Plain Agricultural type, and they have experienced less out-migration. This county type is also much less densely populated and less of its land is devoted to agriculture. And it is a poor region, exemplified by a per pupil investment in public education that is well below the state average.

The lack of economic development in this region is a problem for its residents but the maintenance of a supply of open space is a great advantage for the state. The marshes of the coast and the slopes of the mountains are not notably conducive to agriculture or attractive to manufacturing industries. Recently more economic activity has centered around tourist-related ventures, which represent both the region's opportunity and its greatest vulnerability. Given the seasonal nature of tourist-related activities and a tendency for much of it to be controlled by interests outside the area, it is questionable whether or not these activ ties really offer much to the resident population.

These more remote and scenic edges of the state have in recent decades come within easy reach of a more affluent, mobile, and urban population. More and more people can and want to enjoy these resources, but in the very act of doing so, they threaten their existence. The sometimes frantic buying of beach-front properties and mountain lots often results in the despoiling of the land and destruction of the isolation that was part of its original attraction. The Recreational Fringe counties are feeling much of the pressure of recent growth without gaining much benefit from it. They in turn are relatively unprepared to contrcl this growth that is generated from other areas.

Each of the four types of counties forms a region that has its own problems and opportunities. The steady growth of a changing population calls for new or more vigorous planning efforts if the problems are to be solved and the opportunities realized. At the same time, it must be recognized that the regions are not separate entities and that what happens in one has some effect on the others. Continued growth of the Dispersed Urban counties will no doubt place greater pressure on the recreational resources of the Recreational Fringe counties, for example. This interdependency requires that planning should proceed from a statewide perspective, but that it must simultaneously take into account regional and local variations within the state.

Planning Efforts for the Future

Throughout North Carolina's history, this "goodliest land" has been regarded as a land of almost unlimited resource use. As was the case in most states, large segments of the land were owned originally by government, and the policy was to turn the land over to private use so it could be made economically productive. Since North Carolina has been historically a farming state, private land ownership with complete freedom to use the land has been a basis for economic growth and development.

The potential for major public investment in North Carolina's land eventually did come about as an outgrowth of the 1911 Weeks Law that provided for public acquisition of land for national forests, and over a million acres of land were acquired eventually for that purpose. The creation of the Great Smoky Mountains National Park took place in the late 1920s through the dedicated efforts of a number of North Carolinians. Other federal and state park and recreational lands have been established since in locations throughout the state (Figure 16.1). The increased public interest in land use led states to adopt other measures to allow for better planning. Of major significance was the practice of zoning, begun also in North Carolina during the 1920s. Like many other states, North Carolina enacted legislation permitting the zoning of property for specific uses. As a matter of convenience—rather than for any constitutional reason—the zoning responsibility was given to local government. However, there has been little inclination since that time for local governments to take full advantage of their zoning responsibility. This is especially the case on the county level in North Carolina, where only eleven of the one hundred counties have zoning in effect for the entire county and only twenty-eight counties have subdivision ordinances. The situation is somewhat different among the larger towns and cities: all cities with a population of more than ten thousand have zoning controls, and all but one have subdivision regulations; all but two of the cities with a population of more than three thousand have zoning ordinances, and most of those have subdivision regulations. Among the smallest towns, zoning is not as frequent, and even where ordinances exist, enforcement administration is more difficult because of a general lack of professional staff. As a result, local government land use planning is inconsistent across the state.

There are numerous examples of how growth and land use problems have afflicted various parts of North Carolina because of the lack of zoning or of planning in general. The so-called critical areas of "more than local significance" are especially prevalent in a state with the natural scenic endowments of North Carolina. The Mountains provide recreational and tourist resources for all the state's citizens, yet this western portion of the state is rapidly being sold off and developed in a patchwork of small parcels—without any particular plan. The Outer Coastal Plain is losing to private development similar areas such as the Atlantic shoreline, marshlands, and estuaries that are critical to fish, wildlife, and ecological systems. Many of the watersheds and lakes in the Piedmont region are being developed piecemeal.

Figure J. N.C. Urban Clusters, 1970

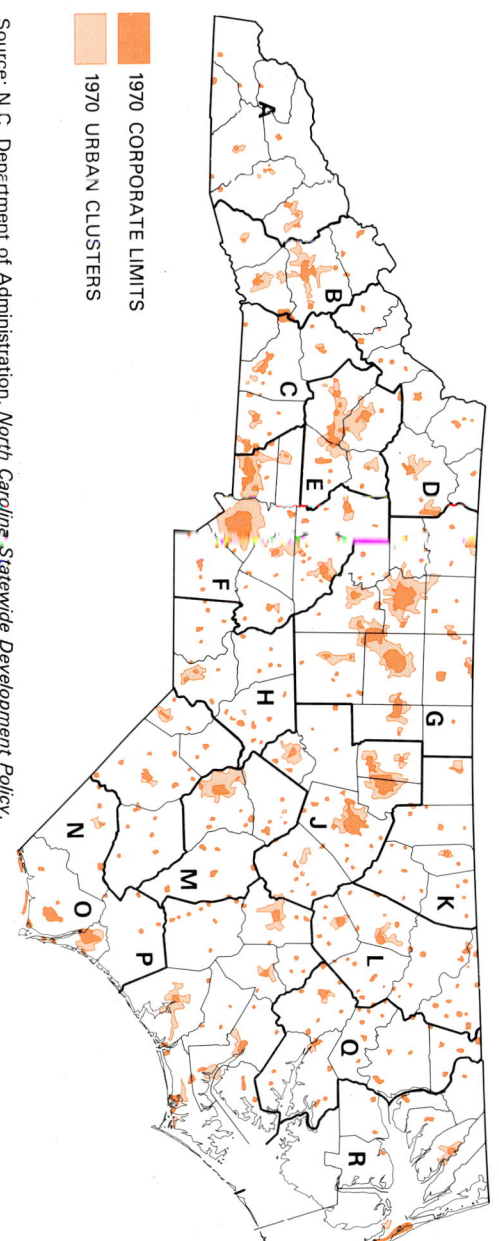

1970 CORPORATE LIMITS
1970 URBAN CLUSTERS

Source: N.C. Department of Administration, *North Carolina Statewide Development Policy,* 1972.

Figure K. N.C. Growth Centers

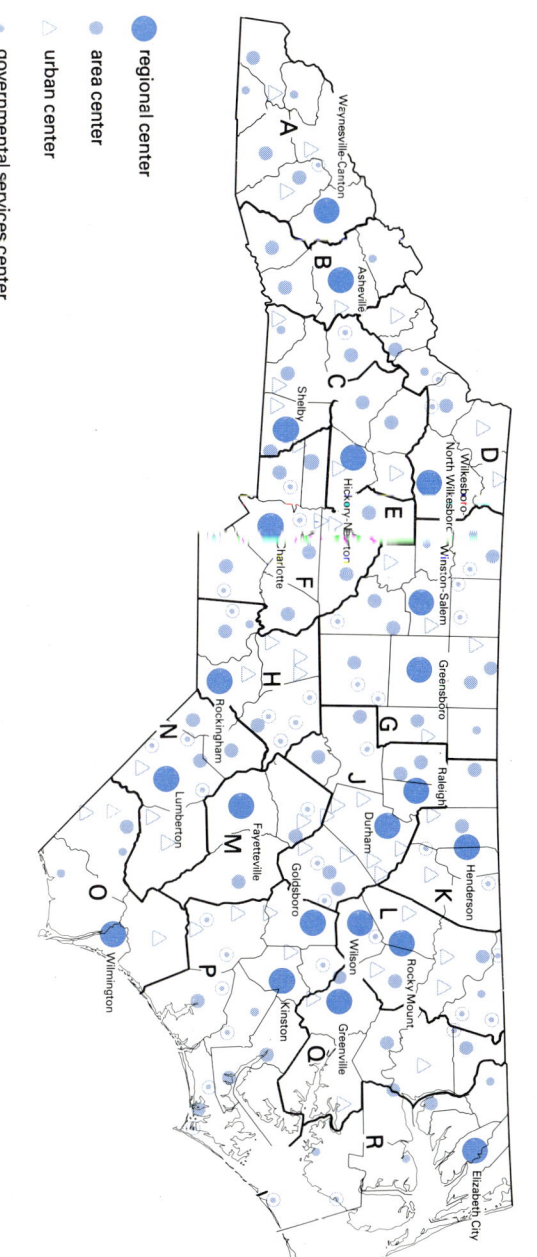

- regional center
- area center
- urban center
- governmental services center
- employment center

Source: N.C. Department of Administration, *North Carolina Statewide Development Policy,* 1972.

The Charlotte area provides a prototype of another kind of unchecked development. There, thousands of people who work in Charlotte have sought out "country living" just across the county line where no zoning or subdivision ordinances exist in the seven surrounding counties. The school systems, roads, and utilities in the counties are not equipped to take care of the sudden overload, while commuter traffic into Charlotte builds to unmanageable proportions. Similar instances are becoming common elsewhere in the state and the nation.

Current Planning Efforts Yet a number of planning efforts hold great promise for a more rational pattern of growth in the state. The North Carolina Municipal Annexation Law has been praised as a model for orderly urban development. The annexation statutes, adopted in the late 1950s and later modified, operate on the principle that what has become urban must be incorporated into a municipality. The standards of development for annexed areas vary according to the size of the adjacent city, but for areas adjoining major cities, at least 60 percent of the land must be in use for other than farming, and at least 60 percent of the residential acreage must be in lots of five acres or less.

An important measure of a developing sentiment among the populace of North Carolina was the overwhelming approval in the November 1972 general election of the Environmental Bill of Rights as an amendment to the North Carolina constitution. Passage of this amendment calls on the state and its local jurisdictions to "acquire and preserve" those critical areas of the state that because of unique environmental or historical character are of "benefit to all its citizenry."

Major progress toward a state land-use policy came in March 1972 when the state government's Department of Administration released the *North Carolina Statewide Development Policy.* It puts forth a strategy of balanced growth throughout the state, supporting the growth of smaller centers of population, and stating that "this policy is based upon recognition of the fact that many of the state's social and economic problems result from an imbalance between where people choose to live and where job opportunities and public services are located. It also is based upon the fact that opportunities for a better way of life in the 1970s come from a clustering of people, jobs, and public services around urban centers." The report defines 368 urban "clusters" in the state (Figure J), ranging in size from 100 persons to 318,832 persons (Charlotte) as of the 1970 census. Slightly more than 3.1 million people live in these clusters, accounting for 61 percent of the state's population. However, roughly half of the people were located in a relatively few large urban clusters with a massive concentration of people "within an extended Piedmont Crescent" (generally, the aforementioned Dispersed Urban type of region).

323

Since such a concentration threatens the likelihood of keeping North Carolina a state of reasonably dispersed and moderate-sized urban centers, the development policy would seek to direct a larger share of state investments of all kinds into designated "growth centers" throughout the state, encouraging the growth of small and medium-sized communities rather than overloading the larger municipalities. In the process, it will try to increase the relative concentration of people outside of the denser Piedmont region. These growth centers would be simply a selected and dispersed group of the urban clusters, and would be classified into a hierarchy of types as shown in Figure K. Modifications in the classifications would be expected as centers underwent change and expansion. At the same time, a policy of jobs and population dispersal poses certain dilemmas. As pointed out in Chapter 9 (Labor and Income), the state's per capita income would improve more rapidly if new job opportunities were located in urban centers rather than in rural areas. Whether or not the current growth-center plan or some subsequent variation of the concept takes effect, it may be an appropriate spatial approach to dispersing the state's growth and land development. Not unlike the American Institute of Architects' "growth unit" idea, it is a concept that is drawing increasing attention in many states.

The major geographic framework for implementation of any statewide development plan would be the seventeen Multicounty Planning Regions and their lead regional organizations (Figure F in Chapter 1). They represent North Carolina's approach to "regionalism." As noted in the development policy report, the Multicounty Planning Regions should be ideally an extension of both local and state planning; that is, state planning that is oriented toward policy development and the setting of statewide goals and priorities, and local planning that is primarily operational in laying out the specific program details. Thus regional planning would be a "marriage of those two efforts, within a smaller area closer to local government than the state can achieve alone." It is anticipated that coordinated planning at the regional level can immediately apply to such things as land-use development, water, sewer, and waste treatment systems, housing, transportation, open space, and recreation. In the longer run, regional planning can also have a role in human resources planning in areas such as education, manpower development, health care, family planning, and child development. So far, however, the state's Multicounty Planning Regions and their lead regional organizations have not been completely accepted by the local municipalities. There have been problems concerning the division of responsibility between the two levels, dissatisfaction with regional boundaries, calls for a weighted voting by size of member municipalities, and a lack of adequate funding.

Meanwhile, there are additional efforts in land-use planning for North Carolina that hold considerable potential. The North Carolina Land Policy Council was established by the governor's 1973 executive order and given permanent status by subsequent legislative action. Composed of eight state cabinet officials, the council is developing components of an overall state land policy, including a statewide land-use information system, the designation of "areas of particular public concern," and a land classification system that will allow particular parcels of land to be classified according to their potential land use for industrial, agricultural, or recreational purposes, or for some combination thereof, or to maintain wilderness areas. It reports to the governor semiannually and is given core staff support by the Office of State Planning. Also enacted recently was the Coastal Area Management Act, which establishes a Coastal Resources Commission to oversee a program of land-use controls for that region. The commission designates those areas on the coast judged to be critical areas (beaches, dunes, marshes, and estuarine waters) and thereafter permits must be obtained from the commission before any development within the areas can be carried out. In conjunction with local governments, the commission is preparing a comprehensive conservation and development plan for the entire coastal zone. Finally, the recent creation of the North Carolina Land Conservancy Corporation enables the state to acquire property of future interest to the public—such as parklands—as an independent public corporation. This would allow the state to compete quickly and effectively in the marketplace for land whenever it is available. The inability of the state to act quickly in the past—to purchase Smith (Bald Head) Island, for example—is often cited as the type of situation to which a land conservancy corporation could have responded.

Fundamental to effective planning efforts is the participation by an interested citizenry. North Carolina includes several citizens' movements dedicated to better state land-use planning. For example, the North Carolina Land Use Congress is a public interest group formed in 1969 to help stimulate public interest in effective statewide land-use planning. It sponsors annual conferences to discuss land-use issues and includes in its membership a mixture of professionals—planners, architects, academicians, soil conservationists, private developers, and public officials. The Piedmont Urban Policy Conference, founded as a nonprofit corporation in 1970, is comprised of a group of private citizens who share a common interest in and concern for the urbanization of the Carolinas' Piedmont region. It meets each fall and holds a series of daylong sessions during the spring months.

Citizen movements across the country are making an effort to peer at least a quarter of a century ahead, and to set goals for the kinds of communities and states they desire. Citizen goal setting has had notable success in the cities of Dallas and Seattle, and in the states of Hawaii and Iowa. In North Carolina, Charlotte and its county of Mecklenburg began in 1973 a citizen's goal-setting program called Dimensions for Charlotte-Mecklenburg. Some 121 goals in thirteen different categories have been established and a process of promoting and monitoring goal achievement is underway. Greensboro, Raleigh, and Durham have similar goals programs. On a statewide basis, the legislature has established a permanent North Carolina Council on Goals and Policy. This is a citizen's advisory group with members appointed for four-year terms by the governor. The council members held a series of public hearings across the state in 1972, its first year of operation, to allow citizens to express their views about possible state goals. The council submits a report to the governor by November 30 of each year to assist him in the preparation of a "state of the state" report. In its report, the council may identify goals for state action, recommend policies for their achievement, suggest short-run priority goals, evaluate the present structure and activities of government and recommend improvements, and identify areas of urgent concern. In its most fundamental form, the council is simply helping to give direction to priorities, advice for which is much needed by any level of government.

In the context of a rapidly changing South, North Carolina has been working with its neighboring southern states on a variety of fronts. Of special recent significance has been the Southern Growth Policies Board, one of the fastest-growing regional organizations in the country. The idea for the board was first advanced in 1971 by former North Carolina governor Terry Sanford. In October 1971, representatives from thirteen southern states attended a planning meeting, and during the next year, governors of those thirteen states signed executive orders joining their states to the Southern Growth Policies Agreement. Member states are Alabama, Arkansas, Florida, Georgia, Kentucky, Louisiana, Mississippi, North Carolina, Oklahoma, South Carolina, Tennessee, Virginia, and West Virginia. Most have since become permanent members through their state's enabling legislation, and all are expected to be members by state law by the end of 1975. Headquartered in North Carolina's Research Triangle Park, the board is envisioned as "a regional planning agency, formed by and for Southern states, to help direct the growth of the South." Each state furnishes five members to the board, including the governor, two state legislators, and citizen members. In 1974, the board organized the

Commission on the Future of the South, which developed a statement of regional objectives concentrating on four areas of concern relating to the future of the southern states: regional transportation, land and natural resources, human resources and public services, and growth management policies.

As southern states face the last quarter of this century, it is indeed appropriate that they plan their future goals in concert. And it is noteworthy that North Carolina is involved in an integral way in this regional effort. Although statistical indexes indicate that North Carolina, like the rest of the South, has lagged behind other parts of the nation in its overall growth and development, this economic retardation is not without its advantages. As has been pointed out often, there does exist a "lead time" for North Carolina to avoid proceeding down the course toward urban sprawl followed by states elsewhere. Yet that lead time is swiftly evaporating because the state and the region now grow much more rapidly than does the nation as a whole.

As North Carolina is confronted with the inevitability of growth and change, it is challenged to find ways to direct these forces. There is little question that the task will be extremely difficult. There are so many factors affecting North Carolina's future patterns, about which the state can do very little—worldwide inflation, migration habits, consumer preferences, cultural traits, the leisure-time boom, and the countless private decisions made every day that also play a part in shaping the future.

In addition, there is the need for balancing the two counterdemands in the definition of quality of life—natural and traditional tranquillity on one hand and economic and social opportunity on the other.

Consequently, the state must set its goals realistically and marshal what family of controls it possesses toward a cohesive policy direction. It can also reinforce the considerable existing advantages it has. For example, while much of the nation is already clustering into overcrowded urban centers, North Carolina—and most southern states—do have a highly desired dispersal pattern of small- to medium-sized population centers. Although there are troublesome signs that this pattern is breaking down, the many aforementioned planning efforts are a recognition of some of the problems. In fact, the sense of energy, optimism, and opportunity prevalent throughout the entire South today affords southern states the chance to be a model of growth and urbanization for the rest of the country. And, perhaps most of all, the state and the region can draw upon a heritage that includes a strong sense of place, of purpose, and of shared bonds of community.

Index

A

Administrative and auxiliary units, 212–13. *See also* Manufacturing
Administrative reorganization of government. *See* Chief executive
Affiliate Artists Program, 309
Age-sex profiles, 39–41
Agencies of government. *See* Government
Agribusiness, 196
Agricultural products: crops, 190–93; livestock and poultry, 193–95; retail value of, 196; exports, 197
Agriculture: soil relationship, 140; land in, 141; gross income from, 189; size of industry, 189–96; in overall economy, 196–98; future challenges for, 200–201
Air pollution dispersion, 107, 109
Air quality, 106–11
Alcoholic rehabilitation centers, 286
American Revolution, 22–23; Provincial Congress at Halifax, 22; Battle of Kings Mountain, 22; Howe, Major General Robert, 22; Gates, General Horatio, 22; Greene, General Nathaniel, 23; Battle of Guilford Courthouse, 23
Anticyclones, 97, 108
Apparel industry, 207–9
Apples: soil association, 141; production of, 193
Architectural styles, 304–5; historical features, 304
Arts and artists, visual, 305
Asbestos mining, 121, 122, 124
Asheville-Biltmore College, 260
Autumn, 101
Aviation and airports, 226–30
Aycock, Governor Charles B., 29

B

"Baby boom": post–World War II, 41, 43
Banking, 22–22
"Barrier islands," 113; vegetation of, 140
Battle of Alamance, 22
Beaches and dunes: vegetation type, 128
Beef, 193
Bermuda High, the, 93, 103
Birthrates, 43–44
"Big Three" industries, 202
Black Creek formation, 119
Black voting patterns. *See* Sociodemographic analysis of interparty competition
Blacks. *See* Population; Population distribution
Blueberries: soil association, 141; production of, 193

Board of Higher Education, 260
Boreal Conifer forest, 134–35
Branch plants, 212
Brevard belt, 119, 120, 121
Bricks, 211
Broiler chickens, 194–95
By-product labor, 205, 208, 210

C

Camping, 296
Capital intensity, 202
Carlyle Commission Report: on higher education, 260–61
"Carolina Bays," 113, 157
Carolina slate belt, 119, 120; crushed stone, 123; vegetation, 132
Carowinds ("theme" park), 297
Castle Hayne limestone, 119
Cement, 124
Central business district (CBD), 67, 219
Charlotte College, 260
Chemicals industry, 211
Chestnut-oak forest, 134
Chief executive, 73–75
Cigarette industry, 209
Citizen participation: in elections, 85–86
City: size of, leading, 58–60
Civil War, the, 24–26; Sherman's march, 25; Stoneman's raid, 25; surrender at Bennett's farmhouse, 26
Clay, 124
Clean Air Act, 109
Climate, 92–106; effects on soil, 140
Climate controls, 92–93, 94, 95, 99
Climate type, 93
Coal, 124
Coastal Area Management Act, 324
Coastal erosion, 177
Coastal marshes, 129, 130
Coastal vegetation, 128–30
Coastline, 171, 172
Coe, Jeffrie L., 12
Coets Scarp, 139, 140
Colonial North Carolina, 21–22
Commercial fishing, 175–76
Commission on the Future of the South, 325
Community colleges: locations, 263–65; financial considerations, 265–67; enrollment, 263–65; financial considerations, 261–62; and sixth-grade assessment study, 255–57. *See also* Community colleges; Higher education; High school graduates; Public schools
Coneret series, 309
Congressional districts, 78
Conservation: of land, 146
Corvette of 1835, 23

Corn: soil association, 141; production of, 191
Cotton: soil association, 141; production of, 193
Cotton mill campaign, 204
Cove hardwood forest: characteristics of, 134; soil association, 141
Crafts: displayed, 305
Cretaceous system, 117
Cropland: percent of state's total land, 146
Crushed stone, 123
Cucumbers, 193
Culpeper's Rebellion, 22
Cultural arts: summary and outlook, 311
"Culture Week," 311
Cumnock formation, 119
Cyclonic storms, 93, 96

D

Dairy, 194
Dance, 311
Daniels, Jonathan, 313
Daniels, Josephus, 29
Dan River basin, 119
Davidson College, 28–29, 259
Death: causes of in North Carolina, 273–74. *See also* Mortality
Deciduous forests, 134
Deep River basin, 119; coal, 124
Democratic party. *See* Party politics
Dentists, 280–82
Department of Community Colleges, 260
Department of Public Instruction, 250
Department of Social Services, 284–85
Desegregation, 31
Dikes and sill, 112, 119
Dimensions for Charlotte-Mecklenburg, 324
Dispersed cities, 219
Diversification: industrial, 202
Draft rejection rates: for physical and mental disabilities, 287
Drainage and erosion control, 143, 146
Drama, 310
Duke Endowment, 29
Duke University, 29, 259, 269
Duke University Press, 307

E

Earnings gap, 183–84
Education: kindergarten program, 253–55; sixth-grade assessment study, 255–57. *See also* Community colleges; Higher education; High school graduates; Public schools
Eggs, 195

Ehringhaus, Governor J. C. B., 30
Electrical equipment industry, 212
Electricity, 244–47
Energy, 241–47
Energy Crisis Study Commission: of the North Carolina General Assembly, 244, 247
English settlers. *See* National origins
Environmental influences, 17–19; communications problems, 17; on patterns of settlement, 18; on economic development, 18–19
Erosion: control of, 141, 143; control needed, 146
Estuarine zone, 171–72
European settlement, 14–16; Pory, John, 14; Berkeley, William, 14; Lords Proprietors, 14; Batts, Nathaniel, 14; Granville, Earl; Davidson, Samuel, 16
Evaporation: mean annual, 103. *See also* Water loss
Evergreen bay tree, 113
Executive Organization Act, 74

F

Factor analysis, 213
Faculty: of higher education, 268–69
Fall line, 112
Family income, 180
Family planning, 44–45
Farm consolidation, 188
Farm income, 189
Farms: structure of, 195–96
Feldspar, 122
Fertility, 43–46
Fertilizer: soil need, 138
Fessenden, R. A., 2
Finance and insurance, 221–23
Fishing: commercial, 175–76; sport, 299–301
Flooding: causes of, 155; major floods, 155; control of, 156; urban, 156, 166; responsibility for control, 157
Folk and country music, 309
Food products industry, 210
Forest industry: naval stores, 135, 136; lumber, 136, 137, 138; tanneries, 137; furniture, 137; pulpwood, 138
Forest resources: land, 135, 210; products, 138; percent of state's land, 146; and agriculture, 193
Friday, William C., 261
Frost, 94; last freeze in spring, 97; autumn, 100; length of freeze-free season, 100

327

Index

Fundamental Constitutions: by the Lords Proprietors, 21
Furniture industry, 209–10

G

Gardner, Governor O. Max, 30–31
Gaston, William, 23
Gem stones, 124
General Assembly. See Legislature
German settlers. See National origins
Gerrymandering: and congressional districts, 78
Geographic units, 5–10; physiographic divisions, 5–10; county units, 6–9; Standard Metropolitan Statistical Areas, 9; Multicounty Planning Regions, 9. See also Regions
Geological history, 118
Geology, 117–22
Gold Hill fault, 119
Goldwater, Barry: presidential candidacy, 77; and the Republican party, 88
Golf, 295
Government, 70–76: activities and powers of, 70–71; local government, 71–72; state legislature, 72–73; chief executive, 73–75; judiciary, 75–76
Governor. See Chief executive
Graham, Frank Porter, 249, 260
Grassbald, 135
Great Depression, the, 30
Great Wagon Road, 17–18
Groundwater resources, 158–61; dissolved solid content, 163, 164; temperature, 167; pollution, 168; classification, 168
Growing degree days, 99
Growth: attitudes toward, 315
Gynecologists, 288

H

Hams: country-cured, 193
Handicapped students, 257
Health care: maldistribution of, 277–82, 287; manpower, 277–83; and allied health professions, 283–84; selected problems, 287–89; training resources, 287; developing future of, 289–90; maintenance organizations, 290
Health education centers, regional, 290
Heath balds, 135; soil association, 141
Heating degree days, 95
Helms, Senator Jesse, 77, 88
Hemlock forest, 134

Higher education: history of, 258–61; types and locations of institutions, 261–63; enrollment in, 263–65; financial considerations, 265–68; faculty, 268–69; libraries, 269; regional comparisons, 263–70; accessibility to, 270–71
High school graduates: proportion graduating, 252; percentage of high school graduates compared to fifth-grade enrollment seven years earlier, 252–53; percentage of high school graduates who continued with higher education, 253
Highways, 233–40
Hodges, Governor Luther H., 31, 179
Hogs, 193
Holden, Governor H. H., 27
Holshouser, Governor James E., Jr., 74, 77
Hospitals, 274–77; accessibility to, 275
Housing: single family, 66; mobile homes, 66; multifamily, 66; SMSAs, 66 rural, 199; urban, 199, 314
Humidity: spring, 97; summer, 98; annual, 101
Hunting: types of, 294–95
Hurricanes, 99, 103, 104
Hydrologic cycle, 150

I

Illiteracy: functional, 187
Income, 180–82
Indians, 12–13; Cherokee, 12–13, 15; Croatan, 12; Chowanoc, 12; Tuscarora, 12; Catawba, 12–13; population of, 39
Industrial regions, 213
Infant mortality, 288; by race, 288
Instruments industry, 212
Insurance companies, 222–23
Irish potatoes, 193

J

James, Hinton, 258
Johnson, President Andrew, 26
Johnston, General Joseph E., 25
Jonas, Congressman Charles, 78
Jonesboro fault, 119
Judicial districts, 75
Judiciary, 75–76

K

Kaolin, 124
Key, V. O., Jr., 76, 78, 84
Kindergarten program. See Education
Kings Mountain belt, 119, 120, 121
Ku Klux Klan, 27

L

Labor force: participation in, 184; blacks in, 185; stoppages, 187; supply, 187
Labor intensity, 202
Lagoons, 113
Lakes and reservoirs: area of, 151; surface, 157-58; temperature, 167
Land use: nonfarm urban, 141–43; in Multicounty Planning Regions, 144–48. See also Urban land
Lapse rate, 92
Lawson, John, 12, 91
Leaching: of soil, 138, 140
Legislative districts: senatorial, 72–73; House of Representatives, 72–73
Legislature, 72–73
Length of daylight, 92, 97
Libraries: university, 269–307; state library system, 307; public libraries, 307
Literary activity, 306–7
Lithium, 120, 122, 123
Local government, 71–72
Longleaf pine: soil association, 140
Longleaf pine—turkey oak—wire grass community, 131
Lumber and wood industry, 210

M

McLean, Governor Angus D., 30
Manufacturing: composition of, 61, 202–3; geographic distribution of, 61, 203–4; value added by, 202; individual industry patterns, 204–13; research and administrative offices, 212–13; regions, 213
Marine terraces, 112, 113
Maritime forest, 128
Maritime shrub thicket, 128
Marshes: coastal, 129, 130; salt, 129; fresh, 130
Marshland, 171–72
Median age, 43
Medicaid, 284
Medical Care Commission, 275
Medicare, 284
Mental health clinics and centers, 285–86
Metallic minerals, 122
Mica, 122
Migration of population, 47; interstate, 48–49; intrastate, 49-51. See also Population distribution
Mills: knitting, 205; yarn and thread, 205; broad woven fabric, 205; paper, 211
Milk, 194
Mineral fuels, 124

Mineral resources, 122–27
Mining: trends and developments, 125; and the environment, 127; surface mining control bill, 127
Monadnocks, 113
Moravian music, 309
Moravian settlers. See National origins
Mortality, 46–47
Murphey, Archibald D., 23
Musical activity, 308–10
Musician-in-residence program, 309

N

National forests, 293
National origins, 16–17; English settlers, 16; Lowland Scots, 16; Germans, 16–17; Highland Scots, 16–17; Scotch-Irish, 16–17; French Huguenots, 17; Moravians, 17; Negroes, 17
Natural gas: potential production, 125; supply and distribution, 241–44
Natural increase: population, 37
Newspapers, 223
Nonelectrical machinery industry, 212
Nonmetallic minerals, 122–27
Noon sun angle, 92
North Carolina Arts Council, 309, 311
North Carolina College for Women at Greensboro, 29, 260
North Carolina Council on Goals and Policy, 324
North Carolina Department of Transportation, 234
North Carolina Division of Archives and History, 305
North Carolina Environmental Bill of Rights, 323
North Carolina Land Conservancy Corporation, 324
North Carolina Land Policy Council, 324
North Carolina Land Use Congress, 324
North Carolina Manpower Council, 187
North Carolina Municipal Annexation Law, 323
North Carolina Museum of Art, 305
North Carolina Office of State Planning, 180
North Carolina School of the Arts: music program, 310
North Carolina State College of Agriculture and Engineering at Raleigh, 259–60
North Carolina State Ports Authority, 232
North Carolina State University (Raleigh), 29, 260

Index

North Carolina State Utilities Commission, 237, 239, 240
North Carolina Statewide Development Policy, 323
North Carolina Symphony, 308
Nurses, 282

O

Oak-hickory forest: Coastal Plain, 131; Piedmont, 132, 133; Mountain, 134; soil association, 140
Obstetricians, 140
Ocean: characteristics of, 173–75
Olivine, 121, 122, 124
Opera, 308
Oral surgeons. See Dentists
Outdoor recreation: classification, 291; total acres, 291; areas, 291–92; selected government-owned facilities, 293; future needs, 301–3; North Carolina's rank in state park acreage, 303
Outer Banks, the. See "Barrier islands"

P

Paper industry, 210–11
Party politics. See Party politics
Pasture: soil type, 141
Peaches: soil association, 141; production of, 193
Peanuts: soil association, 141; production of, 192
Pediatricians, 288
Pee Dee formation, 119
Pekin formation, 119
Per capita income, 180
Petroleum, 125
Pharmacists, 282–83
Phosphate, 122, 124
Physicians, 277–80
Physiographic provinces, 112–13
Piedmont Urban Policy Conference, 323
Pine flatwoods (savanna), 131; soil association, 140
Pine forest, 134
Pioneer people of North Carolina. See European settlement; National origins
Pipelines, 241–44
Planning, 68–69, 322–25
Pocosin (bay), 131; forest, 136; soil association, 140
Poetry. See Literary activity
Political beliefs, 84–85
Political boundaries and units, 19, 21; boundaries of the colony, 19–21
Political development: early history of, 21–27
Political parties. See Party politics
Political partisanship. See Voter characteristics
Polk, William T., 11
Pollution: air, 109–10; groundwater, 160, 167–68; fresh water, 163–68; marine water, 176. See also Air quality; Water quality
Polynucleated urban region, 56
Population: growth, 32–33, 314; white-nonwhite differentials, 37–39; components of change, 43–51; projections, 51–52
Population distribution: regional, 33; county, 33–34; rural-urban, 34–36; by race, 39
Poverty level, 182
Precipitation: autumn, orographic, 93, 101; winter, 96; summer, 99; annual, 101
Presidents: from North Carolina, 23
Printing and publishing industry, 211
Primary and fabricated metals industry, 211
Prohibition, 29
Projections: population, 51–52, 314; income, 180; employment, 183
Property: private, 316
Public health programs. See Department of Social Services
Public schools: national rankings, 250; expenditures, 250–51, 258; enrollment patterns, 257; special services, 257; budget outlook, 258
Pulpwood: soil type, 141
Pyrophyllite, 124

Q

Quaternary system, 119
Queens College, 258

R

Radio, 223
Railroads, 230–31
Reconstruction (Civil War), 27–28
Recreation: percent of state land used, 146
Regional medical program, 290
Regions: physiographic divisions, 5–6; Multi-county Planning, 9; industrial, 213; general, 316–22. See also Physiographic provinces
Reins Insurance Facility, 223
Republican party. See Party politics
Research Triangle Institute, 182
Research Triangle Park, 30, 57, 267, 324
Reservoirs, 293

Retail sales: gross, 214; per capita, 215; deficits, 215–18; surpluses, 215–18
Retail trade, 214–19
"Rip Van Winkle" state, 3, 23
Rocks: classes of, 113
Royall, Kenneth, 31
Rubber, plastic, and leather industry, 210–11
Runoff: streams, 152–53
Rural areas: quality of life in, 198–200; housing in, 199; development of, 201; industry in, 208–9, 211, 213

S

Salt marshes, 113, 129
Sand and gravel, 123
Sanford, Governor Terry, 77, 260, 324
Sanford formation, 119
Savings and loans associations, 222
Scotch-Irish settlers. See National origins
Scott, Governor Robert, 261
Scottish settlers. See National origins
Seasons: winter, 94, 95, 96, 97; spring, 97; summer, 98; autumn, 101
Sedimentation, 164; causes of, 166; legislation, 166
Settlement, patterns of, 17–21
Sharecropping, 196
Shellfish, 131
Shopping centers, 67, 214
Simons, Furnifold M., 29
"Sit-in," lunch counter desegregation demonstration, 31
Skiing, 296
Slavery: extent of slaveholding, 26; and the plight of the black man, 26–27; life-style, 27
Small grain: soil type, 141
Snap beans, 193
Snow, 96
Sociodemographic analysis of interparty competition, 79–81
Soils, 138–48; sandhills, 138; effects of vegetation, 138; effects of rock type, 138; effects of Ice Age, 139; effects of topography, 139; catena, 139; classification, 140; effects of climate, 140; deficiencies, 141; associations, 141; influence on agriculture, 141; influence on land use, 141–42; influence on nonfarm urban percolation, 141, 143; local resources, 144
Southern Growth Policies Board, 324
Soybeans: soil association, 141; production of, 192

Special care systems for health needs, 284–87; Division of Vocational Rehabilitation, 284; Department of Social Services, 284–85; Department of Mental Health, 285–86; voluntary associations, 286
Spectator activities: facilities available, 297
Spring, 97
Spruce-fir forest, 134; soil association, 141
Standard Metropolitan Statistical Areas (SMSAs): defined, 9; population, 35, 58, 60; housing, 66; land use, 68; wholesale trade, 221
Stanly, Governor Edward, 25
Stone, clay, and glass industry, 211
Strawberries, 193
Streams: flow characteristics, 152–58; temperature, 167; classification, 168
Suffolk Scarp, 139
Summer, 98
Sunshine, 92; spring, 97; winter, 97
Surface water resources, 152–58
Surry Scarp, 139
Swamp forest: gum-cypress, 130–31; hardwood swamp (Coastal Plain), 131; Piedmont, 133
Sweet potatoes, 193
Symphony orchestras, 308. See also North Carolina Symphony
Synthetic fibers, 211

T

Talc, 124
Task Force on Land Use and Urban Growth, 316
Teacher qualifications, 252
Technical institutes: locations, 261–62; enrollment, 263–65; financial considerations, 265–67
Telephone service, 224
Television, 223
Temperature: average January, 94; January mean maximum, January mean minimum, January range, 95; spring, 97; July average, 98; autumn, 100; vertical distribution, 107
Temperature inversions, 107–8; nighttime, 109; upper level inversion and anticyclones, 109; ridge and valley, 109
Tennis, 295–96
Tertiary system, 119
Textile industry, 204–7
Textile machinery, 212
Theater. See Drama
Thermal belts, 97

Index

Third party movements, 86–88; Dixiecrat movement, 86; George Wallace, 86, 88
Thunderstorms, 99, 103, 104; summer, 99
Thurmond, Strom, 86
Tobacco: flue-cured, 190; burley, 190–91; manufacturing industry, 209
Tomatoes, 193
Topography: effects on soils, 139
Tornadoes, 103, 106
Towns: growth of, 61; industry in, 205
Trade: centers, 214–18; areas, 218–19
Transpiration. See Water loss
Transportation: historical development of, 225–26; present system, 226; urban, 240–41
Transport equipment industry, 212
Travel: revenue, 217–18, 301; sources of tourist trade, 301
Triassic basin, 119; coal, 124; uranium, 125
Tryon, Governor William, 22
Turkeys, 195

U

Unemployment, 187
Unions, trade, 189
U.S. Census Bureau, 52, 53, 58
University of North Carolina: founding of, 23, 258–59; consolidation, 29, 260; restructuring of, 261; Board of Governors, 261, 271
University of North Carolina at Chapel Hill, The, 23, 29, 258–59, 269
University of North Carolina at Charlotte, The, 260; creative arts program, 310
University of North Carolina at Greensboro, The, 29, 260
University of North Carolina Press, The, 307
Uranium, 125
Urbanized Areas: population, 58, 65; land use, 68
Urban land: conversion to, 63, 314; use of, 65–67; changes in, 66; industrial, 66; residential, 66–67; commercial, 67; public and institutional, 67; transportation, 67; management, 68–69; soil, 141; percent of state land, 144
Urban pattern: evolution of, 53–56; present, 56–58; fringe areas, 58; North Carolina as an urban anomaly, 61; assessment of, 62; new forms, 67–68
Urban population density, 63–65

V

Value added, 202n
Vance, Zebulon, 24, 28
Vegetation, 128–38; plant succession, 133; relationship with soil type, 138, 140–41
Visual arts, 305; display of, 305
Vocational training, 187
Voter characteristics, 81–83
Voting trends: 1948–1974, 76–79; presidential, 77; gubernatorial, 77–78; congressional, 78; state offices, 78–79
Voting turnout: See Citizen participation

W

Wage rates, 183–84
Wake Forest University, 28–29
Water balance, 101–3
Water-based outdoor recreation, 297–301
Water loss: by lake evaporation, 150–51; by evapotranspiration, 150–53
Water quality: groundwater, 160, 164; chemical, 163–64; physical, 164–67; biological, 167–68; standards, 168–70. See also Pollution
Water transportation, 232–33
Water use: groundwater, 158; withdrawal uses, 162; consumptive use, 163
Wheat, 192
Wholesale trade, 220–21
Wildlife areas, 293
Wilmington College, 260
Winds, 103–4: low wind speed and air quality, 109
Winter, 94, 95; precipitation, 96–97
Wolfe, Thomas, 1
World War I, 29
World War II, 30
Writers. See Literary activity

Y

Yellow poplar: soil association, 140
Yorktown formation, 119

Credits for Photographs

Don Aldridge, p. 178.

Charlotte (N.C.) *Observer*, pp. 167, 228, lower center front cover.

Department of Geography and Earth Sciences, The University of North Carolina at Charlotte, back endpapers.

Duke University, p. 261.

Maury Faggart, Chapel Hill, N.C., lower right back cover.

Alan Guggenheim, Charlotte, N.C., pp. 53, 115, 306.

Hugh Morton, Linville, N.C., pp. viii, 2, 102, 129, 133, 173, 295, 297.

Joel Nichols, p. 291.

Clay Nolen, courtesy of North Carolina Department of Natural and Economic Resources, Travel and Promotion Division, Raleigh, N.C., pp. 74, 299, 316.

North Carolina Collection, The University of North Carolina Library, Chapel Hill, N.C., pp. 10-11, 12, 13, 17, 21, 23, 24, 25, 26, 28, 29, 30, 90-91, 188, 202, 225, 259.

North Carolina Department of Conservation and Development, Travel and Promotion Division, Raleigh, N.C., pp. 179, 307, left and right front cover, upper right back cover.

North Carolina Department of Transportation, front endpapers.

Bruce Roberts, Charlotte, N.C., p. 37; courtesy of Rapho Guillumette Pictures, New York, N.Y., pp. vi, x, 1, 45, 105, 123, 125, 194, 230, 245, 248, 254, 273, 285, 309, 325, upper center front cover, left back cover; photo from *You Can't Kill the Dream*, John Knox Press, © M. E. Bratcher, 1968, p. 249; photo from *The Goodliest Land: North Carolina*, Doubleday & Co., © Bruce and Nancy Roberts, 1973, p. 317.

J. F. Scott, Manteo, N.C., title page, pp. 312-13.

Robert Sulkin, Chapel Hill, N.C., p. 315.

Tom Walters, Charlotte, N.C., p. 106.

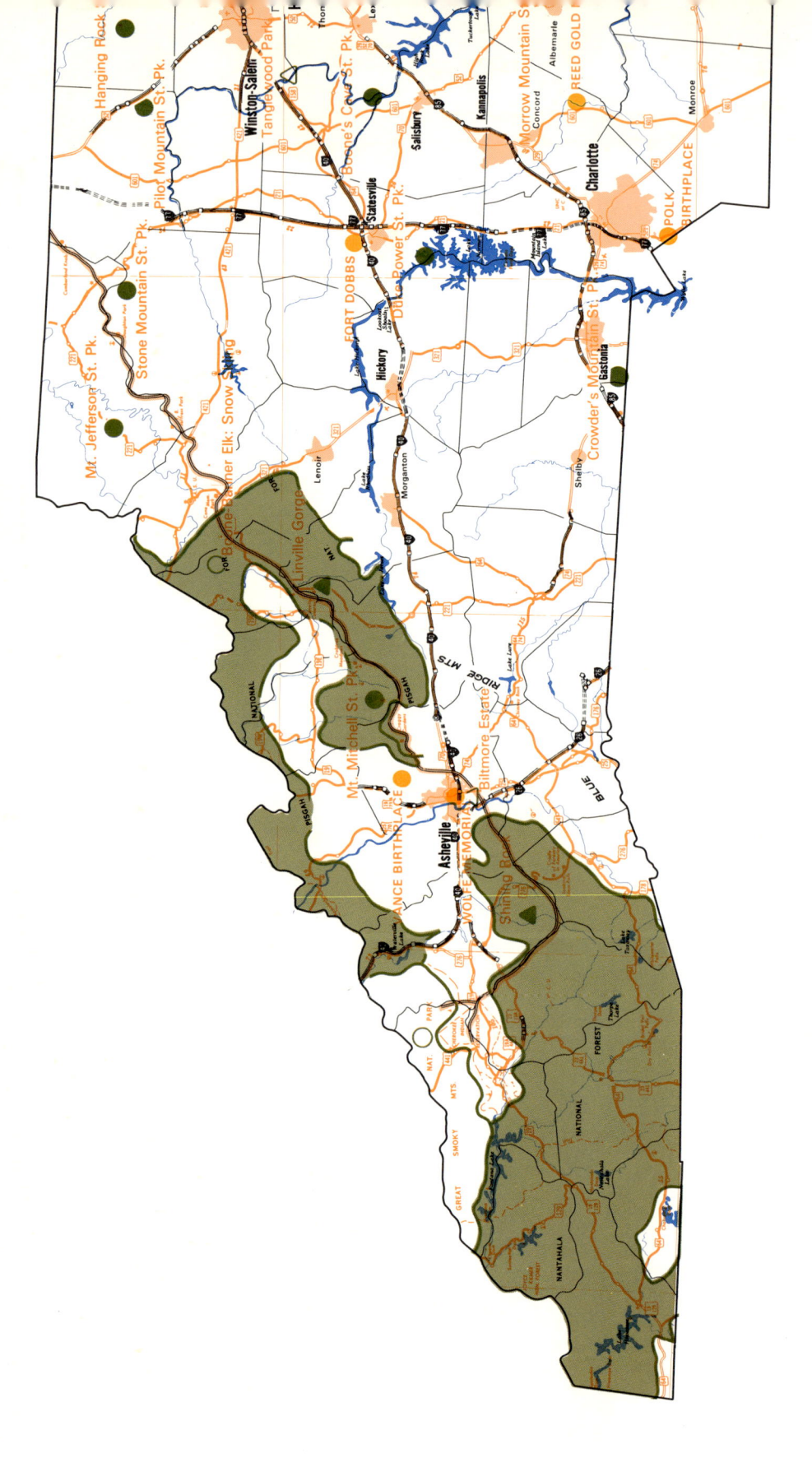